Service Charges for Leasehold, Freehold and Commonhold

Service Charges for Leasehold, Freehold and Commonhold

by

Gerald Sherriff

Associate solicitor with TLT LLP

with additional comments
on tax from Steve Hasson
PricewaterhouseCoopers

Tottel
publishing

TOTTEL PUBLISHING LTD, MAXWELTON HOUSE, 41–43 BOLTRO ROAD, HAYWARDS HEATH, WEST SUSSEX, RH16 1BJ

© Tottel Publishing Ltd 2007

A CIP Catalogue record for this book is available from the British Library.

ISBN 13 978 1 84592 120 0

ISBN 10 1 84592 120 8

Typeset by Phoenix Photosetting, Chatham, Kent

Printed and bound in Great Britain by Antony Rowe, Chippenham, Wilts

Preface

Everyone is naturally concerned about expenses and costs. If a landlord spends money and wants to recover that money from the tenant by way of a service charge then both parties have an interest in ensuring that the arrangements are satisfactory. In a tough financial climate, service charges are important to both landlords and tenants, and the money involved can be substantial. This is perhaps reflected in the point that the majority of service charge cases are from the last three decades. It is, unfortunately, a topic with an in-built conflict, as the landlord wants to recover as much as possible and the tenant does not want to be over-charged. With high figures at stake, the parties are more disposed to litigate, and perhaps particularly so when financial times are hard.

I have tried to make this book the most comprehensive there is on the topic. It covers all legal and practical aspects of service charges, and has sections on rentcharges (which are usually for freeholds) and the commonhold equivalent of service charges in the form of the commonhold assessment. I have illustrated throughout the book the way the courts and tribunals treat service charge disputes. There seems lately, for example, to be a trend away from close interpretation of the words used (for leasehold service charges) and towards a more purposive interpretation.

This book includes all the elements discussed in my book *Service Charges in Leases*, published in 1989. The latter included comments on drafting and negotiating leases, and remedies for recovery. This book includes all that was covered in the earlier book and much additional material, as well as the major legislative changes and cases since that date. Extra items include a chapter on disposing of property affected by service charges (concentrating on suitable contractual provisions), the relationship between service charges and rent, and chapters on estate rentcharges and on commonhold assessment.

The review of statutory provisions affecting dwellings has been expanded and brought up to date to reflect the enormous changes over the last decade or so. The book also discusses the new right to manage introduced by the Commonhold and Leasehold Reform Act 2002. There is expanded information about public sector service charges and such matters as the position following exercise of the 'right to buy'. There are lots of new precedents, including precedents for enquiries and contract provisions, and rentcharge precedents as well as lease provisions.

As it is probably the most important aspect for many people advising on service charges, I have included separate chapters on maximising the service charge recovery and on challenging a service charge demand. These, to some extent, bring together information scattered throughout the book, but in view of the importance of these aspects it seems appropriate to give them each their own chapter.

One of the most important developments in service charges in the last decade or so is the introduction of codes of practice. The separate codes for commercial and for residential service charges are compared and contrasted in Chapter 11.

What of the future of service charges? I have pointed out that commercial leases are now often much shorter than they used to be, and I suppose that if commonhold becomes really successful (as I hope), then long leases of residential premises may become less frequent. The concerns tenants used to have over continuing liability after disposing of their leases is now largely ameliorated by the Landlord and Tenant (Covenants) Act 1995. If leases become very short (eg for three years) as is often the case in Europe, then it may be that landlords will choose to charge an inclusive rent and service charges will be immaterial. Even if there is such a trend, leasehold service charges will continue to be material for those cases where there are existing long leases, and also where tenants of commercial property require a longer lease so that they can use the premises for long enough to justify their outlay on fitting out etc. Some tenants prefer the comfort of longer leases, which are certainly preferred by funders. A short lease is poor security for a long-term loan. Accordingly, unless all leases become very short, it is hard to see leasehold service charges ceasing to be relevant.

After publication of the first book and various articles, I gave a number of lectures on the subject of service charges. I wish to express my thanks to my various fellow speakers, and also to those delegates who raised queries or comments on relevant points. It is slightly depressing that, however much one thinks one knows a topic, it is usually the case that, at a seminar, a few points arise which are new, or perhaps put a different slant on some aspect or other. In addition, I am grateful (now) to those members of the legal profession who have made novel amendments to draft leases which make one re-think the principles or details of what can often be a complicated arrangement. (At the time they seem to be a nuisance!)

I am grateful to Steve Hasson of PricewaterhouseCoopers for his review of tax aspects. It is an incredibly complicated topic, and I hope his clear analysis of the position will be useful to readers.

In addition, I should like to express my thanks to Tottel Publishing and my wife, Jancis, for their patience and help, and also my firm, TLT (incorporating the former Lawrence Jones), for their encouragement. Patience has been needed because publication has been delayed long beyond the intended date, as I have been awaiting publication of certain regulations needed under the Commonhold and Leasehold Reform Act 2002 (which received royal assent in May 2002). These are still not available, but the decision has been made to publish.

The law is believed to be accurate as at 1 July 2006.

Gerald Sherriff

Contents

Table of cases

N

O

Table of statutes

Note: The statutory provisions affecting service charges are discussed in Chapters 9 and 10. Paragraph numbers in bold are where the sections are primarily discussed.

Table of statutory instruments

CHAPTER 1

The origins of service charges

Why so large cost,
Having so short a lease,
Dost thou upon thy fading mansion spend?

William Shakespeare

WHAT ARE SERVICE CHARGES?

1.1   This book is not about the 10% which is added to your restaurant bill even when you ordered a baked potato and were given chips. Nor is it about indictments at a court martial. (And it is certainly not about stud fees!) What this book considers is charges for services made to tenants under provisions in leases. It also deals with service charges in commonholds, and rentcharges affecting freeholds.

1.2   The main definition used (for dwellings) is s 18 of the Landlord and Tenant Act 1985, but the better statutory definition of service charges is in s 87(8)(c) of the Leasehold Reform, Housing and Urban Development Act 1993. It reads:

'(c)   "Service charge" means an amount payable by a tenant … as part of or in addition to the rent –

   (i)   which is payable, directly or indirectly, for services, repairs, mainte- nance, improvements, or insurance or any relevant person's costs of management, and

   (ii)   the whole or part of which varies or may vary according to the costs or estimated costs incurred or to be incurred by any relevant person in connection with the matters mentioned in sub-paragraph (i).'

The words omitted near the start refer to a 'dwelling', but by deleting those words the definition applies equally to non-residential property. In s 87(8)(a) the 'relevant person' mentioned in the definition means 'any landlord [of residential property] or any person who discharges management functions in respect of such property, and for this purpose "management functions" includes functions with respect to the provision of services or the repair, maintenance, improvement or insurance of such property'. (The square brackets are added: for general pur- poses these words can be omitted.) The main terms of charge mentioned are thus services, repairs, maintenance, improvements, insurance and management costs. It will be seen later that service charges sometimes include items such as interest that would not strictly come within the statutory definition, but the main service charge items are as mentioned.

1

1.3   Service charges can be used where part of a building is let (such as an office in an office block, a shop in a shopping centre, or a flat in a block), or where the whole building is let. Although the above definition (which only affects dwellings) indicates that service charges can be 'part of the rent', this is unusual, except perhaps where they are reserved as rent. The definition also refers to insurance. Buildings insurance is subject to complex lease provisions normally covered by separate provisions in the documents (affecting such matters as reinstatement, insured risks, sometimes rights to determine, repayment of loss where damage is caused by the tenant, and so on).The cost of third party insurance and insurance of equipment used for the services and a few other similar items may sensibly be recovered through the service charge, but the author's preference is for the main buildings insurance to be left entirely separate from service charges where possible.

1.4   The above definition contemplates a tenant and property subject to a lease or leases, as well as services affecting the property. The service charge is a charge to enable the landlord to recover all or at least part of his costs for services relating to the premises.

FREEHOLD COMPARED TO LEASEHOLD

1.5   An owner/occupier of a freehold property (other than the owner of a commonhold unit) can carry out such repairs as he chooses (or can afford), or he can allow the property to fall into disrepair (subject to the requirements of any mortgage on the property and to certain statutory obligations affecting public health matters). In the case of other services, such as decoration, cleaning etc, the freeholder can have them done or not as he wishes – if he wants the benefit of the services and is prepared to pay for them he is the only person concerned. (There are exceptions where the freehold is sold subject to an obligation to contribute jointly with owners of nearby property to costs of common items (such as access roads) by way of an estate rentcharge or otherwise.) Rentcharges are discussed in Chapter 16. Commonhold units are held as freeholds and the repair aspects are mentioned in Chapter 17.

1.6   By contrast, where the property is leasehold there are at least two parties who are concerned, and the terms of the agreement between them (ie the lease or tenancy agreement, and occasionally statutory implied repairing obligations) are material. Nearly all such agreements contain express provisions as to repair, decoration, cleaning, etc. These are set out in the document to show whether what has to be done is to be done by the landlord or the tenant. If the landlord agrees to do work (eg maintenance of the structure, external decoration or lighting the halls) but wants to recover the cost from the tenant, he can either ensure that the rent is large enough to cover the estimated cost of the items in question, or alternatively charge a lower rent and recover the actual costs of the works separately by way of service charge provisions.

LEASEHOLD OBLIGATIONS

1.7   The agreement between landlord and tenant is usually a lease, although it can be a tenancy agreement or a licence. A lease or tenancy agreement gives a right for a tenant to occupy premises for a period subject (usually) to payment of a rent. A licence can have the same effect, although licences tend to be short-term arrangements which rarely contain full service charge provisions. (More common would be a licence at a licence fee of £X plus £Y per quarter as a fixed contribution towards costs for services. Occasionally licences require the licensee to repay to the licensor whatever the licensor pays by way of service charges to his landlord, apportioned for the period of the licence. The term 'tenancy agreement' is normally only used for residential property whereas a lease can be for either residential or commercial property. Many people think of a lease as a more important or longer-term arrangement, although tenancies can continue for many years and a lease can be for a short period. In either case the obligations of the landlord and the tenant continue throughout the term, and (as will be shown later) both the landlord and the tenant can have a liability extending after they dispose of their respective interests.

STATUTORY MATTERS

1.8   The obligations of the parties differ from lease to lease, although there are some statutory provisions that can affect the written terms. For commercial properties there are no specific statutory provisions relating to service charges, other than limitations on recovery of arrears of service charge under the Landlord and Tenant (Covenants) Act 1995. In the case of residential premises there are numerous statutory provisions. Those specifically affecting service charges are considered in Chapters 9 and 10.

1.9   A significant statutory provision affecting leases of residential premises is the provision that for such property let for a term of less than seven years there is a specific repairing obligation on the landlord. (Landlord and Tenant Act 1985, s 11 et seq.) (This covers main structural matters and also plant. Where the section applies a provision seeking to make the tenant repair the items covered by the section, or to pay the cost of them, is of no effect (s 11(4) and (6)) unless the parties obtain a court order to contract out of the obligation (s 12).)

TIMESHARE

1.10   Timeshare is not specifically referred to in this book. As far the author is aware, there are no specific statutory provisions directly affecting service charges for timeshare premises. There have been suggestions that the European Union will introduce regulations on matters that must be disclosed in contracts for purchase of timeshares, and these will include (inter alia) details of the services the vendor/landlord will be providing, and the principles under which maintenance, repairs and management will be arranged. Subject to these proposed matters, the author is not aware of any body of statute law specifically governing service charges for timeshares, as service charges are not covered by the Timeshares Act 1992. However, there seems no reason why the principles examined elsewhere in this book should not apply to services provided in respect of timeshare premises. Since most timeshares are residential premises presumably the statutory obligations outlined in Chapters 9 and 10 will be material, although only when the law applicable is that of England. (Value added tax in relation to timeshare service charges was discussed in *Clowance Holdings Ltd v Customs and Excise* (No 17289) LTL 19/9/2001, and in *Clowance Owners Club Ltd v Customs & Excise Comrs* (2004) V & D Tr (London) 8/10/04.)

HISTORICAL

1.11   There are differing views on this, but a history of service charges is as set out here. Most early leases were drawn so as to enable the landlord to receive a rent which was intended to cover the cost of any work that the landlord had to do as well as an element of profit. This was, for example, common in the Victorian days of long rows of terraced houses let on payment of a weekly sum. The profit repaid the landlord for the cost of building the houses (or buying them) over a long period.

1.12   Some of the early leases (although by no means all) included a provision that, in addition to rent, the tenant would repay to the landlord the cost of repair of items, such as party walls or party drains, which were used in common by the landlord's property and adjoining properties. These provisions were put in because they covered the type of expense that the freeholder would have had to pay if he was in occupation, and the clause made it clear that when such expense arose the financial burden would be on the tenant and not the landlord.

1.13   The 'items used in common' provisions mentioned in the previous paragraph were intended to act as a cushion to the landlord, but were (and still are) relatively rarely implemented. The change to proper service charge provisions arose to cover the costs which the landlord incurred in respect of works etc. to the landlord's own property which he carried out for the benefit of the tenant, and sometimes for other tenants of his as well.

1.14   Particularly after the First World War, building techniques improved and developers were able to build blocks of flats rising many stories. In earlier times (eg the Georgian period), tall buildings had been built in terraces, in places such as Bath, but these were intended to be grand houses for the occupation of a single family, rather than initially being divided into series of units of accommodation. The builders of the 1920s and 1930s were not so content as the Victorians had been to allow the cost of buildings to be repaid over a long period. They used the method of letting properties on long leases at a low rent and on payment of a premium. The premium helped repay the building costs (or the amount borrowed to enable the building to be built) and gave the landlord his profit. The rent was often a nominal amount, but as the building had common areas that needed maintenance, decoration, cleaning, gardening etc, the tenant was called on to pay a contribution to the costs of those matters. This additional sum, of course, was the service charge.

1.15 The first of such leases provided for the tenant to repay the landlord after the work had been done. Later, landlords started to seek payment in advance, usually on the basis that there would be an adjustment at the end of the year when the precise figures were known. This is now the normal arrangement.

1.16 Service charge provisions over the years began to cover more and more expenses that the landlord might have to pay. This partly followed buildings becoming more complex. For example, the early blocks of flats did not have communal heating systems, but now this is common, and in the case of modern offices and shops the equipment can include lifts, air conditioning or climate control, escalators, security and other highly technical aids.

1.17 Leases now are often drawn in an attempt to enable the landlord not to have to use any rent towards the cost of repair or other services. Such a lease is called a 'clear lease'. For obvious reasons these types of lease are preferred by the institutions who lend money to landlords: they can calculate the return on their investment in the knowledge that (subject to periods when there are no tenants or where the tenants default) the income will be that represented by the rents payable (a known figure) without deductions of fluctuating amounts for repairs or other services.

1.18 Service charges are not common abroad. Foreign leases are frequently of a much shorter length than that common in the United Kingdom. (At some point there will probably be a European Union Directive seeking to harmonise property, although what a 'Eurolease' might have to contain boggles the mind! In Australia (strata title) and America (condominiums) premises are held on systems somewhat similar to commonhold. As these are using areas in common they have service charges. Some in America are called Camcharges – common area maintenance charges.)

MODERN USE OF SERVICE CHARGES

1.19 There are four common types of property where the landlord carries out services for which he seeks to recover costs. They are:

(a) blocks of flats or other buildings divided into a number of dwellings;

(b) shopping areas, whether a small parade or a shopping complex on a number of floors, or a set of retail warehouses;

(c) offices in a building; and

(d)   industrial estates where there are factory or warehouse units and computer technology parks.

1.20   Quite often some of the above are combined, for example in a parade of shops with living accommodation or offices (or both) over the shops.

ESTATE RENTCHARGES

1.21   The above examples are mentioned in relation to service charges in leases. In the case of freeholds it is possible to recover costs of maintenance of items used in common, through what is called an estate rentcharge. This is largely on the same lines as a leasehold service charge but is payable out of freehold properties and tends to cover a much smaller range of works and services than the modern service charge lease provisions. The use of estate rentcharges mostly seen by the author is for industrial units where the purchasers of individual factories on an industrial park enter into an agreement to cover the cost of common services. In particular, the services include the maintenance of the roadway leading to the units, common service yards, unadopted drainage systems, refuse disposal compactors or equipment, and the landscaped areas. A similar arrangement is also used sometimes for retail parks where large retail units are sold as freeholds with an estate rentcharge covering the costs of maintenance of the access roads and car parks and drains. An estate rentcharge is used because it is difficult to enforce positive covenants (such as to carry out repairs or pay for repairs) against successors in title of freeholders. The rentcharge is created as a charge on the property (like a mortgage) to secure the recovery of the payments for the services, and is enforceable against successors in title. (The scheme is referred to in Chapter 16.) Most of the comments in this book are directed towards leasehold service charges, but many of the principles and cases should provide guidance for estate rentcharges.

COMMONHOLD

1.22   Commonhold is a system under which several parcels of land are held in common. The parts are called units and whatever is not within the definition of a unit is common parts. The freehold interest in the units is held by unit-holders, and the freehold of the common parts is held by the Commonhold Association (which is owned by the unit-holders). The commonhold scheme requires unit-holders to pay a 'commonhold assessment,' which has similarities but it is not the same as leasehold service charges. The scheme for commonhold service charges is discussed in Chapter 17.

MODERN SERVICE CHARGES

1.23   Since the early days, service charges have become more common and more sophisticated. In an attempt to cover all the services and permutations of works and accounting involved in service charges leases have become physically bigger.

> 'Most lawyers start with precedents, then add what is needed for the particular transaction ... Lawyers are better at addition than subtraction.' (National Consumer Council *Plain English for Lawyers*)

The provisions frequently occupy a very substantial portion of the lease itself, and the amount payable is always a major concern of tenants.

1.24   The tenants are very conscious that the lease creates a right for the landlord to spend other people's money (the tenants' money) on his (the landlord's) property. Because of the scope for conflict between landlord and tenant the service charge provisions need careful handling. There are a few general principles that can be discerned, which are set out in Chapter 2, but each service charge has to be interpreted from the words used in the lease itself (or the document creating the rentcharge: in the case of the commonhold assessment the relevant document is the Commonhold Community Statement, although it does not set out details in the same way as a lease or rentcharge deed would do – see Chapter 17) and thus there is a great onus on the landlord (who drafts the lease) and the first tenant (who negotiates the terms) or on the original parties to the rentcharge arrangement to get the balance between the parties as fair as possible, while accepting that the service charge provisions are included to enable the landlord to recover some or (more often) all of his costs. There is little scope for negotiating the terms of commonhold service charges, as the commonhold is registered at HM Land Registry as a whole, and units are sold as registered titles, with all the rights and obligations in place.

CHAPTER 2

General principles and elements

You will never find an Englishman in the wrong. He does everything on principle. He fights you on patriotic principles; he robs you on business principles; he enslaves you on imperial principles.

George Bernard Shaw

GENERAL PRINCIPLES

2.1 There seem to be three general principles of service charges as follows:

1. The lease terms are paramount.

2. There is considerable statutory interference with residential lease arrangements.

3. Reasonableness.

The principles are examined below.

Principle I – The lease terms are paramount

2.2 The terms of the contract between landlord and tenant are those set out in the lease. There can also be material provisions in Deeds of Variation, licences, separate waivers etc. References to 'lease' in this book refer to all such material documents collectively. The basic rule of leasehold law is that (subject to statutory matters) the only factors which affect the parties are those set out in the document. Relating that to service charges results in the clear position that the landlord can only recover costs for works or services:

(a) if they are shown in the lease to be matters for which the landlord is entitled to be reimbursed; and

(b) if the lease makes it clear that it is the tenant who is obliged to pay; and

(c) where the actual charge required by the landlord is shown to be the correct proportion payable; and

(d) the landlord can show he has complied with any preconditions to recovery contained in the lease.

The principle has been beautifully expressed in the following terms:

'The landlord seeks to recover money from the tenant. On ordinary principles there must be clear terms, in the contractual provisions to enable him to do so. The lease, moreover, was drafted by the landlord. It falls to be construed contra proferentem.'

2.3   The obligation of the tenant is to pay the correct amount. Accordingly, the landlord (and presumably the tenant) can seek to recover moneys which by mistake were not claimed (or were overpaid), even in the case of a landlord who demanded money on an incorrect basis (the wrong rateable value figure) for several years. See *Universities Superannuation Fund Scheme Ltd v Marks & Spencer Ltd* [1999] 04 EG 158, discussed at **4.6**. A House of Lords case in the previous year had held that money paid under mistake could be recovered, whether the mistake was of fact or of law: *Kleinwort Benson Ltd v Lincoln City Council* [1999] 2 AC 349. Previously, money paid under a mistake of law was not recoverable, but the distinction between a mistake of law and a mistake of fact was hard to identify. There are a number of aspects of this critical principle illustrated below.

THE RENT IS INCLUSIVE EXCEPT FOR PROPER SERVICE CHARGE COSTS

2.4   The landlord cannot require the tenant to pay sums in addition to the rent unless the lease makes such an obligation absolutely clear. The rent is deemed to be inclusive and thus all the sums that a landlord might incur in relation to the premises are payable by the landlord without a right to recover from the tenant unless the lease provides otherwise. If the landlord cannot bring the costs in question within the lease provisions he cannot recover them.

2.5   For example, in *Riverlate Properties Ltd v Paul* [1975] Ch 133, the landlord covenanted in the lease to carry out various works described in clauses 6(a), (b), (c) and (d). The tenant covenanted to pay towards the costs of the works described in clauses 6(b), (c) and (d), thus not including the costs of external repair which was the subject of clause 6(a). The landlord was not entitled to rectification of the lease to enable it to charge for costs under 6(a). There was evidence that the tenant had understood, before the lease was completed, that she would not be responsible for contributing to the cost of external repair, and the landlord was not entitled to rectification to change the agreed terms of the lease. (It may help to remember this as the Hamlet case – '2(b) or not 2(b)'!) For a more recent case where rectification was also refused, see *Church Commissioners for England v Metroland Ltd* [1996] EGCS 44. The latter related to a case where the centre, of which the buildings were part, had been changed since the original conception.

2.6   Other examples of cases where a landlord could not recover because the lease did not specify the items in question are mentioned elsewhere in this book, but these include:

(a)   repair of a parapet: *Rapid Results College Ltd v Angell* [1986] 1 EGLR 53 (see **2.9** below);

(b)   replacement of windows: *Mullaney v Maybourne Grange (Croydon) Management Ltd* [1986] 1 EGLR 70 (see **5.206** below);

(c)   bank interest: *Frobisher (Second Investments) Ltd v Killoran Trust Co Ltd* [1980] 1 All ER 488 (see **3.88** below) and *Boldmark Ltd v Cohen* (1985) 19 HLR 136.

2.7   A useful example of the general principle came to court in 1988. A land-lord owned a block of flats with its surrounding grounds. It granted rights to use the roads and parking spaces, but without including provisions for recovery of service charges for maintenance of those roadways and parking areas. Subsequently, the reversion was split, with the grounds transferred to someone other than the landlord of the flats. The (new) landlord of the roads tried to impose charges for parking, but the tenants obtained a declaration that they were entitled to park freely. The tenants had been granted rights to park and use the roads in their leases: there was no express provision entitling the landlord to charge, and no right to charge would be implied. (See *Papworth v Linthaven* [1988] EGCS 54.) A more recent example is *Earl of Cadogan v 27/29 Sloane Gardens Ltd* [2006] 24 EG 178. This was a Lands Tribunal hearing from a lease-hold valuation application and was simply on interpretation. The judge said that the words in dispute (relating to the intermediate landlord's right to charge a notional rent for a caretaker's flat) were clear and must apply. There was no scope for seeking to imply contra proferentem. The interpretation was relevant for value on enfranchisement.

NO IMPLIED FULL RECOVERY

2.8   Perhaps a different way of making the same, vital, point is that where there are service charge provisions in a lease, the mere presence of such provi-sions is not enough to imply that the landlord is entitled to recover the whole of his expenditure.

2.9   A specific example where the point was raised in court was *Rapid Results College Ltd v Angell* [1986] 1 EGLR 53. This is the author's favourite service charge case. The dispute revolved around the need to repair the parapet of commercial premises. The latter was constructed on top of some of the exter-nal walls, although the building extended backwards at a lower level where there was no parapet. The word 'parapet' was not mentioned in the lease. The landlord tried unsuccessfully to claim from the tenant of the second floor part of the cost of repairs to the parapet. The lease permitted the landlord to recover 50% of certain costs incurred by the landlord in respect of the premises on the first and second floors, including 'maintenance of the exterior'. The tenant was also liable for 25% of expenses for 'all other parts of the building ... of which the tenants have the use in common ...' with other tenants. The Court of Appeal, agreeing with the court below, would not accept that either of these provisions entitled the landlord to recover. The parapet was neither part of the exterior, nor was it part of the building used in common. In the lower court, as a third point, the landlord had sought to raise a presumption that, regardless of the actual wording of the lease, the clear intention was to enable the landlord to recover a proportion of any expenditure he had incurred in respect of the building. This was evidently rejected in the lower court and not pursued in the Court of Appeal. In the result the landlord failed to recover. (Having seen the property, the author considers that the landlord was very unlucky to lose, but remember that the key point was that the word 'parapet' was not in the lease.)

2.10   More recently, in *Postel Properties Ltd v Boots the Chemist Ltd* [1996] 2 EGLR 60, there was a dispute about service charges running to £1.6m. There were a number of items in dispute, but the court held that the landlord could not recover a sum of £22,000 in respect of one item which was not properly chargeable under the lease, even though, in the context, it might be considered to be de minimis. Either a sum is properly chargeable or it is not.

Principle 2 – Beware statutory interference

2.11   Until a few years ago, it was possible to say that there was no statutory provision directly affecting service charges in relation to commercial premises, but that there is an enormous amount of legislation affecting service charges in the residential sector. This refers to statutory provisions directly relating to service charges. Many statutory provisions affect what can or cannot be done to a property and thus may indirectly affect service charges. In Chapter 5 a common service charge provision is discussed under which a charge can be made for complying with statutory obligations. One can no longer be so sweeping, because the Landlord and Tenant (Covenants) Act 1995 now provides in s 17 that service charges cannot be recovered from former tenants without serving notice on the former tenants, and even then there is a time limit. (See **9.9** et seq.) This provision affects all leases, whether of commercial or domestic premises.

2.12   There is a huge body of legislation which affects service charges for residential property. It is discussed in detail in Chapters 9 and 10. The provisions are so significant that if the author is ever asked to advise on a service charge matter, the first question has to be 'are the premises commercial or residential?' If they are commercial the terms of the lease are paramount, but if they are residential then care is needed to ensure that the landlord has complied with all the necessary hurdles to enable recovery, as well as reviewing the lease terms.

2.13   The statutory provisions cover such important matters as a statutory implication of reasonableness in three respects, an obligation on the landlord to consult with the tenant in respect of items where there are significant cost implications for the tenant, a trust imposed on money paid by a tenant towards service charges, and there is to be an obligation to hold that money in a special type of account. The parties cannot contract out of these provisions. In very brief terms, it is worth commenting that in all the vast panoply of material legislation there are virtually no provisions for the benefit of a landlord at all (the limited exceptions are set out at **9.5**) - the provisions are for the protection of tenants.

Principle 3 – Reasonableness

2.14   In the case of leases of dwellings which contain service charges s 19 of the Landlord and Tenant Act 1985 implies various aspects of reasonableness. (This section is discussed more fully at **9.38** et seq.) There has, however, for three decades been held to be a general implication of reasonableness affecting service charges which applies to all types of lease following the Court of Appeal decision in *Finchbourne Ltd v Rodrigues* [1976] 3 All ER 581, although, as indicated later, *Finchbourne* has not always been applied by courts in respect of the amount payable by a tenant.

2.15   In the *Finchbourne* case the Court of Appeal made it clear that the total costs to be charged to the tenant by the landlord must be no more than is reasonable. In the words of Lord Cairns, who gave the leading judgment, and with whom the other two judges agreed: 'It cannot be supposed that the [landlords] were entitled to be as extravagant as they chose in the standards of repair, the appointment of porters etc ... the parties cannot have intended that the landlords should have an unfettered discretion to adopt the highest conceivable standard and to be able to charge the tenant with it.' Two out of the three judges specifically said that there should be implied in the lease a provision that the costs charged must be 'fair and reasonable'. The third judge agreed.

2.16   A 1994 first instance decision specifically referred to the *Finchbourne* decision in a way that suggests it may be less all-embracing than had previously been thought. In *Havenridge Ltd v Boston Dyers Ltd* [1994] 2 EGLR 73, the main judgment cited various passages from *Finchbourne*, but the court failed to apply it so as to reduce high insurance premiums. In the *Havenridge* case the tenants of commercial premises in Leicester were liable to pay insurance premiums 'properly' payable for insurance for specific risks through a reputable insurer. The cost charged by the landlord was £14,000 but the tenant said it could be as little as £3,000. Applying the earlier decision (also specifically on insurance premiums) in *Bandar Property Holdings Ltd v JS Darwen (Successors) Ltd* [1968] 2 All ER 305 (which was decided before *Finchbourne*) the court in *Havenridge* would not imply the word 'reasonable' in the obligation as regards the cost of the insurance, and said that provided the insurance complied with the landlord's obligations (ie, it was with an office of repute, was for the correct risks etc), it was 'properly' chargeable, and the court would not reduce the cost. The cost paid by the landlord would be 'properly' paid provided it was agreed in arm's-length negotiations, in the ordinary course of business, and where there were no special factors.

It could be said that *Havenridge* turned on the meaning of the word 'proper', and therefore was a decision on a different point, but a concern is that although *Finchbourne* was referred to the court it would not imply reasonableness to reduce the cost to the tenant. (This is perhaps another example of Principle 1, that the words of the lease are the crucial factor, but in *Havenridge* reasonableness was effectively ruled out in relation to cost.)

2.17   While the *Finchbourne* case held that a provision should be implied that the costs to be claimed by the landlord are to be 'fair and reasonable', that case did not address the question of the proportion paid by the tenant. However:

(a)   the amount paid by the tenant must be a proportion of a sum which should be fair and reasonable; and

(b)   the lease will provide what proportion the tenant is to pay: if it is a fixed percentage then the tenant has to pay a fixed percentage of a reasonable total. If the tenant has to pay a 'fair proportion' (or similar wording) of the costs then (a) the total costs have to be reasonable and (b) the tenant has the opportunity of challenging whether the percentage he is being charged is a 'fair proportion'.'

2.18   In 1997 the Court of Appeal again considered reasonableness in a residential case, *Berrycroft Management Co Ltd v Sinclair Gardens Investments (Kensington) Ltd* (1996) 75 P & CR 210. The main point was somewhat similar to *Havenridge*, in that the issue was the cost of insurance premiums. Here, instead of a simple complaint about the amount the landlord of some blocks of flats charged, the case was that the landlord put the liability to insure on the management company but the insurance was to be with such insurers as the landlord directed. Following a change of landlord the new landlord required the management company to insure through nominated insurers (as it was entitled to do under the lease terms). The new insurance was much more expensive and the tenants objected. Bedlam LJ, giving the sole judgment, considered the *Finchbourne* and *Bandar* cases but refused to imply any term of reasonableness. He said the management company and tenants were 'protected by the qualification that the insurance office must be of repute'. The property being residential the judge also considered s 19 of the Landlord and Tenant Act 1985, implying reasonableness. He said 'in so far as the insurance charges are incurred by the tenant as part of the service charge, they would not, in my view, be regarded as incurred by or on behalf of the landlord and therefore not "relevant costs"' within the Act.

2.19   Section 19(1) and (2) of the Landlord and Tenant Act 1985 deal with reasonableness in respect of dwellings from three aspects:

(a)   the costs of the works must be reasonable;

(b)   the standard of work must be reasonable; and

(c)   advance payments requested from the tenants must be no more than is reasonable.

It is only the first aspect that is addressed in the *Finchbourne* and *Berrycroft* cases, and thus only that part that can be said to be a principle reflected in cases.

It is, however, probably fair to say that the second and third limbs (standard of work, and amount of advance payments) are matters that a dissatisfied tenant of commercial property could raise as part of an objection to a charge made by a landlord, if a tenant considered either of these matters were material to the amount he was asked to pay.

2.20   Both *Havenridge* and *Berrycroft* (one commercial and one residential) had some qualification in the lease – in the one case the costs had to be '*properly*' incurred and in the other insurance had to be in an office of repute. It is hard to see how these decisions fit any implication of reasonableness and so the analysis must be as follows:

(a)   Where the lease contains some qualifying words the court will treat these as representing the bargain (ie Principle 1 above). In such cases the courts will not imply reasonableness in addition.

(b)   If the lease contains no qualifying wording then presumably the courts would feel able to imply reasonableness under *Finchbourne*. If reasonableness is to be implied in those circumstances it would seem to be implied not in relation to the cost (which seems consistently to have been rejected as a consequence of the implication), but to some other aspect such as the actions of the landlord. Perhaps it would work this way: if it is reasonable for the landlord to replace the roof he can do so and can charge; if it is not reasonable for the landlord to replace the roof then he cannot charge for it.

2.21   The above interpretation is based on the fact that the courts seem reluctant to imply reasonableness to the amount charged by the landlord despite *Finchbourne* and s 19 of the 1985 Act. It is hard to see that this interpretation reflects the *Finchbourne* case or s 19 as both seem to relate to actual cost rather than carrying out the works, but it is an author's job to try to reflect the way he sees a significant aspect of the subject. Two decisions at the turn of the century have suggested that a further aspect of reasonableness could be the length of the term. (See Chapter 5 discussing *Scottish Mutual Assurance plc v Jardine Public Relations Ltd* [1999] EGCS 43 (**5.41** below) and *Fluor Daniel Properties Ltd v Shortlands Investments Ltd* [2001] EGCS 8 (**5.134**). Chapter 9 discusses cases under s 19 of the 1985 Act at **9.45** et seq.)

MISREPRESENTATION

2.22   A misleading statement as to the amount of probable service charge liability can entitle a purchaser to damages for misrepresentation. (See *Heinemann v Cooper* (1987) 19 HLR 262.) The purchaser of a recently refurbished flat in London paid £77,500 for the lease. He had been told that the initial service charge liability was likely to be in the region of £250 to £350 per year. The figure turned out to be nearer £625 per year. The landlord tried to argue that there was no diminution in value of the leasehold interest as a result of the misrepresentation, but the Court of Appeal accepted the realistic view that a prospective tenant would be likely to pay less for the lease if the cost of services was higher. The purchaser was awarded damages of £3,000 representing the difference between the value of the property with a service charge of £625 pa and the value if the service charge had been only £250.

2.23   Under the Property Misdescription Act 1991, s 1(1) it is a criminal offence to make 'a misleading statement about a prescribed matter in the course of an estate agency business or a property development business.' Under the Property Misdescription (Specified Matters) Order 1992 one of the 'prescribed matters' is – '22 Amount of any service or maintenance charge or liability for common repairs.'

2.24   Although the author is not aware of any case on the point other than the *Heinemann* case there seems little reason to doubt that where there is a duty of care owed by one person to another a misrepresentation as to the level of service charges, and perhaps as to the extent of the works intended to be carried out by the landlord in the near future, can give rise to a claim for misrepresentation. In the case of a contract for sale this could presumably entitle the party to whom the representation is made to rescind the contract in the case of a deliberate misrepresentation, or as an alternative to seek damages in the case of an innocent misrepresentation. (Misrepresentation Act 1967, ss 77 and 88.)

2.25   Where a landlord claimed forfeiture on the basis of non-payment of rent and service charge, the tenants obtained relief from forfeiture when it appeared that the landlord seemed to be plucking figures from the air rather than supporting his claim with facts and evidence. The tenants not only obtained relief, but also were awarded most of their costs (see *Woodtrek Ltd v Jezek* (1981) 261 EG 571, which was a residential case).

Elements of service charges

2.26   This part of this chapter is intended to indicate the general pattern of provisions in leases which set out the service charge scheme.

THE MATTERS USUALLY COVERED

2.27   The service charge provisions are usually drawn to cover the following aspects:

(a) details of the services which the landlord is to provide, and an obligation on the landlord to carry them out, often coupled with a disclaimer if the landlord fails to carry out the services;

(b) details of those services for which the tenant is to contribute (if this is other than the whole of the services which the landlord provides);

(c) the way in which the tenant is required to pay for the landlord's services (eg whether it is quarterly in advance or half yearly in arrear), and whether the service charge is reserved as rent or not;

(d) the proportion of the total costs the tenant is to pay (eg either '4.25%' or 'a fair proportion');

(e) how the adjustment at the year end is to be calculated (ie who is to work it out, and what certificate or other evidence is to be given to the tenant, and, if a certificate is needed, who is to give it);

(f) whether the year end adjustment is to be effected by carrying forward any amount paid in excess of the actual sum needed, or by payment of the difference by one party to the other;

(g) the details of any reserve or sinking fund, and the provisions applicable to such fund; and

(h) what disputes procedure there is to be (if any).

WHERE DO THE PROVISIONS APPEAR?

2.28   When trying to review service charge obligations the reader needs to look at the whole lease. There are quite a few places in a lease where service charges are mentioned or which may be material to interpretation. In addition, there may be relevant provisions in Deeds of Variation, or Licences, or in waivers given by the landlord to the tenants by deed or side letter.

2.29   The normal parts of the lease which contain relevant provisions (and which may be affected by Deeds of Variation etc) are:

(a) The main service charge provisions and the services to be performed tend to appear in a special schedule. This is obviously the most important part.

(b) The definitions are crucial, as indicated later, both in respect of the services to be performed and the property over which services are to be performed, as well as enabling the tenant clearly to identify what is let to him and what he is responsible for. There is often a definitions section, which will include a definition of common parts under some name or other, as well as other definitions material for interpretation.

(c) Covenants are important. The tenant will covenant to pay and the landlord should covenant to carry out the services for which the charges are to be made.

(d) The reddendum, where the rent is reserved, can be material to see if the service charge is reserved as rent, although (as will be mentioned later) this may appear from other indications in the lease.

(e) The declarations in a lease often contain provisions seeking to qualify the landlord's liability to provide the services (eg where non-performance is

17

because of reasons beyond the landlord's control). There can also be other declarations such as the intention of the service charge provisions (which may appear with other declarations or in the service charge schedule), and provisions entitling the landlord to vary or reduce or alter the services.

Different approaches

2.30   One highly respected speaker on service charge matters (John Samson, partner in Nabarro Nathanson) suggests (quite correctly) that one can divide service charges into three categories:

(a)   *Narrow range* This is where the service charge is for recovery of a limited spectrum of costs – eg only cleaning and lighting common parts.

(b)   *Standard range* This is the most common service charge (certainly for commercial premises and long leases of residential property) and is the one where the landlord seeks to recover all his costs of actual services from the tenants (ie the 'clear lease'). In reality recovery in such cases is, of course, less than full where some of the premises are vacant.

(c)   *Extended range* This is where the service charge goes beyond reimbursement of normal services and maintenance etc, and includes additional items such as promotional costs and/or improvements. Promotional items can be said to be a service for the benefit of the tenants but they are not essential for the premises. Improvements are generally thought of as capital items, whereas service charges normally relate to income (revenue) expenses.

These items are discussed later.

2.31   This does seem to be a useful analysis. It will not be relied on elsewhere in this book, but is mentioned as a thoughtful evaluation of the major types of service charge.

2.32   In an article about a survey by Loughborough University Business School (*Estates Gazette* 12 November 2005), Dr John R Calvert suggests that service charges, as operated in practice, are not 'joined up' because service charges are:

(a)   described by lawyers drawing up the lease;

(b)   incurred by building managers;

(c)   paid for by accountants; and

(d)   allocated to tenants by managing agents.

This has an element of truth in some (mostly commercial) cases, and is included as another analysis of the process.

Avoiding the use of service charges

2.33   Landlords and those lending money to landlords tend to prefer a regular and consistent income stream. This is obviously easier to achieve with a fixed rent and a service charge. If the rent is inclusive of the cost of services, the net annual income the landlord receives will vary from year to year, depending on the cost of the works and services which the landlord carries out.

2.34   A landlord can prepare his lease without a service charge at all. He would then charge a higher rent to reflect the lack of direct recovery of the costs of works and services, but all the service charge difficulties and general hassle highlighted in these pages would be immaterial. Inevitably there are some problems with such an arrangement:

(a)   A landlord would normally base an inclusive rent on the rent proper plus an allowance for anticipated expenditure. It is difficult to assess the probable costs accurately one year ahead and even more so for subsequent years. Consequently, the inclusive rent figure is likely to represent the rent proper plus an estimated figure for the cost of works and services plus a contingency figure in case the assessment of costs is insufficient. The longer the lease the higher the contingency figure may be. It will be appreciated that in such a case the tenant will always pay the contingency figure whether any contingency arises or not. In the case of a service charge lease the tenant will pay the rent and the estimated service charges (which will often include a contingency element), but if no contingency arises the tenant will not have to pay for it, and will be entitled to an adjustment at the end of the year. (It is perhaps fair to say that if there is a service charge dispute then there may be costs arising from that dispute.)

(b)   The landlord is taxed on rents. If the rent is £X plus a service charge then the landlord will pay less tax than if the rent is taxed on £Z, the inclusive figure. With an inclusive rent the landlord has to pay tax on the higher figure (£Z rather than £X) but the costs of services which the landlord has to set against that income are the same in each case.

(c)   One may conclude from the above that the landlord always pays more and the tenant usually pays more where the rent is inclusive, rather than the lease being at a rent and a service charge.

CHAPTER 3

Drafting and negotiating service charge provisions

Which of us ... is to do the hard and dirty work for the rest – and for what
pay? Who is to do the pleasant and clean work, and for what pay?

John Ruskin

THE PROBLEM

3.1   Service charges, being variable amounts which the landlord requires
the tenant to pay, inevitably have the potential to cause friction. The landlord
wishes to be reimbursed by the tenants (usually) all that he pays out towards
maintenance etc of the development, and the tenants are concerned not to
give the landlord a blank cheque for each year of the lease. There is scope
for a fraudulent landlord to make a profit by a lease drawn too widely in his
favour, and, while tenants usually accept that they will be required to pay
towards the upkeep of buildings and the facilities properly provided, they are
wary of allowing the landlord too much latitude. Negotiators have to achieve
a balance to enable the recovery of reasonable and legitimate expenses on the
one hand, while excluding unreasonable items or excessive claims on the
other hand.

3.2   It would be good to be able to provide the perfect service charge precedent. The reality is that each lease needs to be a tailored document, designed for
the particular premises and transaction concerned. While most solicitors have
several standard leases stored (and hopefully updated regularly) on word processing systems, such standard leases should be the basis only of a draft, and
should always be adapted to the actual circumstances. To any landlord who says
that this takes more time and costs more in fees, the solicitor should be able to
say that getting the lease right is the key to preventing potentially costly disputes
throughout the length of the term, and should aid maximum service charge
recovery from all the tenants over the years.

DRAFTING

3.3   This chapter comments on some important general aspects of drafting
the service charge provisions in leases, as well as giving some tips to landlords
and tenants. These include comments on service charges in relation to lease
renewals. Drafting aspects issues of estate rentcharges and commonhold are
covered in the chapters relating to those topics. In the next chapter are comments

21

about the mechanics of accounting, and Chapters 5 and 6 cover specific services and other items which appear in the lease and affect service charges.

3.4   The lease is invariably drafted by the landlord's solicitors. This is because it is an agreement under which the landlord is permitting someone else to occupy the property of the landlord. In addition, and at least as importantly, the landlord has details of the rights and obligations that affect the property, and the lease needs to take account of these. The other reason why the landlord drafts the lease is because any arrangement which provides for repair and works or services to other property owned by the landlord has to be reasonably consistent for all the tenants of the landlord who are subject to similar obligations. If the system is inconsistent management becomes more difficult and therefore of course more expensive. The point can be illustrated easily in the case of service charges. If one part of the landlord's property is subject to a service charge where the tenant pays a fixed percentage and another part is subject to payment of 'a fair proportion' of the costs there is a risk that the landlord would charge the tenants between them, for example either 110% or 90% of the actual costs. Neither is illegal, but it would not be sensible or reasonable for the landlord or the tenants.

3.5   Another aspect is the collection system: it would be uneconomic and far from sensible for some leases to provide that the service charge year is from 1 January where others say it is from 25 March, or where some tenants pay half yearly in arrear and others quarterly in advance. As a negotiating point it is worth the landlord pointing out that variations to the service charge system will inevitably result in extra administration costs which will be payable by all of the tenants.

INSPECT WHERE POSSIBLE

3.6   It is not always practical, but it is well worthwhile, to inspect the premises before drafting the lease, where possible. An inspection can bring to mind matters that should be specifically mentioned, and may not be obvious, even from architects' drawings.

3.7   Look at the outside of a building. There can be numerous features. For example, there could be a flagpole, a statue, a clock, a canopy, a safety ladder, a parapet, guard rails, a security camera, a balcony, a satellite dish and a burglar alarm. All these items may need repair, maintenance, replacement or decoration. If the items which can be seen are mentioned specifically in the lease then the landlord should be able to recover the reasonable costs of maintenance etc (within the terms of the lease): if not, he may be unable to do so. (Remember the parapet! – *Rapid Results College Ltd v Angell* [1986] 1 EGLR 53, see **2.9** above.)

3.8   A block of flats may, for example, have a swimming pool (which will usually have a pump and a filter and possibly a cover), or a tennis court (with repairs of tennis nets and the surrounding netting, the surface, and marking out to be considered), as well as security gates, and various outbuildings. The pool and courts may well need maintenance under a maintenance contract.

3.9   The above are all features that can be seen from outside a building. They are mentioned to illustrate some matters that may need to be considered and, if possible, specifically mentioned in the lease. Inspection of the property could reveal other matters that need special mention. In addition, it helps other aspects of drafting the lease to show:

(a)   how the different parts of the property can be divided up (ie exactly which parts of the property should be included in the demise);

(b)   what rights are needed (eg access); and

(c)   what type of construction has been used, and therefore what type of repair or decoration is necessary. (Obviously, if the only external part of a shop let by a lease is an aluminium shop front a covenant to decorate the shop front 'with three coats of good quality paint' is totally unsuitable).

AGREE THE SCHEME WITH THE LANDLORD AND HIS AGENTS

3.10   Solicitors usually have standard forms that set out a particular type of service charge recovery scheme. These usually require estimates of the anticipated cost for the year; payment quarterly in advance on the usual quarter days; certificates from the landlord's agents of actual cost at the year end, and carrying forward of any amount overpaid. However, this standard arrangement may not suit the agents who are going to manage the property, or the landlord. They may prefer half yearly payments on 1 January and 1 July, or refunds of overpayments, and they may well have their own scheme for the accounting aspects. The landlord may want the accounting year to be the same as his own financial year. The lease must fit the proposed arrangement; do not make the arrangements fit a standard document.

3.11   Ideally, the arrangements should be agreed in advance between the landlord, his proposed managing agents who will have to operate the scheme, and the solicitors. Obviously, if the client and the agents require recommendations it will be entirely appropriate for the solicitors to put forward one of the schemes envisaged by their standard forms, assuming it is not completely inappropriate.

Definitions

3.12   To a large extent this follows from what has been said before, but it is impossible to emphasise too strongly the need for accurate definitions in the draft. The relevant definitions are in respect of (a) property (both the demised premises and the landlord's premises), and (b) the works or services for which charges can be made.

The premises concerned

Complete premises

3.13   The lease must make it clear what is being let. It is one thing to say that the landlord is letting *'Humpty Dumpty Cottage, Newland, Westshire,'* and another to be absolutely certain what is within that description. If Humpty Dumpty Cottage is clearly identifiable and is surrounded by a garden, is the garden included? If the garden is included, does the letting include the whole of the wall on the east, the fence on the west and the hedges on the north and south? If the cottage has a front open to the roadway where does the line of the boundary fall? These are all questions that are material for all sorts of reasons. For example, is the boundary wall the tenant's responsibility, or the landlord's, or is it a party boundary or the neighbour's property? The precise boundary is also material if, for example, the tenant wants to make alterations or attach something to a fence or wall.

3.14   The previous paragraph outlined some obvious reasons for concern about the extent of the property in a demise. The need for certainty is because the tenant needs to know where his responsibility lies, and where it ends. It is also important in leases because, depending on the property concerned, there may well be rights of access needed and for the use of pipes etc. If Humpty Dumpty Cottage does not have a frontage to a publicly adopted road how does the tenant reach the property? If he needs to pass over a private roadway he will need a right to use that road. For service charge purposes the mention of a private road obviously draws attention to a possible obligation to contribute to the maintenance of the road. When the lease is drawn it should show the rights granted (and those which the landlord may want to reserve), and thus the responsibility for payment can be considered and specified.

Joined properties

3.15   Humpty Dumpty Cottage was a single property, freestanding in its own grounds. Many properties, however, are joined to others and in such cases exact definitions of the property included are at least as vital. Such properties can be, for example, a shop in a parade, or an office or flat in a block.

3.16   Where the property let is attached to other property there are numerous permutations of the precise line of the boundary between the property let and other property, apart from the other rights that might be needed. The author feels very strongly that it is a matter of preference for the landlord where he fixes the line of the boundary. The important thing is that the exact line is unequivocal and therefore does not give rise to those unsatisfactory arguments where the lease is not clear and there is genuine doubt as to whether a particular feature is in the demise or not. The draftsman must try in particular to ensure that all the property of the landlord is covered by repairing obligations of either the landlord or the tenant. The failure to clarify an item can result, for example, in neither or both parties being under an obligation to repair it.

24

3.17   A property such as an office suite within a building or a flat in a block can have different boundaries as follows:

(a)   walls solely within the demise (internal);

(b)   external walls, fronting eg on to the street;

(c)   walls separating the demised premises from premises demised to other tenants;

(d)   walls separating the demised property from common parts of the building;

(e)   walls separating the demised premises from property not owned by the landlord (ie next door);

(f)   there can also be walls that have a combination of two or more of the above characteristics;

(g)   there can also be a flat roof over one demise but used by the occupier of other premises. (Some cases on this point are mentioned below at **3.22**.)

3.18   Where a landlord retains the structure and lets on internal repairing leases the leases should make it clear where the boundary is between the structure and the demised internal parts. Some leases refer to the demise as including the plaster on the walls, and the landlord retaining the structure, comprising the whole of the walls except the plaster. This may not be appropriate for premises that have some construction not involving plaster. The point should be checked with the landlord and his managing agent.

3.19   For a wall there are, again, various choices which the draftsman can make to define the property to be let. Apart from the above mentioned option of including in the demise just the plaster, other possibilities are (a) that the landlord could include one half, severed vertically, of all walls separating the demised premises from other property let to tenants or neighbouring property, and the whole of internal walls, or (b) the landlord could include just the plaster for walls which are external walls or walls between the demise and the common parts. The main point is to decide the most practical way to treat the actual physical structure. The draftsman should try to take account of how the party responsible for maintenance can obtain access to the part he is to repair. It is not always possible to put this in the lease, particularly if the landlord is responsible for the structure and the tenant for plaster etc, but the point should be considered in case there is some obvious solution.

3.20   It has already been mentioned that a parapet which rested on top of walls of part of a building (and where the lease did not mention parapets at all) was held in one case, *Rapid Results College Ltd v Angell* [1986] 1 EGLR 53, see **2.9** above, not to be part of the exterior or of the common parts. Any such item should ideally be mentioned specifically. It probably does not matter whether it is in the demise and therefore the tenant's responsibility, or is treated as part of the common parts so that the landlord has the responsibility but can recover cost. My plea is simply to ensure such items are mentioned in the lease one way or another so that there is no scope for doubt.

3.21   Similar points affect floors and ceilings. It is not uncommon to see the tenant responsible for the floorboards and the joists which support the floor-boards of the floor, and just the plaster of the ceiling above from the under side of the joists. Inspection may show whether the building is constructed with joists and floorboards or with a steel and concrete frame. Again, the division could be simply halfway through the floor/ceiling divided horizontally, or the tenant could be responsible just for the floorboards/ floor screed and the plaster on the ceiling, leaving the landlord with the main structure. Inspection again may assist and the landlord and his agents should advise on the most practical division, which should be reflected in the lease.

3.22   The following are examples of cases where courts have considered aspects of definitions:

(a)   In *Tennant Radiant Heat Ltd v Warrington Development Corporation* [1988] 1 EGLR 41 a judge at first instance held that the roof was not within the demise, but the Court of Appeal said that it was. Such cases reinforce the advisability of as much express clarification as possible – if the roof is to be included in the demise and the lease says so there should not be a problem, but if the reference is to 'the structure' or the 'main walls' there could be doubt. Other items that should be specifically mentioned are doors and door frames, and windows and window frames. There are frequently doubts about such items and it is so simple to clar-ify it at the first stage of the draft lease. These latter items were dis-cussed in *Reston Ltd v Hudson* [1990] 2 EGLR 51 mentioned at **3.44** below.

(b)   In *Campden Hill Towers Ltd v Gardner* [1977] QB 823 a reference in a statutory obligation of a landlord to repair the exterior (Housing Act 1961, s 32) was held to apply not to the exterior of the whole of the block, but only to that part of the structure immediately round the flat in question.

(c)   In *Elmcroft Developments Ltd v Tankersley-Sawyer* [1984] 1 EGLR 47 the landlord was obliged to 'keep the said entrance hall stairs and passages well lighted during the hours of dark'. This was held to include an obligation to light the external access to the basement flat.

(d)   In *Twyman v Charrington* [1994] 1 EGLR 243, approved by the Court of Appeal at (1994) 1 EGLR 243, the Court of Appeal, agreeing with the judge below, held that the roof came within a reference to 'mutual or party structures' in respect of the subject premises, which had a basement and three floors above. The tenant of the basement and ground floors was therefore liable to contribute to roof repairs. Of course, if the lease had mentioned the roof there would have been no need for a court case. It would have been clearer if this unusual phrase had been separately defined.

The obligation for repair of a roof terrace above a flat was litigated in three cases at the turn of the new century.

(a) The first was *Hallisey v Petmoor Developments Ltd* [2000] EGCS 124. The landlord was liable for repair of the 'main structure of the Building including the principal internal structures and the exterior walls and the foundations and the roof of the Building not included (in) the demise of any flat'. The ceramic tiles of the flat roof (the flat had been let to the tenant of the upper area) moved and let in water, largely because the asphalt layer (under the tiles) had been affected by heat. It was held that it was proper to construe 'main structure' as including whatever additional surfaces were created in order to make the otherwise bare concrete shell an effective structure for maintaining the flats within the development. Accordingly, the landlord could not avoid liability for repair.

(b) In a similar set of circumstances and in a case decided at almost the same time it was held that the wording was sufficient to put the liability for the roof terrace on both landlord and tenant! The court decided that it was best to avoid such a stalemate and held that the lease should be construed as far as possible to avoid overlapping liability. It held that it could interpret the words 'main structure' in a restricted way and thus exclude the roof terrace, which left the responsibility with the tenant: *Petersson v Pitt Place (Epsom) Ltd* [2001] EWCA Civ 86, [2001] EGCS 13.

(c) In the third case where there was a roof terrace over flats below, the decision was that the roof terrace was effectively part of the main structure, where the demise to the tenant of the flat below included 'the ceiling of the flat below the level of the bottom of the beams or joists immediately above'. The case is *Ibrahim v Dovecorn Reversions Ltd* [2001] 2 EGLR 46.

3.23   The above all illustrate aspects of drafting, and they are recorded because they show that if the lease is unclear the very important issue of whose responsibility it is to do work or to pay for work can be genuinely disputed, at the cost of good landlord/tenant relations and sometimes heavy legal costs. My preference is to make sure the definitions are clear so that such disputes are unnecessary.

3.24   On the subject of roofs a Court of Appeal case, *Abbahall Ltd v Smee* [2002] EWCA Civ 1831, [2003] 1 All ER 465, considered a dispute over freehold property. It was between the owner of the lower part (ground floor) of a mews property and the owner (by adverse possession) of the upper two floors. The dispute was over the responsibility for the roof. As the owner of the upper part had acquired it by squatters' rights, there was no documentary agreement about maintenance. The Court of Appeal said it had to find a fair, just and reasonable result, the key to which was 'reasonableness between neighbours'. The Court considered the roof served the flat and shop equally and thus a fair proportion was 50: 50. It also said that the comments regarding the cost of repairs were confined to the facts of the case, but (like *Twyman v Charrington* [1994] 1 EGLR 243, see **3.22** above) shows that the courts are prepared to find the owner of the bottom part of building liable for a proportion of roof costs, even with premises in between the ground floor and the roof.

3.25   Finally, in this section about joined properties a case where the premises were changed should be highlighted: *Stapel (Ernst) v Bellshore Property Investments Ltd* [2001] 2 EGLR 7. In this case the landlord had acquired some premises in the 1970s which were adjoining premises he already owned. He sought to argue that the service charge costs should cover both the old and new property. The original premises had six flats and five of them paid one sixth of the costs each. The clear implication was that the proportion was related to the original building. (See **4.18** for assessing shares of costs.)

Mixed use buildings

3.26   The definitions are at least as important, and certainly become more complex, where the building is one of mixed use, particularly if part is residential. Because residential parts are subject to the Landlord and Tenant Act 1985 and the obligations for consultation etc therein, it has become common to deal with a multi-purpose building by having different service charge provisions for the separate parts.

3.27   Take the case of a parade of shops, which we can call Easter Parade, above which is a block of flats which we shall modestly call Sherriff Towers. The usual way to deal with service charges is for the Easter Parade shops to be let on rack rent (ie full rent, not a nominal rent) leases with the tenant liable for service charges affecting Easter Parade only. The individual flats in Sherriff Towers will each be subject to leases under which the tenant will pay a premium and a nominal rent, plus a service charge primarily relating to the service costs for Sherriff Towers and not the remainder of the building. (This is not invariable, but it is very common). The point is mentioned to emphasise that if this scheme is followed the exact demarcation between Easter Parade and Sherriff Towers needs to be clear, or there could be a costly dispute as to whether either the residential tenants or the commercial tenants are responsible for contributing to the costs, or indeed whether neither has any liability. The situation can also be addressed by having the services set out in schedules where the commercial part contributes X% of the costs of some of the works and the residential tenants the remainder. The tenants then pay their lease percentage of the commercial (or residential) part of those costs. (An example of unsatisfactory leases for a mixed use building is *Alton House Holdings Ltd v Calflane (Management) Ltd* [1987] 2 EGLR 52, discussed in Chapter 12 (on management companies) at **12.30**.)

Common parts

3.28   The other matter where definitions need particular attention is the common parts. These are the areas over which the landlord is to carry out services. In the case of Sherriff Towers, for example, the tenants will need access from the ground floor to the upper floors. This may be by lift or by stairs or both. Normally the stairs or lift will be common parts, although occasionally they will be included with the lease of one of the flats. There may well also be corridors and perhaps a garden or other utility area for storage of rubbish or washing lines, and perhaps parking areas.

3.29   All such items should be defined as clearly as possible, so that the land-lord and tenants are aware beyond doubt what areas are to be in common use and which are to be the subject of service charges. An obvious question is 'are the walls of the lift shaft (or stairs) part of the upper part, or the lower part, or are they treated as (retained) parts not included in any lease?' Whichever is the case, a well drawn lease will make it clear. (The room housing the lift motor also needs consideration, and (on a different drafting aspect) rights of access for repair of the lift motor.)

3.30   In the Rapid Results case it may be remembered that the parapet which was not mentioned as such in the lease was held not to come under the description of common parts. (*Rapid Results College Ltd v Angell* [1986] 1 EGLR 53, see **2.9** above.)

Flexibility

3.31   The desirability of precision in drafting is, however, subject to the further recommendation that there must be a reasonable degree of flexibility in case circumstances change. For example, the landlord may have to lose part of what were previously common parts as a result of road widening. It would be unrealistic for a tenant to be able to claim that a landlord was in breach of his covenant to cut the grass if part of the former lawn had been replaced by a public road. Again, if the landlord acquires additional property immediately adjoining the existing premises it is unreasonable for a tenant to object to that extra land or property being included in the repairing and other obligations provided that the new property lies reasonably satisfactorily with the old and, if there are lettable buildings or areas on the extra land and the tenants of those extra buildings are to have the benefit of the same facilities as the existing tenants, then the new tenants should contribute to the expenses as well. Also, if the lease has a service charge with a fixed percentage the landlord should ensure that there is power to vary that percentage if circumstances change. (See **4.24** et seq.)

3.32   In a case with only county court authority (*Merrick Corporation Ltd v John Milsom Properties Ltd* (LTL 11.2.2002)) a landlord added penthouse flats to a building after leases had been granted for the existing flats. It was held that the service charge liability was for the building as it was and as it might law-fully become, and thus the tenants of the original flats were liable to contribute to the expenses relating to the penthouses jointly with the penthouse flat owner. The judge held this even included making good defects in the original construc-tion of the penthouses, as the repairing covenant had covered renewal as well as repair.

Golden rule

3.33   The golden rule is to ensure that no part of the property owned by the landlord is not clearly within the description of either the demise or another letting or common parts. (The Commonhold Act neatly deals with this by saying that whatever is not described as one of the commonhold units is automatically

part of the common parts: Commonhold and Leasehold Reform A
s 25(1).)

Plans

3.34 It is obviously helpful if the lease contains a plan showing the prop,
let, and if possible the remainder as well. For leases of over seven years plans a
needed so that the lease can be registered at the Land Registry. In the case of a
property on more than one floor there can often be more than one plan. Again, it
is good practice, and fairly common in the case of property which is part of a
large area, for there to be one plan showing the whole of the development (eg the
shopping centre, with the position of the shop itself indicated by red edging) and
another plan showing the actual shop in greater detail, with staircases and internal division walls etc.

Items included in the charge

3.35 In the next few chapters a number of normal items that are covered by
service charge provisions in many leases are mentioned. The purpose of this part
of this chapter is again to emphasise the importance of defining as far as is practical the actual services in question.

3.36 The lease should, normally, cover a number of specific aspects as
follows, assuming the landlord is prepared to carry out such services and wants
to be reimbursed the cost. If these items are included as general items they may
assist in cases where a service is not otherwise clearly specified. Some major
aspects that should normally be covered are:

(a) Repair.

(b) Maintenance.

(c) Contracts for maintenance (eg for gardening or for a lift).

(d) Renewal. This can be contentious and is mentioned in the next paragraph.

(e) Cleaning.

(f) Decorating.

(g) Replacement of (a) tools or equipment for use in carrying out the maintenance etc, or (b) the plant used for the premises (lifts and boilers etc). This
is another potentially contentious aspect and is explored below.

(h) Electricity or other fuel for lighting and, where applicable, heating.

(i) Insurance of plant and equipment.

(j) Costs of management.

These and other types of cost are explored in Chapters 5 and 6.

Renewal and replacement

3.37   This is one aspect of leases that causes the most discussion and difference of opinion among those negotiating leases. In a 1911 case, *Lurcott v Wakeley and Wheeler* [1911] 1 KB 905, it was said 'repair is restoration by renewal or replacement of subsidiary parts of a whole. Renewal, as distinguished from repair, is reconstruction of the entirety, meaning the entirety not necessarily of the whole but substantially the whole subject matter under renewal'. In a much more recent case, *Regis Property Co Ltd v Dudley* [1958] 1 QB 346, it was made clear that provision for depreciation or replacement should be included in the computation of a reasonable charge for services.

3.38   Tenants are naturally worried if a landlord can use the terms of the lease to make them pay for the cost of renewal or replacement of something that does not need renewal or replacement. It must, however, be recognised by tenants that renewal or replacement may be (a) cheaper than repair and (b) in some cases the only way in which an item can be put in reasonable condition. For example, it is not possible to repair a light bulb or glass in windows – the only realistic approach is replacement. (There is an good summary of this topic in Section D2 of the commercial Code mentioned in Chapter 11.)

3.39   As an example imagine that the Clark Centre, a little shopping centre, has a forecourt which is owned by the landlord. When the Clark Centre was built in 1970 the landlord put up five lamp standards on the forecourt. By 2003 they are a danger and the supporting posts are in need of some repair. A quotation is obtained that such repair as can be carried out would cost £550. The company that made the lights in 1970 is no longer in business and so it is impossible to obtain identical copies although a near equivalent could be obtained at a cost of £400. What can be done? It must make sense for the landlord to be able to replace the lights at a cheaper cost than simply repairing the old ones. A lease can be drafted to accept an obligation to pay for replacement rather than repair where it is more economical to do so.

3.40   Many cases illustrate that there are different approaches which can all be valid. In 1965, *Manor House Drive Ltd v Shahbazian* 195 EG 283, the Court of Appeal considered a case where a landlord had taken advice on repair to a roof. The roof had leaked and the zinc covering had been patched, although after a few years it needed to be patched again. The landlord took a surveyor's advice and was told that by removing and replacing the zinc the roof should be free of maintenance for many years. The landlord had a choice of continuing the old patching arrangement or replacing all the zinc and thus saving the need for further repairs for many years, although at a greater initial cost. It was held that the landlord was entitled to replace the zinc in accordance with the advice given to it. In other words it could replace the zinc because that was a reasonable course of action that had been advised by a suitably qualified person.

3.41   In another case on roofs, *Murray v Birmingham City Council* [1987] 2 EGLR 53, the opposite situation arose. The landlord carried out periodic patching, but the tenant wanted the landlord to replace the roof. The Court of Appeal would not order the landlord to replace the roof. It held that the evidence did not show that piecemeal repairs to the roof had become so impracticable that the time had come where replacement of the roof was imperative.

3.42 In a third case on roofs, *New England Properties plc v Portsmouth New Shops* [1993] 1 EGLR 84, the court felt it not unreasonable for a badly designed roof (damaged in a storm) to be replaced in a slightly different and more robust design. Similar decisions were reached in *Postel Properties Ltd v Boots the Chemist Ltd* [1996] 2 EGLR 60 and *Wandsworth London Borough Council v Griffin* [2000] 2 EGLR 105.

3.43 These cases and others illustrate that the courts will tend to allow the person with the responsibility for repair to deal with repair/replacement in the way that person chooses, subject of course to the landlord acting reasonably, which, usually, entails following proper advice. The landlord must, however, be able to show that the lease specifically permits the works. (See, for example, *Jacob Isbicki & Co Ltd v Goulding & Bird Ltd* [1989] 1 EGLR 236 where the landlord tried unsuccessfully to recover costs under a sweeping-up clause, discussed later at **5.199**.)

3.44 An illustration of the point is *Reston Ltd v Hudson* [1990] 2 EGLR 51, where a number of the window frames of a block of flats were defective. Although on the face of it the lease was carefully drawn, it was hard to be sure whether the lease actually demised the external windows or not. In the event the judge decided that the demise did not include the windows, and as they were part of the property for which the landlord was responsible, the judge was able to decide on the further question about replacement of those windows by the landlord. The court had to decide if it was reasonable for all the windows in the block to be replaced at the same time, or whether only those that were actually defective should be replaced. The court made a declaration that it was reasonable for the landlord to replace all the frames at the same time. The judge was satisfied under s 19 of the Landlord and Tenant Act 1985 that incurring the expense was reasonable, and under s 20 of the same Act that the landlord had complied with the (residential) statutory consultation procedure then in force.

Declaration of intention

3.45 One aid to interpretation is a statement of the intention of the provisions. For example, it could say that the intention of the service charge is to enable the landlord to recover from the tenants of the landlord's property (a) all the reasonable costs of the services mentioned in paras A to D of the 5th Schedule (ie repair etc) or (b) all the costs of paras A to D (repair decoration and cleaning etc), and such of E to G as are actually incurred (ie discretionary items such as promotional expenses), or (c) the total expenditure by the landlord without limit.

3.46 Tenants are suspicious of such provisions, but they can assist the parties and the court, and so, subject to safeguards for the tenant to ensure it does not give the landlord a blank cheque, they are recommended for use. When negotiating, it could be useful to include such a declaration (a positive statement) if a tenant seeks to include a declaration that the service charge is not to include particular items. A useful example of a declaration which was held to clarify the intention is *Church Commissioners for England v Metroland Ltd* (1996) EGCS 44, although in the same year, in *Postel Properties Ltd v Boots the Chemist Ltd* [1996] 2 EGLR 60, a provision that the expenses of repair etc included partial but not wholesale replacement did not seem to be accepted by the court.

Use of specific words

Reasonable

3.47   This word is mentioned ad nauseam throughout this volume (see eg **2.14** et seq). On the whole judges use it to enable them to achieve what they see as the fair decision on the dispute. As the judges say, it is a matter of the 'factual matrix', or, in other words, the judge can decide on what he sees as the just interpretation of the facts before him. Readers are reminded that for residential premises s 19 of the Landlord and Tenant Act 1985 deals with reasonableness under the three headings of the costs being reasonably incurred, the reasonable standard of works, and a reasonable amount for advance payments. (See **9.38** et seq.) Readers are also referred to the Index for numerous other references. While it seems to the author that s 19 is intended to hold a balance between the parties so far as the amount of costs is concerned, it is not interpreted as implying cheapness. The word has its uses in both commercial and residential leases, as it gives both parties the opportunity to persuade a court that what they have done is appropriate, and gives the court discretion to decide between the opposing views.

Proper

3.48   In the 1990s the Court of Appeal, in *Havenridge Ltd v Boston Dyers Ltd* [1994] 2 EGLR 73, considered a dispute about insurance premiums where the tenant was to repay premiums 'properly' incurred. That word, too, was held not to mean 'cheapest'. The judge at first instance held that 'properly' meant 'legitimately'. The landlord was able to recover what he had paid, even though the tenant had demonstrated that he could have obtained identical cover from the same insurers at a much lower cost. The court said that what the landlord had paid had to be reimbursed provided the landlord could show that the premium had been negotiated (a) at arm's length, (b) in the ordinary course of business, and (c) without any special circumstances applying. Again, 'proper' is a useful expression to use, but marginally less useful than 'reasonable': it is probably most effective used jointly with 'reasonable'. An example of the use of 'all proper costs' is *Primeridge Ltd v Jean Muir* [1992] 1 EGLR 273 (see **5.191** below).

Reasonable and proper

3.49 In service charge negotiations it is common for a tenant to seek to ensure that the service charge costs are 'reasonable' and that individual items of charge (such as professional fees for services arising during management) are 'reasonable and proper' costs. The difference can be demonstrated as follows: it may be 'proper' to obtain counsel's opinion on interpretation if a dispute arises, but the expense of a senior QC for an opinion on a straightforward question (particularly where not much money turns on the answer) may not be 'reasonable'. Using both words gives comfort. Again, it may be 'reasonable' to sandblast the outside of the building every 20 years, but the cost may well not be a 'proper' service charge expense. This is a useful phrase to use.

3.50 The following cases, which are mentioned elsewhere in this book, illustrate the interpretation of some specific words or phrases:

(a) 'Reasonable and proper' is a phrase used in *Postel Properties Ltd v Boots the Chemist Ltd* [1996] 2 EGLR 60 (**5.15** below); and in *Skilleter v Charles* [1992] 1 EGLR 73 (**3.95** below).

(b) 'Properly and reasonably' appears in *Sun Alliance and London Assurance Co Ltd v British Railways Board* [1989] 2 EGLR 237 (**5.68** below).

(c) 'Reasonably and properly' is in *Isbicki (Jacob) & Co Ltd v Goulding & Bird Ltd* [1989] 1 EGLR 236 (**5.199** below).

(d) 'Reasonably and properly incurred' coupled with a reference to 'total costs', appears in *Woodtrek Ltd v Jezek* (1981) 261 EG 571 (**2.25** above).

Reasonable endeavours

3.51 A commitment by a landlord (or tenant) may be expressed so that he has to use 'reasonable endeavours' to perform the service. This is a less full obligation than 'best endeavours'. (See at **3.53**). It induces an air of reasonableness and thus has some comfort for both covenantor and covenantee. In a 1992 case, *Baring Securities Ltd v DG Durham Group plc* [1993] EGCS 192, the expression was considered when a tenant agreed to use reasonable endeavours to obtain the landlord's consent to an assignment. The intended assignee was to receive a reverse premium. The landlord requested a guarantee from the parent of the assigning tenant (or some other form of security) which the assignor would not agree. The court held it was not a breach of the reasonable endeavours obligation for the proposed assignor/tenant not to obtain a guarantee from its parent company. As the proposed assignor/tenant was not in default, it was entitled to repayment of the reverse premium it had paid. The phrase denotes an obligation which has to be implemented provided it is possible to do it reasonably.

Reasonably practicable

3.52 This expression was considered in *Jordan v Norfolk County Council* [1994] 4 All ER 218, where the council was required to replace certain landscaping 'as far as reasonably practicable'. The case followed a judgment against the council which had built a sewer through the plaintiff's land, destroying trees etc and preventing the plaintiff from selling the land for development at a particularly advantageous time. The scheme put forward (by an independent expert) to replace the lost trees and generally to landscape the area would have cost between £230,000 and £300,000 to implement, although at the time of the hearing the value of the land was only £25,000. In this (admittedly extreme) example, the court ordered that a fresh scheme should be prepared under which the new landscape architect should 'prescribe items in so far, but only in so far' as their cost would be reasonable 'having regard to the nature and value of the site'. The judge also said that in this context the phrase 'so far as reasonably practicable' was 'sufficiently general for it to embrace matters additional to the feasibility of planting replacement trees of the same maturity. In this area there is very little nowadays which is not physically feasible if enough money is spent. Hence in this context the phrase is apt to include financial considerations'. This is very similar in effect to 'reasonable endeavours', and the guidance in the *Jordan* case as to the financial consequences is, it is suggested, helpful to all parties.

Best endeavours

3.53 This is a much greater obligation than 'reasonable endeavours' and 'reasonably practicable'. It was held in *Terrell v Mabie Todd & Co Ltd* (1952) 69 RPC 234 to be the standard of a reasonable and prudent board of directors acting properly in the interests of their company, but it does not extend to actions which would be a breach of other covenants. In similar vein to the *Baring Securities* case (see at **3.51** above relating to 'reasonable endeavours') seeking consent to assign a lease was the issue in *Bickel v Courtenay Investments (Nominees) Ltd* [1984] 1 All ER 657, where the covenant was to use 'best endeavours'. There it was held that 'best endeavours' did not oblige the party who had so covenanted to apply to the court for a declaration that the landlord had unreasonably withheld consent. Thus, while this is a higher level of commitment than 'reasonable endeavours', it is not an absolute commitment. On the whole, however, most solicitors tend to advise against agreeing 'best endeavours' obligations. It was certainly generally thought at one time that the obligation involved the covenantor having to carry out the obligation even if it involved an expenditure of money. This does not seem to be the case now, but caution is perhaps advisable when this phrase is put forward. 'Best endeavours' is also used in the following cases which are referred to in this book: *Lloyds Bank plc v Bowker Orford* [1992] 2 EGLR 44; *Parkside Knightsbridge Ltd v Horwitz* [1983] 2 EGLR 42; *Capital and Counties Freehold Equity Trust Ltd v BL plc* [1987] 2 EGLR 49; and *New Pinehurst Residents Association (Cambridge) Ltd v Silow* [1988] 1 EGLR 227.

'Incurred,' 'provision,' and 'anticipated expenditure'

3.54   The word 'incurred' is discussed at **4.12** and in Chapter 13 at **13.38** (in relation to apportionment and termination), and the word 'provision' is discussed in connection with firefighting equipment (at **5.123**). 'Anticipated expenditure' is referred to in Chapter 7 (at **7.14**) in the section on principles of sinking funds.

Certificates

3.55   Certificates are discussed in depth in the section on certificates at **4.78** et seq.

Negotiating tips for tenants

3.56   The draft is normally sent to the tenant's solicitors and so the tenant is the first to seek to negotiate. Accordingly, we will deal with tips for tenants first. A tenant will often find it easier to persuade a landlord to qualify what is in the draft lease than to change it. The landlord drafts the lease, and there is usually (although not necessarily) other property affected by similar service charge provisions. Landlords have better reason for seeking to insist that the service charge provisions are consistent with other leases than they have on many other parts of the lease. The service charge, after all, affects the recovery of costs from all the landlord's premises, whereas standard prohibitions on change of use or on alienation or rent review provisions etc can often be varied for one unit without affecting others. If the service charge provisions are left (at least relatively) untouched, but qualified, it is harder for the landlord to refuse amendments. What should the qualifications be? The following are suggestions for items which can be added to most service charge schedules as provisos. Obviously, the references to 'Common Parts', 'Building', etc must reflect the definitions in the draft lease.

DECLARATION OF PRUDENT ECONOMY

3.57   Some of what is said in this book by way of detail could be ignored if the tenant can persuade the landlord to agree a proviso to his service charge schedule that the total expenditure by the landlord chargeable to the tenant is 'no more than prudently economical'. It is more likely to be acceptable if it recognises that the landlord has to carry out his obligations under the lease, so the words added could be such as 'the Landlord will use reasonable endeavours to ensure that the works and services described in this Schedule are carried out in as economical a manner as is practicable consistent with his obligations herein'. (See precedents in Appendix 2 – Precedent 7, Part 5.) Such an insertion will not involve major redrafting but will influence interpretation of the whole of the service charge provisions. (An alternative is to say that the costs are to be no more than is reasonable, but, as illustrated in Chapter 2, this does not necessarily imply that the costs are to be kept down, and the reference to prudent economy is put first, as the most important general qualification that a tenant can seek.)

CAPITAL COSTS

3.58   Most tenants object to paying capital costs through the service charge. Clearly, if the property is a new one it is not reasonable for the landlord to charge via the service charge the costs of creating the building, the original decoration, or fitting out by the landlord (as opposed to the tenant's fitting out costs). A qualification on this point could be phrased:

> 'Provided That notwithstanding the provisions set out above the Landlord shall not be entitled to include in the Service Charge any of the costs (a) of the construction of [the Building] [the Development] or (b) of the fitting out or initial decoration of [the Building] [the Development] by the Landlord or (c) of the installation or provision by the Landlord of any plant or machinery in [the Building] [the Development] prior to the date of this Lease.'

Most landlords will accept such a provision or give a warranty that such costs are not to be included. If they are not prepared to agree obviously the proposed tenant will be on notice as to the landlord's attitude, and will be entitled to take a view on the implications for the other costs that might be incurred, and at the worst may decide not to proceed.

3.59   The Commercial Code (see Chapter 11) in para 29 says the service charge shall not include 'any initial costs (including leasing of initial equipment) incurred in relation to the original design and construction of the fabric plant or equipment'.

REFURBISHMENT COSTS

3.60   More difficult is the question of the costs of refurbishment. A tenant (who may have a lease for 15, 20 or 25 years) must accept that if he requires the landlord to decorate and maintain common parts there will come a time when refurbishment is needed. The interest of the tenant should be to ensure that the landlord cannot take advantage to go further than is reasonably necessary, and charge the cost of a major improvement (rather than a full overhaul) to a tenant who may, at the time, have only a few years of his lease to run. Even if the tenant is a business tenant who is likely to renew his lease at the end of the term, the tenant is entitled to seek protection against the landlord improving the property at the tenant's expense to a standard beyond what might be expected. (The key, of course, is 'at the tenant's expense'. If the landlord wants to improve the property at his own expense then that is a different matter, subject to the tenant's concern about the effect of the landlord's improvements on rent review.) This again can be protected by a proviso on the following lines:

'Provided that the costs of renewal and decoration and maintenance [of the Common Parts] [of the Development] shall not exceed the proper and reasonable cost of necessary repair maintenance and decoration in the course of normal wear and tear of any such items And the costs recoverable from the Tenant shall not include any costs representing improvement of [the Common Parts] [the Development] to a standard or specification superior to that at the date hereof other than as required under building regulations or the installation therein of any new plant or furniture or equipment other than necessary replacements of existing plant furniture or equipment which are beyond economic repair.'

3.61   Refurbishment is covered in various parts of the Commercial Code (see Chapter 11), including 29(C) and 30.

ENVIRONMENTAL EXPENSES

3.62   This is a more difficult matter to persuade a landlord to agree, but the costs of putting right some environmental problems can be enormous. Where a tenant has agreed to take a lease (particularly a short lease) it is hard to see that it can be fair for him to be expected to pay a share of the cost of putting right something arising from the state of the premises before the lease commenced, unless this was expressly agreed (or notified to the tenant) and thus taken into account in the rent, for example clean-up work needed in the case of premises that were built on contaminated land. It is to be noted that most leases require tenants to comply with statutory obligations. In so far as clearing a site of contamination may be an obligation under the Environmental Protection Act 1990, such clearing up might fall within the scope of a tenant's covenants, although a tenant would often only have part of a building and the contamination would usually relate to the land on which the whole building stands. Protection against a charge by the landlord could again take the form of a proviso perhaps as follows:

'Provided that the Landlord shall not be entitled by virtue of the above provisions to include in the Service Charge costs any part of the costs of action taken under the provisions of the Environmental Protection Act 1990 in respect of contaminated land.'

INHERENT DEFECTS

3.63   The repair of a defect is not impliedly excluded from the repairing obligation of either landlord or tenant on the ground simply that it is an inherent defect; it is a question of fact and degree. (See eg *Quick v Taff Ely Borough Council* [1986] QB 809.) The only major qualifications to this liability are that:

(a)   a tenant is not obliged by his repairing covenant to give back to the landlord something different from that which was demised to him; and

(b)   the service charge provisions (or the repairing obligations) can contain material exclusions.

3.64   Where a tenant is liable to repair the premises demised to him and to pay the service charge for repairs etc carried out by the landlord over common parts then both these elements are material. The provisions of the tenant's general repairing obligations are outside the scope of this book, but for service charges a proviso on the following lines would be the type of protection that a tenant might seek:

> 'Provided That the Landlord shall not by virtue of the above provisions be entitled to include in the Service Costs the costs of any works needed to repair or replace or make good any defects in [the Building] [the Common Parts] [the Development] arising as a result of defective construction or defective design or the use of defective or unsuitable materials in the construction of [the Building] [the Common Parts] [the Development] [or any part of them].'

A shorter alternative description would be reference to 'inherent or latent defects'.

GOOD ESTATE MANAGEMENT

3.65   There are two opposing schools of thought on good estate management. One is that a clause requiring the landlord to act in accordance with the principles of good estate management is a curb on the landlord's freedom to act in any fashion he thinks fit. The other is that such a clause may entitle the landlord to carry out acts on his property which may not be specifically covered by other terms of the lease, and is thus more beneficial to the landlord. The effect of 'good estate management' and whether or not any works or services come within that description, are a matter on which evidence may need to be given to a court. However, compliance (or non-compliance) with the Codes of Practice referred to in Chapter 11 would be sufficient evidence in many cases to show whether or not an act (or omission) is or is not good estate management, as the case may be. The evidence would have to be to the effect that the work (or service) is such as is normal and appropriate for the type of property concerned. Clearly, if the lease requires a landlord to act in accordance with the principles of good estate management and he can prove that such works or services are indeed normal and proper, he may be able to charge for them, which he may not without such a provision. The tenant must therefore ensure that the principles are applied only to the services and works which the landlord has agreed to perform. Subject to this warning, if a tenant wants protection on this score a proviso could be on the following lines:

> 'Provided That the services to be provided by the Landlord hereunder shall be carried out in accordance with the principles of good estate management.'

An alternative could be:

> 'Provided That the services to be provided by the Landlord hereunder shall be carried out in accordance with the principles set out in the Code of Practice for (Commercial) (residential) property dated … and prepared by …'

Landlords need to be wary of agreeing this: they are probably happy with 90% of the Code, but as to the other 10% they may not be content, but the clause would accept the Code in full.

TENDERING

3.66   While not being needed as a lease provision in the case of a lease of residential property (see Chapter 9 and s 20 Landlord and Tenant Act 1985) for commercial property it may be worth seeking an obligation requiring the landlord to seek tenders for major works, or even an obligation to put significant continuing contracts (such as cleaning, security, gardening, or even management) out to tender. This is to ensure that the cost of such items is competitive. (The Commercial Code (see Chapter 11) in para 34-37 recommends tendering and/or benchmarking.) A landlord should not object to such a provision, but would normally want to reserve his right not to accept the lowest tender. Factors such as timing and the quality of work are relevant when deciding to accept or reject a tender. (Landlords could also be asked to agree that the tenant has the right to be told the result of all the tenders.) A suitable provision would be:

> 'The Landlord will seek not less than three tenders from companies or individuals independent of the Landlord suitably experienced in similar work in the area:
>
> (a)   for all regular contracts affecting the Centre (including for the avoidance of doubt management of the Centre cleaning gardening and/or security); and
>
> (b)   for all repair or decoration of the Common Parts of the Centre;
>
> [where the cost is reasonably expected to exceed (£X) (Z% of the total Service Costs) in any single Accounting Year].'

This could also be adapted to provide that for major works the tenants (acting by a majority in number or a majority in terms of service charge obligation) should be entitled to nominate a contractor to be asked to tender. (A landlord may take the point that if only one lease on the development has this provision the other tenants will not have similar rights, making the clause toothless. Compare the new rules under s 20 of the Landlord and Tenant Act 1985, referred to in Chapter 9.)

ASSOCIATED PARTIES

3.67   The tenant may want to seek a provision prohibiting contracts for works being given to a company which is a holding company or subsidiary of the landlord, or a subsidiary of the landlord's holding company. A blanket prohibition is unlikely to be accepted, but it could be coupled with an obligation on a landlord to seek several tenders (as in the previous paragraph). This should make it acceptable: if the associated company gives the best tender offer at least the tenant will have had some protection from abuse as a result of the other independent tenders. (For residential property (under s 20 of the Landlord and Tenant Act 1985), the landlord, when consulting on proposed works, must provide at least one independent estimate. The landlord must also (now) always give each tenant of a dwelling the opportunity to propose the name of someone the tenant would like the landlord to approach for an estimate. This is not necessarily appropriate for commercial property, but is mentioned as another point that could be considered.)

EXCLUDING COSTS RECOVERABLE FROM OTHERS

3.68   In many cases landlords can recover costs of works and services from tenants through a service charge. There are some cases where the landlord might alternatively be able to recover some of those costs from others, such as insurers or other tenants, or sometimes owners of adjoining property, or (for new properties) under construction warranties. The following proviso is intended to ensure that where the landlord can recover from another party he will not include those costs within the service costs charged to the individual tenant:

> 'Provided That the Service Costs will not include any sums which the Landlord is entitled to recover from any insurers or other tenant or any other third party whether such sums are recovered by the Landlord or not.'

3.69   The landlord is referred to above as being 'entitled to recover ...'; a landlord, if he is prepared to agree such a qualification, is likely to want to revise it to relate to any money 'actually recovered' from others. If this is proposed, it is probably something the tenant should accept but coupled with an obligation on the landlord to seek recovery from third parties when this is possible at reasonably economic cost. A landlord might have a legal right to recover but it may be expensive to recover, and the other party might be insolvent or hard to identify. Some landlords agree to pursue claims, provided the tenant who asks indemnifies the landlord against the costs. This is probably not reasonable unless perhaps there is only one tenant. Where there are a number of tenants the amendment the landlord seeks would require one tenant to indemnify the landlord against costs for recovering a sum for the benefit of all tenants.

RESTRICTING FREQUENCY OF REGULAR WORKS

3.70   One way to keep costs down is to ensure that the landlord is not able to carry out services more often than strictly necessary. For example, in the case of decoration the normal lease will provide that a tenant must decorate internally at specified intervals (eg every five years): by contrast the landlord's obligation to decorate externally is usually at unspecified intervals (or 'when necessary'). A protection to the tenant can be to restrict the landlord's ability to charge for external decoration by reference to the frequency of decoration. This can also be applied (sometimes as significantly) to cleaning of common parts and window cleaning, and inspection for the purposes of insurance. Before making any changes of this sort to a draft lease, the tenant's solicitor should check with the tenant: he may not want such restrictions and may be disposed to rely on the landlord to act responsibly. Requiring cleaning to be no more than once a week could be totally unsuitable in some cases. Again, a restriction on the number of valuations for insurance purposes may seem inconsistent with the tenant's need to ensure that the landlord's property is insured to the full reinstatement value. (If there is no inspection how can the landlord be expected to know the proper figure for which to insure, and if he cannot charge for inspection is it reasonable for him to be required to commit himself to insure for full value?). A proviso for tenants who want to cover the above points could be on the following lines:

'Provided That notwithstanding the above provisions the Landlord shall not be entitled to charge in the Service Costs

(i)   for decoration or treating of [the exterior of the Building] more than once in every [four] years and the interior of the Common Parts more than once in every five years

(ii)   for the cost of cleaning the [interior of the Common Parts and staircases and landings] more than once in each week

(iii)   for the cost of cleaning the windows of [the Common Parts] [the Development] more than once in each month

(iv)   for the cost of inspections of [the Development] for the purposes of insurance more than once in every two years.'

THE SERVICE CHARGE CAP

3.71   A solicitor should not put a service charge financial limit on the amount his client has to pay in his amendments to a draft lease unless he has specific instructions that it has been agreed. (It is one very easy way to set the negotiations off on a bad footing.) There are various ways of capping service charges:

(a)   The first is the straightforward limit to a specific maximum amount.

(b)   The second is a limit on increases over a particular figure, or over a particular percentage, as the years go by.

(c)   The third is a limit by relation to either the rent or the Retail Prices Index. The problem with the Retail Prices Index is that it relates to many costs, not just building costs. Although there is an index of building costs it is little used in leases, and in any event the landlord's services will usually include items other than just building works.

(d)   Relating the increase in service charge to increases in rent is not realistic unless the rent is increased every year: obviously the service charge could be restricted to a percentage of the rent payable but this is not a proposal likely to be acceptable to a landlord.

These permutations can be worded as follows:

1. 'Provided That the Service Charge payable by the Tenant shall not exceed £5,000 [plus VAT] in any Accounting Year [in any of the first five years of the term].'

2. 'Provided That the Service Charge payable by the Tenant in any Accounting Year shall not exceed the amount payable by the Tenant in the preceding financial year by more than [3%].'

3. 'Provided That the Service Charge payable by the Tenant for any Accounting Year shall not be increased by a greater percentage over the amount payable in the preceding Accounting Year than the increase over the same period in the Retail Prices Index.'

4. ' Provided That the Service Charge payable by the Tenant in any Accounting Year shall not exceed [25%] [130%] of the rent first reserved herein.'

Note:

(a) A landlord agreeing any such provision must recognise that he may face a shortfall. Setting the percentage at a realistic figure helps, but is not infallible.

(b) The words 'shall not exceed' have been used to avoid the danger of the service charge cap of, say, increases of 5% pa becoming an agreement to pay 5% over the previous year's payment, even if only 2% is appropriate.

(c) The expression 'payable in the preceding Accounting Year' has been used in case the service charge has not actually been paid. If the tenant has only paid part of what is due a reference to a percentage etc of the 'amount paid' would unreasonably benefit a tenant in arrear.

PERSONAL WAIVER

3.72   If the landlord and tenant are unable to agree that the draft lease can be revised in the way the tenant would like there is a further option, namely giving the named tenant a waiver from some aspects of the service charge. For several reasons this is not the best thing from the point of view of the tenant but it is a further approach that is available if other attempts at change fail. The main reason why it is not entirely helpful from a tenant's point of view is that the waiver affects the tenant alone and cannot be passed on to an assignee. Therefore, if the point is one of great concern and which the tenant genuinely feels affects his pocket substantially, it is also something that might make assigning the lease more difficult or less beneficial to the tenant. It has to be said that on the whole when a person takes an assignment of a lease he accepts it as it is, although if the premises in question seem to have unusually high service charge costs the point may be apparent to a proposed assignee when he looks at the accounts. (It could thus affect any premium payable by the assignee.)

3.73   In the event of a waiver being granted, should it be by a separate document, or in the lease itself? It is probably best for both parties for it to be by a separate document. Any provisions in the lease are going to be seen by a proposed assignee. Such assignee may wish to seek a similar concession from the landlord. If the waiver is by a separate document the assignee may not become aware of the point and thus it may not affect his views. A separate deed can be effective and is not necessarily invalidated by s 2 of the Law of Property (Miscellaneous Provisions) Act 1989. (See *Tootal Clothing Ltd v Guinea Properties Management Ltd* [1992] 2 EGLR 80.)

3.74   One matter which is often the subject of a waiver is the sinking fund or reserve fund. (Waivers in respect of sinking funds and reserve funds are discussed in detail at **7.60** et seq.) Some large organisations object to contributing to a sinking fund on the basis that they can find a large sum when required, and in the meantime they can use their money more efficiently in running their business than if it is simply accumulating in a fund. Sinking funds are relatively rare in practice in commercial leases and so it is not too much of a problem, but if a tenant is able to persuade a landlord to give him a waiver from contributing to such a fund the tenant should accept that it will (a) pay its share of the costs when replacement is needed (ie as if it had been contributing during the time since it became tenant), and (b) at the time of assignment or underletting or parting with possession the tenant will pay into the fund the amount it would have contributed up to that time. After all, at that point the reason for the waiver will have ended.

ITEMS NOT BENEFITING TENANTS

3.75   There are sometimes items which the landlord wants to put into a development after it has been completed which are of no benefit to some of the existing tenants. Perhaps the best example is some new construction within the boundaries of the development, such as a car park or access way, which are intended to be used just by some tenants and the landlord, or for the tenants of the present development and some adjoining property, or for a proposed new development adjoining the current development and which will not be part of it. To enable him to claim the cost for maintenance, etc, the landlord would, as ever, have to show that it was within the terms of the lease (for example, that it permitted the landlord to charge for improvements). Assuming the lease contained some provision for that purpose then a tenant might seek a proviso on the following lines:

> 'Provided That the Landlord shall not be entitled by reason of the above provisions to include within the Service Charge the cost of providing maintaining or replacing any items from which the Tenant [the tenants of the Development] derive no benefit.'

For two examples of cases where there were changes to the landlord's property after the leases were first granted, the reader is referred to *Church*

Commissioners for England v Metroland [1996] EGCS 44 and *Pole Properties Ltd v Feinberg* [1981] 2 EGLR 38. Both are mentioned elsewhere in this book.

INCOME FROM LETTING OF COMMON PARTS

3.76   Many tenants feel that if an area, for example a shopping mall, or a car park, is used for the common benefit of all tenants then income received from lettings of it (eg displays of double glazing, pictures, motoring organisation's displays, will writers, etc) should be credited to the service charge fund. Many landlords feel it is their property and that thus they are entitled to the income. If the use is on property which is genuinely intended to be only for the use of the tenants in common then perhaps there is logic in saying that the tenants are (temporarily) deprived of the use of that part of the common parts and so they should be compensated by receiving part of the income generated by way of credit to the service charge. This is more or less the approach in the Commercial Code (see Chapter 11) and see **5.91** et seq.

HOLDING MONEY ON TRUST AND IN AN INTEREST BEARING ACCOUNT

3.77   Holding service charges on trust is implied for residential property (Landlord and Tenant Act 1987, s 42) but for commercial property (where the money is likely to be larger) a tenant may wish to include a provision that 'money paid by the tenants of the Development towards the Service Costs will be held on trust in an interest bearing account with the interest being credited to the Service Charge'. The new Commercial Code and the Residential Code referred to in Chapter 11 contemplate that interest shall be credited to the service charge fund.

MAKE SURE THERE IS A COVENANT TO DO THE WORKS

3.78   This is not an exclusion, but the tenant's solicitors should look carefully to make sure there is an onus on the landlord (or management company) to carry out the repairs and other services for which he wishes to charge. If there is no actual covenant it is unlikely that one will be implied: *Alton House Holdings Ltd v Calflane (Management) Ltd* [1987] 2 EGLR 52 (see **9.52** below), and see also Chapter 12 on Management Companies. (It is advisable in the case of a lease where the services are to be carried out by the management company for the landlord to be under an obligation to carry out the services if the management company defaults.) Another (minor) point to note is that schedules of services often contain intended services such as repair, as well as references to items which are not services, such as bank interest, VAT, etc. The obligation should be for the landlord to carry out the real services (eg 'the services referred to in paras

1 to 8 of the Fourth Schedule'). The tenant need not be concerned about the ancillary items – there is no point in obliging the landlord to charge VAT.

OBTAIN ALL POSSIBLE INFORMATION

3.79   An intended tenant, whether of a new lease or an existing one, should make enquiries to check past, current, and possible future service charge liability. Draft enquiries appear among the precedents. (Both parties need to remember that misrepresentation on this point can give rise to a claim for damages (see **2.21** above).)

RENT SUSPENSION TO INCLUDE SERVICE CHARGE

3.80   This is discussed in Chapter 8. Most leases provide that the rent is to cease to be paid, or to be reduced, where the premises are wholly or partly destroyed. If the tenant is to have a similar benefit in reduction or removal of liability to pay service charges while the premises cannot be fully used, then it should be specifically stated in the rent cesser clause, which is usually either one of the 'Agreements and Declarations' or in a section of the lease devoted to insurance. As will be seen from Chapter 8 (at **8.18**), a reference in the rent abatement clause to 'rents' as opposed to 'rent' may not be sufficient, even when that term is defined: *P & O Property Holdings Ltd v International Computers Ltd* [1999] 2 EGLR 17.

COMBINED DECLARATION OF INTENTION

3.81   Finally in this section, there is no real inconsistency in combining a landlord's declaration that he intends to recover all his expenses with the saving qualifications mentioned above. Such a clause could start something like this:

> 'It is hereby declared that the intention of this Schedule is to enable the Landlord to recover all his expenses of any type mentioned in this Schedule relating to the Development save that the Landlord shall not be entitled to charge within the Service Charge any costs relating to the design or construction of the Development ...'

Negotiating tips for landlords

3.82   The previous section of this chapter discussed provisions which a tenant might negotiate to improve a draft lease from the tenant's viewpoint (or at least to restrict the amount he can be charged). (It seemed appropriate to give the tenant's exclusions first as he is the first to see the draft. The landlord's tips below in some cases reflect some of the possible revisions sought by the tenant in the previous section.) What can the landlord do to assist himself?

Include all necessary items clearly

3.83 The main point is to be absolutely certain that the standard service charge provisions really do cover all that is needed. This is another way of saying that the landlord should ensure that the definitions are ample and accurate. (Remember the parapet!; see *Rapid Results* case at **2.9** above.)

Inspect, and agree the scheme

3.84 Solicitors should always confer with the managing agents and the landlord when drafting the lease, and should inspect the premises wherever possible to see what is needed and how it is to be managed. This is relevant for rights and reservations as well as for service charges, and it is good client relations.

3.85 Points to agree on the scheme for recovery include:

(a) What is the preferred financial year?

(b) Does the landlord (or the managing agent) want the service charge collected quarterly in advance on the usual quarter days, or do they want some different arrangement?

(c) Are year end excess amounts to be carried forward or repaid?

(d) Are there to be certificates? If so, are they certificates of total cost or the tenant's proportion or both? Who should prepare accounts and give certificates?

A Checklist appears as Appendix 1 and can be used as an aide memoire for these purposes.

3.86 When tenants have a strong bargaining position in a weak market, getting the lease right is more important than ever. If the landlord does not make it clear in the lease (a) what property is to be maintained etc and paid for through the service charge, and (b) precisely what services are to be provided by the landlord, then the tenant will have the opportunity to argue about the validity and/or amount of the charge. With rents at a low level, the last thing the landlord wants to see is an unexpected shortfall in recovery from the tenant of what he pays out on providing services.

3.87 While most solicitors have standard leases which include a wide range of possible items in the description of the 'common parts' which the landlord is to maintain, and an equally wide description of the services to be provided, there is no substitute for inspecting and walking the site with the managing agents and the landlord and discussing their instructions to see what is appropriate.

3.88 There have been many cases showing potential difficulties that should be avoided, but a few cases may suffice as examples.

(a) In *Tennant Radiant Heat Ltd v Warrington Development Corporation* [1988] 1 EGLR 41 various judges differed over whether the roof was included in the demise or not: clearer definitions would have made the case unnecessary.

(b) In *Embassy Court Residents' Association Ltd v Lipman* [1984] 2 EGLR 60 the landlord had covenanted to have the windows cleaned: it was held as matter of interpretation of the relevant lease that this included cleaning all the windows, and not just those in the common parts. Such problems could be avoided by a few extra words of clarification.

(c) The landlord in *Frobisher (Second Investments) Ltd v Killoran Trust Co Ltd* [1980] 1 All ER 488 was not able to charge bank interest where the lease did not refer to interest and only contained vague expressions such as 'general management and administration of the property'. Obviously, doubt on any such aspects can lead to disputes and loss.

Use a sweeping-up clause

3.89   Ideally a lease will refer to all the services and will cover all necessary property. In case something is overlooked, or there are changes after the lease is granted, there should in every lease be a sweeping-up clause. These are, unfortunately for the landlord, not an answer to a major omission, but a sweeping-up clause may assist where there is some doubt. The majority of cases where a sweeping-up clause has been the subject of a dispute have shown that the sweeping-up clause cannot be relied upon to fill a big gap. It has been described as 'more of a sticking plaster than a crutch'. The sweeping-up clause is discussed in more detail in Chapter 5 at **5.196** et seq.

Avoid landlord's conditions precedent

3.90   This paragraph is just a brief reminder that a landlord should not make life more difficult for himself than necessary. He could create unnecessary problems by including in the draft (or permitting a negotiated revision to a lease) imposing on himself an obligation to carry out some act as a preliminary to being able to recover the cost. For example, in *Northways Flats Management Co (Camden) Ltd v Wimpey Pension Trustees Ltd* [1992] 2 EGLR 42, a landlord had agreed that it would provide specifications and estimates to the tenant for major works before carrying them out. When the landlord failed to do so it was unable to recover the cost. There are details of the wording at **6.42**. A similar result arose in *CIN Properties Ltd v Barclays Bank plc* [1986] 1 EGLR 59 (discussed at **14.22**), where there were very substantial figures.

3.91   On the converse side, it has been held in a number of cases that a condition precedent to be fulfilled by the tenant (such as where the landlord's covenant to provide services commences with words such as 'subject to the lessee paying the Maintenance Contribution') is not effective, eg *Yorkbrook Investments Ltd v Batten* [1985] 2 EGLR 100. In any event, if the landlord fails to provide the services to a non-paying tenant he may well be in breach of his obligations to those tenants who have paid. In *Yorkbrook* the landlords, in effect, sought to claim that the tenant could not sue for breach of the landlord's covenants because he had not paid the service charge. The landlord failed in this respect.

Make the service charge terms reasonable

3.92   If the draft lease terms are basically fair and reasonable, the landlord is more likely to have them agreed by a negotiating tenant than if the landlord starts from a very tough precedent. It is only where the market is such that a landlord can insist on a tenant signing a lease in the form submitted that the terms as drafted are likely to be accepted. Even in such cases many solicitors for tenants will want to make alterations to cover matters that particularly concern the proposed tenant, or are matters on which the solicitor in question foresees problems. If the lease is drawn as fairly as possible there is more chance of the majority being acceptable. (Views on fairness often differ depending on which side of the desk you sit!)

3.93   In this context, including in a lease of commercial premises provisions giving the tenant some protection on the lines of that in the Landlord and Tenant Act 1985 (which applies to leases of dwellings) is worth considering. The three provisions are:

(a) *Section 20 of the 1985 Act* – a provision that, at least for substantial items, the landlord will obtain a minimum number of estimates. He could go further to ensure that at least one will be independent. The clause could also go on and provide that copies of specifications (or plans) should be supplied to the tenants before work commences, with the tenant having an opportunity either to make representations on the specification or the proposed costs, and/or to suggest other contractors who should be asked to give estimates. (This may seem contrary to the comment above that the landlord should not make life more difficult for himself by including a condition precedent, but if the leases all contain similar provisions the managing agents should be able remember to follow the system proposed in the lease.) Obtaining estimates is recommended in the Commercial Code – so a clause offering it helps to show a reasonable attitude on the part of the landlord.

(b) *Section 22 of the 1985 Act* – a provision that the tenant will have the right to inspect vouchers on reasonable notice in respect of works done. There should be a sensible time limit – perhaps inspection within two months of the account for the year end adjustment being sent by the landlord. If the tenant does not inspect (or object) within that period he can be assumed (in the lease) to agree the service charge accounts. This is not a major concession by the landlord because if a dispute comes to court the tenant will usually be able to require production of material papers.

(c) *Section 42 of the 1987 Act* – to provide that the payments by the tenant are held in trust. This is not unreasonable, but some landlords take the view that they cannot agree unless all the leases are on the same basis.

49

ENSURING THAT MANAGEMENT CHARGES CAN BE RECOVERED

3.94   There are many items a landlord should ensure are included in the service charge recovery provisions. Management costs include the costs for arranging for works and services, collecting service charge contributions, as well as the accounting side of a landlord and tenant relationship, and complying with any applicable legislation. In the case of commercial premises the costs can be substantial and are more or less unavoidable; it is therefore important to ensure that they are recoverable wherever possible. As with other service charge matters one key to the recovery of such costs is to express them as one of the matters for which a charge can be made. There are a few problems, however, where management is carried out by the landlord. These are the subject of comment in Chapter 5 (see **5.169** et seq). A draftsman should be aware of the problems and should try to avoid, or at least warn the landlord of, the potential difficulties.

3.95   It has been held that in-house management costs can rarely be recoverable: *Cleve House Properties Ltd v Schildof* (1980) CLY 1641. Here, the directors of the landlord company carried out management, and the landlord company included a 15% management charge which was disallowed in a case under the first statutory residential service charge protection for residential tenants (s 91A of the Housing Finance Act 1972) as the management charge did not represent a liability the landlord had incurred or actually paid. By contrast, management by the parent or subsidiary of the landlord company can be the subject of a valid charge: *Parkside Knightsbridge Ltd v Horwitz* [1983] 2 EGLR 42, where the parent company managed a number of properties. This case was three years after the *Schildof* case. A similar decision was reached in 1992 where management of a number of blocks of flats owned by an individual was carried out by a company owned by the individual, and the court was satisfied that the company was not simply a sham – *Skilleter v Charles* [1992] 1 EGLR 73. Where the management (in this case providing a certificate) was supposed to be carried out by the landlord's surveyor but was actually carried out by the landlord himself under another name this was easily held to be a sham in *Finchbourne Ltd v Rodrigues* [1976] 3 All ER 581.

3.96   A number of cases (eg *Regis Property Co Ltd v Dudley* [1958] 1 QB 346; *Perseus Property Co Ltd v Burberry* [1985] 1 EGLR 114) have indicated that profit can be charged as well as management charges, but this needs careful handling to achieve. It may also be particularly hard to persuade a tenant to agree in a bad economic climate. Again, if the landlord wants to be able to charge a profit it should be set out in the lease so that the basis on which a charge is to be made is apparent to a reader.

3.97   If a tenant asks for a cap on management charges, remember that what may be acceptable, today, as a charge for managing may not be so in five years time, when circumstances may be very different. (The same point applies to any service charge cap.) It is also important for both landlord and tenant to remember that if the management charges are restricted by reference to a percentage of the cost this could lead to a shortfall, particularly if the landlord is providing relatively few services in which event the costs of providing those services may seem relatively high compared to the rent. Different ways of assessing management charges are mentioned in Chapter 5 (at **5.173** et seq).

STATEMENT OF INTENT

3.98   Interpretation of any document can be helped by a statement in the document setting out what is intended. (The author is a great believer in recitals in documents, as well as front sheets that give real information.) If the intention is for the landlord to be able to recover 100% of all his expenses, a statement to that effect within the service charge provisions can assist in case of a dispute. A clause could be such as: 'It is hereby agreed that the intention of the service charge provisions in this Lease is to enable the Landlord to recover [all its] [its] reasonable and proper] costs of management and maintenance of the building.' The 'reasonable and proper' alternative may encourage tenants to accept the clause, although they may seek to expand the clause by adding exclusions (inherent defects, etc) as suggested above.

SERVICE CHARGE CAP

3.99   If the parties agree to the service charge being restricted, the drafting needs to ensure that the cap clearly reflects the arrangement reached (see **3.71** above on this). Points for a landlord to watch are:

(a)   Is it personal to the original tenant? (It normally would be, as it is that tenant who has negotiated a cap, although this is not necessarily the case). Assuming it is personal, this should be clearly expressed and, for example, the provision should make it apparent whether it is only to apply while the named tenant is trading from the premises (or occupying them in the case of a residential tenant), so that the cap will cease to apply where the premises are assigned, underlet or become vacant.

(b)   If the cap is to a specific percentage of rent then the clause should clarify what is to happen on rent review. One alternative is for the service charge to be reassessed each time there is a rent review and the cap reimposed at the new figure. Another possibility is for the cap to be increased by the same percentage as the rent.

COVENANT FOR TENANT TO PAY

3.100   The landlord should include a covenant by the tenant to pay the service charge – it is sometimes overlooked. The landlord was just able to recover against a former tenant in *Royton Industries Ltd v Lawrence* [1994] 1 EGLR 110, where the property was demised to the tenant 'yielding and paying' the service charge, but without an actual covenant for him to pay. However, it is clearly best to have a proper covenant. And in *Hafton Properties Ltd v Camp* [1994] 1 EGLR 67, the tenant had covenanted to pay the service charge to the management company, not the landlord. The landlord sought possession on the basis of non-payment and it was held his claim did not stand up.

Service charge on lease renewal

Service charge on business lease renewal

3.101 Under s 24 of the Landlord and Tenant Act 1954, a business lease continues until determined in accordance with the Act. Thereafter, with certain exceptions, the tenant can apply to the court for a new lease. Most are renewed by agreement, but a few reach a court hearing and thus give rise to case law.

3.102 One of the most significant landlord and tenant cases of recent decades was *O'May v City of London Real Property Co Ltd* [1983] 2 AC 726. This was a House of Lords decision. A business lease of an office suite in a large block in the city of London had expired. Under the expired lease the tenants (a firm of solicitors) had paid a rent inclusive of services. On renewal the landlord sought a rent exclusive of service charges, ie a lease at a rent with a separate service charge. The tenant objected to the change and the matter came to court, ultimately reaching the House of Lords. The tenants relied, in part, on s 35 of the Landlord and Tenant Act 1954 under which, on renewal, the court has to 'have regard' to the terms of the existing lease. The Court of Appeal and the House of Lords both agreed with the tenants, and thus held that the landlord could not impose a service charge where there had been none before. Similarly, in *Roux Restaurants Ltd v Jaison Property Development Co Ltd* [1996] EGCS 118 the landlord was held to be unreasonably refusing consent to assignment where (in effect) licence was made conditional on a variation to the lease under which the landlord could recover all outgoings.

3.103 Many tenants, in similar circumstances, are prepared to negotiate a new lease to include a service charge provided that the rent is reduced to reflect the extra financial burden (various concessions were offered in the *O'May* case but the tenants would not agree), but the *O'May* case is useful ammunition for any tenant who wants to say 'no'.

3.104 In a very unusual case, *Amarjee v Barrowfen Properties Ltd* [1993] 2 EGLR 133, business premises had been let on a verbal tenancy. Following service of the landlord's notice to terminate the verbal tenancy, the tenant applied for a new lease. The verbal tenancy had, not unnaturally, been imprecise and the parties disagreed over a number of matters to be included (or not) in the new lease. These included upward only rent reviews, dealings with part, and the release of liability on assignment. The service charge dispute was as to how much of the landlord's adjoining property was to be material for the tenant's service charge responsibility. The tenant's furniture warehouse (in Tooting) was part of a terrace of commercial property owned by the landlord. The shops in the parade (other than numbers 210 to 214, the subject of the tenant's verbal tenancy) were each subject to a service charge calculated by reference to the whole parade. The tenant wanted the service charge to cover: (a) the exterior and common parts only of his property (210 to 214) and of 204 to 208 (next door); (b) a proportion of the sprinkler costs for the whole parade, and also of the car park; and (c) fire escape maintenance of the whole block. The landlord wanted the service charge to be consistent with the other leases in the block which all related to the whole block. The court agreed with the landlord. The judge said:

> 'There are in my judgment sufficient common features in the parade to make sense of the joint service charge, namely the sprinkler system, fire escape routes and the access and car park. I do not see, even now, how an alternative system acceptable to all tenants can properly be devised until such time as they are all subject to the same arrangement.'

Note that the judge supported the landlord's position, but there was no prior written lease with which any new lease terms could be compared.

3.105   In *Kruger Trading Ltd v Global Network Holdings Ltd* [2004] EWHC 1396 (Ch), interpretation was needed for a rectification claim. Interpretation in normal circumstances and interpretation for rectification can be different. (See eg the article on the *Kruger* case by Jennifer Shilton in *Property Law Journal* 1 November 2004.) In the *Kruger* case one factor in deciding that a lease was a lease of part and not of whole was that the tenant was to pay a fixed service charge percentage.

SERVICE CHARGE ON RESIDENTIAL CONTINUATION

3.106   At the end of a lease of residential premises for more than 21 years at a low rent (ie a lease within Pt 1 of the Landlord and Tenant Act 1954, per s 2 of that Act) the tenant is entitled to remain as a statutory tenant. Where the landlord of such a lease served the appropriate notice (in *Blatherwick (Services) Ltd v King* [1991] Ch 218) the tenant became entitled to a statutory tenancy. The tenant tried to persuade the court that under s 10(1)(b) of the Landlord and Tenant Act 1954 the liability for service charge was not continued during the statutory tenancy, but the contrary view of the landlord was upheld in the Court of Appeal. (This case is discussed further at **10.53**.)

RENEWAL OF PART

3.107   If a tenant has granted an underlease of part of business premises special considerations apply. In effect, at the end of the term, the sub-tenant of part can apply for a new lease of the part he occupies. (A business tenant is not entitled to renew a lease unless he occupies and the intermediate tenant may not be the 'competent landlord,' leaving the superior landlord and undertenant to deal direct (Landlord and Tenant Act 1954, s 44)). If, for example, Unit K had been divided into three equal segments K1, K2 and K3, and the tenant had (as part of the negotiations) agreed that the sub-tenant of K3 should pay only one quarter of the total service charge charged to Unit K (rather than one third) what happens on renewal? There are no citeable authorities, but it seems that the court would have to look at the subdivided unit on renewal as a proportion of the whole of the landlord's property as if it were an original letting. On that basis on renewal of the lease of Unit K3 alone the service charge percentage would be based on whatever apportionment basis is used. If floor area is used, it would be the proportion of the floor area of Unit K3 compared to the floor area of the whole of the landlord's property, and thus would be likely to be the equivalent of one third of the percentage charged for Unit K as a whole.

UPDATING

3.108   It is generally accepted that a landlord on renewal of a lease can update the lease, at least to some extent. (This was accepted in *O'May* (see **3.102** above).) How far the terms can be revised is largely a matter of negotiation and negotiating strength. The age of the expiring lease is material. If it was only granted three years ago, there is less scope for saying its terms are significantly out of date than if it was 21 years old.

3.109   Two common updating items, material for service charges, are VAT and interest. Leases before 1989 did not normally mention VAT – an amendment to refer to it now must be acceptable. Older leases often failed to impose an interest penalty on late payments: again most parties will accept that such an obligation is a normal feature of modern leases, although some tenants resist or only agree if the interest rate is less than that used in new leases.

3.110   For service charge purposes the following need to be remembered:

(a)   A lease granted many years ago may have referred to services that are no longer needed, or may have not have referred to services which are actually provided. (Examples of items not referred to in older leases might be an intercom system, air conditioning, a security system or Internet connections.) It should be possible to persuade a court to agree to update the lease on such factual matters where there is evidence that the services are no longer needed, or have been provided since the old lease commenced and paid for, as the case may be. The only likely problem would be where the tenant objects to the 'new' services, but if they exist and have been paid for in the past, they should be properly included in a renewed lease.

(b)   The landlord's property, over which the services are carried out, may have changed since the earlier lease was granted. Again, it is hard to see why revised definitions reflecting reality at the commencement of the new term should not be accepted.

(c) A landlord should beware of trying to change the service charge terms of one lease where others are not changed. If there is a dispute and the service charge provisions of the leases are not consistent, there is likely to be a shortfall. (There are provisions under which tenants of long leases of dwellings can apply to the court to vary leases. The service charge consequences are discussed in Chapter 10 (**10.2** et seq).)

CHAPTER 4

The procedure for collection

The art of taxation consists of plucking the goose so as to obtain the largest quantity of down with the least possible amount of hissing.

Jean Baptiste Colbert

FORMER SYSTEMS

4.1   Originally, contributions to the repair of items used in common were collected as and when they were incurred. If a party wall or a party drain needed to be repaired, the landlord would arrange for it to be done and then, where his lease permitted him to do so, would call on the tenant to repay the amount spent (or the relevant proportion). In those cases where a landlord also owned the adjoining property and had agreed to carry out works such as external decoration, it became more customary for the landlord to expect to be repaid each year, and originally, such reimbursement tended to be annually in arrear. Later, it became more normal for the landlord to expect the tenant to pay first, before the work was done, and the current custom is for most service charges to be paid by the tenant in advance.

4.2   It was at one time unlawful for a landlord of residential tenancies to require payment in advance. (Housing Finance Act 1972, s 91A. This was discussed in *Frobisher (Second Investments) Ltd v Killoran Trust Co Ltd* [1980] 1 All ER 488). This is not now prohibited.

4.3   In *Daiches v Bluelake Investments Ltd* [1985] 2 EGLR 67, the court was asked if the lease permitted the landlord to collect money in advance. The court was not required to decide the point, as it happened, but indicated that if it had been required to do so it would have said that the relevant lease did not permit the landlord to call for advance payments for repairs and, in effect, the judge implied (obiter) that if the lease was silent there would be no implied right to advance payments. The case was an application for the appointment of a receiver of residential property, and was heard before the power to appoint a manager under Pt 11 of the Landlord and Tenant Act 1987 came into force. The point was that if the landlord was unable to call for advance payments he would not have been able to afford to carry out the repairs. Although lack of money to repair is no excuse for a landlord not to carry out repairs (*Francis v Cowcliffe Ltd* (1976) 33 P & CR 368), the inability to obtain payment before the event could have been a material factor in deciding whether or not the appointment of a receiver was appropriate.

NOT OPERATING THE LEASE SYSTEM

4.4   What is the effect where the payment system contained in the lease is not used? This was the position in *D'Jan v Bond Street Estates plc* [1993] EGCS 43. There the normal service charge contribution for some industrial units, after the first year, was to be equivalent to what the landlord had spent in the preceding year. Over a period the system changed and the landlord claimed regular expenditure at the end of each quarter plus amounts for which he had invoices. At one point the tenant was dissatisfied with an invoice but agreed to make payment by post-dated cheques. Later, he cancelled one cheque and substituted a smaller cheque. The landlord distrained. The Court of Appeal held that the distress was unlawful. The change to the system laid down by the lease simply had the effect of waiving the strict obligations under the lease. Distress would only be lawful (assuming the service charge is reserved as rent) if it could be shown that it was part of the revised arrangements, and accepted by the tenant, that failure to pay in accordance with the varied practice could give rise to distraint.

4.5   By way of comment it is worth noticing that, although it is often said that a deed can only be varied by a deed, the court accepted that a course of conduct created an effective variation in this case.

4.6   In a recent and significant case, *Universities Superannuation Fund Scheme Ltd v Marks & Spencer Ltd* [1999] 04 EG 158, the landlord of commercial property had claimed service charges based on wrong figures. The leases on a large shopping centre at Telford shared costs on the basis of comparable rateable values. The landlord had based his demands on an assumed rateable value for the M&S store of £348,600, rather than the correct figure of £848,600. When the landlord realised his mistake, he tried to recover what should have been the balance but failed at first instance. Under the lease the tenant had 42 days to object to a demand: the lower court held that it was unreasonable for the tenant to have to a strict time limit for objections but for the landlord to have unlimited time to vary his incorrect demand. A second important point arose. As is the way of rateable values, this one was subject to appeal by the tenants, and the appeal was successful in reducing the rateable value to £700,000. The tenant argued that if the landlord had been able to backdate the demands then the calculations should be based on the revised rateable value figure. The lower court said it was unreasonable (after what might be several years) for a landlord to have to adjust the whole of the service charge figures because of a change. This decision was reversed by the Court of Appeal. Although the tenant had paid what it had been asked to pay, the actual obligation of the tenant is to pay the correct amount it is liable to pay under the lease. The payment of a smaller sum was not performance by the tenant of its obligation under the lease. The certificate simply had to certify the landlord's expenditure: it did not certify the amount payable by the tenant. It was in any event not expressly or by implication final and conclusive. The effect was that the service charge could be reassessed. (This could perhaps be seen as another case where the court made a reasonable decision on the facts. Whether it would have been different if the certificate needed had been a certificate of what was payable is open to question, but the point about the tenant's obligation to pay the correct amount seems to suggest that if the certificate had been of the amount payable it would still have been overturned.)

4.7 In a different twist a management company agreed to accept a lower service charge from the tenant if the tenant carried out certain functions in place of the management company. It was held that the tenant had not done so (failing to remove graffiti) and the management company was held justified in reverting to the original percentage: *Malt Mill Developments Ltd and Anchor Brewhouse Management Co Ltd v Davis* [2002] EWCA Civ 440.

4.8 In a separate aspect where a tenant did not follow the lease system, a tenant holding a long lease of a flat in Shortlands, Kent replaced the windows in her flat without landlord's consent: *Broomleigh Housing Association Ltd v Hughes* [1999] EGCS 134. The landlord replaced other windows in the block, and the tenant argued that she should only be liable for her proportion of the costs of replacing windows in the common parts, not the windows of other flats. It was accepted that the landlord had waived the breach caused by her carrying out works. However, that did not mean that all the other rights had been waived, and the payment of service charge by the tenant was not affected by the prior waiver of a different lease provision. (See also *Metropolitan Properties Ltd v Wilson* [2002] EWHC 1853 (Ch), [2003] L & TR 15, discussed at **5.44**.)

4.9 The common factor in all these cases seems to be that the court tries to achieve the result which most closely resembles the system laid down by the lease. It seems to be the case that informal variations are treated almost as severed from the rest of the lease. For comments on varying fixed percentages see at **4.24** and **6.45**.

CURRENT COLLECTION PROCEDURE

4.10 In modern leases the most usual collection method is as set out below:

(a) *Assessing next year's requirements* The landlord or his agent will assess what works and services are expected to be needed for the coming financial year, ie the accounting year, which is often identified in the lease. These will be costed, and the estimate should include all costs which the landlord expects to incur in the coming year based on the rolling programme of work which should be prepared for those properties where there is more than merely a nominal amount to be done. A contingency element should also be included where it is considered appropriate.

(b) *Estimating next year's proportions* The landlord's agent (the managing agent) will then calculate what proportion of that total estimated figure (and any reserve or sinking fund contribution) is properly payable by each tenant. For residential property the landlord may, at this stage, need to consult with the tenants under Landlord and Tenant Act 1985, s 20 (see **9.56**).

(c) *Sending demands* The managing agent will send out demands for payment, usually quarterly in advance. The agent will divide the estimated total payable by the tenant for the year by four, and the demand will be for that figure. The demand is usually sent at the same time as the demand for rent. Depending on the terms of the lease, the demand may need to be accompanied by some form of certificate, although it is unusual at this stage.

(d) *During the year* The premises are managed, with works and services being carried out, and service charges on account demanded in each of the following quarters.

(e) *Year end adjustment* After the end of the accounting year, the managing agents will calculate the actual expenditure on service charge items (or sums incurred) and the amounts received in that year. At the same time, they should assess whether costs have been incurred for which no bill has been received.

(f) *Preparing accounts* The agent will then need to prepare accounts (or have them prepared) to show the balance in hand at the start of the year, the amounts paid out, the receipts from the tenants, and the amount of any reserve. The accounts will normally be audited at this stage.

(g) *Sending accounts to tenants* Once the accounts are prepared, the managing agents should send copies to the tenants with a separate bill indicating the amount of any balance due to or from the tenant. (Notes to the accounts to clarify aspects are also considered beneficial and recommended in the Codes of Practice.) This will often be accompanied by some form of certificate. See later in this chapter (**4.78** et seq). What happens to any difference between the amount paid on account and the balance shown at the year end depends on the provisions of the lease – it may be refunded, or held as a credit, or overpayments in excess of a certain figure may be liable to be repaid.

(h) *Start again* The procedure is then repeated for following years.

An illustrative timetable

4.11   The following has been suggested (with thanks to Gordon Farrow) as a suitable timetable for managing agents for the accounting procedure for commercial property, based on a service charge year commencing on 25 December.

(a) *October/November* Collate expenditure information for the previous nine months. Adjust by deleting non-recurring costs, and updating the regular costs to assess the 12-month total. Adjust for inflation and non-recurring costs anticipated in the next 12 months. On the basis of this information prepare an estimate for the year from 25 December, and consult with the tenants or tenants' association prior to confirming the budget for the year.

(b) *December* Notify the tenants of the estimate for the year from 25 December and demand on-account service charges for the quarter starting on that date. Ensure the collecting system has the same figure for the next three quarters.

(c) *February/March* Prepare statements of expenditure for the year to 25 December just past. Carry out service charge audit/reconciliation. Calculate balances owing by tenants or refunds/credits due to tenants, and issue demands.

(d) *October/November* Start again.

Miscellaneous points on accounts

4.12   Time is not of the essence for production of accounts according to *West Central Investments Ltd v Borovik* [1977] 1 EGLR 29. There the service charge was fixed for the first three years, after which accounts were to be prepared. No accounts were prepared for the years 1970 to 1973, but this did not prevent the landlord being able to recover. Such a delay cannot, however, be recommended, and if the lease had made time of the essence for producing accounts the landlord would have lost.

In residential cases there is a prohibition on recovering costs incurred more than 18 months before unless the tenant has been notified about the costs (Landlord and Tenant Act 1985, s 20B) and there is possibly going to be an obligation on the landlord to provide a statement within six months of the end of the financial year, certified by an accountant (Landlord and Tenant Act 1985, s 21) and a right for the tenant to withhold payment until it is produced (Landlord and Tenant Act 1985, s 21A). The landlord may also, in due course, need to send to the (residential) tenant a prescribed summary of rights and obligations (Landlord and Tenant Act 1985, s 21(4)). All these are discussed in Chapter 9. The Commercial Code recommends producing accounts within 4 months of the year end.

If the lease refers to accounts of 'costs paid' it means what it says. It is better to refer to costs 'incurred'. They give a fairer picture, as well as enabling recovery sooner rather than later. Costs 'incurred 'include sums paid, but also items where a bill has been delivered but not paid, or work done for which no bill has been delivered.

Computer aids

> *To err is human: to really foul things up requires a computer.*
>
> Bill Vaughan

4.13   There are a number of computer programs to aid the process. Anyone seeking a computer program needs to make sure it has sufficient capacity for the number of tenants and information to be held (with ample room for expansion). It also needs to be able to prepare accounts and regular statements (eg monthly or weekly) showing the budgeted figures and the actual income and expenditure. It also helps if this can show how these compare with the previous year's performance. The program should be able to generate the demands containing all pertinent information and (for residential) ensure that the demands comply with statute. The program needs to be able to cover leap years, arrears, interest payments, and in particular to be able to prepare figures showing what each tenant is liable to pay at any time, bearing in mind the differences between the obligations of different tenants (eg where ground floor tenants are not liable for lift expenses, or concessions granted to individual tenants). In choosing a system a recommendation from someone who uses a particular program is probably the best guide. Larger firms tend to have their own custom designed systems.

Initial estimated figure

4.14   Sometimes a lease contains a provision that the service charge for the first year is a particular figure. This is intended to assist tenants, although it may have unexpected stamp duty land tax consequences. It should be made clear whether it is a figure for a whole year, apportioned for the initial period, or is subject to adjustment during the initial year. (The initial period just mentioned is of course from the date the service charge first becomes payable to the last day of the first service charge year).

Holding the payments made by tenants

4.15   Unless the lease specifically so requires, there is no obligation in the case of commercial property on the managing agents to hold the advance payments received from tenants on interest bearing accounts. It is, however, recommended in the Commercial Code, para 58 for sinking funds (see Chapter 11). The Landlord and Tenant Act 1987 provides that payments by tenants of dwellings are held on trust, and it is proposed that they must be held in a designated account (Landlord and Tenant Act 1987, ss 42 and 42A).

4.16   A commercial tenant may do well, when negotiating, to seek a provision that the money is placed in an account earning interest, with the interest, less tax if any, being credited to the service charge account. It has been commented that such a provision can be unfair as between the tenants if one pays before the others, and that the interest earned should be credited to the individual tenants for the period from the date of receipt from them. It is suggested that except in very simple cases (or very high service charges), the costs of making any such calculation would outweigh any real benefit. The accounts are continually being debited and credited, and such calculations might thus need to be made for a large number of tenants with different payment percentages virtually on a daily basis.

Rent or service charge paid by a third party

4.17   If rent, or service charge reserved as rent, is received from a third party the landlord or his agent needs to take care. A common clause in the lease to the effect that acceptance of rent is not to be treated as a waiver of a breach of covenant is normally considered to be ineffective. If there is a known breach and the rent is accepted it is likely that the breach will be waived unless it is a continuing breach (such as lack of repair). (An unauthorised assignment is a one-off breach. Accepting rent from the assignee after knowledge of the breach could be treated as a waiver of the breach, or could in some circumstances be treated as creating a new tenancy.) The problem about accepting rent from a third party in such a case is that if it creates a waiver it prevents the landlord from being able to forfeit the lease. A landlord will still, however, be able to sue for damages. It is reasonably safe in most cases to accept rent that is tendered by someone who is apparently the wrong person unless the landlord wants the ability to forfeit the lease. If the landlord is not really concerned about the identity of the tenant, or if market conditions are such that finding a new tenant is going to be difficult, a landlord may decide to accept the payment. The best route may well be to acknowledge the payment saying that it is accepted as a payment on behalf of the tenant. Unless the payer disputes that the payment was made on behalf of the tenant (in which case the landlord will have to consider the position further), the letter can be used to assist a landlord should it later be alleged that the receipt created a waiver of a breach of covenant.

ASSESSING SHARES OF COSTS

The tenant's proportion of costs

4.18   In some cases the lease provides that the tenant pays a fixed proportion, eg X% of the costs, or X% of some costs and Y% of other costs. The latter is usual where there is a lease of a property within a building that is itself within a development or larger area for which the costs are chargeable. For example, if the tenant is one of five tenants of a building he may pay one fifth of the costs relating to that building (decoration, repair, the lift, etc) but only one twentieth of the costs of managing the grounds (gardening, the maintenance of the access roads, security gates, etc) where there are other buildings sharing the same grounds.

4.19   The alternative is payment of a *'fair proportion'* or some similar phrase.

4.20   In the past residential tenants tended to have fixed percentages and commercial tenants tended to have *'fair proportion'* provisions, although now commercial leases are more often on the basis of specified percentages.

How do you calculate the fair proportion?

4.21   There does not seem to be any express court authority on the way to calculate the fair proportion save that the final words of the judgment in *Jollybird Ltd V Fairzone Ltd* [1990] 2 EGLR 55 (which related only to heating costs) supported the tenant's contention that the proportion should be the same as the area of the demised premises compared to the total lettable floor areas supplied with central heating by the landlords. This may suggest that the percentage should be assessed depending on the benefit for the various tenants, and could thus differ for heating as compared to other services such as lift costs or repairs, where some tenants benefit and some do not.

4.22   Assessing the proportion payable is the subject of the next major section in this chapter (**4.30** et seq). Section D5 of the Commercial Code mentioned in Chapter 11 covers the various means of apportionment.

4.23   Using a fair proportion enables the landlord to adjust payments so as to charge tenants only for those items that directly affect them, whereas the fixed percentage is a *'swings and roundabouts'* arrangement. For example, the tenant of the ground floor may not feel he has any direct benefit from the roof, and the tenant of the top floor may not feel he has any direct benefit from the foundations, but charging a fixed percentage means that the tenants of both the ground floor and the top floor contribute to the repair costs of both roof and foundations.

VARYING A FIXED PERCENTAGE OR SET AMOUNT

4.24   The way the proportion is calculated is described below, but where the percentage is fixed the landlord should reserve the right to change the percentage in case of need. There is very limited scope for varying a fixed percentage otherwise. Remember that a change can as often benefit a tenant as a landlord.

4.25   In *Pole Properties Ltd v Feinberg* [1981] 2 EGLR 38 the court held it had an inherent power to change a fixed percentage, but only where the circumstances had changed so dramatically that the basis on which the original figure had been assessed was no longer material. The case concerned heating costs for a flat. The tenant was liable to pay the excess of heating costs over a fixed rate. The flat was in a house converted into flats. The landlord later bought the adjoining house and converted that into flats as well. The landlord then changed the heating systems so that one system heated not only both houses but also areas that had not formerly been heated (eg the halls and stairwells). The court held that the change in circumstances justified the court in changing the fixed percentage. Clearly, there was a very great change, and more subtle changes may not be sufficient to permit such variation by the court. (See also **5.146** and **5.147** below, and **3.32** above.)

4.26   A further attempt to change a fixed percentage also concerned heating costs. In *Jollybird Ltd v Fairzone Ltd* [1990] 2 EGLR 55, the premises were commercial premises in Cricklewood Broadway. In clause 2 of the lease the tenant covenant to pay:

> 'a fair proportion (being not less in any event than the rate of 1/3d per square foot of the floor area of the demised premises) of the cost of supplying central heating

... such proportion to be calculated in accordance with the ratio of the floor area of [X] to [Y] .... Provided That the sum payable may be increased proportionately ... if the cost of fuel for supplying such heating shall at any time exceed the cost thereof at the date of the lease ...'

At the date of the lease it seems the landlord would have been able to recover more than 100% of the cost by applying the floor area ratio to the then cost of the fuel. After argument the case went to the Court of Appeal which reviewed the alternative interpretations in detail. It came down in favour of saying the proper interpretation was the charge should be a fair proportion of the actual cost (calculated on the basis of the comparative floor area) 'but subject to a minimum charge at the rate per square foot' stated in the lease.

4.27   In a case mentioned briefly before (at **3.25**), a tenant held a lease of five out of six flats over commercial premises in Marylebone Street London (Block A). In the 1970s the landlord acquired the premises next door (Block B), which included three flats. The two properties were connected internally. The landlord wanted to treat 'the Building' for which service charges were payable as both Blocks A and B. Apparently 'the Building' was not defined in the lease, but there were six flats in Block A. Four of the flats contributed one sixth each and the fifth contributed one quarter. The other flat was, in effect, for occupation by the landlord, free of service charge. A tenant taking a lease would have been aware there were six flats in Block A and three in Block B. Being asked to pay a contribution of one sixth of costs of the building seemed to imply this was in relation to Block A only. The court held that 'the Building' must be just Block A. The landlord's proposal would put an undue burden on the tenants of Block A. (*Stapel (Ernst) v Bellshore Property Investments Ltd* [2001] 2 EGLR 7.)

4.28   For some residential cases there is specific power for the court to vary percentages (see **10.2**, and the comments on s 35(2)(f) of the Landlord and Tenant Act 1987.)

4.29   There is limited authority for the proposition that if a document says the charge for an item can be reviewed the document is likely to be construed to enable either party to call for a review. This follows from the case of *IVS Enterprises Ltd v Chelsea Cloisters Management Ltd* [1994] EGCS 14. A television system was provided for a block of flats under the provisions of an agreement between the freeholder and the management company. The agreement provided for a basic charge (initially £5.60 per flat) but said the basic charge 'may be reviewed with effect from 1st July 1987 and each subsequent 1st July ... to such sum as shall be reasonable having regard to comparable charges for similar services...' A dispute arose as to whether the basic charge was reasonable and, if it was more than reasonable, whether the management company was entitled to seek a review. The Court of Appeal held that the agreement did not give one party alone the right to call for a review. As the premises were dwellings, the management company was bound by the 'reasonableness' provisions of s 19 of the Landlord and Tenant Act 1985, and was under a duty to ensure that the amounts charged to the tenants were reasonably incurred. The court also made the point that the management company could not recover over-payments made under a mistake of fact (a rule which was changed by a subsequent decision). It was, however, entitled to treat the money received from the tenants in excess of the proper amount as held on trust for the tenants and not the TV company, and so it could set off against future payments those sums it could show had been overpaid.

WAYS TO CALCULATE THE TENANT'S SHARE

4.30   Whether the tenant's proportion of the service charge is expressed in the lease as a fixed percentage or not, in practice the landlord always calculates the sum due from the tenant on the basis of a percentage (or different percentages of different costs). (See also paras 41-47 and Section D4 of the Commercial Code mentioned in Chapter 11.) Dividing the cost of services is like a restaurant party. The costs of the meal can simply be shared equally regardless of the actual cost of the food and drink consumed by individuals. Alternatively, the cost can be split so that the chap eating boeuf stroganoff and drinking claret would probably pay more than the man with egg and chips and lemonade. So long as the parties are happy to agree the manner of dividing the bill, it does not matter whether one method is used or the other.

4.31   The normal methods to assess the appropriate percentage of service charges (which are discussed more fully below) are:

(a)   a simple division of the number of units (ie if there are ten flats then each pays one tenth) – the equal shares method;

(b)   a percentage based on the total floor area of the premises let by the landlord (usually excluding common parts) compared to the property let – the floor area method;

(c)   a percentage based on the rateable value of the unit let compared to the total rateable value of the premises in the development – the rateable value method;

(d)   a percentage based on the comparative rents payable by different parts of the property (extremely rare);

(e)   a percentage based on floor area, but giving a discount for those premises with larger floor areas – the weighted floor area basis.

The simple fraction

4.32   Basing the service charge percentage on the number of units is relatively rare, and usually only happens in the case of a set of flats of similar size. This is a simple concept and easy to calculate. It is rough and ready because it does not for example take allowance of the fact that a ground floor tenant will not need to use the stairs or see the beautifully decorated stairway or upper halls. Over a period the costs may well even out, with a tenant paying what might seem an unreasonably high figure in one year for matters of no direct concern to him, but a lower figure in another year where the costs relate to matters of more direct concern. The author is not aware of any case where a fixed share of this type has been challenged in court (for example by a ground floor tenant objecting to an equal share where the lift costs are high), but in the case of flats let on long leases ss 35 to 37 of the Landlord and Tenant Act 1987 permit variations to the lease and could, perhaps, be used to vary a percentage. This is discussed at **10.2-10.12** below.

The floor area basis

4.33   This is the most common method of calculation. It does not have the sophistication of the weighted floor area system, but it does ensure that as between the various tenants the costs are divided so that tenants of the larger units pay larger proportions. Such party may, for example, have a longer frontage to be cleaned or more windows that need to be decorated.

4.34   As with the other methods relating to percentages, it is important for the arrangements to be consistent as between the tenants. A landlord would be open to criticism if he charged some tenants on a floor area basis and some on a rate-able value basis. This may be unavoidable for a period if the development is changing from one system to another, but otherwise it should be avoided. If not, it will be difficult for anyone to be sure whether the costs are properly and fairly apportioned as between the tenants. There could also be cases where the landlord will make a profit by recovering more than 100% where there is a mixed form of recovery. This is not illegal, but it is unsatisfactory to tenants. It may perhaps be possible to persuade a judge that charging tenants on different bases was an appropriate method to achieve fairness, perhaps if some premises are commercial and some residential and are affected by the same services, but this cannot be recommended.

4.35   The floor measurements should be consistent. There are several codes of measuring that are used: whichever one is used should be applied to all the premises or there will be distortion in the figures. The measurements should all be for either gross internal areas or gross external areas. Whether the floor area of the individual unit is calculated by reference to the total floor area of the landlord's property or by reference only to all the areas which are let does not really matter: the proportions as between the let units should be the same either way.

4.36   It is also important to take into account internal changes made by tenants when seeking to compare like with like. For example, when using net internal measurements the figures will be distorted if one tenant has installed extra toilets compared with otherwise equivalent units. Such alteration could not affect the services being provided. Using gross internal areas avoids creating such an anomaly.

4.37 For commercial tenants the sales floor area may be the relevant area. However, some tenants take the view that their service charge percentage should not be increased if they increase their own floor area, eg by installing at their own expense a mezzanine floor. It is likely to be the case that such extra floor space does not involve the landlord in having to provide any more services (assuming the tenant is responsible for internal repair and decoration). A landlord asked to agree a provision clarifying the point should feel able to agree that unless the extra floor space results in the need for extra services it should not affect the service charge percentages.

4.38 On business parks tenants sometimes have freestanding units on a plot, and the service charge is sometimes based on the size of the plot rather than the floor area of the buildings on it. This is because the services are for the benefit of the (tenant's) site, and as it is freestanding the tenant could alter the shape and size of the building and still only require the same services as before. Services in such parks are often only for external matters such as landscaping, road maintenance and security: for such services the size of the buildings on plots is unlikely to be relevant.

4.39 A very important point is the date on which the floor measurement is taken. If the tenant of Flat 3 Hambrook House has to pay 4.287% of the total costs and that percentage is based on the floor area the percentages will need to be changed if the floor areas change as a result of alterations. If, for example, the tenant who owns both Flats 4 and 5 Hambrook House knocks the two flats together and incorporates into the combined flat what had formerly been the end of a common corridor, this will affect the measurements. The floor area for Flat 3 will be a different proportion of the total area of Flats 3, 4 and 5 before and after the alterations. Accordingly, if the lease says the percentages are based on floor areas the landlord needs to recalculate the percentages because of the change. By analogy with the rateable value basis of apportionment (see below), it may be that the landlord should calculate all the service costs and receipts every time there is an alteration, which could mean several sets of calculations each year. (See *Moorcroft Estates Ltd v Doxford* [1980] 1 EGLR 37 discussed below at **4.45**.) This would be very time consuming, and is to be avoided if at all possible. If it is desired to specify in the lease that the tenants' share of costs is to be based on floor area then it is best to make sure it is the floor area on a specified day in each year – either the first or last day of the financial year or 1 January or some other specific date. That means the calculations need only be done once each year, and yet there is flexibility to adjust the figure.

4.40 If the lease does not state how the percentage is to be assessed then it is not necessary to change the percentage unless circumstances substantially change. If the lease provides for payment of a 'fair proportion' then the landlord should consider whether circumstances have changed requiring an adjustment either up or down.

4.41 It is recommended that the managing agents who are first employed (and who thus normally set the first service charge percentages) keep records showing how the figure was reached. Obviously, if floor area is used the areas in question will usually be known and could be recalculated if needed, but the calculations should be readily available. Where floor area is the key, a record of all the floor areas in question is available and sometimes is shown in the accounts. Areas are needed for rent review and other management matters. As and when circumstances change and a new percentage needs to be calculated the change can be demonstrated to the tenants (and the landlord) by reference to the former statistics. It is good practice in such cases for the service charge accounts to have notes explaining the reason for the change.

The rateable value basis

4.42   The basis here depends on the relative rateable values of the properties, in the same way as the floor area method is based on relative square footages. Most of the same matters are material. In particular, if the lease is to mention that the tenant's share is to be based on rateable value ideally it should provide for the calculations to be revised (following a change in the rateable value of one or more units) on a specified day each year.

4.43   The rateable value method of apportionment has a number of drawbacks. The rating system is a highly complex system intended for taxation. The factors used to assess the rateable value have no bearing on the services provided by a landlord. Theoretically, it was originally intended to bear some relationship to the amount a tenant would pay to rent the property. For example, at one time the presence of double glazing or central heating would add to the rateable value of a dwelling as compared to another similar property which did not have these features. It looks as if something on these lines may be introduced again. Neither is likely to affect the service costs, but if rateable value is the yardstick then the tenants of otherwise similar properties will pay different proportions of service charges for reasons unrelated to the services.

4.44   At least as important is the point that an appeal against a rating assessment causes uncertainty, particularly as changes of rateable value (if made) are backdated. This makes an apportionment between tenants calculated correctly on one day wrong some time later, because of the backdating of the rateable value of one of the units. All the figures will need to be adjusted, and of course if tenants have vacated, or assigned or underlet in the meantime such adjustment can be hard to achieve.

4.45   There are two cases in which rateable value has been a key issue. The first is *Moorcroft Estates Ltd v Doxford* [1980] 1 EGLR 37, where a mixed block of commercial and residential property in Kensington was subject to leases containing obligations on tenants to pay a share of costs based on comparative rateable values. The service charges were collected on the basis of the same percentages for some years and there was then a rating revaluation. As the premises were partly residential and partly non-residential, the rateable values for the two different types of units were altered by differing percentages, thus altering the relative proportions paid. The court held that the reference to rateable value must, as a matter of common sense, have meant the rateable value from time to time: alternatively, the landlord could simply have included a fixed percentage (based on the rateable value at the date the leases started) without stating how that percentage was calculated. That settled the point for deciding the tenants' percentages. The second point concerned calculation of landlord's expenses. The court went on to say 'as what is to be calculated is a due proportion of various expenses paid or incurred by the lessors, the rateable values for calculating the due proportion are to be taken at the times when each item was paid or incurred'. The effect was that all the tenant's percentages needed to be reassessed each time there was a change, and the costs incurred need to be apportioned for that period. Accordingly, there would have to be (very time consuming) calculations to apportion the costs for all the leases concerned on several different sets of figures during each accounting year in which there were changes of rateable value for any of the let properties.

4.46 The next major rateable value case was 20 years later. In *Universities Superannuation Fund Scheme Ltd v Marks & Spencer Ltd* [1999] 04 EG 158, Marks & Spencer were tenants of a commercial property in a large shopping centre in Telford which had a rateable value of £848,600. The lease required service charges to be based on rateable values, but by error the landlord calculated the M & S percentage as if its rateable value was £348,600 – half a million pounds difference! When the landlord became aware of the error an application was made to the court. As stated in **4.6**, on appeal the landlord was held able to reopen the assessments, because the tenant's obligation was to pay what was due under the lease. The fact that it had been incorrectly calculated and claimed by the landlord did not affect this primary obligation. The tenants of the shopping centre would presumably have had a claim for the sums for the past year or two to be adjusted generally. As there are many tenants at the Telford Shopping Centre, this would have been a very difficult task.

4.47 The net effect of the two cases above is that there is clear authority that:

(a) rateable values are the rateable values from time to time;

(b) the figure for receipts and outgoings should, strictly, be apportioned every time there is a rateable value change, unless the lease has provisions to say otherwise; and

(c) a mistake in calculation based on a wrong rateable value can be corrected when discovered.

4.48 In the last 25 years or so, rateable values have either not changed (lack of funding causing the intended five-yearly reviews to be postponed from time to time) or have been subject to major changes in the principle of what is being valued and how. For example, residential general rates became the community charge (the 'poll tax') and have now become council tax. With council tax the rateable value is now set in a number of broad bands based on the assumed capital value of the property (in contrast to the earlier system based on the estimated rental value) and it is a much more broad based figure than the former general rates which varied (as indicated above) as a result of such matters as central heating or double glazing. Accordingly, such figures are even less precise under the council tax regime than under the former rating system. For businesses the charge is now uniform business rates. The current trend seems to be to implement the five-yearly reviews, which entails more changes to rateable values and more appeals and generally more uncertainty for all concerned. The latest proposals are intended to lead to fewer appeals, but on past form this may be unduly optimistic.

4.49   Some landlords and tenants like to use rateable values because the figure is set by the District Valuer, an independent official, and it is not a proportion invented by the landlord. However, it is a system that the author would urge is not used for service charges. It has no relation to the services to be provided, and the backdating effect of changes is extremely difficult to deal with fairly as between different tenants.

The comparative rent basis

4.50   This is very rare, but not unknown, and is where the tenants pay service charges in the same ratio as they pay rent. It is slightly more sophisticated than simple equal division among units purely on the number of units. It means that the tenants with the more expensive premises pay more service charges as well as more rent. To the extent that the premises may have more rent because they are larger and may need more services (eg it may have more windows to clean or a larger area to be decorated) this has slight merit, but apart from such matters is it not directly related to the actual services needed for the premises. In addition, some tenants may pay a larger rent for premises where the rent has no relation to the need for services. For example, they might have the flat with the best view, or an office convenient for other offices they already use.

4.51   The arrangement cannot be recommended. As the service charge is related to the rent the relevant proportions payable by the tenants could vary if the tenancies have rent reviews at different times. (The author has only come across this in a residential long lease without rent reviews.) It is hard to see that a change in the rent of one unit is a good reason for adjusting all the service charge percentages.

The weighted floor area basis

4.52   This is probably the second most important of the more scientific apportionments of service charge percentages. (The most important is the floor area basis.) It is usually only material in retail developments where there are a number of units of considerably varied size. The weighted floor area basis is achieved by notionally adjusting the size of the premises let to achieve some parity.

4.53   The justification for the weighted floor area basis is that simple size does not accurately reflect the use of services. For example, take the Jolly Trolley Shopping Centre – a shopping mall consisting of ten small-sized shops and an anchor unit. If the only service provided by the landlord is cleaning the mall it could be fairly said that the part of the mall opposite the large unit takes longer to clean than the mall opposite a standard-sized unit. But that only reflects the frontage to the mall, whereas the anchor unit also extends back further than the other units. The extra amount of the service (cleaning the frontage) for the anchor unit is not proportionate to the total floor area of that unit. (A fairer percentage would be one based on frontage, rather than floor area.) The landlord will need to send out only one set of accounts, certificates etc for each tenant, regardless of the area occupied.

4.54   For other services the floor area is not necessarily a suitable guide. Take Bamford's Paperworks, a shop in the Jolly Trolley Shopping Centre which has both front and side windows. If the landlord is to decorate the exterior, and paint and clean the windows, he will have to do much more for Bamford's Paperworks than for Ellis Island, the shop unit next door which only has a single frontage. But they both have identical floor areas. Is it reasonable for Ellis to pay the same as Bamford's? Weighting can address that type of problem: eg in the case of Bamford/Ellis weighting could be based on comparative length of frontages. This could be the fairest approach where the services only affect frontages.

4.55   In the weighted floor area basis the real floor areas are calculated and then adjusted, and the service charge percentages are based on the adjusted floor area.

Example of weighted floor area basis

4.56   The simplest system works something like this:

(a)   The landlord assesses the size of the standard shop unit in the Jolly Trolley Shopping Centre. Assume that most shops are between 2,000 and 5,000 square feet. (Square feet are used in these examples, but the principle is the same whether square metres or square feet are referred to.) They are all treated as standard units and their service charge percentage is calculated purely on the square footage, on the basis that each square foot counts as one whole when the totals are added.

(b)   Next the size of the larger units is considered. It is usual to create several bands of size but if there is only one large unit then in practice the decision is simply how much discount to give. In the case of the Jolly Trolley Shopping Centre assume one anchor unit (Safesco) of 25,000 square feet. The banding system could work so that each of the first 5,000 square feet per unit are treated as 5,000. Each of the next 5,000 square feet (ie up to 10,000) could be treated as multiplied by 0.8 and thus treated as 4,000 square feet. Each of the next 5,000 square feet (up to 15,000) could be multiplied by 0.6, and thus be treated as 3,000 square feet, and the remainder over 15,000 square feet could be multiplied by 0.4 – thus the final 10,000 of the anchor unit would be treated as equivalent to 4,000 square feet. Safesco's 25,000 square feet unit, on the adjusted basis, would be treated as 5,000, plus 4,000, plus 3,000 plus 4,000, giving a revised (notional) area of 16,000 square feet.

(c)   The final step is to add together all the standard unit areas and the notional areas to arrive at the total. In the case of the Jolly Trolley Shopping Centre the ten smaller units might have, say, a total of 45,000 square feet between them (ie the actual floor areas added together) and the adjusted figure for the anchor unit is 16,000. The total adjusted floor area for the whole Centre is thus 61,000 square feet. The Safesco unit is treated as having 16,000 square feet out of 61,000 square feet, and its service charge percentage would thus be 22.22%. If there was no weighting the anchor unit would have to pay a percentage based on 25,000 square feet out of 70,000 square feet which works out at 35.71%. For a 4,500 square foot standard unit its percentage of the adjusted area (61,000 square feet) is 7.37%. If the areas had not been adjusted it would have a percentage of 4,500 out of 70,000, ie 6.42%.

There is a similar example in Section D4 of the Commercial Code referred to in Chapter 11.

Other weighting factors

4.57   The above is a deliberately simple example, partly because mathematics is a weak point of mine, but mainly to show the way the system works in its basic form. Like all other aspects of service charges, however, the calculations are an intensely practical matter, and the scheme needs to take account of the real services and the real buildings.

4.58   For example, different percentages could be applied to different premises which have the benefit (or not) of different services. In addition, the percentage to be paid could be assessed using different multipliers for different parts of the property included in the individual leases.

4.59   Developing the latter point, if there is a development on several levels some tenants may have several different floors in their demise. If the premises are shopping premises the ground floor is obviously the most attractive part of the premises for shoppers and (mostly) the upper or lower floors are of less importance. (This is not so marked in the case of a department store, where equal trading is often done on several floors.) The normal system seems to be to treat the ground floor as the standard unit (subject perhaps to size weighting as above), and to apply some discount to the other floors. Adding these together gives the total adjusted floor area of the premises let. Some systems are even more sophisticated and give a greater discount where the arrangement of upper or lower floors is not convenient. For example, a basement area may normally be rated at 0.5% for service charges compared with 1 for the ground floor, but the basement area may only be treated as, say, 0.25% where there is no direct connection between the ground floor and basement. While this (lack of connection) does not, of itself, necessarily affect the cost of the services, it gives premises which are less convenient a slightly lower service charge percentage than for what might otherwise be identical premises.

4.60   The latter principle is one to be considered when any such scheme is being devised for a particular centre. The actual services provided is another area where the percentages could be adjusted in an attempt to achieve equity between the tenants. An obvious example is an adjustment for those tenants who use the lift and those who do not. Any such adjustment needs to be carefully worked out, however. It would be possible to give double benefit if those not using the lift were given a smaller service charge percentage to pay, and if the accounts were then prepared so that the tenants not using the lifts were not charged for its use. This would obviously be unsatisfactory.

4.61   The key, it seems, is to consider what factors are unusual in the development as a whole (particularly where there are many standard units and a few which are very much bigger (or even very much smaller) than the others); whether the layout has any effect on the provision of the services or the use of the various parts which are to be let; whether there are some tenants who have no benefit from some of the services, etc. The service charge system should be reviewed to take such matters into account with a view to preparing an equitable scheme. Small units such as kiosks need to be looked at very carefully when weighting is planned. Sometimes the rent for such units is at a much higher rate per square foot than normal units. The service charge needs to reflect a minimum of cost (eg for preparing accounts etc). Based on square footage, a kiosk might have such a small percentage that it would not even cover accounting costs without some upward weighting. Sometimes kiosks are let on terms under which they do not contribute, but in such cases it is recommended that the landlord allows a notional credit to the service charge account (ie some of the rent is credited).

4.62   Two final crucial points need to be made on weighting.

(a)   Whatever the scheme, it must be applied consistently throughout the centre. This is, if there are two large 25,000 square feet units, then subject to any factors such as basements etc that apply to one but not the other, they should both be assessed on the same weighting principles.

(b)   Whether the scheme is notified to the tenants in advance or not the landlord (or the managing agents) should ensure they keep records of (i) the basis on which the percentages are calculated and (ii) the reasons for any particular differences. This point is made for two reasons. First, if circumstances change (eg units are joined together or split up) then the service charge percentage may need to be adjusted and the managing agents will need to know the basis of the original calculations for that purpose. Secondly, records are vital in case at any time the landlord is put to proof that the 'fair percentage' he is seeking to justify is indeed fairly assessed. The presence of a recorded scheme which can be shown to be consistently applied, and where there are reasons for reducing or increasing what would otherwise be a straightforward apportionment of the floor area, must aid the landlord in showing he has indeed acted reasonably.

4.63   It would probably be easiest to be able to show a consistent scheme if the leases all set out the weighting scheme, although not only does this increase the length of the document but some tenants may seek changes if they consider their own particular premises are unsatisfactorily prejudiced by the scheme. If a change is agreed in one lease consistency of approach cannot be shown. This means that it is best for the scheme to be kept out of the draft leases unless the landlord is absolutely sure he will not be obliged to change it when negotiating with any tenant.

Apportionment for mixed use premises

4.64   In the not uncommon case of mixed properties (for example shops with offices and/or flats above), the most satisfactory treatment is notionally to divide the building into blocks (retail, office and residential), and divide the costs relating to separate parts of the building among the tenants of that part. For example, there may be common air conditioning in the offices but not the shops. The air conditioning costs should be divided among the tenants of the offices only. This is particularly material bearing in mind that numerous obligations affect residential premises but do not apply to commercial premises. Keeping the service charges for the residential part separate enables the statutory requirements to be dealt with for the residential tenants without having to involve the non-residential tenants. There may well be items used in common by the different parts of the building such as lifts or service yards or common entrances. The easiest way to deal with such factors is to charge a specific proportion of such costs to each segment of the building. For example, with a lift there would be no charge to the ground floor shop units, but, say, 25% would be divided among the tenants of the offices on the first floor and, say, 75% among the tenants of the flats on the 2nd to 6th floors. There may well need to be quite a few different items for which suitable proportions need to be decided. Draftsmen should also consider whether the proportions themselves between various parts of the building should be capable of being changed if, for example, some offices are changed to residential use or vice versa.

PAYMENTS IN ADVANCE

4.65   In the case of residential property the amount payable in advance must be 'no greater amount than is reasonable'. (Landlord and Tenant Act 1985, s 19(2).) For non-residential property there is no similar statutory requirement, but in both cases the advance estimate needs to be strictly in accordance with the terms of the lease. If there is no provision in the lease payments cannot be validly claimed in advance (*Daiches v Bluelake Investments Ltd* [1985] 2 EGLR 67; see **4.3** above), although the parties can always agree to make payment in some other fashion.

4.66 The lease should say who is to give the estimate. A tenant negotiating a lease would do well to try to ensure that if the estimate is to be prepared by the landlord's surveyor, which is very common, the surveyor acts impartially and professionally. Ensuring that the definition of the landlord's surveyor (often defined in general terms in a lease) states that he must be a fellow or associate of the Royal Institution of Chartered Surveyors is a help to a tenant, and then in the provision about estimates some qualifying words such as 'acting impartially' or 'acting reasonably and professionally' should give further comfort to a tenant.

4.67 Provided that the demand for advance payment is made within the terms of the lease, it is not necessarily fatal to the landlord's claim that the preparation of the year end accounts is delayed. For example, in *Peachey Property Corporation Ltd v Henry* (1963) 188 EG 875, the landlord's agents had given a certificate of a reasonable interim payment in 1959, but had not provided new certificates for subsequent years. It was held that the landlord was entitled to claim the advance payment for 1963 on the basis of the 1959 certificate which had not been revised. Under the lease the adjusted figure was to be certified by 6 April in each year, or as near after that date as possible. The judge pointed out that while the adjustment was to be done within a timescale the interim payment certificate was not qualified in the lease by a time limit, and interim payments were not the result of exact computation. The landlord would have to make a proper adjustment for the previous years when the accounts were finally completed. In the case of residential premises the landlord may in due course have to provide accounts within six months of the end of the financial year if new s 21 of the Landlord and Tenant Act 1985 is implemented (see Chapter 9). For commercial property the new Commercial Code (see Chapter 11) recommends that accounts should be prepared within six months of the end of the service charge year.

4.68 The timing of sending estimates is a matter for the managing agents. Not many leases put an enforceable obligation on the landlord to send the estimated figure by a certain date. Such a provision would probably only be enforceable if time was expressed to be of the essence, which is not a provision the author has seen in this context. From a pure cash flow point of view, however, the managing agents should try to send out the estimated demand for the advance payment in good time before the commencement of the service charge year. (See **4.10** and **4.11** for suggested timetables.) It should be possible to plan the year's work so that the planning for the forthcoming service charge year is done a month or so before the year starts, which should give ample time to work out the figures for each tenant. Remember, also, that for residential premises there is a consultation procedure to follow with the tenants whereby the tenants must be given a total of two months to make observations. (Landlord and Tenant Act 1985, s 20.) Time for the consultation must be allowed where this is a requirement. In some commercial cases there is also an obligation to consult, and if so the programme must take this into account.

4.69   The managing agents should follow the wording of the lease: if it calls for a certificate they should prepare it as a certificate, to be certified by the correct person. If there are any other special provisions they should be followed. If not, the managing agent may find himself being held to be negligent and responsible to the landlord for any loss arising. Even if the position can be rectified by, for example, a proper certificate being served, there could still be cash flow problems if the lease procedure is not used and the tenants object.

4.70   When calculating the estimate, the managing agent needs to take account of all the material factors. These will include:

(a)   the obligations under the lease (in particular obligations which may have to be done in specific years, such as external decoration);

(b)   the anticipated costs for the normal running expenses (eg electricity for the lights in the common parts and maintenance contracts for lifts or gardening);

(c)   items shown for that year in the cyclical programme that should be prepared (covering work over periods of say three, five or ten years, such as replacement of carpets);

(d)   a modest contingency figure for unexpected costs;

(e)   the credit, if any, already in hand from previous years;

(f)   any sum that is considered proper towards a reserve or sinking fund (where the lease provides for one); and

(g)   (if there is a reserve or sinking fund) – whether any of the work to be done in the forthcoming year should be paid from that reserve or sinking fund.

4.71   When these calculations of the costs for the coming year are assessed the total which is payable by the tenants as a whole should be worked out (if it is less than the whole). Then the proportions for the individual tenants can be calculated and the demands for the advance payment can be made.

Receipts to be held in trust

4.72   This is just a brief reminder that in three cases receipts from tenants must be held on trust. The main purpose of holding money on trust is to ensure that the money cannot be claimed by creditors of the landlord (because it is not his money – it is held by him on trust for the tenants). The three cases are:

(a)   For residential property s 42 of the Landlord and Tenant Act 1987 makes it clear that all receipts from tenants towards service charges are held on trust. (It may also need to be held in a designated account (s 42A); see Chapter 9.)

(b) Many leases of non-residential premises provide that sinking fund and reserve fund money is to be held on trust.

(c) Where the lease provides that service charge money is to be held on trust.

4.73 The professional organisations for some agents require money to be held in bank accounts separate from their own money (client accounts) so that it can be identified and, again, it will not be available for creditors of the agent.

END OF THE YEAR ADJUSTMENT

4.74 Once the financial year has ended, the landlord or his managing agents must prepare the accounts for that year. This involves collating details of all payments and receipts, and then setting them out with as much detail as is needed to enable the tenants to see what the money has been spent on. Again this involves including details of the money received as well as the money paid out.

4.75 The accounts must reflect the lease terms. If the lease refers to costs 'paid' or 'expended' then the accounts can be prepared more quickly (because the information will all be available) than where the lease referred to costs 'incurred' (because this can include future commitments which are not exactly quantified). (See **3.47** et seq for comments on words used, and **7.14** for references to 'anticipated expenditure'.) The 'incurred' basis provides a more accurate comparison with costs in earlier years: the costs *'paid'* system depends on dates of receipt of bills as well as the payment of those bills. Once the accounts have been worked out the landlord must consider the arrangements for claiming the balance (or accounting to the tenant for any excess). This, of course, depends on the terms of the lease, but in the case of residential premises the landlord must also ensure that he complies with the statutory obligations (see Chapter 9).

The accounts

4.76 The Commercial Code discussed in Chapter 11 recommends various matters for accounts which are all, in the author's opinion, very helpful and practical. If and when the statement of account for dwellings becomes a requirement it will have to include prescribed information. (Landlord and Tenant Act 1985, s 21; see Chapter 9.)

4.77 The main points are that accounts should include, in reasonable detail, particulars of the amounts spent on the various items. These should be broken down to show what the items are (repairs, cleaning, etc) and should, where practical, compare the figures with the budget figures and the previous year's actual figures. The accounts should be supplemented by notes on material matters to assist tenants to understand them and to explain, for example, why this year's figure for repairs is 15 times that of last year's, or why the percentage being charged to the tenants is not as it was last year. The accounts should be audited and, where required under the lease, should be certified by the appropriate person nominated in the lease. While it may seem an obvious point the accounts should show (a) the premises to which they relate ('The Clark Centre') and (b) the period covered ('Accounts for the year ending 24 March 2009'). It is also useful to state who prepared the accounts (which is a chance for the managing agents to have their name and logo displayed). If computer printouts are used with the accounts, make sure they are intelligible to the tenants. (For a case where muddled accounts caused tenants to apply to a Leasehold Valuation Tribunal and both the LVT and the Lands Tribunal penalised the landlord in costs, see *Maryland Estates Ltd v Lynch and Wilson* LTL 19.3. 2003, and **4.114** below.)

CERTIFICATE OF COST

4.78   Very often the lease will require the landlord to arrange for a certificate of either the total costs spent by the landlord on service charge matters, or the proportion of that total which the tenant has to pay, or both.

4.79   To recover the costs, obviously the landlord must comply with the terms of his own lease. If it requires a certificate to be given by an accountant, then a landlord is asking for trouble by arranging for a certificate from a chartered surveyor. A tenant will usually be entitled to refuse to pay until the proper formalities are observed. For residential property, when s 21 of the Landlord and Tenant Act 1985 is brought into force it may be that with limited exceptions the accounts will have to be certified by a qualified accountant.

4.80   The tenant is entitled to expect that where a certificate is to be given by the 'landlord's surveyor' or 'the landlord's managing agents' it is given by someone other than the landlord himself (*Finchbourne Ltd v Rodrigues* [1976] 3 All ER 581). This fairly short Court of Appeal decision has for three decades been treated as one of the most important service charge cases in the law library. One of its facets was that the lease required payment of service charges as 'ascertained and certified by the landlord's managing agents acting as experts and not arbitrators'. A certificate was given by Pinto and Co, whose sole proprietor was Mr Pinto, who was effectively also the landlord. The court held that the certificate was not valid: it had to be given by someone other than the landlord.

4.81   In other cases certificates have been held to be valid where:

(a)   given by the parent company of the landlord (*Parkside Knightsbridge Ltd v Horwitz* [1983] 2 EGLR 42);

(b)   given by a management company set up by the landlord and his wife to manage both the block in question (where they lived) and some other premises (*Skilleter v Charles* [1992] 1 EGLR 73 (see **5.171**)).

Both were cases where the management was carried out by what was genuinely a separate legal entity, and in a fashion that was not a sham.

4.82   In another important service charge case, *Concorde Graphics Ltd v Andromeda Investments SA* [1983] 1 EGLR 53, the tenant's covenant 2(3) was to pay a 'rateable or due proportion of the costs ... of making repairing ... (items) used for the demised premises in common with other premises such proportion in case of difference to be settled by the landlord's surveyor whose decision shall be final and binding'. A dispute arose and the landlord was held not able to rely on the certificate. As the court said the surveyors 'must act impartially and hold the balance equally between the landlord and the tenant ... they must not simply obey the instructions of the landlord ... Parties are entitled to rely upon him (ie the surveyor) as a professional man to exercise an independent judgement'. The judge went on to say that on a literal construction of the clause:

> 'all that was referred to the landlord's surveyor is the rateable or due proportion of the costs ... But to my mind it is impossible to suppose that the reference to the landlord's surveyor should be so limited. The words "such proportion" can be read as an elliptical reference to the amount of the total expenditure on matters within clause 2(3) which is fairly proportionate to the demised premises. The ascertainment of the total expenditure is just as much within the special province and expertise of a surveyor as the ascertainment of the proportion which ought to be borne by the demised premises.'

(Following *Nikko Hotels (UK) Ltd v MEPC plc* [1991] 2 EGLR 103 (see **4.86**) this last comment may now be too wide – ascertaining the total expenditure was not the question directly asked of the landlord's surveyor by the lease. In addition, *Nikko* and the similar rent review cases all needed an independent expert.)

4.83   Section 27A(6) of the Landlord and Tenant Act 1985 makes it clear that such a certificate cannot be used to oust the jurisdiction of the court or Leasehold Valuation Tribunal in residential cases. Apart from court or lease-hold valuation tribunal proceedings, only post-dispute arbitration is an accept-able means of settling disputes for residential premises: other provisions are expressly made void.

Is the certificate binding?

4.84   How far a certificate can be binding on the parties is a matter which has taken up much time in court. A certificate will not be conclusive if a tenant can show that it has been incorrectly calculated. (*Dean v Prince* [1954] Ch 409.)

4.85   As mentioned above certificates have been treated as not binding in a case where the certificate was given by the landlord himself, *Finchbourne Ltd v Rodrigues* [1976] 3 All ER 581, and where the court considered the surveyors were acting for the landlord rather than acting impartially. (*Concorde Graphics Ltd v Andromeda Investments SA* [1983] 1 EGLR 53.)

4.86   The comments above refer to a certificate of the amount payable by a tenant. A certificate given by an expert impartially of what is a fair proportion (ie whether a particular tenant should pay 6% or 9% of the total) can be binding. (*Nikko Hotels (UK) Ltd v MEPC plc* [1991] 2 EGLR 103.) This was a rent review case where it was held that the court would not set aside the decision (which the lease had said was to be conclusive) on the grounds that the expert had wrongly interpreted the law, although it would do so if it could be shown that he had not performed the task assigned to him.

4.87   Generally, the courts seem more prepared these days than previously to let an expert's decision stand, provided the expert has made a decision on the question referred to him. However, for service charge purposes (a) s 27A(6) of the Landlord and Tenant Act 1985 makes such procedure void for residential leases, and (b) there has not been a case specifically on service charges where the validity of such a certificate has been in issue since the *Nikko* case was heard, except *Universities Superannuation Fund Scheme Ltd v Marks & Spencer Ltd* [1999] 04 EG 158 (see **4.46**), where the landlord was held entitled to set aside his own (incorrect) certificate. Accordingly, it may be too soon to say dogmatically that the courts (in non-residential cases) will always allow the expert's determination to stand provided he has carried out his instructions. Traditionally, courts have been reluctant to allow matters that would normally be within their jurisdiction to be decided by others, and, particularly where they did not like the determination, always looked for reasons to be able to set it aside. If a certificate has to be given by the landlord's surveyor or the landlord's accountant the court may well feel able to set it aside on the basis of lack of independence.

Who should the lease appoint to give the certificate?

4.88   Who should give the certificate? Different professionals have different skills:

(a) *Accountant* – Can be relied upon to certify that the figures reflect the vouchers, but not necessarily that the costs are within the provisions entitling the landlord to recover, nor that the costs themselves are reasonable for what was done. Similar points apply to auditors. Note that in due course an accountant will have to certify the statement of account for residential property, when the new version of s 21 of the Landlord and Tenant Act 1985 is brought in.

(b) *Solicitor* He may be able to add up (although mathematics is not a strong point for many lawyers) and carry out the auditing exercise, although not many do so. With the aid of time and a calculator a solicitor can prepare accounts and also interpret the lease. However, he would not be able to comment authoritatively on whether the costs were reasonable for the services.

(c) *Quantity surveyor* Although not ideal for interpreting the lease provisions a quantity surveyor is good at figures and would also have first-class knowledge of relevant levels of building costs. This is helpful for many types of work but not all, and a quantity surveyor does not normally give advice on the cost of services (such as cleaning and gardening) as opposed to building works.

(d) *Surveyor* The surveyor is the normal choice for giving the certificate. Most surveyors have the ability to deal with most aspects of certificates, although lease interpretation is not always their forte. The main point to watch (as with the other candidates) is impartiality. If it is important to have a certificate it is best if it is not given by the landlord's own managing agents, but by an independent surveyor, both for reasons of tenant confidence and for the reasons indicated above.

4.89 It has been suggested (by Gordon Farrow) that there could be merit in having two certificates (at least for premises where there are substantial service charges). One (perhaps from an auditor) would be to confirm the accuracy of the figures ('yes, the cost was £80,500'). The other certificate (perhaps from a quantity surveyor or a surveyor) would be to confirm that the £80,500 was a reasonable cost for what was done, or, as the Commercial Code referred to in Chapter 11 would say, was value for money. Such a system would give comfort to the tenants but would obviously cost more. To be even more fully covered, there could even be a third certificate from a solicitor that all the items charged for were legitimate items of charge under the lease terms. Obviously, double or triple certificates would increase management costs and cause some delay in preparation of accounts, but for really large developments they could be thought to be helpful to landlords and tenants.

REMEDIES FOR RECOVERING SERVICE CHARGES

4.90 There are several remedies for recovering service charges when the tenant does not pay. The main ones are as follows:

Distraint

4.91 If the lease reserves the service charge as rent, or if the wording of the lease is such as to make it clear that the service charge is treated as rent (*Escalus Properties Ltd v Robinson* [1996] QB 231) the landlord can (at the moment) distrain, ie send in a certificated bailiff to sell the tenant's goods. This cannot be done:

(a) where there is a dispute (*Concorde Graphics Ltd v Andromeda Investments SA* [1983] 1 EGLR 53, **4.85** above); or

(b) for arrears from a former tenant (*Wharfland Ltd v South London Co-operative Building Co Ltd* [1995] 2 EGLR 21); or

(c) for residential premises (because under s 42 of the Landlord and Tenant Act 1987 the service charges for dwellings is held on trust, and is therefore not the money of the landlord); or

(d)   where the lease lays down a system for payment which is varied, at least unless it is clear that it is intended by both parties that a breach of the varied procedure can lead to distraint (*D'Jan v Bond Street Estates plc* [1993] EGCS 43 (see **4.4**)); or

(e)   where the service charge is not reserved as rent.

There are moves afoot to make distraint less helpful to the landlord by requiring, for example, advance notice of the intention to distrain, which gives a tenant time to remove goods. Distraint is also discussed in Part 10 of Chapter 6.

Forfeiture and peaceable re-entry

4.92   The lease can usually be forfeited for breach of covenant. If the service charge is not reserved as rent the landlord must serve a notice under s 146 of the Law of Property Act 1925 first, giving the tenant a reasonable time to pay. This notice is not needed for commercial property if the service charge is reserved as rent. There are, inevitably, different considerations for residential property: see s 81 of the Housing Act 1996 (see Chapter 9). In particular, forfeiture can only be used once the liability has been agreed or determined. A case heard this century suggests that the reasonableness provisions of s 19 of the Landlord and Tenant Act 1985 do not apply to costs of s 146 notices claimed under the lease. (*Forcelux Ltd v Sweetman* LTL 7.8.2001.)

4.93   Forfeiture has its drawbacks because it means the lease comes to an end (unless the tenant or someone else obtains relief from forfeiture) and the landlord is without a tenant. There is likely to be a period when the landlord is not receiving either rent or service charge from the premises. However, if there is no prospect of the tenant paying there is little reason to keep the lease alive. A tenant will normally be entitled to relief from forfeiture if non-payment is the result of a genuine dispute which is decided by the court, although the relief would be subject to the tenant paying the amount which the court decides is proper. If the landlord has accepted a lesser sum in payment of rent and/or service charges he may have waived the right to forfeit. As an alternative, landlords can sometimes peaceably re-enter, but it is hard to comply with the numerous qualifications to ensure that peaceable re-entry is not unlawful, giving rise to a potential claim from a dispossessed tenant. The Law Commission recommended (in 1985, 1994 and 1998) that the law is changed so that peaceable re-entry in its present form is abolished, but a similar effect could be achieved by a notice procedure coupled with a court possession order (a 'termination order') which would give a right to possession where the tenant fails to remedy the breach within a specified period. The proposal for requiring a court order is repeated in the Law Commission Consultation Paper 174 of January 2004 ('Termination of Tenancies for Tenant Default'.) It emphasises that it recommends that the landlord must serve notice and obtain a court order to end the lease, and (inter alia) recommends that this procedure cannot be used if the lease has more than 25 years to run.

Rent deposit

4.94   If the tenant has given a rent deposit then the landlord will probably be entitled to take funds from the deposit if the tenant fails to pay rent, and he may also be able to use the fund if the service charge is not paid, depending on the terms of the arrangement. There are often terms about days of grace and the giving of notice of some sort. Normally, the terms of the deposit are such that the tenant is required to replace sums taken from the deposit, but if he is not paying the service charge it is unlikely he will top up the deposit account. The deposit provides a fund to avoid a shortfall while the landlord can prepare court proceedings in case there are future defaults. Alternatively, and probably better, the landlord could issue proceedings for an order to make the tenant top up the deposit. Those proceedings would be running while there is no loss to the landlord (because he has used part of the deposit).

Statutory notice

4.95   Service of a statutory notice can be effective in some cases. Where such a notice is served and payment is not made within the short period given by the notice, the person serving the notice can apply to make the defaulter insolvent (ie by bankruptcy or winding up). This can sometimes be a very effective remedy against a debtor, particularly one who is in business.

Bank guarantee

4.96   Some leases (or licences to assign) are completed on the basis that the tenant provides a bank guarantee. If there is one and the terms are such that the landlord can call on the bank to pay if the tenant fails to pay the service charge, then the landlord should consider calling on the bank as one option. One difficulty is that banks are sometimes reluctant to give a guarantee for longer than a short period (say one year) which is not particularly helpful if the tenant is committing himself to a 25-year lease. As in the case of the rent deposit, if this remedy is to be used the landlord must exercise it strictly in accordance with its terms.

Personal contact

4.97   It is not a legal remedy as such, but sometimes the most productive method of obtaining payment from a slow tenant is to contact that tenant, either by telephone or by visiting the premises. Obviously, the first approach is normally the written demand, but thereafter this should be followed up by letters referring, where the lease permits, to the provision for interest on late payment. If these fail a telephone call or visit can be helpful. A diary system (perhaps computer induced) is vital for this, although as all tenants are normally liable to pay on the same dates the easiest system is a diary note to check all receipts on a few specific dates after the due date. A personal visit may enable the collector to assess whether the tenant is in real long-term difficulties, and may also be an appropriate opportunity to inspect to check for other breaches of covenant and dilapidations.

A solicitor's letter

4.98 With some tenants a letter from the landlords or the managing agents will not achieve the desired result, but a letter from a solicitor (that is, a 'Dear Sir, Unless' type of letter) which will show that the landlord is taking the position seriously, can sometimes give rise to a response. The landlord will need to check whether or not he can recover the costs of the solicitor's action from the tenant under his lease (or from the tenants generally through the service charge), but if such a letter results in payment or action which was otherwise not occurring it might be worthwhile, even if the landlord has to pay the costs himself. Such an approach has been known to make tenants think twice before defaulting in future.

Issuing proceedings

4.99 Court proceedings can be expensive and time consuming. The tenant may raise a defence (either genuine or spurious) and if he does the landlord will need to expend time and money in dealing with that defence. (Occasionally, there might be public relations aspects of bringing proceedings in public.) A court can award costs against the tenant, but:

(a) the costs of proceedings which the court ordered were not recoverable from the defaulting tenant, cannot be added to the service charge costs (*Reston Ltd v Hudson* [1990] 2 EGLR 51); and

(b) the tenant of a dwelling can require proceedings to be stayed if he makes an application to the Leasehold Valuation Tribunal as to reasonableness; and

(c) s 20C of the Landlord and Tenant Act 1985 entitles the tenant of a dwelling to seek a declaration that none of the court costs are to be included within the service charge.

4.100 A landlord can also bring proceedings against the tenant's surety (if any) provided that the surety provisions are sufficient to enable a claim to lie – they are usually material for rent, but not always for service charges. The point needs to be checked. (The Commercial Code referred to in Chapter 11 recommends for commercial property the RICS alternative dispute service, for cases where there is a dispute, as opposed to where a tenant does not want to pay.)

Claiming against former tenants

4.101 Subject to the points in the next paragraph, if the present tenant and/or his surety are unable to pay then a claim against former tenants may be possible. Unless the former tenant (or his surety) has been given an express release (or the lease was granted after 1 January 1996, when there is an automatic release under the Landlord and Tenant (Covenants) Act 1995 when a tenant assigns, except where the tenant guarantees his successor with an authorised tenant guarantee) and assuming he can be traced, the landlord can usually claim against the former tenant. (For ease of reading only the former tenant will be referred to, but similar points can apply to a former surety.) If there is a choice of former tenants the landlord can claim against any one or more, leaving the person sued to claim from their successors following any chain of indemnity that applies.

4.102 The law was radically changed by the Landlord and Tenant (Covenants) Act 1995, discussed also at **9.9** et seq. Section 17 of the Act restricts the right to claim arrears of rent or service charges from a former tenant to six months arrears, where they can be claimed. For leases granted after 1995, the immediately preceding tenant is liable only if he has entered into an authorised guarantee agreement, and then only when his assignee is still tenant. For leases granted before 1996 any of the former tenants can be liable as indicated in the previous paragraph, but only for six months arrears. The current tenant remains liable throughout the term for all arrears during the time he is tenant, subject to the relevant limitation period. The latter depends on whether his tenancy is in writing or by deed.

4.103 The landlord cannot recover arrears from a former tenant unless the landlord has given notice that he intends to claim, and the notice must be served within six months of the date the amount claimed became due. The landlord can claim subsequent amounts from the former tenant subject to serving further notices within six months.

4.104 If a claim is to be made the parties need to bear in mind that changes that may have been made to the terms of the lease can create a surrender and re-grant, and if they do the right to claim may be lost. (This is put in formal shape by s 18 of the 1995 Act.) In *Howard de Walden Estates Ltd v Pasta Place Ltd* [1995] 1 EGLR 79, a term of the guarantee provisions that supplemental deeds would not affect the liability of the surety was held to be ineffective.

4.105 Landlords or their managing agents need to have systems to ensure that an early approach is made to those former tenants and former sureties (if any) who can be called upon, when a default by the current tenant is noticed. The landlord cannot sit back and claim years of arrears – he is limited to the six-month period.

4.106 The 1995 Act also provides that where a former tenant is called on to pay for his successor by notice and does so he can call for an overriding lease (s 19). The former tenant will then become the landlord of the defaulter. The advantage to the former tenant is that he will have an estate (rather than just an obligation to pay) and can exercise rights against the current tenant who will become his (the former tenant's) tenant. If the former tenant forfeits the (under)lease, he will hold the overriding lease free of the former lease and can thus assign or underlet the premises if market conditions and the lease permit. He could even occupy again. He will have the burden but he will at least have a legal interest he can use. The overriding lease is basically on the same terms as the lease under which there is a default, but is for a few more days (s 18(2)). Accordingly, the former tenant will have to take on the liabilities of the tenant, including service charge obligations. Obviously, if he remains landlord of the defaulting tenant he will be able to exercise the remedies mentioned in this part of this chapter against the tenant. The right to an overriding lease only arises where a s 17 notice is served and the former tenant pays. If for some reason the landlord does not want the former tenant to become tenant again, he must consider whether or not to serve the notice. He could try to claim by letter rather than notice, but the well advised former tenant will not pay without a formal s 17 notice so that he has the option to improve his position by calling for an overriding lease.

4.107   A former tenant in *Royton Industries Ltd v Lawrence* [1994] 1 EGLR 110 tried to escape liability for arrears of service charge built up by his successor in title. It was claimed that the covenant to pay rent was expressed (in clause 2) to be 'throughout the term', but it was also claimed that this expression did not also apply to the obligation to pay service charges. In the lease the only obligation to pay the service charge appeared in the reddendum (in clause 1) where the property was demised for 110 years at a rent of £1 per year using the words 'and also yielding and paying ... the Tenant's Proportion of the Maintenance Costs'. Tenant's covenant (clause 2) included a covenant to pay rent but did not mention service charges. The judge said he saw no reason to cut down the obligation to pay service charge in clause 1 because in clause 2 obligations were expressed to be for the whole of the term. In effect the landlord was able to claim despite the absence of a direct covenant to pay service charge, although clearly it is far better to ensure that there is a tenant's covenant to pay, rather than having to rely on implication. (The judge cited cases from 1653 and 1832 as authority for the words 'yielding and paying' imposing an obligation to pay.)

4.108   The date from which an assignee is liable was raised in *Mullaney v Maybourne Grange (Croydon) Management Ltd* [1986] 1 EGLR 70, where the lease obliged the assignee to execute a separate deed of covenant for payment of the service charge. The lease was assigned in February 1984. The assignee did not complete a deed of covenant until June. The court had little difficulty in confirming that the assignee's liability for service charges arose in February, not in June.

4.109   Confirmation that an assignee was not liable for arrears of rent that existed prior to the assignment to him was given in *Wharfland Ltd v South London Co-operative Building Co Ltd* [1995] 2 EGLR 21. The House of Lords had a few years previously confirmed a similar point for payment of freehold rentcharges in *David Watson Property Management Ltd v Woolwich Equitable Building Society* 1992 SC (HL) 21 (a Scots case).

GOOD MANAGEMENT PRACTICE

4.110 Readers are referred to Chapter 11, which comments on the two main Codes of Practice, one for residential property and the other for commercial. Between them, they set out what is accepted as good management practice, and (subject to the quibble that the present form of the Residential Code needs to have a lot of statutory references updated) are highly recommended to all those interested in the topic.

4.111 The Codes both highlight keeping tenants informed and consulted on proposals affecting the premises and generally communication with the tenants. This obviously aids good landlord/tenant relations.

4.112 By regular letters or circulars to the tenants (or meetings with tenants) landlord's managing agents can reduce possible future complaints from tenants. Tenants who are kept informed are less likely to complain than those who are suddenly disrupted by the unexpected arrival of workmen. (When one is a child, a surprise is often pleasant, but surprises are best avoided for a landlord or tenant.)

4.113 Clear and full accounts with explanatory notes can also help good relations. This has been expressed as 'the glass pocket' – a good expression for open accounting. Sometimes graphs can make accounts easier for tenants to follow than columns of figures, and certainly information comparing the actual figures to last year's figures and the budget figures.

4.114 In a recent case, *Maryland Estates Ltd v Lynch & Wilson* LTL 19.3.2003, the accounts were held to be confusing, and so although the landlords were able (just) to support their claim, the Lands Tribunal only allowed them to charge half their costs to the service charge. Presumably, if the accounts had been clearer the proceedings might not have been needed.

Setting aside assignments

4.115 For a case where tenants of commercial premises at the Metro Business Centre purported to transfer the leases of two units without the landlord's consent, and the court set the transfers aside on the grounds that the motive was to prevent the landlord from enforcing payment of service charges, see *Beckenham MC Ltd v Centralex Ltd* [2004] EWHC 1287 (Ch), [2004] 2 BCLC 764.

CHAPTER 5

Some specific services and works

It is impossible to enjoy idling thoroughly unless one has plenty of work to do.

Jerome K Jerome

GENERAL

5.1   This chapter records the main items that are usually the subject of a service charge by the landlord to the tenant. The general principles of service charges apply to these items, but for many of them there have been cases which indicate the approach a court may take in disputes. It is hoped that the illustrations of cases will help either to resolve disputes or to ensure that leases are worded to avoid specific problems. In Chapter 6 are items often included in a service charge provision but which are not actually works or services. Such other items include interest, promotional expenses and disputes procedures. Chapter 7 covers sinking funds.

5.2   The actual words used in the lease are crucial for service charge purposes. Accordingly, comment on individual items mentioned in this chapter must be read in the context that the court in each case had to determine the issue before them on the basis of what was in (or omitted from) the lease.

5.3   Some leases, particularly for blocks of flats, provide that the services are to be performed by a management company rather than the landlord. The principles in respect of individual items of service charge expenditure apply in those cases. (Management companies are the subject of Chapter 12.)

PART I – REPAIR AND DECORATION

Introduction

5.4   Repair is probably the most important of the usual items for which a landlord will expect the tenant to pay. The cost of repair of major items can be very high, and the topic gives rise to disagreements over:

(a)   whether the repair was covered by the lease terms;

(b)   whether the repair was necessary;

(c) if it was necessary, whether the costs charged were reasonable;

(d) whether the work done was done to a reasonable standard; and

(e) whether the work was simply repair or whether it included an element of improvement.

5.5 Some types of repair can be affected by insurance. For example, the obligation of either landlord or tenant to repair may exclude insured risks which can include such causes of damage as fire, flood, or impact. If the landlord can recover the cost of some damage through insurance (for which the tenant is probably paying the premiums) it is not reasonable for him to be able to charge the tenant, except where the claim arises from some act or omission of the tenant, or, if the lease so provides, in respect of any excess under the policy. (Aspects of insurance are discussed at **5.34** below and in Part 3 of Chapter 6 at **6.28**.)

5.6 The items a landlord is responsible for repairing should be clear from the lease. There are comments at **3.12** et seq on the importance of definitions, and the details set out in the lease are vital for determining the obligations of the landlord and the items for which recovery can be made. In many service charge leases the tenant is responsible for the repair of the premises let to him, at least internally, and the landlord is responsible for the repair of the structural parts and the remainder of the landlord's property, or at least those parts used in common and not let to other tenants. Where there is damage to an item such as a wall, there may be liability on the landlord for the main structural part and the tenant for the internal plaster part. The cases tend to show that the person responsible for carrying out the repair, whether landlord or tenant, is entitled to do so in his own way, provided he complies with his obligation. (See eg *Plough Investments v Manchester City Council* [1989] 1 EGLR 244.) Although the party with the repairing obligation can normally deal with repairs as he sees fit, that does not, in the case of the landlord, automatically mean he can recover the whole of the cost from the tenant. Such aspects as reasonableness or the length of the lease can be material in such cases.

5.7 In *Lurcott v Wakeley and Wheeler* [1911] 1 KB 905, it was said that: '[R]epair is restoration by renewal or replacement of subsidiary parts of the whole. Renewal, as distinguished from repair, is reconstruction of the entirety, meaning by the entirety not necessarily the whole but substantially the whole subject matter under discussion'. This section of this book refers to repair, but the comments as to renewal may be material in the context of interpretation in individual cases. If the repair clause specifically refers to 'renewal' or 'replacing' then interpretation needs to reflect this factor.

5.8 As well as ensuring the landlord is responsible for repair of the main structure, the tenant may also be well advised to require the landlord to be responsible for repair of the means of access to the demised property (particularly where the demised property is not at ground level or does not front an adopted highway) and also the pipes and cables for services such as drainage, gas and electricity. The latter usually pass to or from the demised premises by way of other property owned by the landlord and therefore outside the direct control of the tenant. Obviously, the landlord will want to be paid for these items through the service charge.

5.9   An excellent summary of the many factors involved in considering a repairing obligation appears in *Holding and Management Ltd v Property Holding and Investment Trust plc* [1990] 1 All ER 938, where the judge said:

> 'Thus the exercise involves considering the context in which the word 'repair' appears in a particular lease and also the defect and remedial works proposed. Accordingly, the circumstances to be taken into account in a particular case under one or other of these heads will include some or all of the following: the nature of the building, the terms of the lease, the state of the building at the date of the lease, the nature and extent of the defect sought to be remedied, the nature, extent and cost of the proposed remedial works, at whose expense the proposed remedial works are to be done, the value of the building and its expected lifespan, the effect of the works on such value and lifespan, current building practice, the likelihood of a recurrence if one remedy rather than another is adopted, the comparative cost of the alternative remedial works and their impact on the use and enjoyment of the building by the occupants. The weight to be attached to these circumstances will vary from case to case.'

Standard of repair

5.10   The words 'good tenantable repair' were said in an early leading authority, *Proudfoot v Hart* (1890) 25 QBD 42, to mean 'such repair as, having regard to the age, character and locality of the house, would make it reasonably fit for the occupation of a reasonably minded tenant of the class that would be likely to take it'. This case concerned a repairing obligation under a three-year tenancy, but the passage just quoted has been cited with approval in many subsequent cases.

5.11   A century later, in *Ladbroke Hotels Ltd v Sandhu* [1995] 2 EGLR 92, a tenant challenged the extent of repairs needed. A hotel in Cheshire was let for 99 years in 1970. The issue of repair arose at the 1991 rent review. In effect, an expert advised that the premises had been badly built, and that £500,000 would have to be spent on repair to give the property an estimated life of 60 years. The tenants claimed that only £60,000 was needed to give the premises a further life of 15 years, which was the commercial life expectancy of such buildings. The court held that the tenant's attempt to restrict repairs to the commercial life expectancy of the property was wrong: the standard of repair had to be determined by the parties' expectations when the lease was granted. For a later view on the costs payable, see *Fluor Daniel Properties Ltd v Shortlands Investments Ltd* [2001] EGCS 8 (and see **5.134**), where the landlord's claim was reduced because only a few years of the lease were left. More recently, in *Riverside Property Investments Ltd v Blackhawk Automotive* [2004] EWHC 3052 (TCC), [2005] 1 EGLR 114, the tenant of an industrial unit who had repairing liability carried out roof repairs at the end of the term. The landlord considered the work done inadequate, and removed and replaced the roof. The judge held, on the evidence, that the work by the tenant was sufficient to comply with his repairing covenant, and the landlord's claim for the cost of replacing the roof failed. It is an illustration of factors influencing a decision on the standard of repair.

5.12   The point that the covenant to repair must be construed by reference to the condition of the premises at the commencement of the term was decided as long ago as 1924 (*Anstruther-Gough-Calthorpe v McOscar* [1924] 1 KB 716). This can be material not only for deciding the appropriate standard of repair, but it can also have a dramatic effect where an underlease is granted many years after a head lease using identical repairing terms. The undertenant's obligation is based on the condition of the premises at the date of the underlease: if the tenant of the head lease thinks he is passing on an identical quality of obligation that he himself has under the head lease he is mistaken.

5.13   The words 'good and tenantable repair' and 'good and substantial repair' mean effectively the same. The exact words are immaterial provided that they plainly express the intention that the premises are to be repaired, kept in repair, and yielded up in repair. (*Proudfoot v Hart* (1890) 25 QBD 42 (**5.10** above) and *Anstruther-Gough-Calthorpe v McOscar* (**5.12** above).)

5.14   For service charge purposes the standard of repair is material in the case of residential premises because the charge that a landlord can make is limited if the services or works are not of a reasonable standard (s 19(1)(a) of the Landlord and Tenant Act 1985).

5.15   Contrasting cases where the roof needed repairing have been mentioned above (*Manor House Drive Ltd v Shahbazian* (1965) 195 EG 283, at **3.40** above, and *Murray v Birmingham City Council* [1987] 2 EGLR 53, at **3.41** above). In the first case, the landlord had been dealing with the roof over the years by patching and had decided (following advice) to replace the zinc: the court supported him. In the second case, the tenant wanted the landlord to replace the roof and the landlord wanted to continue patching and the court again supported the landlord as the person with the repairing obligation: it was held that the roof had not reached the stage where replacement was essential. A more recent case where the roof was a major issue was *Postel Properties Ltd v Boots the Chemist Ltd* [1996] 2 EGLR 604. Again, the court supported the landlord in carrying out the repair (following suitable advice). In the *Postel* case, the advice was for the roof to be recovered in full, in a case where the roofs which had an estimated life of around 20 years were about that age. (The *Postel* case is reported with great detail about the works and reports of what needed to be done.)

5.16   The impression is that the courts will allow a landlord to manage the repair obligation as the landlord considers appropriate, at least provided it is done:

(a)   following suitable advice; and

(b)   within the terms of the lease.

The Commercial Code (see Chapter 11) recommends, in para 21 and Section D1, , performance contracts, which define the standard to be achieved, rather than setting out what is to be done.

The obligation to repair

5.17   Lack of funds is no excuse for a landlord not to repair (*Francis v Cowcliffe Ltd* (1976) 33 P & CR 368) and if the landlord has a liability to repair the tenant can enforce it.

5.18   In *Creska Ltd v Hammersmith and Fulham London Borough Council* [1998] 3 EGLR 35, the tenants of commercial premises were liable to repair (inter alia) all 'electrical heating mechanical and ventilation installations therein which exclusively serve the Premises'. The heating was by underfloor electrical storage heaters. When parts became defective the tenants provided individual storage heaters rather than repairing the whole system. At first instance this was held acceptable, but the Court of Appeal said that it was not. Although expensive and inconvenient the system could be repaired, and, as that was what the lease required the tenant to do, that was its obligation. This case is discussed further in this chapter in the section on heating and hot water.

5.19   Until recently, by a rather odd and unsatisfactory series of cases, the position seemed to be that while a tenant can enforce specific performance of a landlord's covenant to repair (eg *Jeune v Queen's Cross Properties Ltd* [1974] Ch 97, and for residential premises s 17 of the Landlord and Tenant Act 1985), the reverse may not be true, and thus a landlord could not obtain specific performance of the tenant's repairing covenant. (*Hill v Barclay* (1811) 18 Ves 56.) However, a 1998 first instance decision held that specific performance can be available for tenant's repairing default, although it is fair to say that the facts of the case were rather unusual. (*Rainbow Estates Ltd v Tokenhold Ltd* [1999] Ch 64.) This discrepancy has been much criticised over the years. In 1992 a Law Commission Report, Consultation Paper 123, Landlord and Tenant, Responsibility for State and Condition of Property, recommended at para 5.61 that specific performance should be the primary remedy for failure to repair, and it may be that there will be statutory intervention in this at some later date. It may also be that the law of repair as between landlord and tenant will be varied to revise the law in respect of other unsatisfactory aspects highlighted in the Law Commission Report, but this chapter seeks to describe the law as it is at present.

5.20   Repairing obligations relate to premises where there is disrepair, and not where the property has never been in repair. For example, in *Post Office v Aquarius Properties Ltd* [1987] 1 All ER 1055, the floor of the basement of a property was under water for the whole of the term of the lease, and the tenant was held not liable to carry out the work needed to make good the defect.

5.21   There is useful authority for the proposition that under the statutory obligation to repair the exterior of property (imposed by s 32 of the Housing Act 1961, and later replaced by s 11 of the Landlord and Tenant Act 1985), which implies obligations on the landlord of residential property let for not more than seven years, the reference to the *'exterior'* was to the external parts around the flat, and not the whole of the exterior of the building. Similarly, the part of the same section imposing an obligation to maintain plant at the demised premises was restricted to the installations within the physical confines of the flat. (*Campden Hill Towers Ltd v Gardner* [1977] QB 823.) Section 11 of the 1985 Act was discussed in detail by the Court of Appeal in *O'Connor v Old Etonian Housing Association Ltd* [2002] EWCA Civ 150, [2002] Ch 295 (see also at **5.27** below).

5.22   In *Embassy Court Residents' Association Ltd v Lipman* [1984] 2 EGLR 60, an obligation in a lease to clean 'outside windows' was held to cover all the windows of the building and not just those in the common parts.

Where the lease is silent

5.23   If the tenant has not covenanted to repair a particular item the landlord cannot take action because there is no breach of covenant (and vice versa – see *Lloyds Bank plc v Bowker Orford* [1992] 2 EGLR 44, discussed in detail in its own section at **5.203** et seq).

5.24   It is possible that there may be some case for implied covenants but this is of very limited application.

5.25   In *Edmonton Corpn v W.H. Knowles & Son Ltd* (1961) EGD 400, where there was no covenant by the landlord to decorate, it was held that there was an implied obligation on the landlord to do the decoration, and thus to be able to recover the cost, based on a reference in an obligation of the tenant to pay the costs of decorating 'every third year of the term all the outside wood and metal work and other exterior parts of the demised premises'.

5.26   It has been held that there was an implied covenant by a landlord (*Barrett v Lounova* [1990] 1 QB 348) in a case where the tenant had covenanted to repair and decorate the interior, and this was impossible because of the lack of repair of the exterior. The landlord had no express repairing liability, but the tenant could not decorate the interior because the exterior was in such a poor condition that as soon as any decoration was carried out it was ruined by damp. The court held that to enable the tenant to comply with his express internal repairing covenant there must be an implied obligation on someone to keep the exterior in such a condition as not to nullify the tenant's efforts. They held that the landlord should be the one on whom the implied obligation fell in those circumstances. (*Barrett v Luonova* was distinguished in the unusual case of *Adami v Lincoln Grange Management Ltd* [1998] 1 EGLR 58 (see Chapter 12 on management companies at **12.5**).)

5.27   In those cases (probably fairly rare for service charge leases, but material for many protected or assured tenancies), where the tenancy of a dwelling is granted for a term of less than seven years, s 11 of the Landlord and Tenant Act 1985 implies certain repairing obligations on the landlord. Those obligations will apply not only to those cases where a lease is granted for a short term but also to those cases where there is a periodic tenancy. The obligation applies only where the landlord in question is responsible for maintenance of the defective premises. In *Niazi Services Ltd v Van der Loo* [2004] EWCA Civ 53, [2004] 1 WLR 1254, the defects were in pipework in a ground floor restaurant and the (intermediate) landlord of the tenant of the top floor flat had no legal interest in the ground floor. The intermediate landlord succeeded in an appeal against damages awarded at first instance – the occupational tenant of the top floor flat who held a short lease had no redress against his landlord under s 11.

5.28   The fact that a landlord has a right to enter to do certain repairs does not necessarily imply that he has an obligation to carry out those repairs. (*Sleafer v Lambeth Borough Council* [1960] 1 QB 43 (general repairs) and *Duke of Westminster v Guild* [1985] QB 688 (repair of drains).)

5.29   In *Minja Properties plc v Cussins Property Group plc* [1998] 2 EGLR 52, the landlord obtained an interim injunction permitting it to enter to carry out work (replacing defective windows) where the two leases of commercial property contained tenants' covenants to permit entry for repair, even though it was near the end of the term.

5.30   Where the lease did not reserve rights for the landlord to enter to carry out normal (roof) repairs such a right was not implied (*Regional Properties Ltd v City of London Real Property Co Ltd* [1981] 1 EGLR 33) but later it was held that a landlord has an implied right to enter to carry out repairs, at least to comply with the Defective Premises Act 1972. (See *McCanley v Bristol City Council* [1992] QB 134, and also *King v South Northamptonshire District Council* [1992] 1 EGLR 53.)

Defect not known to the landlord

5.31   A landlord may be able to avoid liability for disrepair he does not know about, at least in relation to the property demised to the tenant (*O'Brien v Robinson* [1973] AC 912). Therefore, a tenant should notify the landlord of items not in repair as soon as possible and call on the landlord to carry out the repair.

5.32   The same position may not apply to property other than that demised, notably to common parts. There, particularly if the landlord's covenant is to 'keep' the common parts in repair, the tenant may be able to enforce an obligation to repair and the liability of the landlord may commence when the disrepair starts, rather than after the landlord has been given notice and has failed to comply within a reasonable time. (If the property not in repair is outside the demise it is hard to see a good reason why it should be up to the tenant to put the landlord on notice.) See, for example, *British Telecommunications plc v Sun Life*

Assurance Society plc [1996] Ch 69, a decision which was later approved by the Court of Appeal.

Timing

5.33   When negotiating a lease a tenant could usefully seek a provision to ensure that repairs are carried out at times as convenient to the tenant as possible. For example, a business may well prefer works to be carried out after the close of business, whereas residential tenants may prefer works to be done in the daytime. There is no hard and fast rule, but a provision that repairs affecting the tenant's premises will be carried out on prior reasonable notice and at times previously agreed by the tenant (such agreement not to be unreasonably withheld or delayed) may be acceptable to a landlord. When a landlord carried out external repairs, using scaffolding and leading to a claim for loss of profits from the ground floor restaurant tenant, the Court of Appeal considered the effect of the obligation to repair on the landlord's obligation for quiet enjoyment. Faced with the alternative views of the landlord (that he should, under the quiet enjoyment covenant, use reasonable precautions when carrying out work to prevent disturbance), and of the tenant (that he should take all possible precautions) the court preferred the landlord's approach. The court also indicated that express provisions in the lease (or by agreement where the lease was silent) for the landlord to accept a reduced rent and/or service charge during the disturbance could help establish reasonableness. (*Goldmile Properties Ltd v Lechouritis* [2003] 15 EG 143.)

Insured risks

5.34   In interpreting repairing covenants take care that the repair in question is not needed as the result of damage by an insured risk. If it is, then you should check if there is an exclusion from the obligation of the landlord (or tenant) in respect of insured risks. The wording needs to be examined, and the facts, eg has payment under the policy been refused because of action or inaction on the part of the tenant or landlord? Simple lack of repair cannot be insured against, but damage caused by impact, fire, explosion, flooding or storm could well be covered by the insurance obligation. Clearly, if the repair arises from an insured risk the tenant should not be called on to pay towards the repair (other than any excess on the policy) unless the payment of the policy money is withheld as the result of default by the tenant.

Repair of inherent defects

5.35   Whether the repairing covenant of either landlord or tenant covers inherent defects is a matter of interpretation. There is no rule of law that a tenant is excused from liability under his covenant to repair simply because the work results from an inherent defect. In *Ravenseft Properties Ltd v Davstone*

(Holdings) Ltd [1980] QB 12, external cladding fell off the building owing to the design not including expansion joints. At the time of construction it was not known that these were necessary. The tenant was liable not only for the cost of replacing the cladding but also for inserting expansion joints which were essential to prevent a recurrence of the problem.

5.36   Equally, a landlord can be liable for remedying inherent defects for matters within his repairing obligations. Where a landlord was responsible for structural repairs in *Elmcroft Developments Ltd v Tankersley-Sawyer* [1984] 1 EGLR 47, he was held liable by the Court of Appeal to insert silicone injections into a building, in effect forming a damp proof course. The original damp proof course had been constructed too low down the wall to be effective. The landlord had wanted to repair damp plaster from time to time, but the court said this was not sufficient and the landlord was liable to make good the inherent defect.

5.37   In a case of serious (expensive) damage, *Credit Suisse v Beegas Nominees Ltd* [1994] 4 All ER 803, cladding was constructed in a way that permitted water to enter. To effect a repair the cladding had to be removed and replaced. The tenants wanted the work done, but objected to paying for it through the service charge. The court held that the landlords were in breach of their repairing covenant to *'keep'* the walls in good condition. The clause was also held to cover renewal. (The report included an excellent summary of repair cases to that date.) The replacement of cladding was said to be beyond *'repair'* but not beyond *'renewal'*. As it was the landlord's obligation he was able to recover the costs through the service charge, although the tenants had a cross claim against the landlord for damages for inconvenience.

Repair contrasted with improvement

5.38   The *Elmcroft* case (see **5.36**) – regarding the defective damp proof course – was mentioned in the context of inherent defects. It is perhaps also material as an example of those cases where the obligation to repair can include an element of improvement. In the *Elmcroft* case the obligation of the landlord was to repair, and the only reasonable means of repair involved an element of improvement. The two are not mutually exclusive – an improvement can be a repair and vice versa. Section 18 of the Landlord and Tenant Act 1985 now includes improvements in the definition of service charges for dwellings, and so the statutory provisions on consultation and reasonableness apply. So for dwellings the difference is no longer material.

5.39   It is said, however, that a covenant to repair does not involve a duty to improve a property by introducing something different in kind to that which was originally comprised in the lease. There are, however, various different approaches by the courts. For example, in the *Elmcroft* case (**5.36**) there was a damp proof course at the house, even though it was an ineffective one because it was too low. In a case from the 1940s, *Sotheby v Grundy* [1947] 2 All ER 761, an old house had defective foundations and could only have been saved from demolition by underpinning and the incorporation of new foundations. It was held that this represented an improvement and was beyond the scope of the tenant's repairing covenant. The question is one of degree.

5.40 Changes to the property may, however, be necessary to comply with the covenant. In *New England Properties v Portsmouth New Shops* [1993] 1 EGLR 84, a damaged roof was replaced by a roof with a different pitch and which was otherwise generally strengthened. The landlord had covenanted to repair. The changed design was considered necessary to avoid further problems, as the original design and construction of the roof had been insufficient to stop it blowing off in heavy wind. While holding it to be a borderline decision, the judge held that the changes were not so great as to be an improvement or alteration as opposed to a repair. In another roof case, *Elite Investments Ltd v TI Bainbridge Silencers Ltd* [1986] 2 EGLR 43, the tenant, to comply with its repairing covenant for an industrial unit, was required to replace the roof with a different type of construction and materials. The tenant had claimed this was an improvement rather than just repair, but the court held this was necessary for the tenant to comply with its covenant. The landlord would still be having back, at the end of the term, an industrial building with a roof – it was just a new roof made of modern materials. It was an obligation of the landlord to maintain an industrial building in *Welsh v Greenwich London Borough Council* [2000] 3 EGLR 41. The property was affected by a severe growth of black spot mould. This arose from a structural defect in construction. The Court of Appeal held it was the landlord's responsibility, under the covenant to maintain in good condition, and the tenant was entitled to damages for breach.

5.41 In 1999 a tenant holding under a three-year lease objected to paying the cost of significant roof repairs. The tenant argued that the work (a) was done to put the roof in good repair for a period of perhaps 20 years beyond the end of the lease, and (b) was partly being done at the request of a proposed future tenant of the premises to enable the landlord to let at the end of the short term. It was held that repairs were needed, but, in effect, what was to be done was excessive. The tenant was held liable to make a contribution of only 40% of the cost. (*Scottish Mutual Assurance plc v Jardine Public Relations Ltd* [1999] EGCS 43.)

5.42 In a number of cases landlords have been able to replace defective single glazed windows with double glazed windows, without this being treated as beyond the scope of repair. For residential cases see *Sutton (Hastoe) Housing Association v Williams* (1998) 1 EGLR 56 (see **5.202**), and for commercial property see *Minja Properties plc v Cussins Property Group plc* [1998] 2 EGLR 52 (see **5.29**).

Tenant's self-help

5.43 Finally, a reminder that tenants may have a remedy of self-help. For example, in *Loria v Hammer* [1989] 2 EGLR 249, the landlord of a set of four flats in NW3 was liable for repair of the roof and main water tank etc. The tenants were obliged to pay towards the cost of those specified items. The water tanks (which were not within any part of the building let to a tenant) overflowed, causing considerable damage including both wet and dry rot. The tenants notified the landlord who took no action. One of the tenants therefore had a report prepared by a suitable person and carried out the works recommended in the report. The tenant claimed the cost of those works from the landlord. The landlord said the works were unauthorised and that he had told the tenants that they could have the works carried out at their own expense (which seems to contradict the claim that they were unauthorised!). The court found for the tenant. It was held that the consequential damage was caused by the landlord's failure to attend to the ball valves in the water tank, and also that inadequate gutters allowed ingress of water. A key element was that the damage arose in the water tanks and roof, neither of which were demised to the tenant. The landlord was liable for consequential damage to the tenant's flat, as well as being obliged to repay the tenant the costs of doing the work. In addition, in this case, the tenant was awarded £200 per month for the period while the repairs were being carried out (representing, in effect, the cost of temporary accommodation). Twenty-five years later, another tenant (Mrs Marenco) took firm steps. The case was *Marenco v Jacramel Co Ltd* [1964] 191 EG 433. As tenant of one flat in a block of 12 flats she notified the landlord in writing of many defects which she wanted the landlords to put right. The landlords said they would not do the work until the tenants paid for past works and gave security for costs of future work. Mrs Marenco was prepared to pay her fair proportion of the costs. She sued the landlords who were found to be in breach of covenant. The cost of doing the works was estimated at £384 which Mrs Marenco claimed as the diminution in value of her flat. The matter was taken to the Court of Appeal after the trial judge had awarded Mrs Marenco damages of one twelfth of the costs of the work, and he also said that as she was liable for one twelfth of the cost of the works she had actually suffered no loss! On appeal Mrs Marenco was awarded damages equal to the whole cost of the works. The court pointed out that the landlords might be liable to other tenants in a similar amount. The landlords could reduce that liability at any time by doing the work. Mrs Marenco's property had been diminished in value by the whole cost of the repair, not by one twelfth of it. Judgment was given for the whole sum, subject to Mrs Marenco's agreement to pay one twelfth of the sum as her proper service charge contribution.

5.44   Much more recently, in *Metropolitan Properties Ltd v Wilson* [2002] EWHC 1853 (Ch), [2003] L & TR 15, tenants sought to carry out the landlord's works themselves but ran into difficulty. The premises were a residential block in London. The exterior and interior were in need of repair. The landlord produced a scheme and carried out consultation under s 20 of the Landlord and Tenant Act 1985. The tenants, however, withheld payments and decided to do the work themselves. The tenants set up scaffolding on the exterior of the property. Not only was this on property not demised to the tenants, but it effectively prevented the landlord from entering to carry out the work. The court pointed out that if the tenants carried out the work with their scheme it would have been without formal s 20 consultation. If the tenants did the work and then withheld payment (reflecting the costs they had incurred) this would be contrary to the basis of the lease, and would, for example, supplant the statutory procedures enabling residential tenants to challenge a landlord's service charge on grounds such as the standard of the work.

Decoration

5.45   The landlord's decorating obligation usually relates to the common parts and frequently also to external parts of a building. In the case of an office block or a block of flats the landlord is usually responsible for decorating the outside of the block and the corridors, stairs, entrance hall and other common parts. For industrial parks there is usually little decoration needed by the landlord. In a retail development the landlord may have to decorate entrances, malls and perhaps canopies as well as corridors and other common parts. Most retail tenants are responsible for their own shop fronts, and usually prefer to have control over them.

5.46   One advantage of the landlord dealing with external or common parts decoration is that it is all done at the same time and will be consistent, and thus the block will look better. The managing agents usually try to arrange for external work to be done in the months which (theoretically) have the best weather.

5.47   Many leases oblige a tenant to decorate at specified intervals, but a landlord does not often commit himself to decorate in specific years: more often he simply agrees to decorate 'when necessary'. In the case of leases with reserve funds there is occasionally an assumption that the external decoration will be done in particular years. This is to justify the amount the landlord wants tenants to pay in to the reserve fund, and provides a basis for the calculations. It does not by itself commit the landlord to decorate in those years, although it may be possible to imply a commitment. For example, in *Edmonton Corpn v W.H. Knowles & Son Ltd* (1961) EGD 400 (see **5.25** above) the landlord council did not covenant to decorate the exterior, but the tenant covenanted to pay the cost of three-yearly external decoration. It was held that there must have been an implied obligation on the landlord to do the external decoration.

5.48   The tenant may, however, well be justified in objecting to contributing to a reserve fund intended for decoration if the landlord does not decorate. The reserve fund is most commonly used for decoration. If external decoration is expected to be carried out in each third or fourth year the service charge costs will be higher in those years than other years: the reserve enables the sums claimed from the tenant to be spread more evenly over a few years. (For reserve and sinking funds, see Chapter 7.)

5.49   It is also fairly common (at least in older leases) for a tenant's decorating covenant to require the tenant to burn off old paint and to repaint with a specified number of coats of good quality paint. By contrast, the landlord rarely commits himself to the manner in which he will do the work. If he does it is important that the required method is suitable for the premises. Some types of building are not appropriate for painting and decorating or wallpapering: there is much benefit in a simple obligation such as 'to decorate or otherwise treat in a suitable manner', rather than seeking to specify what that manner should be. For example, the frames of shop fronts used to be mostly made of wood and decoration entailed stripping the old paint and using a primer, undercoat and top coat of paint. Now many are made of aluminium or other materials for which painting is not appropriate, although they may need some form of treatment.

5.50   Where a landlord failed to carry out his repairing obligations, he was liable for damages which included the cost of internal decorations (without any deduction for betterment): *McGreal v Wake* [1984] 1 EGLR 42, where the landlord also had to pay damages to the tenant for living in a house in bad repair, and the cost of temporary accommodation while the premises were repaired. In a similar case, *Stent v Monmouth District Council* [1987] 1 EGLR 59, the tenant was able to claim damages for ruined carpets as well as decorations when the landlords failed to keep a door in good repair and it let in water.

5.51   In an important and more recent case, *Postel Properties Ltd v Boots the Chemist Ltd* [1996] 2 EGLR 60, a delay in painting the window frames was held to be a breach by the landlord, but the court considered it was balanced by the fact that the tenant had not been called on to pay for the decoration. The lack of painting had caused deterioration, and as the frames had not been decorated for a number of years the work extended to stripping and removal of rust etc. A similar point was considered by the Lands Tribunal in *Continental Property Ventures Inc v White* [2006] 1 EGLR 85, where it was held that the tenant had a claim against the landlord for equitable set-off (ie the notional damages the tenant could have obtained for breach of the landlord's covenants).

5.52   Decoration was held not to be covered by a sweeping-up clause in *Lloyds Bank plc v Bowker Orford* [1992] 2 EGLR 44. This case is discussed more fully at **5.203** et seq.

PART 2 – PLANT AND MACHINERY

5.53   Where a development contains machinery or plant which provide services for a number of the tenants it is common for the landlord to be responsible for maintaining, cleaning, decorating, inspecting and insuring it, at the cost of the tenants. The expression plant and machinery can cover a wide range of items. These include major items such as lifts, escalators, boilers and generators, central heating, air conditioning plant, security cameras and sprinkler systems, as well as smaller items such as automatic doors, door entry phones, and sign boards. This section concentrates on the larger items.

5.54   Such items can be extremely expensive to install and to maintain and sometimes, also, to run. Therefore, they can be an important element of the service charge.

5.55 For such machinery it is rarely difficult to identify the equipment for which the landlord is responsible. The landlord will normally retain within the common parts such items as the lift and the lift shaft, or the boiler for the central heating. The only items that may give rise to doubt about responsibility for repair are connections such as pipes or wires from the main boiler to the individual units. It would perhaps be rare for the tenant to be responsible for any of the pipes and wires except where they are within the tenant's demise and/or solely serve some equipment within that demise. Accordingly, let us reiterate that it is important to make clear what is the responsibility of the landlord and what is that of the tenant. In *Campden Hill Towers Ltd v Gardner* [1977] QB 823, the landlord's statutory duty to repair was under the Housing Act 1961, ss 32 and 33. The obligation in relation to pipes etc was held to relate to the pipes etc within the flat only. There is obvious merit in clarifying what pipes etc the landlord has to repair, and which he can charge for through the service charge.

5.56 In 2002 the Court of Appeal decided the case of *O'Connor v Old Etonian Housing Association Ltd* [2002] EWCA Civ 150, [2002] Ch 295, relating to the water supply to flats in Surbiton, Surrey. The flats were let on terms where repair under s 11 of the Landlord and Tenant Act 1985 applied. This included an obligation on the landlord to keep installations for the supply of water, gas and electricity 'in proper working order'. The water supply had been satisfactory for years, but then the water supply to the top flat ceased to work well because the water pressure dropped. Before this, as part of a refurbishment, the landlord had replaced the pipes with pipes of smaller bore. The drop in pressure (caused by greater local demand) was ended when the water authority built a new pumping station. The court reviewed the landlord's obligation to maintain plant, and the principles to apply to any case where the landlord is under an obligation to keep plant in order. The obligation is to keep the equipment in proper working order, and it cannot be in proper working order if it cannot function, even if this is because of a fault in design or construction. An installation 'will be in proper working order if it is able to function under those conditions of supply that it is reasonable to anticipate will prevail'. Reasonable anticipation in that context should be judged by reference to such matters as the statutory obligations imposed on the providers of utilities. The court was unable to lay down precise circumstances in which the landlord may be under an obligation to adapt an installation following unanticipated changes in supply. It seemed clear that the landlord would have to take action after some voluntary change (eg changing the supply from electricity to gas). Additionally, it may be reasonable for a landlord to be obliged to take action if only a modest expenditure might be needed to avoid the tenants being deprived of the service for a long period.

5.57 Repair of the plant is of course important, and a properly drawn service charge provision will make it clear that such repair is one of the items included. In addition to repairing actual defects, it is common for a landlord to have a maintenance contract under which specialist firms check the plant regularly. This is sensible for both landlord and tenant: not only does this help ensure that the equipment continues working properly (which is not of course a factor when considering the repair of a building), but it may be essential to ensure that the equipment in question complies with current statutory requirements as to safety, etc. There are, for example, obligations on a landlord to arrange annual safety checks on gas appliances for dwellings under the Gas Safety (Installation and Use) Regulations 1998. The regulations are too detailed to be covered here, but include some criminal offences. The lease should ideally specifically refer to the right of the landlord to charge for maintenance contracts. It should perhaps be noted that the cost of such repair and maintenance would seem to come within the reference to 'works' within s 18 of the Landlord and Tenant Act 1985 for residential tenancies. Therefore, regular maintenance contracts would need to be the subject of consultation with tenants under s 20 if the total cost is more than £250 for any dwelling. (See Chapter 9.)

5.58 The plant may also require an energy supply. The cost of the energy, whether electricity or gas or oil, again should be an item that the lease should permit the landlord to recover, although it is difficult to see a claim for reimbursement of such energy costs being disallowed on the grounds that fuel costs were not mentioned in the lease because the landlord would not be able to supply the service without using the energy.

5.59 As well as repair and regular maintenance, plant is usually the subject of insurance. Sometimes the plant is included as part of the landlord's buildings policy, and insurance provisions are usually best left out of the service charge, but sometimes it is covered separately. On the assumption that the plant is covered by the buildings insurance the recovery of premiums and all the other provisions affecting insurance can be left out of the service charge provisions, although where any repairs are covered by insurance the landlord should give credit to the service charge fund for the insurance moneys recovered. This is not specifically covered by the Landlord and Tenant Act 1985 for residential tenancies, but it seems hard to see how the cost of a repair which was recovered through an insurance claim could be claimed through the service charge by the landlord: it would surely be held to be not 'reasonably incurred' (s 19(1)). And see **9.237** regarding the Schedule to the Landlord and Tenant Act 1985 and the right of tenants of dwellings to notify an insurer direct of damage. If the tenant does not pay insurance premiums separately from the service charge then consideration should perhaps be given to ensuring that the landlord can recover the cost of premiums for insuring the plant within the service charge.

5.60 Plant and machinery are the most common items for which a sinking fund is set up. For sinking funds see Chapter 7. Obviously, with expensive items of plant the cost of replacing them, when it is necessary, is a particular problem, and the sinking fund builds up a sum to enable replacement to be carried out as painlessly as possible. Again, the question of when a repair is appropriate and when replacement is necessary is important, and the general principles mentioned above concerning repair apply. In *Perseus Property Co Ltd v Burberry* [1985] 1 EGLR 114, it was said that 'once it is conceded … that the plant in question is necessary … to provide the services some provision for its depreciation or replacement must be included in any computation of the reasonable charges for those services'. This seems to imply that even if there is no express right in the lease to call for a sinking fund, where plant is involved the landlord may be entitled to set one up. (Thinking of our own washing machine or car, and reluctant as we are to face the financial consequences, we have to recognise that they will eventually cease to function and will need to be replaced. The point is the same for landlords and tenants in respect of many items of plant.)

5.61   For a case where replacement of plant for cleaning windows was involved, *Sun Alliance and London Assurance Co Ltd v British Railways Board* [1989] 2 EGLR 237, see the next section. For a case on the cost of installation of lights, see *Elmcroft Developments Ltd v Tankersley-Sawyer* [1984] 1 EGLR 47, discussed in the section below on lighting, starting at **5.71**. For thermostats on radiators see the section below on heating (starting at **5.140**), and *New Pinehurst Residents Association (Cambridge) Ltd v Silow* [1988] 1 EGLR 227 . In the same section on heating is a case on replacement of boilers, *Yorkbrook Investments Ltd v Batten* [1985] 2 EGLR 100. Air conditioning is mentioned in *Fluor Daniel Properties Ltd v Shortlands Investments Ltd* [2001] EGCS 8 (see **5.134** below), with comments on the estimated life and actual life of plant. The landlord was prevented from recovering costs for replacement of equipment that had reached the end of its estimated life but was in good condition. The case also refers to what the service is – differentiating between the services to be provided and the equipment needed to provide the service. For a case where the sweeping-up clause enabled a landlord to recover certain capital costs for plant (plant for providing hot water and also replacement of certain electrical plant needed to provide services which the landlord had agreed to provide), see *Lloyds Bank plc v Bowker Orford* [1992] 2 EGLR 44, and at **5.203**.

5.62   A tenant expects that plant for which he is paying via the service charge will perform its functions. However, it is important, in the case of plant, for a landlord to have protection if he has acted responsibly but the plant ceases to work. In *Electricity Supply Nominees Ltd v National Magazine Co Ltd* [1998] EGCS 162, the amount of damages for constant breakdown of the lifts and air conditioning that the landlord was due to maintain was discussed. In part, it was said that the measure of damages was the diminution in value to the tenant of its occupation for the relevant period, and that the rent payable was a guide (on the basis that the rent was based on premises with services that worked).

5.63   Failure of plant is one major reason for exclusion clauses in leases. A non-resident landlord will not know if the plant has ceased to operate unless the tenant tells him. It is, accordingly, quite common to see exclusion clauses provide that a landlord is not responsible for breakdowns in services unless the landlord has been notified of the breakdown and has failed to have necessary repairs done within a reasonable time. While the author feels this not an unreasonable qualification to the landlord's liability, it has to be recognised that it can be difficult for a tenant to know that something is wrong if it not within his demise. Since the landlord has control of the common parts the tenant may well be unaware of a problem until it becomes serious. (See also **5.31** above.)

What is a reasonable time depends on the circumstances and the plant in question. If a 20-storey block only has one lift then a much shorter period for repairs would be appropriate than in the case of a similar building with two or three lifts. Again, in the case of heating, a breakdown in a cold spell is more urgent than in the height of summer. It is hard to see that a landlord negotiating a lease could reasonably object to a qualification to an exclusion clause to reflect the above point (the breakdown to be repaired within a reasonable time of notification of the fault). In the wider context, however, the landlord must take care that any qualification does not purport to ensure that the landlord will at all times provide all the services provided at the date of the commencement of the lease. This could create problems in relation to services that are present at the start of the lease but are not required 20 years later. Exclusion clauses did not help the landlord in *Connaught Restaurants Ltd v Indoor Leisure Ltd* [1994] 4 All ER 834.

5.64 In the case of lifts there may also be a need to employ a lift operator. This is much more rare now than formerly, but if this is necessary the landlord should ensure that the point is recorded in the lease so that he can recover the expenses relating to employing the operator. (See below on employment of staff at **5.93** et seq.)

PART 3 – OTHER WORKS AND SERVICES

Cleaning and window cleaning

5.65 Cleaning is another area where the definition of the premises to be cleaned is important. For example, in *Embassy Court Residents' Association Ltd v Lipman* [1984] 2 EGLR 60, the lease provided that the landlord's services would include 'cleaning outside windows by employing window cleaners'. It was held that this description covered cleaning all the exterior windows of the building, not just those in the common parts.

5.66 The cleaning obligation needs to be related to premises that can be identified. It is often the case that the lease refers simply to cleaning in common parts. This may be sufficient, but be careful that the definition of common parts is sufficient to cover the areas for which cleaning is needed. For example, if the car park needs to be swept but is defined separately from the common parts a general definition of cleaning in common parts may not enable the landlord to recover the cost relating to car park cleaning.

5.67 Service charge provisions ideally should cover replacement of cleaning materials (soaps etc) and cleaning tools (brushes etc) when reasonably necessary. The lease should also permit charging for contracts for cleaning. This will ensure that the landlord can recover the cost of contract cleaning provided that it is otherwise reasonable (and, for example, where material for residential tenants, that any necessary consultation has taken place). (Landlord and Tenant Act 1985, s 20.) For residential premises if the cost of cleaning (or many other elements of cost) is challenged the Leasehold Valuation Tribunal can substitute its own figure if it considers the amount charged by the landlord is unreasonably high. (See eg *Stoker v Urbanpoint Property Management Ltd* (LVT) LON/00AE/LSI/2003/0025.)

5.68 If there is a cleaning cradle or other built-in cleaning aid, this is an item of plant, and the provisions relating to plant mentioned at **5.53** et seq above apply. In 1987 the upgrading of an old window cleaning aid (a trolley) by replacing it with a modern system with a permanent roof cradle and track was the subject of a court case, *Sun Alliance and London Assurance Co Ltd v British Railways Board* [1989] 2 EGLR 237, when the landlord wanted to recover part of the cost of the new system. Although the lease contained some service charge provisions concerning plant and equipment, the original equipment belonged to the cleaning contractors, not the landlord, and thus was not covered by those clauses. It was held there that the landlord could recover part of the cost of the new system by virtue of the sweeping-up clause. ('The cost of providing such other services as the Lessor should consider ought reasonably be provided for the benefit of the building or for the proper maintenance and servicing of any parts'.) The fact that the landlord was not claiming in full, but only £17,500 out of a cost of £70,000, may well have been a factor in the decision, as well as the point that part of the cost included having to strengthen the roof to take the weight of the new equipment. The tenant had pointed out that (a) the works were not needed for safety reasons, (b) the installation of the new equipment had not produced great costs savings for the tenants and (c) the capital costs incurred were out of line with annual expenditure. Despite these observations, the landlord was able to recover the proportion claimed. (Incidentally, the lease provided that the tenant should clean the windows, but as the letting was of upper floors and the windows could not be cleaned from inside the landlords, in practice, arranged for the cleaning.)

5.69 For window cleaning a tenant may seek to clarify in the lease that the cleaning is not to be done more often than, say, once every week or month (or 'not more often than is reasonably necessary'). This is not to prevent the work being done, but to ensure that the landlord cannot claim the cost of unnecessarily frequent cleaning. Any proposed draft amendment on these lines should, of course, be specifically checked with the prospective tenant who may well have his own views on such matters.

5.70 If the cleaning is done by a resident caretaker the lease should permit the landlord to require repayment of the cost of replacing the tools and materials used for cleaning so far as they are used for cleaning premises for which the tenant is obliged to pay.

Lighting and electrical matters

5.71 Again, in the case of lighting, it is material to ensure that the area to be lit is defined to avoid problems. For example, in one case, *Elmcroft Developments Ltd v Tankersley Sawyer* [1984] 1 EGLR 47, relating to a block of flats at Embankment Gardens, SW3, the landlord covenanted to keep the entrance hall stairs and passages well lit during hours of darkness. In the relevant lease the tenant was given rights over the entrance hall staircase and passages 'in or about the said building'. The court was asked whether the lighting covenant included the external common parts or only the internal common parts. The tenant had fixed her own external lights, at the front and back, both of which had been dark areas, and had attached the lights to her own electricity supply. The court held the landlord was in breach of its covenant as to lighting, and that the tenant could recover the cost of installing lights and of the electricity consumed.

5.72   The landlord's obligation to light will almost always cover the common parts, notably corridors, hallways and staircases, but may well also cover such parts as any toilets in use by a number of the tenants. For shopping precincts there may also be a need to consider lighting for the malls or streets, and also the service yards and accesses to the shops, or to any public toilets. As with so many other aspects of service charges, doubts should be removed by referring in the lease as clearly as possible to the areas concerned if there is any possibility of ambiguity or a lacuna.

5.73   It is not usual to state hours for lighting, but in some leases (particularly for offices and shopping precincts) there are obligations by the landlord to keep the common parts lit during the hours when the offices or the shops are normally open for trading, sometimes coupled with a right for the landlord to make a separate charge for electricity to those tenants who want to use the premises outside normal hours.

5.74   As in the case of plant the question of replacement of equipment is material. Light bulbs, tubes, spotlights and floodlights need replacement from time to time. These are normally not a major expense unless they are in places which are particularly hard to reach. The light fittings themselves are often more expensive, but again they have a life which is not infinite, and replacement should be expected in all but the shortest lease terms. (*Perseus Property Co Ltd v Burberry* [1985] 1 EGLR 114.) It must also be remembered that frequently replacement is cheaper than repair (is it possible to repair a light bulb?) and that, as it may not be possible to obtain identical items many years after the originals were installed, a modern equivalent may be needed. This may, for example, include replacing the original bulbs with energy saving bulbs.

5.75   A landlord will normally seek to restrict his liability for breach in respect of matters outside his control. A landlord would be well advised to ensure that his liability for breach does not arise until he is notified of the failure. By comparison with a case concerning heating, *Yorkbrook Investments Ltd v Batten* [1985] 2 EGLR 100, it may well be the case that if a lighting installation is continually failing the landlord may be under an obligation to renew it.

5.76   In some cases (mostly residential), electricity is put through a central meter and the cost charged to tenants based on the figures shown on a sub-meter. In some such cases, the landlord makes a profit on the cost, although the landlord does incur management costs for the accounting and collection, and has the risk of shortfall if the tenants fail to pay.

5.77   In *Lloyds Bank plc v Bowker Orford* [1992] 2 EGLR 44 (reviewed at **5.203** below), the provision of lighting and electrical items was under consideration by the court. The repairs to lighting and also provision of new lighting were held allowable costs. On construction, the cost of rewiring was also allowed 'in so far as the electrical work was required to enable the lessor to comply with its obligation to provide any of the services' which the landlord had specifically covenanted to provide.

Signs

5.78   Signs can be material for service charges in several contexts. For example, in the case of offices or industrial developments there is often a board setting out the names (or trading names) of the tenants, and/or hours of trading. This is usually in the common areas. There can also be signs displaying the name of the development (and opening hours). Secondly, there are signs within the development generally. These can include signs showing what floor you are on, and direction signs, as well as signs in car parks, safety warnings and signs covering statutory matters (for example 'danger' signs, green exit signs, and signs concerning dangerous chemicals). The expression can also be used to cover the marking of parking bays and symbols for disabled spaces or parent and child spaces in car parks (or numbered spaces in some office complexes), as well as lines on the road surface. The marking of the lines in bays may be best mentioned separately in the lease as these may not qualify as 'signs'. Signs can also include a noticeboard for the use of the landlord to give notice to tenants (eg of the dates of intended works), and to use for regulations affecting the building.

5.79   On the basis that these signs are for common use, and usually in the common parts, the landlord will normally be responsible for them. The obligation should extend to having the signs marked up (for example changing the name on the board when a new tenant moves in to an office block), and keeping the parking bays in a car park clearly marked. If a tenant wants a special sign on the names board (perhaps with its logo) it is probably reasonable for the landlord to ask the tenant in question to pay for the addition to the sign board, but thereafter maintenance should be through the service charge.

5.80   The costs of maintenance should include repairing the noticeboard, and keeping it clean, as well as remarking signs when necessary. Since some exit signs are required to be illuminated the cost of the illumination (light bulbs and electricity) is also material.

5.81   The cost of replacement of a noticeboard or manufactured signs when necessary should be covered by the service charge. The same considerations apply in this context as to other plant.

Street furniture and ornaments

5.82   This expression covers such items as seats for the public, litter bins, clocks and also ornaments in the nature of statues or fountains. These are found in particular in shopping centres, where they help the general public, but they can also be in the grounds or other common parts of office developments occupied by multiple tenants. In an office such items can include seats and magazine stands and tables used by people waiting for appointments in a general waiting area. Similar items would be loudspeaker systems for broadcasting music, or for internal shopping arcades advertisements (if the precinct is subject to public rights of way its loudspeakers cannot be used for advertising), as well as public address announcements. The description in this section is also intended to include door entry phone systems in offices and flats. New industrial units are likely to have landscaping and, accordingly, these matters may be relevant.

5.83   Obviously, if the landlord provides these items the maintenance should be a legitimate service charge item. The main points are as follows:

(a)   Unless it is clearly agreed by the parties the initial capital cost of providing the items will not be recoverable, as service charge recovery is normally related to income and not capital expenditure.

(b)   The landlord will needs rights, as with other equipment, to charge for the repair and maintenance of these items and to clean, decorate, inspect, and insure them. It may also be necessary to replace them, in place of repair.

(c)   In the case of such items it is probably appropriate for a landlord to reserve the right to move the features to other positions: this may be needed for operational purposes, or where there is redevelopment, or as a marketing device (eg if the marketing people consider the seats are best together rather than scattered about the shopping precinct). A landlord could, for example, refer to items 'in such position within the common parts as the landlord shall reasonably determine'. A tenant may wish to expand such a provision to include a reference to consultation with the tenants for any such change. (This would be sensible whether it is mentioned in the lease or not.) It must be remembered that the item will normally be on common parts, over which rights are probably granted, rather than on parts let to any specific tenant. It may not always be possible to obtain the agreement of all tenants. Some may prefer not to have the feature near them as it may cause an obstruction to potential customers, while other tenants may be only too pleased to have a feature near them in the hope that those attracted to the feature will also look at the shops nearby.

(d)   For items such as fountains the landlord will be involved in keeping in good order the water supply, filters, pumps and perhaps solar panels so that the fountain works. This would normally be done by way of a maintenance contract, and the service charge provisions should ideally mention charging for maintenance contracts as well any charge for electricity and water needed for the operation of the fountain.

5.84   The most contentious area is the introduction of new items. For example, a landlord may feel that a fountain (where there was none before), or some other artistic feature, such as clock or a statue, would be for the benefit of the shopping centre because it would make the centre more attractive to potential shoppers. (These points are unlikely to be relevant for office or industrial premises, as the tenants of such premises do not usually rely on attracting people to their premises for trade.) In such a case the landlord may wish for lease provisions entitling him to incorporate the new feature at his own expense, with the tenants paying the maintenance costs thereafter, provided that the tenants agree. The proposed tenant of a lease of a unit in a shopping centre may seek a proviso to such clause to enable the landlord to include this new type of item provided that not more than half (or 25%, or some other percentage) of the tenants object. If the feature does indeed add to the numbers of people visiting the centre, then the tenants will benefit from increased numbers of potential customers, even if they also have a minor increase in service charge costs to pay. It could also make an individual shop more attractive if the tenant wants to assign the lease. (The provision of new items is discussed in Section D2 of the Commercial Code.)

5.85   As a corollary to the previous paragraph, the tenant negotiating a lease might wish to incorporate a provision entitling the tenants to require the landlord to construct a new feature in the development on the above lines, with the landlord paying the capital cost and the tenants paying for maintenance, subject to a specified proportion of tenants making the request. The difficulty with an individual tenant negotiating a provision like this is that the provisions will be only in one lease. The other tenants will not be subject to the same obligations and may object if asked to pay for maintenance of new items.

Car parks

5.86   Car parks used by tenants have numerous service charge ramifications. Repair of the surface, for example, is material as well as relining, lighting, gritting and cleaning. There can also be repairs for pipes and cables that pass under the car park, needing lease provisions to ensure the landlord can close the car park (or parts of it) when necessary. In addition, there may be equipment (eg barriers, traffic lights, security cameras, trolley parks, rubbish bins and cleaning equipment), signage, and sometimes staff to man the car park. Other aspects can include landscaping, a kiosk by the barrier, and the maintenance of a sign displaying the names of the tenants and opening hours etc. The above items are mentioned in this book under various headings, but this segment is to remind readers of the factors that can be involved, so that they can be incorporated where necessary in the lease.

5.87   It is also not unknown to see provisions to the effect that the car park shall only be resurfaced with the consent of a certain number of tenants. Resurfacing is normally the major repair expense (the other major item of expense for car parks tends to be staff for manning the barriers), and is a matter of concern to all tenants. It is one item which might encourage a landlord to set up a sinking fund.

5.88   Two specific aspects of car parks are sometimes controversial. These are laying out the car park to a different design, and the use of the car park for income producing events.

5.89   When tenants take premises on a development they can see the way the car park is designed. If at some later stage the landlord (or the tenants) feel that some other layout is more suitable, or efficient, or avoids the queue that occurs at busy times, can it be changed? This is not specifically a service charge point, but where the landlord is responsible for maintaining the car park and charges through the service charge there are sometimes provisions in the service charge schedule (or among the rights reserved, declarations or covenants) which entitle the landlord to change the layout. On the basis that any such change affects the occupiers (ie the tenants) it is not uncommon for the provision either initially, or as amended, to provide that changes to the layout shall only be by agreement of all, or a stated number or minimum percentage, of the tenants. This is not usually controversial, except perhaps where the landlord is itself an occupier of the development, when it may well wish to exercise full control (particularly if it has the largest unit). Clearly, if the landlord is an occupier tenants will want him to share the costs.

5.90   Landscaping is mentioned above. The comments elsewhere in this chapter as to gardening apply. There are often landscaping requirements in the planning permission for new developments, and the running costs of complying with such landscaping obligations should be mentioned in the service charge provisions: the tenant cannot seriously object where the landscaping is a planning requirement. The cost of the initial laying out of the landscaping is, of course, a different bed of roses.

Income from the use of the car park or common parts

5.91   As mentioned above, income from the use of the car park is an issue with many tenants. The point is that the car park is intended for parking and the tenants are required to pay for its repair. If it is used for some income-producing use (eg a display of double glazing, or for the AA or RAC, or an art exhibition for which viewers pay) the tenants can say that the car park is reduced in size (where the third party use is during business hours) and therefore require that income from the use of it should be set against the costs. The counter is that the common parts are the landlord's property, not the tenants', and that so long as the car park is still usable the tenants are not suffering. Indeed, in the case of retail premises the tenants could well benefit from increased numbers of passers by. It is also said that the tenants would not expect to receive income from other units on the development, and temporary uses are simply another way for the landlord to make some money from what is, after all, his property.

5.92   This topic is usefully treated at paras 83–86 and Section D3 to the Commercial Code (see Chapter 11). This recommends that owners should state their policy on such income, and that any income 'derived from the provision of a service or activity, the finance for which is included in the service charge, will be treated as a service charge credit eg photocopy and fax reimbursement'. As to letting spaces in the common parts (for barrows or kiosks in shopping malls) it says that the owner normally retains the income as rent, but in those circumstances 'the space will be included in the service charge apportionment matrix or appropriate equivalent credit give for the costs of that space'. For less substantial fixtures, 'a sum will be credited to the service charge to reflect a contribution to the service charge depending on services utilised and how permanent a fixing the item represents'.

Staff and staff accommodation

5.93   The inclusion in a service charge provision of an obligation for the tenant to contribute towards the cost of employment of staff at the relevant premises by the landlord can be contentious. With larger blocks of flats there may be a caretaker or porter, and in all sorts of premises there may be security personnel and/or car park personnel. More rarely (for serviced offices) there may be staff employed to carry out secretarial services, and sometimes there is a landlord's estate management office.

5.94   To enable a landlord to recover the costs involved the lease must, as usual, be clear. Some leases refer simply to the 'employment' of a caretaker etc, rather than setting out the individual items for which the tenant is to pay. There can be some merit in this, but it can lead to doubt about whether some costs of the employment are included or not: for example, what about the Christmas bonus which is not part of the employee's contract of employment but which is paid by custom? The employee may also be entitled to benefits such as private health insurance and use of a vehicle. If these items are mentioned in the lease there should be little difficulty in a landlord justifying repayment of those items by the tenant, subject to quibbles about the amount. The expenses that are usually mentioned specifically include pay, national insurance contributions, holiday pay, and pension contributions.

5.95   Some tenants seek to restrict pension contributions to statutory pension requirements. While this may be seen as a reasonable qualification, it must be recognised by both parties that, assuming it is necessary to employ a member of staff, in practice he or she will have to be paid what is paid in the marketplace, or the landlord will be unable to employ anyone to do the job. For example, in *Metropolitan Properties Ltd v Noble* [1968] 2 All ER 313, a case where a rent assessment committee's 'fair rent' was under dispute, an appeal against the figure held that, in respect of providing the residential staff, selective employment tax had to be taken into account. The tax no longer exists, but the court said 'it is something the landlords have to pay in providing those services'.

5.96   An employer may be under an obligation to offer particular pension benefits to staff. If not, he will have to pay the 'going rate'. The same point applies to other aspects of salary, and revisions by the tenant need to be considered carefully to avoid the landlord having an unavoidable shortfall. The cost is, after all, the cost, whether it is a statutory figure or not. A tenant may wish to restrict being obliged to contribute to special pension arrangements for directors of the landlord company who may be employed at the premises. Such restriction may be appropriate to avoid a possible way for a landlord to achieve an unfair higher income than might be reasonable.

5.97   If the holiday pay and perks are to be recoverable they should be mentioned, otherwise if there is a dispute the landlord may only succeed if he can satisfy a court that the items in question are part of normal emoluments for the type of employee in question. One item that it is not reasonable to include is bonuses paid by a landlord for benefits which are benefits for the landlord, such as commission for introducing new tenants, as opposed to work specifically for management of the premises. The Commercial Code briefly mentions staff in para 26.

5.98   The 'provision of staff' by the maintenance trustee in *Nell Gwynn House Maintenance Fund Trustees v Commissioners of Customs & Excise* [1994] EGCS 163 was held subject to payment of value added tax. VAT was also the subject of two cases affecting timeshares: *Clowance Holdings Ltd v Customs & Excise Comrs* (No 17289) VADT 14/6/2001, and *Clowance Owners Club Ltd v Customs & Excise Comrs* (No 18787) VADT 8/10/2004.

Resident caretakers

5.99   There have been a few cases regarding resident caretakers. It was held in *Posner v Scott-Lewis* [1987] Ch 25 that specific performance could be ordered of a landlord's express covenant to provide a resident caretaker.

5.100   Two conflicting cases considered whether the conduct of the landlord when granting the lease was sufficient to imply that the landlord would be employing a caretaker. In *Hupfield v Bourne* (1974) 28 P & CR 77, it was held that the landlord's conduct did imply that he would, but *in Russell v Laimond Properties Ltd* (1983) 269 EG 947, it was held that the landlord's conduct was not sufficient. For an appeal against an LVT determination where the leases of flats in a block of seven flats in Mayfair referred to services including cleaning and the costs of maintenance of the services of a porter or porters (see *Veena SA v Cheong* [2003] 1 EGLR 175). The LVT held that the professional management of the block did not require a full-time porter and also a part-time cleaner. It consequently disallowed some of the costs allocated to those items, and the Lands Tribunal upheld that decision.

Staff accommodation

5.101   A lease may also contain a provision entitling the landlord to recover the cost of overheads for staff accommodation, such as a caretaker's flat, or porter's lodge. (Management offices are mentioned separately in the next section of this chapter.) These overheads can include electricity, gas, council tax, water and telephone. Ideally, the costs for the telephone should be split between the personal use of the caretaker and use for the purposes of the building – for this purpose the clause could be qualified to refer to the costs 'only to the extent that the use of the telephone is related to the management of the building'. For negotiating purposes, the tenant could usefully include a provision that the tenant's liability for these items is only to the extent that the caretaker does not pay the overheads himself/herself.

5.102 A clause that is unpopular with tenants is one permitting a landlord to charge to the service charge the cost of accommodation for staff, whether actual or notional. From a landlord's point of view, the position is relatively simple: if providing or paying for accommodation is necessary to attract someone to carry out the necessary job then that is a reasonable charge to make, and is likely to be reflected in the (lower) wages actually paid. If the accommodation is used for the person concerned the landlord will not have it available to let and so produce income. Where the employee is a caretaker or porter whose presence at the premises at all times is important the position is even clearer. Disputes, however, arise when the tenants object to the service charge including a notional rent for the accommodation, or a charge for rent of accommodation for staff that could be outside the landlord's property.

5.103 The question of rent is difficult. It has been held by the Court of Appeal in *Agavil Investments Ltd v Corner* (3 October 1975 (unreported but which has subsequently been referred to favourably in a number of cases, eg *Boldmark Ltd v Cohen* [1986] 1 EGLR 47 and *Lloyds Bank plc v Bowker Orford* [1992] 2 EGLR 44) that the notional cost of accommodation for a caretaker's flat can be a proper charge, provided that the lease contains an obligation on the part of the landlord to provide a resident caretaker, or even a non-resident caretaker, and the service charge is expressed to cover all the costs and expenses to the landlord of performing the services. In *Lloyds Bank Ltd v Bowker Orford*, the landlord was able to recover a due proportion of the notional provision of accommodation for a caretaker within the building. The relevant clause (in a list of items of services to be carried out) read: 'a resident caretaker should be employed housed and uniformed generally to be responsible for the upkeep and security of the building'. The moral is presumably that if a landlord wants to recover such charges he must expressly include the cost of the accommodation (actual or notional) within the service charge, or, if he seeks to rely on more general provisions, he must bind himself in a firm obligation to provide the caretaker. The wording entitling an intermediate landlord to charge a notional rent for a caretaker's flat was discussed in *Earl of Cadogan v 27/29 Sloane Gardens Ltd* [2006] 24 EG 178.

5.104 The Residential Code (see Chapter 11) at para 8.15 simply says 'when accommodation is provided, either for staff or ancillary to the provision of the services, any rent charged should be reasonable'. This may be partly because of the implied reasonableness for residential premises in any event. The Commercial Code does not directly address the question, save as mentioned in

5.97 above, although neither accommodation nor staff costs are mentioned in the definition (17) of those costs to which the service charge should be restricted.

5.105   In *Gilje v Charlgrove Securities Ltd* [2001] EWCA Civ 1777, [2002] 16 EG 182, the lease said the landlord would provide a resident caretaker. The lease also said the landlord could include in the service charge costs the gas, electricity, rates etc for the caretaker's flat but did not mention rent. The landlord was entitled to recover 'money expended'. It was held by the Court of Appeal that the landlord was not entitled to claim a notional rent: on proper construction of the lease it had not been specified as a recoverable item.

5.106   What level of notional rent is payable is of course another question. In *Metropolitan Properties Ltd v Noble* [1968] 2 All ER 313, mentioned at **5.95** above, another issue was the notional rent for the staff accommodation. The court held the rent assessment committee should allow only such rent as they considered appropriate, even though they had not inspected the staff flats. The appeal related to other flats, and rent for the staff flats was simply one factor in determining the fair rent.

5.107   Where the landlord is to recover actual rent payable, then that figure is readily identifiable, but the tenants will be concerned to ensure that the rent payable is reasonable. For example, if the caretaker was housed off the development in a flat owned by an associated company of the landlord which charged a much higher rent than a market rent this would clearly be unsatisfactory. The tenant in such case would want the rent to which he is to contribute to be limited to a 'reasonable market rent', or some similar qualification. In the case of a caretaker housed on the site the landlord will often want a notional rent to be charged to the service charge, on the basis that if the accommodation was not occupied by the caretaker the landlord could let it to a third party at a rent which he would receive. The tenants will again want protection, and a few points are material in this context:

(a)   Whatever the level of notional rent to be charged, it should be remembered that if the flat was occupied by someone other than the caretaker this may make the demised premises less valuable (for rent calculation) because the development would not have a resident caretaker.

(b)   The rent is likely to vary depending on the type of tenancy that could be offered. For example, if the caretaker had been offered the flat on the basis of an assured tenancy the rent might well be slightly higher than if the flat was offered on the basis of an assured shorthold tenancy, under which the tenant has security of tenure for a specified period after which the landlord can guarantee being able to obtain possession.

(c)   Another possibility would be to assume a lease on terms similar to the other in the development. If they are not let on rack rent leases a different assessment arises. For example, if the caretaker's flat was in a block of flats which had each been let at a premium and a small rent, then one would expect the caretaker's flat (if not used for a caretaker) to be let on somewhat similar terms. If this was the assumption for the notional rent then it would be expected the notional rent to be equivalent to the nominal rent. However, doing this the landlord would not receive the equivalent of the premium received on the other flats. One way to assess a figure would, perhaps, be to assume a rent equivalent to the probable income receivable on investment of the notional premium.

(d)   Yet another possibility is that the notional rent could be the equivalent of the reduction in the salary the caretaker might otherwise have. For example, if the caretaker had to find his own accommodation, he might be paid a salary of £X per month, but if the landlord provides accommodation the salary would be the smaller figure of £Z per month. In such a case the value of the notional accommodation could be the difference between these two figures, although it is fair comment that the two are not identical to each other as one represents the value to the employee and the other the value to the employer.

5.108   These possibilities are mentioned to illustrate the difficulties in deciding what a fair basis for a notional rent might be, even before the calculation of the notional rent can be made. As in most service charge matters the most satisfactory solution is to spell out in the lease the basis of the rent or notional rent if at all possible.

Management offices

5.109   The comments in the preceding section of this chapter may be similarly relevant in shopping precincts or office blocks where there are offices for the use of the people who manage the development. In the case of full-time staff the costs would normally be part of the reasonable and proper cost of managing the precinct. Accordingly, such costs would normally be recoverable provided that the lease enables such recovery. The cost of the staff themselves would be similar to the costs of caretakers, porters, etc – national insurance contributions, pension contribution and so on being material. If any of the staff are employed only part-time in relation to the development concerned and, for example, also work for the landlord in relation to other premises, their expenses should be apportioned.

5.110   The Court of Appeal in *Parkside Knightsbridge Ltd v Horwitz* [1983] 2 EGLR 42 considered a case where the parent company of the landlords had carried out management for several blocks of flats. The parent company had carried out an exercise in one year as a result of which they were able to estimate the time spent in relation to each of the blocks and they apportioned the costs between the blocks accordingly. The court seemed to suggest, however, that this exercise should be carried out each year. After reviewing the facts the court said of the landlord's management costs under dispute 'precisely how that amount was arrived at is not, in my opinion, of significance. The question is whether the amount can be said to have been a reasonable charge'. As with so many other aspects of service charges a landlord has to be able to prove what he wants to claim is reasonable: the exercise to apportion time was, surely, a reasonable method of approach. The complaint must have been that in one year that apportionment would be appropriate, but in following years the proportion of time spent on the various blocks would be different, and so the original apportionment might not necessarily reflect time apportionments in later years.

5.111 In the case of the offices within a block for use of management staff, again the cost of the space is material to the landlord. In this case, any notional rent should be on the basis of office space, and if there is other office space in the precinct this should provide some sort of guide to the rent per square foot (or square metre) that the landlord could recover.

Refuse disposal

5.112 Where there are a number of tenants the landlord may make arrangements for refuse collection and charge the cost through the service charge. Formerly local authorities used to collect household refuse from flats and houses free of charge, but now it is sometimes subject to a charge either from the local authority or from private contractors. Tenants of large industrial units may well make their own arrangements with refuse collectors who are licensed under the Environmental Protection Act 1990 and the relevant regulations (eg Waste Management Licensing Regulations 1994). In such a case no service charge obligations or rights will apply. Some of the larger retail units also make direct arrangements for refuse.

5.113 Where a landlord makes the arrangements he has to comply with the 1990 Act. As refuse has to be dealt with under specified conditions (this is 'waste management' whereby the actual types of waste are material, and consideration is given to such matters as reduction or recycling, or, as the final option, disposal – see Department for the Environment Circular 11/94) and, under the Environmental Protection Act 1990, s 34, there is a duty of care on all persons handling waste, whether as producer, storer, carrier or disposer. The cost is therefore higher than before. There are criminal offences under the Act for failing to comply. It has been suggested (see eg a useful article in T Smithers 'The Waste Management Regime' *Estates Gazette*, 2 July 1994) that, as the statutory offences include the phrases 'knowingly causing' and 'knowingly permitting,' a landlord could have a criminal liability if a tenant is responsible for waste management and does not comply. Presumably the reverse could apply, and if a landlord is responsible a tenant could have a criminal liability if he encourages the landlord not to comply with the system. Certainly waste disposal and similar environmental matters are being given a higher profile in the UK and through the European Union than formerly. This usually seems to involve more detailed regulations and (unfortunately) more expense. Recycling is being given a higher profile than previously.

5.114 For service charge purposes the landlord's right to charge should include the costs charged by the local authority or other proper contractor for collection and disposal of waste in accordance with the statutory procedure, and, where necessary, the replacement of the bins and other equipment.

5.115   The rubbish bins or skips or other containers are usually placed on part of the common parts of the landlord's premises. This means that tenants will need to have rights of access and use of the bins. This is normally covered by an express grant of rights in the lease. On negotiating a lease a tenant's solicitor should enquire whether there is a refuse area and ensure that there are suitable rights included.

5.116   In addition to normal rubbish bins or containers, some developments have compactors, bottle banks and recycling plant. All these items need to be maintained, kept clean and hygienic, and must comply with the relevant regulations, and from time to time may need to be replaced. The principles for replacement of these items are the same as replacement of other plant. (See **5.53** et seq.) Tenants may also wish to ensure (if such items are used by others) that any income generated is credited to the service charge account. Income would be rare from such a source, but could apply, perhaps in relation to recycling.

5.117   As there are specific provisions governing who is entitled to deal with waste disposal under the Environmental Protection Act 1990 it may assist recovery of costs if the lease makes it clear that the tenant is to refund the cost to the landlord (inter alia) of complying with the Environmental Protection Act in respect of disposal of normal rubbish. A tenant should try to resist a blanket obligation to pay for any work required under the Act. This could include very extensive and expensive work where, for example, the premises are on contaminated land. An exclusion of capital costs arising under the Act would be appropriate for this purpose.

5.118   A tenant seeking to keep the costs to a low level may wish to insert a qualification that the collection is not to be more often than, say, once per week. The tenant's views should be sought before such an amendment is made to a draft lease. If such a qualification is agreed, then, even if the landlord does arrange for collections more often than the stated interval, in the absence of further agreement he will only be able to charge on the basis of weekly collections. Such a provision is only likely to show a minimal saving, if any. The more important aspect, of course, is how frequently collections should be made for practical reasons and in accordance with statutory requirements (if any). Obviously, a large shopping centre or office may need collections daily, whereas a small office may not need a collection more than once a week.

Fire fighting equipment and safety plans

5.119   When premises are occupied by a number of tenants, particularly where there are several storeys or where there are many people employed or living in the premises, fire regulations will apply. The local fire office will be entitled to make recommendations or requirements for safety and, in addition, the insurers sometimes have their own requirements. For some premises there is a new oblig-ation (replacing fire certificates). The effect is that there has to be a person (or more than one) responsible for preparing and keeping up to date, a safety plan (see **5.121** below). This obviously has financial consequences.

5.120 Some of the obligation to provide the services or equipment or to prepare and maintain the safety plan will be on the tenant and some on the land-lord. On the whole, tenants will be responsible for whatever is needed within their demise, and the landlord will be responsible for the remainder of his prop-erty (normally the common parts). Tenants normally expressly agree to comply with statutory requirements in respect of the property let to them, and often to comply with the requirements of fire officers or insurers. In that case, of course, there are no service charge consequences, but the relevant clauses clarify who is responsible for the works and thus for the cost. So far as the landlord is con-cerned, he will not always covenant to comply with statute in respect of the common parts, but he will have to do so in any event – there is no one else who could. In a service charge lease, however, he will normally expect the tenant to reimburse the cost of complying.

5.121 The requirements for safety can cover such matters as ensuring that doors are fire resistant for a specific period of time (30 minutes, etc). This is material for repair and replacement. They can also include requirements for the premises to have a certain number of fire extinguishers, the installation of smoke alarms, sprinkler systems, and other items such as keys in glass cases ('break glass in case of emergency'). Some sprinkler systems are specific to individual premises (eg a large supermarket or department store in a centre) but others are joint and shared by various units (eg in a small row of shops or a collection of offices). The service charge provisions should reflect reality. If the system is the landlord's system the service charge provisions should enable recovery, inter alia, of power and water supplies, and there should also be rights of access for inspection and repair. The system under which certain business premises needed to have a fire certificate is being abolished from 1 October 2006 (Regulatory Reform (Fire Safety) Order 2005 (the Order)). There will be a system under which the onus is put on owners and occupiers to prepare a plan for fire preven-tion. This has to be prepared, and updated as necessary, and the local authority will be entitled to inspect the plan and make recommendations. The object is to protect 'relevant persons,' who are basically those lawfully at the premises, and also people in the immediate vicinity who are at risk from a fire on the premises. The onus for complying is on the 'responsible person', who is usually the employer (in places of work), or otherwise the person who has control of the premises (as occupier or otherwise) or the owner. The effect of the definitions in the Order is likely to mean that the person with responsibility for maintenance or safety is likely to be the responsible person. The responsible person has to appoint a 'competent person' to assist in relation to the obligation. This pushes the responsibility from the local authority on to individuals. Such a scheme causes some possibility of duplication or of a lacuna where several occupiers each have responsibility for different parts of a building. It is likely that the land-lord will have responsibility for the common parts and the tenants for the parts let to them. The parties would be well advised to get together to have an agreed plan for the whole building, but obviously a landlord will expect to recover the costs he expends in this respect. This is an area where managing agents should perhaps take a lead to ensure all parts of the building are subject to a risk assessment. Alternatively, the tenant may save money by agreeing to take on the responsibility, although the tenant needs to be aware of the heavy liability of the responsible person. The Order requires the responsible person to co-operate with others (eg a landlord responsible for common parts would need to co-operate with the tenant responsible for internal repairs and safety). It may be simplest for the managing agent to be responsible for the whole building, although this needs careful checking to ensure the costs can be charged. Measures to be adopted relate to reducing the risk or spread of fire; securing and maintaining means of escape; means of fighting fire and means for detecting fire (eg smoke alarms), and arrangements for fire drills and for evacuation in case of fire. Failure to comply can lead to a criminal penalty which can include imprisonment.

5.122   As so often in service charge matters, one of the major issues is whether the landlord can charge for the hire or purchase of the equipment, maintenance and in particular the testing of it, and in due course replacement. Most service charge leases are fairly clear about the obligations. Tenants on the whole are reasonably phlegmatic about the cost, as it relates to the safety of their staff and customers and property. Many of such matters are covered by contracts for maintenance and inspection. There may be scope for a plan agreed by tenants and landlords in respect of shared equipment etc.

5.123   Some tenants object to leases that refer to the 'provision' of fire fighting equipment such as extinguishers (and the use of the same word for other items). They argue that the landlord should provide the initial items and the tenants should only be concerned with costs of testing and maintenance and, only later, replacement. The author is not convinced by this approach. The equipment is there because it is needed (or required by fire officers or insurers). If it is needed to enable tenants to use the premises (to live or trade there) then it seems not unreasonable for the tenants to have to pay the initial costs and not just later costs. Others have different views, but the author would treat fire equipment as different to other items such a central heating or air conditioning. In the latter cases the landlord will install such items to increase the value of the premises, not to enable it to be lawfully used. The actual fire fighting requirements, in any event, differ from time to time, and are usually based on the use by the tenants.

5.124   The significant point to be concerned about in this area is the capital cost of major work. The installation of a few fire extinguishers and maintenance contracts for them is usually a relatively small cost. If the plan for the building, or an insurer or fire officer requires a new sprinkler system or fire escape to be installed this can be expensive. In one case in the 1970s, premises were intended to be used as a nursing home, but could not because of a requirement to install smoke alarms, which at that time were going to cost several thousand pounds and made the proposed purchase not viable. That was a case where the proprietor would

120

have had to bear the whole cost: in the case of service charge property there would usually be a number of tenants to share the cost.

The moral for the tenant is to be careful about the capital cost of items such as sprinkler systems or new fire escapes. For such items the tenant should negotiate that he is only responsible for his proportion of the cost of maintenance and repair or replacement of items already at the property, but not the capital cost for new items that are not replacements. Landlords often try to resist such amendments: if new items are needed, particularly to enable the tenant to occupy the premises for his purposes, and the tenants are to pay all costs, then that is simply one of the costs a tenant must bear. Where a tenant is taking a new lease he may seek a warranty or at least information about anticipated expenditure on such items. The potential tenant can always check with the local authority or fire officer about probable requirements before entering in to a lease. Many tenants of modest means do not do so because such an enquiry can lead to expensive requirements, not all of which the proposed tenant could realistically expect the landlord to bear.

5.125   A fire escape may be required for some properties. If this already exists at the property then repair and decoration of it would normally be covered by the terms of the lease. Some fire escapes are included in the letting, and thus the responsibility of the tenant, but often they are common to several premises and the landlord will be responsible and will seek to recoup costs via the service charge. On the same basis as in the previous paragraph, the question of creation of a new fire escape may arise from time to time as a result of new requirements. This would normally apply in such cases as where a new part of the upper part of the premises is to be occupied for the first time. If a landlord is, for example, creating a new flat, then the tenant taking the new flat should check that the premises comply with fire regulations. If enquiries indicate that a new fire escape is needed then, at least in those cases where the tenant is paying a premium for the lease, the tenant should try to ensure that the landlord installs the fire escape at the landlord's cost. If the landlord does not agree to do so and the terms of the lease are such that he can recover the capital cost of building the staircase then at least the tenant will take the flat with knowledge of what he will be asked to pay. If the cost is high, the tenant might, for example, seek to reduce the premium he is paying. Once it is built, the cost of repair and maintenance of the fire escape is a reasonable service charge item.

Pest control

5.126   Some areas have periodic infestations of pests. This can apply perhaps particularly to places where there are restaurants or shops selling non-packaged food. If the pests appear as the result of the activities of one tenant, there may well be a breach of that tenant's lease, and the landlord should be able to require the tenant to remove the pests or pay the cost the landlord incurs in doing so. In other cases, if the landlord is called on to seek to eradicate pests from common parts he should be able to recover the costs of doing so, provided that pest control is mentioned. (Even the Pied Piper of Hamelin tried to agree the basis of payment in advance.) In the alternative, he may be able to recover under a general provision relating to contracts for management purposes, or one for complying with statute, or perhaps (less certainly) under a sweeping-up clause. Pest control is in the interests of all the tenants. Only where the pests appear as a result of the landlord's action (or inaction), or that of a particular tenant, would it seem unreasonable for the landlord to be able to recoup the costs of ridding the premises of pests. This may involve contractors or poisons or perhaps traps.

Gardening and landscaping

5.127   Where the landlord's property includes grounds, whether small or large, the question of gardening arises. This is most material in the case of blocks of flats, where the tenants naturally wish the garden to be either pleasant or at least useable. Industrial estates often have obligations in planning permissions for certain areas to be kept landscaped and for trees to be planted and, if the trees die within a few years, to be replaced with similar trees. Offices sometimes have gardens surrounding them, and in those cases the tenants will want the grounds to be kept neat and sometimes suitable for staff to use for al fresco eating etc. Some offices and blocks of flats also have plants indoors in common parts.

5.128   As usual the major points to note are the definitions of the areas concerned, and the right to charge for maintenance contracts and replacements. Tenants would normally resist allowing the service charge to entitle the landlord to recover the cost of the original landscaping, which is a common planning requirement for new premises. However, the replacement (under a planning condition) of the plants or trees which were initially provided by the landlord and which have died or become diseased seems to be a proper service charge cost. So far as definitions are concerned, the normal lease will refer to gardening in the common parts. The tenant should check that this seems correct and whether these are areas over which the tenant has any rights (if needed). If the lease puts an obligation on the tenant to pay for the gardening works but without any right for the tenant to have any direct benefit from the garden area the position should be made known to the tenant.

5.129   Where the landlord owns several blocks with grounds used in common then the cost to any one of the blocks should be part only, and a tenant should ensure that the lease makes this clear. Particularly in the case of residential property, a tenant in one block which bears all the cost of gardening for grounds surrounding three or four blocks would presumably have a good case for saying that the charges made to him were not reasonable. (Landlord and Tenant Act 1985, s 19.) The normal solution is for each block to be responsible for its appropriate percentage of the total costs relating to gardening.

5.130   Leases often simply refer to 'gardening' without any further definition. This is probably adequate and presumably includes all such works as are normal for any garden such as grass cutting, weeding and pruning. Gardening costs can also include water charges (eg for hosepipes (when they are not banned)).

Presumably, normal costs would also include providing new bulbs and seeds and materials such as weed killer, and probably maintenance and replacement of normal gardeners' tools. For example, in the case of very large area a 'sit-down' type of mower will be appropriate. This would need fuel, servicing and eventual replacement. For a large enough area this seems a reasonable charge, but in the case of smaller property such cost may not be reasonable. As usual, to avoid the growth area of litigation and weed out possible prickly problems, mentioning these items in the lease should save disputes.

5.131   If the premises are large enough to require the employment of a gardener who perhaps requires accommodation, the points mentioned at **5.93** et seq are material.

5.132   In *Yorkbrook Investments Ltd v Batten* [1985] 2 EGLR 100 (one of the major service charge cases), one of the tenant's complaints was that the gardening had been so unsatisfactory over many years that he claimed that nothing should be charged for it. The lower court disagreed that nothing should be paid, but agreed to a deduction of one seventh of the charge because the work was unsatisfactory. The Court of Appeal did not disagree with this approach. This related to flats (at Chiswick) where the tenants had been unhappy with many aspects of the work for which charges were made. Unfortunately, the report of the case does not give details of the way in which the work was considered unsatisfactory, but it shows that tenants can obtain reductions in charges for unsatisfactory work. As the premises were residential statute assisted the tenant. In the case of residential tenants, s 19 of the Landlord and Tenant Act 1985 now specifically provides that costs of work 'shall be taken into account in determining the amount of a service charge payable ... only if the services or works are of a reasonable standard'. In the *Yorkbrook* case the parties referred to similar provisions in s 91A of the Housing Finance Act 1972.

Air conditioning

5.133   Air conditioning and/or climate control is a form of plant/equipment, and the general comments at **5.53** et seq above, accordingly, apply. See also later in this chapter at **5.140** et seq.

5.134   In 2001 a dispute over £2 million required by a landlord of commercial premises at Hammersmith for a significant air conditioning system became the case of *Fluor Daniel Properties Ltd v Shortlands Investments Ltd* [2001] EGCS 8. The equipment was the largest of its kind (variable air-volume) when installed in 1980. The landlord was liable to maintain it. The lease also permitted the landlord to vary the services, and a sweeping-up clause allowed it to recover the reasonable cost of other services. The landlord wrote to the tenants saying it intended to expend £2 million on what was described as 'air conditioning and structural repair'. The cost was to be recovered from the tenants by (a) an additional £750,000 reserve fund contribution, (b) a similar contribution, retrospectively charged, and (c) a contribution of £500,000 from the reserve fund. The tenants challenged the demands and were successful. A significant point was that, although the air conditioning had reached the end of its estimated life, it was not actually in disrepair. The landlords had had the plant regularly serviced and it was working satisfactorily. The power to vary the services was held not to help the landlord, 'as the relevant service was the treated air, electricity or hot water that the landlord had covenanted to provide. The landlord did not provide a service by renewing or improving plant that was capable of delivering such a service.'

Computer systems and the Internet

5.135 One aspect of management that is increasing is the use of computers for various purposes. Such uses include use by managing agents of programs for management, but this section relates to the use of computers in buildings. In 'hi-tech' buildings where the energy consumption is monitored and heating, air flow and other aspects are controlled by a computer system there can be considerable savings in the overall costs to the benefit of the tenants.

5.136 This is mentioned because, in practice, such systems need maintenance (with regular checks from computer personnel who will often require a maintenance contract) and, more significantly, 'upgrading' may be needed.

5.137 The maintenance contracts are, it is suggested, a normal and reasonable element of a service charge cost, and unlikely to be controversial unless the bottom line figure is excessive. Upgrades are, however, another matter. They are, in effect, improvements, and all the observations about improvements and how far a landlord can and should charge them to the service charge are material. For example, the computerised system might cover the heating in a building where it operates through thermostats etc to keep temperatures at particular levels in different parts of the buildings. If the computer firm puts out a new computer program under which it can cease heating all those areas where there are no people (by means of sensors etc) this could result in a saving of fuel costs in the long run, at the expense of an initial capital cost for upgrading the system. This can be very expensive, and over the past 20 years or so computer companies seem to have produced new improvements to their programs every few months. In other cases the upgrade simply makes what is already being done more efficient (eg it works more quickly). Whether a landlord should be able to charge for such upgrades is frankly hard to say. But attention should be drawn to the point and it is suggested that where such properties are concerned this point should be borne in mind by those negotiating the lease. The tenant may seek to exclude any liability to pay for upgrades at all (if they are not mentioned in the lease), or revise the reference so that they agree to pay for reasonable upgrades provided a majority (or a certain percentage) of tenants agree in advance. Perhaps the right approach is to allow a charge for updated versions which perform the same functions but in some way more efficiently (eg being quicker or cheaper), but to refuse to pay for upgrades which introduce entirely new functions except where a specified percentage of the tenants agree, or where it is required to comply with some new government-imposed obligation, for example such matters as systems which control temperature being upgraded to control humidity as well. Consultation with the tenants is probably the key.

5.138   If the system becomes obsolete it will need replacement, and the original system will not only no longer be available but would not be appropriate. The replacement would need to be suitable rather than identical. Again, making the replacement of an obsolete or otherwise unsatisfactory system chargeable through the service charge subject to a majority of tenants agreeing is perhaps the safest protection for an individual tenant against abuse. For large buildings (over 1,000m2) the changes to Part L of the Building Regulations may require a different system to reduce CO_2 emissions.

5.139   Landlords often find it advantageous in serviced offices or other multi-let office buildings to provide a connection to the Internet as a facility. This can be done most economically for all the units in a building at the same time by the landlord, who not only makes his building more attractive to potential tenants (who simply have to plug in and get on with it rather than each having to set up his own system), but would be able to charge for the service. It is suggested the comments above would need consideration should the landlord decide to charge for Internet connection as a service. One concern is likely to be a change from narrowband to broadband connection. This may involve a capital expense, and a claim for reimbursement of the cost should be treated as with any other similar claim under the lease.

Heating and hot water

5.140   Landlords sometimes provide heating or hot water or both for offices and flats. This might be provided to the demised premises or to common parts (eg to toilets used in common in office blocks and heating common areas). The service charge provisions should of course mention these items if the landlord wishes to recover the cost. A survey by Jones Lang Wootton around 1995 suggested that energy costs are the 'biggest single component of service charges in air conditioned buildings and comprise about 21% of the overall bill. If the cost of maintenance of heating and air conditioning systems is thrown in almost 40% of the service charge has been accounted for.'

5.141   The landlord will normally covenant to provide the heating. The service charge provisions ideally will refer to the heating and also to the fuel costs and the maintenance of plant (eg boilers, pumps, pipes, flues, radiators, grilles and any other equipment used). Clearly, there will be maintenance from time to time, and thus a need for maintenance contracts, particularly for boilers and generators. For replacement of the boiler or other large items there may be a sinking fund. (See Chapter 7.)

5.142   Some leases provide that the landlord will supply hot water all the year, or, in the case of offices, during specified hours. (If the office tenants require lighting or heating outside the specified hours then clearly the tenant requiring the extra service should pay for it. The cost needs to be apportioned for this purpose.) If timing is mentioned for heating it tends to be in respect of a period of the year (for example from 1 October to 31 May). It is important, on a practical level, to ensure that there is a right for the landlord to provide these facilities at other times at the request and cost of the tenant. Given a really cold August, as is not unknown in the United Kingdom, it would be ridiculous for tenants to shiver simply because the lease does not permit heating to be put on before a particular date. (The tenants not unnaturally sometimes get steamed up about these matters!) Because of the importance of these items the tenant should require that the lease has an obligation on the landlord to restore the heating and hot water service as soon as possible in case of breakdown. Business premises may have to close if the temperature is below a statutory minimum. Some tenants seek a rent reduction for days when the premises cannot be used as a result of the landlord's default.

5.143 Particularly where the boiler etc is covered by a maintenance contract for which the tenant is paying, there is no good reason for a tenant to have to put up with lack of hot water or heating for long periods. A landlord should be prepared to agree to this, although he can reasonably require a proviso that he is not liable until he has notice of the breakdown. A tenant could also usefully seek an obligation on the landlord to obtain competitive tenders for energy supplies periodically, at least for large systems (it is now possible to buy gas from the electricity board, etc). If it is thought desirable to change the type of fuel, this will need careful handling by the landlord. If gas is cheaper than electricity to operate the particular heating system the parties need to remember the capital costs for changing the system, and if a landlord is to be obliged by the tenants to change the system then he should, surely, be entitled to recover the conversion costs. That may make the exercise less attractive to tenants.

5.144 A landlord should ensure that the lease excludes his liability for matters beyond his control. This was the subject of the most useful example of a case concerning heating, *Yorkbrook Investments Ltd v Batten* [1985] 2 EGLR 100, which related to four blocks of flats in Chiswick. They had one boiler between them. The flats were let on different types of tenancy under which some tenants were liable to contribute to the cost of heating and some were not. The landlords in those circumstances tried to keep the maintenance costs to a minimum. The result was that the boilers and heating system kept breaking down. The tenants complained about many breaches of the landlord's covenants, including a breach of the obligation to provide heating. The relevant clause opened with the words 'unless prevented by mechanical breakdown or failure of fuel supply or other cause beyond the control of the lessor to provide and maintain a good sufficient and constant supply of hot water …'. The Court of Appeal held that the tenants had bought the flat and pipes and radiators, but not the heating system. The landlord was in breach of its obligation to provide constant hot water: in view of the state of the equipment such a constant supply could only be ensured by replacing the boiler (a crucial part of the heating system) and the landlords had not done this. Referring to the exclusion provision mentioned above the court said:

'the inclusion of the word "other" indicates to us that the phrase "beyond the control of the lessor" governs the earlier two phrases. If one analyses the causes of breakdown, they were all, save for the strike of tanker drivers for a few days and the consequent disruption of the fuel supply, the result of antiquated and unserviceable equipment which should have been replaced to enable the plaintiffs to comply with their obligations ... the breakdown of the system could and should have been avoided by the plaintiffs. The solution was within their control.'

In other words the landlords should have replaced the faulty system, and as they had not done so the tenants obtained damages. The exclusion provision was not sufficient for the landlord to avoid liability.

5.145 The temperature of the water is not usually mentioned and it would seem risky for a landlord to commit himself to any specific temperature, particularly in a long lease where fashions and, for example, better insulation and concern over energy waste may make a specific goal unattainable or unwanted. In the *Yorkbrook* case (see **5.144** above), the level of a reasonable temperature for flats in 1985 was the subject of evidence. In the case of hot water, the judge at first instance and the Court of Appeal all agreed that 115°F was a reasonable temperature, and an expert giving evidence for the tenant suggested that the landlord should 'aim at 120°F at the tap ... better to let the tenants reduce temperature'. For heating the radiators the Court of Appeal accepted the expert's view that a room temperature of 55°F with an outside temperature of 32°F was a reasonable test.

5.146 Heating was also the issue in *Jollybird Ltd v Fairzone Ltd* [1990] 2 EGLR 55, which is reviewed at **4.26**. The case related to a provision which linked the amount paid by the tenant to increases in cost above a certain level. Another case concerning heating, *Pole Properties Ltd v Feinberg* [1981] 2 EGLR 38, is mentioned at **4.25** in relation to variation of fixed percentages payable by tenants. The circumstances were unusual. The premises were a flat in a house in Kensington. The problem arose when the landlord bought the adjoining property and created a new combined heating system. Professor Feinberg was a tenant who was liable to pay for heating and for increases in fuel costs over a stated limit. When he became a tenant, the house he was in was partially heated. After the landlords acquired the adjoining premises, they enlarged the heating system so that, for example, the common hallways and staircases of Professor Feinberg's property were heated, whereas before they were not. In addition, the new heating system provided heating to both the original and the new premises. Before the change the Professor was liable for two sevenths of any increase in fuel costs over the original stated price. The landlords wanted to vary this to 19.33%, a figure they based on the floor areas of the two buildings that benefited from the heating. It was held that there was such a major change to the circumstances that it was right for the fixed percentage to be revised.

The court revised the percentage to 12.08% to reflect the use by the tenant, rather than the floor area. It considered that in the absence of a direction in the lease to vary the percentage, the court was free to adopt a fair and reasonable approach, although only where there was a significant change in circumstances.

5.147 A year or so later the courts considered an application for a judicial review of the decision of a Rent Assessment Panel in relation to heating. *R v London Rent Assessment Panel, ex p Cliftvylle Properties Ltd* [1983] 1 EGLR 100 related to 102 flats in East London. Originally, all were let on rack rent tenancies, but then the landlords started to sell some flats on long leases. The flats which were sold had their own heating and hot water. The landlords thereafter provided hot water only for the rented flats. Because the heating system provided heating for fewer flats, the cost per flat became relatively high. It was not possible for an expert to adopt normal calculating criteria for assessing an appropriate charge, because the system was used for some flats, although not all of them. In assessing a registered rent (which can include a reference to the cost of services – Rent Act 1977, s 71(1)), the cost applicable to the heating is material. The court agreed that it was proper for the Rent Assessment Panel to use its own experience to determine a fair figure for heating and hot water, where the actual cost was not a proper charge to the tenants as a result of changed circumstances.

5.148 Improvement by the addition of thermostatic radiator valves to radiators was considered in *New Pinehurst Residents Association (Cambridge) Ltd v Silow* [1988] 1 EGLR 227. The residents of flats bought the superior interest and managed the flats themselves. One tenant fell out with the others. One of her grumbles was that the new landlords (ie the residents' company) had fitted thermostatic valves to the radiators. They had installed a new boiler for the heating system which made the premises too hot. Having found that thermostatic radiator valves aided cost control, the landlords arranged for them to be fitted to control the heat. These were an improvement, as they did not replace anything there before. The court held that the cost of the valves was a valid charge. There was an obligation on the landlords to use 'best endeavours' to provide sufficient and adequate heating, and the valves helped ensure that this was the cheapest and most efficient way of performing that obligation.

5.149 Changes were also considered by the Court of Appeal in *Creska Ltd v Hammersmith and Fulham London Borough Council* [1998] 3 EGLR 35. The tenants of commercial premises covenanted to keep in repair the pipes and 'all electrical heating mechanical and ventilation installations' solely serving the premises. The premises had under-floor heating and some cabling was within the concrete floors. Some of the cabling became broken or had damaged insulation. The tenants decided to install storage heaters (thus avoiding the need to replace or repair the broken cabling). The tenants considered this was a substitution for repairing the cables, and was a way of repair by a modern equivalent of the original, and that repairing the original heating system was not a sensible and practical way of performing its obligations. Repairing the cables would mean excavating the concrete floors, making the premises unavailable for use for a period. The Court of Appeal disagreed with the tenants' view. The tenants had covenanted to maintain the system in good order. This could be done, even though it was costly, and even if the repairs would need to incorporate some improvements to the design.

Common toilets

5.150   In multi-occupied offices and some shopping centres the landlord provides toilets and washrooms for general use. These, like other common parts, need
to be repaired, maintained, decorated and insured, and the landlord may pay rates
for them. The requirements for cleaning are more stringent in these areas than for
other parts of the common parts. The landlord will need to provide water to wash
basins and usually soap (perhaps in dispensers) and towels or driers in some form,
and sometimes sanitary disposal units. Toilets for public use have some special
requirements (eg usually male and female toilets are separate, and there are special
requirements for toilets for the disabled). In addition, there can be building regulation requirements such as a lobby or two sets of doors. These requirements
need to be borne in mind (other than the initial cost of building) when drafting
service charge provisions. Ideally, there should be a mention of replacing soap
and towels, or cleaning of cloth towels, and the general level of cleaning needed.
The hygiene regulations are being tightened up regularly. For example, a regulation from the late 1990s appears to require the installation of coat hooks on doors
in all lavatories used by the public. The cost of complying with ever increasing
statutory and sub-statutory obligations relating to all matters affecting hygiene
needs to be borne in mind by landlords and tenants and their advisers.

Carpeting and floor covering

5.151   Carpeting and floor covering are mentioned as items that can be material for service charges, and which can be contentious and expensive. For industrial developments and most shopping developments these are rarely material,
but for offices and residential blocks they are often essential. Carpet or other
floor covering is usually found in common corridors, lobbies and on stairs. It is
worth remembering that for shopping centres the malls (or part of the malls) may
well need floor covering, and if the landlord has office accommodation in the
shopping centre for the staff running the centre, floor covering or carpets will
usually be present.

5.152   In the usual way the service charge concerns revolve around repair (or
mending), replacement, insuring and cleaning. Repair of the carpet or flooring
will sometimes be covered by a maintenance contract.

5.153   Cleaning can be a major expense. A large carpet can be cleaned in
various ways and with varying degrees of thoroughness, and this will sometimes
lengthen its life as well as making it look better. If a tenant is asked to consider a
lease including a reference to carpets then a restriction on the number of times a
carpet can be cleaned may be appropriate ('not more often than is reasonably
necessary', or 'not more frequently than the period recommended by the manu-
facturers'). Most modern flooring is relatively easy to clean by washing with
mops and disinfected water. More substantial cleaning may be needed from time
to time for some other types of flooring, and the lease should address this if the
landlords want to recover the cost. If the flooring needs sanding, or some special

treatment by way of particular periodical polishing, then mentioning this in the lease should make the position clear to tenants. The word 'treating' is a useful general expression for such items.

5.154 Carpeting and floor covering are similar to the extent that they cover floors, but they are different in nature and thus slightly different considerations apply. If there are both, then the two sets of comment are relevant. The main difference is in permanence. For example, it is possible to lift a carpet and take it away for repairs (at least in some cases), whereas the more solid type of floor covering cannot be removed as a whole and is usually either replaced or patched in situ. Carpets can, of course, also be patched if necessary, although it may be sensible for a section (perhaps one corridor) to be replaced if there are a number of bad patches rather than having smaller inserts. The carpet will normally wear out much sooner than a vinyl floor cover or solid tiles.

5.155 The capital cost of putting in the carpet or flooring initially will usually fall on the landlord. Occasionally, the tenant will include them as part of the fitting out of their own unit, in which case the tenant will be responsible, but the tenant would not normally have any involvement with carpeting the common parts. Thereafter, the landlord will want to recover the cost of repair (where repair is practical) or treatment, and of replacement when this is necessary. It is in this latter field that problems can be foreseen. The replacement of a large, long-lasting carpet covering many square metres of corridors and stairs is very expensive. Tenants may be reluctant to commit themselves to the expense of replacing these items (as with other high cost items). If the carpet has lasted, say, 20 years, it is unlikely that an identical carpet can be found and, in any event, the design is likely to be thought out of date. Tenants can feel that the landlord is seeking to improve the premises by replacing the carpet at their expense. For the tenant the appropriate revision to the draft lease is to seek to ensure that the replacement of the floor or carpet is only 'when reasonably necessary' or 'when repair (or mending, in the case of a carpet) is not economically possible'. It is as well to mention replacement, but it should be remembered that an obligation to repair can imply depreciation provisions: *Perseus Property Co Ltd v Burberry* [1985] 1 EGLR 114.

5.156 For common areas of residential premises and offices, the style of the carpet (or flooring) is important. Accordingly, the tenants might wish to provide that, in the case of replacement being necessary and an identical carpet (or flooring) not being available, they should be consulted about the new one as to colour and design. Landlords may be reluctant to agree any restriction on dealing with what is, after all, their own property, but need to remember, however, that the tenants are being asked to pay and will be living or working in the premises in question. It could be a goodwill gesture by the landlord to offer to consult, even if he is not required to do so under the lease or under statute. An amendment by the tenants providing for a replacement carpet to be in a 'style, design, and colour previously approved by the tenant [or a majority of the tenants] (such approval not to be unreasonably withheld)' may be worth trying to include. For a large carpet a sinking fund is worth considering.

5.157 The quality of the carpet (or flooring) is of importance. Replacing a worn-out carpet with a cheap carpet may save the tenants a few pounds at the time, but it is likely that the new carpet will need repair or replacing more quickly than a better quality carpet. Carpets in different parts of a building receive different amounts of wear. There can be difficulties if the carpet in the corridor on the fifth floor is virtually pristine whereas the carpet in the ground-floor lobby is in urgent need of replacement because it is worn out. It is a practical decision for the landlord (or his managing agent) whether it is more appropriate to replace all the carpet (on the basis that the carpets will all be identical and a larger purchase may give cost savings), or to replace only those parts in urgent need of replacement, with the probability that the new carpet and old ones will not match exactly. The decision may well turn on the type of premises and the area, but a landlord should perhaps think twice before embarking on full replacement without consent of the tenants, or at least with prior consultation to explain why the whole carpeting is being replaced where only part is beyond repair. Consultation is necessary for residential units and recommended for other property. The author is not aware of any cases where carpeting was an issue, and so it is not possible to indicate the probable attitude of the courts, although for residential cases seeking a declaration of the court, as in *Reston Ltd v Hudson* [1990] 2 EGLR 51 (see **3.44** above, on replacing windows), may be worthwhile.

Compliance with statutory obligations

General

5.158 Whether a property is used for commercial or residential purposes there are statutory provisions that affect its use. Perhaps the most significant (expensive) relate to safety, hygiene and planning, although there are many others. The lease normally obliges the tenant to be responsible for statutory provisions affecting the demised premises. The landlord will be liable for those statutory obligations which concern the common parts and those parts of the landlord's property not subject to leases. If the landlord wants to recover costs from the tenant for any expenses involved in complying with statute he should make this clear in the service charge provisions.

5.159 Among many Acts of Parliament with which landlords and tenants are concerned are the Offices, Shops and Railway Premises Act 1963. This includes obligations such as the minimum temperature at which offices must be kept, and keeping such parts of buildings as staircases in a safe condition. Use of a property is also affected by the Town and Country Planning Acts. The Public Health Acts (particularly the Health and Safety at Work etc. Act 1974) include other statutory provisions likely to cause potential expense, and more recently the Environmental Protection Act 1990, the Disability Discrimination Act 1995, the Control of Asbestos at Work Regulations 2002, and the recent European Union Directive on the Energy Performance of Buildings. The last three items are discussed in more detail at **5.164** below. The pace of new statutory interference in property (as well as other aspects of life) has quickened in recent years, and land-lords and tenants and their advisers need to be aware of changing requirements. All the Acts mentioned above, and many more, can impose on a person an oblig-ation to do (or refrain from doing) something. In so far as such statutory obliga-tions cause expense, the cost is something a landlord will usually transfer to the tenants through the service charge.

5.160 Many such statutory provisions relate to the use of premises. Normally, the tenant would be responsible under his lease covenants to comply with statute in respect of the property let to him, because the provision concerned normally only applies because of the actual (or proposed) use by the tenant. An example is where a shop selling books is assigned to a tenant who wants to sell food. There are numerous different statutory obligations that need to be complied with in relation to food sales. These will include, for example, ensuring that there is somewhere for staff to wash their hands. This can involve expense if there is no washbasin in the premises. Where the tenant is responsible for the costs himself service charges are irrelevant.

5.161 The example at **5.160** above is a clear case for the tenant to be responsi-ble. Where such statutes affect the common parts it falls to the landlord to comply. Unfortunately, for determining whether the works or services are ones for which recovery of costs can be achieved, the obligations tend to fall into two categories:

(a) In the first, there is a statutory obligation to do something specific, for example to provide illuminated signs saying 'Exit', the provision of safety rails on stairs, and signs in car parks for ensuring a safe circulation of traffic. They can also cover fire precautions and refuse disposal, mentioned elsewhere in this chapter, as well as hygiene requirements affecting toilets for common use.

(b) The second category is much more difficult as it is not precise. For example, such obligations as under the Disability Discrimination Act 1995, where the statute does not say 'you must provide X, Y and Z,' but requires a person to achieve an object (making the premises more capable of access and use by disabled people) which, in reality, can be achieved in several different ways. Because of this the costs implication differ, and so landlord and tenants need to be aware of the scope for disputes over whether what is proposed be done is (i) necessary under the Act, and (ii) unduly expensive.

See **5.164** below for comments on three major concerns, namely the Control of Asbestos at Work Regulations 2002, The Disability Discrimination Act 1995, and the European Directive on Energy Performance for Buildings.

5.162 The cost of compliance with statutory obligations is a common item within a service charge schedule. Clearly, the landlord must comply, and on the assumption that he requires reimbursement there is little scope for disagreement with a lease containing such a provision, except where the work can be done in different ways at different costs, or in some cases, arguably, does not need to be done. Most preliminary enquiries ask whether the premises comply with various statutes, and one reason is to see if there is likely to be expense in changing premises to make them comply. If so, the tenant may seek to avoid being charged with the costs of known expenses for such matters. This could be very important where, for example, the landlord is under an obligation to comply with require- ments to install a new fire escape, or a sprinkler system. Work needed to remedy contamination in the landlord's property is another potentially expensive item about which enquiry should be made. It does not, however, help in cases where statutory provisions change during the term.

5.163 Health and safety requirements are being revised and tightened on a very frequent basis. These are becoming a major item of expenditure. Such requirements can involve expenditure on new equipment or signage or modifica- tions to buildings, or in some cases periodic inspections. They tend to impose a liability on a party to carry out the works etc and, occasionally (as, for example, with the Gas Safety (Installation and Use) Regulations 1994) may provide that a landlord is responsible for what goes on in the demised premises. To cover such circumstances the lease should contain an indemnity to ensure that the landlord is not out of pocket as a result of the tenant's failure to comply with statutory obligations imposed on the tenant.

Three examples

5.164 There are a large number of statutes affecting property and they do not always operate in the same ways. However, there are currently three recent major statutory (or similar) obligations that operate in different styles, and these are discussed below. The three relate to asbestos in commercial buildings, the Disability Discrimination Act, and requirements for energy saving measures. They are all alleged to be for public benefit. The asbestos regulations are intended to make buildings safer for people to work in; the Disability Discrimination Act is intended to aid disabled people to have access to shops and offices etc which were previously difficult for them to enter; and the energy saving measures are intended to assist slowing down global warming for the benefit of mankind as a whole. The asbestos regulations are perhaps more of a benefit to occupiers than to landlords, but will help the latter when the premises are for sale. The disability rules, similarly, are alleged to assist occupiers on the basis that they will have a larger catchment of visitors to whom they can sell or provide services. They also help landlords on sale, as a building that clearly can be accessed by more people should command a higher capital value. The energy saving measures help both occupier (by keeping down bills for fuel) and also landlord as a building with a bad energy rating may in future be more difficult to sell, or may have a lower value, than a building with lower fuel costs.

(a) *Asbestos* The Control of Asbestos at Work Regulations 1987, which only affects commercial premises although, of course, there may be changes in the future, require that people with an obligation to maintain non-residential premises must investigate whether asbestos is present in a building. If it is, they must monitor its condition and set up a system to ensure that people such as workmen who may disturb the asbestos while working, are notified of the risk. It is not a requirement of the Regulations that all asbestos must be removed: the requirement is to ensure that every person who needs to know (eg occupiers or workmen) can check whether there is asbestos in the building and, if so, where it is and what type of asbestos it is. Not all types of asbestos are equally dangerous to health. In some cases where works are being done to part of a building which has asbestos in it, it may be sensible to remove the asbestos, and in other cases it may not be necessary or it can be encased so that it is fully covered. There are two service charge points. First, the landlord needs to have a survey made to comply with the Act, and needs to keep copies available for inspections and to update it. As this is a clear obligation it is difficult to see that there can be an objection by the tenant to the costs being included in the service charge, subject to any qualification to the individual's liability in the lease or other documents. Secondly, there may be additional costs for works done by a landlord to remove or encase asbestos. Whether a landlord can charge for such additional work is matter of interpretation of the lease. If the work is done as part of improvements, the lease should be checked to see whether it permits the landlord to recover the cost of improvements, and, if he can recover, whether there is any cap or qualification. If the asbestos work simply arises during ordinary repair work for which the landlord can usually charge, then it would normally be recoverable. It may add to the costs but if is simply part of the repair then it would be chargeable, subject to a challenge that the repair was not necessary or cost too much.

(b) *Disability discrimination* The Disability Discrimination Act 1995 is another statute which may require works, but here the obligation is far vaguer and open to different interpretation. Basically the requirement is to ensure the building is capable of use by disabled people. This covers not only people in wheelchairs, where ramps and wide doors and larger toilets may be needed, or wider lift doors, but also assistance, for example for people with visibility or hearing problems. For example, there are recommendations that colours could be used for floors or walls to aid partially sighted people to see what part of the building they are in (eg green for the medical parts or yellow on the fourth floor), or to emphasise where the access routes are. In addition, lifts may need to have recorded verbal messages saying what floor has been reached and that the doors are opening or closing, as well as visual signs. There can be help for those with hearing difficulty. There are many recommendations about what can be done, and new buildings are being built with the Act in mind, but for old buildings changes may be contemplated, and here the question of cost and charging tenants (or not) arises. As previously mentioned, this is a statutory obligation, but the statute does not say you must do this or that. The Act provides that if the landlord's consent is needed for work to make the building compliant with the Act then the landlord's consent is not to be unreasonably withheld. It is probably fair to say that there is no such thing as a DDA compliant building: provided disabled people can have access to the services in the building they require then there is compliance with the Act. For example, if the concern is for wheelchair access to an office on the sixth floor but where the building does not have a lift large enough for wheelchairs, it is still possible for transactions to be carried out with people in wheelchairs if, for example, the business arranges to use a room on the ground floor to see such customers. The business is then complying with the Act. This may give rise to different problems if there is no ground floor access to toilet facilities, but hopefully the principle is clear. The Act gave nine years for buildings to comply, and the obligation is now in force. As ever the question is whether a landlord can charge the tenants for making the building comply. If the work contemplated is actually required by the Act then clearly it is a statutory obligation and will be covered by the normal service charge provision relating to recovery of cost for such items. As previously stated, however, the Act does not require carrying out specific works and thus it is a matter for the landlord and tenant to agree. In practice, many good landlords are consulting with tenants about what can or should be done, and seeking agreement on the work and the cost. Enforcement can include claims for damages from a person who is able to show he has been discriminated against: this may highlight the advantage of landlords and tenants co-operating to comply with the Act. This is the best way to do things, particularly as the tenants may have better ideas than the landlords in some cases, and may, for example, be able to agree among themselves something that suits themselves and for which they are content to contribute, as opposed to something the landlord feels obliged to do simply to comply with the Act, but which the tenants do not like. Tenants may be able to persuade a landlord that the costs for alterations should be shared between the landlord and the tenants, as the landlord will have the benefit of a building that will comply with the Act, and this is particularly so where there are short leases and the tenants thus have limited benefit from any physical changes that are made.

(c) *Energy saving* Recently there has been a European Directive on the Energy Performance of Buildings. The EU and the UK government are seeking to reduce carbon emissions, and as buildings create a large percentage of such emissions the intention is to control buildings to help reduction. The detail is too specific for this work, but for service charge purposes, the main provisions of the Directive needing review by landlords and tenants are (a) energy certification of all buildings, (b) regular mandatory inspection of boilers and air conditioning systems, and (c) an obligation to carry out further works when alterations are in hand. There will also be other requirements, such as one for new buildings to be constructed with energy saving in mind, but these would only seem to affect initial capital costs. There will be a requirement for buildings to have a certificate showing an energy rating. Obtaining the certificate will obviously cost money, and the question of who pays will arise. Since it is a statutory obligation, it would seem likely that the cost will be recoverable under a lease in which costs for complying with statute can be recovered. The certificate will be for the whole building: if the tenant occupies part only he should only pay part of the cost. If he has a fixed percentage then, to apply, and otherwise he should pay a fair proportion. A building with a good rating may be worth more in rental terms because the fuel costs will be lower, and it may attract a higher quality tenant who wants a prestige building. The cost of regular inspections of the boilers and air conditioning is likely to be an obligation within the service charge, regardless of the statutory element. However, if it is not in the service charge as a normal item, the new statutory obligation may enable a landlord to recover costs that he could not have recovered before. More difficult for service charge advisers will be the provisions under which there are requirements to spend additional money when works are being carried out to large commercial buildings. The proposal is, at present, only in relation to commercial buildings that exceed 1,000m^2. The obligation is to the effect that where the cost of the relevant works exceeds £8,000 (which seems a small figure) the person carrying out the works must spend an additional sum of at least 10% of that cost on improving the energy efficiency of the building. The relevant works include alterations and upgrading of the building. Whether the cost of the main works can be recovered or not is matter of interpretation in the usual way. So far as the compulsory extra sum is concerned, this is different, to the extent that it is a statutory obligation to incur a cost. As in some other cases it may be that the landlord can recover this additional sum through the service charge under the 'statutory obligations' provisions, even if he could not have recovered the cost of the main work otherwise under the lease. This could give rise to landlords in such cases providing a specification of works (non-recoverable) excluding the heating or air conditioning which they would normally have included, on the basis that they can then add it in as part of the 10% requirement and recover the costs under the statutory obligations provisions of the lease. The obligation to incorporate cost-effective energy efficiency measures may require the replacement of old plant with new. As indicated elsewhere, the landlord cannot usually charge for the whole of replacement costs via the service charge if the equipment is not in disrepair. (See eg *Fluor Daniel Properties Ltd v Shortlands Investments Ltd* [2001] EGCS 8.) The obligations here may call for just that. It remains to be seen what a court would say in the event of a dispute, but it is to be hoped that landlords will consult with tenants before incorporating the energy saving measures. The tenant will benefit (if he is at the property long enough) by having reduced fuel bills, and so he may be content to encourage the change. As with so many aspects, consultation may help both parties. The tenant may have a preference for a different type of, for example, air conditioning from the one the landlord may be proposing. It also needs to be noted that the 10% limit could be a very large sum in the case of a great expenditure as building works do not come cheaply. For the smaller cost of works that are just over the £8,000 limit it may well be that the cost of doing something effective will have to be higher than 10% of the cost of the other works. In such a case might a tenant have an argument that the obligation in the lease was restricted to 10% of the main costs? Unfortunately, this is probably not the case: the statutory obligation seems to be to spend a minimum percentage to incorporate energy efficiency measures. If 10% of the costs is £800 but the measure costs a minimum of £1,200 then the landlord spending that is complying with the statute and thus the tenant would seem obliged to pay. It is to be hoped that the landlords will consult with the tenants in good time to decide on the most effective way to comply with these obligations for the benefit of both parties.

PART 4 – MANAGEMENT CHARGES AND LEGAL COSTS

5.165   It is a fact of leasehold life that management of property involves expenditure of time and often expertise. When premises need action taken someone has to do it. For a freehold property the only person who can do it is the freeholder: for leaseholds there are several parties involved. Clearly, the tenant must make his own arrangements for such work and obligations as are imposed on him. For other work, particularly in respect of parts not let, and those parts of let property for which responsibility is retained, the landlord must take action. Depending on the size of the property the management can take a very little time or could be virtually a full-time job, but for any property, where service charges are payable there is work involved in preparing estimates and accounts and collecting the contributions from the tenants, as well as arranging for the services. For a landlord of property where there is a lot of work to do management is usually left to managing agents. Although the need for a managing agent may be clear, that does not necessarily mean the landlord can recover their charges through the service charge. The same consideration applies to audit and accountancy fees. In the absence of an express mention of management charges as such, a landlord has difficulty in recovering management charges.

5.166   For his fee the managing agent carries out a wide range of services. These can include:

(a)   preparing budgets and estimates;

(b)   preparing year end accounts;

(c)   sending demands and collecting the service charge;

(d)   considering what works need to be done;

(e)   arranging tenders or quotations, and placing and monitoring contracts for works or services;

(f)   ensuring costs stay within the budget;

(g)   complying with the lease and statutory requirements;

(h)   accounting for money demanded from tenants;

(i)   sometimes employing staff (eg porters, gardeners, security personnel) or arranging contracts for such matters;

(j)   keeping the tenants informed of relevant matters;

(k)   sometimes setting up and managing sinking funds and reserve funds; and

(l)   checking standards and cost of work and services.

Management charges contrasted with legal costs

5.167   In *Sella House Ltd v Mears* [1989] 1 EGLR 65 (where the tenant was a practising solicitor named Martin J P Mears) the lease contained a reference to the 'costs of computing and collecting the rents and the service charge'. It was held that this entitled the managing agents to charge for management, but did not permit the landlord to charge for legal costs in collecting service charges etc. In effect, Sella House was followed in *St Mary's Mansions Ltd v Limegate Investment Co* [2002] EWCA Civ 1491, [2003] 05 EG 146, although in the later case the Court of Appeal emphasised that the key was to interpret the terms of the lease. In the *St Mary's* case there were two clauses that the landlords relied on. One was a sweeping-up clause and the other referred to costs of auditors and fees of managing agents, but the court was satisfied that neither, on a proper construction, would allow the landlord to recover legal costs as a part of the service charge.

Implied right to charge for management

5.168   The costs of management were held to be recoverable in *Embassy Court Residents' Association Ltd v Lipman* [1984] 2 EGLR 60, where the building had been let to a residents' association subject to leases of individual flats. The residents' association, comprising the tenants of the flats, was thus the landlord of the flats and subject to the landlord's repairing obligations. Members of the residents' association had personally carried out management, but after a time none were prepared to do so. In those circumstances the court was prepared to imply a provision that management charges could be recovered to aid business efficacy. This is a rare example of a court implying such a covenant, but without the power to employ an agent (who would require to be paid) management would simply not have been carried out, and the lease system would fail. The residents' association had no income other than rent, which it had to pass on to the landlord.

Management by the landlord and landlord's profit

5.169   Where the management is carried out by the landlords themselves, tenants can be suspicious about the landlord making charges. Charges by a landlord for in-house management are unlikely to be recoverable except where the lease is worded very carefully on the point. (*Cleve House Properties Ltd v Schildof* [1980] CLY 1641). However, if the management is carried out by a subsidiary company of the landlord (which is thus technically a separate entity), the landlord may be able to recover costs. For example, in *Parkside Knightsbridge Ltd v Horwitz* [1983] 2 EGLR 42 (see **5.110** above), the costs of the parent company for management were calculated and apportioned on a time basis in one year between the various properties managed by the parent company. The same percentages were applied in later years. The court accepted the principle of the landlord being able to charge, but pointed out that the material factor was whether the actual figure charged was a reasonable one. In other words the time spent had to be recalculated every year.

5.170   Management charges can also include an element of profit to the land-lord, particularly where management is carried out by the landlord himself. This, it is to be noted, is in addition to the rent which the tenant pays. Presumably, the reason is that the rent is the charge for the right to use and occupy premises, whereas the management charges are the cost of carrying out necessary manage-ment work, needed for the premises to operate properly. In *Metropolitan Properties Co (FGC) Ltd v Lannon* [1968] 1 All ER 354, it was said: 'there is plenty of authority for the proposition that management costs, and indeed in appropriate circumstances management profit, may be properly admitted.' In *Perseus Property Co Ltd v Burberry* [1985] 1 EGLR 114, a case concerning flats in Hove, the court referred back to the Rent Assessment Committee their deci-sion not to include in registration of a rent a figure which included an element of profit to the landlord for the provision of services. The court said such charges should not be disallowed unless there were special circumstances.

5.171   More recently, in *Skilleter v Charles* [1992] 1 EGLR 73, a block of 13 flats in Littlehampton was owned by an individual. Management was by a company run by the landlord and his wife. The company had been formed to manage the block in question and some others. The tenants challenged the man-agement charges, citing *Finchbourne Ltd v Rodrigues* [1976] 3 All ER 581, where certificates of cost were to be given by the 'landlord's managing agents' and it was held that the agent had to be someone other than the landlord. The court in the *Skilleter* case held that the management by the landlord's company was a proper subject for a charge, on the basis that the management company was not a sham: in *Finchbourne* there clearly was a sham.

5.172   In *New Pinehurst Residents Association (Cambridge) Ltd v Silow* [1988] 1 EGLR 227, flats in a block of flats were let on long leases which envis-aged management by a managing agent. In practie the tenants managed the block themselves through a committee of tenants. The leases provided for service charges to be estimated and certified by 'the lessor's managing agents as experts and not as arbitrators'. A challenge was made to the service charge being certi-fied by the committee of tenants on two grounds:

(a)   the certificate was given by people who were themselves tenants and thus financially interested in the result; and

(b)   the committee were not professional managing agents.

The challenge failed in the Court of Appeal. On the question of independence the court said the issue was that the person giving the certificate as a landlord's agent should be independent of the landlord. The committee represented the tenants, rather than the landlord. The committee arrangement was 'likely to operate for the benefit of the tenants themselves, and in no way liable to cause any mischief'. On the question of expertise, the Court of Appeal held that 'since no professional qualification is required where the words are quite general, as they are here – there is no reference for instance, to accountants, surveyors, estate agents etc – it follows that on the judge's findings this management committee could also comply with the requirement that they were to act as experts'. As ever, the moral for drafting is clear: if the landlord (or tenant) wants certificates to be given by someone with a particular professional qualification or experience then the lease should say so. It is fairly common for leases to say that the landlord's surveyor must be a fellow of the RICS. If a lease provides that the surveyor can be an employee of the landlord the clause often requires that the surveyor shall act 'fairly and impartially,' or ' professionally and impartially'.

Amount of management charge

5.173   Many years ago, the Royal Institution of Chartered Surveyors had scales of charging, but these no longer apply. *Thameside Properties v Brixton Estates* [1997] NPC 5 held that where a lease referred to the charges being on the RICS scale it should be interpreted as a right to charge a reasonable fee, and not a charge based on the final RICS scale.

5.174   Charges now are on a wide variety of bases. The *Parkside* case (see **5.169** above) contains a useful passage which sets out various methods of charging which were used by some managing agents at that time. Current bases of charging now include charges:

(a)   Based on a percentage of rents.

(b)   Based on a percentage of the service costs (see **5.178**). This is much more normal. The actual percentage varies from perhaps 5% to 10% for managing large shopping centres to 20% to 25% where there are limited services but a management system is still needed to run those services. Sometimes a percentage is agreed subject to a minimum charge. The management cost can be based on the service costs either with or without VAT, but whichever system is chosen the agent should remember that where VAT is charged this involves extra work.

(c)   Based on a combination of the above.

(d)   Based on a percentage of some service charge costs. This arrangement normally excludes charging based on the cost of large items such as major refurbishment costs for which a separate charge is agreed, or excludes a fee on service costs exceeding an agreed figure.

(e)   A fixed fee. This is one of the most common arrangements these days. There can also be a fixed fee which is discounted by a percentage where there are vacant units and thus (at least in theory) less management.

(f)   There can be a fee on an incentive basis (see **5.179**).

Restricting the amount payable

5.175 What can the tenant do to restrict the charges to an acceptable level? (Apart from reading this book?) Ensuring that the lease has a general reference to 'prudent economy' or some similar qualification affecting the total service charge costs is one aid, leaving the landlord to justify the actual charge made as being reasonable. An alternative way would be to seek a limit on the management charges, by reference to a stated percentage of the total service charge costs. This has its difficulties for landlords, however. If the premises are, for example, a house divided into three flats each held on a long lease with a nominal rent the management costs may be relatively high (because the same, perhaps limited, amount of work has to be done and there are only three tenants to share it). Another factor is that if the lease is for a long term it is hard to predict what a normal level of management charges might be in the later years of the term. For example, if the lease restricts the charge to 10% of the total service charge costs, that may be a reasonable figure for 2010 but it might not be appropriate in 2015 or 2025 or 2060.

5.176 Commercial leases used to be commonly for 25 years with five-yearly reviews. This was the preference of those lending money to the landlord, who knew their investment had the benefit of an obligation to pay over a long period. Some tenants also liked the certainty and some needed a long term to justify their fitting out expenses. Many parties are now agreeing much shorter leases. The change was first partly sought because of concerns over the continuing liability of the original tenant and assignees during the term where there was of default by a successor (although this is now not so important), and partly because businesses, like people, tend to be much more mobile than they used to be, and their space and facilities requirements change much more frequently than in former times. The shorter the lease, the more reluctant tenants are to accept responsibility for such aspects as replacement of items. Shorter leases are, accordingly, likely to lead to even harder negotiations on both sides on the service charge provisions.

5.177 New materials and techniques for repair and so on may be such that the service charge costs for such items can reduce dramatically, but the administrative side will be just as time consuming. (Use of such materials as aluminium or UPVC can reduce maintenance costs, and many new premises are being designed with a view to keeping maintenance and energy costs as low as possible.) Where the actual repair costs are lower, the 10% limit suggested above would be based on a much smaller figure and might be insufficient to cover the actual cost of management. In the final analysis, if the cost of management is not recoverable in full it may be hard to find managing agents to take on the work, at least without the landlord agreeing to pay the balance of a fair charge. Accordingly, a landlord would be well advised to resist a tenant's amendment to restrict the management charge to a maximum percentage of the service charge costs, if at all possible.

5.178 In many cases the management charge is based purely or largely on the total cost of the services. Tenants may feel that this method of charging is not conducive to keeping the service charge costs down. It is hard to know what to do about this. Incentive charges mentioned in the next paragraph are one option but they are a landlord's option, and not a tenant's option. Tenants of dwellings must be consulted in many cases. When they are consulted they have a right to nominate someone from whom a quotation can be requested. Accordingly, it may pay the tenants to make a few enquiries of other agents if they are consulted. Tenants and any Recognised Tenants' Association have the right to be consulted on the appointment of a managing agent and his terms of employment under the Landlord and Tenant Act 1985, s 20. (See Chapter 9). A tenant can ascertain from the landlord the basis of charging by the agents at the commencement of the lease. However, the landlord will want the freedom to change the managing agents from time to time if he thinks fit, and so even if the tenants are happy with the basis of charging at the lease commencement this basis may not apply after a change of agent. With so many different methods of assessing management fees it can be difficult to compare the quoted charges of two or more potential agents. The tenant should seek to ensure that the charges must be a reasonable amount, but can rarely influence the choice of managing agent directly.

Incentive basis for management charges

5.179 One useful aid to charging is the *'incentive basis'* under which the managing agent's fee is X%, but is X% plus more if the service costs are kept below an agreed level. For example, if the service charge costs have been about £100,000 per year the agent might charge a fee of, say, 5% of the costs incurred, but 7.5% if the service costs incurred are not more than, say, £90,000. On that basis if the costs were £100,000 the agent's fee would be 5% (£5,000) giving a total charge to the tenants of £105,000. On the other hand, if the agent is able to keep the charges to £90,000, his fee (at 7.5%) would be £6,750, giving a total payable by the tenants of £96,750, to the benefit of the tenants and the agent.

5.180 Arranging such basis needs care. For example, the initial benchmark level of costs on which charging is to be based should be one that is fairly standard. For example, if the service costs in the previous year were £112,000, did this figure include the periodic external decoration costs, or some other unusual large item? Assessing the average over three or four years (with a suitable allowance for inflation and contingencies) or the estimated budget for the three- or five-year programme is probably best. Another aspect to watch is to make sure that the agent is not so keen on keeping the costs down as to fail to have the necessary work carried out. The managing agent acts as a buffer between landlord and tenant. As they say, it is hard, if not impossible, to please all of the people all of the time! Additionally, there are many cases where some tenants have different views to their neighbours on what should or should not be done. This is mentioned only to emphasise that many managing agents earn their fees and more.

Collection of rent

5.181 One management item that causes friction when negotiating leases is that part of the costs that relates to collection of rent. Whether the costs are to be chargeable to a tenant or not can be covered by express wording in the lease. Some tenants' solicitors object to references in the service charge provisions to payment towards the cost of recovering rent on the basis that the rent is the landlord's income, and has no relation to the provision of services. Another point is that some agents used to charge landlords for separately collecting rent, but later included those costs in the service charge.

There is some merit in this, but, in practice, the landlord usually claims them both at the same time. It is relatively rare for a tenant to dispute the amount of rent he is supposed to be paying, but some tenants raise objection to the service charge. If a tenant decides to pay his rent but not the service charge then the costs of recovery will relate to service charge not rent, and the point is not material. If the tenant pays neither rent nor service charge (the tenant risks forfeiture) then the costs will be incurred to recover both items, and it is not realistic to try to split the cost between the two. For this reason, the author does not consider it totally unreasonable for the lease to record that the service charge recovery includes costs of recovering rent, but it is probably better practice not to do so. Perhaps a final (and not very satisfactory) compromise would be to qualify the clause to refer to 'the cost of collection of rent but only in those cases when the landlord is also claiming service charges'.

5.182   The Codes of Practice (see Chapter 11) are not particularly helpful on management charges. The Commercial Code (para 82) says the fee should be 'reasonable for the work properly done in relation to the operation and management of the services and have due regard to work necessary to fulfil the principles of this Code'. Paragraph 39 says the 'management service will be regularly tendered or benchmarked against the market'. The Residential Code, in para 3.2, says the agent's charges 'should be appropriate to the task involved' and says changes should be subject to reasonable notice, and if the charges are subject to indexation the index should be specified. It discusses in para 2 the duties of a managing agent. In para 2.5 it indicates that, subject to the terms of any written agreement, 'for a basic fee the managing agent should normally …' and then sets out items which include the collection of rent. In clause 2.6 it sets out items which a managing agent may consider to be outside the basic fee. These include preparing specifications and obtaining tenders and 'supervising substantial repairs or alterations'.

Legal costs of management and court actions

5.183   Section 20C of the Landlord and Tenant Act 1985 permits the tenant of residential property to apply to the court for an order that costs incurred in relation to court proceedings are not to be included in the service charge costs. (See Chapter 9, at **9.145** et seq.) In case of a genuine dispute, or even simple doubt, an application can be made by tenants under this section.

5.184   In *Boldmark Ltd v Cohen* [1986] 1 EGLR 47, the Court of Appeal considered a case (affecting flats in Golders Green) where the judge in the lower court had made no order for costs in a service charge dispute (where the landlord had wanted to charge interest and the lease did not permit this) apparently by analogy with the Landlord and Tenant Act 1954. The Court of Appeal said this was wrong and a court was entitled to make an appropriate order for payment of costs.

5.185   Service charge provisions will often mention legal costs as well as management charges. This is perfectly proper. As with most aspects of service charges, if it is accepted that the basis of the charge is reimbursement of payments by the landlord needed for the proper running of the relevant development, then legal costs can in appropriate circumstances be a proper charge. The question, of course, is: what are the appropriate circumstances?

5.186   When the lease is granted the landlord will (unless he is very brave) use the services of a solicitor. The costs for the granting of the initial leases and, for example, registration of the landlord's title at the land registry would not be proper for inclusion in the services for which the tenant pays. They are simply the necessary expenses for setting up the scheme. However, when the lease has been granted and the term is running there may be a need to employ solicitors, or (more rarely) barristers. The obvious examples are for advice on service charge disputes or help with collection of money owed by tenants to the landlord or enforcement of other breaches of covenant, but there are others. There are occasions where the land owned by the landlord is subject to some form of trespass. This would include major matters such as squatters occupying a flat or a shop, or (what may be slightly less critical) matters such as a wall or fence being built partly on the landlord's property. There could also be claims against the landlord, for example that the landlord had built partly on an adjoining owner's land, or that the landlord's development (or the use by the tenants) blocked a right of way or a right of light, or damaged pipes or cables. There may be need for legal advice on receipt of a summons alleging breaches of planning laws, health and safety matters, disputes with those carrying out services or works at the property, claims for personal injury (usually passed to insurers in more serious cases), insurance claims following damage to the premises, and other matters affecting the property. When the problem arises as a result of some action of a particular tenant the landlord will often be entitled to recover the costs arising from the tenant in question. This is not always possible in relation to proceedings affecting only the common parts of the premises.

5.187   How far the charge is a proper charge is a matter of fact and degree. For example, if the landlord has built a wall which is partly on adjoining land, it is hard to see any justification for including in the service charge legal costs for defending an action by the neighbour. This does not, realistically, represent a service performed for the tenants: it is a service for the landlord as a wrongdoer. On the other hand, the costs to protect the landlord's property in the converse case (where a neighbour has built on the landlord's property) would presumably be a reasonable charge, as it is to protect the land over which the landlord's services are to be performed, and over which tenants may have rights.

5.188   Turning to the costs of recovering service charge from recalcitrant tenants, the position again depends on the terms of the lease and the reasonableness of the action taken. If there are 44 tenants subject to similar service charges and 43 have paid in full without protest, the fact that the 44th has not paid could mean recourse to legal assistance. If that tenant has not paid because of lack of funds, rather than as a result of an objection to the amount requested, it is surely right that a landlord could recover the costs through the service charge, as the costs were incurred in an attempt to bring into the service charge pot the full amount for the cost of the services provided for the benefit of tenants. (Others would argue that the landlord should bear the loss, but (a) he has presumably lost his rent and (b) the service charge is for services performed for the property, rather than for the landlord.)

5.189 Where the tenant refuses to pay because of a dispute over the sum claimed different considerations could apply. The other tenants might take the line that the landlord should not charge to the service charge the costs of resolving a dispute. Perhaps the only real answer is that, where matters reach the court, at least the court (subject to s 20C of the Landlord and Tenant Act 1985: see **5.183**) can decide whether the landlord or the tenant should pay the costs of the action. It should be noted that (a) even an order for costs does not mean that all the costs incurred by the landlord are recoverable from the other side, (b) there may well be costs incurred before the proceedings were commenced which are not included in the court order, and (c) the balance of court costs not awarded by the court are not recoverable through the service charge. (For point (c) see *Holding and Management Ltd v Property Holding and Investment Trust plc* [1990] 1 All ER 938: see **5.193** below.)

5.190 If the lease does not specifically mention legal costs then they may not be recoverable. In *Sella House Ltd v Mears* [1989] 1 EGLR 65, the Court of Appeal heard a claim concerning damage to the common parts and claims and cross claims between landlord and tenant. In effect, it was held that where the lease did not mention legal costs they were not recoverable under such general words as 'costs of computing and collecting the rents and service charge'. Possibly, if the solicitors had been instructed by the managing agents rather than directly by the landlords the claim for the legal costs through the service charge might have succeeded. The end result was that the landlord was not able to recover through the service charge the legal costs that he had not been awarded by the court. A sweeping-up clause was not sufficient in *St Mary's Mansions Ltd v Limegate Investment Co* [2002] EWCA Civ 1491, [2003] 05 EG 146.

5.191 In the later case of *Primeridge Ltd v Jean Muir* [1992] 1 EGLR 273, concerning commercial premises in Bruton Street, London W1, the level of costs recoverable was considered by the court. The lease provided that the landlord could recover 'all proper costs charges and expenses (including professional advisers, costs and fees) incurred by the landlord in connection with any breach of covenant by or the recovery of rent due from the tenant'. These are very widely expressed terms. The tenant in this case had made a payment into court, and the court was asked by the landlord to award costs on the 'indemnity basis' applicable to court costs, rather than the less favourable 'standard basis' because of the terms of the lease. It was held that the judge had a discretion which could not be fettered by a contractual term of the lease, although he was entitled to take account of the relevant clause. Despite the apparently very wide terms of the lease, the judge decided the 'proper costs' meant nothing more than such costs as the landlord was entitled to recover under the rules, and he made an order for costs on the standard basis. This seems consistent with the interpretation of the word 'proper' in *Havenridge Ltd v Boston Dyers Ltd* [1994] 2 EGLR 73. As the premises were commercial there was no statutory assistance.

5.192 However, by contrast, in *Church Commissioners v Ibrahim* [1997] 1 EGLR 13, where there was a reference in the lease to the tenant being liable 'fully' for legal costs (the issue being possession proceedings following a breach by the tenant), the Court of Appeal said that the court's discretion on costs should reflect the contractual terms. Costs were awarded on the indemnity basis, rather than the (lower) standard basis.

5.193 Legal costs were considered in 1987 (as well as fees for consulting engineers) in *Holding and Management Ltd v Property Holding and Investment Trust plc* [1990] 1 All ER 938. The costs were incurred in relation to a scheme for major works that was not carried out. The landlords had incurred legal costs as well as costs of consulting engineers for a scheme likely to cost about one million pounds. The tenants refused to pay and said they had their own scheme which would only cost a quarter of that sum. The landlords then arranged for another scheme to be planned which would have cost about £0.5 million. In due course (at the hearing) a compromise scheme (the fourth!) was adopted, costing about £250,000. The court said that the legal fees and engineers' fees relating to the first (most expensive) scheme, which was not going to be carried out, could not be recovered from the tenants. The same case had an issue related to court costs. Holding & Management Ltd (as maintenance trustee who carried out the landlord's functions under the leases) had asked for an award of costs. The court held that as the main point at issue had been settled by agreement it would make no order as to costs. (Order 62 of the Rules of the Supreme Court and s 30(2) of the Trustee Act 1925 were called in aid, but the court said they did not assist in this case.) The court also made it clear (as in *Reston Ltd v Hudson* [1990] 2 EGLR 51 and *Sella House Ltd v Mears* [1989] 1 EGLR 65) that the maintenance trustee could not recover through the service charge the legal costs it was not awarded by the court. A covenant in the lease in the *Holding and Management* case for payment of 'all legal costs incurred by the Maintenance Trustee ... in the enforcement of the covenants ...' was dismissed by the Court of Appeal, who said: '[r]ead fairly, this paragraph embraces legal costs reasonably and properly incurred ... I have already indicated my view that the costs were not reasonably or properly incurred.'

5.194 A landlord claimed forfeiture *in Iperion Investments Corporation v Broadwalk House Residents Ltd* [1995] 2 EGLR 47, following breach of covenant by the tenant, who carried out alterations without consent. An order for relief from forfeiture was given to the tenant with costs against the landlord. However, the landlord sought to recover the costs of the proceedings from the tenants via the service charge. The Court of Appeal, not surprisingly, said that the landlord could not recover through the service charge those costs awarded against the landlord in the exercise of the court's discretion. On the terms of the lease it is arguable that if the landlord had been awarded part of its costs in the proceedings it would have been able to recover the balance through the service charge. A somewhat similar case, where there was a consent order for the landlord to pay the tenant's costs and the landlord rather cheekily tried to recover the costs through the service charge, had a similar outcome for the landlord. (*Morgan v Stainer* [1993] 2 EGLR 73.)

5.195   An alternative (and useful) approach to legal costs was applied in *Reston Ltd v Hudson* [1990] 2 EGLR 51 (other aspects of which are mentioned at **3.44** and **5.200**). In *Reston* none of the tenants appeared in the court proceedings, and (on the understanding that the landlord would not seek an order for costs against them in court) the court agreed that the costs of the landlord's application were reasonably incurred. The court made a declaration that the costs of the court application were properly recoverable through the service charge. The moral seems to be that the landlord was able to recover because it was said to have acted reasonably by going to the court for a declaration that what it wanted to do was reasonable rather than rushing ahead, doing the work, and arguing about it afterwards.

PART 5 – SWEEPING-UP CLAUSES

General

5.196   In an ideal service charge lease, if there were such a thing, the specific items mentioned would include all the services actually needed and provided. In the real world this is not always possible, and most leases have a clause which tries to cover any items inadvertently omitted but which are essential: this is the sweeping-up clause (or 'sweeper'). This is included as the last specific item in this chapter for obvious reasons. In the next chapter are references to items which are often included in service charge schedules that are not services as such. The other major service charge item (sinking funds) deserves a chapter to itself, and in this book it is Chapter 7.

5.197   The biggest problem with sweeping-up clauses is making them effective. As will be shown below, a sweeping-up clause is far from being a cure for all defects or omissions in the lease. The author agrees with one conference speaker who said a sweeping-up clause is more like a sticking plaster than a crutch. In other words it can be a help, but it is not a complete remedy.

5.198   Such provisions are construed against the landlord. This emphasises, again, in my view, the importance of making the lease fit the premises, rather than hoping that a standard form will be sufficient if it includes a general provision seeking to allow the landlord to charge for 'any other services' or some similar wording.

Examples

5.199   As an example of the limited benefit of sweeping-up clauses, *Isbicki (Jacob) & Co Ltd v Goulding & Bird Ltd* [1989] 1 EGLR 236, is worth recording. The case was a construction summons concerning some (presumably) commercial premises. The lease set out details of services to be carried out by the landlord in the usual way. It is material that the specified services did not include repair of the external walls. At the end of the list of services was a sweeping-up provision. In *Isbicki* it took the form of a proviso that the landlord could 'at his reasonable discretion hold, add to, extend, vary or make any alteration in the rendering of the said services or any of them from time to time if the Landlord at his like discretion deems it desirable to do so for more efficient conduct and management of the building.' The landlord decided to sandblast the external walls and attempted to recover the cost from the tenants. The landlord failed. In a key passage in the brief judgment the judge said: 'within the limits of the work for which the landlord can recover, the landlord has his admitted right to alter those works, but not, as I see it, wholly to extend and make the tenant liable for a kind of work that was never intended by (the service charge) clause.' The reference to the limits of the work for which the landlord could recover costs makes it clear that a sweeping-up clause is an aid to specified services, but not the source of a new right to claim.

5.200   A sweeping-up clause was held to have some merit in *Reston Ltd v Hudson* [1990] 2 EGLR 51. There, a problem over windows (an ever popular topic of legal cases) was considered by the court. The question in part was whether or not replacement of all the windows in the block at the same time (where a large number were defective) was an obligation of the landlord covered by the service charge provisions. The right to recover the court costs was held by the judge to come either under 'the cost of management of the estate' or under the sweeping-up clause: 'all outgoings, costs and expenses whatsoever which the lessor may reasonably incur in the discharge of its obligations under clause 4 of the Lease and not otherwise hereinbefore specifically mentioned.'

5.201   In *Holding and Management Ltd v Property Holding and Investment Trust plc* [1990] 1 All ER 938 (see also **5.193** above), a scheme was prepared for dealing with significant defects. The Court of Appeal held that the scheme went beyond repair in the meaning of the main repair covenant, and disallowed the engineers' and legal costs relating to that scheme. An attempt was made to suggest that those costs might have been covered by the sweeping-up clause which related to such works as the maintenance trustee 'shall consider necessary to maintain the Building as a block of first-class residential flats or otherwise desirable in the general interests of the tenants'. This was also rejected by the court. Nicholls LLJ, giving the judgment of the Court of Appeal, said: 'I cannot read this paragraph as giving the plaintiff a free hand to require the residents to pay for all the works, whatever they might be, which the plaintiff might consider necessary to maintain the building as a block of first-class residential flats.' He went on to say: 'it is necessarily implicit in this paragraph that the plaintiff will act reasonably ... Either the works proposed to be done to the exterior walls fell within the ambit of the tenants' repairing obligation to keep such walls in good repair or they did not. If they did not, the residents could not be required to pay for these works by recourse to [the sweeper].'

5.202   In *Sutton (Hastoe) Housing Association v Williams* [1988] 1 EGLR 56, the housing association landlord was able to recover the costs of replacing defective single glazed wooden windows in flats with double-glazed UPVC windows. Windows were not mentioned in the repairing covenant. The landlord succeeded on a reference in the lease to 'carrying out such additional works and providing such additional services as may be considered necessary by the lessor in its absolute discretion from time to time'. This was backed up by a schedule (needed because this was a right to buy lease: see **10.98**) of condition in the lease which showed that the windows would need to be renewed within ten years of the grant of the lease. It was also an improvement rather than a repair, and at that time no consultation with the tenants was needed and the works were not subject to the usual implication of reasonableness applying to dwellings. This approach was followed, for example, by the Lands Tribunal in *Re Bedfordshire Pilgrims Housing Association Ltd* LTL 20.3.2002, although now improvements come within the definition of service charges in s 18 of the Landlord and Tenant Act 1985 and so consultation and reasonableness would apply in future in similar circumstances.

The Bowker Orford case

5.203   An even more striking example of the uses and limits of sweeping-up clauses is *Lloyds Bank plc v Bowker Orford* [1992] 2 EGLR 44. This Chancery Division decision of Mr Justice Neuberger, as he then was, is worth reviewing in detail because it had many facets relating to interpretation of sweeping-up clauses. In that case there were two more or less similar leases of parts of a commercial building in Cavendish Place, London W1. The leases were unusual in two respects as regards the service charge provisions. First, the tenants had agreed to pay a due proportion of what were described as the 'total costs' of providing the services 'specified in s 2' of the relevant part of the schedule. Secondly, s 2 itself was also unusual in consisting of five short paragraphs:

'1. Two lifts for the use of the occupiers of the demised premises shall be provided and maintained in good repair and proper working order.

2. A resident caretaker should be employed housed and uniformed generally to be responsible for the upkeep and security of the building ...

3. The entrance halls corridors staircases lifts and all parts of the building used in common with the other tenants thereof and lavatories ... shall be cleaned and after dark ... lighted

4. Constant hot water shall be provided in the lavatories ...

5. Any other beneficial services which may properly be provided by the lessors.'

This provision is slightly unusual in giving a specific but rather brief list of services. The sweeping-up clause in this case was, of course, para 5.

5.204   There were quite a few points at issue in the *Lloyds Bank* case, where the sweeping-up clause was considered.

(a)   *External repairs* The first point was whether or not the landlord could claim for the cost of a proportion of external repairs. The specific items of charge mentioned in s 2 of the Schedule did not include repair. To succeed in a claim the landlord therefore had to rely on the sweeping up-provision ('any other beneficial services'). The landlord failed in this claim. It had covenanted elsewhere in the lease to carry out external repairs. The court considered this would, for example, be inconsistent, because the express clause was a positive obligation, while the sweeping-up provision related to works which were discretionary – the landlord was not obliged to carry them out.

(b)   *Internal repairs* The second claim was for the cost of internal decoration and repairs to the common parts of the building. Item 3 of the second section related to cleaning and lighting common parts, but did not mention repair or decoration of those parts. So, again, the landlord had to try to rely on the sweeping-up provision, and again the landlord failed. The judge considered this was a more difficult point. Arguments were put that the first four parts of s 2 were of a similar type, so that the fifth item (the sweeping-up clause) should be construed eusdem generis with the earlier items. The court did not agree, but pointed out that it would have been easy to have provided that the fifth item was to be construed in a different manner to the others. The court laid more stress, however, on the point that the lighting and cleaning of the common parts were mentioned (item 3) and so the common parts were clearly in the contemplation of the parties when drafting s 2. The parties could have mentioned repair and decoration of the common parts if this had been intended, but did not. The sweeping-up clause was not adequate to enable the landlord to justify its claim.

(c)   *Different external repairs provisions* One of the two leases in *Bowker Orford* had a different provision for external repair to the other lease. The tenant was specifically liable to pay a fair proportion of the expense of repair and decoration etc of party walls, fences, gutters, drains etc used in common with any other person. The landlord questioned whether it could (by virtue of the sweeping-up clause) recover costs of repairs of the building beyond the express terms of the clause. The court said that it would be 'unrealistic to read para 5 in the second defendant's lease in such a way as to enable the lessor to add to the service charge over and above what the parties had specifically agreed as to the extent of the lessees' liability under (the specific clause)'. In other words, again the sweeping-up clause was not enough to enable the landlord to succeed in recovering the costs.

(d)   *Electrical system* The landlord sought to recover the cost of replacement of the electrical system in the building. Referring to the provisions of s 2 the judge said: 'The repairs to the old lighting in the common parts clearly falls within para 3 of Sch 2. Although the defendants argue to the contrary, it seems to me clear that the provision of new lighting also falls within that section. Paragraph 3 is not worded in such a way as to exclude the possibility of the landlords having to provide, and being able to charge for, further lighting in the common parts, where appropriate. In so far as the electrical work was required so as to enable the lessor to comply with its obligation to provide any of the services in paras 1–5 of s 2, the cost is recoverable for reasons already given.'

(e) *In relation to other claims by the landlord in relation to capital expenditure* In so far as the electrical work was for any other purpose, the plaintiff has to argue that it falls within para 5. For the reasons already given in relation to the second question (see (b) above), it was not considered that it did. Accordingly, the landlord could recover, through the sweeping-up clause, the costs of electrical work needed to enable the landlord to carry out its specific obligations, but not further.

It is noticeable that the landlord failed on each of the first three points, and succeeded only to a limited extent on the final point. The moral, again, is that if a landlord wants to be able to recover the costs for a specific item he should express it clearly in the lease: the sweeping-up clause will not enable a landlord to claim for something entirely fresh or contrary to specific provisions. It is intended to amplify other provisions, rather than to create new items of charge – the salt in the soup, not the main ingredient.

Use of the sweeping-up clause

5.205　It is important to a landlord for the lease to include a sweeping-up clause unless the landlord and tenants have agreed that the service charge is to cover only a few specific matters. Even then it is advisable. Without one the landlord has to rely on the express words of the services to be provided, with no scope for inadvertent omissions. Where a lease is incorrect there is very limited scope for rectification (*Riverlate Properties Ltd v Paul* [1975] Ch 133: see **2.5** above). The sweeping-up clause seems to be upheld only when it is used to amplify the services the landlord is required to provide.

Unsuccessful sweeping-up clauses

5.206　The following is a summary of cases where the sweeper has failed to enable a landlord to charge:

(a) In the *Isbicki* case (see **5.199** above) the landlord had not covenanted to repair external walls: the sweeping-up clause did not enable him to charge for sandblasting those walls.

(b) In *Lloyds Bank plc v Bowker Orford* [1992] 2 EGLR 44 discussed above (at **5.203** et seq), the sweeping-up clause did not enable the landlord to recover costs of external repair where it had not covenanted to repair; nor internal repair and decorating internal parts where cleaning and lighting were mentioned but not repair or decoration; nor repairs beyond the extent of the express obligation to repair specified items used in common. It permitted recovery of that part, only, of the cost of electrical rewiring needed to enable the landlord to perform the defined services.

(c) In *Mullaney v Maybourne Grange (Croydon) Management Ltd* [1986] 1 EGLR 70, a landlord failed to recover the cost of replacement windows under a sweeping-up clause which referred to 'providing and maintaining additional services and amenities'.

(d) In 2003 a sweeping-up clause ('cost of all other services which the lessor may at its absolute discretion provide or install in the said Building for the comfort and convenience of the lessees') was not sufficient to enable the landlord to recover legal costs for advice. (*St Mary's Mansions Ltd v Limegate Investment Co* [2002] EWCA Civ 1491, [2003] 05 EG 146.)

Successful sweeping-up clauses

5.207 The landlord did succeed with a sweeping-up clause in *Sun Alliance and London Assurance Co Ltd v British Railways Board* [1989] 2 EGLR 237 discussed at **5.68** above, where the clause entitled the landlord to charge for 'costs of providing such other services as the lessor shall consider ought reasonably and properly be provided for the benefit of the building or for the proper maintenance and servicing of any parts'. The landlord was able to recover the proportion claimed (it did not claim the whole) of the cost of replacement of the external system for window cleaning with a more up-to-date system. The landlord was partially successful in *Lloyds Bank plc v Bowker Orford* [1992] 2 EGLR 44, but only to a very limited extent (see **5.204**). The sweeper was used successfully in *Reston Ltd v Hudson* (see **5.200** above).

Sweeping-up clause summary

5.208 It is to be noted that landlords have failed far more often than they have succeeded in these cases. It would seem that a sweeping-up clause may be successfully used in these circumstances:

(a) To enlarge or vary the manner of carrying out a specified service. For example, if the landlord had been under an obligation to repair external walls in the *Isbicki* case (**5.199**) then a sweeping-up clause might have permitted sandblasting, if worded to refer to additional services.

(b) To cover replacement of items needed to carry out the chargeable services. For example, the electrical works in the *Bowker Orford* case (**5.204**).

(c) Where the lease permits the landlord to carry out new services or works with the consent of the tenants. For example, if the tenants of a shopping mall agreed to the installation of a new clock the maintenance could be covered by the sweeping-up clause, in relation to the item which was not present before. (By analogy with varied services as in the *Sun Alliance* case: see **5.207**.)

(d) Assuming the lease contains the usual provisions for variation of the area covered by the definition of the common parts, then the sweeping-up clause might assist to avoid a dispute that the landlord cannot charge for services in relation to property added on.

(e) A sweeping-up clause should enable a landlord to charge for repair etc of innovations not contemplated at the time the lease was granted. For example, leases of flats granted in 1925 will not mention common television aerials or door entry phones. Many tenants these days would want such items, and where they are put in, certainly with the consent of the tenants, the sweeping-up clause may well come into play to enable the landlord to recover the cost of maintenance of such items.

5.209   Charging and being paid over a period could presumably lead to some form of estoppel, so that if demand and payment for maintenance etc of particular items was made for a number of years with the tenant's knowledge and without objection from them, the tenants may be estopped from later suggesting the landlord had no right to charge. A tenant who is unhappy about any charge is recommended to take the matter up sooner rather than later for any point on service charges. Sitting back might lead to the implication that the tenant accepted the position.

CHAPTER 6

Other service charge provisions

Reading the fine print may give you an education – not reading it will give you experience.

V M Kelley

INTRODUCTION

6.1   This chapter covers a number of lease provisions affecting service charges, but which are not actually services or works. Some items are included in the lease as a matter of convenience along with items such as repair, decoration, heating etc. Sometimes leases provide that the landlord will carry out the services described in, for example, paras 1–18 of the Schedule, and on inspection it is seen that some are items such as interest. These extra items are not ones the landlord should covenant to carry out, and for good drafting the reference to the numbered paragraphs should be adjusted. Sinking funds are covered in the next chapter.

PART I – INTEREST

Bank interest and bank charges

6.2   Charging bank interest and other bank charges can be contentious. Where the landlord can call for payment in advance some tenants take the view that there is no reason why the landlord should also be able to charge the cost of borrowing money. The answer is, as usual, a practical one: advance payments are to cover the costs that are anticipated, but if major works which were not expected have to be done urgently, or if a major item of plant has to be replaced urgently and there is no sinking fund for the purpose, then the advance payments will not cover the costs. (The problem is better resolved by allowing the landlord the right to call for a supplementary service charge contribution in case of need.)

The obligation to pay interest

6.3   From a technical point of view, the most important point is that interest must be clearly mentioned to be chargeable. For example, the expressions 'general management and administration' and 'other outgoings payable by the lessors in respect of the property' were not sufficient to enable the landlord to charge bank interest in *Frobisher (Second Investments) Ltd v Killoran Trust Co Ltd* [1980] 1 All ER 488. In the *Frobisher* case the premises were flats for which, at that time, s 91A of the Housing Finance Act 1972 prohibited advance payments of service charges. This is not prohibited now, although s 19 of the Landlord and Tenant Act 1985 requires advance payments to be no more than is reasonable. The landlord wanted to borrow money to pay for works before collecting contributions from tenants, but was unable to satisfy the court that the lease permitted charging bank interest.

6.4   General wording was also ineffective for this purpose in *Boldmark Ltd v Cohen* [1986] 1 EGLR 47, where the lease referred to 'general administration and management'.

6.5   Where interest is mentioned, it can be charged. In *Skilleter v Charles* [1992] 1 EGLR 73, the lease referred to interest, but the clause omitted a few words which made the actual clause ungrammatical. The Court of Appeal held that the clause was sufficient to indicate that the landlord was intended to be able to charge interest, and to give business efficacy to the lease the court confirmed that interest could be charged. The clause said 'any interest charges payable by the lessor on his bank account or accounts in respect of any for the purposes of the maintenance charge'. Either something was omitted after 'in respect of', or those words should not have been included. However, the clause clearly referred to bank interest. Parker LJ, giving the only judgment of the Court of Appeal, said that the interest liability arose because the tenant had not paid the maintenance charge. He then said 'no question of reasonableness can arise', although he did not expand on that comment.

6.6   It must be remembered that interest is not the only charge made by banks for lending money. There can also be 'arrangement fees', and charges made by banks for managing the account. If interest is to be mentioned, it is as well for the clause to cover all amounts charged by the bank.

6.7   Sometimes, the right for a landlord to charge bank interest etc is proposed by tenants as an alternative to a sinking fund. There is some merit in this if the sinking fund is intended for replacement of a specific item such as a lift, or where urgent and expensive repairs become apparent which were not taken into account in calculating advance payments. It would not help for a reserve fund, which simply evens out expenditure.

Negotiating an interest provision

6.8   A tenant negotiating a lease should seek to agree:

(a)   That bank interest can only be charged in specified circumstances. For example, 'interest on money necessarily borrowed by the landlord to comply with his obligations under this lease in respect only of unanticipated major items of repair'. This restricts the entitlement to charge to those matters where an unexpected but major expense arises.

(b) To restrict the amount to a reasonable commercial rate of interest. The clause could refer to 'a normal and reasonable rate of interest charged for loans for similar purposes and for similar periods by clearing banks to customers'. It is important to give some detail of the type of lenders whose interest is to be treated as a yardstick: a loan shark would charge many times more than would be charged by a high street bank. The reference to similar purposes and similar periods is also important, so that a fair comparison can be sought.

(c) (To ensure that the interest does not become a permanent feature) that 'the loan is to be taken out for no longer than is reasonably necessary, and is to be repaid as soon reasonably practicable'. It is difficult to be more precise in such cases because the length of a loan depends on the terms agreed with the bank and the purpose. Generally speaking, the shorter the period of the loan the higher the interest rate, which can make such a provision counterproductive. However, the sooner the loan is repaid the sooner the obligation to pay interest ceases.

(d) To ensure that the landlord does not include in the service charge costs bank interest on his own overdraft which is, perhaps, working capital and is nothing to do with the service charge.

6.9   Agents who manage accounts for landlords and who are members of the Royal Institution of Chartered Surveyors need to remember that they are bound by the RICS accounts regulations. In similar fashion to the Law Society regulations for solicitors, the RICS regulations prohibit overdrawing on the client account.

Entitlement to interest

6.10   See **3.77**, above, recording that the Codes of Practice both contemplate that interest earned on the money in the account is credited to the account, although interest payable on late payment may be payable to the landlord if the service charge is reserved as rent (see at **6.15** below).

Interest on late payment

6.11   Because it is important that service charge payments are made regularly, so that the money needed for works and services is available for those purposes, most leases provide that interest is payable if the payments are late. This is common sense and not a matter that is normally controversial as a principle, although tenants often seek to lighten the potential burden on their pocket in one way or another.

6.12   There is, in most modern leases, a general provision that interest is payable if any payment due from the tenant to the landlord is overdue. The provision is usually among the tenants' covenants, although sometimes it appears in the agreements and declarations or even in the redendum. The exact wording of the provision needs to be checked before interest is charged. A landlord would be well advised to ensure it covers service charges.

6.13   Where a tenant is required to pay service charges in advance there is no excuse for a tenant to delay. The only exception may perhaps be for the first payment at a new estimated rate, and then only if the landlord has been slow in producing the estimated figures. The days of payment will be set out in the lease and the amount payable is also known in advance. The effect is that a tenant will know when and how much he has to pay, usually well in advance, and if he feels the figures are too high (or otherwise wrong), he will be able to consider what rights are open to him under the disputes procedure (if any) in the lease or otherwise.

6.14   Interest penalties for late payment for leases of dwellings are an 'Administration Charge' under Schedule 11, para 1(c) to the Commonhold and Leasehold Reform Act 2002. They are accordingly subject to challenge if they are unreasonable (see Chapter 9 at **9.37**), and there is a right to make an application to a Leasehold Valuation Tribunal to vary the lease if a fixed administration charge (or a formula for calculating it) is unreasonable.

6.15   If interest is not chargeable, the effect is that those tenants who pay properly on the due dates are subsidising those tenants who pay late. The interest received should normally be credited to the service charge fund on receipt. However, the Court of Appeal, in *St Mary's Mansions Ltd v Limegate Investments Ltd* [2002] EWCA Civ 1491, [2003] 05 EG 146, perhaps surprisingly, held that the landlord was entitled to keep the interest where the lease provided that the interest was payable 'by way of further rent'. Presumably, the same point would apply whenever the service charge is reserved as rent. The court had sympathy with the view that interest (for dwellings) should accrue to the fund under s 42(2) of the Landlord and Tenant Act 1987, but said the position must be subject to the terms of the lease.

Drafting interest provisions

6.16   A few points need to be assessed regarding interest provisions:

(a)   the date from which interest becomes payable;

(b)   the date for commencement of the interest calculation;

(c)   the interest rate;

(d)   whether the tenant can require interest to be paid by the landlord on amounts the tenant has paid in advance in excess of the amount actually needed;

(e)   value added tax; and

(f)   excluding apportionments.

The date for calculating interest

6.17   The interest permutations are well known. The landlord drafting a lease (or the parties when negotiating) have to decide whether the interest is to be paid if the payment is late at all, or only if it is delayed by a period such as 7, 10, 14, 21 or 28 days. A draft lease sometimes starts with the provision for interest to become payable if the payment is in arrears to any extent, and is then negotiated to refer to interest payments when arrears are late by more than a specified period. Once the acceptable period of delay in payment is agreed, it is necessary to decide the date from which the interest is payable. If, for example, the lease provides for interest to be payable if the tenant is 21 days late in paying, should the interest be calculated from the date on which it should have been paid, or from 21 days after the payment is due, or indeed from some other date such as ten days after the payment should have been made? The author's view is that as the payment is properly due on a known date (usually the usual quarter days) the tenant should not be entitled to any leeway. On that basis, if a tenant persuades a landlord to agree to give him, say, 14 days' grace for payment, it seems right that interest should be paid from the date on which the payment should have been made (ie from the quarter day). Any other arrangement would mean that the tenant has a double benefit from his delay: he has been given days of grace which he has more than used up, and has still not paid within the extended time given to him. Such delay in payment causes the service charge fund to be unbalanced, and possibly insufficient at a critical time. It is important that the service charge payments by tenants should be made in good time and it is hard to see why a tenant should not be penalised in interest if he fails to pay within the time specified.

Interest rate

6.18   What the interest rate should be is another matter of discussion at the negotiating table. Normally, interest is expressed to be at a certain percentage rate above the base rate for the time being of a specified high street bank. (Currently, the range seems to be between 3% and 5% over the base rate.) The author has seen drafts where the tenants tried to amend the interest rate payable to be a specified percentage of the base rate (eg 125%). This was suggested as fair on the basis that if interest rates reduced substantially (as they did in the early 1990s) the base rate might be a very low figure and a specified percentage over that base rate might be unreasonable. The theory was that if base rates reduce to, say, 2%, and the interest penalty was 4% over the base rate this would make the interest payable unreasonably harsh, as it would be three times the base rate. The author's view is that the interest provision is intended to be a penalty for a tenant who is not complying with his primary obligation of paying what he owes the landlord on time. If the base rate becomes very low there is little penalty involved if the tenant's formula is followed. This is mentioned, however, as an approach that can be considered.

Should the landlord pay interest?

6.19   Another major question is whether the landlord should pay interest when repaying amounts overpaid by the tenant. This depends on the terms of the provisions for adjustment at the year end. On the basis that the excess held by the landlord is carried forward to the next year (which is a common provision), the question of interest does not really arise, although tenants may seek to ensure that the lease provides that payments by them should be held in an interest bearing account and that interest earned on those payments is credited to the service charge account. In the last year of the term, the question of a refund to a tenant may arise, or where the lease requires the landlord to pay any excess (or any excess over a stated amount) to the tenant. In such circumstances, provided the interest earned on the service charge fund has been credited to the fund, the tenant will have the benefit of some interest within the amount calculated as his refund. If the lease provides for the landlord to make such refund within, say, 28 days of the amount being ascertained, it seems not unreasonable for the landlord to be required to pay interest on the amount due if it is not paid within the specified period. It is worth noting that the time limits could reasonably be shorter for this payment: the money is actually in the hands of the landlord (or the managing agents), and once the amount is calculated there seems no reason for delay in repaying the tenant his own money. The author would recommend that tenants negotiate that where a refund is payable it should be made within a short time (perhaps ten days) of the amount being ascertained, and that interest thereafter should be payable by the landlord himself (not out of the service charge fund) at a rate equal to the amount that the tenant is required to pay on late payments. In such cases, interest should commence from the end of the time allowed for payment (ten days in this period), as the landlord will be aware that a payment is due, and will be actively considering the figures. He will also have control over when the figures are produced to the tenant.

Value added tax

6.20   Where value added tax is payable on service charges the interest calculation should be based on the gross figure (£100 plus £17.50 VAT), but VAT should not be added to the interest so calculated.

Apportionment of interest

6.21   There is a particular problem on apportionment of interest which is based on the decision in *Moorcroft Estates Ltd v Doxford* [1980] 1 EGLR 37 (see also at **4.45**). By analogy with the rateable value apportionment, it would seem that, strictly, interest credited to the service charge account, for example from interest bearing accounts, has to be apportioned as between tenants based, in effect, on the actual dates of payment by each tenant to the fund. Thus if tenant A pays his contribution on 1 April but tenant B does not pay until 15 April the interest to be credited to each should be calculated taking account of the period during which interest has been accrued. Tenant A would thus have the benefit of his proportion of the total interest for 15 days more than tenant B. If possible, it is best to avoid any need to carry out this exercise by a suitable provision in the service charge clauses. While the correct position is perhaps strictly the fairest arrangement, so that a tenant paying in good time receives a credit for a larger slice of interest, the costs of making the calculation are likely to outweigh the benefit in most cases.

PART 2 – PROMOTIONAL EXPENSES

Promotional expenses and publicity

6.22 Attracting the public to the development can benefit retail precincts. The more people who come to the precinct the more potential customers there are for the occupiers. This is obviously to the advantage of the retail tenants, and if it helps the precinct to thrive it also benefits the landlord as he will have a more buoyant investment. Accordingly, publicity and promotional activities can become material. These are not directly works or services provided by the landlord for the benefit of the tenant's premises, but they are sometimes offered as additional attractions to tenants (particularly the smaller retailers). When promotional matters are included, they usually appear among the service charge services. These issues are not normally relevant to offices, flats or industrial units. The Commercial Code (see Chapter 11) covers promotional activities in paras 77–82. At one time there was a difference in the VAT treatment of promotional expenses and other expenses, and some landlords accordingly put provisions for promotional expenses separate from the main service charge provisions in an effort to ensure that tenants obtained the benefit of the VAT treatment. They are no longer treated differently for VAT.

6.23 Publicity for a shopping centre is normally by way of newspaper and magazine advertisements and posters, but can also be by way of radio or television advertisements, and postal 'mail shots' or handouts and free gifts, and displays or decorations in the common parts. Publicity is a very nebulous thing, and there are now many outlets (including internet websites) that are easy to set up for the direct benefit of the individual businesses, rather than the development. Some of the larger shopping precincts do have their own websites, and points mentioned below apply to those as well as other forms of advertising.

6.24 If the landlord wants the tenant to pay for publicity, this should be clearly expressed in the lease. It is hard to see that a landlord could successfully reclaim publicity costs on the strength of a sweeping-up clause, because the latter usually relates to works or services on the landlord's premises. Publicity is not 'works', and publicity is hard to reconcile with 'services' as it does nothing for the fabric of the landlord's property, although it may benefit businesses there.

6.25 The tenant should be alert to ensure that the lease does not give the landlord an unreasonable opportunity to spend the tenant's money for no real benefit. A tenant should try to ensure that both the publicity scheme and the budget for it are agreed in advance by the tenants, or at least a majority of them. This is the recommendation of the Commercial Code. Although the landlord will have some benefit it is primarily the retailers who should be the objects of the advertising and it should be primarily relevant to them.

6.26 Some larger retailers object to contributing to publicity costs on the basis that they have their own advertising scheme and budget. The point about the advertising for a landlord's property, however, is that it is directed to advertising the shops in the precinct in question, whereas the multiple retailers normally advertise on a more general basis. It is unreasonable for the smaller retailers to subsidise the large retailers, and if the large retailers are reluctant to join with the others they should be asked to make sure that their own advertising campaign specifically advertises the precinct in question. Many multiple retailers take the practical view that the publicity will benefit their shop as well as the others, since it is advertising for the precinct, even if it not solely for their own branches. (Many adverts mention the larger units specifically as an attraction.) If the point becomes a crunch point in negotiations any waiver should be expressly limited to the named tenant, so that on assignment future tenants have the same liability as others on the development.

6.27   A tenant negotiating a lease should try to ensure that the tenants are to be consulted (or can decide) the budget, and style or methods of advertising. They should not be required to contribute to advertising to find new tenants of the precinct, as this is a matter for the benefit of the landlord, not for the general benefit of the precinct.

PART 3 – INSURANCE

6.28   Insurance is mentioned here, although it would seem best for the main insurance provisions and the service charge provisions to be kept separate. An acceptable exception is a provision for insurance of plant and machinery and third party risks in the service charge schedule. These are suitable items for a service charge, but the main building insurance is not. The reason is that building insurance has many aspects that are customarily covered in leases, and if they are to be covered it is unsatisfactory to clutter up the service charge schedule (which is usually long enough as it is!) with yet more provisions. Buildings insurance liability in a lease usually involves:

(a)   an obligation to insure for full reinstatement value (by landlord or tenant);

(b)   (if the landlord insures) a provision for the tenant to reimburse the premium;

(c)   frequently lengthy descriptions of the risks against which insurance is to be taken out;

(d)   an obligation for reinstatement in case of damage or destruction;

(e)   rights for the tenant to cease to pay rent in the event of total or partial damage to destruction of the building (rent suspension in case of destruction is discussed in Chapter 8); and

(f)   sometimes rights for either or both parties to determine in the case of destruction.

All these provisions are usually covered in detailed clauses relating only to insurance aspects, and are thus not really suited to a position within the myriad provisions primarily related to service charges. Unfortunately, in the author's view, s 18 of the Landlord and Tenant Act 1985, which defines the elements of service charges affecting dwellings, includes insurance. Thus for dwellings the statutory provisions affecting service charges, notably reasonableness and consultation, apply to insurance. (It is a pity, particularly as the Schedule to the 1985 Act deals solely with insurance and could have given the same protection without jumbling service charges and insurance together.)

6.29 Insurance against damage to plant needed for the services the landlord is to provide is a reasonable service charge object. A simple provision that providing and maintaining such insurance is one of the services the landlord is to carry out, the premium for which can be recovered through the service charge, is sensible. The aspects of buildings insurance mentioned at **6.28** above are not really appropriate for insurance just of plant or third party risks. The tenant will wish to ensure that the risks covered are appropriate, and the amount of cover and the premium are reasonable, and the insurance only applies to plant and equipment necessary for the services for which the landlord is responsible.

6.30 If the landlord has to insure the building for full reinstatement value he is entitled to have regard to inflation, and to charge the tenant the premium for reinstatement at today's value plus an inflation element. (*Gleniffer Finance Corporation v Bamar Wood and Products Ltd* (1978) 37 P & CR 208.) For insurance of plant and equipment, the inflation element is probably unnecessary: for buildings, replacement will usually take a few years, with the need for insurance claims to be settled and often a need for planning permission.

6.31 Third party risks are another matter suitable for inclusion in the service charge provisions, at least where the landlord is responsible for common parts. It is to cover claims made against the landlord for injury arising on premises the landlord is liable to repair, or under the landlord's control. Such claims sometimes need to be resisted, and this costs real money if it is not insured. Some tenants consider this is a matter for the landlord to pay for out of his own pocket. However, if the landlord does not carry such insurance and a large claim has to be paid by the landlord, it could put him in financial difficulty, and thus unable to manage the property properly (eg if there are vacant units, or where he has to contribute a specific part of the costs). This cannot be in the interests of the tenants. Claims for personal injuries seem to be increasing in number and level of damages, following the compensation culture that seems to have been growing in recent years. The premiums for third party cover are in any event fairly small, and usually insignificant when divided among the tenants.

6.32 In *Beale v Worth* [1993] EGCS 135, an insurance claim was made following damage to a block of flats in Enfield. The landlord claimed she was refunding the sum recovered from the insurers to each of the tenants by way of set-off against amounts owed to her. The brief report shows that the court held the insured sum was due to the residents' association jointly, so that the landlord was not entitled to set off the refunds against the service charge demands made to individual tenants.

6.33 If a landlord agrees that the insurance charged to the tenant is that 'properly incurred', *Havenridge Ltd v Boston Dyers Ltd* [1994] 2 EGLR 73 (discussed at **3.48**) qualifies the ability of the landlord to charge, but does not imply that the premium must be 'reasonable' in amount. This follows the earlier case of *Bandar Property Holdings Ltd v JS Darwen (Successors) Ltd* [1968] 2 All ER 305.

6.34 Should a landlord charging insurance premiums through the service charge give the benefit of any discount? The answer seems to be that if reimbursement is intended the landlord should only charge the tenants what he has paid, and the tenants would, in effect, get the benefit of any discount. In the absence of a provision in the lease covering commission, however, it has been said that if a landlord obtains commission for entering into a contract for a number of years (as opposed to the normal 12-month arrangement) then he can retain the commission. (For residential premises such an arrangement would be a 'long-term agreement' and so subject to consultation under s 20 of the Landlord and Tenant Act 1985.)

6.35 In an unusual case, *Williams v Southwark London Borough Council* [2000] EGCS 44 (where many properties had been let on 125 years created under the right to buy scheme, and where there had been two successive insurers and special insurance schemes) the landlords were held entitled to retain such part of the insurance discount as was attributable to remuneration to them for the services that the council had carried out by handling claims on behalf of the insurers. It seems to have been conceded that the tenants were entitled to the benefit of the (5%) discount representing a loyalty payment by one insurer, and the whole of the discount (36.5%) from the other insurer where there was no arrangement for the landlords to handle claims. This was followed in a residential case, *Ionic Properties and Lessees of Melcombe Regis Court* (LVT) LON 00BK/LSL/2003/0015, by a Leasehold Valuation Tribunal where the commission was payable by a tenant to the head landlord, and the tenant could not pass on that element of the premium to the residential undertenant.

PART 4 – RATES AND TAXES

Rates

6.36 If the landlord is obliged to pay rates on common areas he will want to recover the sum concerned from the tenants. Rates are payable on usable spaces, and these may include such areas as (sometimes) covered malls, and management offices, or kiosks for car park attendants. The charge is relatively straightforward. The amount is fixed by the local authority based on the assessment by the District Valuer, an independent official, and so the amount payable may be an irritation but is not something about which a landlord can do much (although he can appeal an assessment).

Taxes

6.37   Leases normally exclude from what the landlord can recover the tax that the landlord has to pay on his income from the letting. Such a charge would be totally inappropriate. The only tax relevant to the tenant may be on the interest earned on the income created by the service charge fund. Tenants simply have to accept that the interest (which should be credited to the fund) will be reduced by the tax payable.

Tax on parking spaces

6.38   If parking spaces become taxable (a political suggestion mooted from time to time), treating the tax fairly will be more difficult. If the parking space is let to the tenant then the tax should fall on him under the ordinary lease provisions. If the tenant simply has a general right to use the parking area then different considerations apply. In such a case one would expect the tax to be payable by the landlord, as it is his property and not let. Whether or not he could recover through the service charge would depend on the wording of the lease. If the space is not demised but the tenant is give the right to park in a specified space it is hard to see what is the fair approach. It could be said that it is close to being demised and that thus the tenant should pay the tax, but on the other hand it is not demised and so the landlord retains it. The author recommends that the point is considered by the landlord and his managing agent when the lease is granted. It may be that the fashion would be to include specified spaces in the letting rather than granting general rights (so that any tax would be the tenants' responsibility) but if the landlord wants the tenant to be responsible for the tax on a nominated space the lease should specify this. If such a tax is introduced the legislation may cover these permutations.

PART 5 – CONDITION PRECEDENT

6.39   On the whole, a provision that the performance of the services by the landlord is subject to the tenant first paying the service charge is not very practical. (See at **6.41** below.) This is a fairly common provision, but if a landlord finds a tenant whose solicitor insists on removing the provision from the draft lease the landlord's solicitor need not lose too much sleep. Apart from any other consideration, if one tenant out of ten fails to pay his service charge contribution the landlord would be in breach of his obligations to the nine who have paid if he refuses to provide the services.

6.40   Even where there is an effective condition precedent the landlord cannot rely on that as a defence in a dispute as to the landlord's performance. An example of this is the Court of Appeal case of *Gordon v Selico Co Ltd* [1986] 1 EGLR 71, where a flat was affected by wet rot and dry rot. There was a history of complaints by tenants of the block and lack of action by the landlord. The landlord's builders, instructed by the management company running the building for the landlord, did work which covered up the defects but did not cure them. The builder had been given instructions to do work to flat C 'to bring it up to a very good standard for the purpose of selling'. The plaintiffs bought the flat, but their survey failed to discover the dry rot. It was held that the builder's work had been fraudulently done (to disguise the problem), and that the landlords were liable for the default of their own agents. The tenants refused to pay the service charge because of the dispute. The court held that as the landlord was not doing the works he was supposed to do, the lease provision that his obligation was 'subject to the payment by the lessee of the maintenance contribution' did not enable him to avoid his liability. The court considered the landlord's defence based on the condition precedent was 'without substance'. In this case the land-lords and the management company both acted in a highhanded manner, ignor-ing their responsibilities, and the court had no sympathy for them. Because of the state of the building there had been local authority notices requiring works to be done, etc, which the landlord had not complied with. The courts seem to dislike conditions precedent and will construe them against the landlord where it can. For example, in *Yorkbrook Investments Ltd v Batten* [1985] 2 EGLR 100(see also at **5.132**), the Court of Appeal considered the lease of a flat in Chiswick Village. The relevant clause commenced 'the Lessor hereby further covenants with the Lessee that subject to the Lessee paying the Maintenance Contribution pursuant to the obligations under clause 4 hereof the Lessor will ...'. After dis-cussing the lease and the principles the court said: 'in our judgment it is abun-dantly clear that the parties to this deed did not intend that the words at the beginning of clause 6 should be a condition precedent.' The judgment seems to be based partly on the fact that the obligation of the tenant to pay the mainte-nance contribution was included in clause 4, and the obligations of the landlord to carry out the services were in clause 6. The court considered that the mainte-nance contribution covered matters in addition to those set out in clause 6, 'and therefore ... the covenant by the landlords forms only part of the consideration for which the tenant is making payment under the maintenance contribution'. This seems a surprising decision in view of the express words of the clause, but it is recorded here as a Court of Appeal decision showing a dislike by courts of a landlord being able to escape liability on a technicality. The court also said that 'the lease should be construed contra proferentum', ie against the landlord who sought to rely on it. It may be that at some time there will be an objection to such a provision on the basis that such a provision is not a fair provision. This could be something that might be subject to challenge under European regulations as being unfair, one day, at least for non-commercial properties.

6.41   The *Yorkbrook* case was discussed in useful detail in *Bluestorm Ltd v Portvale Holdings Ltd* [2004] HLR 939, [2004] 2 EGLR 38. The defaulting tenants of a block of flats on the seafront in Brighton had acted very badly. The defaulters held about 35 flats and the others about 22. A subsidiary of the default-ers had formerly been the landlord, but when they were sued for breach of repair-ing covenants the company was wound up, leaving the property with no landlord. After a time, a company (Bluestorm) was found by tenants of the other flats to take over the freehold. The defaulters not only refused to pay service charges on the basis of non-repair, but, when sued, counter-claimed for damage to their interest caused by the lack of repair (which had been started originally by their subsidiary). The dispute came to the Court of Appeal, following Leasehold Valuation Tribunal and county court decisions in favour of the (new) landlord. On the main claim, the tenant's claim to set-off would have been an equitable claim, and the actions of the tenant were such that equity should not be exercised in their favour. The other point in the case, which did not need to be decided, related to the clause saying that the provision of the services was 'subject to the receipt by the Lessor of the Maintenance Contribution'. *Yorkbrook* had held a similar provision not to be a condition precedent. While not needing to decide the point the Court of Appeal judges all discussed it. The first judge (Buxton LJ) said:

> 'I think it may well be an acceptable approach to … say that it deprives the non-payer of the right to complain of the landlord's breach when there is a direct connection between the non-payment and the breach. Thus some, but not all, and probably not very many, defaults in payment would disqualify action by the tenant. Applying that view of it, the single tenant with a genuine grievance in Yorkbrook would not be disqualified. On the other hand, a tenant such as Portvale, refusing to pay for the reasons it did, would be.'

Maurice Kay LJ preferred not to address the *Yorkbrook* issue, which had stood for 20 years. The third judge, Sir Martin Nourse, said the purpose of the words 'subject to receipt' etc were to link the landlord's obligation to carry out services with the tenant's obligation to pay. He also said 'It may be – I express no view – that the lessor would not be able to disclaim liability under its obligation where a tenant was substantially in arrears with its maintenance contribution, but nevertheless accepted its obligation to pay it. That is not this case'. The line of argument in *Bluestorm* is very attractive. In effect, but without deciding the point, the judges suggest that wording linking performance of the landlord's obligations to the tenant's obligation to pay service charges is what one might call a 'qualified condition precedent', ie it is probably unenforceable against someone disputing the basis of liability to pay, but enforceable against a tenant who is simply unable to pay but accepts that the sum is payable.

6.42   A condition precedent was held valid against the landlord in *Northways Flats Management Co (Camden) Ltd v Wimpey Pension Trustees Ltd* [1992] 2 EGLR 42, where the covenant for payment of the service charge was qualified by the phrase 'Provided that in respect of major or substantial repairs the landlord shall before carrying out such works submit a copy of the specification of works and estimates obtained upon such specification to the tenant for consideration and if the tenant shall not have raised any objection thereto within 21 days of the same having been served upon the tenant the tenant shall be deemed to have accepted the specification and estimates as reasonable.' The landlord had carried out major works and sought £36,700 from the tenant, but failed because it had not served specifications and estimates before carrying out the works, in accordance with the terms of its own lease. A similar case is *CIN Properties Ltd v Barclays Bank plc* [1986] 1 EGLR 59, where the amount the landlords failed to recover was £166,254.

6.43   The above indicates that the courts dislike conditions precedent imposed on a tenant by a landlord, although the tenant will be given the benefit of a condition precedent which the landlord has imposed on himself.

PART 6 – SET-OFF

6.44   The general tenor of interpretation of set-off provisions is that a court will allow a tenant to set off against the landlord any sum that the landlord owes to the tenant wherever it can. Even the common provision that the tenant must pay rent etc to the landlord 'without any deduction' may be considered unenforceable if it is considered to be an attempt to oust the jurisdiction of the court. (*British Anzani (Felixstowe) Ltd v International Marine Management (UK) Ltd* [1980] QB 137; see also *Connaught Restaurants Ltd v Indoor Leisure Ltd* [1994] 4 All ER 834.) Set-off is discussed further in Chapter 15. (See also the *Bluestorm* case at **6.41**.)

PART 7 – WHERE THE LEASE ANTICIPATED CHANGES IN THE LAW

6.45   The decision of the Court of Appeal in *Investment & Freehold English Estates Ltd v Casement* [1987] 2 EGLR 112 revolved around unusual provisions in the lease of a flat in a block in Kensington Park Gardens. Because of what was (incorrectly) thought to be a prohibition on charging premiums for assignment of leases where the rent exceeded two thirds of the rateable value, the lease contained a special provision. It was that the ground rent and service charge 'will in no event exceed two-thirds of the rateable value of the premises'. That was not an unusual provision at the time, but the clause went on to say that if the rent and service charge were likely to exceed that figure 'the lessor shall not be under any obligation to carry out any work or perform any duties notwithstanding his covenant which would impose upon him a liability in excess'. The lease also said that if the Leasehold Reform Act 1967 was amended or there was a court decision that service charges were not included within the expression 'rent' for the purposes of calculating the rateable value limits then the proviso mentioned above would be of no effect, and the landlord was entitled to claim the full service charge, even if that brought the rent and service charge over the two-thirds limit. The original statutory provision (Leasehold Reform Act 1967, s 39) had included service charges within the definition of rent for calculating the limit. This was later varied (by s 80 of the Housing Act 1969) by removing service charges from the calculation. The lease had been executed after the amendment in the 1969 Act came into force, although the parties to the lease appeared to be unaware of this. There was doubt whether the landlord was entitled to claim the full amount of the service charge where the total was over the two-thirds limit. The Court of Appeal held that the landlord could claim the whole sum: the parties had contemplated what would happen if the law was changed, having been unaware that a change was already in being.

PART 8 – SUNDAY TRADING

6.46   This is a topic that (currently) only affects retail premises, although some of the principles are analogous to those of offices let under leases that refer to normal business hours.

6.47   Under the Sunday Trading Act 1994, the former restrictions on shops opening on Sundays in the Shops Act 1950 were replaced. Large shops can now open on Sundays for up to six hours and small shops all day. For individual shops, or for shops in a precinct where all the shops open (or all close) on Sundays, there is no service charge problem. Where some open and some do not there can be difficulty in apportioning the costs associated with the opening among the tenants, at least for leases existing before the Act came into force. In many cases the larger shops can open as they have sufficient staff, but small shops find it hard as they may well have to employ extra staff to work on Sundays and they may prefer to stay closed. However, many shops do now open, not only on Sundays but often for much longer hours than formerly. The old system, with shops opening from 9.00 am to 5.30 pm from Monday to Saturday and with early closing on Wednesday, seems a distant memory.

6.48   Under the 1994 Act 'keep open' clauses, requiring the tenant to trade during the normal trading hours of the centre, are not to be regarded as requiring the tenant to open on a Sunday. In other words, even if there is a 'keep open' clause and the landlord and/or tenants decide to open on Sundays, this will not oblige an individual tenant to open on Sundays if he chooses not to.

6.49   When landlords address the point they can adopt one of two approaches:

(a)   Charging only those tenants who open with the total cost of the Sunday opening (divided between them on an apportioned basis).

(b)   Charging the Sunday opening costs among all the tenants in the same way as other costs, regardless of whether the individual tenant opens or not. Landlords might adopt this procedure where a tenants' association has voted in favour of Sunday opening, thus exercising a modicum of democracy.

6.50   The additional costs of opening tend to relate to cleaning, security and electrical costs for lighting, heating, as well as extra wear and tear on lifts, automatic doors etc. Security (and other staff) may well need to attend and will cost more at the weekend, and this needs to be reflected in assessing the total cost.

6.51   There are other management problems arising from Sunday trading. Perhaps the most significant is that where a centre is busy on Sundays the landlord is prevented from using that day for carrying out noisy or disruptive works. They have to be scheduled for other times, perhaps at night, and this can cause great problems for some properties, for example those in a residential area, or where there are flats above the shops. It can also affect the cost. There will also be more management work liaising with tenants to ensure that the work is carried out in the least disruptive way.

6.52   Where the centre has a sinking fund it may need to be taken into account that Sunday trading is likely to increase the wear and tear on such items as lifts and escalators and automatic doors. If all the tenants contribute to both Sunday opening costs and the sinking fund, it may be thought unfair to require those tenants who do not open up on Sundays to contribute fully to a sinking fund for items that are deteriorating more rapidly as a result of use by people who are not that tenant's customers. Obviously, a mechanism to adjust the contributions to reflect this could be worked out, but sinking fund calculations are difficult enough without such refinements. A tenant (particularly a tenant of a very small unit in a big centre) may wish to seek some concession or limited waiver in respect of the sinking fund aspects.

PART 9 – CHANGES TO THE ACCOUNTING YEAR

6.53   Tenants negotiating leases are sometimes concerned by the provision entitling a landlord to change the date for commencement of the service charge year. It is mentioned here simply to say that, apart from rare circumstances indicated below, the tenant is unlikely to be prejudiced by this provision.

6.54   Most landlords have an accounting year for tax purposes which could start on any date in the calendar. It is not uncommon for a landlord to want to have the service charge year the same as the tax year for his business. This can save apportionments of income and outgoings for his tax returns. If such a landlord acquires the reversion after the leases were granted he might well want to change the service charge year. Again, some landlords like to have the service charge year starting on a day on which service charge is due (eg one of the usual quarter days). This also saves apportionments of receipts from tenants in one year where the payment out is in another. The payment date is the best date for the start of an accounting year in the author's view. Other people like the last day of a period for payment, ie the day before the quarter day.

6.55   The change of landlord, or a change by the landlord of his own tax year, is fairly infrequent, and so the tenant will be unlucky if the service charge accounting year is changed at all.

6.56   The risk to a tenant is only where he has a fraudulent landlord or one who uses a change of accounting year to gain some advantage. There seem to be two risks, one minor and the other serious:

(a)   The landlord may change the accounting year so as to bring some particular expenditure in one year rather than another so that he can gain some tax or other advantage, perhaps being able to claim against a more substantial tenant if a lease has been assigned, or for capital allowance purposes.

(b)   A fraudulent landlord might seek to change the accounting year to enable him to collect a larger amount from the tenants in one year prior to disappearing with the money.

Landlord's tax advantage

6.57   A change to give the landlord a greater tax benefit is not a major problem for a tenant. The situation where this might arise would, perhaps, be where the accounting year is changed so that capital allowances can be claimed in one year where a landlord has a larger profit against which the allowances can be set. Such a case would not arise often, and provided that the tenant is not obliged to pay more frequently than before (eg his quarterly payments should continue) it is hard to see that the tenant suffers. If a tenant considers such changes might adversely affect his cash flow, which could happen if the service charges are suddenly heavier than the tenant had budgeted for, the remedy is for the lease to say that the financial year shall not be changed more than once in, say, any period of three years. Another alternative would be to provide that the accounting period can be changed at any time but not so that any accounting year exceeds, say, 15 months, or is less than nine months. These suggested revisions restrict the frequency of change and aid the tenant in budgeting. A landlord who really wants to change the year for tax purposes can do so but, depending on the change, might have to take two or three years to do so (eg changing from January to 24 June). For residential service charges, s 21(9) and (10) of the Landlord and Tenant Act 1985 (inserted by s 152 of the Commonhold and Leasehold Reform Act 2002) has the effect that an accounting period cannot be greater than 12 months.

The fraudulent landlord

6.58   Where a landlord changes the year to entitle him to a larger figure which he can steal the position is obviously much more serious, but the change of year end is likely to be the least of the tenant's problems. Residential tenancy service charge payments are already held on trust and may need to be in a designated account (Landlord and Tenant Act 1987, ss 42 and 42A), but this will not prevent the determined fraudster from running off with the money. The only remedy the tenant has in such a case is to ensure that the service charge contributions are paid to a third party (eg the managing agents) on behalf of the landlord. There is also the risk of the managing agents being fraudulent, but this is very rare and if the fraudulent agents are members of the RICS or other reputable body the tenants may have recourse to an indemnity scheme set up by these bodies. The difficulty in agreeing a provision of this nature is that a landlord (whether fraudulent or not) will be unwilling to agree to the payments being made to named agents, as this will commit him to use those agents for the whole of the term. In the case of a 99-year lease the agents might not still be subsisting, and even for shorter leases the landlord may prefer to keep his options open to change agents for financial or other reasons. A recognised tenants' association has a right to make representations about managing agents for residential property (Landlord and Tenant Act 1985, s 30B). In due course, service charges for dwellings may have to be held in a designated account, when s 42A of the Landlord and Tenant Act 1987 is brought into force (see at **9.260** below). The original proposal requires a bank to be notified that the account holds (only) money relating to the service charge for a particular property. However, there is no statutory obligation on the bank to check payments out, and it is difficult to see how there could be. Save only, perhaps, in the case of a cheque in favour of the landlord closing the account, one cannot see any onus on the bank to query any payment. There are, of course, times when a payment is made to the landlord himself legitimately – for example to repay sums he has paid out. Accordingly, although the money is to be held in a designated account, the protection against fraud seems slender.

6.59 The tenant's answer to being suspicious that his landlord may be fraudulent is to be vigilant and to take action for breach of covenant sooner rather than later. The tenant's remedy of set-off (when available), under which the tenant holds back payments due to the landlord against amounts which the landlord could be responsible for by breach of covenant, is perhaps even more effective – if no payment is made the landlord cannot run off with it.

PART 10 – RESERVING THE SERVICE CHARGE AS RENT

6.60 In many leases service charges are reserved as rent. This sometimes appears in the service charge schedule and sometimes in the reddendum (ie the part of the lease referring to payment of rent). The service charge has similarities to rent, being a regular payment by the tenant to the landlord in respect of the use of the premises. (The two are compared in Chapter 8.) It seems hard, accordingly, to see why it should not be treated in the same way as rent. To do so it may need to be reserved as rent, although in 1995 the Court of Appeal in *Sinclair Gardens Investments (Kensington) Ltd v Walsh* [1996] QB 231 held that a provision in the lease that the service charge was to be deemed to be additional rent was sufficient for this purpose, even when not expressed to be reserved as rent. (The report was in respect of four appeals and the decision has also been reported under the name *Escalus Properties Ltd v Robinson* [1996] QB 231.)

6.61 There are three benefits to a landlord of commercial property who reserves service charge as rent:

(a) where there are arrears the landlord of non-residential premises can distrain, ie send in certificated bailiffs without a court order; and

(b) the landlord does not need to serve a notice under s 146 of the Law of Property Act 1925 before being able to forfeit the lease on grounds of non-payment of rent; and

(c) where the service charge is reserved as rent the effect may be to entitle the landlord to retain interest on the late payments (see at **6.15** above).

See **6.63** below regarding residential premises.

6.62   The fact that the service charge is reserved as rent does not automatically entitle the tenant to the benefit of the rent suspension, or rent cesser, clause. (See at **8.16** et seq.)

The effect on distraint

6.63   A landlord can only distrain for items which are 'rent'. Therefore, to be able to apply this remedy to the service charge the landlord must reserve the service charge as rent in the lease. The ability to distrain is qualified by three factors:

(a)   The landlord of residential premises can never lawfully distrain for service charge arrears because s 42 of the Landlord and Tenant Act 1987 states that all service charge payments by tenants are to be held on trust: the receipt can therefore never be rent. Apart from this, the landlord of property subject to regulated and assured tenancies, which include assured shorthold tenancies, cannot distrain without the consent of the court. (Rent Act 1977, s 147 and Housing Act 1988, s 19.)

(b)   Distraint for service charges is unlawful where there is a dispute between landlord and tenant over the service charges. (*Concorde Graphics Ltd v Andromeda Investments SA* [1983] 1 EGLR 53.)

(c)   Distraint to recover arrears owing by a former tenant is unlawful. (*Wharfland Ltd v South London Co-operative Building Co Ltd* [1995] 2 EGLR 21.)

6.64   In the *Concorde* case, cited at **4.85**, the court said:

> 'it is clear that when the amount of the service charge properly payable by the tenant has been agreed or otherwise ascertained (that is when both the due proportion of the costs, charges and expenses incurred by the landlord and properly chargeable to the tenant and the amount of those costs, charges and expenses have been agreed or otherwise finally ascertained) the amount chargeable to the tenant will be "recoverable as rent in arrear" and will then properly be the subject matter of distraint …it is to my mind equally clear that neither the due proportion of these costs, charges and expenses nor the amount of the costs charges and expenses have been either agreed or finally ascertained and that the landlord is not entitled to distrain for the amount now in dispute.'

The landlord's managing agents had distrained after a dispute which they had endeavoured to resolve by certifying (under the provisions of the lease) that the amount in question was due: the court held that the certificate by them (as agents for the landlord) was not 'final and binding' on the tenants and thus the amount was still in dispute, despite the certificate.

6.65   The right to distrain is therefore limited in its effect, but could be of use, in the case of commercial premises, where the amount is not disputed but the tenants are slow to pay. Distraint is much quicker and can be more effective than court proceedings in many cases. There are moves afoot to make distraint less helpful to landlord, with, for example a requirement for the tenant to be given a few days' notice of the intention to distrain, which many commentators consider will draw the teeth from this ancient remedy.

The section 146 notice and forfeiture

6.66   Reserving service charges as rent for non-residential premises can speed up the landlord's recovery process by avoiding the need for serving a notice under s 146 of the Law of Property Act 1925 before forfeiting a lease. However, a landlord is not entitled to forfeit a lease for breach of any covenant other than non-payment of rent without serving a s 146 notice (s 146(11)). (See at **9.288** et seq for residential aspects.)

6.67   The s 146 notice needed for breaches of covenant other than non-payment of rent has to set out details of the breach, require the breach to be remedied, and also requires the tenant to pay compensation to the landlord. In addition the tenant has to be given 'a reasonable time' (s 146(1)) in which to remedy the breach. Service charges are, in the lease, usually due on specified days. If forfeiture is under consideration clearly the tenant must be already in breach. If the payment provisions, or the proviso for forfeiture, permit the tenant to have 14 days' or 28 days' grace after the due date before forfeiture can commence it is galling for a landlord to have to serve yet another notice before he can forfeit for a breach. In a case where the breach is non-payment of rent (or of service charges reserved as rent) for commercial property, the landlord can at least avoid the delay (and expense) entailed in having to serve a notice giving the defaulting tenant yet further time.

Conclusion

6.68   There seems no good reason why a landlord should not reserve the service charge as rent. There are cases where it does not help a landlord (where the premises are residential or where there is a dispute so that the landlord cannot distrain) but in other cases it assists, notably, where distress can be properly used, and saving time before forfeiture can be implemented. Since the tenant can rely for help on the points above relating to distraint, and there seems no good reason why forfeiture should be delayed by a notice period when a tenant is slow to pay, it would be unreasonable for a tenant of commercial premises to object to the service charge being reserved as rent.

PART 11 – DISPUTES ARRANGEMENTS

6.69   For residential properties no provision for settling disputes other than through a Leasehold Valuation Tribunal, a court, or by arbitration is valid.

(Section 27A(6) of the Landlord and Tenant Act 1985.) For other properties there are various possibilities. This section of this chapter highlights the normal schemes for dispute.

Application to court or Leasehold Valuation Tribunal

6.70   Either party can apply to the court to seek guidance on general construction of a point at issue. There is specific power for either party to the tenancy of a dwelling to apply to the Leasehold Valuation Tribunal for a declaration on reasonableness in s 19 of the 1985 Act. The application to the Leasehold Valuation Tribunal can be made either by a tenant after he receives a demand, or by a landlord after sending a demand or, in advance, for a declaration that what the landlord proposes to do is reasonable and that the cost of that work is reasonable. If either landlord or tenant issues proceedings the court will adjudicate, but has power to refer disputes affecting service charges for dwellings to a Leasehold Valuation Tribunal. (Commonhold and Leasehold Reform Act 2002, Sch 12, para 3.) For commercial property, the usual route for disputes is through the courts or arbitration or alternative dispute resolution.

Arbitration

6.71   Leases often contain arbitration provisions. These can be either in general terms, or, for this book, can be specific provisions permitting service charge disputes to be referred to arbitration. Service charge disputes for dwellings will be ineffective: the only form of arbitration is a 'post-dispute arbitration', ie an arbitration agreement made 'after a dispute about the matter has arisen'. (Landlord and Tenant Act 1985, s 27A(6) and Commonhold and Leasehold Reform Act 2002, s 155(2).)

6.72   Most arbitration clauses provide for the arbitrator who is to act either to be agreed by the parties when the dispute arises or (if they are unable to agree), then to be appointed by the President for the time being of the Royal Institution of Chartered Surveyors. This is very sensible, for the majority of service charge disputes which tend to revolve around the practical problems dealt with daily by managing agents. Many of the more sophisticated arbitration clauses provide for a reference to the RICS but, if the dispute is over interpretation of the lease rather than other aspects, then the person to appoint the arbitrator could be the President of the Law Society. Some clauses (in leases of large and complicated properties) go further and give alternatives such as reference to bodies covering, for example, building construction or mechanical and electrical works for disputes affecting those aspects.

6.73   The Arbitration Act 1996 now replaces the 1950 and 1979 Acts. Under the 1996 Act the parties can say how they want the arbitration to run. Arbitration can be either by written representations by the parties or by a hearing similar to a court hearing. The arbitrator has power to award costs as he sees fit. It is also usually open to a party against whom proceedings have been issued to apply to the court to stay the proceedings if there is an arbitration provision in the lease, provided that the application is made promptly. Appeals against arbitration awards are now limited to appeals on a point of law. The court can make orders covering security for costs and matters of evidence etc while the arbitration is proceeding. Once the award is made, it can be enforced through the courts. This is mentioned because, apart from ensuring that the arbitration provisions refer clearly to arbitration (see eg *Fordgate Bingley Ltd v Argyll Stores Ltd* [1994] 2 EGLR 84, where there were three references in the lease in different terms which were, or could have been, references to arbitration under the Arbitration Acts) and who is to make the appointment, there is little need for the draftsman to go into detail about the arbitration unless particular matters (such as timing of written representations) are of particular concern to the parties negotiating the lease. Provisions as to who is entitled to appoint the arbitrator and as to fresh appointments if the appointed arbitrator dies or fails to act are helpful. It is good practice to require that the arbitrator is a person experienced in dealing similar properties (or similar properties in the same area), although this needs careful consideration if the premises are unusual, as there may not be anyone who could fit the description.

6.74   Arbitration was set up as an attempt to find a quicker and cheaper alternative to the courts. It is probably quicker than the courts in many cases, but it may not be much cheaper. The courts have increased the jurisdiction of the county courts to keep legal costs lower than if cases were heard in the high court, but with more cases to be heard in the county court it is doubtful whether the courts are quicker than arbitration. If they choose arbitration, the parties can set their own procedure, within limits, to save time and costs. Another advantage (to some) is that arbitrations are private, whereas court proceedings are public, with limited exceptions.

6.75   Parties could agree in the lease that arbitrations shall be run in a particular way, but one may doubt the wisdom of trying to anticipate what type of dispute might arise, other than providing for disputes on particular aspects to be referred to an expert rather than an arbitrator (as in **6.78** below).

6.76   Arbitration clauses often provide for the arbitration procedure to start within a specified period, for example within two months of the tenant receiving the accounts. There is limited power in the Arbitration Act 1996 to apply to the court for an order permitting the arbitration to take place despite being out of time.

Expert

6.77   Analogous to appointing an arbitrator is a lease provision for disputes to be resolved by an expert. Such a provision would not be valid for residential property. (Section 27(A)(6) of the Landlord and Tenant Act 1985, and **6.71** above.) Frequently, the provisions are similar to arbitration provisions (eg who should make the appointment, power to seek a substitute if the appointee dies, etc), but they usually provide that the expert shall give his decision as an expert rather than as an arbitrator.

6.78   There are several consequences of the appointment of an expert. An arbitrator must have regard only to the submissions put to him by the parties: by contrast an expert is entitled to use his own (expert) knowledge and experience in coming to his decision. For that reason, the expert's qualifications ('not less than ten years' experience in the management of similar types of property') should always be mentioned: it is after all more important where the parties will have to rely on the expert's expertise. Leases sometimes set out a procedure requiring the parties to make submissions (sometimes within a timescale) and for the making of counter representations where an expert is appointed. If the parties think it desirable for the expert to be able to direct how the costs of the reference to him are to be paid the lease should say so, because the Arbitration Act power for the arbitrator to award costs does not apply to the expert.

Arbitrator and expert compared

6.79   There are differing viewpoints within the legal profession as to whether (or when) to provide for an expert and when to require an arbitrator. Some think an expert can be more helpful than an arbitrator where the premises are unusual (eg particularly large, or constructed of unusual materials, or in a unique setting). It is also thought by some that an arbitrator may be better for a landlord because the landlord has all the information about the whole development readily to hand and is thus able to put forward a more complete detailed submission to the arbitrator. (This aspect is more significant for rent review than service charges.) The advantages of control over the manner in which the dispute is decided, and as to privacy, apply to both systems. Another factor can be that it is possible to appeal to the courts against the decision of an arbitrator (on a point of law) but it is harder to appeal against an expert's decision. As an expert is not covered by the Arbitration Act in the absence of fraud his decision is virtually impossible to appeal, unless it can be demonstrated that the expert did not decide the point he was asked to decide (ie he did not follow his instructions). (See eg *Nikko Hotels (UK) Ltd v MEPC plc* [1991] 2 EGLR 103.)

Landlord's surveyor's decision

6.80   Provisions entitling the landlord's surveyor to certify matters relating to the service charge have been commented on in detail at **4.78** et seq. The two main points to reiterate are:

(a)   the courts will not be prepared to accept a valid certificate from a landlord's surveyor who is not independent of the landlord (see eg *Finchbourne Ltd v Rodrigues* [1976] 3 All ER 581, and *Concorde Graphics Ltd v Andromeda Investments SA* [1983] 1 EGLR 53); and

(b)   s 27(A)(6) of the Landlord and Tenant Act 1985 makes any such reference ineffective for residential property.

Alternative Dispute Resolution

6.81   In recent years the legal profession has tried to encourage the use of Alternative Dispute Resolution ('ADR'). The courts now require parties to state, at a very early stage, whether they have considered ADR.

6.82   The expression covers many types of procedures and can have advantages of time and costs over arbitration or court procedures. One simple form is for the landlord and tenant to agree that any dispute can be determined either by a named individual (rare, and subject to problems if the named person is not available or not willing to act) or by a particular type of person, such as a surveyor or a solicitor, with a minimum amount of experience in the field. This is, in effect, the reference to an expert mentioned above. If the parties agree to ADR it can be the quickest and cheapest form of dispute resolution, and has the advantage of privacy. (Courts are at least in theory open to the public and cases may appear in law reports.) To ensure that a party can have his case fully heard, however, this scheme should only be available provided both parties agree, so that for major disputes a party has a right to apply to the court.

6.83   ADR appears in other forms including mediation, conciliation and even mini-trials. Some of these may be of help in some service charge disputes, but it seems best to consider whether ADR is appropriate when a dispute arises, rather than impose it in the lease. Much depends on the nature of the dispute and the inclination of the parties at the time of the dispute to want to settle their differences. If it is unlikely that one or other party will 'listen to reason', ADR is probably not suitable except in cases where both parties agree in advance to be bound by the outcome. (This is not universal in ADR matters.) If they do not, then ADR could be an expensive and delaying step. If both parties do not agree to be bound then, despite the effort put into the ADR procedure, the dispute may later have to be taken to court for resolution. This would duplicate the effort and costs and would delay an outcome. An ADR decision/agreement can be enforced through the courts if it is embodied in a court order.

6.84   Some disputes may be more suitable for ADR than others. Unfortunately, the parties do not know in advance what will be the nature of the dispute. Accordingly, it seems unsatisfactory simply to provide that disputes must be settled by ADR in all cases. Where a dispute arises it should certainly be considered.

Summary

6.85   It is not essential for a lease to include provisions about resolution of service charge disputes. There are statutory provisions affecting service charges for dwellings, and for commercial property the courts will always be available, as well as other possibilities. As such disputes are sometimes about amounts that do not justify the expense of court proceedings, and as proceedings are often slow, so that the result of the hearing is not known for months or even years, many parties prefer to include some provision for settling disputes in a way that should be cheaper and quicker.

6.86   The usual ways are to include an arbitration provision or to allow disputes to be decided by an expert. If there is an arbitration provision any court action would be stayed, so that the arbitration can proceed.

6.87   The above reflects the considerations when drafting a lease. If a dispute arises the parties can agree to adopt any of the above means to settle the difference, subject (a) to the statutory requirements for dwellings and (b) the ability of a court to stay court proceedings if there is a valid arbitration provision.

6.88   Since this chapter was written the new Commercial Code (see Chapter 11) has been issued. The RICS, who led discussions leading to the new Code, recommend the use of the RICS dispute resolution facilities.

PART 12 – TAXATION COMMENTS BY STEVE HASSON

6.89   Whilst tax matters are rarely straightforward, in the area of services charges there is, at least, some area of common interest between the tax objectives of the landlord and the tenant. Both parties will want certainty of tax treatment, the minimum tax cost and straightforward compliance.

6.90   It is important to recognise that there are no unique tax provisions as far as services charges are concerned. The tax treatment will be entirely dependent upon the provisions of the individual lease other than in situations – most notably s 42 of the Landlord and Tenant Act 1987, where the law operates to impose a statutory treatment. Precision in the drafting of the lease provisions is therefore essential if the objective of certainty of tax treatment is to be achieved. However, as we will see, the tax authorities will often choose to ignore precise drafting in favour of simplicity. Whilst in many cases this is very welcome, it is, of course, not something which can be relied upon for the future.

6.91   Despite the areas of common interest as far as landlord and tenant are concerned, there are some differences and therefore we will consider the position landlord both from the point of view of direct (income or corporation taxes) and indirect (primarily VAT). The tax treatment of sinking funds is rather more complex and this is dealt with in the taxation section of Chapter 7.

Landlord – taxation of income

6.92   The correct tax treatment of the receipt of service charges should follow the provisions of the lease. In practice, HMRC may not enquire deeply into the precise wordings and may follow historic precedent or the industry practice of treating almost all service charges received as additional rental income.

6.93   In fact, there are a number of possibilities from the point of view of services charges received directly by the landlord. It may very well be that service charge income is reserved as additional rent, but in other circumstances it may be that the income is received as a result of a covenant to reimburse the landlord for appropriate expenditure. As noted above, reserving the service charge as additional rent has some potential advantages and this is certainly the case for taxation. Unsurprisingly, service charges treated as additional rent will be taxed in the same way as the rental income (either liable to corporation tax or in the case of an individual income tax). The landlord will then be able to deduct actual expenditure allowable under the relevant provisions. For routine annual expenditures subject to the occasional non deductible item, this should provide a perfectly satisfactory arrangement where the service charge is taxed in exactly the same way as the rental income and the landlord can obtain deductions for tax purposes for expenditure.

6.94   The potential difficulty here is when a sinking fund is required, as the symmetry of the income and expenditure may be denied. This is considered in more detail in Chapter 7.

6.95   Technically, there is a good tax argument that where income is received under a covenant to reimburse, it should not be taxed in the same way as rent. It is very unusual for this point to be taken and HMRC will normally tax all service charge income in the same manner as rent. The effect of the technical tax argument is that, where there is a reimbursement under covenant, the income might attract a less flexible tax arrangement as it would fall into a special category of income, taxable under Schedule D Case VI, which would limit loss offsets and the carry back of any tax loss. Although the risks may be remote, it nonetheless represents another good reason to reserve the service charge as rent.

Management companies

6.96   In some cases the service charge is, of course, paid to a management company rather than direct to the landlord. Whilst this arrangement is very common in respect of residential property, it is somewhat more unusual for commercial buildings. A separate management company nonetheless can represent an elegant solution to some of the tax issues which arise. The management company would be carrying on a trade of providing property services. However, provided the company can be set up so as to be viewed by HMRC as a being a 'mutual trader', any profit on the activity of providing services would not be taxed. Whilst we are not usually expecting large amounts of profit to arise in relation to the provision of management services, the use of a mutual company will avoid the mismatch between surpluses and deficits in a particular year. This is, of course, exactly the position where, in order to smooth expenditures, a reserve fund has been established. Reserve funds are dealt with in Chapter 7. The point here is that, where a reserve fund is set up to smooth costs over a few years, there may be a mismatch of income of expenditure for tax purposes. The result of income arising in advance of allowable expenditure would be for that surplus to be taxed. The mutual trading concept may avoid this issue. Under the mutual trading provisions, the surplus in any year would be free from tax. Mutual trading can be established where a member makes a contribution to a common fund in which he and his co-members are interested. In order to demonstrate the common interest and, crucially, the division of assets on a winding up, it is very common for each tenant to hold a share in the company. It should be noted that the concept of mutuality does not extend to investment income whereas typically interest received which remains taxable.

6.97   The position of residential flat management companies is, unfortunately, rather more complex as, technically, they are unlikely to fall within the mutual trading arrangements, for example where they are entitled to ground rents. As from a taxation point of view there is little or no tax at stake, HMRC have wherever possible adopted a pragmatic view and will often accept by concession that no tax is payable by owner controlled flat management companies where over a period (often five years) income and expenditure where broadly matched. As the position of flat management companies has become more complex by virtue of the provisions of s 42 of the Landlord and Tenants Act 1987, which require that service charge moneys received in relation to most residential property are to be held on trust, HMRC has issued guidance in the form of Tax Bulletins Nos 37 and 48. These deal primarily with the position as far as sinking funds are concerned and this is addressed in Chapter 7 below.

The tenant

6.98   The position of the business tenant obtaining a tax deduction for service charge payments should be relatively straightforward. Certainly, if the service charge is reserved as additional rent or reimbursed under covenant, the payment will be deductible under normal tax principles. If the payment is to a management company, notwithstanding the possible mutual trading arrangements, it seems clear that the service charge should be a deductible expense.

6.99   The position of payments into a sinking fund which is established as a trust is rather more complex. There is a possible argument that sinking fund payments may be capital in nature and could be denied a deduction. Again, this is dealt with further in Chapter 7 below.

The landlord – indirect taxes

6.100   As far as value added tax is concerned, as with income tax, the technical position is that the VAT treatment will depend upon the provisions of the lease. However, in practice HMRC's policy – and this is set out in VAT Notice 742 – is to apply the same VAT status to service charges as to rent regardless of how it is described in the lease. It should be noted that this is a concessionary treatment and if you are seeking to rely on this you should ensure that the service charge comes within the terms of the VAT Notice broadly that the charge is 'connected with the external fabric or the common parts of the building or estate as opposed to the demised areas of the property of the individual occupants' and that is paid for by all the occupiers through a service charge.

6.101   The practical effect on these concessions is that the VAT treatment for service charges will be the same as the lease – exempt if the option to tax has not been exercise and standard rated if it has. This is because service charges are viewed as additional consideration for the right to occupy. The consideration of the option to tax is beyond the scope of this book.

6.102   Nonetheless, there are a number of VAT pitfalls to consider and a landlord would be well advised to consider both the VAT treatment of the services he is planning to provide and the effect on prospective tenants.

6.103   The experienced practitioner will have noted that the terms of the HMRC concession may create a difficulty where services are supplied to the demised area occupied by the tenant, such as office cleaning. This means that if services are supplied to the tenants' individual premises, HMRC regard that part of the service charge as a separate supply from the accommodation, with the result that VAT needs to be added to that part of the service charge except to the extent that it relates to zero rated items such as energy where the benefit of the zero rating may be passed on to the tenant.

6.104   The areas of apportionment and composite supplies are notoriously difficult for VAT and specific advice must be sought in this area.

6.105   Perversely, the practice of HMRC in relation to services offices is rather different and, typically, whilst the office might come with the shared used of business centre staff, the current HMRC approach is to treat this as a straightforward lease. Whilst this may not be a particular issue for the landlord, it could result in the loss of the right to recover input tax as far as the tenants are concerned.

6.106   The overall effect of this is that there is a clear tension in the VAT treatment of buildings for which the option to tax has not been exercised and the drafting principles we have outlined for service charges more generally. In order to create a separate supply on which the tenant can recover the VAT charged (assuming the tenants are VAT registered traders who can reclaim input tax), it might be desirable to make the service charges entirely separate from the rent. However, as we have already seen, there are many benefits in relation to the collection of service charges to provide that it is indeed additional rent.

6.107   Service charges supplied by a third party, such as a management company, will always be standard rated because they are not supplied with the right to occupy land.

Tenant – indirect taxes

6.108   One must assume that any tenant has given careful consideration to their own VAT position in relation to the primary lease and whether or not the option to tax has been exercised in respect of this building. Clearly, the VAT on the rent will be a much more significant consideration than the VAT position of service charges. Nonetheless, as service charges increase, the landlord may be faced with a tenant increasingly focusing on the irrecoverable VAT. It is clearly commercially desirable that the landlord seeks to minimise this 'tax leakage' as much as possible. The point here is that where a landlord incurs VAT on costs associated with the provision of services which are then bundled with rent (where that rent is exempt), the tenant may incur a higher cost than if they had contracted for the services themselves and recovered the VAT.

Indirect taxes – other issues

Managing agents

6.109   Services supplied by managing agents directly to the landlord in managing the property will invariably be standard rated for VAT purposes. Where the managing agent is responsible for providing services directly to the tenant, the VAT treatment will vary according to the terms negotiated. Where, for example, a managing agent is provided with funds by the landlord to pay for services provided to the tenants on their behalf, the VAT incurred on such services is the input tax of the landlord. If, on the other hand, the managing agent acts as the principal, incurring costs and recharging them to the landlord, it will normally be appropriate for the managing agent to recover the VAT on its costs as well as charging VAT on its invoice to the landlord. In practice, most managing agents will have considered their own VAT position.

Interest

6.110   Interest on arrears of rent (and, by implication from the concessions noted above, service charges) is exempt from VAT, whether or not the option to tax has been exercised in respect of the building.

6.111   The only stipulation here is that HMRC requires that the interest charge be shown separately on any invoice.

6.112   As with so much of taxation, the devil is most certainly in the detail. However, the main issues to consider are whether there will be any significant mismatch between income and expenditure (invariably this will happen where a sinking fund is required), and whether the services to be provided create any VAT issues (clearly this is the case with serviced offices, but in many other cases the actual services being provided may create a need to account for VAT separately on services going directly to tenants in their premises).

CHAPTER 7

Sinking funds and reserve funds

The Sinking Fund's unfathomable sea,
That most unliquidating liquid, leaves
The debt unsunk, yet sinks all it receives.

Lord Byron (Don Juan)

PART I – INTRODUCTION

What are sinking funds and reserve funds?

7.1   There is a difference between sinking funds and reserve funds. Accordingly, the manner of calculation of the amount payable by the tenant differs. (See at **7.27** below.)

7.2   A sinking fund, strictly, is a fund set up to enable a major item to be replaced at the end of its life. The most common examples are lifts, generators, boilers, and occasionally roofs. If a lift costs, say, £100,000 to replace and there are ten tenants they would each have to pay £10,000 when the lift needed replacement: if that cost was covered by a sinking fund they might (in simplistic terms) pay £500 a year each for 20 years and there would then be sufficient to replace the lift without a huge one-off payment in the twentieth year.

7.3   By contrast, a reserve fund is one that builds up a cushion so that expense is evened out over a few years. The intention is similar to that of a sinking fund, namely that the tenant does not have to find a much larger sum in one year than in others. The reserve fund is usually of help for such items as external or common parts decoration which the landlord carries out every few years. Without a reserve fund the tenants may have been paying, say, £1,000 per year in most years, but in the year when the landlord's decoration is carried out that figure might increase to £3,000. If the expense is covered by a reserve the tenants might, for example pay £1,500 in each of four years. This would give a total of £6,000, amounting to the same total over the four-year period. Sinking funds for commercial premises are discussed in the Commercial Code (see Chapter 11) at paras 58-63 and Section D6, and sinking funds and reserve funds in the Residential Code, para 10. The confusion between sinking funds and reserve funds is made worse for commonholds where the term 'reserve' is used for what seems to be a sinking fund.

General

7.4   Both methods are like PAYE tax: the major cost is taken in (relatively) small bits and therefore is not so painful as paying one large amount when the tax is due.

7.5   That analogy is fair as far as it goes, but tax relates to the earnings of an individual or company. In the case of leases there can be assignments and sub-lettings, particularly over a long period of years, and the original tenant who signs the lease in year 1 may not be there when the lift is replaced in year 20. That means some annual contributions are paid by parties who do not, apparently, have a direct benefit from part of the contributions (ie the sinking fund part) unlike tax, where the taxpayer gets some benefit (even if he does not like the way the government spends his money).

7.6   For that reason, and the tax reasons indicated below, the sinking funds and reserve funds do not meet with complete approval by either landlords or tenants. In practice, sinking funds are relatively rare in the case of commercial premises, although much more common for residential property. It seems that reserve funds are more common for commercial premises, although often in an informal way. In other words they arise by judicious use of the carry forward provisions of the lease, rather than as a formal arrangement.

Tax problem

7.7   The tax difficulty used to be such that neither landlord nor tenant got full tax credits. This was because in year 1 the tenant pays money to the land-lord, but the money is not spent until year 20. HMRC have sometimes said this is not an allowable expense for the tenant as the money is not spent within the same tax year as the money is paid. So the tenant pays for 20 years and the payments are not treated as an allowable expense until year 20, when the sinking fund is finally used. Conversely, HMRC have sometimes taken the view that as the money is paid to the landlord but not used in the tax year, it is actually simply extra rent and taxed as such. Therefore the landlord is taxed on rent plus the sinking fund receipts, but only has the same outgoings to set against that combined figure. Neither aspect is satisfactory and for this reason landlords have been reluctant to invoke sinking funds except for residential property where (a) the tenants usually cannot use the annual payment as a tax credit, and (b) the need for a sinking fund is greater, as it may well be much more difficult for an individual to find a large capital sum when needed than a business. This may be different with an understanding Inspector of Taxes, and may clearly be easier if the sinking fund is expressed to be held on trust, but the problem can arise.

PART 2 – PRINCIPLES OF SINKING FUNDS AND RESERVE FUNDS

7.8   As a sinking fund is for replacement of worn out items and reserve funds are for keeping expenditure to a fairly even amount over a period the principles, although similar, are not identical. They are dealt with together here because they have similarities and are often treated the same way. Many funds have elements of both.

7.9   Assuming the lease permits the setting up of a reserve fund or a sinking fund, there are a number of matters that the parties need to bear in mind including the benefits of having a fund, tax problems, and ensuring that the fund is not available for the landlord's creditors.

7.10   The first point to make is that the landlord is not automatically entitled to operate a sinking fund or a reserve fund without the authority of the lease. There is authority that the landlord is entitled to include something for depreciation of plant in normal service charge calculations, but this only applies to depreciation, ie a sinking fund, and not to a reserve fund. It merely means that, when calculating what is reasonable for a landlord to charge, the depreciation of an item that needs maintenance must be taken into account: it is not strictly authority for setting up a proper sinking fund. In *Regis Property Co Ltd v Dudley* [1958] 1 QB 346, it was said 'once it is conceded ... that the plant in question is necessary in order to provide the services, some provision for its depreciation or replacement must be included in any computation of the reasonable charge for those services'.

7.11   There is authority to the effect that a landlord cannot require payment in advance unless the lease expressly permits this: *Daiches v Bluelake Investments Ltd* [1985] 2 EGLR 67. This was stated obiter in the case, but has not been disputed and this is entirely consistent with the usual service charge principle that a landlord is not able to call for any payment unless the lease contains a right for him to do so. In the *Daiches* case there was a provision permitting the setting up of a reserve fund (although there was no such fund), but no provision for payment of service charge in advance for normal repairs. (See at **4.3**.)

7.12   *Fluor Daniel Properties Ltd v Shortlands Investments Ltd* [2001] EGCS 8 (and see **5.134** above) shows that a landlord cannot automatically call for replacement of an item of equipment for which a sinking fund has been set up simply because it has reached the end of its estimated life. The air conditioning in that case was not, at the time, in disrepair.

Two major cases

7.13   Sinking funds were the subject of two significant and fairly recent cases to which readers are referred. The first is *Secretary of State for the Environment v Possfund (North West) Ltd* [1997] 2 EGLR 56. The court held that payments to a sinking fund, amounting to one million pounds over the years, for a commercial property were not impliedly held on trust. The payments were effectively an indemnity against the cost actually and irreversibly incurred by the landlord each year by virtue of depreciation of the plant. The effect was that the tenant could not recover the payments it had made towards the depreciation fund for the air conditioning, even though the air conditioning had not been replaced during the term of the lease.

7.14   The Court of Appeal decision in *St Mary's Mansions Ltd v Limegate Investment Co* [2002] EWCA Civ 1491, [2003] 05 EG 146 covered various points relating to a residential block in Maida Vale, London. Among other matters the landlord could recover 'expenses and outgoings' and also 'a sum or sums of money by way of reasonable provision for anticipated expenditure'. The landlord used money in hand, charged to tenants in effect towards future expenses, to assist cashflow for ordinary service charge expenditure. The Court held that the landlord was entitled to apply the 'anticipated' element towards the actual expenditure certified under the lease, and any surplus should be subject to repayment to the tenants at the year end. It was a breach of s 42(2) of the Landlord and Tenant Act 1987 for a landlord to retain money overpaid in respect of one identified expense for other, unidentified, future expense.

PART 3 – SAFETY FROM CREDITORS – TRUSTS

7.15   One reason tenants are unhappy about sinking funds is that they run the risk that they may pay money to build up a fund which might be taken by creditors if the landlord becomes insolvent. It will then not be available for replacement of the item in question. The best way to ensure this does not happen is for the sinking fund/reserve fund to be held on trust for the contributing tenants. In this way the fund is not the landlord's money and, accordingly, not available for his creditors.

7.16   For residential properties all service charge receipts, whether for sinking funds or otherwise, are held on trust automatically under s 42 of the Landlord and Tenant Act 1987. (See below and Chapter 9.)

7.17   In non-residential leases the point can be dealt with by suitable provisions in the lease, setting up the trust. The lease can, although rarely does, cover such matters as who the trustees are, their powers of investment, appointment of new trustees, and the shares in which tenants are entitled to the fund. Normally, of course, although the fund is held for the tenants, because they have paid the money, they are not entitled to call for it. The money is to be held for the replacement of the item in question, and only if the amount paid is too much or the replacement is not necessary, for example the building is destroyed, is there any question of the tenants being entitled to a refund of sums they or their predecessors paid.

7.18   In the 1980s it was held in *Re Chelsea Cloisters Ltd (in liquidation)* (1980) 41 P & CR 98 that the fact contributions were held in a separate bank account would be enough to imply a trust, but even if this may help save the money from the creditors of the landlord it does not assist with assessing the terms of a trust.

7.19   A well-drawn sinking fund provision for commercial premises should ensure the trustee has full powers of management and investment. For residential premises, s 42 of the Landlord and Tenant Act 1987 gives some statutory assistance as to investment. (See Chapter 9.)

7.20   Readers are reminded that if the service charge is held on trust the landlord cannot distrain for arrears of service charge, because trust money cannot validly be reserved as rent.

PART 4 – EFFECT ON INSURANCE CLAIM

7.21   If premises are destroyed the landlord and tenant will look to the building insurance policy for the cost of rebuilding and replacement of the premises. Most leases contain an obligation, usually on the landlord, to rebuild. This point is mentioned here because if there is a sinking fund for replacement of a specific item when a property is destroyed, the insurers may refuse to pay for the item in question under the policy. Insurance is an indemnity against loss, and in such case the landlord has not suffered a loss – he has the money in hand for that very purpose. This unsatisfactory state of affairs, where the tenants have not only paid into the sinking fund but usually have also refunded the insurance premiums and yet do not benefit, can be avoided if the lease provides that, in the event of destruction of the premises by an insured risk, the tenants will be entitled to repayment of their share of the sinking fund. In those circumstances the sinking fund is not the landlord's money, and he can validly claim on the insurance. Similarly, he does not have money which is held in trust.

PART 5 – LANDLORD'S CONTRIBUTION

7.22   Where there is a sinking fund or a reserve fund, and even where there is simply a service charge, it is advisable for a tenant who pays a 'fair proportion' of service charge costs to ensure that the lease provides for the landlord to contribute to the fund in respect of vacant units (flats, shops, offices, etc). If the landlord does not agree to do so there is the risk, in the case of sinking funds, that the landlord will seek the total replacement cost, when needed, from those tenants who are at the property, even if only 25% is occupied. If a tenant pays a fixed percentage the point does not arise. For a tenant paying a fair proportion, the landlord may seek to claim that the only tenants benefiting from the replacement are those at the property, even though some units are empty, and that therefore they should bear the costs between them. A residential tenant or commercial tenant whose lease contains wording to clarify that the amount payable is to be no more than is reasonable may be able to challenge this sort of demand. This seems a specious argument, but one best avoided by an obligation in the lease on the landlord to pay the share that would be borne by vacant premises.

7.23   If there is a shortfall arising from empty units, the landlord should meet it. It is, after all, his property, and he is the only person able to let the vacant units. For ordinary service charge expenditure this is important, but for sinking fund replacements it is vital. The renewal of such items as lifts benefits the landlord's property. The sinking fund therefore benefits the landlord, even if he does not use the lift himself.

7.24   Take the case of a lift in a block of 20 identical offices. If the lift needs replacing and, assuming the landlord is entitled to recoup the cost, the 20 offices would between them need to find the total replacement cost of, say, £100,000. If the tenants had all contributed throughout the period, or the tenants and the landlord for vacant premises, and the calculations had been reasonably accurate the sinking fund would stand at more or less £100,000. The sinking fund would have done its job and the tenants would not have to find a large sum for the lift in addition to the other service charge costs for the relevant year. If, during the 20 years or so of the life of the lift, some of the offices had been vacant then in year 20 the fund would be less than £100,000, unless the landlord contributed for empty premises. If, say, 15% of the offices had been vacant during the whole term on average then the 20 tenants would have to find a further £15,000 between them for replacement of the lift when they, but not the landlord, had been paying the sums requested from them over the period.

7.25   An alternative provision, which is probably the most satisfactory, is for the landlord to agree to contribute to the sinking fund, when replacement is needed, the share that would have fallen on those parts of the premises that have been vacant. Many precedents seek to exclude from the costs chargeable to the service charge the costs applicable to units that are designed or intended to be let, and such wording can have a similar effect. The tenant looking at the draft lease should, however, read the lease with this point in mind.

PART 6 – AN ALTERNATIVE TO SINKING FUNDS

7.26   An alternative to sinking funds, which does not have the tax disadvantages of an ordinary sinking fund, is for the landlord to pay in advance. For example, if the landlord pays for the lift in year 1, and is advised it has a 15-year life, he could seek reimbursement over a 15-year period, and could then start again. As the payment has already been made the tax disadvantages outlined above do not arise. There are, however, a number of problems:

(a)   The landlord will have to pay for the equipment himself in advance.

(b)   Many tenants negotiate to ensure that they are not liable for capital costs of construction. Such a tenant is unlikely to agree to the reimbursement scheme, even if it is better for tax purposes than a normal sinking fund.

(c) With inflation taken into account it is perhaps unlikely that the cost of a lift in year 1 will be the same as the replacement in year 15. Accordingly, although the landlord may be reimbursed the original cost, the total recovered may be either more or perhaps less than is needed in year 15 to replace the lift.

(d) An actual calculation may have to take account of money borrowed to provide the item, and the repayment of the borrowing costs, thus increasing the base figure. This might make the total unreasonably high for the item in question and thus potentially subject to challenge.

PART 7 – CALCULATIONS

Calculations for the sinking fund

7.27 Imagine a block of 30 flats: in a sinking fund simply for the lift the basic calculations are something like this:

(a) Assume the cost of the lift today is £150,000. If the lift is replaced today each tenant would pay £5,000.

(b) Assume the estimated life of the lift is 20 years.

In practice, it seems that sinking funds are not normally calculated for periods in excess of ten years. The calculations are hard enough over a short period because of the numerous variable factors, and the longer the period of calculation the more hypothetical the figure is likely to be. The calculations are likely to be adjusted every few years to make them more near the final figure. On a straight line calculation, each flat should contribute £250 in each of the 20 years. Ignoring voids and tax and interest, this would build up a fund of £150,000 in 20 years, in time to replace the lift when its expected life ends.

7.28 The above is the simplistic basis of calculation. In practice, managing agents, whose job it is to calculate these figures, have to assume many other variables. These are primarily:

(a) What is the realistic estimated life of the item?

(b) The lift would cost £150,000 today – is it likely to cost either more or less in 20 years time? If so, what is that revised cost likely to be, based on today's cost?

(c) Apart from changes in cost (sometimes technology brings the price of items down, and sometimes factors such as changing safety or other statutory requirements increase costs), the agent needs to take account of inflation. If it can be assumed that the cost of the lift will reduce by 2% per year, or increase by 4% per year, the actual cost in terms of money will be different if inflation affects the value of money.

(d)   Having decided what the anticipated cost of a lift will be in cash terms at the end of its anticipated life, it is then necessary to recalculate the annual sum needed from each flat. This, however, should be done, again with the aid of a giant crystal ball, adding, notionally, the interest that will accrue to the amounts received (changing as interest rates change and becoming compounded), and deducting, notionally, the tax that will be payable on the interest received each year (again changing as tax rates change).

(e)   To make the calculation even fairer the person making the calculation should perhaps take account of the fact that the tenants of the building at the start of the 20-year period may have little direct benefit from the sinking fund as they may not be tenants in 20 years' time. Accordingly, there is something to be said for having the contributions not evenly spaced out over the period, but starting lower and increasing over time.

7.29   As stated above, I am glad I do not have to attempt these calculations. There are, I believe, various computer software programs which can calculate the relevant figures, but these still require the managing agent to input assumed interest rates etc.

7.30   In practice, it seems that many agents recalculate the figures every few years and adjust them as the fund goes along to make them more realistic in accordance with the latest information available from time to time.

Calculations for a reserve fund or a mixed fund

7.31   The calculations for a sinking fund are difficult as indicated above. The calculations of a reserve are perhaps easier as the period is usually much shorter. The way these are calculated is usually based on a rolling programme of works. The managing agents will have a programme covering a number of years. Many of them will have a series of programmes covering such aspects as (a) work needed every year, (b) works anticipated in the next five years, and (c) the dates at which specific items of plant or equipment, or even parts of the building, are likely to need replacing.

7.32   Having decided on a programme of works, the costs are estimated for each of the next few years (often on a three- or five-year cycle). These are then added together and divided by the number of years in the cycle (three or five years, for example). This shows the average cost anticipated over each of the next three or five years as the case may be. As an example, if the cost per flat for each year of a five-year cycle was estimated to be £1,500, £850, £1,600, £3,300 and £1,200 respectively this would add up to £8,450 for the five-year period. This equals £1,690 per year. If this amount is charged to the tenants for each of the first three years the tenant would be paying more than was actually required, but would not have to find more than approximately double that figure in year 4 (which is probably the year of external decoration). The agents might choose a gradually increasing rate to achieve the total at the end of the five-year cycle, and also to make the adjustment into the next cycle smoother. It is critical that the agents should take account of cashflow and organise the carrying out of the works to be after the money is due to be received, not before.

7.33 The actual calculation of the yearly contribution to a reserve can be more subtle than indicated above, and, again, could take account of interest earned on the income and tax on that income as well as contingencies and elements representing inflation. It must be remembered that all receipts from residential tenants are held on trust and, in effect, must be invested (Landlord and Tenant Act 1987, s 42; see Chapter 9). These funds therefore give rise to income. It is recommended in the Code of Practice that interest on service charge receipts from commercial property is also added to the fund (see at **3.77** above).

7.34 The principles for calculating a sinking fund contribution for a single item, and the calculations for a reserve fund are set out above. Very commonly, the managing agents are asked to combine the two (and in the case of sinking funds for a number of different items with different estimated lives and costs). The calculations are based on the above ideas but simply banded together. For example, in year 1 the tenant of a flat may be asked to pay £1,450 which is made up of £275 for a sinking fund contribution to the lift which has an estimated life of a further seven years, £140 sinking fund contribution to a boiler with an estimated remaining life of four years, and a reserve fund (evened out for the next few years) of £1,035. In year 2 the total contributions may be £1,550 with each of the constituent parts increased by a figure representing inflationary increases in the estimated costs of the works and services and perhaps the capital costs of the sinking fund items.

PART 8 – PURPOSE TRUSTS

7.35 This is technical matter of concern to company tenants. A 'purpose trust', as the name suggests, is a trust created for a particular purpose. Such a trust could be the maintenance of a building. It is mentioned here because sinking funds are often trusts (and are recommended to be trusts for commercial property as well as residential, where a trust is implied) and there is a problem with purpose trusts. Such a trust cannot be validly created other than for charitable purposes if it does not have individual beneficiaries. (*Re Denley's Trust Deed* [1969] 1 Ch 373.) Trusts which are not charitable trusts must be drawn up so as to come to an end within the perpetuity period which is now usually 80 years under the Perpetuities and Accumulations Act 1964, s 1. The deed setting up the trust (in this case the lease) can set out what the perpetuity period is to be, provided it does not exceed 80 years. Accordingly, doubt has been expressed as to whether or not a sinking fund or reserve fund can be a valid trust. The point may be settled where the lease contains provisions under which at some stage (usually on destruction of the building, or where there is a surplus after replacement of an item) the fund is to be paid either to the landlord or to the tenants, or a combination of both. In addition, it should be relevant that leases are for a specific term, and leases for more than 80 years are in a minority other than for residential premises where there is a statutory trust regardless of length. Many leases these days include a specific perpetuity period.

7.36   The point is immaterial for residential premises following s 42 of the Landlord and Tenant Act 1987 under which all service charge contributions (sinking fund and other contributions) by tenants are held on trust. Clearly, as s 42 imposes a statutory trust there seems little scope for arguing that the trust is invalid. Most residential tenants are in any event individuals and not companies, but for the company tenant of a dwelling the Act resolves any doubt.

7.37   In those comparatively rare cases where there is a sinking fund for commercial property, the problem over purpose trusts may be material because the tenants are unlikely all to be individuals or charitable bodies. Commercial leases for more than 80 years are infrequent, except perhaps long leases at a peppercorn where the tenant has built the premises, which are leases that can include service charges. If such a lease contains a sinking fund without an express trust, under which the fund is at some stage payable to the tenants, or the landlord and the tenants, there is a possibility that the trust could be held invalid unless (a) there is a perpetuity period in the lease, and (b) there are provisions for the fund to come to an end within that period. If such circumstances arise the parties may wish to consider entering into a deed varying the lease to include provisions of the type just mentioned so that the trust is not invalid.

7.38   A reserve fund may also be subject to challenge on the same basis. The point is perhaps less likely to be a problem than for a sinking fund. This is because for a reserve fund the lease will normally provide that at the end of the financial year, or at least at the end of the lease, the service charge payments will be adjusted. This ensures that the tenant is entitled to a refund of any amount overpaid within a short period, although it does not affect the basic principle in the case of tenants who are not individuals.

7.39   If the sinking fund or reserve fund is held invalid for the above reasons the tenants may wish to call for their contributions back. It was formerly the case that payments made under a mistake of fact were not recoverable unless they were made under duress (eg the threat of distraint). *Maskell v Horner* [1915] 3 KB 106 and *Sharp Brothers and Knight Ltd v Chant* [1917] 1 KB 771 is not now a true statement of the law (see eg *Universities Superannuation Fund Scheme Ltd v Marks & Spencer Ltd* [1999] 04 EG 158) but the invalidity of the trust would not prevent the landlord from being able to call for contributions to the replacement of sinking fund items when needed, or to the cost of work covered by the reserve fund. The illegality is only in the building up of the fund. In practice, it may be that the landlord and tenant would prefer to follow the system set up by the lease even if it is not a valid trust, or, as indicated above, consider a variation to remove the illegality.

PART 9 – PROBLEMS WITH THE TREND TOWARDS SHORTER LEASES

7.40 Residential properties (at least those where service charges are imposed) are often let on long leases, but there is a trend for commercial leases to be for shorter terms, and in recent years there are often rights for tenants to determine the lease early. This is for two main reasons. One is that when the country is in a poor economic state tenants are reluctant to commit themselves to a long-term obligation to a landlord. In many cases they will in any event have the right to apply for a new lease at the end of the term under the Landlord and Tenant Act 1954.

7.41 The second reason for commercial tenants to seek shorter leases, at least before the Landlord and Tenant (Covenants) Act 1995, was that the tenant remained liable for rent etc owed by his successor after he assigned the lease. The longer the lease the greater the potential liability following assignment. Now there is a six-month time limit for claiming and a former tenant can call for an overriding lease, and so this second reason is much less significant than it used to be. (The steep increase in stamp duty land tax over recent years is a third reason.)

7.42 The effect of shorter commercial leases on service charges is on the whole slight. Obviously the precise effect depends on what services are to be provided. Even for a lease of, say, five years, which at one point seemed to be becoming fairly common in place of the former 25-year lease with five-yearly reviews, virtually all the services needed for a longer lease will still need to be performed. These include repair, cleaning, decoration, maintenance of plant, security and so on. Indeed the only two items likely to be subject to any real doubt are:

(a) sinking funds for replacement of items which are unlikely to need renewal within the lease term; and

(b) decoration of parts which may not be needed within the period of the lease.

7.43 Dealing with both of these items, my feeling is that the landlord should insist upon the standard provisions remaining in place. There are two reasons:

(a) The work (or replacement) will be needed at some time, and if the lease does not provide for the renewal or decoration, as the case may be, the tenant may find his lease is less valuable if he wants to assign. Although replacement, for example of the boiler, may not be anticipated within the short term it may still be necessary during that time, and definitely will at some time.

(b) Except in limited circumstances, the business tenant will be able to renew at the end of the term: if he does he will have the benefit of a longer occupation than the initial short term. On renewal the court must 'have regard to the terms of the current tenancy'. (Landlord and Tenant Act 1954, s 35.)

If the first lease does not include these provisions the landlord will have difficulty in insisting on them being included on a renewal. (See *O'May v City of London Real Property Co Ltd* [1983] 2 AC 726 at **3.102** above.) Including the provisions may, perhaps, be even more difficult on a second or third renewal, even though some of the provisions may be even more relevant then.

7.44   The answer is for the landlord to insist on the usual provisions being included in the lease, but, in case of need, agreeing a waiver in favour of the tenant under which the landlord agrees not to charge the tenant during the short term for the sinking fund contribution. The waiver should be personal to the tenant and on the basis that it is not repeated if the lease is renewed, whether under a court order or otherwise, because the waiver is only being given because of the short term. Another option would be a waiver (personal to the tenant) to last for a fixed period of years. If this is agreed the landlord may find sinking fund expenditure needs to be made during the term of the initial lease, in which case he will not be able to recover it from the tenant, depending on the terms of the waiver. (For waivers see at **7.60** et seq.)

7.45   Apart from the limited matters mentioned in the previous paragraph, I can see no good reason for any other change to the service charge provisions in a short lease. The main point must be that most of the services that are provided by the landlord are to be carried out frequently (eg cleaning, lighting, heating) or when necessary (eg repairs, external decoration or replacement of plant). As the lease should cover services that are needed then there should be no good reason for a tenant to seek to remove or qualify items in a short lease in any way other than he would for a longer lease.

PART 10 – AT THE END OF THE LEASE

7.46   Tenants sometimes think that because their lease has expired they are entitled to the return of any balance standing to their credit in the reserve fund or sinking fund.

Reserve funds

7.47   In the case of a reserve fund they are correct: such a fund is to even out expenditure, and at the end of their term there should be an adjustment, similar to that at the end of the financial year. If they have paid into the reserve more than is needed, apportioned to the end of the lease, then they are entitled to a refund as part of the normal adjustment, subject to any special terms in the lease. For residential tenants the year end adjustment should reflect the requirement for advance payments to be no more than is reasonable. (Section 19(2) of the Landlord and Tenant Act 1985. See also *St Mary's Mansions Ltd v Limegate Investment Co* [2002] EWCA Civ 1491, [2003] 05 EG 146 at **7.14** above.)

Sinking funds

7.48   Where a lease with a sinking fund comes to an end the tenant will not normally be entitled to a refund, see eg *Secretary of State for the Environment v Possfund (North West) Ltd* [1997] 2 EGLR 56, at **7.13** above. The point is that the sinking fund is being built up to provide for the replacement of an item at the building. It is paid for that purpose, and not as a means of saving, even though HMRC sometimes seem to want to tax it as if it is. If the item that is the subject of the fund is not replaced at the end of the tenant's lease, then the fund will need to continue until it is. A landlord should find it easier to find a new tenant where there is a fund available for use when the item needs to be replaced. While the lease exists, for the same reasons, a tenant should be able to obtain a better premium on assignment. The tenant whose lease comes to an end, of course, has not had the benefit of the payments made other than the possibility of it improving the premium on assignment where that is a possibility, but equally he has not been called upon to pay what might be a very large sum at very short notice during the term.

Mixed funds

7.49   Where the fund is partly a sinking fund and partly a reserve fund the position is a combination of the above. That part representing a continuing sinking fund will not be repayable, and that which represents a reserve should be apportioned to the end of the lease.

Destruction

7.50   If the lease ceases because the premises have been destroyed the lease may provide for the sinking fund to be repaid to the tenants, to prevent potential insurance objections to a claim for the cost of replacement of the relevant item. Clearly, the tenant can call on the landlord to release the tenant's proportion of the sinking fund in such case. If the lease does not contain a provision under which the sinking fund is repaid if the premises are destroyed, then the other provisions of the lease will prevail, or s 42 of the Landlord and Tenant Act 1987 for residential tenants (see Chapter 9).

7.51   The lease provisions may well put an onus on one or other party to rebuild in case of destruction following the happening of an insured risk. If the landlord is liable to rebuild, which is the normal provision, he could claim under the insurance policy for the cost of rebuilding:

(a)   If the sinking fund is repayable to the tenants the insurance claim will be for reinstating the building including those items for which the sinking fund was building up.

(b)   If the sinking fund is not repayable under the lease terms after a disaster the insurers may say the landlord cannot claim for the item in question as he has not made a loss, because there is money in hand for replacement, namely the sinking fund.

(c) If he is not going to rebuild then the sinking fund is not needed and should be refunded, even if this is not specifically stated in the lease. The fund is for replacing an item: if it is not to be replaced at all then there can be no justification for the landlord keeping the sum built up solely for that replacement.

7.52 On balance there seems no disadvantage to the landlord in agreeing that the sinking fund should be repaid if the premises are destroyed. It would keep the tenant (or his solicitors) happy, and the landlord does not suffer because the full reinstatement value should be recoverable from the insurers, even if the fund is only half built up when the disaster occurs.

Surrender

7.53 There are not many leases that contain specific reference to surrender. Some contain an obligation on the tenant to offer to surrender to the landlord if the tenant wants to assign, but otherwise surrender is not usually mentioned in the lease, and so any terms are only negotiated when the surrender arises. This paragraph is simply to remind readers that if a lease is surrendered the service charge provisions need consideration. In particular the question of sinking funds should be reviewed. The final agreement will depend to some extent on the bargaining position of the parties and who most wants the surrender to happen.

7.54 If the tenant approaches the landlord to accept a surrender, either because the tenant cannot trade successfully from the premises or has found more suitable premises, then the tenant has little bargaining power. In such a case he will be unlikely to be able to persuade the landlord to refund any part of the sinking fund.

7.55 By contrast, if the landlord approaches the tenant, perhaps so that the landlord can redevelop, the tenant may be in a strong position to negotiate for the return of sinking fund contributions. The fund would not be needed in any event if the building is being demolished. The tenant may also look for payment of a premium and costs and even other benefits such as removal costs, stamp duty land tax and land registry fees for other premises and printing of new stationery and so on, to reflect the cost to the tenant of having to move.

PART II – DRAFTING AND NEGOTIATING SINKING FUNDS AND RESERVES

For landlords

7.56 As usual, the most important point is to ensure that operation of the sinking fund and reserve fund are clearly set out. The usual points, as to making clear what is the subject of the services and what those services are to be, apply as in the case of all other service charge provisions.

7.57   The additional points for sinking funds and reserve funds are:

(a)   The lease must include provisions for payment by the tenant in advance.

(b)   The money paid by the tenants should be expressed to be held on trust. In the case of residential property this is implied but it may be worth including and amplifying the trusts for commercial property. For residential property, see the detailed comments in Chapter 9 on s 42 of the Landlord and Tenant Act 1987. The Commercial Code recommends that sinking funds are held on an interest bearing account, separate from the landlord's own money, and that the interest should accrue to the fund (paras 58 and 64).

(c)   The lease for non-residential premises should ideally set out:

    (i)   Who is to be the trustee (usually the landlord, but it could usefully be a third party or up to four individuals).

    (ii)   Who are to be the beneficiaries (usually the tenants, but sometimes the tenants and the landlord, and occasionally just the landlord).

    (iii)   The items for which the tenant's sinking fund contributions are to be paid (eg 'the renewal or replacement of the lift shown edged in green on plan 3 and the generator shown hatched in yellow on plan 4 and the cost of replacement where necessary and where repair is not economical of other plant machinery and other equipment used or from time to time used for the benefit of the Building').

    (iv)   Any appropriate assumptions of the periods for which the fund can be kept eg 'the cost of replacement where necessary and where repair is not economical of items of plant machinery and other equipment and other capital items calculated on such life expectancy of the said items as the Landlord or the Landlord's managing agents shall from time to time reasonably determine and on the assumption that the future decoration or other treatment of the exterior of the Building shall be carried out in every third year'. (The latter is to cover the reserve fund element.)

    (v)   The lease should provide that when the item for which the fund has been set up needs to be replaced, the cost of doing so shall be paid out, as far as possible, from the sinking fund during the relevant financial year.

    (vi)   It is helpful to show what is to happen to the interest on any income. In this context a provision that money in the fund will be held in an interest-bearing account with interest being added to the fund is simplest and fairest.

    (vii) For the reasons mentioned above, it is sensible to make it clear that in case of destruction of the property, or of the specific items for which a sinking fund is building up, the fund is to be repaid to the tenants in the proportions in which they are liable to contribute. The landlord should, of course, also be entitled to a refund of his contributions, if any, in such circumstances.

(viii) If the landlord is disposed to grant a waiver, excluding the tenant from liability to contribute to the sinking fund or reserve fund, it is recommended that the waiver follows the points made below at **7.60**, and in particular that the tenant agrees to contribute to the fund in certain specified cases.

(ix) The lease should permit the landlord to pay tax on the interest of the sinking fund or reserve fund from the fund. This may not be strictly necessary in the case of a fund held on trust where this must be the case, but the provision clarifies the point.

For tenants

7.58   Again, most of the normal points about drafting service charges apply similarly to sinking funds. For example the primary object of the tenant in negotiating the lease should be to ensure that any sums he is asked to pay for a reserve or sinking fund are reasonable and justifiable, and that the fund is not simply a way for a landlord to line his pocket.

7.59   So far as sinking funds and reserve funds are concerned, the tenant should seek to ensure that the lease contains protection for a tenant as follows:

(a) The tenant should ensure that the fund is held on trust. This is implied by s 42 of the Landlord and Tenant Act 1985 for residential premises but there is no statutory implied term for non-dwellings.

(b) Consider who is the trustee and who has the right to appoint new trustees. From the point of view of the tenant if the fund is held independently of the landlord this is extra protection to a tenant against the landlord running off with the money. If it is held in trust it is not available for creditors of the landlord. Other than a management company it is hard to see the obvious trustee. No doubt go-ahead agents and bankers or even solicitors could set up trustee companies for the purpose.

(c) Make sure who the beneficiaries of the trust are. The tenants should be beneficiaries of the trust, and one point is whether the tenants are to benefit in the same ratio as they are due to pay, or as they actually pay. The latter would seem fairer. It may be that the landlord will be one of the beneficiaries where he contributes to the fund.

(d) Try to ensure that the lease provides for the landlord to contribute to the fund for empty properties. Where a tenant pays a fixed percentage he cannot be called upon to pay more than that percentage simply because some of the premises are empty. However, he runs the risk that the fund may not be sufficient for provision of adequate services if the landlord does not contribute in this way. (If there are lots of voids and the landlord is insolvent, the fund may not suffice.) Where the tenant pays a 'fair proportion', then in the absence of a specific provision making the landlord contribute for vacant properties, the tenant may find himself being asked to pay a higher percentage than otherwise. The clause is usually to the effect that the landlord will bear the service charge costs of the empty premises, rather than having to actually put the money into the fund: the effect is much the same except that the landlord does not have to pay in advance, but the fund does not in such event obtain interest from those parts where payments are made periodically.

(e) The provision should entitle the tenants to the return of their contributions if the premises are destroyed by an insured risk for the reasons outlined above (see **7.21**).

(f) Try to ensure that items to be replaced through the sinking fund are not to be replaced before the end of their normal economic life, or until repair is less economic than replacement. A brave tenant in a good bargaining position may consider seeking a provision that no major item is to be replaced during the last two years of the term. This may well be counter-productive, as by that stage the tenant will have been paying into the fund for years (unless he has an exemption), and an item may actually need to be replaced at that time, regardless of what the lease says.

(g) It is helpful to ensure that the lease provides for the fund to be held in an interest earning deposit with interest to be credited to the fund.

(h) The tenant should try to ensure that the lease says that if the item for which a sinking fund has been set up needs to be replaced, then the fund will be used first, before the tenants are asked to contribute more. This is probably the most important point.

PART 12 – WAIVERS

7.60   Commercial tenants (particularly large companies) often object to paying to a sinking fund or a reserve fund. They do so on the basis that they will be able to pay their share when it is needed, and in the meantime they can make much better use of the money in their own business. While this is often stated, particularly by the larger companies, landlords need to be conscious that financial circumstances change, and the company which is making millions of pounds profit this year may be struggling in eight years' time. Sadly, there have been many examples in the last few decades of well-known major companies having financial difficulties.

7.61   While landlords often agree to give waivers in the case of large companies, such waivers should only be given subject to conditions. Such waivers are normally given by letter rather than by variation to the deed. Side letters are acceptable as variations to leases. There was a doubt about whether the Law of

Property (Miscellaneous) Provisions Act 1989 made such letters ineffective, but this doubt was resolved by the Court of Appeal in *Tootal Clothing Ltd v Guinea Properties Management Ltd* [1992] 2 EGLR 80. To ensure they are enforceable such letters need to be signed by both parties. The advantage of a letter rather than a deed is that it does not necessarily come to the notice of assignees who will therefore not necessarily seek similar concessions from a landlord. The disadvantage is that the points may be forgotten or the letters lost. This may be a problem particularly in the case of a long-term arrangement such as a sinking fund. Such letter, ideally, should be in duplicate and copies kept with the lease and counterpart. It could best be in the form of a letter from the landlord to the tenant setting out the terms of the waiver which is acknowledged by the tenant signing and returning a copy.

7.62   The main points are that the waiver:

(a)   should be personal to the tenant in question;

(b)   must be on the basis that if the named tenant assigns or underlets (or ceases to occupy) it will immediately pay in to the sinking fund the total of what it would have paid during the period in which the waiver operated;

(c)   must make it clear that the tenant will contribute to the cost of repair of the items (replacement etc in the case of a sinking fund) when called upon to do so: this will include the amount that it should have contributed to the sinking fund prior to the date when the money is needed.

A landlord will perhaps need to consider whether to call on the tenant also to pay interest when called on to contribute: after all the contributions by other tenants will usually have been earning interest and thus creating a larger sum towards the money needed. Precedent 11 in Appendix 2 has some suggested forms of waiver.

Disposal

7.63   A reserve or sinking fund needs careful attention if the lease is assigned or if the reversion to the lease is transferred. The relevant issues are discussed in Chapter 13.

Taxation comments by Steve Hasson

7.64   As noted above, sinking and reserve funds both raise a number of tax issues. For both sinking and reserve funds we have to consider whether, for tax purposes, it is possible to match income and expenditure, but for sinking funds, there are much more fundamental issues, particularly in relation to residential property.

Reserve Funds

7.65   As we have seen a reserve fund is one that builds up a cushion so that expense is evened out over a few years. Whilst this is undoubtedly commercially wise, it is unsurprising that as far as Her Majesty's Revenue and Customs are concerned, in general the income in the hands of the landlord will taxable when received, or receivable, whereas it may not be possible to obtain a deduction for expenditure until it takes place. The position for the tenant is rather more straightforward in that payments, be they additional rent or under covenant, should be deductible when paid. In practice, most landlords seem able to manage a situation where, for tax purposes, they may have a small taxable profit in one year arising because relief is not available for expenditure until a later date and a small loss when that expenditure takes place.

7.66 The position in respect of capital allowances and who is entitled to claim allowances is a complex one and beyond the scope of this book.

7.67 As we highlighted in Chapter 6, where the service charge is treated as additional rent it should be possible, with judicious planning, to avoid any significant mismatch of income and expenditure and consequent tax cost. However, arguably where the service charge is received under a covenant, if the special tax treatment under Sch D, Case VI is invoked by HMRC, any loss cannot be carried back and, equally, could not be set against other income such as rents.

Sinking Funds

7.68 As we observed in para **7.07** as a sinking fund potentially arises over a longer period and may involve larger sums, the mismatch of income or expenditure may be very significant and no doubt for this reason sinking funds in relation to commercial property are relatively rare. It is, however, the case that occasionally a sinking fund arrangement will be put in place, but the reserve fund element is payable to a trustee. This is clearly intended to protect the larger sums at stake and the greater periods involved, although that protection may be limited in the case of a rogue landlord, since the trustee invariably is the landlord himself.

7.69 The use of trusts either under the provisions of the release or, in the case of residential property, by virtue of s 42 of the Landlord and Tenant Act 1987 introduces a further series of tax difficulties.

7.70 As we saw in Chapter 6, s 42 overrides the provisions in the lease in relation to service charges and creates a statutory trust, albeit it is far from clear precisely what the terms of that trust may be. The essential point here is that if the sinking fund element of the service charge (confusingly in relation to residential property this may still be described as a reserve fund) is payable under the terms of the lease by the tenant to a trustee, then that trust is a completely separate taxable entity. This is a source of real difficulty and the reason why HMRC has issued its tax bulletins in relation to residential service charges.

7.71 In principle a trust will receive these fund contributions as capital, which would not be taxable, but the income generated over time from the investment of such funds is clearly taxable and, in recent years, the tax regime applying to trusts has become more onerous. It does not help in deciding how to apply the trust tax regime to a statutory trust established by virtue of the Landlord and Tenant Act 1987, that it is not always clear what type of trust we are dealing with. Indeed some commentators have gone so far as to suggest that, since trusts always have inheritance tax consequences, specific advice needs to be taken in relation to this aspect of residential property and conceivably commercial property as well.

7.72 HMRC in its tax bulletin on the trust implications of service charge funds and sinking funds, acknowledge that it is possible for funds to be held under a bare trust, interest in possession trust, discretionary trust or accumulation trust arrangement. This is a very unhelpful state of affairs and represents something of a pitfall for the unwary.

7.73 It is clear that, unless there is good reason, the commercial landlord will wish to steer clear of trust arrangements, giving rise to issues not only of the matching of income and expenditure, but more fundamentally, the creation of a separate taxable entity which may well be subject to an onerous tax regime. In relation to residential property, the practitioner may not have the luxury of avoiding what has been imposed statutorily.

7.74 For resential property all parties should be very clear that, under current HMRC guidance, it will be necessary for the trust to file a tax return with the specialist trust office. Full details are provided in the tax bulletin. In addition, it would be advisable to consider whether or not a separate VAT registration will be required.

CHAPTER 8

Service charges and rent

Who paid rent for Mrs Rip Van Winkle when Rip Van Winkle went away?

Alfred Bryan

THE DIFFERENCE

8.1   Rent is a charge by a landlord for use and occupation of a property (the 'demised premises'). The rent is based on the size, position and convenience of the premises and the potential use. By contrast service charges are a charge, usually by a landlord, for works and services mostly carried on outside the demised premises. Rent for commercial premises is usually fixed for a few years and then subject to review. For long leases of flats rent is often fixed for a long period such as 25 or 33 years, and then subject to fixed increases or increases in accordance with an Index. Some leases or tenancy agreements of dwellings are subject to frequent review. Service charges are, however, usually adjusted annually to reflect what works and services have been carried out.

8.2   In an unreported Lands Tribunal case, Minster Chalets Ltd v Irwin Park Residents Association LTL 9/7/2001, there were leases with a fixed base rent and a 'site fee' intended to bring the rent to a fair rent. The tenants argued that the site fee was a service charge and thus subject to reasonableness under s 19 of the Landlord and Tenant Act 1985. The landlord only covenanted to keep the site clear, but there were facilities such as a swimming pool. It was held that the site fee was not a service charge. In particular it did not increase on account of the cost of services.

8.3   The history of service charges was commented on earlier (at 1.11 et seq). In effect, they developed from 'common parts' contribution clauses to today's detailed provisions for advance payments and sinking funds and so on. Originally, landlords charged a rent which was intended to provide an income for the landlord and also to cover all expenses the landlord might have by way of repair etc. Later, landlords sought to recover some expenses from the tenants separately and subsequently increased the extent of what they tried to recover. The difference can sometimes be blurred, and this chapter reflects some aspects of the differences and the relationship between rents and service charges.

8.4   As in so many other aspects of landlord and tenant law and relationships, there is often a difference between the position affecting residential tenancies and that affecting commercial tenancies. Residential tenancies where there are service charges are often by way of a long lease at a premium and a relatively nominal rent. It is quite common to find a 99-year residential lease where a tenant has paid a premium of, say, £50,000 and thereafter pays a rent of £100 per annum and a service charge. In such leases the premium is paid when the lease is granted, and thereafter, other than mortgage payments, the regular outgoings for the tenant are the rent and the service charge. The rent is often relatively small but the service charge can be many times the amount of the rent, and is thus often a more significant outgoing than the rent. For example, in a bad year the rent might be £100 and the service charge £3,500. For commercial leases the relative difference in amount of the rent and the service charge is often not so marked. In the case of a small shop a typical lease may be for 20 years at an initial rent of £15,000 and with five-yearly rent reviews. It would be surprising for the service charges to be as much as the rent, by contrast to the residential lease quoted in the previous paragraph.

COMPARATIVE TABLES

8.5   These tables are inevitably pure generalisations. Circumstances vary from property to property, and on how much the landlord actually provides by way of services. If a house is divided into two flats, there may be no common expenses other than, say, external decoration every three or four years: in a large block of flats or an office block there may be regular lift and boiler maintenance, heavy repairs at intervals, and weekly gardening and cleaning. Again, for a high street shop there may be virtually no common parts for which the tenant is to contribute, whereas in a shopping mall there could be much, including car park expenses and security. These contrasts are made because a few organisations publish tables comparing the rate of service charge per square foot within different shopping centres. While these are obviously of interest, they need to be treated with some caution. It must be remembered that if a landlord does absolutely nothing the service charge will be nil and reading the figure off a table may make it look good – but is the centre being well managed? As in so many cases it is important to compare like with like. They are becoming more sophisticated now, with a breakdown of different types of expense in some cases, but it seems the compilers have difficulty with making these consistent, as different centres use different expressions for what is charged.

8.6   Tenants should look at the total outgoings they will have to pay for a property before committing themselves to taking a lease. A sensible prospective tenant will want to see details of the service charge estimates for the present year and the accounts for the last few years, as well as an indication of what they are likely to be in the next few years. It is for that reason that prospective tenants make preliminary enquiries. If the grand total of rent and service charge is more than the tenant would have to pay for equivalent accommodation elsewhere the tenant may decide not to proceed, although his ability to withdraw also depends on the market at the time. Alternatively, he may seek to reduce the asking rent or price.

SERVICE CHARGES RESERVED AS RENT

8.7   The consequences have been discussed at 6.60 et seq. There are three advantages to a landlord of commercial property in reserving the service charge as rent:

(a)   In case of default the landlord can distrain.

(b)   There is no need for a landlord to serve a s 146 notice (under s 146 of the Law of Property Act 1925) leading to forfeiture.

(c)   Interest on late payments may belong to the landlord, not to the service charge fund.

8.8   While the above aspects are slightly helpful to a landlord of commercial premises they are hardly critical. They have little benefit for a landlord of residential property. For example, distraint cannot be exercised for service charges of residential leases unless the amount is agreed or determined (Housing Act 1996, s 81), which removes the benefit of distraint being a prompt remedy, and a s 146 notice cannot be served until 14 days after agreement or determination of the service charge liability. Reserving service charges as rent does not guarantee that it will cease to be payable if the premises are destroyed, even if the rent suspension clause mentions 'rents': see 8.18 and P & O Property Holdings Ltd v International Computers Ltd [1999] 2 EGLR 17.

8.9   A landlord cannot distrain if there is a genuine dispute. (See eg Wharfland Ltd v South London Co-operative Building Co Ltd [1995] 2 EGLR 21 and Concorde Graphics Ltd v Andromeda Investments SA [1983] 1 EGLR 53.) In addition, it is widely expected that the right to distrain will be removed soon in respect of service charges generally, as well as being made less effective as a remedy in respect of rent. In view of these drawbacks, it is hard to see reserving the service charge as rent as a major negotiating issue.

EFFECT FOR STAMP DUTY LAND TAX

8.10   Service charges payable under a lease are not taken into account in assessing the stamp duty land tax payable on the lease unless it is reserved as rent, and then only in the unusual case of a lease which sets out a specific sum for service charges. In that event, the specific sum is added to the rent, and stamp duty land tax is calculated as if the total was all rent.

RENTS TREATED AS INCLUSIVE OF SERVICE CHARGES

8.11   Whether the service charge is actually part of the rent has been aired in a few cases. The following cases illustrate points considered by the courts. The first, Investment & Freehold English Estates Ltd v Casement [1987] 2 EGLR

112, revolved around a long tenancy and whether the rent included the service charge or not. If it did, it would take the rent to more than two thirds of the rateable value and thus bring the tenancy within the Rent Acts. Shortly before this time, it was considered to be unsatisfactory to allow the rent to exceed two thirds of the rateable value, because this would bring into effect the Rent Acts, which at that time prohibited the charging of a premium for assignment. Tenants wanting to assign, and mortgagees of the leasehold term, were concerned to ensure that the Rent Acts did not come into play and thus prevent the charging of a premium. The lease was badly drafted, and indeed misconceived, because it not only purported to ensure that the rent and service charges combined would not exceed two thirds of the rateable value, but also tried to cover a potential change in the law which had already been brought into effect. Section 80 of the Housing Act 1969 had been brought into force and made it clear that service charges were not included in the definition of rent for Rent Act calculations. The most unsatisfactory part of the lease was that it provided that the rent and service charge were not to exceed two thirds of the rateable value, and went on to say that if they did 'the lessor shall not be under any obligation to carry out any work or perform any duties notwithstanding his covenant which would impose on him a liability in excess'. (Such a provision could give rise to the situation that eg external repairs were not the responsibility of either landlord or tenant.) The lease further provided that if the law was changed so that service charges were not to be included in the calculation of rent (ie the change that had already occurred), the provision excluding the landlord's obligation to carry out services 'shall be of no effect and the lessor shall be at liberty to demand a full contribution from the lessee … notwithstanding that such contribution together with the ground rent hereby reserved exceeds two thirds of the rateable value'. The judge, not unnaturally, had difficulty in interpreting the provisions, but in the end decided to hold that the two provisos should have no operation. The circumstances are unlikely to arise again, but this case is of some assistance in interpretation on whether rent includes service charge or not.

8.12 More recently, in Eaton Square Properties Ltd v Ogilvie [2000] 16 EG 143, the services were provided by a management company and the landlord had no obligation to repair. The management company's obligation was in a document separate from the lease. The question was whether the service charge was part of the registered rent under s 71(4) of the Rent Act 1977. It was held that they were not.

8.13 R v Beverley Borough Council Housing Benefits Review Board, ex p Hare (1995) 27 HLR 637 concerned housing benefit, and service charges needed to be considered. The applicant paid £40 for his room with a further £34.84 service charge. The regulations (regs 10 and 11 of the Housing Benefit (General) Regulations 1987) provided for housing benefit to be paid in respect of rent, but where the rent paid was excessive the rent should be treated as reduced, and thus the benefit was also reduced. The regulations provided that rent for the purpose of benefit included service charge payments (reg 10(1)(e)). The regulation which sought to reduce benefit if the rent was unduly high by comparison with other rents (reg 11(2)(c)) did not refer to service charges as such. The Queen's Bench

Division, in an application for a judicial review, said the reference to comparable rents should include service charges, even though they were not mentioned specifically, so that the total payments for accommodation were fairly compared. The application was referred back to the benefit review board for further consideration.

8.14   In Sinclair Gardens Investments (Kensington) Ltd v Walsh [1996] QB 231, which involved mortgages, the Court of Appeal held that where the lease referred to service charge being 'deemed to be … additional rent', then such provision had the effect of conferring the attributes of rent on the service charge, even though the service charge was not reserved as rent in the reddendum (ie the part of the lease which reserves the rent).

8.15   A somewhat similar point arose in the Court of Appeal in Khar v Delbounty Ltd [1997] EGCS 183, where it was held that service charges were the equivalent of rent for the purposes of forfeiture and relief from forfeiture. The landlord had forfeited the long lease of a flat following service of a s 146 notice, and had then granted an assured shorthold tenancy to a third party. Eleven months after the forfeiture, the former tenant applied for relief. The tenant had argued that arrears of the maintenance charge should be treated in the same way as arrears of rent in relation to an application for relief. The judge did not agree, but the Court of Appeal did, and exercised its discretion in favour of the tenant. The order was for the lease to be sold (after the shorthold tenant's occupation) and the proceeds, after deduction of the arrears owing to the landlord, were to be paid to the tenant.

CESSER OF SERVICE CHARGE CONTRIBUTIONS ON DESTRUCTION

8.16   One material factor relating to the difference between service charges and rent is whether or not the usual cesser of rent provision should apply to service charge contributions as well as the rent. The cesser of rent provision normally appears within the Agreements and Declarations if it is not a specific insurance section of the lease. The usual clause provides that the tenant does not need to pay rent if the premises (or accesses to it) are destroyed by an insured risk and cannot be used or occupied. It usually provides that rent is reduced to a fair proportion if the premises (or common areas or accesses to the demised premises) are so damaged that the demised premises are not capable of full beneficial use. Sometimes the cesser is for an unlimited period, ie until the damage is made good, and sometimes it is for a maximum period, often three years, reflecting the period for which the landlord insures loss of rent. For the purpose of this book, the issue is whether the rent cesser or reduction applies to service charges as well as rent.

8.17   The right to cease paying rent normally applies only where the damage has been caused by one of the insured risks, and the tenant needs to be satisfied that the risks against which insurance is carried are sufficient: it can be short-sighted to restrict the risks against which the landlord is to insure, even though the tenant pays the premiums. In Manchester Bonded Warehouse Co v Carr (1880) 5 CPD 507 the lease said the rent would cease to be payable if the premises were destroyed or damaged by 'fire storm or tempest'. When the building collapsed as a result of overloading on one of the floors, the rent cessation did not apply. If overloading had been one of the insured risks and if the cesser provision had referred to 'all insured risks', the tenant could have claimed the benefit.

The P & O case

8.18   Suspension of service charge payments was the subject of an important and detailed judgment of Mr Justice Neuberger in P & O Property Holdings Ltd v International Computers Ltd [1999] 2 EGLR 17. The case followed significant damage to the Arndale Centre in Manchester caused by an IRA bomb. P & O were landlords, and the dispute was whether the tenants were liable to pay service charges during the rent suspension period. The rent suspension clause did not mention service charges, but it permitted suspension of 'rent,' and the service charges were reserved as rent. The judge took account of this, but nevertheless held that the service charges were not intended to be suspended. The decision followed a detailed analysis by the judge and is not capable of easy summary, but the judge made it clear that it was necessary to look at the lease as a whole. There were a number of inconsistencies throughout the lease in the use of the words 'rent' and 'rents'. Sometimes references were clearly intended to refer to rent alone, and sometimes references were more relevant to rent and other payments. If the rent suspension clause had mentioned service charges there would have been no need for the case. The key for new leases is obviously to spell out what is intended. The fact that the service charge is reserved as rent is apparently not sufficient.

SUSPENSION GENERALLY

8.19   There are often negotiations as to the length of time during which the rent is to cease – should it be for a maximum fixed period, or for the duration of the insurance against loss of rent, or indeed without limit? This is a straightforward matter for negotiation. The point that is explored below is what the tenant might reasonably expect to be able to cease paying.

THE ALTERNATIVES

8.20   In a commercial lease (and many residential leases) the tenant frequently pays three separate items to the landlord: the first is the rent proper, the second is the insurance premium, and the third is the service charge contribution. The rent proper is not usually a controversial item when looking at the rent cesser clause, because if the tenant cannot use the premises and he has been paying insurance to include loss of rent insurance nobody loses: the insurers, who have been receiving premiums for the purpose, pay the landlord and the tenant does not have to do so. The clause usually allows the tenant to cease rent payment 'to the extent' that the premises are not capable of being used, or some such wording. This covers partial destruction, for example where a two storey shop is damaged by a fire in the upper part the tenant may well still be able to trade from the lower floor: although this will obviously not be as beneficial as using the whole building, he may still be able to have some benefit and the rent reduction would take this into account. The amount of the reduction is normally subject to arbitration in case of disagreement. The Court of Appeal decided a 1993 case where the lease had a provision for cesser of rent for so long as the premises were destroyed or damaged by an insured risk. One insured risk was impact damage, and the premises, which were car showrooms in Tottenham, were damaged by the impact of a van driven by the defendant. The tenant was relieved of his liability to pay rent to the landlord for about eight weeks. The landlord claimed from the van driver the rent which the tenant did not have to pay and was successful: Ehmler v Hall [1993] 02 EG 115. If the whole of the premises are destroyed, there is no building to insure and thus the landlord would not pay a premium for which he would require reimbursement. If only part has been destroyed the insurance premium should reflect the value of what is left, and should thus be smaller than if the whole property was standing. The tenant does not, in such circumstances, need further protection in the cesser clause to cover the tenant's liability for the insurance premium. Turning to the service charge, the position is somewhat different. The rent is payable in respect of the premises which the tenant occupies. If the premises cease to exist (or to be usable) there is nothing to pay rent for. By contrast, the service charge payments inevitably relate to premises other than those let to the tenant. Unless the whole of the landlord's property is destroyed, there will still be works and services being be provided by the landlord. In such a case automatic agreement to allow the tenant not to contribute at all to service charges if the tenant's property is destroyed may be unwise. There seem to be four possibilities which are outlined in the next paragraph.

8.21   To achieve fairness it may be that the cesser of rent clause needs to be expanded to cover an agreed position in relation to each of the permutations:

(a)   If the whole of the landlord's property is destroyed it seems reasonable to agree that payment of service charge should cease. (Indeed, there will presumably be no services provided, except such items as rates for which there may be some rating relief.)

(b)   If part of the landlord's property is destroyed but the tenant can still occupy and use the premises let to him, then there seems no reason why the tenant should not pay service charge contributions, to cover those services which are supplied.

(c)   If the premises let to the tenant are destroyed, or damaged so that he cannot use them at all, it would seem right for the tenant to be excused the liability to pay for services, even if the landlord has to supply them to other parts of the landlord's property. This is on the basis that the tenant's service charge contribution is a part payment for services from which, in the case of total destruction of his unit, he can have no benefit.

(d) If the premises let to the tenant are damaged but still capable of beneficial use by the tenant he should still pay a proportionate part of the service charge. Thus if the premises are capable only of 50% beneficial occupation perhaps the tenant should only pay 50% of the contribution he should otherwise make.

SERVICE CHARGES AND PRICE INDEXES

8.22   For tenants of flats on the Chelsea Embankment in Cumshaw Ltd v Bowen [1987] 1 EGLR 30, the service charge was originally assessed at £100, and this figure was to be increased in accordance with increases in the Retail Prices Index. (This is an unsatisfactory way of assessing service charges as it bears no real relation to the actual expenditure, but the leases were so drafted.) The leases also provided that if the Index ceased to be published, or was no longer available to the public, the tenants would pay service charges based on £100 plus 'a fair proportion of any increase from time to time in the cost incurred by the landlord in providing the services ... above the cost incurred by the lessors in respect of the same as at the date hereof'. After a number of years, the basis of the Index had changed several times and the base figure of the Index had twice been brought back to 100. The landlords sought a declaration that because of the changes the Index no longer represented the basis on which the lease was granted, so that the service charges should henceforth be based on the fall-back position (ie £100 plus the increase in actual costs). The court would not grant the declaration. The Index still subsisted. The increase could be calculated by taking the 1956 Index figure as the base.

8.23   In a highly technical case, Coventry City Council v Cole [1994] 1 All ER 997, an index was also a material factor. The case revolved around a 'right to buy lease'. The latter is a 125-year lease which a public sector residential tenant of a flat can acquire under the Housing Act 1985, where the tenant pays a reduced premium depending on the length of his occupation as a qualifying tenant. The terms of the lease are governed by Sch 6 to the Housing Act 1985. (See 10.76 et seq.) In a somewhat similar way to the Cumshaw case at 8.22 above, the tenant was required to pay a fixed service charge of £208 per year and, by clause 5(2), 'By way of additional charge a sum bearing the same proportion to the said sum as shall be borne by any increase in the Building Cost Information Service Tender Price Index ...' The tenant alleged that the requirement to pay the additional amount was unlawful within the terms of the Housing Act 1985. The claim suggested that the amount was unenforceable under para 18(a) of Sch 6 (which prohibits recovery of service charges under right to buy leases except in respect of certain defined matters) or, alternatively, that if the sum was not an unauthorised service charge it must be rent which was restricted

(Sch 6, para 11 to the Housing Act 1985) to £10 per year. The Court of Appeal rejected both arguments. The rent restricted to £10 was the ground rent, and the indexation provision was not rent. The judge giving the sole judgment held 'after some hesitation' that the indexation figure was not a service charge payment either. He said:

> 'Schedule 6 and the protection which it confers on a tenant have to be looked at in the context of the statutory control relating to variable charges. The reasonableness of a fixed charge can be examined at the time when the long lease is being negotiated. Assuming that the fixed charge is reasonable, the tenant is protected over the whole period of the lease from fluctuating and unpredictable costs. His only exposure to risk is in the risk attendant on a clause which depends on inflation. I consider the judge was right to uphold the clause and to treat clause 5(2) [the index provision] as falling outside paragraph 16 A and therefore outside the scope of paragraph 18 of Schedule 6.'

The effect, therefore, was that the index sum was held not to be rent, not surprisingly, but was also held not to be a service charge, which is perhaps less expected. (It is perhaps fair comment that the service charge here was largely for repair of structural items – ie items which involve building. If there were non-building items (gardening, security, cleaning etc), the decision would be, it is suggested, unsatisfactory.) As it was held that as the index payment was not a service charge the 'reasonableness' provisions affecting service charges for residential premises (s 19 of the Landlord and Tenant Act 1985 for private tenants and s 47 of the Housing Act 1985 for right to buy tenants) did not apply to that sum.

8.24   Using an index seems an unsatisfactory way of proceeding. During a long lease clearly the level of service costs will change, and coupling a fixed sum which was fair at the start of the tenancy with an index will undoubtedly mean that within a few years the total of the indexed sum and the fixed sum will bear less and less relation to the actual costs incurred.

Service charges and registered rents

8.25   Rents of residential premises can be registered with a variable amount for services under the Rent Act 1977, s 71(4) in appropriate circumstances (see Chapter 9). The courts have been called upon to review several aspects of such registration and the following are cases that indicate judicial thinking on significant aspects.

8.26   In a leading service charge case, Firstcross Ltd v Teasdale (1982) 47 P & CR 228, affecting some furnished and some unfurnished flats registration was one of the two main issues. (The other issue related to the construction of a covenant to keep premises in 'good and tenantable condition.) The tenants of the unfurnished flats were liable to pay a proportionate part of the cost of certain expenses as outlined in Sch 4, which contains provisions relating to items such as porterage, gardening, repairs, lifts etc. The Rent Assessment Committee, which determined the registration, decided to register a fixed rent and decided not to register the service charge element as a variable amount, although it had power to do so. The landlords appealed and won. The judge said:

> 'The proper approach, as it seems to me, is first to value the "occupation" element in the rent of the subject flat, next to consider the services provided by the landlord ... and to determine whether or not the contractual terms for that variation are reasonable and, if not, to assess, having regard to all the relevant circumstances, the annual rental value to be attributed to them as part of the "service" element to be included in the inclusive fair rent. Finally, to consider, as s 71(4) requires, the cost of the landlord's maintenance and repair obligations when chargeable to the tenant.'

The judgment is a very detailed and closely reasoned one, and usefully reviews the Rent Act registration provisions and the effect of reasonableness under the statutory provisions then applying and also Finchbourne Ltd v Rodrigues [1976] 3 All ER 581.

8.27   In a case where the relationship between rent and service charge was peripheral, Legal and General Assurance Society Ltd v Keane (1978) 38 P & CR 399, a rent was registered which, in effect, was an all inclusive and non-variable figure. The landlords wanted to increase the registered rent. There was no obligation on the tenant to pay a service charge, although the landlord was to carry out certain services. In those circumstances, the court decided that the tenants were not entitled to an order for discovery of information relating to the costs of the services. This had been requested by the tenant, as the figures put forward as the costs of services seemed to be somewhat inconsistent.

8.28   In *Wigglesworth v Property Holding & Investment Trust plc* (1984) 270 Estates Gazette 555, a rent assessment panel incorrectly registered a rent and the case was referred back to another panel by the court. The lease had provided for a rent of £550 p.a. plus 0.8% of any increase in the costs of certain specified services in 1959. In due course a new rent fell to be registered. The rent officer had registered £2,295 as a fixed rent with no variable element. An appeal was made to the rent assessment panel, and after evidence of the cost of services had been given the panel registered £2,350 as a variable rent. On review by the court, it appeared that this figure was made up, in effect, of £1,470 for rent and £880 for services. The court held that as the rent figure included the proportion for services it was not right for the whole to be treated as a variable rent and remitted the case to a different panel.

8.29   The decision in Perseus Property Co Ltd v Burberry [1985] 1 EGLR 114 on registration of a registered rent raised two useful points. First, was that it was proper to consider, in registering a variable rent, including an element for depreciation. Secondly, that the registration could include an element for landlord's profit. The case was referred back to the Rent Assessment Committee for reconsideration.

8.30   The final case to be mentioned in this section on registered rents is R v London Rent Assessment Panel, ex p Cliftvylle Properties Ltd [1983] 1 EGLR

100. There the dispute related to the element to be taken into account to reflect the cost of heating. (The facts are set out at 9.51.) The committee assessed what they considered was a reasonable figure for the heating costs rather than the actual costs, and the court supported this approach.

Service charges and rent review

8.31 This section relates to the effect on rent review of service charges. The two are strictly separate matters.

8.32 Tenants look, and are well advised to look, at the total outgoings of a property when deciding to take a lease. Where the rent is subject to review the tenants are entitled to see whether the rent review provisions need any adjustment because of service charge factors.

A rent review assumption

8.33 There grew up a fashion in the late 1990s for a few years for some tenant's solicitors, when considering draft leases of commercial premises containing rent review provisions, to add in the rent review terms a disregard of items for which the tenant has contributed through the service charge. The disregard just mentioned was on the following lines: 'Disregarding ... any effect on rent of any item for which the Tenant has contributed through the service charge.' At first sight this is not unreasonable. In rent review clauses landlords normally accept that they should not increase the rent in respect of items for which the tenant has paid (eg improvements by the tenant). That said, it is not necessarily the case that a service charge disregard is appropriate except in very limited circumstances. No court decisions on the clause are available, but the following is intended to analyse some aspects if such a clause is being negotiated:

(a) The main fallacy is that it is intended to be the equivalent of those cases where the tenant actually pays the cost himself – eg his own improvements. The case envisaged by the proposed disregard ignores the point that the tenant has not paid for the whole of the item – he has merely paid his X% but seems to want 100% of the amount disregarded on review. A more fair disregard might be to disregard the effect of the item 'in so far as (or to the extent that) the tenant has contributed to the cost.' This would enable the valuer, in appropriate cases, to seek to disregard X% of the value to the whole building of the item in question. This seems, to a lawyer, a difficult but slightly more acceptable proposition. It is not clear how it works. Does the valuer assume a value for the item of £Z and somehow capitalise this to find the rent? Perhaps he can assume the building does not have the factor in question and can hypothesise on the amount of rent a tenant would pay for the demised premises if the feature was not present. This would give the tenant 100% benefit even though he only contributed X% of the cost. Another alternative is to disregard on rent review 'those items for which the whole capital cost has been recovered by the landlord through the service

215

charges paid by the tenants of [the building]'. They would only be disregarded if the tenant could show that the landlord had not paid any part of the cost of the item.

(b) If a tenant has been able to negotiate a provision that the landlord will not charge the capital cost of new items through the service charge the tenant will have had protection against the setting up costs. However, the item may well be a sensible and necessary item (eg a replacement lift or new escalator) and it seems hard to see why the rent payable by the tenant on review should not reflect the physical state of the premises. The rent review is to reflect what a tenant taking the premises would be likely to pay, and he, of course would see the condition of the lift or escalator. (Although a prospective tenant does not normally have a survey of the common parts carried out.) Taking the point further, it could be argued that the wording just mentioned would require the valuer to assume that the premises did not have a lift: that seems taking unreality too far.

(c) If the disregard on the rent review is very wide the tenant might obtain the benefit of a reduction in rent for each rent review after some change, even though the change only has effect for part of the lease term. An example might be a change to the gardens. Perhaps they need to be re-laid after 15 years. The tenant might be able to object to contributing to the cost of such relaying (on the basis that it went beyond normal gardening; although the point is clearly arguable – if good gardening practice requires relaying every 15 years and that is what the landlord does, he is only carrying out normal garden maintenance), in which case the rent review disregard would not be material. If it was accepted that it was the tenant's liability to pay service charge for the relaying, would it be reasonable for the tenant to be able to use this as a way of restricting rent on each subsequent rent review? Fifteen years later it would need to be done again! The fact, of course, is that the tenant (and the notional tenant assumed in the rent review) has the benefit of the grounds as laid out and should be prepared to pay rent to reflect that. Any disregard should not entitle the tenant to reduce the rent on a false assumption that there is no garden, or that the garden is in a state other than it is in. (Courts are currently leaning against artificial assumptions in rent review clauses, and adopt reality as far as possible.) Another example of temporary benefit might be some form of treatment of a material (eg polishing or some form of re-covering such as new carpets) needed every seven years: it would not be reasonable for the rent review to disregard the presence of the material.

(d) If the tenant pays through the service charge towards an item which is hired (eg security cameras), the disregard would seem to require the building to be valued without security cameras at all. This would reflect a considerable departure from reality. If there were no security cameras at the start of the tenancy perhaps the tenant would have reflected this in his rental bid and thus had a benefit at that time.

(e) On construction of rent review clauses there may be provisions which, for example, disregard improvements where the tenant or its predecessors have contributed to the cost. The usual wording of the disregard is in relation to improvements to the demised premises (which is all that the tenant is entitled to improve). However, in a few (probably very few) cases, the tenant may be able to rely on that wording to reduce rental increases on the basis of the cost of improvements to the main building/centre by the landlord for which the tenant has been charged through the service charge.

(f)   It is only in those cases where the landlord introduces something entirely new, such as a cradle for external cleaning which was not present before, and where the tenants between them have paid the full capital cost and have paid the full maintenance costs as well which demonstrate sympathy with this clause. The clause mentioned above is much wider than that. The suggested disregard takes the lease away from reality, but seems fair in those limited circumstances. It is tentatively suggested that if such a provision is required it should be in a limited form of the disregard as follows: 'Disregarding ... the effect on rent of each new service or new facility for the [Building] in respect of which the capital cost and maintenance costs have been paid in full by the tenants of [the Building] through the service charge.'

Effect on review of high service charge liability

8.34   One significant aspect of rent review and service charges worth recording is the possible effect severe service charge provisions may have. The rent review is intended to ascertain what a potential new tenant would pay for the property on the basis of the lease terms. If the service charge provisions in the lease are unduly harsh and are such that the landlord can charge whatever he chooses without the tenant being able to challenge the amounts concerned, so that the tenant may have to pay unduly high service charges, a tenant, on rent review, is entitled to point out that the hypothetical tenant would take account of those lease terms when making his bid for the property. The fact that the service charges are higher than may be expected for similar properties is the subject of comment in representations to the arbitrator or expert. After all the hypothetical tenant would look at the overall sum he expects to have to pay – if the service charge level is too high it would affect what he was prepared to pay by way of rent.

Rent, service charge and the internet

8.35   If the tenant's proposed use of the premises is for e-commerce there could be two service charge consequences, namely: (a) assessing the 'fair proportion' if the tenant pays a turnover rent; and (b) the landlord's additional set-up costs.

8.36   Turnover rents are rare other than for retail shops, but if a landlord wants to use the potential massive turnover from a new venture to increase the rent payable he may consider a turnover rent for such businesses as call centres. The landlord may also agree a turnover for such businesses and try a turnover rent to see whether it would provide a greater rent than a conventional rent.

8.37   The normal system is for the first year's rent to be agreed, and for future rents to be a fixed percentage of the initial rent (as a base rent) plus a proportion of profits. The rent will, accordingly, go up and down according to the profitability of the tenant, but never below the fixed amount. There is a problem, however, with the internet when assessing profits. Although the tenant may be trading from the premises, there can be great doubt about where the business was transacted. If it was not transacted at the premises should the profit be included within the figures for calculating the rent? This may sound like an exam question: there may be computers and internet connections in the demised premises in Loughborough, but if a customer in Leeds telephones to Loughborough to arrange delivery of goods to Luton which will come from the tenant's warehouse in Launceston, and payment is made by a credit card credited to the tenant's accounts department in Liskeard, it may be hard to say quite where the contract is made. The tenant has three sets of premises involved in the transaction. This is only relevant to service charges if the service charges are based on the turnover figure. The author has never seen a provision of this sort and would strongly advise against it because of the potential for dispute, unless the lease sets out very clearly the basis on which e-commerce deals are to be treated. Apart from the difficulty of finding a satisfactory solution to the above problem, it is right to say that the service charge works and services affect the demised premises, and apart from the point mentioned in the next paragraph are not in any way affected by what the tenant does at the premises.

8.38   Apart from the possibility of a turnover rent, the internet aspect that the landlord will be concerned with is ensuring the premises have the right cabling and possibly also internet connections in the first case. Such costs could include providing broadband connections to the internet so that tenants can 'move in and plug in'. This is an initial cost and will no doubt be reflected in the initial rent. Tenants would probably resist any attempt to include the cost of providing the connection in the service charge – it is a set up cost which the landlord should bear. It is to be expected that the landlord be responsible for the cabling in the building leading to the outlets in the demised parts of the building, and for the service charge to reflect this. (See also 5.135 et seq.)

CHAPTER 9

The main statutory provisions affecting service charges

The Statute Book, which is a vast jungle of strange and primitive things.

A P Herbert

PART I – INTRODUCTION

9.1 The difference between dwellings and other property is crucial in interpreting leases and the effect of the law on any given service charge problem. There are many statutory provisions directly and indirectly concerning service charges, but, apart from the Landlord and Tenant (Covenants) Act 1995, the provisions solely affect residential property. It has been held, at first instance (*Electricity Supply Nominees Ltd v IAF Group plc* [1993] 3 All ER 372) that the Unfair Contract Terms Act 1977 does not apply to leases, so that even this limited aid to interpretation will not assist. (It relates to exclusion clauses only.) If the premises are mixed, such as flats over shops or offices, the tenants of the flats can claim benefits under the legislation which are not open to the commercial tenants.

9.2 It is not possible to contract out of the statutory obligations.

9.3 The protection for residential tenants originally appeared in the Housing Finance Act 1972, and has been amended, replaced and enlarged from time to time since. The main body of legislation is now in the Landlord and Tenant Act 1985, with amendments and further important provisions added by the Landlord and Tenant Act 1987, the Leasehold Reform, Housing and Urban Development Act 1993, the Housing Act 1996 and most recently by the Commonhold and Leasehold Reform Act 2002. These are described in this chapter. Originally the relevant provisions of the Landlord and Tenant Act 1985 affected 'flats'. This was helpfully changed by the 1987 Act to refer to 'dwellings' which of course makes the relevant provisions apply to houses as well as flats.

9.4 The majority of the statutory provisions affect all residential premises. Certain other provisions apply solely to long tenancies or secure tenancies or other special tenancies. The statutory provisions which affect only some types of leases of dwellings are the subject of Chapter 10.

9.5 The legislation is very one-sided. None of the provisions which relate to service charges is of any benefit at all to the landlord, apart perhaps from:

(a) Section 27A of the 1985, added by the 2002 Act, under which either party can apply to the court for a declaration whether or not the service charge costs for works or services are reasonable, either for past or future costs; using this procedure a landlord can obtain clearance of his plans in advance.

(b) (Perhaps) the discretion given in s 20ZA of the 1985 Act to waive consultation requirements if it is reasonable to do so. This is the only place in the legislation where discretion is given to waive a landlord's obligation.

(c) The change to s 35(4) of the Landlord and Tenant Act 1987 under which a landlord, as well as the tenant, can apply to vary a lease if the total recoverable service charge is less than 100%.

(d) The right under the Schedule to the Landlord and Tenant Act 1985 for the landlord, as well as the tenant, to seek an order about whether a policy with a nominated or approved insurer is unsatisfactory or the premiums excessive.

9.6   Obviously, any such legislation is an interference with the rights of the parties to contract as they think fit. However, it would be no more an interference with commercial leases than it is an interference with residential leases or tenancies. Governments of varying political colours over the years have always sought to protect the tenants of residential premises, and have given them various rights. By contrast governments have put forward relatively little legislation that springs to mind as a benefit specifically to tenants of commercial premises, other than the major right to renewal at the end of the term under the Landlord and Tenant Act 1954, Pt 2. It is hard to see any legislation giving any benefit at all to landlords for many years. The government has indicated that it may decide to legislate in respect of alienation provisions in leases of non-residential property, and perhaps banning upward-only rent reviews. As far as the author is aware, they do not seem to be contemplating introducing service charge legislation for commercial leases, and we can but wait and see what, if anything, transpires.

9.7   In a development the author finds unwelcome, the 2002 Act has changed many of the material provisions and provided for important aspects (such as details of the consultation procedure) to appear in regulations. In addition, instead of perhaps introducing replacement provisions by repealing s X of the 1985 and replacing it with para Y of the umpteenth Schedule to the Commonhold Act, the 2002 Act has replaced many important sections, so that we have two versions of the same section, depending when the change comes into force. The changes appear in various parts of the 2002 Act. As this is written, there are a few sections still not yet in force, four years after the Act received royal assent. This means it is difficult for both professionals and the parties themselves to be sure exactly what the relevant provisions are at any time.

Summary

9.8   In the interests of completeness, all the statutory provisions affecting service charges have been included. They appear in this chapter for those provisions that affect all leases, and those that affect all dwellings. Chapter 10 deals with the provisions relating to a limited number of leases, for example only long leases, or those with particular landlords. In both chapters the provisions are, with limited exceptions, included chronologically. The most important provisions affecting all dwellings can be summarised thus:

Section 18 of the 1985 Act The principal definition of service charges.

Section 19 of the 1985 Act The requirement for reasonableness.

Section 20 of the 1985 Act Obligation for the landlord to consult with the tenants concerning works and services.

Section 20B of the 1985 Act An 18-month time limit on claiming costs.

Section 21 of the 1985 Act The obligation of the landlord to provide a summary of costs.

Section 22 of the 1985 Act A right for tenants to inspect receipts etc.

Section 23 of the 1985 Act Obligations on superior landlords to provide information.

Section 25 of the 1985 Act Criminal penalties.

Section 27A of the 1985 Act Service charge disputes to be decided by a leasehold valuation tribunal.

Section 30B of the 1985 Act The right for 'Recognised Tenants' Associations' to be consulted about the employment of managing agents.

Section 3 of the 1987 Act The former landlord to remain liable until the tenants are notified of change of ownership.

Section 42 of the 1987 Act All service charge payments by tenants are held on trust.

Section 42A of the 1987 Act All trust money is to be held in a designated account. (This provision is not in force at the time of writing.)

Sections 76 to 84 of the Leasehold Reform, Housing and Urban Development Act 1993 Tenants' right to an independent audit of service charge costs.

Section 87 of the 1993 Act Providing that Codes of Practice can be used as evidence.

Section 81 of the Housing Act 1996 Prohibition on forfeiture or re-entry for failure to pay service charges unless the amount is agreed or has been determined.

Of the above, the three most important are ss 19 and 20 of the 1985 Act and s 42 of the 1987 Act.

PART 2 – LEGISLATION AFFECTING ALL SERVICE CHARGES

Landlord and Tenant (Covenants) Act 1995: the position of former tenants and landlords

9.9   The basic effects of the Act have been described at **4.101**-**4.106** above. Readers are referred to those paragraphs for the general scheme for protection of former tenants against being required to pay service charges after they are no longer concerned with the premises. The Act 1995 covers other aspects affecting service charges, such as release of tenants and landlords from liability. There are other material provisions affecting landlords and tenants mentioned separately below.

Section 17 of the Landlord and Tenant (Covenants) Act 1995

Six months' limit for claims against former tenants

9.10   In the case of all leases, whenever granted, there is now a six-month time limit for recovery of arrears from former tenants, or the guarantors of former tenants. The limit applies to both (a) what are known as 'old tenancies', ie tenancies granted before the Act came into force (1 January 1996) and (b) 'new tenancies', ie granted after 1995 (other than following an agreement for lease before that date), but, in the latter case, only when a former tenant has given an authorised guarantee agreement ('AGA').

9.11   The restriction applies where the former tenant is liable for payment and a successor in title has defaulted. Under an old lease, if Tenant A is expressly released by the landlord when he assigns, then the landlord cannot claim from Tenant A for arrears caused by one of his successors. By contrast, if Tenant B assigned the same lease but was not released on the assignment, he can be pursued for payment when the current tenant defaults. Claims against current tenants and their guarantors are affected by normal limitation periods.

9.12   The limits for the recovery under s 17 work by notice. The notice has to state that the amount is due and that the landlord intends 'to recover from the former tenant such amount as is specified in the notice and (where payable) interest calculated on such basis as is so specified'. Section 17(2) says that the former tenant is not liable to pay any 'fixed charge payable under the covenant unless, within the period of six months beginning with the date when the charge becomes due, the landlord serves on the former tenant a notice'. Under s 17(6), 'fixed charge' includes rent, a liquidated sum mentioned in the lease for breach of covenant, and also 'any service charge as defined by section 18 of the Landlord and Tenant Act 1985 (the words 'of a dwelling' being disregarded for this purpose)'. Accordingly, the provisions apply to service charges for commercial premises as well as residential. Section 17(3) goes on to prohibit recovery from the guarantors of a former tenant without a similar notice.

9.13 There is provision in s 17(4) for the amount in the notice to be revised upwards, provided that the notice makes it clear that there may be some later adjustment. A second notice must be served within three months of the adjusted figure being known. Subject to this the amount to be recovered cannot exceed the amount in the original notice. Therefore, where a notice claims service charges as well as rent and the year end adjustment has not been made before the notice has to be served, it is vital that the landlord should, in the notice, notify the tenant of a possible increase, and then serve the second notice within three months of the adjustment being made.

9.14 The landlord can, of course, serve notices every few months, and indeed will have to do so if he wants to be able to continue to recover from a former tenant while the lease continues. The sensible course for a landlord with a current tenant who is not paying service charge, or appears unlikely to be able to do so, is probably to serve notice on the former tenant at about the time the service charge payments are due. He should do this each time another payment becomes due. If the current tenant pays, well and good: if not, the landlord will have the mechanism in place to claim against the former tenant (or guarantor). This is subject to the comments below.

Variations

9.15 The right to recover from a former tenant may be lost or restricted where there have been changes. Section 18(2) of the 1995 Act limits claims against former tenants and guarantors of former tenants where the lease has been varied 'to the extent that the amount (claimed) is referable to any relevant variation of the tenant covenants of the tenancy effected after the assignment'. In other words, if the lease has been varied and the variation would increase the sum otherwise payable, the former tenant is only liable for the arrears excluding the increase. An obvious example is higher service charges following alterations to the building. Examples affecting rent might include changes to the permitted use from a very restricted use to an open use, or changes to the form of any rent review. Section 18(4) states that a variation is a relevant variation 'if either the landlord has, at the time of the variation an absolute right to refuse to allow the variation', or (b) it is a variation where the landlord would have had a right to refuse the variation immediately before the assignment by the former tenant, but where the lease was varied later. Accordingly, the former tenant is, in effect, only liable for payments of the type contemplated by the documents which he executed.

Overriding lease

9.16 Where a s 17 notice has been served on a former tenant and the amount claimed is paid in full by that former tenant, then the former tenant can call for an 'overriding lease' under s 19 of the 1995 Act. This is a lease inserted between the landlord's interest (whether freehold or leasehold), and the lease under which the payment is made. It is for the term of the lease plus three days, unless this is more than the landlord's own reversion, and is on the same terms, other than any personal covenants (s 19(2), (4)). If the former tenant takes an overriding lease he becomes, again, the tenant of the landlord, but at the same time he also becomes the landlord of the defaulting tenant. So far as he is landlord of the defaulting tenant he can forfeit the lease or exercise the other remedies available to any landlord. In particular, if he forfeits the original lease the former tenant will then hold an interest, the overriding lease, which he can assign or underlet free from the forfeited lease. He could even occupy the premises again. This avoids the previous position under which a former tenant could be made to pay rent throughout the residue of the term where his successor had defaulted but with no real recourse to the property (unless the tenant became insolvent and the lease was disclaimed, when the former tenant could seek an order for the lease to be vested in him) and only a remedy against successors in title, at least one of whom was, ex hypothesi, a defaulter.

9.17   Points to note are:

(a)   The right to an overriding lease only arises when a s 17 notice has been served and the sum claimed has been paid by the former tenant. Accordingly, if the landlord does not want the former tenant to have the right to an overriding lease he must consider whether or not to serve the s 17 notice on that tenant. If the former tenant was one who would, for example, use the premises for a use competing with other premises of the landlord, or was for some reason or another undesirable, the landlord should weigh the advantages of being possibly able to recover arrears from this former tenant against the potential disadvantages of being obliged to grant the former tenant an overriding lease.

(b)   If the landlord seeks to avoid the position highlighted in the preceding sub-paragraph he could seek recovery of arrears without serving notice, eg by request in a simple letter, but the well advised former tenant will refuse to pay without the proper notice.

(c)   Where there are a number of former tenants against whom a landlord could claim he is entitled to claim against any one or more of them: he is not obliged to proceed in any particular order, nor to exhaust all possible remedies against the current tenant before suing a former tenant. (*Cheverell Estates Ltd v Harris* [1998] 1 EGLR 27.) So where there are several former tenants the landlord could serve s 17 notices only on those former tenants he would not object to have as tenants again.

Other provisions of the 1995 Act

Covenant obligations to cease

9.18   Although mercifully short for a Landlord and Tenant Act, there are other provisions in the Act that touch on service charges. The main general provisions affect the continuing, or non-continuing, liability of former tenants and former landlords in respect of new leases.

9.19   The Act seeks to provide that for new tenancies (ie post-1995 tenancies: see at **9.10**) the liability of tenants under the lease covenants will normally cease on assignment, although the liability of a landlord will continue unless he is released.

9.20   The benefit and burden of all 'landlord and tenant covenants' is annexed to the premises concerned and passes on assignment (s 3(1)). 'Landlord covenant' and 'tenant covenant' are defined in s 28 and effectively relate, as one would expect, to the covenants by those parties.

9.21   As mentioned above, the six-month rule for recovering service charge arrears from a former tenant applies where the former tenant remains liable. For old tenancies that liability normally continues throughout the term. For new tenancies the former tenant is not liable for arrears created by a successor at all, save only where the tenant enters into an 'authorised guarantee agreement' under s 16. This is a guarantee by a tenant of his own successor. Under s 16, although if the original tenant gives an AGA he will be liable to Act as guarantor for the tenant to whom he assigns, his liability ceases when there is a further assignment. The same applies to the various successors – a tenant under a new tenancy can only be liable for his immediate successor and no further.

Release of landlord after assignment of the reversion

9.22   The position of the landlord of a new tenancy has been changed. For the author's purposes it is material to remember that the landlord will almost certainly have entered into specific obligations, or there would be no service charge to collect. (In many non-service charge leases the landlord only covenants for quiet enjoyment and perhaps insurance.) In contrast to the tenant's position, if the landlord assigns the reversion to a new owner the former landlord is not automatically released from liability for the landlord covenants. The consequence is that in case of a breach of a landlord covenant a tenant may have a right to make a claim against either the current, defaulting, landlord or against a previous landlord who has not been released.

9.23   Section 6 entitles the landlord to apply to be released from future liability when he assigns the reversion, and s 7 gives a former landlord a right to apply for a release when his successor assigns the reversion. When the release is given the landlord ceases to be bound by the landlord covenants and no longer has any benefit from the tenant covenants. The release is given by the tenant to the landlord on request by the landlord, either before the assignment of the reversion or within four weeks after. In the case of a former landlord, the timing is based on the subsequent assignment.

9.24   When a notice requesting release is served:

(a)   the release is granted if the tenant does not object within four weeks;

(b)   the release is granted if the tenant objects but is overruled by the court; or

(c) the release is granted if the tenant writes agreeing, or withdraws an earlier objection.

(Section 8(2).)

9.25   For service charge purposes a landlord would do well to seek a release unless the leases are virtually at an end. If his successor fails to provide the services the tenants could, at least in theory, claim against a former landlord. As the former landlord is no longer owner of the premises he has no legal right to enter the premises to carry out works etc, although he could in reality presumably instruct agents to manage the premises and could fund the works. The agents may feel reluctant to accept instructions in such cases. On assignment of the reversion he may need to consider reserving rights of entry to do the works if he is unable to obtain a release.

9.26   Can he recover costs he pays in such cases via the service charge in the lease? The answer seems to be that he can, because until he has a release of his landlord covenants he still has the benefit of the tenant covenants. Section 6(2)(b) makes it clear that the benefit of the tenant covenants is lost when the landlord is released: the corollary is surely that the benefit continues until that time. The current landlord also has the benefit of the tenant covenants, but if he does not spend money on providing services he will not have anything to recover from the tenants.

Benefit of arrears

9.27   The final section of the 1995 Act that can be singled out as material for service charges is s 23(1). This section states that on an assignment the person entitled to the burden or benefit of a covenant does 'not by virtue of this Act have any liability or rights under the covenant in relation to any time falling before the assignment'. Section 23(2) permits rights to be assigned expressly. The effect is that an assignee of the reversion cannot claim for breaches arising before the assignment, for example non-payment of service charges, unless the right to sue for previous arrears is expressly assigned.

PART 3 – THE MAIN LEGISLATION AFFECTING DWELLINGS

Section 18 of the Landlord and Tenant Act 1985

Definitions of 'service charge' and 'relevant costs'

9.28   Section 18(1) defines 'service charge' as:

'an amount payable by a tenant of a dwelling as part of or in addition to the rent:

(a) which is payable, directly or indirectly, for services, repairs, maintenance, improvements or insurance or the landlord's costs of management; and

(b)   the whole or part of which varies or may vary according to the relevant costs.'

('Relevant costs' are defined in s 18(2): see at **9.35**.)

9.29   The key point here is the reference to a 'dwelling', emphasising that the legislation does not affect commercial property. The expression 'as part of or in addition to the rent' makes it clear that the provisions apply whether or not the service charge is reserved as rent, and also that it applies, eg to those cases where there is a rent registered as a variable amount under s 71 of the Rent Act 1977. (See Chapter 10.)

9.30   The section refers to a figure that can vary, and so it does not apply if there is a fixed service charge, whether expressed as a specific amount, or simply included within the fixed rent.

9.31   The word 'dwelling' is defined in s 38 of the 1985 Act. (See at **9.234** below.) It encompasses a whole house, as well as a separate part of a house used for living, such as a house divided into flats. Equally, it covers flats in a purpose built block. There are no service charge exemptions for resident landlords, and so the provisions of that Act apply, for example, to a landlord company owned by the tenants. There are exemptions, mentioned later, in respect of landlords who are local authorities etc. (See s 26, at **9.196** below.)

9.32   Section 18 and the other service charge sections refer to 'the landlord'. The alleged definition in s 30 merely provides that '"landlord" includes any person who has a right to enforce payment of a service charge'. Thus, for the purposes of the Act, a management company may in appropriate circumstances be 'the landlord'. (See, however, at **9.51** and the comments on *Berrycroft Management Co Ltd v Sinclair Gardens Investments (Kensington) Ltd* [1997] 1 EGLR 47, where the relative positions of the real landlord and the management company within the Act were reviewed.)

9.33   It would seem from the wording of s 18(1) that the service charge provisions can apply if there is only a variable service charge payable without a rent. It has been held that a rent is not essential for a tenancy (eg in *Bostock v Bryant* [1990] 2 EGLR 101, where the tenant paid only for gas, electricity and rates) and, accordingly, it would be possible for there to be a tenancy to which the Act could apply even if no rent is payable, as for example where the tenant pays towards repair and maintenance only.

9.34   The provisions are said to apply to insurance. There is, however, specific protection for tenants in respect of insurance separately in the Schedule to the 1985 Act (added by s 43 of the Landlord and Tenant Act 1987; see at **9.236**), which will be more useful for insurance disputes than the other 1985 Act provisions. In reality, the parties or the managing agents probably do not think of insurance in the same way as they do service charges.

9.35   Section 18(2) states that the 'relevant costs are the costs or estimated costs incurred or to be incurred by or on behalf of the landlord, or a superior landlord, in connection with the matters for which the service charge is payable'. The reference to 'relevant costs' appears throughout the later sections of the 1985 Act. It is to be noted that it includes costs already incurred and also future costs, and that the expression, in addition to referring to costs of the landlord, can include the costs of a superior landlord, where these are material. Thus, in addition to a charge levied by a landlord for work already done, it can include estimated costs of a superior landlord where these are payable by the tenant. (See at **9.32** for the definition of 'landlord'; the position of the superior landlord is also reflected in s 23; see at **9.178** below.)

9.36   Section 18(3) states that 'costs' includes 'overheads'. It goes on to make it clear that costs are 'relevant costs' whether they are 'incurred, or to be incurred, in the period for which the service charge is payable or in an earlier or later period'. This clarifies that provisions, for example, for reasonableness and consultation, cover all permutations and therefore in a dispute the whole of the costs can be taken into account, whether for the current year, the previous year, or indeed the following year. The 'later period' could also cover a sinking fund payment for replacement of some plant years ahead. When considering earlier periods the reader needs to take account of s 20B of the Act (s 20B has an 18-month time limit; see at **9.130** below) as well as the Landlord and Tenant (Covenants) Act 1995 referred to in Part 2 of this chapter, at **9.10**.

9.37   The reference to 'overheads', which does not appear elsewhere in the service charge provisions, seems to be included to make it clear that if a landlord charges for his own time for managing the property those charges are affected by the statutory provisions, even though the sum to be claimed is not money paid out by the landlord. This has perhaps at least partly been overtaken in practice by the introduction in Sch 11 to the Commonhold and Leasehold Reform Act 2002 of specific protection for tenants in relation to administration charges. Administration charges are to be no more than is reasonable. They are charges by or on behalf of a landlord arising in four circumstances: (a) charges for consents; (b) charges for providing information; (c) penalties for late payment of service charges; and (d) other penalties.

Section 19 of the Landlord and Tenant Act 1985

Reasonableness

9.38   This section, along with s 20 (consultation) and s 42 of the 1987 Act (money to be held on trust), is the key statutory service charge provision. Section 19 provides for reasonableness of service charges for dwellings in three circumstances. Section 19(1) says that:

> 'Relevant costs shall be taken into account in determining the amount of a service charge payable for a period –

(a)   only to the extent that they are reasonably incurred, and

(b)   where they are incurred in the provision of services or the carrying out of works, only if the services or works are of a reasonable standard,

and the amount payable shall be limited accordingly.'

Section 19(2) goes on to say that where advance payments of service charges are payable 'no greater amount than is reasonable is so payable, and after the relevant costs have been incurred any necessary adjustment shall be made by repayment, reduction or subsequent charges or otherwise'. It is important to remember that the first alternative relates to the costs having been reasonably incurred: it does not say that the costs themselves must not be more than is reasonable. So it has to be reasonable to have incurred the costs, and, once that is established, then the amount payable is to be 'limited accordingly'. It is not clear that this slightly tortuous process reflects what Parliament thought it was doing.

9.39   Section 19(2) also states that where service charges are payable in advance there must be an 'adjustment' after the costs have been incurred. The adjustment can be by repayment, reduction or subsequent charges, or otherwise. The manner of adjustment is not described further, and perhaps the 'otherwise' is intended to cover such cases as those where any excess is to be carried forward unless it is over a particular figure, or perhaps where the parties reach an arrangement affecting other financial dealings amongst themselves.

9.40   Section 19(2) gives no time limit for the adjustment to be effected. If there is no adjustment by the time the next year's accounts are prepared, the tenant will be able to rely on this provision to assist. If there is no adjustment by that time, the landlord would surely be in breach of this provision, which requires advance payments to be no more than reasonable. This section was not in force when *Peachey Property Corporation Ltd v Henry* (1963) 188 EG 875 was decided (see at **4.67** above). In that case certificates for interim payments given in 1959 were accepted as still applicable some years later in the absence of later certificates. If s 19 had been in force before the case the landlords might have had difficulty in persuading a court that the 1959 certificate was a valid 'reasonable' estimate for a year for which it had not been prepared.

9.41   There is, perhaps surprisingly, no obligation on the landlord of private sector tenants to produce annual accounts. In due course there may be a provision requiring accounts to be provided within some specified period of the end of the accounting year. The Commonhold Act was to introduce this, but see the notes regarding s 21, at **9.149** et seq.

Disputes to be heard by Leasehold Valuation Tribunal

9.42   The Housing Act 1996 added new provisions to the 1985 Act. The provisions added to s 19 were to the effect that service charge disputes were to be decided by a leasehold valuation tribunal ('LVT'). Appeals from the LVT are to the Lands Tribunal with the consent of either the LVT or the Lands Tribunal. (Lands Tribunal Act 1949, s 3; and see at **9.208** below regarding possible judicial review.) New subsections were added as s 19(2A), (2B) and (2C). These were repealed by the Commonhold and Leasehold Reform Act 2002 but replaced with new s 27A to the 1985 Act (see at **9.201** et seq below). Some points of principle have been litigated, as indicated in the following paragraphs.

9.43   It was held by the Court of Appeal in *R (on the Application of Daejan Properties Ltd) v London Leasehold Valuation Tribunal* [2001] EWCA Civ 1095, [2001] 43 EG 187 that the Leasehold Valuation Tribunal has no jurisdiction to consider the reasonableness of service charges once the amount has been paid. The effect of the decision is modified by the new form of s 27A(5) to the 1985 Act, under which payment of an amount is not an admission that the amount is agreed.

9.44   In *Cheverell Estates Ltd v Harris* [1998] 1 EGLR 27, the Lands Tribunal held that a tenant who had made an application for a declaration under s 19 and had then assigned her lease was still entitled to pursue her request for a declaration.

9.45   In *R (on the application of Sinclair Gardens Investments (Kensington) Ltd v Lands Tribunal* [2004] EWHC 1910 (Admin), [2004] 47 EG 166 (the facts are set out at **9.208** below), landlords sought judicial review of the decision of the Lands Tribunal not to allow an appeal. The court said that Parliament had clearly intended there should be no right of appeal to the Court of Appeal against such a refusal by the Lands Tribunal. The Administrative Court had power to judicially review decisions, but applications for judicial review could only be made in exceptional circumstances. Here the landlord seemed to be seeking the opportunity to argue the case anew. The judge reviewed the authorities in detail. Exceptional circumstances would be limited to such matters as those where there were procedural irregularities of a kind which constituted a denial of the applicant's right to a fair hearing. The judge said:

> 'It is plain that the claimant was seeking permission from the Lands Tribunal to re-argue the merits of the LVT decision to disallow certain costs. The criticism of the LVT decision raises a mix of factual, legal and valuation issues. They are precisely the kind of issues that Parliament wished to be dealt with in a non-legalistic way and "left to the good sense of the LVT under the expert supervision of the Tribunal".'

9.46   Reasonableness may now be sometimes easier to prove in some cases as a result of s 87 of the Leasehold Reform, Housing and Urban Development Act 1993, which gives the Secretary of State power to approve specific codes of practice relating to residential property for the purpose of evidence. The question of whether or not an Act or omission is reasonable may, accordingly, be judged against the code. Codes are discussed in Chapter 11. It remains to be seen how cases will be decided where the matter in question is contrary to the code but specifically permitted in the lease.

Declarations

9.47   The numerous amendments to the 1985 Act seem to have left in place
s 19(4), which gives county courts a right to make a declaration concerning any
of the three strands of reasonableness 'notwithstanding that no other relief is
sought in the proceedings'. See the comments on s 27A below as to whether it is
necessary to issue two sets of proceedings.

Reasonableness – cases

9.48   As this is such a critical matter, a few cases where reasonableness was
material are now highlighted. In Chapter 2 (at **2.14** et seq), various cases where
reasonableness was an issue in a case were commented on. The statutory provisions on reasonableness have been specifically considered in a number of cases,
of which the following illustrate some significant approaches that may assist
those seeking to prove or disprove reasonableness.

9.49   In one of the leading cases on service charges, *Yorkbrook Investments
Ltd v Batten* [1985] 2 EGLR 100, the judge giving the judgment of the Court of
Appeal and commenting on s 91A of the Housing Finance Act 1972 (s 91A was
the predecessor of s 19 of the 1985 Act and covered the standard of work, stating
that the costs incurred by the landlord should be reasonable) said that 'we can
find no reason for suggesting that there is any presumption for or against a
finding of reasonableness of standard or of costs'. Thus, the party alleging that
something is or is not reasonable must satisfy the judge on the point. The court
clearly reserves its rights to decide all matters on the basis of the evidence put
to it.

9.50   How does the section work? In *Yorkbrook v Batten* the court decided
that the tenant had proved that the services provided were not of a reasonable
standard. The effect was that the tenant was entitled to a deduction from the
amount claimed by the landlord to reflect the poor standard of service. The case
was remitted back to the lower court to assess damages, but the effect was as
indicated. Tenants seeking their own audit under Chapter V of the Leasehold
Reform, Housing and Urban Development Act 1993 (see Chapter 10) and recognised tenants' associations appointing a surveyor under s 84 of and Sch 4 to the
Housing Act 1996, have rights to inspect common areas, which can assist in
ascertaining whether works are or are not of a reasonable standard. This is the
main sanction of s 19: the fact that costs are limited by the three elements of reasonableness should be a powerful incentive to a landlord to comply with the Act.
The services or works in dispute were, after all, ordered by or on behalf of the
landlord, and if he is not reimbursed by the tenants he will be responsible himself
for payment. He may have a remedy against the contractors for sub-standard
work, or even the managing agents for poor supervision.

9.51   The relation of landlord and management companies and s 19 was
raised in *Berrycroft Management Co Ltd v Sinclair Gardens Investments*

(Kensington) Ltd [1997] 1 EGLR 47 (also mentioned at **2.17**). This was an important Court of Appeal residential case, where the issue was the cost of insurance. A development of 14 purpose-built blocks of flats was created and the developers created management companies to carry out services for the blocks. The management companies were owned by the tenants. The leases put an obligation on the management company to insure for such sum as the landlord thought fit 'in some insurance office of repute and if directed by the landlord through a company nominated by the landlord and if required through any agency of the landlord in that company'. The developers had arranged insurance through two companies, but when the reversion was sold the new landlords nominated new insurers (Commercial Union) where the cost was considerably higher. The management company, inter alia, sought a declaration under s 19 that the insurance premiums from the new insurers were excessive and irrecoverable. In a lengthy judgment the Court of Appeal discussed issues including the relationship of landlord, management company, and tenant, as well as a claim for 'reasonableness' under *Finchbourne Ltd v Rodrigues* [1976] 3 All ER 581 and under s 19 of the 1985 Act. Beldam LJ, giving the only judgment, said that he did not think it possible in the circumstances of the case and 'having regard to the terms of the Act to regard the (management) company as the tenant's landlord to the exclusion of the landlord as defined in the lease'. He pointed out that the tenant had covenanted directly with the landlord for payment of the service charge to the management company, and thus the landlord was entitled to enforce payment of the service charge and thus was the landlord under s 30. He went on to say that costs under s 18 were those to be incurred by or on behalf of the landlord. Although the insurance was payable by tenants as part of the service charge it was not incurred by and on behalf of the landlord and therefore not 'relevant costs'. He also said that the judge below had concluded that the quotations from Commercial Union were competitive, compared to the quotation obtained by a single management company acting alone, and 'the active and responsible management of the agency nominated by Sinclair was, taken overall, beneficial to the lessees. Consequently, the costs of the insurance were neither unreasonable nor excessive and were negotiated in the ordinary course of business'. This is a warning that the reasonableness provisions seem limited to actions of landlords, and do not seem to apply where management is not by the landlord.

9.52   The provisions of s 19, and its predecessors, were discussed in the case of a mixed use building in *Alton House Holdings Ltd v Calflane (Management) Ltd* [1987] 283 EG 844. Premises in north London consisted of a block of 55 flats together with garages in the basement, some offices, and a showroom and petrol station. In effect, the repairing obligations were carried out by a management company, but (a) the management company did not covenant to carry out repairs etc, but merely to apply such sums as they received from the tenants of the flats towards repair etc, and (b) the fixed percentages in the residential leases and garages totalled 100% of the costs for the building, while the offices etc. did not pay service charges at all. After carrying out substantial works the management company found itself out of pocket. It was not entitled to claim from the tenants of the offices and petrol station, and tried to claim under s 19 for a contribution from the landlord. The management company tried, and failed, to persuade the court that where there was a shortfall in these circumstances the landlord should make up the balance. They failed, as the landlord had no obligation to contribute at all to the service charge, and had not covenanted to carry out any repairs itself, and neither had the management company. As the management company had no obligation to make any payments itself (it merely held the payments actually made by the tenants on trust to use to pay for repairs), it was under no obligation to 'put its hand into its own coffers (and so) there can be no implied covenant by the landlord to fill up the coffer again'. One interesting aspect is that s 19 was considered, and although the residential tenants had to pay 100% of the costs between them for works that benefited other tenants who had no obligation to contribute, the court apparently did not consider that s 19 justified either some change to the terms of the leases or some reduction in the total payable by the residential tenants. There are now powers under the Landlord and Tenant Act 1987 for parties to obtain court orders to vary residential leases in certain circumstances (see Chapter 10). These provisions may perhaps give tenants or landlords some help in similar cases.

9.53   A case illustrating the effect of change is *R v London Rent Assessment Panel, ex p Cliftvylle Properties Ltd* [1983] 1 EGLR 100. It revolved around the reasonableness of charges for heating in some Rent Act tenancy cases. The heating system had been designed for a whole building and originally supplied 102 flats. Later, the heating was used for less than the whole building. Over a period, many of the flats were sold off on long leases to tenants who thereafter had to provide their own heating. The effect was that the remaining tenants were being asked to pay the costs of the whole heating system which was supplying fewer flats. This gave a much larger cost per flat. Because of the change it was not possible for an expert to adopt a normal approach to calculating that part of the costs reasonably payable by each of those remaining tenants who were liable to pay. The court said 'it is only fair in fixing a rent (the application related to the proportion of heating costs to be included in a registration of a Rent Act rent) to make a discount for the additional costs which are incurred because of the way the property is managed'. In the event, the court supported the Rent Assessment Panel, which had included a figure for the heating based on what they considered a fair amount would be. In other words, they based the amount of a reasonable figure, not on some formula related to the actual cost of the heating, but on what, in their experience, they considered was appropriate. Although the decision was not based on apportionments of actual costs, it would be surprising if the same attitude was not taken where there are voids. There were changes to a heating system at issue also in *Pole Properties Ltd v Feinberg* [1981] 2 EGLR 38 (see at **4.25** above).

9.54   A much more recent example raising two aspects of reasonableness (use of guarantees, and additional expense caused by the landlord's default) is a Lands Tribunal appeal from an LVT determination. In *Continental Property Ventures Inc v White* [2006] 1 EGLR 85, relating to flats at Buckingham Gate:

(a)   Part of the amount claimed was over £55,000 for damp proofing and redecoration. The LVT accepted that the cost of the damp proofing was not 'reasonably incurred' because it could have been covered by a guarantee given in 1994. If this had been used the tenants would not have had to pay anything.

(b)   The decorating had been costed at over £17,000, but the LVT reduced this to £3,500 on the basis that the decorating was necessary because the landlord failed to repair a leaking pipe within a reasonable time. On appeal the Lands Tribunal approved both points.

On point (a) the LVT had found as a fact that the landlord could have had the damp proofing carried out at no expense. It concluded that to carry out works at a cost was to incur a cost other than reasonably. On appeal the Lands Tribunal said that unless there was evidence of some disadvantage, or good reason to reject the availability of the works without cost, the LVT's attitude seemed incontrovertible. On point (b) there was a more technical discussion, with the landlord arguing that, on a strict construction of s 19(1)(a), the Act enables a landlord to recover the costs 'reasonably incurred' and does not go on to say that the liability to incur those costs must also be reasonable. The LVT had given credit to the tenant for the fact that the decoration cost more than it would have done if the landlord had repaired the leak sooner. The Lands Tribunal agreed with the result, but based its approval on the LVT treating this as an equitable set-off (ie a tenant's claim against the landlord for the landlord's breach). The Land Tribunal considered that the LVT had jurisdiction to consider equitable set-off, although it could have directed that aspect to be decided by a court if it had preferred.

Summary of cases

9.55   The above cases illustrate aspects of reasonableness under the Act:

(a)   The first (at **9.49**) shows that there is no presumption for or against reasonableness. The charge was reduced because the works were not of a reasonable standard: *Yorkbrook Investments Ltd v Batten*.

(b)   The second case (at **9.51**) is a useful discussion on the relative positions of landlord, tenant and management company, and shows that interpretation can depend on whom the covenant is given to: *Berrycroft Management Co Ltd v Sinclair Gardens (Kensington) Ltd.*

(c)   In the third case (at **9.52**) the court would not imply a covenant by the landlord to contribute. In addition, the fixed percentage payable by tenants was not reduced although the services were used in part by non-contributors: *Alton House Holdings Ltd v Calflane (Management) Ltd.*

(d)   The fourth case (at **9.53**) was where a service (heating) had originally been provided to all the flats and was subsequently provided to a smaller number of flats. The court had discretion to fix a reasonable figure, rather than having to assess a mathematically correct one: *R v London Rent Assessment Panel, ex p Cliftvylle Properties Ltd.*

(e)   The fifth case (at **9.54**) highlights the practical approach where a guarantee could be used to save payment, and also the ability of the LVT to reach a reasonable conclusion taking account of equitable set-off where a landlord himself is in breach: *Continental Property Ventures Inc v White.*

So what is the effect of s 19? Reasonableness in general has been commented on above and in Chapter 2. The main point to make is that despite wording which states that 'the amount payable shall be limited accordingly', the courts have frequently refused to interpret this as meaning that the sum payable by the tenant is to be reduced even where a similar service could be provided at a lower cost. The impression is that the reasonableness is not of the cost, but of the way the landlord manages the premises – if what he does can be said to be reasonable the court will not reduce the charge he wants to make, even where the tenant is able to obtain identical services at a cheaper cost. Section 19(1)(a) does say costs are taken into account 'only to the extent that they are reasonably incurred', and where a landlord can persuade a court that the costs have been reasonably incurred then no reduction in the actual sum payable seems to be made. Was this really what Parliament was trying to achieve?

Section 20 of the Landlord and Tenant Act 1985

Consultation – general

9.56   This section, which was wholly replaced by the 2002 Commonhold Act, is perhaps the second most significant statutory provision and backs up the reasonableness provisions of s 19. It requires the landlord to consult with the tenants in three main cases, and a number of subsidiary cases. The provisions came into effect on 31 October 2003. The main cases where consultation is now needed are:

(a)   before carrying out expensive works; or

(b)   before entering into a 'long-term agreement' which is not excluded; and

(c)   before carrying out works under a long-term agreement which will cost over a limited amount. (See **9.61** below for long-term agreements.)

In addition, there are alternative types of consultation where works are advertised in the Journal of the European Parliament (called 'public notice' in the Regulation) and during the short transitional period. In addition, no consultation is needed in the first 31 days of a right to buy lease.

9.57   The tenant's obligation to pay is limited if the consultation provisions have not been either (a) complied with or (b) dispensed with by a Leasehold Valuation Tribunal. (Section 20(1) of the Landlord and Tenant Act 1985 as replaced by the 2002 Act.) The amount payable is limited to the minimum figure of £100 or £250 payable by any tenant, in accordance with s 20(7) and the Regulations. The latter have now been published as the Service Charges

(Consultation Requirements) (England) Regulations 2003 (the Regulations). Regulations 4 and 6 prescribe the figures above which consultation is needed as below.

9.58 The section is substantially different to its predecessor. The section as enacted ran to about two pages and set out the system for consulting and the right to apply for dispensation. The new version has more or less the same length, but says the procedure is to be described in regulations, and the latter run to nearly 30 pages with procedures set out in four separate Schedules, one of which is divided into two parts. The Regulations were published during the summer of 2003, and were brought into effect at the end of October 2003. They differed in a number of significant effects from the drafts on which there had been consultation. The main differences between the procedure as set out in the Regulations and the provision set out in the 1985 version of s 20 are:

(a) consultation is required in three main sets of circumstances, instead of the former single case,

(b) the new section introduces the concept of a 'long-term agreement' (see at **9.61** below);

(c) there is a new and heavier burden on the landlord to justify what he is seeking to do at every stage;

(d) all tenants are now given the right to nominate someone to give an estimate.

The latter was limited previously to some tenants in restricted circumstances:

(e) the Regulations make it clear that if there is a Recognised Tenants' Association the landlord must consult with it and also with all the tenants;

(f) the power to dispense with the consultation requirements is slightly widened;

(g) 'public notice' (in the sense of matters advertised in the Journal of the European Union) have suddenly become a factor giving rise to a different form of consultation; and

(h) there is a special provision affecting right to buy leases.

9.59 The Regulations have four Schedules (one divided into two parts) which include the details of the consultation procedure in each case. Paraphrasing the titles of the Schedules they are, in effect, as follows:

(a) *Sch 1* – requirements for consulting when entering into a long-term agreement, where there is no 'public notice';

(b) *Sch 2* – requirements for consulting when entering into a long-term agreement where public notice is required;

(c) *Sch 3* – requirements for consultation (a) for works to be carried out under a long-term agreement, and (b) where the transitional provisions apply; and

(d) *Sch 4* – requirements for consulting on other qualifying works (ie not under long-term agreements or under transitional provisions): Pt 1 – Where public notice is required, and Pt 2 – Where public notice is not required. (Pt 2 of Sch 4 is thus the normal type of consultation.)

9.60   The Regulations seem unduly long, but if it is necessary to have so many different reasons for and methods of consultation it is, perhaps, best for the system for each type of consultation to be set out in a separate Schedule, as has been done.

Long-term agreement

9.61   This is an agreement, lasting more than 12 months, entered into by or on behalf of the landlord or a superior landlord, towards the costs of which the tenant is to pay (new s 20ZA(2)). Consultation is not necessary if the long-term agreement is one exempted by regulations (new s 20ZA(3)).

9.62   The exemptions (where consultation is not needed for a long-term agreement) appear in reg 3(1) and are:

(a) a contract of employment;

(b) a management agreement made by a local housing authority and (i) a tenant management organisation or (ii) a body established under s 2 of the Local Government Act 2000;

(c) agreements between a holding company and one or more of its subsidiaries, or between two or more subsidiaries of the same holding company; and

(d) an agreement entered into when there are no tenants (eg on completion of a building, before letting), and for a term of no longer than five years.

The exclusion for consultation where there are no tenants is sensible, but the reference to a five-year period (added after consultation) gives rise to the question of how one consults with non-existent tenants if you do want to enter into such an agreement.

9.63   It may be assumed that as the intention is that as the landlord has no ability to consult in such a case such long-term agreement will not be binding on the tenants when some appear on the scene. The regulations do not comment on the point, and the provision is aimed at consultation rather than enforceability. Presumably, the landlord is intended to consult (after the event) with the first tenant. He would surely be complying with the Regulations by doing so, as he would be consulting with the full body of tenants as they exist at that point.

9.64   It seems unsatisfactory that there is no obligation to consult on a long-term agreement which is an employment contract. This would mean, for example, that the landlord does not need to consult when appointing a resident caretaker for a three-year term. The fact that the landlord is not obliged to consult of course does not prevent him from doing so if he thinks fit, but he is not obliged to do so, and if he does he does not have to go through the whole process, nor does he have to 'have regard' to the tenants' observations as in other cases. The author is also less than enthusiastic about the exemption for companies in the same group, which seems to lend itself to unsatisfactory practices, although the tenant will still have the right to apply to the LVT if he considers the charges to be unreasonable.

Where consultation is needed

9.65   The first subsection of the revised version of s 20 (as replaced by s 151 of the Commonhold and Leasehold Reform Act 2002) shows that the sanction for not complying with the provisions is that the excess is not payable ('the relevant contributions of the tenant are limited'). The section applies where:

(a)   the cost of the works to be carried out exceeds either a total sum to be set out in regulations, or the total payable by the landlord, as set out in regulations, (s 20(5)); and

(b)   the landlord enters into a long-term agreement which is not exempt (s 20(4)); or

(c)   the cost of works under a long-term agreement are going to exceed a sum set out in regulations (s 20(2)).

Financial limits

9.66   The financial limits are now (as a result of the Regulations):

(a)   for works (other than under a long-term agreement) costing any tenant more than £250 (reg 6); and

(b)   for works to be carried out under a long-term agreement costing any tenant £100 (reg 4(1)).

9.67   The main figure is effectively £250 inclusive of VAT, since reg 2(2) says that value added tax shall be included where applicable in relation to any estimate. This makes sense because most tenants of residential premises are unable to recover VAT paid, and so the figure which comes out of their pocket is the inclusive figure.

9.68   The Regulations refer to consultation where 'any' tenant has to pay over the limit. Accordingly, all tenants will need to be consulted even if only one out of six will be paying more than the minimum. The notes to the draft Regulations correctly said that the tenants are not really concerned with the total cost of the works, but only what they will be paying. This is the reason for a single figure, rather than a figure per dwelling and another for the total cost. From the landlord's view, however, the position is less satisfactory. To decide whether works need consultation the landlords or their managing agents will need to calculate for each separate block what total cost will cause the tenant paying the highest service charge to pay more than £250 or £100. It could well be a different figure for each block.

Dispensing with consultation

9.69   Tucked away in this section (new s 20ZA(1)) is a provision that the Leasehold Valuation Tribunal is given discretion to waive all or any of the consultation requirements if the tribunal is 'satisfied that it is reasonable to dispense with the requirements'. This is the only section in the whole of the service charge range in which the court is given the power to waive the rules. Before the 2002 Act changes the dispensation only applied where the landlord had acted reasonably: the new wording is accordingly slightly wider. The notes to the consultation paper leading to the Regulations say the provision 'is intended to cover situations where consultation was not practicable (eg for emergency works)'. Presumably the court would be influenced by arguments that the landlord genuinely did not expect the cost to exceed the limit, and that this was a reasonable assumption. Obviously, if the cost is excessive the reasonableness provisions of s 19 are also likely to be material. Alternatively, where the landlord has discussed the proposals at a meeting of tenants but without actually serving the notices, or if he had written to the tenants with some details but not precise costings, the tribunal may perhaps be prepared to consider giving dispensation. However, in view of the new emphasis on the landlord having to give reasons and allowing the tenants several opportunities to make representations, if consultation is not in writing as required by the Regulations then the LVT may have difficulty in being able to dispense with consent.

Some cases on dispensing with consultation

9.70   The discretion was exercised by the judge in *Broadwater Court Management Co Ltd v Jackson-Mann* [1997] EGCS 145 and the discretion was not disturbed by the Court of Appeal. The landlord of a set of only six flats was a management company owned by the tenants. The report is brief, but no doubt each tenant was aware of what was proposed, even if no formal consultation took place. If the tenants also own the freehold between themselves they are still under an obligation to consult: there is no exemption and they would have to rely on the tribunal exercising discretion if they fail to follow the consultation provisions.

9.71   Discretion was exercised in *Wilson v Stone* [1998] 2 EGLR 155, where a house had been divided up into three flats. The landlord lived in one flat and tenants in the other two. The tenant of one flat was doing works in his own flat when major structural problems were discovered, needing urgent attention. After consulting with the landlord the necessary works were completed, but the third occupier was away and they could not contact him. He later refused to pay. Discretion was exercised in favour of the landlord.

9.72   In *Martin v Maryland Estates Ltd* [1998] 25 EG 169, the Court of Appeal considered a case of partial consultation. The landlord had consulted in the usual way on various works. The tenants, through solicitors, questioned whether the work was really necessary and the total cost. The correspondence seems to have petered out, but the works were started and the tenants objected. The works were delayed (partly because the tenants wanted to enfranchise) but then continued. However, while the works were being carried out the builders discovered defects in the roof needing additional work, not covered by the original consultation and requiring considerable extra expense. Following the earlier history of the consultation the landlord decided to have the additional works completed without the further delay (and aggravation) which further consultation would entail. The tenants sought a declaration that the costs of the extra works were not reasonably incurred and the landlord requested dispensation. The Court of Appeal did not accept that discretion should be exercised in favour of the landlord: he should have consulted again regarding the additional works. As he had not done so he could not recover more for the extra work than the statutory financial limit of the time. Whether the works were one set of works or two was a matter of common sense, although in this case there was only one contract. The court had first to decide if the landlord had acted reasonably. (Now it would have to decide if it was reasonable to exercise the discretion.) If it decided the landlord had acted reasonably it could then decide whether or not to exercise the discretion.

9.73   In *Heron Maple House Ltd v Central Estates Ltd* [2002] 13 EG 102, the question revolved around a head lease and underlease of a block and separate sub-underleases of flats in the block. Works were done by the superior landlord (who was the freeholder) but no consultation took place. The right to recover costs was challenged. The superior landlord argued that s 20 of the 1985 Act did not apply because the head lease was not of 'a dwelling' but of lots of dwellings and other premises (the common parts). It was held that s 20 did apply: the 1985 Act referred to the 'tenant of a dwelling', not the 'tenant of the dwelling and nothing else'. Accordingly, as there had been no consultation the costs were not recoverable.

New features

Long-term agreement

9.74   As explained above, consultation is needed (a) on entering into a long-term agreement unless it is exempt, and (b) where works are to be carried out under an existing long-term agreement and at least one tenant has to pay £100. A long-term agreement is 'an agreement entered into by or on behalf of the landlord or a superior landlord, for a term of more than 12 months', towards the cost of which the tenants are to pay (new s 20ZA(2)). Consultation is not necessary if the long-term agreement is one exempted by regulations (new s 20ZA(3)). As a result of an amendment, the Service Charge (Consultation Requirements) (Amendment) (No 2) (England) Regulations 2004 insert new para (3A) into the

Regulations, relating to cases where accounts have not been made up between 31 October 2003 and 12 October 2004. In that case, if the landlord intends to enter into a long-term agreement after 12 November 2004 the 'relevant date' (the start of the period for which accounts need to be made up) will be 'the date on which begins the first period for which service charges referable to that intended agreement are payable'. Thus consultation will be needed if 'any tenant' is liable to contribute more than £100. Under paras 4(2) and (4) of the original Regulation, the effect is that once an accounting period has started each subsequent accounting period will be 12 months from the end of the prior accounting period. (The No 2 Amendment Order replaced the defective original amendment Order made one month earlier.)

9.75   The four exemptions, where consultation is not needed for a long-term agreement, appear in reg 3(1) and are set out in **9.60** above.

9.76   There is no financial limit applicable when the landlord enters into a long-term agreement. Accordingly, if it is not a prohibited type of agreement, the tenants must, strictly, be consulted before a landlord enters into such an agreement, even if the cost in due course would be only £1 per year per tenant. By contrast, when works are to be carried out under a long-term agreement consultation is needed (reg 4(1)) where 'any tenant' is to pay more than £100. The reference to 'any tenant' makes it clear that, if tenants pay different percentages, consultation is needed with all of them where the tenant paying the highest service charge proportion has to pay more than the minimum figure.

Nominations

9.77   In two cases the initial notice of intention to carry out works must invite the tenants and the recognised tenants' association ('RTA') if there is one, to nominate someone 'from whom the landlord should try to obtain other estimates'. (Section 20ZA(5)(c) and regs 8(3) and 35(3).) The landlord must seek an estimate from those persons nominated by the tenants and by the RTA. These are not alternatives – if both make nominations the landlord must seek one from each. The landlord will have complied with his obligation by requesting an estimate even if the person approached is not prepared to give one – he does not have to keep trying lots of alternative potential estimators.

9.78   There is a scale of preference as to whom the landlord should approach, which, in keeping with the Regulations, is perhaps unduly complex:

(a)   If a single nomination is made by a single tenant or by the RTA the landlord must seek an estimate from that nominee or those nominees.

(b)   Where there is more than one nomination from tenants (and not more than one nomination from the RTA) for someone to give an estimate, the landlord should seek an estimate from: (i) the person with the most nominations, (ii) if there is no person with the most nominations but two have equal top votes the landlord must seek a quote from one of the two (the landlord's choice), and (iii) in any other case the estimate can be sought from any nominated person. This applies where the tenants make a nomination whether the RTA does as well or not.

(c) If both the tenants and the RTA make more than one nomination the land-lord has to try to get quotes from one person nominated by a tenant, and also one from a person nominated by the RTA, other than a person nominated by a tenant who the landlord is approaching. This seems to mean that if the RTA nominated A Ltd and B Ltd and the tenants also do the landlord must approach A Ltd (as RTA nominee) and B Ltd (as tenants' nominee).

(See reg 38(1)–(4) for consultation on ordinary works, and reg 11 for entering into long-term agreements when public notice is not material.)

Connected parties

9.79 Regulation 38(7), in Sch 4, Pt 2 sets out criteria for deciding if the estimates are independent, or, as the Regulation puts it, 'wholly unconnected with the landlord' in relation to consultation on ordinary works. There are similar definitions of connected parties in other Schedules to the Regulations. (Sch 1, para 12(6), Sch 2, para 19(3), and Sch 4, Pt 1, para 31(3).)

The Regulations assume that there is a connection in certain cases. There are references to five categories and several include a mention of a 'close relative'. 'Close relative', as used in the Regulations, is very widely defined in reg 2(1) to include spouses or co-habitees, and a wide range of relatives including parents and children, in-laws, step-parents or step-children, and 'co-habitee' includes people of opposite sexes living as husband and wife, and also people of the same sex living in a comparable relationship. The five cases where a connection is assumed in reg 38(7) are:

(a) Where the landlord is a company and the other party (the person giving an estimate) is 'a director or manager of the company or is a close relative of any such director or manager'.

(b) Where the landlord is a company and the estimator is a partner in a partnership, there is assumed to be connection 'if any partner in that partnership is, or is to be, a director or manager of the company or is a close relative of any such director or manager'.

(c) If both landlord and estimator are companies then there is a connection 'if any director or manager of one company is, or is to be, a director or manager of the other company'.

(d) Where the estimator is a company there is a connection 'if the landlord is a director or manager of the company or is a close relative of any such director or manager'.

(e) Finally there is an assumed connection if the estimator is a company 'and the landlord is a partner in a partnership, if any partner in that partnership is a director or manager of the company or is a close relative of any such director or manager'.

242

The fact that the landlord and the contractor may be connected under these rules does not mean that the landlord cannot employ the contractor – merely that within the consultation procedure the tenants must be made aware that there is a connection. Failure to give this notification would mean that consultation had not been properly carried out. In similar vein the landlord can employ associated companies (see at **9.72** above) without the need to consult, as that is one of the exemptions for long-term contracts.

Public notice

9.80   Where this applies, slightly different forms of consultation are set out in Schs 2 and 4, Pt 1 to the Regulations. Regulation 2 defines 'public notice' as 'notice published in the Official Journal of the European Union pursuant to the Public Works Contracts Regulations 1991, the Public Services Contracts Regulations 1993, or the Public Supply Contracts Regulations 1995'. Accordingly, 'public notice' is unlikely to affect any landlords other than public sector landlords. Under s 26 of the Landlord and Tenant Act 1985, the main statutory provisions of the 1985 legislation applying to service charges only apply to public sector landlords where the tenant holds a long lease.

The consultation procedure

9.81   As stated at **9.56** above, there are three main cases where consultation is needed, and two subsidiary ways of consulting. Each has slightly different rules, but the main type of consultation is likely to be that in respect of ordinary works which are going to cost any tenant more than £250. The new procedure is going to be illustrated first in respect of such consultation. In brief there is a two- or three-stage procedure for consultation. In Stage 1 the landlord puts forwards proposals and invites comments, and also invites tenants to suggest the names of people from whom estimates should be sought. At Stage 2 the landlord puts forward estimates of the cost of the works, responds to tenants' observations from Stage 1, and the tenants are given a further opportunity to make representations. Once a contract is in place the landlord may have to deal with Stage 3, which involves justifying his choice of contractor and possibly responding to observations made at Stage 2. The differences between the five separate forms of consultation are sometimes subtle, but to consult properly, so that he does not run the risk of being unable to recover more than a minimum figure, a landlord will need to follow the correct procedure. Despite the complications of the process, there are no prescribed forms of notice: Some drafts are included in Appendix 2, Precedent 13.

Part 1 – consultation on normal works

9.82   This refers to works where there is no long-term contract or public notice involvement. Consultation in these cases is needed where the contribution of any tenant is to be more than £250 (reg 6).

The Regulations do not set out an alternative for the total cost of the works as in the original section: managing agents therefore need to calculate for each set of service charges what total cost is going to give rise to the tenant of that building with the largest service charge percentage having to pay more than £250. Getting that wrong can mean no consultation, and failure to recover.

THREE STAGES

9.83 For normal works consultation is in three stages. This is set out in the Regulations, paras 35 to 40, being Sch 4, Pt 2.

STAGE ONE (THE INITIAL APPROACH)

9.84 This is the initial notice to be given to each tenant and also any recognised tenants' association with details of the work to be done (reg 35(2) and (3), and s 20ZA(5)(e)). Notice has to be given to all the tenants and also to any RTA: these are not alternatives. The initial notice must:

(a) describe 'in general terms' the proposed works, or it must specify 'the place and hours at which a description of the proposed works may be inspected'; and

(b) state the landlord's 'reasons for considering it necessary to carry out the proposed works'.

The notice must also:

(c) 'invite the making, in writing, of observations in relation to the proposed works' from the tenants within 30 days of the date of the notice (30 days is defined as the 'relevant period' in reg 2(1));

(d) specify the address to which observations can be sent;

(e) state that any observations 'must be delivered within the relevant period', and the date of expiration of the consultation period; and

(f) 'invite each tenant and the (RTA) (if any) to propose, within the relevant period [30 days; reg 2(1)] the name of a person from whom the landlord should try to obtain an estimate for the carrying out of the proposed works' (reg 35(3); see at **9.77** for nominations).

9.85 If the notice says particulars of the works are available for inspection the notice must specify a place and hours for inspection, and 'a description of the proposed works must be available for inspection, free of charge, at that place and during those hours'. The place and time must be reasonable. If copying facilities are not available at that time the landlord is to provide to any tenant, 'on request and free of charge a copy of the description' (reg 36). The landlord is to 'have regard' to the tenants' observations (reg 37 and s 20ZA(5)(d)).

STAGE TWO (CONSULTATION WITH ESTIMATES)

9.86 After the 30-day period for making objections and for making nominations has passed the second stage (reg 38) is for the landlord to obtain estimates.

Where the tenants have nominated someone to estimate, the landlord must request an estimate, but cannot, of course, oblige the party concerned to give one (see at **9.77**). When the landlord has his estimates, reg 38(5) says he shall supply, free of charge, to each tenant and the secretary of the RTA, a 'statement ('the para (b) statement') setting out … as regards at least two of the estimates, the amount specified in the estimate as the estimated cost of the proposed works'. If the landlord has received observations as part of the Stage 1 consultation he is also to set out in the para (b) statement 'a summary of the observations and his response to them'. The requirement for a summary of responses was not part of the original 1985 provisions, although it seems a sensible extension of the obligation on a landlord to 'have regard' to those representations. The statement is referred to in reg 38(5)(b) – hence the name. It is called a statement, but in effect it is a second notice. (Under reg 35(5)(c) the landlord must 'make all of the estimates available for inspection'.)

9.87   'At least one of the estimates must be that of a person wholly unconnected with the landlord' (reg 38(6); see at **9.79** as to whether there is assumed to be a connection) and if the landlord has been able to obtain an estimate from a nominated person 'that estimate must be one of those to which the para (b) statement relates' (reg 38(8)). In similar vein to the initial notice, the landlord must give written notice of a place and times where each tenant, or the RTA, can inspect the estimates. In many cases, photocopies of the chosen estimates will probably be supplied to tenants. Note that the landlord does not have to supply copies of all the estimates he has obtained. He can obtain six estimates, but is only obliged under the rules to include two in the statement.

9.88   The tenants and RTA have a second period of 30 days to make further representations, and the landlord must 'have regard' to those representations. The invitation to make observations can be separate from the para (b) statement, although there seems little point in creating even more paperwork. The invitation to give observations must, again, give an address, and state that the observations must be given in time and specify the end date for the (second) consultation period (regs 38(10) and 39).

STAGE THREE (AFTER CONTRACTING)

9.89   Stage 3 applies when the landlord has placed the contract for the works. Regulation 40 requires the landlord, within 21 days of entering into the contract, to give to each tenant and the RTA notice in writing stating 'his reasons for awarding the contract or specify the place and hours at which a statement of those reasons may be inspected'. He does not need to give this (third) notice if 'the person with whom the contract is made is a nominated person or submitted the lowest estimate'. If the tenants or RTA have made any representations at Stage 2 to which the landlord is required to have regard, the landlord must 'summarise the observations and set out his response to them' (reg 40). In some other forms of consultation under the Regulation, the response need only be the tenant or RTA who made the observations.) If the landlord specifies a place and time for inspection similar provisions apply as to the initial notice – see at **9.85**. The effect is that if (a) the estimate that has been accepted is from a nominee or is the lowest, and (b) there have been no observations from the tenants at Stage 2, then there is no Stage 3.

Part 2 – Consultation on entering into a long-term agreement

9.90   Long-term agreements have been mentioned at **9.71**, and the exemptions from the need to consult in **9.72**.

9.91   Schedule 1 to the Regulation sets out arrangements for consulting with tenants before a landlord enters in to a long-term agreement, other than one that is affected by public notice. The provisions for the latter are set out in Sch 2. Both have similarities to the procedure outlined above, but they are not the same and are not identical among themselves. The procedure for consultation on entering into normal long-term agreements are described below, and after each stage the differences where the works or services are subject to public notice are set out.

STAGE I – INITIAL NOTICE

9.92   There must be an initial notice to the tenants, and also to the RTA if there is one, where the landlord proposes to enter into a long-term agreement which is not of a type excluded by regulations. The initial notice describes in general terms 'the relevant matters' which are defined in reg 2(1) as the 'goods or services to be provided or the works to be carried out (as the case may be)' under the long-term agreement. It should be noted that this refers to works and services, whereas the main consultation only refers to works. Services are perhaps more likely to be material for a long-term agreement. Where the notice includes 'qualifying works' it must 'state the landlord's reasons for considering it necessary to carry out the works'. As in the case of the main type of consultation (see at **9.84**), if the initial notice does not describe the works to be carried out, it must state a place and time where such a description can be inspected. The notice does not need to specify the names of the proposed parties to the agreement. The notice will invite each tenant and the RTA to make written observations within 30 days, must specify an address to which observations are to be sent, and must specify the date on which the period for observations ends. The notice also must invite each tenant and the RTA (if any) to nominate someone, within the 30-day period, from whom the landlord should seek an estimate for the 'relevant matters', ie works or services. (See at **9.77** for nominations.) The landlord has to 'have regard' to the observations, and has to try to obtain an estimate from the person(s) nominated. Where the landlord has given details of where the proposals can be inspected, rather than setting out the proposals in the notice, the times and place for such inspection must be reasonable, and the description must be available for inspection, free of charge, at that place and times. If copying facilities are not available at that time the landlord is to provide a copy of the description to the tenant free of charge on request. (Sch 1, paras 8-10.)

246

9.93   For long-term agreements where the subject matter is one (for works or services) that has to be the subject of 'public notice' the provisions are in Sch 2. (See at **9.80** for public notice.)

9.94   Under Sch 2 the first stage of consultation is virtually identical to the procedure for other long-term agreements. The difference is that the notice has to 'state that the reason why the landlord is not inviting (the tenants or RTA) to nominate persons from whom he should try to obtain an estimate for the relevant matters is that public notice of the relevant matters is to be given'. (Sch 2, para 16(2)(d).) The wording just quoted implies that the notice has to be given before the public notice is put in the Journal. This no doubt reflects the position that the landlord has to give reasons why he considers the works are needed (if works are the subject of the consultation), and if the tenants, in response, satisfy the land-lord that the works are not necessary then the public advertisement may not be needed. It is likely that this is contrary to the practice in many local authority housing departments, and they will either have to change their practices or take account of the fact that the carefully worked out timescale they may have adopted in the past may not be suitable in the case of public notice matters.

STAGE 2 – CIRCULATION OF PROPOSALS

9.95   The second stage for consulting on normal long-term agreements (ie where public notice is not a factor) under Sch 1 to the Regulations is again similar to that for works. The landlord must seek estimates including (if possible) one from the person nominated on behalf of the tenants or RTA. There is a sliding scale of preference, as in the case of ordinary consultation (see at **9.78**) for the person from whom such estimate should be sought. The landlord must then put forward 'at least two proposals' for the long-term agreement. At least one of the proposals must be for an agreement with 'a person wholly uncon-nected' with the landlord. (Being 'unconnected' in this sense is similar to that for consultation for ordinary work: see at **9.79**.) The provisions are similar to the general consultation procedure, in that if the tenants or RTA have nominated someone then any estimate given by that person must be put forward as part of the proposal. (Sch 1, para 12(3).)

9.96   If 'it is reasonably practicable' the proposal should also include an esti-mate of the costs to be paid by each tenant. If an estimate for each tenant cannot be given the proposal should set out details of the total cost for the building. If neither of these is possible but it is possible to ascertain the 'current unit cost or hourly or daily rate', then the proposal must include these. (Sch 1, para 12(7)–(9).) This is not a provision that appears in any of the other consultation procedures. In the other cases the tenant is given details of estimates of the total costs, leaving the tenant to assess the amount he is likely to pay.

9.97   Each proposal must also include a statement of the intended duration of the proposed agreement, and also 'a statement as to the provisions (if any) for variation of any amount specified in, or to be determined under, the proposed agreement'. This would presumably include provisions for annual reconsideration of the hourly or daily rate for example. Importantly, if the landlord has received observations from the tenants or RTA as part of the Stage 1 consultation 'each proposal shall contain a statement summarising the observations and setting out the landlord's response to them'. (Sch 1, paras 12(11)–(13).)

9.98 As with consultation on ordinary works, notice of the proposal for the long-term agreement is to be supplied to the tenants and RTA, or details given of where they can be inspected, observations must be invited, and an address must be given for observations which are to be made within 30 days of the date of the notice. The landlord must specify the date on which the period for observations expires. The landlord has to have regard to the observations. (Sch 1, paras 13 and 14.)

LONG-TERM AGREEMENTS TO EMPLOY MANAGING AGENTS

9.99 There is a special provision applying only where the proposed long-term agreement is for the appointment of managing agents. It is the only type of contract specified in the Regulations. In such cases the proposal must state that the proposed agent is or is not a member of a professional body or trade association and, if he is, the name of the professional body or trade association. Unusually, it must also state that the proposed managing agent 'subscribes or, as the case may be, does not subscribe, to any code of practice or voluntary accreditation scheme relevant to the functions of managing agents'. (Regulations, Sch 1, para 12(10).) Regulation 12(10) seems in line with the philosophy of giving tenants the opportunity of ensuring that managing agents are (a) competent and (b) subject to some professional control.

VARIATIONS WHERE THERE IS PUBLIC NOTICE

9.100 Stage 2 is basically much the same as for ordinary long-term agreements except that the landlord is only obliged to put forward one proposal which is likely to be in respect of the long-term agreement originally proposed, as the tenants do not have rights to require the landlord to seek alternative estimates. The proposal has to state the name and address of the other party to the contract and a statement of any connection (apart from the agreement) between the landlord and the other party. The description of the manner in which a connection is assumed is as before. (See at **9.79** for connected parties.) The statement is to include an indication of the actual cost to the individual tenant or, if this is not possible, details of the total cost. If neither is possible the statement should include details of the current unit cost or hourly or daily rates. Where none of these is possible then, in the case of consultation where there is public notice, but not for other long-term agreements, the proposal must state why the landlord cannot do so 'and the date by which he expects to be able to provide an estimate, cost or rate'. Under reg 23 he must provide the information on hourly rates etc within 21 days of receiving sufficient information to enable him to estimate the amount, cost or rate. The statement of the proposal must indicate the duration of the agreement, but the regulation does not require mention of provisions for variation. If representations are made at Stage 1, the landlord's proposal must summarise these and respond to them. The provisions relating to managing agents mentioned at **9.99** also apply to these long-term agreements. (Sch 2, para 19.)

STAGE 3 – AFTER THE LONG-TERM AGREEMENT IS MADE

9.101   The landlord must within 21 days of entering into the ordinary long term agreement state to the tenants and the RTA his reasons for making that agreement, or specify a place and time where such reasons can be inspected, except where the long-term agreement is made with the person who was nominated by the tenants or RTA, or was the person giving the lowest estimate. Where he has received representations in the Stage 2 process to which he has to have regard he has, within the 21-day period, to summarise the observations and set out his response to all the tenants and the RTA. (Sch 1, para 15.)

VARIATION FOR LONG-TERM AGREEMENT WITH PUBLIC NOTICE

9.102   After entering into the contract the landlord does not need to notify the tenant that he has done so, but if any of the tenants has made observations to which the landlord has to have regard he is obliged, within 21 days of receipt of those observations, to state in writing his response to the person making them (not to the tenants at large). (Sch 2, para 22.)

Part 3 – Consultation on works under a long-term agreement (and transitional cases)

9.103   Schedule 3 to the Regulation sets out, in paras 24–27, the consultation procedure where a long-term agreement exists and works are to be carried out except where public notice applies. This relates to consultation on works, not on services, and is required where the cost to be incurred under that agreement by any tenant is to exceed £100 in any financial year (ie the service charge financial year) (reg 4). For works under a long-term agreement where public notice has been given, other than the transitional case, consultation is under Pt 1 of Sch 4 to the Regulations. Schedule 3 also applies to the cases mentioned in reg 7(3). These are the two transitional cases, which are now probably obsolete. They are:

(a)   where the landlord or superior landlord had entered into an agreement before 31 October 2003 (the date the Regulations came into force) for works to be carried out by 31 December 2003; and

(b)   where the landlord or superior landlord had entered into a long-term agreement before 31 October 2003 and works were to be carried out for which public notice had been given before 31 October 2003.

9.104   In the cases covered by Sch 3 consultation is a more limited type of consultation, somewhat similar to Stages 1 and 3 for consultation on ordinary works above. (See **9.84** and **9.89** above.)

9.105 The landlord must consult by giving to all tenants and any RTA written notice of intention to carry out the works. As in other cases the notice must describe in general terms the works intended, or specify when and where details can be inspected. The notice must also 'state the landlord's reasons for considering it necessary to carry out the works', as well as containing a statement 'of the total amount of the expenditure estimated by the landlord as likely to be incurred by him on and in connection with the proposed works'. Tenants are to be invited to make observations within 30 days, with a note of the end date of the period, and the landlord must have regard to the observations. The place for inspecting the description of the works must be reasonable and the position about copying is as in the case of ordinary works. (See at **9.85** above.) The difference between this and consultation on other works is that, because it is known who is to do the work, the landlord is not obliged to invite the tenants to nominate someone else to give an estimate. (Sch 3 paras 24–26.)

VARIATIONS WHERE THE WORKS UNDER THE LONG-TERM AGREEMENT ARE SUBJECT TO PUBLIC NOTICE

9.106 Schedule 4, Pt 1 contains the provisions for consultation in these cases. In effect, the procedure for public works aspects is a three-stage process, much as for ordinary works, whereas the procedure for ordinary works under a long-term agreement has what amount to Stages 1 and 3 only.

9.107 For public notice cases, Stage 1 is for the landlord to give notice to the tenants and the RTA of the intention to carry out qualifying works, describing them or saying where a description can be inspected. He must also state his reasons for considering it necessary to carry out the works. The difference between this and the non-public notice works consultation is that the notice has to 'state that the reason why the landlord is not inviting recipients of the notice to nominate persons from whom he should try to obtain an estimate for carrying out the works is that public notice of the works is to be given'. The tenants are to be invited to make observations. The provisions for inspection and copying are as in other cases. The landlord is obliged to have regard to the observations. (Sch 4, Pt 1 paras 28–30.)

9.108 Stage 2 is for the landlord to put forward a statement in respect of the long-term agreement under which the works are to be carried out. The statement gives the name and address of the person with whom the landlord proposes to contract (which seems odd, as the long-term contract is already in place, but it could be material if there are several long-term agreements in place) and particulars of any connection between the landlord and the contractor other than the long-term agreement itself. These are in similar wide to terms to those mentioned above in relation to ordinary works. (See at **9.79**.) The reference to connected parties appears where the works are under a long-term agreement and public notice is relevant, but not for works under other long-term agreements. This aspect should have been dealt with when the landlord consulted on entering into the long-term agreement, at Stage 2, in both cases. (See at **9.95** and **9.100**.) The Regulations do not require a landlord to notify the tenants of a connection where there has been a change since the long-term agreement came into place. The landlord is to give an estimate of the amount payable by the tenant and the total cost of the works, or if that is not reasonably practicable, details of the unit rate, or hourly or daily rate. If the landlord cannot give an estimate of the unit cost or hourly or daily rates he must state the reasons why he cannot comply, and the date by which he expects to be able to provide figures. He is also under an obligation to provide the figures within 21 days of being able to do so. (Sch 4, Pt 1, paras 28–32 and 34.)

STAGE 2 – LANDLORD'S RESPONSE TO OBSERVATIONS (ORDINARY WORKS UNDER LONG-TERM AGREEMENT)

9.109   There is no obligation on the landlord under Sch 3 to notify tenants of the contract (because it already exists), but where observations have been made at Stage 1 to which the landlord is to have regard he must notify in writing 'the person by whom the observations were made' of his response to them. This must be within 21 days of receipt of those observations. (Sch 3, para 27.)

VARIATION FOR WORKS UNDER LONG-TERM CONTRACT WITH PUBLIC NOTICE

9.110   The same obligation to respond to observations from individuals (or the RTA) within 21 days of receiving them applies in cases where the works under the long-term agreement are subject to public notice. (Sch 4, Pt 1, para 33.)

Comment

9.111   The consultation procedure is, in the author's view, the most important of all the major statutory protection given to tenants of dwellings. The original single scheme has been complicated enormously by the Commonhold Act changes. It will make management more expensive, particularly if the landlord has to give several different types of notification at the same time, each with different requirements and different rights for the tenants, for example where ordinary works are to be done and at the same time works under a long-term agreement. It would be possible to do a combined notice, but it would perhaps be simpler to do two notices (each with their different subsequent follow-up procedures). A cheaper alternative may be to use the most complete form of notice procedure, eg under Sch 4, Pt 2, and give the notice under that for all items. This would give tenants greater rights, in some cases, than under the Regulations. It means the landlord may have to offer to allow the tenants to nominate someone to give an estimate when he does not need to do so, but there will only be one type of consultation. By doing more rather than less surely the landlord cannot be criticised, unless he is criticised by the tenants who think this increases the management costs!

9.112 To the extent that the new system increases costs it is a step in the wrong direction. The complications previously existing, making management not very profitable, was a major reason why many of the major firms of surveyors decided to drop management of residential premises in the early 2000s. The new rules will not encourage them to change their minds.

9.113 The new system does give greater rights to tenants, accompanied by a heavy obligation on the landlord to justify what he wants to do before, during and sometimes even after the consultation process. The right for each tenant to be able to nominate someone to give estimates is new, although some had this right before. The concentration on the cost of the work to the tenant, rather than the alternatives of the cost to the tenant or the cost of the whole, seems a good practical approach from the tenant's viewpoint. It has the disadvantage that with no stated maximum cost per building the landlord must calculate for each separate block what minimum figure of total costs will trigger the need for consultation.

9.114 The author is not convinced that the idea of a long-term agreement is particularly helpful. Such an agreement can often be for the benefit of both the contractor and person paying, if the contractor will discount what would otherwise be his figure to achieve the benefit of a contract for a few years.

9.115 Contractors give quotes on different bases, making it more difficult for tenants as well as landlords to consider and compare. One can foresee likely problems with landlords consulting on a single basis rather than several, either by mistake or as a matter of convenience. Realistically, tenants are unlikely to suffer if they do, although the relevant costs figure where consultation is needed for long-term agreement works is a lower figure than for ordinary works.

9.116 Presumably, the reference to public notice was included at the request of local authorities or public bodies, but they may well find that it does not cover all their works, and so they will probably have to use several different procedures for consultation for works in the same accounting year.

9.117 The procedure is likely to lead to more disputes alleging that the landlord has not consulted properly. The penalty for failure to consult properly is that the landlord is unable to recover more than the minimum sum (£250 for ordinary works or £100 for works carried out under a long-term agreement) unless he is able to obtain dispensation. For example, what if the landlord consults under Stages 1 and 2 but does not respond to the representations made to him after entering into the contract, ie he misses out Stage 3? There is a time limit for this, but is he going to be able to persuade an LVT that he should have dispensation for failing to follow up Stages 1 and 2 with Stage 3, which is after the event? What if the landlord has received representations and genuinely does not believe that they are such as to require a response?

9.118 One can foresee a boom in applications to the LVT on the basis of improper consultation, and cross applications for dispensation.

9.119   The author believes that the system, as changed in 2002, is unnecessarily complicated and will lead to lots of problems. It is to be hoped that it will be simplified in a few years time. It must be better for tenants as well as landlords to have either a single system, or at least not one that needs pages of explanations of minor differences between five different types of consultation for one basic purpose.

9.120   It would be good to see the obligation to consult, in a reasonably simple fashion, extended to all services as well as works.

9.121   It seems an excellent idea for a landlord to have to justify in writing what they want to do, although the author is less enthusiastic about the need to do so in Stage 3. This should concentrate some landlords' minds, and would provide evidence when issues of reasonableness are called in question.

9.122   When a tenant or RTA is nominating someone from whom an estimate is to be sought, perhaps the tenant or RTA should be obliged to provide information about the nominee:

(a)   as to whether he is a member of a relevant trade body;

(b)   as to whether he has suitable public liability and negligence cover;

(c)   as to whether he has adequate staff (or arrangements in force) to cover emergencies; and

(d)   as to what experience he has in dealing with similar types of property.

Contractors should be able to provide the information relatively easily and may be happy to provide their promotional literature to the landlord which may have most of the above information. It may also make it more apparent why some estimates are lower than others, thus aiding choice and the giving of reasons.

9.123   Exempting contracts of employment from consultation over long-term agreements is, in the author's view, very unsatisfactory (reg 3(1)(a)). The Regulations are a blanket exemption. Surely it is unreasonable for the employment contract of someone working solely in respect of those matters for which the service charges are payable not to be the subject of consultation, even if a tenant has to pay over the minimum figure? Consider someone such as a caretaker: on the basis that such a person performs 'services' rather than 'works' Sch 1 does not apply, but the appointment is surely relevant if the cost to an individual tenant will be more than £100 per year? One can understand a local authority not wanting to have to consult about the salary of a person who deals with numerous sets of premises rather than a single property, but if a person is employed to be responsible solely for the one set of premises and his salary is included in the management charge (or 100% of his salary is deemed material for service charge calculations) then why should it not be included, but perhaps without the right to propose an alternative, in a similar way to consultation over works where there is to be a long-term contract? The technical answer will be that new s 20ZA(2) defines qualifying works without reference to services, but, if this is the preferred interpretation, it seems to defeat the object of the legislation.

9.124 The above summarises the statutory obligations. A landlord can, of course, consult on a voluntary basis where the statutory criteria do not apply. If he does, the requirement to allow the tenants to nominate contractors and the giving of landlords' reasons for decisions would not be compulsory. Landlords of commercial property could operate a similar system if they so chose, although one would expect them to consult and perhaps invite tenants to nominate someone to quote but without too much of the rest of the consultation formalities. The code of practice for commercial property does recommend consultation and obtaining competing estimates, but the statutory provisions only apply to residential premises.

9.125 The requirement in each of the Schedules to the Regulations that the landlord must 'have regard' to observations of the tenants is generally felt to be somewhat weak, although this is the wording from the original version of the procedure. It is up to the landlord to manage, and it is right that he should have the major say. Although the tenants will often be paying the whole of the cost of the items in question, the work should only be what the parties have contracted that the landlord will do at the expense of the tenant. A landlord can note the tenants' comments and then proceed, although if the tenants often make representations objecting and the landlord ignores them all the tenants may in some cases have grounds to consider seeking the appointment of a manager or could consider exercising the Right to Manage (under the Commonhold Act) where these remedies are open to them. While this may help where it applies it is unfortunately only likely to be of benefit after a series of unsatisfactory events. Again, one can foresee more applications to the LVT on whether the landlord has 'had regard' to observations and/or whether any response from the landlord is adequate or justifies the cost.

9.126 In *Sutton (Hastoe) Housing Association v Williams* [1988] 1 EGLR 56, under rather similar provisions in the Housing Act 1980, the consultation procedure was followed. The tenant and other tenants 'strenuously objected' to the proposal to replace wooden windows with UPVC windows. Despite these strenuous objections by some of those who were to pay, the landlords were able to replace the windows and recover the cost. This case may be contrasted, perhaps, with *O'May v City of London Real Property Co Ltd* [1983] 2 AC 726, where the House of Lords considered s 35 of the Landlord and Tenant Act 1954. Under that section, in setting the terms for a new business lease on the expiration of the former lease, the court has to 'have regard' to the terms of the former lease. It was held that the landlord could not insist on replacing a lease that had no service charge at all with one with a full service charge. Although these cases came to totally different decisions, it is perhaps right that each case must depend on the view the court or LVT takes of the facts. For service charge purposes, a court should accept that the landlord has the obligation to manage, and unless what he wants to do is totally outrageous and/or perhaps contrary to the professional advice he has been given, the courts will tend to allow the landlord to manage as he thinks fit. The *O'May* case revolved, not around management, but seeking to renew a lease on a different basis – in other words changing the contractual terms.

Section 20A of the Landlord and Tenant Act 1985

Grants to be taken into account

9.127   The first part of this section (first added by the Housing and Planning Act 1986) makes the very reasonable requirement that, 'where relevant costs are incurred or to be incurred on the carrying out of works for which a grant has been or is to be paid ..., the amount of the grant shall be deducted from the costs and the amount of the service charge payable shall be reduced accordingly'. This seems to be a simple provision under which if, for example, the landlord receives £8,500 from the local authority by way of grant that sum must be deducted from the total amount to be charged to tenants through the service charge.

9.128   The second subsection deals in similar fashion with certain grants concerning external works under what are called group repair schemes, under Pt VIII of the Local Government and Housing Act 1989.

Comment

9.129   The provision is perfectly sensible but does it go far enough? It is limited to certain specified grants that a landlord could obtain. It seems rather odd to require a landlord to take account of a grant if it is obtained under s X of statute Y, but not if it is obtained under s A of statute B. Subject to the comments below, it would surely be reasonable for the provision to provide for the tenants to be given the benefit of any grant that is obtained from a local authority or public body for works to the property? It may be thought unreasonable for the tenants to have to pay for something that the landlord could reasonably obtain from another source. (If the lease excludes from costs charged to tenants amounts the landlord obtains from third parties, then the tenant may be protected.) Presumably, the section will need to be amended as and when new grants become available:

(a)   The section would be better if it: (i) required the landlord to credit the service charge with any grant from whatever source, preferably after deducting proper costs of obtaining the grant, except where the grant is subject to an obligation for repayment if there is a disposal within a limited period, and/or (ii) encouraged landlords to consider the possibility of obtaining a grant where one is reasonably likely to be available. This might encourage keeping the stock of buildings in repair or, in some cases, improving them. For example, there are some grants being offered for some energy saving arrangements such as for cavity wall insulation or for more efficient gas boilers, either of which should save the occupier some expenses for energy costs.

(b)   The major difficulty may be that with some grants there is an obligation for it to be repaid in whole or in part if the property is sold within a limited period. If the landlord has put the grant into the service charge pot he would not have the money to repay the grant. Such grants, accordingly, are difficult to cater for with fairness to both landlord and tenant. Provisions in Acts or leases seeking recovery of such sums from the tenants could be difficult, particularly where tenants have assigned or become insolvent since the adjustment was first made. When the grant is obtained it may not be known whether the property will be sold within the period that requires repayment of the grant.

Section 20B of the Landlord and Tenant Act 1985

Time limit for demand

9.130   The purpose of this additional provision (brought in by the Landlord and Tenant Act 1987) is to ensure that a landlord cannot make a charge to a tenant a long time after work has been done without prior notice to the tenant. Under s 20B(1), 'the tenant shall not be liable to pay so much of the service charge as reflects the costs so incurred'. It applies if the relevant costs 'were incurred more than 18 months before a demand for payment'. Section 20B(2) says the restriction in s 20B(1) does not apply 'if, within the period of 18 months beginning with the date when the relevant costs were incurred, the tenant was notified in writing that those costs had been incurred and that he would subsequently be required under the terms of his lease to contribute to them by the payment of a service charge'. (This should not be confused with the provisions of the Landlord and Tenant (Covenants) Act 1995 giving a six-month limit for claiming arrears from former tenants.)

9.131   On the whole this seems a very sensible and proper provision. It is worth commenting that the landlord can easily bring himself within the section by giving notice, and it would seem that, provided he has done so, he need not serve a demand for payment for years afterwards, subject presumably to normal Limitation Act time limits. (It can rarely be in the interests of the landlord to delay claiming the amount deliberately.)

9.132   The section refers to notification to the tenant after the costs have been incurred. Accordingly, it is no defence for a landlord to say that the tenant knew that the works were done, even in those cases where the landlord has served prior notice of proposal to carry out the works and estimates under s 20. The section does not give the court (or LVT) discretion to dispense with notice.

9.133   In *Gilje v Charlgrove Securities Ltd (No 2)* [2003] EWHC 1284 (Ch), [2004] 1 All ER 91, tenants who had paid on account for the years ending March 1999 and March 2000 called the section in aid when accounts were not produced until 2001. Those accounts showed an overpayment by the tenants. The tenants claimed the accounts represented a demand, and as that demand was sent more than 18 months after the work was done s 20B prohibited the landlord from recovering the costs so incurred. It was held that s 20B does not apply where (a) payments are made on account, (b) the actual expenditure is not more than the sum paid on account, and (c) the landlord does not request any further payment from the tenants. The court said the accounts and certificates delivered were not a demand for payment in such circumstances. The amounts paid on account were clearly payment of service charges, and where there was no further payment to be made by the tenants there was no demand at the adjustment stage – there was nothing to demand. The court pointed out that the tenants can challenge payments on account if they are more than is reasonable. Clearly, this case shows a tenant cannot seek to recover money paid on account under s 20B in such circumstances, although the position might be different if the landlord did seek a further payment in addition to that paid on account. Unfortunately, the judgment does not address the latter point.

9.134 The section refers to costs 'incurred' more than 18 months before the demand, not to works 'carried out' at that time. This could create unexpected problems where a contract for works is entered into, and thus the costs 'incurred', but those works are not carried out until later. It would be a brave tenant who tried to rely on s 20B where work was carried out more than 18 months after a contract was placed, but within 18 months of subsequent notice by the landlord. One might expect the courts to treat the carrying out of the works as 'incurring' the costs in such a case, perhaps in addition to any earlier event which could also be treated as 'incurring' the costs.

9.135 The section refers to 'relevant costs' which, under s 18(2), covers both works and services.

9.136 Whether the tenant pays in advance or not, one would expect the landlord normally to include some amount in the charge for the following accounting year, even if the final figure is not known (or at least a note in the accounts). Provided this is sent within the 18-month period the tenant will then have been given notice within the meaning of the section. Where the tenant pays in arrears it is likely that some charge to the tenant would be made in the year after the works, and so the position of the landlord would be thus protected. Delay in charging can rarely be in the interest of the landlord.

9.137 The reason for the provision is twofold:

(a) It avoids the possibility of the landlord seeking to make a charge long after what was done is forgotten, or has perhaps even become covered up by later works, and where, perhaps, there are new tenants.

(b) It would enable a landlord who has not been given details of the contractors' charges, or perhaps where there is a dispute over the cost, to give notice that a charge will be made and to recover it when the cost is known.

9.138   Since originally writing this section, the author has heard of a county court judge who took the view that the section requires the landlord to notify the tenant of the actual amount to be charged. The author does not read the section this way (the section uses the expression 'the tenant was notified in writing that those costs had been incurred' – not 'the tenant was notified of the amount'), but the author is not aware of any reported cases on this aspect. If actual figures are not available it is to be hoped that a court would accept a tenant had been given due notice if the landlord gave at least a reasonable estimate of the amount concerned within 18 months: in many cases he will have given an estimate when consulting, if it was something where consultation was compulsory. One would expect the landlord to want to recover as soon as possible, and delays may be due to the landlord not having received an account, or, at least as likely, there being a dispute over the amount of the contractor's bill, so that the precise amount is not known.

9.139   Readers are reminded that the Act does not give the court discretion to dispense with the requirement (to achieve justice the courts might try to find an inherent discretion in suitable circumstances) and, like all these provisions, it applies only to leases of dwellings.

Criticism

9.140   Although the section requires the landlord to give a notice that a charge will be made, it does not state that the charge, when made, must be demanded within any specific period. It would seem a landlord could notify a tenant within 18 months that a cost had been incurred, but not actually make a charge until six years after the work was done. This could arise if the cost of the works, or perhaps the standard of work, was under dispute. Obviously, the normal periods of limitation will apply. If a landlord did delay, the author would recommend notes in the accounts, and in successive years if necessary, to say 'the account with (Ron's Roofers) for the (roof works) has not yet been agreed and will be included in the accounts, once the figure is settled', or something similar.

9.141   It seems odd that the court has discretion to give a dispensation for failure to consult with tenants under s 20 before carrying out work, but not for a landlord who has acted reasonably, perhaps using the consultation procedure, but has failed to serve notice after the event. An express power to exercise discretion would surely be appropriate.

Section 20C of the Landlord and Tenant Act 1985

Court costs

9.142   This section gives the tenant a right to apply for 'an order that all or any of the costs incurred or to be incurred, by the landlord in connection with any proceedings are not to be regarded as relevant costs to be taken into account in determining the amount of any service charge payable by the tenant'.

9.143   The application is either to the court or, more normally, to the Leasehold Valuation Tribunal in the course of proceedings (s 20C(2)(a)). If made after the proceedings are concluded it is to the county court (s 20C(2)(b)). The application for an order is easy to make and can be made at the same time as an application to determine reasonableness.

9.144   It is put sufficiently widely to cover costs that would otherwise be charged to A relating to proceedings by B against C, if they might be included in the service charge that A has to pay. This is perhaps most likely to be material if tenant A discovers that the landlord (B) has incurred legal costs in respect of proceedings against tenant C, perhaps for non-payment of rent or some other breach of covenant, and wants to include the balance he cannot recover from tenant C as part of the total service charge costs. Such costs may not strictly be recoverable according to a number of cases (for example, *Reston Ltd v Hudson* [1990] 2 EGLR 51, at **5.157** above; *Sella House Ltd v Mears* [1989] 1 EGLR 65, at **5.167** above; and *Morgan v Stainer* [1993] 2 EGLR 73) but the section permits the tenant to seek an order which a landlord would have to accept. The tenant would have a good defence to proceedings by the landlord seeking to recover the costs through the service charge. By giving the court the right to make such order as is just and equitable, the court could entitle the landlord to recover the whole of such costs in suitable cases.

Some cases

9.145   The section was considered by the Court of Appeal in *Iperion Investments Corporation v Broadwalk House Residents Ltd* [1995] 2 EGLR 47. The landlord wanted to forfeit the lease for flagrant breaches of covenant by the tenant. The landlord peaceably re-entered, after which the tenant sought an order to regain possession. The tenant was largely successful in the proceedings, and the judge at first instance ordered, under s 20C, that the costs of the proceedings for forfeiture and relief from forfeiture were not to be payable by the tenant as part of the service charges. The landlord took the case to the Court of Appeal and lost – ie it was not entitled to claim the court costs through the service charge. The appeal court pointed out that although the tenant had acted badly, this was reflected in the order of the lower court where the successful tenant was awarded a lower proportion of its own costs than might have been expected had it behaved correctly throughout.

(a)   The Lands Tribunal heard an appeal against an order under the section in *Maryland Estates Ltd v Lynch and Wilson* LTL 19.3.2003. Works had been carried out and the tenants challenged the surveyor's charges of 15% of the contract sum. It appeared, however, that the amount being challenged, which related to a costs overrun, had actually been paid by the contractors. The landlord's accounts, however, were such that this was not apparent. 'Confused and complicated service charge figures, involving apparently inexplicable adjustments.' As the amount had been paid by the contractors the Lands Tribunal agreed with the landlords that the LVT had no jurisdiction to hear the application. However, as the confusion had arisen from the landlord's accounts the Tribunal exercised its discretion so that the landlord could only include in the service charge accounts half its costs of the proceedings.

(b) As examples of the way the section is applied in the Leasehold Valuation Tribunal see *Ionic Properties and Lessee's of Melcombe Regis Court (LVT)* LON/BK/LSL/2003/0015, where, considering the success and faults of the parties in the Tribunal, it ordered that 70% of the costs incurred by the landlord were not to be regarded as relevant costs, and *London Borough of Sutton v Leaseholders of the Benhill Estate (LVT)* LON/OOBF/LSC/2003/0011, where the Tribunal considered it as not just and equitable to make an order under s 20C in the circumstances of that case. (The report is only in relation to the s 20C application, but shows factors that influenced the outcome.)

9.146　In 2001 tenants applied to the Leasehold Valuation Tribunal on disputed service charges. They then sought an order that the landlord's costs of the application would not be charged through the service charge. The Leasehold Valuation Tribunal would not make that order. The tenant sought leave to appeal, first from the Leasehold Valuation Tribunal and then from the Lands Tribunal, but was refused in both cases. The Lands Tribunal awarded the landlord his costs (or at least a part of them) relating to the cost of the application for leave to appeal: they had jurisdiction to do so. (*Barrington Court Developments Ltd v Barrington Court Residents Association* [2001] 29 EG 128.)

9.147　In *Ibrahim v Dovecorn Reversions Ltd* [2001] 30 EG 116, there was a dispute about whether a flat roof over a flat (Flat 8) was the responsibility of the tenant or the landlord. Flat 8 was underneath a flat roof used by the tenants of the flats above. The tenant of Flat 8 joined the tenants of the upper flats into the action. The judge held the flat roof was the responsibility of the landlord. On the question of costs, on appeal, it was held that the judge was right to make an Order under s 20C, but that the tenant of Flat 8 should pay the costs of the tenants of the other two flats.

Costs and fees of LVT proceedings

9.148　Although it is not in chronological order, it is worth mentioning here the provisions of Sch 12 to the Commonhold and Leasehold Reform Act 2002 regarding costs and fees. Paragraph 9 provides that Regulations may include provisions to entitle an LVT to order one party to pay the fees, up to £500, of the other party. In addition, para 10 of Sch 12 entitles an LVT to order payment by one party to another of the costs of that party where the application to the LVT is dismissed on the ground that the application is frivolous, vexatious or otherwise an abuse of process, or where one party has acted similarly or otherwise unreasonably in relation to the proceedings. The latter provision was the subject of a number of differing Leasehold Valuation Tribunal decisions. One, *Staghold Ltd v Takeda* [2005] 3 EGLR 45, was taken to appeal on various issues, one of which was that the tenants claimed that para 10(4) of Sch 12 to the Commonhold and

Leasehold Reform Act 2002 has the effect that landlords cannot recover any costs at all from tenants relating to LVT proceedings. Paragraph 10(4) reads 'A person shall not be required to pay costs incurred by another person in connection with proceedings before a (LVT) except by a determination under this paragraph or in accordance with provision made by any enactment other than this paragraph.' The judgment, although it has only limited authority because it is a county court case, followed a carefully argued case, and the judge gave a detailed judgment, reviewing a number of LVT decisions on the point. Here the tenant had argued numerous points with a bundle of 734 pages. On the Sch 12 point, the judge held against the tenants. He said:

> 'I cannot think that Parliament intended that though a tenant whose behaviour had in no way contributed to the (landlord's) incurring costs in the LVT proceedings was properly required to pay by way of service charge, a proportion of those costs, a tenant whose actions led to the costs being incurred should be excused from paying his or her appropriate proportion.'

Section 21 of the Landlord and Tenant Act 1985

Summary of relevant costs – statement of account

9.149   The current provision entitles a tenant to call for a written summary of service charge costs. That section was to be entirely substituted by s 152 of the Commonhold and Leasehold Reform Act 2002, with a new version requiring the landlord to provide 'a written statement of account'. The government, following consultation, has decided not to implement the new section as originally intended. This chapter will, accordingly, review the present provisions, and then comment on the extremely important proposals, which are likely to be reintroduced in an amended form when parliamentary time allows.

Summary of relevant costs

9.150   The current section is still in force. Under s 21(1): 'A tenant may require the landlord in writing to supply him with a written summary of the costs incurred … and which are relevant costs in relation to the service charge payable or demanded … in that or any other period.' The summary is to be of the service charge costs in the last completed 12-month period 'or if the accounts are not so made up, in the period of 12 months ending with the date of the request'. This could assist, for example, where the landlord has not prepared accounts for some time, although s 20B, with the 18-month limit will assist a tenant in such cases.

9.151   The landlord is to comply within one month of the request or, within six months of the end of the period mentioned in the preceding paragraph, whichever is later (s 21(4)).

9.152   Under s 21(5) the summary has to state whether any costs relate to grant work –

'and, in addition shall summarise each of the following, namely –

(a)   any of the costs in respect of which no demand for payment was received by the landlord within the period referred to in sub-s(1)(a) or (b) [see **9.150** above],

(b)   any of the costs in respect of which –

   (i)   a demand for payment was received, but

   (ii)   no payment was made by the landlord within that period, and

(c)   any of the costs in respect of which –

   (i) a demand for payment was so received, and

   (ii) payment was made by the landlord within that period,

and specify the aggregate of any amounts received by the landlord down to the end of that period on account of service charges in respect of relevant dwellings and still standing to the credit of the tenants of those dwellings at the end of that period.'

9.153   Under s 21(6) if the service charges 'are payable by the tenants of more than four dwellings the summary shall be certified by a qualified accountant' as 'a fair summary, complying with the requirements of (s 21(5)), and ... being sufficiently supported by accounts, receipts and other documents which have been produced to him'.

9.154   This is a fairly useful weapon for a tenant who is dubious about the accounts he has seen. For example, if there is a grant and it is simply not mentioned in the accounts a certificate of the above sort would require the point to be at least considered. Where there are four or more tenants the certificate has to be certified by a qualified accountant, who will be under a duty to review the papers. Section 25 provides that it is a criminal offence to breach s 21, and so giving a false certificate could have serious consequences. Apart from cases where the tenant is concerned about the accounts he has seen, the summary could be helpful if accounts have not been produced at all. If the tenant has doubts about the accounts he can always raise queries with the landlord or managing agents, but in cases where the answers seem unsatisfactory this is another approach.

Proposed statement of account provision

9.155   The new section requiring the landlord to provide a statement of account has not been brought into force and, according to a press release from the Office of the Deputy Prime Minister dated 29 July 2005, it is being reconsidered. The relevant part of the press release said:

'New rights for leaseholders to receive regular statements of their service charges are to be delayed following concerns raised by social landlords in a recent consultation. The new rights under the Commonhold and Leasehold Reform Act 2002 would have required landlords to supply service charge payers with a regular statement of account, an accountants' certificate and a summary of a tenant's rights and obligations relating to service charges. However, the ODPM has concluded it is not possible to introduce the new measures without imposing considerable extra costs on social landlords and their leaseholders. Proposals are being developed to amend the legislation to ensure both public and private sector leaseholders receive appropriate information that does not incur a disproportionate cost to them. Housing Minister Baroness Andrews said the Government remained committed to improving the rights of all leaseholders in obtaining key information about their service charge payments. "This will prevent fraud and provide much needed assurance as to whether they are obtaining value for money. Many leaseholders in both private and social sectors receive very good levels of information, however, it is important all leaseholders receive a decent level of information and protection." The ODPM does not expect progress on other outstanding accounting provisions in the 2002 Act to be delayed and that a further announcement on the commencement of these provisions will be made in due course.'

No announcement about the other accounting provisions, on designated accounts (s 42A of the 1987 Act has been made at the time of writing. It may be that, in due course the replacement section will be re-enacted as a watered down version of what was in the Commonhold Act, and the section, or perhaps more likely the regulations under the section, may include some of the better suggestions from the consultation carried out in 2005. The following is a brief summary of the points, but with a warning that the section may, when brought in, be totally different.

9.156   The landlord's obligation was to be in three parts: (a) the landlord was to provide the statement of account within six months of the end of the financial year, incorporating prescribed information: (b) the accounts were to be accompanied by the certificate of a qualified accountant, also incorporating prescribed information; and (c) the accounts were to be accompanied by a prescribed summary of the rights and obligations of residential tenants. (See at **9.159** about the accountant's certificate and **9.169** in respect of the summary of rights and obligations.) The obligations, subject to any exemptions in regulations, were to apply equally to a house divided into two flats, and a purpose-built block of 100 flats. Failure to comply was to be a criminal offence, and there was no right to obtain dispensation. In addition, the tenant was given a new right to withhold payment until the three items were produced.

9.157   The consultation paper suggested that an accountant's certificate should not be needed in four cases:

(a)   Where there are four or less dwellings.

(b)   Where no service charge costs have been incurred.

(c)   Where a local authority is under an obligation to give a certificate of cost.

(d)   Where the tenant waives the right.

9.158   Although in the case of well-run blocks where there are no problems, the six-month time limit should be easily achieved, one can foresee cases where circumstances will make it hard to comply, eg where there are works in course of being carried out at the year end for which the figures are not available or are under dispute. Readers are reminded that failure was to be a criminal offence.

9.159   The statement of account was to be certified by a qualified accountant and accompanied by a prescribed summary of the rights and obligations of tenants of dwellings in relation to service charges. The accountant's certificate was to state that in the opinion of the qualified accountant the statement of account deals fairly with the matters with which it is required to deal and is sufficiently supported by accounts, receipts and other documents which have been produced to him.

9.160   So what matters were to be covered by the statement of account? They were set out in proposed replacement s 21(1), which says the statement must deal with:

(a)   Service charges of the tenant and the tenants of dwellings associated with his dwelling.

(b)   Relevant costs relating to those service charges.

(c)   The aggregate amount standing to the credit of the tenant and the tenants of those dwellings:

    (i)   at the beginning of the accounting period, and

    (ii)   at the end of the accounting period.

(d)   Unspecified related matters.

The consultation paper from 2005 suggested in great detail the items to be covered in the statement of account, and also the approximate form of the accountant's certificate.

Criticism of the proposals

9.161   The section on the whole seemed reasonably good, although is a pity that, yet again, the detail was to appear in great detail in regulations rather than in the Act. The suggested exemptions from the need for an accountant's certificate seem sensible and are welcome. It would mean, however, that the accounts for a house divided into five flats would need to be audited by an accountant, regardless of the sum involved unless the tenants agreed to do without a certificate. It all seems to be adding to the costs. This is presumably a large part of the reason why the social landlords (and surely many private sector landlords) objected to the proposals. It seems one of those cases where, with a view to protecting all (residential) tenants (whether they have a problem or not), a considerable length of red tape would need to be used, leading to more work for landlords and considerable expense to the tenants the provision seeks to benefit.

Proposed s 21A of the Landlord and Tenant Act 1985

Power for tenants to withhold service charge

9.162   As well as the main proposed new s 21 on statements of account, there were two subsections also to be added. Again, neither of these subsections (21A and 21B) has been brought into force. (See at **9.155** above.) However, on the assumption that something similar is likely to be introduced, the following comments on the proposals can be made. There are only limited rights under current legislation permitting a tenant to withhold payment of service charges. (Sections 47 and 48 of the Landlord and Tenant Act 1987, at **9.275** and **9.278** below.) Section 21A was to amplify the proposed new s 21 by entitling a tenant to withhold service charges. The right was to apply where:

(a)   the landlord had not supplied any one of the documents required under proposed s 21 (ie a statement of account, an accountant's certificate or the summary of tenants' rights and obligations) within the timescales in s 21, or

(b)   documents had been supplied which do 'not conform exactly or substantially' with the requirements in s 21 or the regulations under it.

There was to be power in s 21A(4) for a Leasehold Valuation Tribunal to determine whether or not the landlord had reasonable excuse for a failure. The right to withhold was to cease to apply after a finding that there is reasonable excuse.

9.163   Where a tenant could lawfully withhold service charges under s 21A penalties for late payment ceased to be exercisable. Service charges were not, however, to be withheld after the document (or a satisfactory replacement document, where the original was defective) had been supplied to the tenant. The tenant was to be entitled to refuse to pay the service charges on receipt of a perfect set of accounts accompanied by an accountant's certificate, if the landlord forgot to include the prescribed summary.

9.164   The Act proposed that the maximum the tenant could withhold was a sum equal to the aggregate of:

(a)   'the service charges paid by him in the accounting period' in question; and

(b)   the amount standing to his credit at the start of the accounting period in question.

9.165   Note that the reference is to amounts 'paid', and not to amounts 'payable'. If the tenant had £250 standing to his credit carried forward from the previous year, and had paid £500 per quarter on account during the accounting year in question he could withhold up to £2,250 until the statement of account, accountant's certificate and summary of rights were all produced in a proper form. If the tenant pays quarterly in advance he may well have paid two more quarters before he is aware that the landlord is in breach of the section and that he can lawfully start withholding payment.

Criticism

9.166   The power to withhold payment seems a good practical remedy to force a landlord to produce certified accounts within a reasonable period. Obviously, if the accountant is unable to certify the accounts the problem will presumably come to light at an earlier stage than may otherwise be the case. If so, the tenant would, at least, have the benefit of the section, when in force, to hold back further payments until the problem is sorted out. That would probably be the most useful aspect of this provision. On the other side of the coin, if the tenants withhold payment it could make the running of the development difficult or impossible, which will not be in the interests of tenants or landlords. There would be clear onus on landlords to ensure accounts were produced promptly, fully, and distributed to tenants without undue delay.

9.167   The amount the tenant can withhold is related to historic figures, but it is hard to see any other sensible yardstick. Difficulties could arise if there are ongoing disputes over previous years' service charges, as the reference is to the amount 'paid'. If the tenant has not paid then he will be unable lawfully to exercise this right, although he will already be withholding informally.

9.168   The proposed wording opens the door to potential disputes as to whether documents conform 'exactly or substantially' to the requirements. This would cover both the accounts, which would have to address specific aspects, and the accountant's certificate, as well as the summary of the tenants' rights and obligation. It remains to be seen whether any small error or omission will be used to enable a tenant to withhold payment: as is common in many areas it may well be the reasonable tenants who do not take advantage and the usual suspects who do. It would be preferable for the right to be linked to the production of the accounts only, and not the summary of rights, but clearly a legal right to withhold is a useful tool for the tenant.

Proposed s 21 B of the Landlord and Tenant Act 1985

Notice accompanying demands for service charge

9.169   This is the section, to be inserted by the Commonhold Act, but not yet brought into force, requiring the landlord to send a 'summary of the rights and obligations of tenants of dwellings in relation to service charges' when sending accounts. This proposed new subsection entitles the tenant to 'withhold payment of a service charge which has been demanded from him' if this summary does not accompany the accounts. The author does not view this proposal with any enthusiasm. The suggested 'summary' in the consultation paper ran to four A4 pages. The idea was that this would have to be sent to each tenant at least once a year (with the accounts), and, depending how the regulations turned out, possibly also with each service charge demand. Under the Act, the summary would have to be sent again and again, even where the tenant remains the same and has read it umpteen times before. This is likely to lead to a huge waste of natural resources: for example in a block of 100 flats, if the summary has to be sent each quarter that is 400 copies each year of the same thing. Will the tenant read it once, let alone four times a year? It is probably accepted that people are less likely to read the summary if they see it on a regular basis. However, Parliament decided this was necessary.

Section 22 of the Landlord and Tenant Act 1985

Inspection etc of documents

9.170   This is another section which is intended to be replaced (by s 154 of the Commonhold Act), but where the replacement has not yet been brought into force. The replacement section was introduced, in effect, to make consequential amendments following the proposed introduction of statements of account, which are now being reconsidered. The present section entitles a tenant who has obtained a summary of costs under s 21 above (see at **9.150** above) to inspect certain items. Accordingly, it does not apply to all tenants of dwellings. The right is for qualifying tenants, or the secretary of an RTA, 'within 6 months of obtaining the summary (to) require the landlord in writing to afford him reasonable facilities, (a) for inspecting the accounts, receipts and other documents supporting the summary, and (b) for taking copies or extracts from them'.

9.171   The landlord is to 'make such facilities available to the tenant or secretary for a period of two months beginning not later than one month after the request is made'. (The new section had a 21-day period.) Under s 22(5) the landlord is to make inspection free of charge 'where such facilities are for the inspection of any documents', and where the 'facilities are for the taking of copies or extracts, be entitled to make them so available on payment of such reasonable charge as he may determine'. Section 22(6) goes on to say that the requirement imposed to make facilities free of charge 'shall not be construed as precluding the landlord from treating as part of his costs of management any costs incurred by him in connection with making the facilities so available'. This is not further defined, but would presumably include the time cost of the managing agent for producing the actual receipts, accounts, etc.

9.172   Breach of this section is a criminal offence (Landlord and Tenant Act 1985, s 25).

9.173   The request is to be made by the tenant, or by the secretary of a recognised tenants' association, within six months of obtaining the summary of costs under s 21. The request is treated as served on the landlord if it is served on the agent named in the rent book or the person who receives the rent on behalf of the landlord. If the demand is served on the agent of the landlord or receiver of rent that person 'shall forward it as soon as may be to the landlord'. (Landlord and Tenant Act 1985, s 22(3).) In practice, the person collecting the rent will often be the person with custody of the accounts, etc.

Cases

9.174   For a case where a predecessor of this provision (Housing Finance Act 1972, s 90) was referred to, and which influenced the outcome of the case (the landlord having failed to allow inspection), readers are directed to *Woodtrek Ltd v Jezek* (1981) 261 EG 571 (see at **2.25** above).

9.175   For a 1978 case where s 90 of the 1972 Act was considered and inspection not ordered, because it was not material for registration under the Rent Acts in the circumstances, see *Legal and General Assurance Society Ltd v Keane* (1978) 246 EG 827(see at **8.27** above).

Criticism

9.176   The summary of costs, particularly if it has been duly certified, should surely be sufficient in the absence of fraud or perhaps confusing accounts, although the possibility of the latter may be the reason why the right to inspect is given. This limited right is only available to tenants of residential premises who have obtained a summary of costs under s 21. Not giving a summary of costs, when required to do so, is a criminal offence. If the summary is unsatisfactory the tenants can seek inspection of the vouchers. If the landlord does not co-operate with inspection, that, too, is a criminal offence. It is probably fair to say that a tenant could probably obtain inspection, in commercial as well as residential cases, by way of disclosure in court proceedings. This section gives a quicker, and certainly cheaper, statutory alternative.

9.177   Section 22(2) permits inspection of accounts, receipts or other documents 'supporting the summary'. While this covers the documents recording what actually was spent it does not seem to include, for example, estimates which were not accepted or the specifications on which estimates were sought. Both the summary of costs and the inspection can show that the actual cost was, say, £10,000: the Act does not, in this section, necessarily seem to enable the tenant to go behind the actual figures to see what the contractor was asked to do, and what the various quotations were. This may be one of the most important elements of any enquiry on behalf of the tenant. There may well have been a number of proposals which at the end of the day were not brought to fruition. To inspect the latter may not necessarily be particularly helpful to anyone, but the responses to the quotations that the landlord is bound to seek under s 20 are, one imagines, a different matter. The landlord could obtain six quotations, but under s 20 need only disclose two to the tenants.

Section 23 of the Landlord and Tenant Act 1985

Request for information held by superior landlord

9.178   This is another section that was to be replaced by the Commonhold and Leasehold Reform Act 2002 (s 152 and paras 1 and 2 of Sch 10). The replacement provisions referred to statements of account which, as indicated above, are not being enacted as originally proposed, and the new provision is accordingly not in force. The present section applies where a request for a summary of relevant costs under s 21 'relates in whole or in part to relevant costs incurred by or on behalf of a superior landlord, and the landlord to whom the request is made is not in possession of the information'. The (immediate) landlord 'shall in turn make a written request for the relevant information to the person who is his landlord (and so on, if that person is not himself the superior landlord)'. The superior landlord 'shall comply with that request within a reasonable time, and … the immediate landlord shall then comply with the tenant's or secretary's request, or that part of it which relates to the relevant costs incurred by or on behalf of the superior landlord, within the time allowed by s 21 or such further time, if any, as is reasonable in the circumstances' (see at **9.150**).

9.179   The section continues, in s 23(2), by referring to a request for inspection of accounts etc under s 22 (see at **9.170** et seq). If such a request is made the intermediate landlord 'shall forthwith inform the tenant or secretary of that fact and of the name and address of the superior landlord, and … section 22 shall then apply to the superior landlord as it applies to the intermediate landlord'.

9.180   Breach of the section is made a criminal offence by s 25.

Proposed replacement section

9.181   The proposed replacement s 23 is also in two parts. The first part of s 23 was to give a landlord the right to request from the superior landlord information which the landlord does not have, and as to arranging inspection of vouchers. Proposed new s 23A, not reflecting anything in the original 1985 provisions, was to apply where a landlord or superior landlord disposes of his interest. In effect, the former landlord was still obliged to co-operate under s 21 (summary of costs), s 22 (inspection), and s 23 (passing requests to the superior landlord), to the extent to which he is able to do so. Breach of either section, again, was to be a criminal offence under s 25 of the Landlord and Tenant Act 1985.

9.182   The reason new s 23 is not in force is that it was to apply to a 'statement of account' under s 21. As stated above, the latter is not being brought into force. The section was to apply 'if a statement of account which the landlord is required to supply … relates to matters concerning a superior landlord and the landlord is not in possession of the relevant information'. The immediate landlord was to be able to give written notice requiring the superior landlord, and so on further up the chain if applicable, to provide the relevant information. The superior landlord is to comply within 'a reasonable time'. The immediate landlord is then in a position to comply with a request for information or inspection. Similarly, as in the current version, where a request to inspect vouchers has been made under s 22 and the vouchers are held by a superior landlord the intermediate landlord is to 'immediately' inform the tenant, or the secretary of an RTA, of that fact and give them the name and address of the superior landlord. Thereafter, s 22 applies to the superior landlord.

9.183   Proposed new s 23A was to create a new right, which would also be a criminal offence. It was also to apply when any duty owed by a landlord or superior landlord under ss 21, 22, or s 23, remains outstanding, and the landlord or the superior landlord 'disposes of the whole or part of his interest as landlord or superior landlord to another person'. Under the proposed s 23A(2) if 'the landlord or superior landlord is, despite the disposal, still in a position to discharge the duty to any extent, he remains responsible for discharging it to that extent'. The following subsection was to provide that if the 'other person' (ie the person to whom the interest has been disposed) 'is in a position to discharge the duty to any extent, he is responsible for discharging it to that extent'. Where a landlord transfers his interest other than on the last day of a financial year, there will be apportionments between vendor and purchaser. The transferor will at that stage have the information for the period up to the date of transfer, and the transferee for the period after. The proposed obligations were not limited to information in the year of transfer of the reversion. There is no obligation in the Act on anyone to retain records for any period, although this is good practice, and professional managing agents and others will usually retain records for some time.

Criticism

9.184   The present section is sensible, and the author's only criticism is the slightly eccentric timing. Under s 23(1) an intermediate landlord is to seek information and the superior landlord has to respond within 'a reasonable time'. Under s 23(2)(a) the landlord is to notify the tenant 'forthwith' of the name of the superior landlord. These are, however, very minor defects in a sensible and practical provision. The qualification of wording on the intended criminal liability means it is not an absolute liability, and is intended only to apply where someone has information and refuses to co-operate. Under the Landlord and Tenant (Covenants) Act 1995, a landlord who assigns his reversionary interest can seek a release from the tenant(s), and if it is not given can apply for a release through the courts. A landlord or superior landlord who has failed to comply with his obligations under the 1985 Act may find it harder to obtain a release under the 1995 Act than one who has complied.

Section 24 of the Landlord and Tenant Act 1985

Effect of assignment

9.185   This simply provides that if a lease is assigned the assignment 'does not affect the validity of a request made under s 21, 22 or 23' (summarised at **9.149**, **9.170** and **9.178** above). The section sensibly goes on to say that a person, ie the landlord or superior landlord, is 'not obliged to provide a summary or make facilities available more than once for the same dwelling and for the same period'. This is yet another 1985 Act section intended to be completely replaced (by the Commonhold Act, s 157 and Sch 10, para 3). The replacement section says the landlord or superior landlord is not required to comply with more than a reasonable number of requirements imposed by any one person. No clue is given as to what a 'reasonable number' of requirements may be, but the proposal gives limited (and rare) protection to the landlord.

Sections 25 and 33 of the Landlord and Tenant Act 1985

Criminal offences and liability of directors etc

9.186 Section 25 states that it is 'a summary offence for a person to fail, without reasonable excuse, to perform a duty imposed on him by section 21, 22 or 23'. A person found guilty is liable to a fine not exceeding level 4 on the standard scale. The fine at the time of writing is up to £2,500. (Criminal Justice Act 1991, s 17(1).)

9.187 There are also criminal offences for failure without reasonable excuse not to comply with the provisions of the Schedule to the 1985 Act regarding insurance of dwellings (Landlord and Tenant Act 1985, Sch, para 6; the Schedule is reviewed at **9.236** below) and, when it is brought in, it will be an offence to fail to comply with s 42A of the Landlord and Tenant Act 1987, which is the requirement to hold service charge money for dwellings in a 'designated account'.

9.188 Neither s 25 of the 1985 Act nor proposed s 42A of the 1987 Act indicates what might be considered to be a 'reasonable excuse'. There are hardly any reported cases, but for a case on s 25, see *R v Marylebone Magistrates' Court, ex p Westminster City Council* (1999) 32 HLR 266, which was an application for a judicial review. A summary of costs under the original s 21 had been provided, but it was defective. The landlord was prosecuted in the magistrates' court under s 25 of the 1985 Act, but as the defect was held to be trivial the magistrates decided to stay the proceedings. In proceedings for judicial review the court held that as the defective summary was a criminal offence the court should not have stayed the proceedings as an abuse of process – it could, for example, have given no penalty but ordered costs to be paid. Judicial review was not appropriate as, by then, the tenant had the information he wanted, and in any event could inspect the relevant documents under s 23.

9.189 Perhaps where the vouchers etc have been accidentally destroyed in a fire, or where the landlord has unknowingly employed a rogue managing agent, a landlord may be able to persuade a court he has reasonable excuse for non-compliance.

9.190 Remember that although the duty is primarily on the landlord to take action there is also a duty on others and thus a potential criminal penalty for failure. For example, a request to inspect vouchers or to pass on requests to a superior landlord can be validly given to 'the person who receives the rent on behalf of the landlord'.

9.191 The current level of fine seems to have been in place for a long time. A maximum fine of £2,500 may be relatively insignificant compared to the possible sums involved in many cases.

9.192   Criminal penalties do not arise from failing to consult under s 20 of the Landlord and Tenant Act 1985. The penalty is the landlord's inability to be able to obtain reimbursement of the money he has spent on works and services.

Criminal liability of directors etc

9.193   Directors and secretaries of companies also have personal criminal liability, as well as the company, under s 33 of the 1985 Act in relation to breaches of the 1985 Act. The section is widely phrased in s 33(1)(a) to apply to give personal liability in cases where an offence is proved to have been committed 'with the consent or connivance of a director, manager, secretary or other similar officer of the body corporate, or a person purporting to Act in any such capacity', or, s 33(1)(b), where the offence is attributable 'to any neglect on the part of' such person.

9.194   Section 33(2) extends similar liability to members of a company which is managed by its members. This obviously applies where tenants own the reversion and the directors prejudice a minority by not complying with the formalities. This is separate from the right of a tenant perhaps seeking to obtain the benefit of the 'oppressed minorities' provisions of the Companies Act 1985.

9.195   The criminal liability of directors etc under s 33 (see at **9.193**) is repeated in virtually identical wording in proposed s 42B of the Landlord and Tenant Act 1987 in respect of failure to use a 'designated account' under s 42A. (Commonhold and Leasehold Reform Act 2002, s 156.) Section 42B(5) provides that 1987 Act proceedings are to be brought by a local housing authority as defined in s 1 of the Housing Act 1985.

Section 26 of the Landlord and Tenant Act 1985

Exemption for certain public sector tenancies

9.196   Section 26 provides that ss 18-25 do not apply to tenants of local authorities, new town corporations or the Development Board for Rural Wales unless they hold under a 'long tenancy, in which case sections 18 to 24 apply but section 25 (offence of failure to comply) does not'. The effect is that only public sector tenants with long leases have the protection of the provisions for reasonableness, inspection of vouchers, etc given to tenants of other landlords, but the relatively modest criminal penalty applying to other landlords do not apply.

9.197   Subsections (2) and (3) of the section define long leases, ie those cases where the main sections apply. These are, in effect, leases 'granted for a term exceeding 21 years', tenancies subject to perpetual renewal, and right to buy leases. Tenancies subject to termination on death are only treated as long leases in certain specified circumstances. (Section 26(3); service charge aspects of public sector tenancies are reviewed in Chapter 10.)

Summary of criminal offences

9.198   The following sections currently provide for a criminal penalty for breach:

(a)   *1985 Act, s 21* Landlord's obligation to provide a summary of relevant costs. (See at **9.150**.)

(b)   *1985 Act, s 22* Not co-operating with inspection of vouchers. (See at **9.170**.)

(c)   *1985 Act, s 23* Not passing on a request to a superior landlord, or the superior landlord not co-operating. (See at **9.178**.)

(d)   *1985 Act, Sch* Insurance provisions. (See at **9.236**.)

(e)   *1985 Act, s 3* Failure by landlord to notify the tenant of the landlord's name and address. (See at **9.273**.)

9.199   This is a reminder that the criminal provisions can apply to directors and secretaries etc of companies. (1985 Act, s 33, at **9.193** et seq above.) In addition, while ss 18-24 apply to tenants holding long leases from local authorities, new town corporations and the Development Board for Rural Wales, the criminal penalties do not apply. (1985 Act, s 26, at **9.196** above.)

Section 27 of the Landlord and Tenant Act 1985

Registered rents

9.200   Rents can be registered under s 71(4) of the Rent Act 1977 to include service charges. (See Chapter 10, at **10.54** et seq.) This short section in the 1985 Act makes it clear that where a rent is registered under the Rent Acts and the registered rent includes a service charge, the main sections (ss 18-25 of the 1985 Act above) relating to service charges do not apply 'unless the amount registered is, in pursuance of s 71(4) (of Rent Act 1977) entered as a variable amount'. The registration shows that the tenant pays either a fixed contribution to service charges, in which case the rights for estimates etc are unnecessary as the tenant knows exactly what he has to pay, or as a variable rent, when the sections above will apply and the tenant will be entitled to the protection afforded to other tenants.

Section 27A of the Landlord and Tenant Act 1985

Liability to pay service charges: jurisdiction

9.201   The new s 27A, inserted by s 155 of the Commonhold Act, contains much more precise provisions for determining service charge disputes than the earlier provisions, which had formerly been added as new subsections of s 19. Like the previous version it entitles a Leasehold Valuation Tribunal to make a determination whether a service charge is payable either after a demand (s 27A(1)), or before works etc are carried out (s 27A(3)).

9.202 In the case of future expenses s 27A(3) says the application is for 'a determination whether, if costs were incurred for services, repairs, maintenance, improvements, insurance or management of any specified description, a service charge would be payable for those costs ...'. The items specified are those in the definition of service charges in s 18. The section does not say who is entitled to apply, and so it could be (a) the tenant faced with a bill he considers too high, (b) a landlord, either where he wants to carry out substantial works and seeks clearance in advance, or where he has consulted under s 20 and has had adverse observations, or (c) a management company. This right for a landlord to seek advance approval to carry out works is one of the few provisions that benefit a landlord. (For costs of the application see s 20C of the 1985 Act, at **9.142**.)

9.203 The new aspect introduced by the 2002 Act is that when an application is made, after a demand, the LVT is required to determine five things, namely:

'(a)   the person by whom it is payable

(b)   The person to whom it is payable,

(c)   the amount which is payable,

(d)   the date at or by which it is payable, and

(e)   the manner in which it is payable.'

(Section 27A(1).) Where advance clearance is sought the LVT determination has to cover the same points, grammatically adjusted, under s 27A(3).

9.204 The section was the subject of a useful Lands Tribunal decision in 2006, from Judge Huskinson, which held that the LVT had no discretion to set a timetable for payment different to that within the lease. The case was *Southend-on-Sea Borough Council v Skiggs* [2006] 21 EG 132, where an application to test reasonableness of some charges had been made by several tenants. The LVT decided largely in favour of the landlord, but made a direction the 'payment should be made by the Applicants to the Respondents three months from the date hereof without any interest being charged during that period. The Tribunal hope that during this period the (parties) can achieve a satisfactory manner in which payment is to be made'. If not, the parties could apply to the LVT again 'to determine this issue of the manner in which the payment is to be made'. The appeal to the Lands Tribunal was solely on the issue of the timetable. It is worth recording some of the points made:

(a)   The right to buy leases of some flats in Southend, required the tenants to pay service charges annually in advance on 1 April. The LVT had suggested the parties have three months in which to agree a scheme for payment. The judge referred to s 20C(3), on costs (see at **9.142**) under which the LVT is given specific discretion 'to make such order ... as it considers just and equitable in the circumstances'. The judge pointed out there is no similar reference in s 27A.

(b) In the key paragraph (15) the judge said: 'The first and fundamental reason for my decision … is based upon the wording of section 27A itself. I do not consider that this section can be construed as conferring any such discretion on the (LVT) …The section confers on the LVT … a jurisdiction to make a "determination" as to whether a service charge is payable and, if it is, as to certain other matters. … The expression "a determination" … is appropriate language to confer jurisdiction on the LVT to reach a decision as to what liabilities actually exist between the parties. It is not appropriate language to confer a jurisdiction for the LVT to decide what liabilities it concludes, in its discretion, should exist between the parties.'

(c) In para 16 he said: 'The wording of section 27A, especially subsection (1), …is incapable of being read as conferring a discretion on the (LVT) to give such time to lessees as it thinks reasonable to make payments for service charges. It has jurisdiction to determine only the rights existing under the terms of the lease, but, of course, such rights must be determined having regard to the limitation on service charges as contained within the statute (for example in section 19).'

(d) The judge (at para 18) quoted from the explanatory note to the Commonhold and Leasehold Reform Act 2002, which says that the 2002 Act 'extends the jurisdiction of LVTs so that they can determine whether or not leaseholders are liable to pay service charges as well as the reasonableness of (them)'. He went on to say he considered this 'to be confirmation that section 27A was introduced to confer jurisdiction on LVTs to decide the legal rights of parties on points that previously could have been dealt with only by the county court. This is quite different from conferring a discretion on the LVT to adjust these legal rights in such manner as the LVT may think just and reasonable.'

(e) Counsel for the landlord had pointed out that, although the LVT had jurisdiction under s 35 of the Landlord and Tenant Act 1987 (see at **10.2**) to vary a lease, no application to vary had been made. It is not stated in the judgment, but this comment seems to contemplate that such a variation could be temporary.

(f) The Lands Tribunal determination was thus that the sums determined by the LVT were payable by the appellants named in the LVT determination, 'and that such sum is payable at the date and in the manner provided for in the lease under which the respective respondent holds his or her premises'.

9.205 Section 27A(2) makes it clear that the jurisdiction under sub-s (1) applies whether or not any payment is made. Section 27A(5) amplifies this by saying that a 'tenant is not taken to have agreed or admitted any matter by reason only of having made a payment'. This could apply to general payments on account, and it would permit a tenant to make a payment under protest and then seek an LVT determination. A tenant would be wise, however, to make sure that any payment under protest is made accompanied by a letter (a copy of which is kept), making it clear that the sum is not admitted, so that there is no misunderstanding.

9.206 An application to the LVT under sub-s (1) or (3) cannot be made (s 27A(4)) in respect of a matter which:

(a) 'has been agreed or admitted by the tenant'; or

(b) 'has been, or is to be, referred to arbitration pursuant to a post-dispute arbitration agreement to which the tenant is a party' (a 'post dispute arbitration agreement' is defined in s 27A(2) adding to s 38 of the 1985 Act, to be 'an arbitration agreement made after a dispute about the matter has arisen'); or

(c) has been determined by a court; or

(d) has been determined under a post-dispute arbitration agreement.

9.207 The reference to a determination of a court is backed up by s 27A(7) recording that the jurisdiction of an LVT under s 27A 'is in addition to any jurisdiction of a court in respect of the matter'. In other words, it is possible to make an application to a court rather than an LVT. It may be that for straightforward service charge disputes the application will normally be to an LVT. However, where there are separate issues such as applications for damages or forfeiture on account of breaches other than non-payment of service charges, it may be that the application will be started in court, and the court may or may not refer the service charge aspects to an LVT under s 174 and Sch 12 para 3 of the Commonhold and Leasehold Reform Act 2002. The latter Schedule gives details of LVT procedure. Procedure of LVTs on specific aspects introduced by the Commonhold and Leasehold Reform Act 2002 were put in place by the Leasehold Valuation Tribunals (Procedure) (Amendment) (England) Regulations 2004.

9.208 Appeal from an LVT is to the Lands Tribunal, with consent of either the LVT or Lands Tribunal. An application for a judicial review to challenge the refusal of both LVT and Lands Tribunal to allow an appeal against an LVT determination was heard by the Court of Appeal in 2005. (*R (on the application of Sinclair Gardens Investments (Kensington) Ltd v Lands Tribunal* [2004] EWHC 1910 (Admin), [2004] 47 EG 166.) The dispute related (inter alia) to damp proofing. The LVT had held that the cost of damp proofing in the basement was a recoverable cost, but that the cost of damp proofing in the lobby was an improvement, which was not recoverable. LVT and Lands Tribunal both refused leave to appeal. The judge at first instance held that judicial review would be available because an appeal against refusal of permission lay to the Court of Appeal under Lands Tribunal Act 1949, s 3(4), but that this would only be granted in exceptional circumstances, which did not apply here. The Court of Appeal agreed, and added that it did not consider the arrangements under which service charges for dwellings can be challenged in an LVT whose decision in turn is capable of being reviewed by the Lands Tribunal breached the European

Convention on Human Rights. For judicial review to be obtained the person applying for leave to appeal would have to show (a) that the refusal was wrong in law, and (b) that the error was sufficiently grave to justify the case being treated as exceptional. In other words judicial review cannot be treated simply as a further means of challenging the LVT decision – there must be some exceptional feature.

9.209   Tucked away in s 27A(6) is the very important provision (the equivalent of the former s 19(4)) making void any agreement relating to a dwelling to determine a service charge dispute except in accordance with the Act. The section reads:

'(6) An agreement by the tenant of a dwelling (other than a post-dispute arbitration agreement) is void in so far as it purports to provide for a determination –

(a)   in a particular manner, or

(b)   on particular evidence,

on any question which may be the subject of an application under subsection (1) or (3).'

(Section 27A(1) and (3) are service charge disputes for matters already carried out and to be carried out respectively.) Although the wording is not the same as in former s 19(4), the effect is the same: provisions in a lease, agreement for lease, licence or deed of variation etc affecting a dwelling which purport to set out ways to decide a service charge dispute are void unless they simply repeat the statutory provisions. In particular this means provisions to the effect that a certificate of the landlord's surveyor or accountant is final and binding are of no effect.

Criticism

9.210   These provisions are inserted to enable the LVT to make orders for payment, where before they could only make a determination which had to be enforced by a separate court. The section is partly a response to cases such as *Gilje v Charlgrove Securities Ltd* [2001] EWCA Civ 1777, [2002] 16 EG 182, where there were comments on the need for several sets of proceedings, and *Daejan Properties Ltd v London Leasehold Valuation Tribunal* [2001] EWCA Civ 1095, [2001] 29 EGCS 122, holding that the LVT could not investigate the reasonableness of service charges that had been paid.

Section 28 of the Landlord and Tenant Act 1985

Meaning of 'qualified accountant'

9.211   This is the section which records who is entitled to certify, under s 21(6) of the 1985 Act, the summary of information about relevant costs. (See **9.150** et seq.) The person must be duly qualified by being eligible for appointment as a company auditor under s 25 of the Companies Act 1985, and must not be disqualified. The provisions referring to the Companies Act were added by the quaintly named Companies Act 1989 (Eligibility for Appointment as Company Auditor) (Consequential Amendments) Regulations 1991. The people who are disqualified are described in s 28(4). Paraphrasing the subsection they are:

(a)   an officer, employee, or partner of the landlord, or of an associated company of a company landlord;

(b)   a partner or employee of any such officer or employee;

(c)   'an agent of the landlord who is a managing agent for any premises to which any of the costs covered by the summary in question relates'; and

(d)   'an employee or partner of such managing agent'.

Section 28(6), however, says that for a local authority, new town corporation, or the Development Board for Rural Wales, the disqualification for employees does not apply. It also adds members of the Chartered Institute of Public Finance and Accountancy to those qualified.

9.212   Section 28(5) clarifies references to an 'associated company' by reference to s 736 of the Companies Act 1985 as 'the landlord's holding company, a subsidiary of the landlord or another subsidiary of the landlord's holding company'. Section 28(5A) expands further on the question of who is a managing agent without really adding anything.

Criticism

9.213   It seems sensible to ensure that the certificate and summary is given by a professionally qualified and independent person. It is perhaps a pity that the former provisions which set out named professional bodies whose members were entitled to act have been replaced by reference to people qualified under a statute relating to another topic. The obligations in s 21 do not extend to requiring the qualified accountant to certify that the costs are reasonable, merely that the statement covers what it should cover, and is supported by vouchers. Tenants have the comfort that the figures are accurate, backed up by paperwork, and verified by an independent and suitably qualified person, although the works or services may still be subject to challenge.

Section 29 of the Landlord and Tenant Act 1985

Recognised Tenants' Associations

9.214   This section defines, in a somewhat vague way, those groups of tenants who are 'recognised tenants' associations' ('RTA'). The RTA has rights beyond those of individual tenants. The changes to the 1985 Act by the Commonhold and Leasehold Reform Act 2002 have given ordinary tenants some rights that had been restricted to recognised tenants' associations, although s 29 itself was one of the few sections of the Landlord and Tenant Act 1985 not amended at all by the Commonhold Act. Section 29(1) says:

'(1) A recognised tenants' association is an association of qualifying tenants (whether with or without other tenants) which is recognised for the purposes of the provisions of this Act relating to service charges either –

(a)   by notice in writing given by the landlord to the secretary of the association, or

(b)   by a certificate of a member of the local rent assessment committee panel.'

9.215   The RTA has to be an association of 'qualifying tenants'. In this case a qualifying tenant is simply one who 'may be required under the terms of his lease to contribute to the same costs by payment of a service charge' (s 29(4)). The tenants do not have to hold long leases, or be Rent Act tenants, or have any qualification other than contributing to the same service charges.

9.216   The section gives no direct guide to the grounds or qualifications under which an RTA might be recognised or where a refusal to recognise is appropriate. Section 29(5) entitles the Secretary of State to make regulations as to procedure, material factors, duration and other matters, but at the time of writing no such regulations have been introduced. Guidelines from October 1980 for the assistance of rent assessment panels were prepared for the purposes of the earlier equivalent section in the Housing Act 1980. They recommend a minimum of 60% of the total number of tenants should be members of the association before it could be certified by the panel, and that there should only be one vote per flat (dwelling). They also recommended certain matters concerning the constitution of the association, suggesting that it should be set up on a reasonably formal basis, and that the certificate of the rent assessment committee should be for a period of four years.

9.217   Section 29(2) provides that the landlord can withdraw his approval by six months' notice, and s 29(3) that 'a certificate given (by the rent assessment committee) may be cancelled by any member of the local rent assessment committee panel'.

9.218   In *R v London Rent Assessment Panel, ex p Trustees of Henry Smith's Charity Estate* [1988] 1 EGLR 34, recognition of an RTA was considered by the court. Eight houses known as numbers 1 to 8 Onslow Gardens, London, SW7 had been converted into five blocks of 34 flats. Numbers 1 and 2 Onslow Gardens formed one block, 3 and 4 another, 5 another block, 6 and 7 another, and number 8 was the fifth block. The tenants of all five blocks formed an association and were given a certificate of recognition by the president of the London Rent Assessment Panel. The president was asked by the landlord to cancel his registration on the basis that the certificate had been wrongly given. The court application was by the landlord for judicial review of the decision of the president not to cancel the certificate. The landlord succeeded. He argued that there were five blocks and the tenants argued that there was one block consisting of the eight former houses. It was clear that each block had its own service charge arrangements. The judge said:

> 'it seems to me to accord with the scheme of the legislation for recognised tenants' associations to be formed for each block of flats with its own service charge regime. It is really those words which are important, though of course there is nothing to prevent such associations from federating, or otherwise co-operating, one with the other.... In the present case there is no … interrelation … either in terms of services supplied or charges payable. In such a case it is, in my judgment, not permissible to give the certificate under section 29(1)(b) in the way it has been done.'

The concentration was on an association for each set of service charges: if the services were not common there was no place for a recognised tenants' association. In evidence the president had recorded that between 1980 and 1987 108 certificates had been issued by his panel, and of those seven had been cases where there had been a number of blocks which were physically separate, but which shared services, such as porters, refuse collection or hot water. Section 29(1) originally referred to an association of tenants of flats in a 'building', but this was later varied to refer to an association of qualifying tenants.

9.219   Section 20(1) contemplates that there can be qualifying tenants who are not part of the association. Before the Commonhold Act changes the original provisions of the 1985 Act (eg s 21(2)) were worded in such a way that the benefits accrued to those tenants 'who are represented by a recognised tenants' association'. Therefore, strictly, the landlord had to deal separately with those who were not so represented, although the non-member individuals were not then entitled to the same rights, for example to nominate a contractor to give estimates. The Commonhold Act changes give individual tenants several rights similar to those formerly the sole province of an RTA, and now the only real difference in rights are those mentioned below at **9.226** (managing agents) and **10.15** (appointment of a surveyor for a tenant's audit). Section 29 does not spell out the position of tenants who are not members, and does not require the RTA to notify the landlord which tenants are members of the association. The regulation setting out the (new) consultation process makes it clear that a landlord must consult both the association and also all tenants. Even where a landlord recognises an association he would be well advised to obtain a list of those tenants who are represented by the association so that he knows which tenants are not members and can thus deal with them on an individual basis in accordance with his obligations under the Act.

9.220   A recognised tenants' association has the following rights:

(a)   The provisions requiring the landlord to provide details of works to be carried out (as part of the consultation procedure in s 20) require such details to be given to the association where there is one, and to each tenant. (Under the original version of s 20, RTAs were entitled to see specifications in the consultation procedure, but tenants were not. With the changes to consultation this benefit is lost.)

(b)   An association is entitled to nominate a contractor from whom an estimate for works is to be sought during consultation. (See notes on s 20 above at **9.56** et seq. Now all tenants have this right as well.)

(c)   Where estimates are obtained, copies are to be sent to the association as part of the consultation process.

(d)   The association has the right to seek information and copies under s 22(2) of the Landlord and Tenant Act 1985. (Tenants also have this right.)

(e)   The association is entitled in some circumstances to be consulted about the managing agents. This right does not apply to individual tenants. (See s 30B below, at **9.226** et seq.)

(f)   The RTA has rights as to insurance of dwellings in accordance with the Schedule to the Landlord and Tenant Act 1985. (See at **9.236** et seq.)

(g)   The association also has the (exclusive) right to appoint a surveyor to represent the RTA for a tenant's audit, with powers to inspect vouchers and also common parts, under s 84 and Sch 4 to the Housing Act 1996. (See Chapter 10, at **10.15** et seq.)

Criticism

9.221   Most of the original benefits are no longer unique to such associations. However, the author firmly recommends them to all residential tenants. There are some advantages as indicated above, and it is probably a good thing for the tenants to be members of an association for mutual benefit. A landlord can simply refuse, without giving reasons, to recognise the association, and unless the tenants apply successfully to the rent assessment committee for a certificate of recognition they will not have the benefits. It must surely be right that there should be more than half the tenants involved because otherwise theoretically there could be two recognised tenants' associations, both allegedly acting in relation to the same premises, or a minority could purport to represent the whole. The idea of tenants in the RTA having one vote per dwelling may be less satisfactory: if the concern is service charges, should not the votes reflect service charge proportions? It would be useful for statutory guidance to be given on qualifications for recognition, although now that such associations have fewer unique advantages than before it may not be so urgent. In addition, it would be helpful if the section put some obligation on the secretary of the association to specify precisely which tenants were represented by the association from time to time. To avoid fraud or misunderstandings perhaps it would be appropriate to have a prescribed form of request for recognition which was signed by all the tenants who are members, and with an obligation on the association to notify the landlord of changes.

Section 30 of the Landlord and Tenant Act 1985

Definitions of 'landlord' and 'tenant'

9.222   Continuing the series of definition sections the final definitions refer to the landlord and the tenant. Neither is a real definition. Section 30 simply records that the expression 'the landlord' in those provisions of the Act relating to service charges 'includes any person who has a right to enforce payment of a service charge'. (Service charges are defined in s 18.)

9.223   The definition of the tenant is again limited to stating that certain people are included in the expression. In this case the parties included are statutory tenants, and, where the dwelling or part of it is sub-let, it includes the sub-tenant.

9.224   The section was mentioned in a Lands Tribunal case, *Sarum Properties Ltd's Application* [1999] 17 EG 136, where a tenant applied for a declaration that the service charges were unreasonable and then assigned the lease. The landlord claimed the tenant was not entitled to proceed with the application for a declaration, as she was no longer the tenant, but failed. Section 30 did not define 'tenant' in exclusive terms.

9.225   Including sub-tenants is useful, as it enables those sub-tenants who are charged service charges to exercise the same rights as the original tenants. So if a landlord grants a lease which includes an obligation on the tenant to pay service charges and the tenant sub-lets, then by virtue of the definition the sub-tenant has the right to seek information or to inspect vouchers, in his own right, although the Act gives him the same rights via the original tenant. The definition section could be said to clarify that the landlord is obliged to comply with s 23 for the benefit of an undertenant even though the landlord may have no direct contractual relationship with him. (Under s 30B, discussed below, the definitions of both landlord and tenant are changed to refer to the immediate landlord and direct tenant, and thus excludes superior landlords and sub-tenants.)

Section 30B of the Landlord and Tenant Act 1985

Recognised tenants' associations and managing agents

9.226   This subsection (after s 30A, which introduces the Schedule as to insurance, see at **9.236** below) gives an RTA useful rights relating to managing agents. Basically, these entitle the RTA to serve notice on the landlord requesting him to consult the RTA 'on matters relating to the appointment or employment by (the landlord) of a managing agent for any relevant premises', and, later, to be notified at five-yearly intervals after the initial notice of 'the obligations which the managing agent has been required to discharge' (s 30B(1), (4)). Under s 30B(8), 'landlord' is defined as the 'immediate landlord of the tenants represented by the association or a person who has a right to enforce payment of service charges payable by any of those tenants'. It would thus cover a management company that employs the managing agents, or a right to manage company, but not, apparently, a superior landlord if it is he who employs the managing agents.

9.227   Where an RTA serves notice on the landlord requesting the landlord to consult the RTA on the appointment or employment of a managing agent, there are two possibilities, depending on whether the landlord has already employed managing agents or not.

(a)   Where he has not appointed managing agents and the RTA serves notice, 'before appointing any managing agent' the landlord is to give the RTA a notice specifying the name of the proposed agent and details of those 'landlord's obligations to the tenants represented by the association which it is proposed that the managing agent should be required to discharge on his behalf'. The notice must also give not less than one month for the RTA to 'make observations on the proposed appointment'. Thus the appointment needs to start at a later date. (Section 30B(2).) If the appointment is to be for more than one year then the landlord will need to consult with all tenants under s 20 of the Landlord and Tenant Act 1985, on the basis that the appointment will be a 'long-term agreement'. (See at **9.90** et seq.) There are special consultation requirements when appointing managing agents under a long-term agreement. (See at **9.99** and **9.100** above.)

(b)   Where the landlord already employs a managing agent then the RTA can serve notice and within one month the landlord is to give details of the obligations which the managing agent is to discharge. The landlord must also give the RTA 'a reasonable period to make observations on the manner in which the managing agent has been discharging those obligations, and on the desirability of his continuing to discharge them' (s 30B(3)).

9.228   The key to the right of an RTA to make observations is s 30B(7), which provides that a landlord shall 'have regard' to the observations. While in reality this does not mean that the landlord must dismiss managing agents if the tenants say they are not happy, the tenants can make their views officially known, and it may assist to make the managing agents more co-operative to the tenants. If a dispute arises the treatment of requests, and the responses to requests, could be treated as evidence of whether or not the landlord has acted reasonably. (See at **9.125** et seq (relating to s 20) for comments on the expression 'have regard'.)

9.229   Where an RTA has served a notice on the landlord concerning managing agents then every five years the landlord must serve notice on the RTA:

(a)   specifying 'any change occurring since the date of the last notice served by him on the association under this section in the obligations which the managing agent has been required to discharge on his behalf'; and

(b)   giving the RTA a 'reasonable period within which the association may make observations on the manner in which the managing agent has discharged those obligations since that date, and on the desirability of his continuing to discharge them'. In addition, when the landlord is changing managing agents he must serve on the association a notice similar to that required in s 30B(2).

(Section 30B(4); see at **9.227** above for s 30B(2).)

9.230   When there is a change of landlord a notice to the former landlord ceases to have effect, and so the RTA must serve another notice if it wishes to have the benefit of the section. (Section 30B(6).)

Comment

9.231   It seems slightly unsatisfactory for an RTA to have to serve a new notice each time the landlord changes. It would be helpful for the statutory provisions to clarify the position of tenants who are not represented by the association. The author's views about this have been indicated above.

9.232   There is no provision in the Act entitling an RTA to check the relationship of the landlord and the managing agent, or any prohibition on managing agents who are not independent of the landlord, save where there is statutory consultation prior to entering into a long-term agreement. However, the section does permit the tenants, through the RTA, to record their views formally. If in the future managing agents have to be subject to some form of licensing then the RTA can no doubt raise the lack of a licence when making comments.

9.233   So is it worth setting up an RTA? It probably is. Tenants are likely to have more effect as a group, and the right to influence the appointment and obligations of a managing agent would be very important. For example, the RTA might have a number of keen gardeners who would like to do the gardening, perhaps free of charge, and the RTA could notify the landlord of this and ask the landlord not to ask the managing agents to arrange gardening. Of course, tenants who are not part of an RTA could make the same request, but it would surely be more effective from an RTA.

Section 38 of the Landlord and Tenant Act 1985

Minor definitions (including 'dwelling')

9.234   Because some provisions about recognised tenants' associations were added in, the minor definitions in s 38 have become separated from the earlier definitions of landlord and tenant. The definitions in this section are very straightforward, but include a definition of 'dwelling' – see the next paragraph. The other definitions are of 'address', 'co-operative housing association', 'housing association', 'local authority', 'local housing authority', 'new town corporation', 'protected tenancy', 'registered' (in relation to a housing association), 'restricted contract', and 'urban development corporation'.

9.235 A dwelling is defined as 'a building or part of a building occupied or intended to be occupied as a separate dwelling, together with any yard, garden, outhouses and appurtenances belonging to or usually enjoyed with it'. This is quite useful in relation to the demised premises, and the statutory provisions only apply to dwellings. There is, perhaps wisely, no attempt to define common parts or the areas over which services are to be carried out.

Schedule to the Landlord and Tenant Act 1985

Insurance

9.236 This Schedule was added to the 1985 Act by the Landlord and Tenant Act 1987, and has been amended in detail by the Commonhold and Leasehold Reform Act 2002. It is relevant because the statutory definition of service charges includes insurance.

9.237 The Schedule gives tenants of dwellings rights to require certain information and to inspect policies and details. Perhaps more importantly, it also entitles some tenants to notify insurers of a potential claim. There are also obligations on landlords to pass requests for information to superior landlords where appropriate. Breach of the provisions as to information is a criminal offence. The Schedule does not, in itself, provide that the premium the tenant is to repay is to be reasonable, but, as s 18 includes insurance within the definition of service charges, the statutory implication of reasonableness recorded in this chapter applies.

9.238 The Schedule does not apply, para 9, to tenants of a local authority, a National Park authority, a new town corporation, or the Development Board for Wales. For the purposes of the Schedule, para 1 includes a slightly different definition of 'landlord', which 'includes any person who has the right to enforce payment of that service charge', which includes an amount 'payable directly or indirectly for insurance'. The latter reference is unusual, but presumably it is intended to include leases where the landlord covenants to insure, and the tenant pays a rent but not, a separate reimbursement of the insurance premium – in other words, an inclusive rent. It clearly includes those cases where the insurance premium is one of the service charge items.

9.239 Paragraph 2 of the Schedule entitles a tenant, or secretary of an RTA, to give written notice to the landlord requiring a 'written summary of the insurance for the time being effected in relation to the dwelling'. Such notice can be served on the person receiving the rent. Where it is not served on the landlord the notice must be forwarded to the landlord 'as soon as may be', a rather strange expression. The landlord is to respond within 21 days of receipt by him of the notice. In some cases this may be a rather optimistic timescale, as obtaining this information can sometimes be time consuming. The landlord is to provide a summary which, under para 2(4) of the Schedule, is to include details of (a) the insured amount or amounts, (b) the name of the insurer, and (c) the 'risks in respect of which the dwelling, or (as the case may be) the building containing it is insured under any such policy'. The landlord can comply by providing a copy of the policy within the 21-day period instead of a summary, under para 2(6). Leases often contain rights for tenants to see details of the policy, and such provisions apply in addition to the statutory rights. (The Act does not require details to be given of the excesses on the policy, or the amount of any commission paid to the landlord.)

9.240　The Schedule only entitles a tenant to have a summary, not a complete copy of the policy. However, para 3 (as completely substituted by s 157 and Sch 10, para 9, of the Commonhold and Leasehold Reform Act 2002) entitles tenants or the RTA to give written notice requiring the landlord to afford the tenant 'reasonable facilities for inspecting any relevant policy or associated documents and for taking copies of or extracts from them'. Alternatively, the notice can call on the landlord to take copies or extracts, and either send them to the tenant 'or afford him reasonable facilities for collecting them'. 'Associated documents' are defined in para 3(7) as 'accounts, receipts or other documents which provide evidence of payment of any premiums due under a relevant policy in respect of the period of insurance which is current when the notice is served or the period of insurance immediately preceding that period'. The provisions are effectively the same as for taking copies of other service charge documents under s 22. (See at **9.170** et seq.) The landlord cannot charge the tenant for inspection but can include costs incurred within the costs of management, and he can 'make a reasonable charge for doing anything else' to comply with the inspection provisions. (Landlord and Tenant Act 1985, Sch, para 3(5) and (6).)

9.241　The insurance Schedule continues, in para 4, to require landlords to pass on requests for a summary to superior landlords where the 'superior landlord has effected, in whole or in part, the insurance of the dwelling in question, and the landlord on whom the notice is served is not in possession of the relevant information'. The superior landlord is to 'comply with the notice within a reasonable time', and 'the intermediate landlord shall then comply with the ... notice' within 21 days. Where the tenants want to inspect the policy etc the immediate landlord is to notify the tenant, or secretary of the RTA, that he has sent a notice to the superior landlord and the name and address of the superior landlord, and thereafter responsibility for inspection under the Schedule is the direct responsibility of the superior landlord. The Commonhold Act added another provision as para 4A to the Schedule which mirrors the provisions of s 27A of the Landlord and Tenant Act 1985, under which a landlord or superior landlord remains liable to comply with requests, even after assignment, to the extent he is able to do so.

9.242　It is a criminal offence to fail to perform a duty under paras 2 to 4A of the Schedule 'without reasonable excuse' (Sch, para 6). The paragraphs are the ones just discussed covering requests for a summary, for inspection, passing on requests to superior landlords, and the landlord's own liability even after assigning his interest. The penalty is a fine not exceeding level 4 on the standard scale. (See s 25 of the Act above, para **9.186** et seq.)

9.243   Paragraph 7 is possibly the most useful provision in the Schedule. It entitles the tenant to notify the insurer direct of damage. The details are in para 7(2) of the Schedule as follows:

'(2) Where –

(a)   it appears to the tenant of any such dwelling that damage has been caused –

(i)   to the dwelling, or

(ii)   if the dwelling is a flat, to the dwelling or to any other part of the building containing it,

in respect of which a claim could be made under the terms of a policy of insurance, and

(b)   it is a term of the policy that the person insured under the policy should give notice of any claim under it to the insurer within a specified period, the tenant may, within that specified period, serve on the insurer a notice in writing stating that it appears to him that damage has been caused as mentioned in paragraph (a) and describing briefly the nature of the damage.'

9.244   There is an unusual, but useful, provision in para 7(3) to the effect that if the period for notification under the policy 'would expire earlier than the period of six months beginning with the date on which the tenant's notice is served, the policy in question shall have effect as regards any claim subsequently made in respect of that damage by the person insured under the policy as if for the specified period there were substituted that period of six months'. This is to give the landlord ample time to make a claim, but in the meantime the insurer cannot say he had no notice of a claim. It does not entitle the tenant to claim under the policy (although this may be possible under some policies or some leases) but, as the landlord will have time to submit a claim, he should do so – after all, the tenant has paid the premiums. (If he was not liable to pay the premiums, the Schedule would not apply.) If the claim is not made the landlord might seek to charge for works through the service charge that the policy was intended to cover.

9.245   Paragraph 8(2) of the Schedule is another very useful provision. It applies where the lease 'requires the tenant to insure the dwelling with an insurer nominated or approved by the landlord'. The –

'tenant or landlord may apply to a county court or leasehold valuation tribunal for a determination whether –

(a)   the insurance which is available from the nominated or approved insurer for insuring the tenant's dwelling is unsatisfactory in any respect, or

(b)   the premiums payable in respect of any such insurance are excessive.'

(This is not to be confused with the right given by s 164 of the Commonhold Act to the tenant of a house who holds a long lease and has to insure through a nominated insurer, to insure in another way.) Note that the landlord can seek a determination as well as a tenant. The paragraph refers to the insurance being 'unsatisfactory' rather than 'unreasonable'. It could thus perhaps enable a tenant (or landlord) to seek a change where a policy does not include cover for a specific risk, such as flooding. The absence of cover for some risks may mean the tenant could not obtain mortgage finance.

9.246 The order cannot be made if the matter has been agreed by the tenant or is to be referred to arbitration, or has already been determined by a court or arbitral tribunal. (Sch, para 8(3).) The court or LVT can make an order 'requiring the landlord to nominate such other insurer as is specified in the Order', or 'to nominate an insurer who satisfies such requirements in relation to the insurance of the dwelling as are specified in the order'. An order by an LVT under this paragraph can be enforced with leave of the court in the same way as a county court order. (Sch, para 8(4) and (5).)

9.247 The final sub-paragraph, para 8(6), says that:

'an agreement by the tenant of a dwelling (other than an arbitration agreement) is void in so far as it purports to provide for a determination in a particular manner, or on particular evidence, of any question which may be the subject of an application under this paragraph.'

Comment

9.248 For reasons expressed elsewhere, and in particular the numerous aspects that are specific to insurance and not to matters such as repair or security or cleaning, the author's preference is to keep insurance out of the service charge arrangements and deal with them elsewhere. However, in so far as the 1985 Act states that insurance is part of the service charge then this Schedule is, it would seem, helpful in dealing with particular matters such as inspection of insurance policies, and the right to notify insurers of damage, and the right to change unsatisfactory policies. The Schedule is probably not as well known as it should be, but where a lease of a dwelling includes an obligation on a landlord to insure, and certainly where the tenant has to pay towards the insurance, then both landlord and tenant should be aware of the rights and obligations, as well as the potential criminal liability. One practical difficulty is often obtaining a copy policy: reference to the Schedule and the criminal liability thereunder may perhaps assist to give the request more urgency. It is one of the few cases where the landlord has a benefit, in that he can obtain clearance for an insurance charge from the LVT, although only (under the Schedule) where the tenant has to insure through the landlord or his nominee.

9.249 It is not clear how helpful it is in keeping the costs down. Both the *Havenridge* and *Berrycroft* decisions (the second of which was residential) were Court of Appeal cases where the amount of the insurance premium was in issue, and the court failed to reduce the high premium the landlord charged, despite the tenants being able to obtain similar cover at a much lower cost. While in *Berrycroft* the court said the Schedule did not apply (because the insurance was by the management company and it was not the 'landlord',) the general impression is of a lack of either ability or willingness on the part of the court to assist tenants who feel the landlord is paying too much and simply reclaiming it from tenants. This suggests that, at least in relation to cost, the Schedule has limited use. (See at **9.51** re *Berrycroft Management Co Ltd v Sinclair Gardens Investments (Kensington) Ltd* [1997] 1 EGLR 47, and at **3.48** re *Havenridge Ltd v Boston Dyers Ltd* [1994] 2 EGLR 73.)

Section 42 of the Landlord and Tenant Act 1987

Trusts of service charge contributions

9.250   Only two years after the 1985 Act came the 1987 Act. It made changes to the 1985 Act recorded above and introduced provisions about service of notices in ss 47 and 48. However, by far the most important new element was s 42. This provides, in effect, that all payments made by tenants of dwellings towards service charges are automatically held in trust (unless the landlord is a local authority or similar). The provisions of the section prevail over any express trust in the lease where they conflict, unless the lease was granted before the section came into force, in which case the lease terms prevail. Section 42 is the third of the most important service charge provisions, with the reasonableness and consultation provisions of ss 19 and 20 of the Landlord and Tenant Act 1985. This provision is not reflected in earlier versions of the service charge code. (For the avoidance of doubt, it is not affected by the Trusts of Land and Appointment of Trustees Act 1996, as it is not a trust of land.)

9.251   As the money is held in trust, it does not belong to the landlord personally, but only as trustee on behalf of whoever may be the beneficiaries. Accordingly, because of the trust, payments made by tenants for service charge expenditure cannot be claimed by creditors of an insolvent landlord, and similarly the landlord cannot distrain – such payments cannot validly be reserved as rent. Similarly, the money does not belong to the tenants; it is to be used for repair, decoration etc as prescribed in the lease. When there are no more leases, the balance of the fund belongs to the landlord. If the property is, for example, destroyed, it seems the tenants will be entitled to have their proportion of the trust fund back.

9.252   The section originally only applied where tenants of two or more dwellings contributed to service charges for the same services. The Commonhold and Leasehold Reform Act 2002 added the protection where there is only a single tenant.

9.253   Section 42(1) contains various definitions. The only definitions that need special mention are:

(a)   "'The payee" means the landlord or other person to whom any such charges are payable by those tenants or that tenant (ie where there is only a single tenant contributing to the service charges) under the terms of their leases or his lease.' This, accordingly, includes a management company which is responsible for repairs etc and is entitled to receive the payments from the tenants, or manager appointed under the Landlord and Tenant Act 1987, or a right to manage company. It would not include managing agents who just collect the service charge unless the lease requires the service charges to be paid to the managing agent, which would be very unusual.

(b) The expression 'the tenant' does not include tenants of 'an exempt landlord'. Section 58(1) of the Landlord and Tenant Act 1987 defines exempt landlords as various bodies such as local authorities, and public bodies and housing action trusts, housing trusts and registered housing associations. Accordingly, the statutory trust does not apply if they are the landlord.

(c) 'Service charge' is as defined in s 18(1) of the Landlord and Tenant Act 1985 (at **9.28** et seq) and includes service charges registered as variable service charges under s 71(4) of the Rent Act 1977.

9.254   The next two subsections (s 42(2) and (3)) are the key to the provisions. Section 42(2) reads:

'(2) Any sums paid to the payee by the contributing tenants or by the sole contributing tenant by way of relevant service charges shall (together with any income accruing thereon) be held by the payee either as a single fund or, if he thinks fit, in two or more separate funds.'

The significant points are:

(a) That the subsection relates to 'any' sums: it does not just relate to sinking fund payments.

(b) The trust fund includes 'any income accruing thereon', thus clarifying that, for residential tenants, interest earned on payments by the tenants for service charges is treated as part of those payments, and not as a profit for the landlord or the managing agent.

(c) Section 42(2) says the trust fund is to be held as a single fund, or where appropriate, as more than one fund. It may make sense to be able to have more than one fund, eg one for normal payments and one for sinking fund payments. Presumably, so long as each fund is put in a designated account (see at **9.260** et seq) when those provisions are brought in, the landlord has complied with the Act.

9.255   Section 42(3) sets out the trusts. It states that:

'(3) The payee shall hold any trust fund:

(a)   on trust to defray costs incurred in connection with the matters for which the relevant service charges were payable (whether incurred by him or by any other person), and

(b)   subject to that, on trust for the persons who are the contributing tenants for the time being, or the person who is the sole contributing tenant for the time being.'

Accordingly, the money paid by the tenants is automatically held on trust for the purpose for which the money was paid, and subject to that is to be held for the contributing tenants 'for the time being'. The latter phrase clarifies that the fund is not to be held for those tenants who have paid over the years, but for those who are contributing tenants at the time when any question arises. It also makes it clear, subject to s 42(7) (see at **9.256** below), that the fund does not belong to the landlord.

9.256   The remaining subsections are somewhat confusingly laid out, but provide in effect as follows:

(a)   When the lease of a contributing tenant terminates 'the tenant shall not be entitled to any part of any trust fund, and (except where sub-s (7) applies) any part of any such fund which is attributable to relevant service charges paid under the lease shall, accordingly, continue to be held on the trusts referred to in sub-s (3)'. (Section 42(6); for sub-s (7) see (b) of this paragraph, and for sub-s (3) see at **9.255** above.)

(b)   If the lease of a contributing tenant expires and there are at that time no longer any contributing tenants, eg either where all the leases expire together, or in the case of the last lease to expire or a sole lease, the trust fund is dissolved and any assets in the fund are returned to the landlord. (Section 42(7).) The subsection reads:

> '(7) On the termination of the lease of the last of the contributing tenants, or the lease of the sole contributing tenant, any trust fund shall be dissolved as at the date of the termination of the lease, and any assets comprised in the fund imme-diately before its dissolution shall –
>
> (a)   if the payee is the landlord, be retained by him for his own use and benefit, and
>
> (b)   in any other case, be transferred to the landlord by the payee.'

It should be remembered that the fund is to be used to pay for services and so should have been used up in payments for that purpose. In addition, the landlord must not call for payments in advance which are more than rea-sonable. (Section 19(2) of the Landlord and Tenant Act 1985.) If the leases are ending the services may be being wound down, and the fund should be minimal at the end of the period.

(c)   Section 42(4) provides, that:

> '(4) Subject to sub-ss (6) to (8) [sub-s (6) is at (a) above, sub-s (7) at (b) above, and sub-s (8) is at (d) below] the contributing tenants shall be treated as entitled by virtue of sub-s (3)(b) [see at **9.255** above] to such shares in the residue of any such fund as are proportionate to their respective liabilities to pay relevant service charges, or the sole contributing tenant shall be treated as so entitled to the residue of any such fund.'

This would seem to be material only in limited circumstances, such as cases where the premises are destroyed and not rebuilt, or (for financial record purposes) where one landlord replaces another. The subsection refers to 'liabilities to pay the relevant service charges' and thus the proportions would still apply even where a tenant is behind with his payments. In practice if this became material the landlord would be entitled to deduct from any sum due to a defaulting tenant the amount he owes to the fund.

(d) Subsections (4) (6) and (7) are stated by s 42(8) to have effect 'subject to any express terms of his lease (whenever it was granted) which relate to the distribution, either before or (as the case may be) at the termination of the lease, of amounts attributable to relevant service charges paid under its terms'. However, sub-s 42(9) goes on to say that 'subject to subsection (8)' s 42 'shall prevail over the terms of any express or implied trust created by a lease so far as inconsistent with those provisions, other than an express trust' created in leases granted before the section came into force, which was 1 April 1989 (or for a sole contributing lease granted before 28 February 2005). The effect is that the statutory provisions as to distribution of the trust fund apply, unless they conflict with the express terms of a lease granted before the section came into force. This follows the general service charge principle that you cannot contract out of the statutory scheme.

(e) The Secretary of State has power to make regulations as to permitted investment of such funds (s 42(5)). This is helpful because there are strict rules covering investment of trust funds which are not really appropriate for this type of fund, where there are likely to be frequent receipts and payments rather than a fairly steady holding of a single fund. The statutory instruments (Service Charge Contributions (Authorised Investments) Order 1988, as amended by the Financial Services and Markets Act 2000 (Consequential Amendments and Repeals) Order 2001), provide that service charge funds can only be placed in interest-bearing accounts with banks, building societies, friendly societies and credit unions as authorised under Pt 4 of the Financial Services and Markets Act 2000. They can be placed in shares in similarly authorised building societies.

Criticism

9.257 The idea behind the section is excellent, and it is hard to see why it is not also applied to commercial service charges. The author's main criticisms are that the section is confusingly set out and, while it is sensible for service charge purposes, is not consistent with practice for other trusts. For example, it is common in a trust to appoint more than one trustee and to give someone the right to appoint new trustees. Here 'the payee' is, like it or not, turned into a (single) trustee. Since the definition refers to the payee as 'the landlord or other person to whom any such charges are payable ...', there seems to be potential doubt about the identity of the trustee – is it one or the other where there are both? That is probably relatively easy to resolve, as the trustee is presumably the person to whom the fund is actually paid, but it is not clear. In addition, if the trustee is the landlord this means the trustee could be not only an individual, whereas there are normally several trustees to provide a measure of counter-checks, but the trustee of the tenant's service charge money could be a foreign company, or a non-resident individual, as well as a respectable pension fund, or an individual with a real connection with the premises.

9.258   Normally, trusts provide who is to have the power to appoint trustees but here the trust is thrust upon someone, however unsuitable. There is no requirement for any professional qualifications. A requirement for some qualification would add to expense and administration. In any event the protection to a tenant is in reality limited to protection against insolvency of the landlord and then only provided that the actual fund can be traced and identified. (Having an identifiable fund will, to a limited extent, be aided by proposed s 42A with its requirement for a designated account, breach of which will be a criminal offence.) A requirement for an independent trustee, or trustees, with professional qualifications might be a better safeguard, although it would add to costs, and, if the point was overlooked by the parties, the tenant would have no better protection than the section now provides.

9.259   It has been suggested that the trust created by the section contravenes the perpetuity laws because a 'purpose trust', such as this, must be limited to the perpetuity period. While, technically, there may be some force in this view, the fact that it is created by statute surely means that it would not be open to a court to dispute its general validity.

Landlord and Tenant Act 1987

Proposed ss 42A and 42B – Designated accounts

9.260   As explained above these provisions, to be inserted by s 156 of the Commonhold and Leasehold Reform Act 2002, are probably the most important new aspect of the service charge code introduced by the Commonhold Act 2002 after the changes to consultation. The regulations needed to bring the section into force were not available at the time of writing, four years after the Act was passed. It is anticipated that the regulations may be published by the end of 2006, but will not come into force until a year or so thereafter.

9.261   When brought in, the section will require all money held on trust under s 42 of the 1987 Act to be held in a 'designated account'. In default there will be a criminal penalty, and the tenant will be entitled to withhold payment of service charges until given satisfactory evidence of compliance. The provisions of s 42 do not apply to exempt landlords such as local authorities, and so these provisions do not apply to them either. Until the regulations are published it is not certain that there will be any other exemptions, although it would seem unlikely.

9.262   The obligation is that '(1) the payee must hold any sums standing to the credit of any trust fund in a designated account at a relevant financial institution'. (Section 42A(1); s 42 states that all service charge payments by tenants of dwellings are held on trust – see at **9.250** above.)

9.263 Proposed sub-s 42A(2) describes a designated account. The keys points are:

(a) The 'relevant financial institution' has to be notified in writing that sums standing to the credit of the trust fund are to be (or are) held in it; and

(b) no other funds are held in the account,

and the account is an account of a description specified in regulations made by the Secretary of State.

9.264 The Act does not say who has to give the notice. It would seem that notification can be given by anyone, so the tenant could notify the financial institution, although it is hard to see how a tenant can be certain that the account consists only of trust money. The 'financial institution' is to be of a type described in regulations.

9.265 The section says that no other money is to be in the designated account. Two consequences arise:

(a) Managing agents who manage lots of property and are subject, for example, to the client account rules of the RICS, will still have to comply with s 42A(1) and will thus have to use one account per set of service charges rather than putting them all in one client account. Some already do this, but for others new arrangements will be needed.

(b) Strictly, if the service charge fund covers residential and commercial premises, such as for a block with flats over shops or offices, then the service charges for the shops or offices cannot be put in the designated account because they are not 'trust money', as this expression only applies to receipts from 'dwellings'. Many such blocks have separate service charge arrangements for the flats and the commercial parts, but if there is a single fund receipts from the commercial elements cannot be put in the designated account.

9.266 The tenant or secretary of a recognised tenants' association will be able to give notice to the 'payee' (as defined in s 42, see at **9.253**):

(a) to afford him reasonable facilities for inspecting documents evidencing that sub-s (1) is complied with and for taking copies of or extracts from them; or

(b) to take copies of or extracts from any such documents and either send them to him or afford him reasonable facilities for collecting them (as he specifies).

The payee is to comply within 21 days of receipt of the notice. The provisions for service of notice and for the inspection to be free but with the ability of the landlord to include costs incurred within the service charge, are the same as for inspection of documents under s 22 of the 1985 Act. (Section 42A(3)–(8); for s 22 see at **9.170** above.)

9.267   The tenant is to be given a statutory right by s 42A(9) to 'withhold payment of a service charge if he has reasonable grounds for believing that the payee has failed to comply with the duty imposed on him by sub-s (1); and any provisions of his tenancy relating to non-payment or late payment of service charges do not have effect in relation to the period for which he so withholds it'.

9.268   Proposed s 42B will give the provision further teeth by making non-compliance a criminal offence, with a fine not exceeding 4 on the standard scale. This is £2,500, and is the same as under s 25 of the 1985 Act. Section 42B(3) also provide that where an offence:

'committed by a body corporate is proved -

(a)   to have been committed with the consent or connivance of a director, manager, secretary or other similar officer of the body corporate, or a person purporting to Act in such a capacity, or

(b)   to be due to any neglect on the part of such an officer or person,

he, as well as the body corporate, is guilty of the offence and liable to be proceeded against and punished accordingly.'

(Section 42B(5) says proceedings 'may' be brought by a local housing authority within the meaning of s 1 of the Housing Act 1985.)

Criticism

9.269   If the landlord puts all the service charge money into one or more designated accounts (when they are required), it may be easier to trace what has happened than if it was paid in to various different accounts. The fact that a tenant can withhold payment of service charges until satisfied that his money is held in a designated account is a good practical remedy to assist those few cases where there is a fraudulent landlord. Assuming tenants do check, it may enable problems to be spotted early. Subject to those cases where professional managing agents prefer for good reason to have all their service charge payments within one client's account, there would seem no disadvantage to genuine managers and protection for tenants from those who are not genuine. There may be additional bank costs which inevitably will fall to be paid by the tenants.

9.270   Perhaps the biggest flaw is that although the bank is notified that the account is for holding service charges for a particular property it is under no obligation, under the Act, to monitor payments made out. Indeed, it is hard to see how it could be. If the landlord is XYZ SA and a cheque is drawn in favour of that organisation, or its proprietor, Mr K, the bank cannot know whether or not this is not a permissible payment under the lease. It may well be a legitimate refund of money paid out. Unless there is some protocol for banks, or some instruction of a relevant government department, it is hard to see how it actually stops a payment out which is not in accordance with the terms of the lease.

295

9.271 The question mark over whether there could be more than one designated account for parts of the same trust money was mentioned above. It would be useful for that to be clarified at some time. Similarly the payee will have a problem where the tenants send one cheque to pay service charge and also rent or insurance premiums. The money will have to be paid into the account to which it is addressed, and as soon as the cheque clears the payee will need to remember to make transfers to ensure that only service charge receipts are in the s 42A account.

9.272 In the absence of any specific exemption when the regulations appear the rules will apply, except where there is an exempt landlord, to all residential tenancies where service charges are payable. This includes a house divided into two flats where there may be no payments for years, and of course those cases where the tenants own the freehold by way of a management company. In the case of the latter, the provisions are helpful, as they assist the tenants/landlord to keep track of the income for the property, but there are likely to be cases where the requirement is accidentally or deliberately overlooked, and thus criminal penalties can come into play.

Section 3 of the Landlord and Tenant Act 1985

Landlord's notice of assignment of the reversion

9.273 This is the first of three sections mentioned here on the subject of notice which are of concern to both landlords and tenants of service charge leases. It is out of chronological order, but is put here to keep it with the two other material notice provisions. Section 3 puts the onus on the new landlord of a dwelling to give the tenant written notice of the change of landlord and his name and address. This should be done by the next rent day, or at least within two months of the assignment. The new landlord is liable to a criminal penalty, namely a fine not exceeding level 4 on the standard scale, for failure to serve the notice 'without reasonable excuse'. Trustees can give a notice in more general terms ('the trustees of the trust in question'), and the address can be that from which the affairs of the trust are conducted. A simple change of trustee does not need to be notified under s 3.

9.274 It is convenient to repeat here that the former landlord of a 'new tenancy' remains liable under the terms of the lease until he is released, notwithstanding his assignment of the reversion, under the Landlord and Tenant (Covenants) Act 1995. In addition, s 3(3A) and (3B) of the Landlord and Tenant Act 1985 specifically provide that the former landlord 'shall be liable to the tenant in respect of any breach of any covenant, condition or agreement' occurring, not just before the assignment, but before the date when the tenant is notified of the assignment and the name and address of the new landlord. Notice can be given by the former landlord. Section 3(3A) also says that if there is a continuing breach the former and current landlord 'shall be jointly and severally liable in respect of it'.

Sections 47 and 48 of the Landlord and Tenant Act 1987

Notice of the landlord's name and address for service

9.275   These important sections, having somewhat similar aims, are dealt with together. Both sections are within Pt VI of the Act which (under s 46) applies to dwellings. Thus, like s 3 of the 1985 Act, the sections do not affect tenants of commercial property. Breach of these two sections is not a criminal offence, but until they are observed the landlord will be unable to recover any payment if the tenant takes the point.

9.276   Section 47(1) of the 1987 Act requires that 'any written demand given to a tenant of (a dwelling) … must contain … the name and address of the landlord, and, … if that address is not in England and Wales, an address in England and Wales at which notices (including notices in proceedings) may be served on the landlord by the tenant'. The heading to the section in the Act refers to demands for 'rent etc' and s 47(4) says a demand is 'a demand for rent or other sums payable to the landlord under the terms of the tenancy'. If a demand is sent which 'does not contain any information required by virtue of sub-s (1) then (subject to sub-s (3)) (this relates to where there is a receiver or manager responsible for collecting rent) any part of the amount demanded which consists of a service charge (defined in s 18(1) of the 1985 Act) or an administration charge shall be treated for all purposes as not being due', until the 'information is furnished by the landlord by notice given to the tenant'. (Section 158 of and Sch 11 to the Commonhold and Leasehold Reform Act 2002.) Administration charges are payments payable by a tenant (a) for approvals under a lease (b) for information or copies (c) penalties for late payment or (d) penalties for other breaches. The 2002 Act provides that they must be reasonable. A prescribed summary of rights and obligations must accompany a demand for any administration charge, but none has yet been prescribed. (Section 47(2) Landlord and Tenant Act 1987.) Accordingly, a tenant is given a right to withhold payment until he has proper details.

9.277   The provision for service charges not being due does not apply when 'there is in force an appointment of a receiver or manager whose functions include the receiving of service charges from the tenant'. (Section 47(3).) In reality, since the receiver is not the landlord, he must clearly notify the tenant of where service charges are to be paid before he can collect it.

9.278   While s 47 requires names and addresses on demands for payment, s 48 is more general. It provides that the landlord must give notice to the (residential) tenant of 'an address in England and Wales at which notices (including notices in proceedings) may be served on him by the tenant'. This is, as it were, a preliminary notice, separate from a rent or service charge demand. In the case of default in providing a s 48 notice 'any rent, service charge, or administration charges otherwise due from the tenant to the landlord shall … be treated for all purposes as not being due … before the landlord' complies. Again, there is an exception for a receiver or manager appointed by a court or tribunal whose functions include collection of rent, service charges or administration charges. (Section 48(3).) This is a one-off notice, as opposed to the s 47 notice which is needed with each demand.

9.279 Failure to comply with these sections can be very serious, even though ss 47 and 48 do not carry criminal penalties and it is easy to comply with them. If a landlord fails to serve an initial notice he is not entitled to recover service charges or even rent until he does. There is no time limit stated for serving the s 48 notice, but clearly it should be served as soon as the tenancy is granted, or at least before the rent and service charge is due. The notice is, however, helpful, as well as necessary, if the tenancy has been granted on behalf of the landlord by agents, or if his address is outside England and Wales.

9.280 A written agreement normally states who the landlord is. The Court of Appeal in *Rogan v Woodfield Building Services Ltd* [1995] 1 EGLR 72 took the practical view that where the original landlord remained as landlord his name and address in the lease could be treated, in effect, as notice under s 48. This is of course helpful, but only where the original landlord is still the landlord. On assignment of the reversion notices must be served under s 3 of the 1985 Act (see at **9.273**) and such notice gives the information required under ss 47 and 48 of the 1987 Act. In *Drew-Morgan v Hamid-Zadeh* [1999] 2 EGLR 13, the Court of Appeal confirmed that the notices then needed under s 21 of the Housing Act 1988, to terminate an assured shorthold tenancy, gave sufficient particulars to comply with s 48. Accordingly, if there is a default the landlord may be able to find some document or notice that the court will treat as sufficient. It is, however, unwise to rely on this, and there should be no difficulty in serving the proper notice.

Section 87 of the Leasehold Reform, Housing and Urban Development Act 1993

Codes of Practice

9.281 The 1993 Act includes three matters affecting service charges for dwellings. Two of those changes (variation of leases, and the tenant's own audit) only affect long leases and are therefore included in Chapter 10. The third item is the codes of practice which are the subject of Chapter 11.

9.282 Section 87 gives the Secretary of State the right to approve Codes of Practice 'designed to promote desirable practices in relation to any matter or matters directly or indirectly concerned with the management of residential property by relevant persons'. He can approve them in whole or in part, or more than one, can approve modifications and can withdraw approval, and can approve codes which make different provision for different types of case or different areas. He must only approve modifications to a code after suitable publicity. Section 87(6)(b) specifically states that it can cover such matters as resolution of disputes, competitive tendering, and 'the administration of trusts in respect of amounts paid by tenants by way of service charges'.

9.283 Failure to comply with an approved code is not a criminal offence, but the code is admissible in evidence 'in any proceedings before a court or tribunal', and 'any provision of any such code which appears to the court or tribunal to be relevant to any question arising in the proceedings shall be taken into account in determining that question'. (Section 87(7).) The significance is that if a dispute arises as to whether something done or omitted is eg 'reasonable' or 'good estate management', an approved code can be used to support or dispute the claim.

9.284 When leases of residential premises are negotiated, the landlord may be asked to covenant to comply with his obligations in accordance with the provisions of any code approved under s 87 or its successor. It may not be altogether wise for a landlord to agree. Unless a landlord is prepared to commit himself to abide by all aspects of the approved code, he could find himself in breach of covenant for doing, or omitting, something not mentioned in the lease. It would in any event be unwise to agree to observe a code other than in a form that the landlord has seen – not the code 'from time to time'.

9.285 For consultation under s 20 of the Landlord and Tenant Act 1985 on long-term agreements for appointing managing agents, see at **9.99** and **9.100** above. Managing agents are required as part of that process to state whether or not they 'subscribe to' any code.

9.286 Tucked away in the definitions section of the 1993 Act (s 87(8)(c)) is a good statutory definition of service charges, being an expanded version of that in s 18 of the Landlord and Tenant Act 1985. It reads:

> '(c) "service charge" means an amount payable by a tenant of a dwelling as part of or in addition to the rent –
>
> (i) which is payable, directly or indirectly, for services, repairs, maintenance, improvements or insurance or any relevant person's costs of management, and
>
> (ii) the whole or part of which varies or may vary according to the costs or estimated costs incurred or to be incurred by any relevant person in connection with the matters mentioned in sub-paragraph (i).'

Criticism

9.287 Where a lease contains some specific provision, for example as to the date for producing accounts, the treatment of interest, or the person who shall give any certificate, and the code has some other recommendation the provisions of the lease would be expected to prevail, as the bargain between the parties. In such a case the landlord can comply with the lease agreed between the parties but be in breach of the code. If the lease is silent then clearly the code can provide a useful guide: if the lease is not silent, it would be unsatisfactory for the courts to rely on the code rather than the express terms of the bargain between the landlord and the tenant.

Section 81 of the Housing Act 1996

Forfeiture and re-entry

9.288 The most important service charge provision of the 1996 Act affecting all leases of dwellings is the provision in s 81 which restricts the landlord's right of forfeiture. The provision was heavily amended by s 170 of the Commonhold Act, and the former s 82 (affecting s 146 notices) was repealed by Sch 14 of the 2002 Act. There are other changes mentioned later affecting forfeiture for non-payment of small sums including service charges, but as they affect only long leases they appear in Chapter 10.

9.289 Under s 81 the landlord of a dwelling 'may not ... exercise a right of re-entry or forfeiture for failure by a tenant to pay a service charge or administration charge' unless the amount has been either admitted by the tenant, or determined by or on appeal from a Leasehold Valuation Tribunal, or court, or in a post-dispute arbitration. Section 81(3) records that a determination has not been given until appeals have ended, or the time for making them has expired without an appeal. This was upheld in *Mohammadi v Anston Investments Ltd* [2003] EWCA Civ 981, [2004] HLR 88, where the tenant sued his landlord for non-repair, and the landlord served a s 146 notice and issued a counterclaim seeking forfeiture. The Court of Appeal held that the order of the court below (granting forfeiture) was invalid, as the service charges had not been agreed or determined.

9.290 The section continues in s 81(2) and (4A) by saying that the landlord 'may not exercise a right of re-entry or forfeiture by virtue of sub-s (1)(a) until after the end of the period of 14 days beginning with the day after that on which the final determination is made'. Section 81(4A) says reference 'to the exercise of a right of re-entry or forfeiture include the service of a notice under s 146(1) of the Law of Property Act 1925'. Accordingly, s 146 notices cannot be served until after the 14-day period.

9.291 Section 81(6) makes it clear that the section does not affect the exercise of a right of re-entry or forfeiture on other grounds.

Criticism

9.292 Where the tenant has been deliberately difficult this section delays the landlord's right to recover possession, but 14 days is probably not too long a delay. In any event forfeiture takes a long time where a court hearing date is needed. The remedy of forfeiture is likely to be curtailed or completely removed for residential premises in the next few years, and so the provisions of this section may become immaterial fairly soon.

Contracting out

9.293 For commercial leases there is the possibility of contracting out of the Landlord and Tenant Act 1954 provisions relating to the tenant's right to apply for a new lease. (Section 38(4) of the 1954 Act.) There is no equivalent provision for contracting out of the provisions described in this chapter for tenants of dwellings, and only one case where the court is given express discretion to waive the statutory obligations, namely s 20ZA(1) of the Landlord and Tenant Act 1985.

Final reminder

9.294 The statutory provisions mentioned above are the major statutory provisions affecting service charges. Other than the Landlord and Tenant (Covenants) Act 1995 they all relate solely to residential tenancies. Chapter 10 deals with statutory provisions affecting a more limited range of residential premises. The purpose of this paragraph is simply to remind readers that, with the limited exception just mentioned, the statutory provisions have no relevance to commercial leases.

CHAPTER 10

Statutory provisions applying in limited cases

The Common Law is founded on common sense and is the glory of this country. The other law is made by the politicians.

Sir Travers Humphreys

INTRODUCTION

10.1   Chapter 9 dealt with the important provisions affecting service charges for all dwellings. Other statutory provisions apply in more limited circumstances. Some, such as the rights to seek a court order to vary a lease, and the right for a tenants' audit only apply to cases where the tenant holds a long lease. Others apply only where the tenant has a specific type of tenancy such as a Rent Act tenancy or a secure tenancy. Such more limited statutory provisions are the subject of this chapter.

PART I – PROVISIONS AFFECTING ONLY LONG LEASES

Sections 35–39 of the Landlord and Tenant Act 1987

Powers to vary long leases of flats

10.2   Section 35 of the 1987 Act permits 'any party to a long lease of a flat' to seek an order from a leasehold valuation tribunal varying the lease where it 'fails to make satisfactory provision' in certain specified aspects, including two service charge aspects. This is the main section affecting service charges directly, but is supplemented by ss 36 and 37. Under s 36 if a s 35 order is made 'any other party to the lease' can apply for 'an order which effects a corresponding variation of each of such one or more other leases, as are specified in the application'. Section 37 is a slightly more general provision under which a large majority of tenants of long leases of flats who have the same landlord can apply for a variation: the only ground for such application is 'that the object to be achieved by the variation cannot be satisfactorily achieved unless all the leases are varied to the same effect'. (Section 37(5) sets out particulars of what constitutes a majority for this purpose.) Section 35, being the sole provision specifically mentioning service charges, is subject to further comment below, but the other sections are mentioned for completeness.

10.3   The grounds for seeking a lease variation under s 35 are that the lease fails to make satisfactory provision in respect of various stated aspects. The Commonhold Act (s 162(3)) adds a power to create further grounds by regulation. The two grounds which are material to this book are:

(a)   s 35(2)(e) – 'the recovery by one party to the lease from another party to it of expenditure incurred or to be incurred by him, or on his behalf, for the benefit of that other party or of a number of persons who include that other party'; and

(b)   s 35(2)(f) – 'the computation of a service charge payable under the lease'.

10.4   Section 35 applies only to 'long leases' (ie basically a lease granted for over 21 years, a perpetually renewable lease, or a 'right to buy' lease: Landlord and Tenant Act 1987, s 59(3)). Section 35(6) (added by Housing Act 1988 s 119) excludes from the definition of a qualifying long lease premises incorporating three or more flats in the same building, and business tenancies. It will be noted that the section does not apply to the long lease of a house, and, of course, not to commercial premises.

10.5   The application can be made by 'any party' to the lease. Therefore, it could be by the company or individual which is the landlord or the tenant, but it could be a management company.

10.6   Section 38(10) provides that if an order is made for variation of a lease under any of ss 35, 36 or 37 the tribunal can make an order 'providing for any party to the lease to pay, to any other party to the lease or to any other person, compensation in respect of any loss or disadvantage that the tribunal consider he is likely to suffer as a result of the variation'. The reference to 'any other person' is perhaps primarily intended to enable the position of undertenants or superior landlords to be taken into account.

10.7   Section 35(3A), added by s 162(4) of the Commonhold Act, says that 'for the purposes of sub-s (2)(e) the factors for determining, in relation to a service charge payable under a lease, whether the lease makes satisfactory provision include whether it makes provision for an amount to be payable (by way of interest or otherwise) in respect of a failure to pay the service charge by the due date'. This clearly entitles a landlord to seek to add a provision for interest for late payment to a lease that had none. Interest provisions are relatively rare in leases more than a few decades old.

10.8   Section 35(2)(e) (cited at **10.3** above) covers variations to leases that are unsatisfactory in respect of recovery by one party to the lease from another of expenditure incurred for the benefit of that other party or of others. This would cover, for example, simple clauses for recovery of costs of maintenance of party walls or party drains or other common parts. As the section talks of a lease that 'fails to make satisfactory provision', it seems to contemplate the possibility of adding a liability where there was none before, for example on matters such as decoration or repair of the block. The author is not aware of any cases making the point, but it seems contrary to the normal service charge position that a landlord can only recover costs where the lease expressly permits him to do so, if he can vary a lease to charge where he could not under the lease as completed.

10.9   As an example, perhaps an application could be made to reduce the percentage payable by the tenant of a ground floor flat who does not need to use a lift but who pays the same percentage as the tenant on the fifth floor who does use the lift. This would upset the original scheme of recovery. The tenant of the fifth-floor flat might have a claim for compensation under s 38(10) for the increase in his percentage. If an order was made under s 35, the landlord might seek an order under s 36 of the 1987 Act to vary the other leases. Alternatively, all the tenants might apply to vary their percentages under s 37, where an order can be made varying long leases of flats if the object of the variation can only be achieved if the leases are varied to 'the same effect'. While the latter expression suggests the variation must be to make all the leases equal, it is suggested that it would be interpreted to enable changes to be made to achieve a consistent approach, rather than meaning that all the leases will be identical. (See also **10.11** below.)

10.10   Section 35 is intended to permit a variation against the background that compensation is payable to a party whose future position is adversely affected. If a landlord varied a lease entitling him to recover costs where he had been unable to do so before, then the other party to the lease, the tenant, would surely have suffered a 'loss or disadvantage' for which he should receive compensation. This raises the spectre of parties agreeing a lease with no service charge, and the landlord later 'buying' a variation by obtaining an order and paying compensation to the tenant. This could improve the value of the landlord's investment, and the tenant who receives compensation will be better off in cash terms, although what number of years commutation of future service charge liability would be appropriate as compensation, and what the effect on the capital value of the tenant's interest would be on a subsequent sale, is hard to envisage. The converse is the possibility of a tenant seeking to buy out his obligation to contribute to service charges in consideration of a one-off payment (or a rent increase), although it is hard to envisage that this could properly come under the terms of 'unsatisfactory provisions'. It is doubtful whether compensation would be awarded where an old lease is varied simply to include an interest provision where there was none before. Interest would only be payable when a tenant is in default, not as a matter of course.

10.11   Section 35(2)(f) permits an application to vary a long lease of a flat where the 'computation of a service charge payable under the lease' is unsatisfactory. This is amplified in s 35(4), which states that 'a lease fails to make satisfactory provision with respect to computation of a service charge payable under it' where the landlord can recover from all the tenants either more or less than the total of his expenditure. Thus it can only apply where there is a service charge and one with a recognisable percentage or fraction basis. The wording also suggests that this provision can only be used where the service charges payable by the tenants as a whole do not add up to 100%. Originally, the section simply permitted variation of a lease where the landlord could recover more than the expenditure: s 86 of the Leasehold Reform, Housing and Urban Development Act 1993 changed the original wording. The author has been informed that the change was to take account of the fact that if the freehold of some flats was acquired (ie enfranchisement) under the 1993 Act this might mean that the landlord would only be able to recover expenses from a smaller number of tenants, whose percentages would need to be increased on purely mathematical lines. The section does not say so, and is not limited to that effect. (This point was more fully explored in G Sherriff 'More or Less a Service Charge Revolution' *Solicitors Journal* 1 October 1993.) The section thus gives the possibility of changes to leases which could result in service charge percentages for individual flats being greater or lesser than before the variation.

10.12 Clearly, where the landlord recovers from each of 11 tenants one tenth of his expenditure, he can thus recover 110% and make a profit. This is probably not what the tenants would expect, and the right to change such an anomaly seems relatively uncontroversial. The case of changing a lease where the landlord can recover less than 100% is a very different case. If the 11 tenants each pay 8% the effect is that the landlord has accepted that he will recover 88% of his expenditure: why should he be entitled to change the bargain? This may seem inconsistent with previous comments suggesting that tenants paying more than 100% should reasonably be able to call for a change. The difference is that the service charge is normally considered a reimbursement of service costs, and if the landlord can recover more it becomes the equivalent of additional rent. Under s 19 of the Landlord and Tenant Act 1985 payments must be no more than is reasonable. It is hard to square this sensible provision with s 35(2)(f) which appears to contemplate entitling a landlord to recover by way of service charge more than he has paid for services, although that subsection only permits changes where there are 'unsatisfactory provisions'. The 1993 Act change emphasises the prospect of landlords agreeing leases with limited service charge recovery, and then seeking a court order to change those terms, subject to paying compensation. Section 35(2)(f) applies only where there is some recovery of service charges: it cannot apply where there is none.

Criticism

10.13 It is a pity the main section gives relatively little guidance to the parties or the court on the grounds justifying a change. The examples are useful but not comprehensive. The expression failing to make 'satisfactory provision' in some respect or other is rather general. Obviously, the terms of individual leases and the circumstances of the original parties and their successors are as variable as the number of leases in existence, and no doubt the section is worded deliberately to give the maximum scope for the parties to be able to put their views to a tribunal. The author is unhappy about the power of a landlord to be able to create a heavier service charge burden on a tenant than that negotiated, even where the compensation provisions apply, although the author has not heard of this happening. This sits uncomfortably with normal service charge decisions and philosophy. The provision specifically referring to computation of service charges (s 35(2)(f)) does not even give a maximum or minimum basis of change – it would seem that a lease with any service charge percentage at all (eg 0.05%) could be changed to be one enabling the landlord to make full recovery.

10.14   The author's other grouse is that if the power to change is reasonable, why is it restricted to long leases of flats? Should it not also cover single houses? (Section 35(2)(e) applies to a single flat, and s 35(2)(f) envisages a number of flats.) It is probably reasonable for a right to vary to arise only when the lease is of more than a short minimum length, or there would be the prospect of numerous court applications for leases which might expire before the court hearing, but one might wonder whether 21 years is a reasonable minimum. With leases as short as seven years now needing to be registered at the Land Registry perhaps seven years would be a more appropriate period.

Chapter V of Part I of the Leasehold Reform, Housing and Urban Development Act 1993

Management audit for tenants with long leases of dwellings

10.15   This gives some tenants the right to call for their own audit. Usually, the landlord carries out management and arranges for the accounts and any certificates which, even when professionally and independently prepared, are prepared by people appointed by the landlord: Chapter V of Part 1 of the 1993 Act gives tenants the comfort of a right to have someone to inspect the books and the premises etc specifically on their behalf.

10.16   The right to inspect common parts may well prove to be the most significant aspect of the 1993 Act in practice. The 1993 Act as a whole is very wordy and Chapter V (ss 76-84) is no exception. The effect is that, usually, not less than two thirds of the tenants (see at **10.17** below) who must each hold long leases of dwellings, can call on the landlord to permit their own representative ('the auditor') to inspect the books and also the common parts. The object of the management audit is to see whether the obligations of the landlord and the money spent on services have been fulfilled and spent respectively in 'an efficient and effective manner'. The Act gives these useful rights, but fails to state the position if the audit reports less than efficient and effective management. The audit report could be produced in court in case of dispute, but the Act does not require the landlord to refund money or sack the managing agents. (A right to inspect common parts is also given in Housing Act 1996 where a recognised tenants' association appoints a surveyor to act for it. See below.)

10.17   The first section of Chapter V (s 76, of the 1993 Act) sets out the number of tenants of long leases of dwellings needed for an application. Qualifying tenants are a single tenant where the building contains only one qualifying tenant (s 76(4) and(5)), either or both tenants where the building has only two qualifying tenants (s 76(2)(a)) and two thirds of the qualifying tenants if the building has three or more qualifying tenants (s 76(2)(b)). The landlord has to be the same where there are several tenants, although anything else would be unusual.

10.18 The building over which services are performed and which contains the dwellings is described in s 76(3)(a) as the 'relevant premises'. These are defined by s 76(3) to mean 'so much of the building or buildings containing the dwellings let to those tenants, and … any other building or buildings in relation to which management functions are discharged in respect of the costs of which common service charge contributions are payable under the leases of those qualifying tenants', together with 'appurtenant property' which is property not within the relevant premises but over which the same management functions are discharged. The appurtenant property would presumably include a separate garage block or separate garden area managed by the landlord. In so far as premises are partly residential and partly commercial (eg flats over shops) the definition of appurtenant property could apply to parts of the building over which commercial tenants also have rights so far as the landlord is responsible for management, but the commercial tenants cannot be qualifying tenants. Where there is a dispute in a multi-use building the tenants of the commercial parts might consider persuading the residential tenants to apply for a management audit. The chapter does not state the consequences where the management audit shows bad management, but if there is a bad report no doubt the commercial tenants will want to use the result of the audit as evidence in proceedings affecting their part. The Chapter does not give them the right to apply for their own audit, but an unsatisfactory management audit report could presumably be evidence in court proceedings, either through disclosure or by calling the auditor as a witness.

10.19 'Qualifying tenants' are those (ss 77 and 77(1) of the 1993 Act) who hold long leases of dwellings and where 'any service charge is payable under the lease'. These are leases granted for more than 21 years, leases which are perpetually renewable, right to buy leases, and shared ownership leases. Only one lease can qualify per dwelling, and, where there are long leases and long underleases, the underlease is the qualifying lease (s 77(3) and (4)(a)). Joint tenants are treated as one, and a tenant can be a qualifying tenant for more than one flat (s 77(4)(b) and (5)).

10.20 Section 78 defines a management audit. It is an audit carried out to ascertain the extent to which the landlord's obligations 'to the qualifying tenants of the constituent dwellings and … involve the discharge of management functions in relation to the relevant property, or any appurtenant premises (see the definitions mentioned above at **10.18**) are being discharged in an efficient and effective manner', and also the extent to which 'sums payable by those tenants by way of service charges are being applied in an effective and efficient way' (s 78(1)(a) and (b)).

10.21 The use of the word 'payable' may suggest that the tenants could seek a management audit based on the estimated sums they have been asked to pay, or where they have refused to pay the service charge because of dissatisfaction with the way in which the landlord's obligations have been carried out. Section 78(2) spells out that in considering efficient and effective management regard shall be had to any code of practice approved by the Secretary of State under s 87 of the 1993 Act. (See Chapter 9 at **9.281** et seq and Chapter 11.)

10.22 The auditor is defined in s 78(3)–(6). In effect he is a person with relevant qualifications who is not disqualified. The auditor has to be a 'qualified accountant' within the meaning of s 28 of the Landlord and Tenant Act 1985 (see at **9.211** et seq) or a qualified surveyor. A tenant of any of the premises concerned is disqualified from being an auditor (s 78(4)(c)), as are the others who are disqualified under s 28 of the 1985 Act. Section 78(5) provides that a qualified surveyor is a fellow or professional associate of the Royal Institution of Chartered Surveyors or the Incorporated Society of Valuers and Auctioneers, or otherwise satisfies criteria to be prescribed by the Secretary of State.

10.23 Section 79(4) includes the important right mentioned above for the auditor appointed by the tenants, following notice under s 80, to inspect 'any common parts comprised in the relevant premises or any appurtenant premises'. This enables an auditor to inspect works done, eg to the common roof, to ensure that the work has been done and is of a reasonable standard. This right is probably the most useful aspect of the right to a management audit. In any case where tenants are concerned about what has been done this should certainly be one of the points that is considered.

10.24 The right to a management audit is exercised by notice under s 80 to the landlord or to a person who receives the rent on behalf of the landlord. The notice is given by the auditor and must be signed by all the tenants on whose behalf it is given. The notice has to give details of the tenants and the auditor, and specify the documents or types of document which the auditor wants to inspect, and, if the auditor wants to inspect common parts, it should set out a date on which he intends to inspect. The inspection date is to be between one and two months after the date of the notice. (Section 80(4) of the 1993 Act.) Where the relevant documents are with a superior landlord, the Act (s 82, as amended by the Commonhold and Leasehold Reform Act 2002, Sch 10, para 19) requires the immediate landlord to inform the auditor of the name and address of the superior landlord and the auditor can give the notice direct to the superior landlord.

10.25 The 1993 Act is to be amended by the Commonhold and Leasehold Reform Act 2002, s 157 and Sch 10, para 16(3), and the original s 79(2) was to be replaced by new s 79(2) and (2A). These would give rights to the auditor to require the landlord to permit inspection:

(a) (s 79(2)) of 'accounts receipts or other documents relevant to the matters which must be shown in any statement of account required to be supplied to the qualifying tenant under section 21 of the 1985 Act'; and

(b) (s 79(2A)) of 'any other documents sight of which is reasonably required by him for the purposes of carrying out the audit', and to take copies.

The provisions in s 79(5) (intended to be replaced by the Commonhold Act), as to the cost of copies and making facilities available, are similar in effect to those in the 1985 Act. (See at **9.170** et seq.) Because the government is reconsidering its changes to s 21, para 16 of Sch 10 to the Commonhold Act has not yet been brought into force. (See at **9.155**.)

10.26   Several sections of Chapter V make reference to a 'relevant person'. Under s 79(7), a relevant person is one, but not the landlord, who either carries out the service obligations or is responsible for applying the service charge receipts from tenants, and, rather oddly, can be a person with 'the right to enforce payment' of the service charge. The right can thus be exercised against a management company, including one owned by the tenants.

10.27   The Act requires the landlord to react to the s 80 notice. The landlord must within one month:

(a)   comply with the requirement for inspection of documents, and afford facilities for inspection; or

(b)   state whether that landlord objects to producing documents, with reasons for such objection; and

(c)   if the notice requires inspection of premises either approve the date for inspection, or propose an alternative date which must still be within two months of the giving of the s 80 notice. (Section 81(1) and (2). Section 81(1) is due to be revised by the Commonhold Act Sch 10, para 18, when the provisions are brought into force.)

Where notice is given to a 'relevant person', as opposed to the landlord, to inspect accounts etc he must permit the inspection within one month of the notice or give notice, within the same period, of objection and the reasons for objection. (Section 81(3).)

10.28   In the case of failure to comply with the notice within two months of the notice the auditor can apply for a court order. The application for an order must be made not less than two nor more than four months from giving the notice. (Section 81(4)–(7).)

10.29   There are supplementary provisions in s 83 relating to cases where notice has been served and the interest of the landlord changes or a person ceases to be a 'relevant person'. The general effect is that the new landlord becomes responsible for discharging the obligations, although if the former landlord is also still able to discharge the obligations despite the change then he remains liable as well. (This is a point to bear in mind on selling the reversion to leases.) Finally, s 83 also makes it clear that no notice requiring an audit can be given within 12 months of a previous notice.

Criticism

10.30   The Chapter gives another benefit to a tenant who has doubts about the way the building is managed. As all tenants of dwellings now have the right to inspect papers following the landlord providing a summary of costs under s 20 Landlord and Tenant Act 1985, the major benefits are:

(a)   the right to inspect common parts; and

(b)   a slightly wider right to inspect documents other than those directly relating to the statement of account.

10.31   The section signally fails to give any remedy where a bad report is given, although it is obviously useful evidence for proceedings or, for example, an appointment of a manager under the Landlord and Tenant Act 1987.

10.32   It is probably fair that it should be exercisable only by a majority of tenants: this prevents much work and cost that could arise in the case of an individual who took an unrealistic view of the tenancy.

10.33   The section does not say who pays the auditor's costs. As the tenants have employed him they are committed to pay his fee. It might have been helpful to provide that where the auditor's certificate shows an unsatisfactory state of affairs the tenants should be able to set off the costs of the auditor against the service charge demands, but this may be difficult to achieve fairly. In particular, the auditor might indicate satisfaction in some areas and dissatisfaction in others, in which case the fee should not be taken wholly from the landlord. The author's main complaint is that it is restricted to tenants holding long leases of dwellings. As in the case of powers to vary leases mentioned above, a tenant with a lease of over, say, seven years has surely enough interest to qualify for this type of benefit, as has a commercial tenant.

Sections 71 to 113 of the Commonhold and Leasehold Reform Act 2002

The Right to Manage (for long leases of flats)

10.34   This is mentioned here because there are a number of specific service charge consequences of this right for some tenants to take over management. The right is only exercisable by tenants holding long leases of flats, which is why the provisions appear in this chapter, but for the right to be exercised the building also needs to qualify. The right may become more used than the right to appoint a manager in the Landlord and Tenant Act 1987, because under the Right to Manage procedure the tenants do not need to prove any fault. (1987 Act managers are covered at **10.44** et seq.) Provided the tenants and the building both qualify the tenants can take over management through the medium of a company, the RTM Company. The qualifications are effectively identical to those allowing tenants of flats to acquire the freehold collectively under the Leasehold Reform, Housing and Urban Development Act, 1993. In most cases that would probably be more satisfactory, because there are some problems with the Right to Manage, notably that it is also an obligation to monitor covenants, there is no right to forfeit or distrain, and the landlord will still to involved where there are non-qualifying tenants, and to give consents. The landlord, in such case, will also be a member of the RTM Company. Obviously, tenants who enfranchise pay for the freehold, whereas the Right to Manage does not involve payment to the landlord.

10.35   The building qualifications are quite strict. The building, which must contain at least two flats held by qualifying tenants, has to be either:

(a)   detached; or

(b)   a self-contained vertical division of a building which could be 'redeveloped independently of the rest of the building', and where the services provided for the tenants are, or could be independent of the remainder of the building without the need for works that would cause 'significant interruption' to the provision of services for the rest of the building.

Not more than 25% of the internal floor area of the building can be non-residential. If the building has different freehold owners the right does not apply to any part of the building. There is a resident landlord exemption, and the right does not apply where the landlord is a local housing authority, or where the Right to Manage has been exercised within the previous four years. (Section 72 and Sch 6.)

10.36   'Qualifying tenants' are simply those holding long leases of flats, but not tenancies that qualify under the Landlord and Tenant Act 1954 as business tenancies. There is no residence qualification or low rent test. Where a flat has leases and underleases which are all long leases, the undertenant is the qualifying tenant (s 75). The claim to a Right to Manage can only be made if, when the notice making the claim is served, both tenants (if there are only two flats in the premises) are qualifying tenants, or (in the case of more than two flats) the number of qualifying tenants in the building is not less than half the total number of flats (s 79).

10.37   Provided the building and the tenants qualify, the tenants who are interested need to form an RTM Company, which is a company limited by guarantee. They must then invite all the qualifying tenants in the building to join in before they can serve notice on the landlord exercising the right. The notice gives the landlord not less than one month for serving a counter notice, and sets out a date for commencement of RTM which must not be less than three months after the date for the counter notice (ss 73 and 79). Once the process is in hand, the landlord has the right to serve a counter notice, but only either (a) to agree that the right can be claimed, or (b) to dispute that the building or the tenants qualify – there is no other defence by a landlord. If the landlord objects on the grounds that the claim does not fulfil the requirements of the Act (eg that the building or tenants do not qualify) and the tenants disagree, the parties can apply to the LVT for a determination (ss 84 and 85).

10.38 The Right to Manage will usually start four months after the notice exercising the right. At that point the RTM Company will become responsible for the management obligations affecting the building in place of the landlord or management company, as the case may be (ss 80(7), 90 and 96). 'Management functions' for the purposes of Right to Manage relate to 'services, repairs, maintenance, improvements, insurance and management' (s 96(5)).

10.39 This is not the place to go into great detail about management under the right, but in effect the RTM Company steps into the shoes of the landlord and is responsible for management functions. Contrast the position of a manager under the Landlord and Tenant Act 1987 who is an official appointed by the court, sometimes for limited purposes only. In reality the RTM Company will be responsible for the common parts and for the parts occupied by qualifying tenants. The landlord remains responsible as landlord for any non-qualifying tenants, such as commercial tenants or residential tenants with short leases. The landlord will become a member of the RTM Company, once it has become entitled to exercise the right, but not before, representing those parts not occupied by qualifying tenants (s 74(1)).

10.40 The following points relate solely to service charges. Section 93 entitles the RTM Company to require information to enable it to manage. The following section requires the landlord to pay to the RTM Company 'accrued uncommitted service charges'. These are in effect the balance of service charge receipts held by the landlord (or management company or even a manager appointed under the Landlord and Tenant Act 1987) including any investments representing those receipts and the interest on those investments, 'less so much (if any) of that amount needed to pay costs incurred before the acquisition date (ie the date on which the Right to Manage starts) in connection with the matters for which the service charges were payable'. Disputes between the landlord and the RTM Company as to the amount can be referred to the LVT. The landlord is to comply 'on the acquisition date or as soon after that date as is reasonably practicable' (2002 Act, s 94). The RTM Company will thus have money in hand to start managing.

10.41 As the RTM Company is responsible for management it is obviously responsible for collecting service charges. There is a procedure for the landlord to require those people who carry out work for the building to be notified by the landlord of the change of management, and this enables the RTM Company to see who does what, and (if they wish) to re-appoint them (ss 91–92). The Act is silent on what happens to the contracts the landlord has entered into which are for periods that extend beyond the date on which the right to manage is acquired, but presumably such contracts are frustrated, as the landlord no longer has the right to be responsible for such work. It remains to be seen how enthusiastically those landlords who have been deprived of management functions co-operate to notify contractors.

10.42   Resisting the temptation to comment on the intriguing provisions under which the RTM Company has to consider applications for consent from qualifying tenants and also notify the landlord of those requests (s 98) and the obligation to monitor covenants by the tenants (ss 100–101) (this contrasts with the landlord's right to monitor covenants if he chooses) the service charge provision that does need attention is s 103. This is material (a) where a flat or other part of the building (an 'excluded unit') is not held by a qualifying tenant, and '(b) the service charge payable under leases of flats contained in the premises which are so subject fall to be calculated as a proportion of the relevant costs, and (c) the proportions of the relevant costs so payable, when aggregated, amount to less than the whole of the relevant costs'. In such circumstances the landlord is responsible for the service charges of those excluded units:

(a)   If there is only one 'excluded unit', the landlord must pay to the RTM Company the difference between the relevant costs and the aggregate amounts payable under the other leases (s 103(2).) (This is regardless of what (if anything) the landlord is entitled to claim from the tenant under the tenant's lease. Presumably, if the lease of the excluded unit says the tenant pays 5% of the total costs but a calculation under RTM requires payment of 8% then the landlord pays the shortfall.)

(b)   If there is more than one excluded unit, the landlord must pay to the RTM Company 'the appropriate proportion' of the difference (s 103(3)).

(c)   The anomaly is that the 'appropriate proportion' is said to be 'the proportion of the internal floor area of all of the excluded units which is internal floor area of the excluded unit in relation to which he is the appropriate person' (s 103(4)).

The wording of the section seems to be intended to require the landlord to pay the difference between the total costs incurred and the sums payable under leases of qualifying tenants, and that the share of the excluded units is to be based on the relative floor areas of those excluded units. The oddity is that the section ignores any percentages that may be included in any of the leases. Take, for example, Haydon House, a block with ten flats, where RTM is exercised. Only Flats 4, 5 and 6 are not held by qualifying tenants. If the leases of Flats 4, 5 and 6 say the tenants are liable for 6%, 8%, and 10% of the total costs respectively:

(i)   the landlord representing them may be obliged to pay a different amount, which may be more or less than 24% (the combined percentage for the three flats), because his contribution, as landlord of the excluded units, is based not on the figures in the leases, but is the balance of costs not payable by qualifying tenants, and

(ii)   the tenants may be notionally liable to pay to the landlord different percentages to those in their leases, if they do not accord with a floor area measurement. He will only be able to claim what they are liable to pay under their leases – if the leases of Flats 4, 5 and 6 do not contain percentages this is a helpful rule of thumb; if they do, then there seems scope for confusion at the least.

Section 167 of the Commonhold and Leasehold Reform Act 2002

Failure to pay small sums for a short period

10.43   Where a tenant of a long lease of a dwelling owes an amount for rent, service charge or administration charges (or any permutation of them), the landlord cannot enforce the debt if the total is less than a sum set out in regulations, unless it has been outstanding for more than a specified period. The Rights of Re-Entry and Forfeiture (Prescribed Sum and Period) (England) Regulations 2004 provides that the total owing must be under £350, and the period is to be three years. (For administration charges see **9.276**.) Obviously, if the sum is under the relevant figure in the first year but goes over the minimum in the second year the landlord can then take action as needed. Section 167(3) provides that the sum is to be calculated excluding any administration charge payable in respect of the tenant's failure to pay.

PART 2 – PROVISIONS AFFECTING GROUPS OF FLATS

Part II of the Landlord and Tenant Act 1987

Appointment of a manager for a building with flats

10.44   Part II of the 1987 Act (ss 21–24) gives tenants of a building containing two or more flats rights to apply to a Leasehold Valuation Tribunal for appointment of a manager where the landlord is not managing the building satisfactorily. The provisions were changed and amplified, particularly to change the venue to a Leasehold Valuation Tribunal and in respect of service charges, by s 87 of the Housing Act 1996. (The revised form of Part II of the 1987 Act was set out as Sch 5 to the Housing Act 1996.) An alternative to this procedure is the Right to Manage, see at **10.34** et seq above. Under RTM, provided both the building and the tenants qualify the landlord cannot prevent the tenants taking over management through a company. By contrast, the landlord can challenge a 1987 Act application, under which management is by an appointed official, not the tenants.

10.45   The 1987 Act right to appoint a manager only applies where a building contains two or more flats, and thus could include a house divided into flats as well as blocks of flats. This is the only qualification for the building; for the Right to Manage the building has to comply with other criteria. It does not apply to a single flat, or where there is a resident landlord, or where the premises are functional land of a charity, or to a house not divided into flats. The application has to be made by at least two tenants, but it does not need a majority and there is no restriction to long leases. No company has to be formed.

10.46   The right is exercised by the tenants serving notice on the landlord stating that the tenants intend to apply for an order to appoint a manager unless the landlord complies with the requirements in the notice. The notice must specify the grounds for seeking the order. Where the problem is one capable of remedy, the application to the LVT is to be after a reasonable period (stated in the notice) has gone by without the landlord complying (1987 Act, s 22).

10.47   Section 24 gives the LVT the right to appoint a manager to carry out functions in relation to the building in four circumstances:

(a)   where the landlord is in breach of his obligations (or would be), and that it is just to make the order; or

(b)   where unreasonable service charges have been made, or are likely to be made; or

(c)   where the landlord has failed to comply with codes of practice under the Leasehold Reform Housing and Urban Development Act 1993; or

(d)   where there are other circumstances making it just.

The provisions in (b) and (c), being s 24(2)(ab) and (ac), were added by the Housing Act 1996.

10.48   The remainder of s 24 and new ss 24A and 24B expand on the procedure for appointing a manager, but obviously of concern is the reference to service charges in s 24(2)(ab). This is amplified by s 24(2A), which states that 'a service charge shall be taken to be unreasonable' where it conflicts in three ways with reasonableness. For the purpose of an application to appoint a manager, s 23(2A) of the Landlord and Tenant Act 1987 says a service charge is unreasonable where:

'(a)   if the amount is unreasonable having regard to the items for which it is payable,

(b)   if the items for which it is payable are of an unnecessarily high standard, or

(c)   if the items for which it is payable are of an insufficient standard with the result that additional service charges are or may be incurred.'

10.49   These three reasonableness aspects have echoes of, but are not identical to, the three strands of reasonableness for s 19 of the Landlord and Tenant Act 1985 (see at **9.38** et seq). In passing it seems that this is a better way of expressing the three possibilities than in s 19.

10.50   The position following appointment of a manager was considered by the Court of Appeal in *Taylor v Blaquiere* [2002] EWCA Civ 1633, [2003] 1 WLR 379. The court confirmed that the manager was appointed to carry out the functions required by the LVT. He was not the landlord's manager. He acted in his own right as a court appointed official. Accordingly, the tenant had no right to set off claims which the tenant had against the landlord against service charge demands by the manager. It perhaps also illustrates that the appointment can be for a specific purpose (eg just for repair of the roof), whereas the Right to Manage is envisaged as being a permanent arrangement.

Comparing Right to Manage and appointment of a manager

10.51   The power to seek a manager where the landlord is acting unsatisfactorily is a useful weapon in the armoury of the tenant. In some cases it can go on to lead to the compulsory acquisition of the landlord's interest under Part III of the 1987 Act, a very significant remedy, because one ground for compulsory acquisition is the appointment of a manager for a period. The Right to Manage (RTM) is perhaps easier to obtain, because no proof of mismanagement is needed, and the landlord cannot object if the building and tenants qualify, but for RTM:

(a)   the tenants need to form a company;

(b)   it is more onerous for those taking it up, as it includes an obligation to monitor tenants' covenants; and

(c)   the qualifications for RTM are similar to those for enfranchisement, and tenants who are concerned would do well to consider the latter course as the most effective way of ensuring management of the property to their own satisfaction, and it takes the landlord out of the picture.

10.52   The way s 24(2A) is worded infers that the concern is with cost, as one would expect, although various cases on reasonableness mentioned elsewhere in this volume indicate that just because an item could have cost less the charge was not necessarily unreasonable. It remains to be seen how the LVT approach this particular point. A provision on costs appears in s 24A(4). It provides that 'no costs incurred by a party in connection with proceedings under this Part (of this Act) before a Leasehold Valuation Tribunal shall be recoverable except by order of the court'.

The position at the end of a long lease

10.53   When the long lease of a dwelling reaches its end the tenant may be able to continue in occupation under either Pt I of the Landlord and Tenant Act 1954 or Sch 10 to the Housing and Local Government Act 1989. (The tenant thus continues in occupation either as a regulated tenant or an assured tenant.) The Court of Appeal, in *Blatherwick (Services) Ltd v King* [1991] Ch 218, had to consider what happened about the service charge provisions of a long lease when it ended. The service charge was not reserved as rent. In that case the tenancy continued under the 1954 Act and a rent was registered. A dispute arose whether the tenant was liable to pay service charge for the period after the contractual term expired and before the statutory tenancy started. The court held that he was. Section 10(1) of the 1954 Act extinguishes 'any liability … arising under the terms of the former tenancy', subject to three exceptions set out in a proviso. One exception was the 'liability under the former tenancy' in so far as those terms 'related to property other than the dwelling-house'. It was held the proviso applied to service charges which, for example, concerned obligations to repair etc common parts.

PART 3 – PROVISIONS AFFECTING ONLY RENT ACT TENANCIES

Section 71 of the Rent Act 1977

10.54   There are many fewer Rent Act tenancies now than there used to be and there are very limited circumstances indeed in which new Rent Act ('regulated') tenancies can arise. The significance of s 71 is that it provides for registration of a rent (not surprisingly known as a 'registered rent') and the landlord is not entitled to recover more than the registered rent. (Rent Act 1977, s 44.)

10.55   Section 71 sets out that 'the amount to be registered as the rent shall include any sums payable by the tenant for the use of furniture or for services, whether or not those sums 'are separate from the rent 'or are payable under separate agreements'. Section 71(4) specifically deals with service charges. It says that:

'(4) Where, under a regulated tenancy, the sums payable by the tenant to the landlord include any sums varying according to the cost from time to time of –

(a)   any services provided by the landlord or a superior landlord, or

(b)   any works of maintenance or repair carried out by the landlord or a superior landlord'

[the amount to be registered] as rent may, if the rent officer is satisfied, or as the case may be the rent assessment committee are satisfied that the terms as to the variation are reasonable be entered as an amount variable in accordance with those terms.'

The wording in s 74(4)(b) is slightly less full than the definition of service charges in s 18 of the Landlord and Tenant Act 1985, as it does not mention improvements, insurance or management costs.

10.56   According to *Eaton Square Properties Ltd v Ogilvie* [2000] 16 EG 143, the services to be included as part of the registered rent must be provided by the landlord: where the services are provided by a management company and the landlord has no liability for services under the lease the service charge cannot be included within the registered rent.

10.57   Section 71 does not give guidance on what makes variations reasonable or not reasonable. In deciding whether to register a rent as variable or not the rent assessment committee should 'take account of all relevant factors, must not take into account irrelevant factors and (it) must be a decision to which a sensible tribunal, properly directing itself as to the matters which it should take into account, could reasonably come', *Firstcross Ltd v Teasdale* (1983) 265 EG 305.

This contains a useful analysis of s 71(4) of the Rent Act 1977. The comment just quoted (from the *Firstcross* case) was said to be based on the well-known *Wednesbury* decision on tribunals: *Associated Provincial Picture Houses Ltd v Wednesbury Corpn* [1948] 1 KB 223.

10.58 The rent assessment committee should endeavour to give a brief statement of the principles on which the registration was made. (*Metropolitan Properties Co (FGC) Ltd v Lannon* [1968] 1 All ER 354.) The Rent Act 1977 came into force a few years after the first general statutory service charge protection (1972) and so tenants in 1977 were entitled to the benefit of some statutory service charge protection, though this was less extensive than that now available.

10.59 The register of registered rents should set out details of what services are included in the tenancy. The service charge element can include allowances for depreciation, and even an element of profit on the cost of provision of the services. (See *Regis Property Co Ltd v Dudley* [1958] 1 QB 346 and *Perseus Property Co Ltd v Burberry* [1985] 1 EGLR 114.) A good example of registration and factors for consideration is *Metropolitan Properties Ltd v Noble* [1968] 2 All ER 313, which touched on several topics including rents for staff accommodation and central heating costs.

10.60 Where the actual cost of services is unreasonably high, because of changes in circumstances, the rent assessment committee can use its own knowledge and experience to assess a reasonable figure to be included as the variable amount. (*R v London Rent Assessment Panel, ex p Cliftvylle Properties Ltd* [1983] 1 EGLR 100 (see at **9.53** above).)

10.61 A question arose in 1987 whether the amount of service charge payable was to be included when assessing whether or not the rent was more than two thirds of the rateable value, and thus whether the tenancy was protected by the Rent Act or not (*Investment & Freehold English Estates Ltd v Casement* [1987] 2 EGLR 112). Further details appear at **6.45**. The lease was created after certain statutory changes had come into force, but contained provisions (which were then obsolete) seeking to ensure that the combined rent and service charge remained below two thirds of the rateable value. The court held that these provisions did not prevent the landlord recovering the total service charge costs.

10.62 A significant case on registration of service charges, affecting flats in Chelsea, is *Wigglesworth v Property Holding and Investment Ltd* (1984) 270 EG 555. A rent of £2,295 had been registered inclusive of services, ie it was not a variable rent. The tenant had formerly paid a rent plus 0.8% of the increase in certain costs. The tenant appealed to a rent assessment committee which agreed that the provisions in the lease for variation were reasonable. It determined a rent of £2,350 pa subject to variation. The court found that the rent assessment committee had assessed a rent and then added a fixed sum for services to reach £2,350, but had then provided for it to be a variable rent. The court referred the decision back to a different rent assessment committee for reconsideration. The judge said:

> 'the correct approach is to consider the terms as to variability which are to be found in the lease. If the result which the committee wish to achieve can be effected by grafting their determination on to these terms, all well and good. Terms inconsistent with their determination will, of course, be overridden. It is as if they were notionally crossed out. But what the rent assessment committee cannot do is to write additional terms into the lease.'

10.62 It has been suggested the *Wigglesworth* case makes the 'reasonable' implications of *Finchbourne Ltd v Rodrigues* [1976] 3 All ER 581 a rebuttable presumption only. In other words, as the *Wigglesworth* decision is based on the registration having to reflect the actual wording used in the lease rather than what is necessarily seen as reasonable, that means the *Finchbourne* implication of reasonableness is not automatic, and is thus rebuttable. The author does not subscribe to this view for three reasons:

(a) The court has to be satisfied with the terms as variability. If they are not, then the court will not give effect to them for registration. In other words the right to vary itself is subject to reasonableness.

(b) In the earlier case of *Metropolitan Properties Ltd v Noble* [1968] 2 All ER 313 (mentioned at **10.59** above), the Court of Appeal had held that the rent assessment committee could register a lower figure than the full sum where the amount claimed was excessive, thus importing reasonableness. In the 1968 case the committee reduced the figures for management charges, rental for flats for staff, and costs for central heating.

(c) Section 19 of the Landlord and Tenant Act 1985 implies reasonableness for residential property and the parties cannot contract out of the Act.

10.63 Where rent had been registered with an inclusive service charge figure the registration could not be changed, even where the actual costs were less than the amount registered. The tenancy agreement in *Laimond Property Investment Ltd v Arlington Park Mansions Ltd* [1989] 1 EGLR 208 provided for the landlord to carry out certain services, although there was no provision for recovery of service charges as such. Rent was to be £830 pa 'or such greater sum as shall for the time being be registered as the rent for the flat under the Rent Act 1965'. A rent was registered including a specified amount for services (ie not a variable rent). The tenants were not entitled to apply to the court to vary the registration even where the services cost less than the specified sum. The court also refused to allow the tenants to inspect the vouchers, because as the service charge figure was fixed no purpose would be served by such inspection.

10.64 Section 72A of the Rent Act 1977 (added in 1992) invites rent officers, when registering a rent, to indicate the amount, if any, of the rent which is in the opinion of the rent officer 'fairly attributable to the provision of services', except where this is negligible. This is to assist housing authorities with the housing benefit scheme, and presumably is only necessary if the rent is registered as inclusive of service charges, rather than where it is a variable amount, although the section does not say so.

PART 4 – PROVISIONS AFFECTING ONLY PUBLIC SECTOR TENANTS

General

10.65   There are a number of special service charge aspects, affecting only public sector tenants, the main aspects of which are set out in this Part 4. For example, for some secure tenants who exercise the 'right to buy' (see below) there are unique provisions restricting service charge liability for the first five years. In addition, for public sector tenants reasonableness is implied, and they have rights to inspect documents. There can even be criminal penalties in limited cases.

10.66   If a tenant takes a right to buy lease he will normally acquire a 'long lease' for the purposes of s 26 of the Landlord and Tenant Act 1985 and thus will have the benefit of ss 18 to 24 of that Act. Section 26 excludes from the definition of 'long lease' certain leases including leases terminable on death except where they are of a specific type. Perhaps the most significant leases terminable on death which are still treated as long leases under s 26 are those (a) 'granted at a premium calculated by reference to a percentage of the value of the dwelling house or the cost of providing it', or (b) tenancies terminable on death 'granted by a housing association which at the time of the grant is a registered social landlord'.

10.67   To decide what provisions (if any) apply to such service charges needs careful analysis of the identity of the landlord and the nature of the actual lease granted.

10.68   The definition of tenants entitled to form recognised tenants' associations in s 29(4) of the Landlord and Tenant 1985 simply refers to tenants who contribute to the same service charge, and does not qualify the capacity of those tenants otherwise. It would therefore seem that public sector tenants are entitled to form associations within the provision, although s 29 is not mentioned in s 26 which sets out specific provisions which do apply to such tenants.

Secure tenancies

10.69   Secure tenancies are certain types of tenancy granted by public sector landlords. Some secure tenants have the 'right to buy' mentioned in the next paragraph.

10.70   In general terms tenancies other than 'long tenancies' granted to tenants occupying a dwelling as their only or principal residence by local authorities, development corporations, new town corporations, housing action trusts, some housing co-operatives and some statutory bodies having housing functions will be secure tenancies. (Housing Act 1985, ss 79–81.) The tenancy can cease to be 'secure' if, for example, the tenant ceases to use it as his only or principal home. The Housing Act 1996 brought in another form of tenancy called an 'introductory tenancy' (a sort of probationary tenancy) which can become a secure tenancy after one year. (For further details of secure tenancies, see ss 81, 89(3), 91(2) and 93(2) of the Housing Act 1985.) There are many new types of public sector tenancy, but this sets out the position affecting the majority of public sector tenants.

10.71 The different categories of secure tenancy are partly based on the capacity of the landlord (whether it is a local authority, or housing action trust, or the Commission for New Towns), and on the length of the term. The position is further complicated by the arrangement under which it was formerly possible (but not now) for a public sector landlord to transfer its interest to an 'approved person', who then took what had been public sector tenancies into the private sector. There were complicated transitional provisions (far beyond the scope of this book) under which some rights of tenants were preserved even after they passed out of the public sector. Those wanting to see the detail of the arrangements are referred to the Housing Act 1985, Housing Associations Act 1985, Housing and Planning Act 1986, Housing (Consequential Provisions) Act 1985, Housing Act 1988, Local Government and Housing Act 1989, Leasehold Reform, Housing and Urban Development Act 1993, and the Housing Act 1996, as well as the numerous statutory instruments thereunder.

10.72 Specific service charge provisions affect secure tenants, particularly in relation to the right to buy, which is given to some, but not all secure tenants. The rights, when they apply, are not identical in all cases. Set out below are the primary effect of the provisions, with an indication of those cases where significant variations apply. In view of the complexity and length of the provisions, and the various alternatives, space does not permit more than a general indication of the effect of the provisions. Readers are warned that this is a highly technical field, and if a problem arises you must first ascertain exactly which of the various types of secure tenancy is involved, and then read the actual provisions concerned. Even that process is not simple, as quite a few of the provisions in the Acts have been amended by statutory instrument (a process the author finds appalling).

The Right to Buy and service charges

10.73 The qualifications for the right to buy are too complex to set out in full here, but they depend on (a) the status of the landlord (whether it is a local authority, or housing action trust, etc), (b) the status of the tenant (who must have a residence qualification), and (c) the dwelling which must also qualify.

10.74 In general terms there are six different versions of the right to buy. There are three schemes, and different consequences depending on whether the tenancy was created before or after 10 October 1993. The three variants are:

(a)   the ordinary right to buy scheme, the relevant details of which are outlined below; and

(b)   the extended right to buy scheme, where the landlord does not own the freehold; and

(c)   the preserved right to buy scheme, where the property has been transferred out of the public sector.

Significant differences in the separate schemes are indicated in parentheses. At the time of writing there are proposals to change the right to buy provisions, although the concern seems to relate to the level of discount given to tenants. If changes are made they may affect the service charge provisions.

10.75   The 'right to buy' entitles qualifying secure tenants to acquire the freehold or leasehold of the dwelling in which they reside on certain conditions. Where the landlord itself only owns a leasehold interest, then the right is to acquire a leasehold interest. The service charge aspects in this context can relate to both freehold and leasehold right to buy premises.

10.76   The right to buy is exercised by notice. Assuming the landlord accepts that the tenant has established his right to buy, the landlord has to serve a counter notice which must include certain information. This includes special information about service charges (s 125 A of the Housing Act 1985) and also (for flats only) about improvements (s 125 B). There are statutory terms for the conveyance or lease (Sch 6 to the Housing Act 1985). In addition, various other statutory provisions give the purchaser of the freehold or the tenant of the new lease some, but by no means all, of the protection of the Landlord and Tenant Act 1985. The protection is notably ss 47 and 48 of the Housing Act 1985. Under these provisions the service charge obligation of the tenant is restricted, for a period of five years, to the estimated amounts – a unique statutory benefit available only to tenants exercising the right to buy.

Section 47 of the Housing Act 1985

Reasonableness of service charges for freeholds

10.77   This section is similar, but by no means identical, to s 19 of the Landlord and Tenant Act 1985 (see at **9.38** et seq). It applies, under s 45 of the Housing Act 1985, where (a) the tenant has acquired the freehold from a public sector authority which remains liable to carry out works or services, and (b) the conveyance enables the authority to recover service charges from the purchaser. Section 181 provides for disputes to be decided by a county court. Section 47 of the Housing Act 1985 is the section which provides for reasonableness of the (freehold) service charges in three ways. It starts:

'(1) Relevant costs shall be taken into account in determining the amount of a service charge payable for a period –

(a)   only to the extent that they are reasonably incurred, and

(b)   where they are incurred on the provision of services or the carrying out of works, only if the services or works are of a reasonable standard;

and the amount payable shall be limited accordingly.

(2) Where the service charge is payable before the relevant costs are incurred, no greater amount than is reasonable is so payable, and after the relevant costs have been incurred any necessary adjustments shall be made by payment, reduction of subsequent charges or otherwise.'

(Section 47(1) and (2).) This section refers to 'the payer' and other sections refer to 'the payer' and 'the payee', rather than to the tenant and the landlord, but, of course, these provisions relate to freeholds. In s 47(3) there is a provision somewhat like s 27A(6) of the Landlord and Tenant Act 1985 (see at **9.209**) making void provisions for deciding particular aspects of reasonableness other than by arbitration. The effect is very similar but the wording is set out in a varied way. Section 47(4) (added by the Housing and Planning Act 1986, s 24(1)(i) and Sch 5) specifically requires money paid by way of two different types of grant (for works of improvement, repair or conversion) to be deducted from the service charge costs. A somewhat similar provision was added to the Landlord and Tenant Act 1985 as s 20A. (See at **9.127**.)

10.78   Section 48 of the Housing Act is commented on below, but in the meantime it is worth pointing out that, very significantly, the Housing Act does not, for freeholds, follow s 20 of the Landlord and Tenant Act, which requires the landlord to provide estimates and consult about major works (see at **9.56** et seq). Those provisions will apply to right to buy leases (which will be long leases), but not to the freehold equivalent. The Housing Act also does not include equivalents for freehold or leasehold right to buy of s 20B (the 18-month time limit), or s 20C (under which a tenant could apply to court for an order that costs incurred should be disregarded). (See at **9.130** and **9.142**.)

Section 48 of the Housing Act 1985

Information as to relevant costs of freehold service charges

10.79   This section, under which the tenant who exercises the right to buy a freehold ('the payer') can call for a summary of costs, has a certain amount in common with the current version of the equivalent section in the Landlord and Tenant Act 1985. (Section 21 of the 1985 Act; see at **9.149**.) The Housing Act provision permits a purchaser to require a summary of costs. The period to be covered is the last 12 months or the last complete financial year. (Housing Act 1985, s 48(1).) The Housing Act requires the landlord to respond with the summary by the later of one month from the request or six months from the end of the accounting period covered by the statement. (Housing Act 1985, s 48(2).) The statement itself is much less tightly controlled in the Housing Act than in the original Landlord and

Tenant Act equivalent. Apart from stating whether grants have been or are to be paid for works of improvement, repair or conversion (which must be deducted from the costs under s 47(4)), the summary has only to 'set out those costs in a way showing how they are or will be reflected in demands for service charges'. The summary must be certified by a qualified accountant as 'in his opinion a fair summary complying with this requirement', and 'being sufficiently supported by accounts, receipts and other documents which have been produced to him'. Section 51 (see at **10.85** below) shows who can give the certificate. Each Housing Act summary has to be certified by a qualified accountant: for private tenants this only applies where there are more than four tenants.

10.80 The Housing Act continues (s 48(4)) by giving a brief right to the purchaser, within six months of receipt of the summary, to inspect accounts, receipts etc and to take copies. These are to be made available for a period of two months beginning one month after the request for inspection. The Housing Act does not mention the cost of taking copies or of making the accounts etc available for inspection. (Housing Act 1985, s 48(4); compare s 22 of the Landlord and Tenant Act 1985, Chapter 9, at **9.170**.) The Housing Act permits the request for either a summary or for inspection to be served on the person who receives the service charge: that person is to pass on the request to the 'payee'. The section ends with a provision that disposing of the dwelling does not invalidate the requests, but there is no obligation to provide the summary or permit inspection more than once for the same house and for the same period. These provisions are slightly different to the Landlord and Tenant Act provisions. (Section 24 of the Landlord and Tenant Act 1985, at **9.185**.)

10.81 In considering the above simplified provisions it must be remembered that local authorities and other such public bodies are already under considerable statutory obligations to account for money passing through their hands. It is likely that most public landlords have the information for a summary readily to hand, and the obligation to provide a summary on request should therefore not be too onerous.

10.82 The Housing Act provisions do not now contemplate the involvement of a superior landlord, as the Landlord and Tenant Act 1985 does. Section 49 had such provisions, but they were repealed by the Landlord and Tenant Act 1987 (Sch 4, para 5) and tenants of public sector landlords can rely on s 23 of the Landlord and Tenant Act 1985 (see at **9.178**).

Section 50 of the Housing Act 1985

Criminal liability and public sector landlords

10.83 This short section provides for a fine, not exceeding level 4 on the standard scale (currently £2,500: s 17(1), Criminal Justice Act 1991) if 'a person fails without reasonable excuse' to comply with s 48. Section 48 of the Housing Act 1985 is the section covering the provision of a summary of costs and the right of inspection. Section 50 continues by saying that this does not apply where the payee is a local authority, a new town corporation or the Development Board for Rural Wales. Since these are presumably the majority of landlords affected by the Act, it is a significant exclusion.

The effect

10.84   The effect seems to be:

(a)   for those vendors who are not local authorities etc (eg Housing Associations), a fine can be imposed under s 50 for breach of the provisions;

(b)   local authorities, new town corporations and the Development Board for Rural Wales are not liable to a fine for breach of s 48, which covers free-holds created after exercise of the right to buy;

(c)   under s 26 of the Landlord and Tenant Act 1985 local authorities etc as landlords of tenants holding long leases are liable to comply with ss 18 to 24, but are not liable to a fine for breach of those sections; and

(d)   also under s 26 of the Landlord and Tenant Act 1985, local authorities as landlords of tenants who do not hold long leases are not liable to comply with ss 18 to 24 of the Landlord and Tenant Act 1985.

Section 51 of the Housing Act 1985

Qualified accountants for s 48 of the Housing Act 1985

10.85   This section is somewhat similar to s 28 of the Landlord and Tenant Act 1985 (see at **9.211**) other than using references to payer and payee. The change is needed because s 48 refers to freeholds not leaseholds. The section defines who is entitled to certify the summary of costs under s 48(3) of the Housing Act 1985. Such a person is one who is eligible for appointment as a company auditor and who is not disqualified by being associated with the landlord. However, s 51(6) says that members of the Chartered Institute of Public Finance and Accountancy are qualified, and being an employee of the payee does not disqualify a person where the payee is a local authority, new town corporation or the Development Board for Rural Wales. This contrasts strongly with s 28 of the Landlord and Tenant Act 1985 for most tenants, which makes it clear that being associated with the landlord always disqualifies a person from being able to give a certificate.

Section 125 of the Housing Act 1985

Counter notice by landlord when the tenant exercises the right to buy

10.86   This section sets out the information a landlord has to put in its counter-notice when a right to buy tenant has served notice exercising the right to buy.

The counter notice has to be given by the authority within eight weeks for a freehold and 12 weeks for a leasehold. The purpose of the counter notice is to give financial details of how much the tenant has to pay and what discount he is entitled to. The main point for service charge purposes is s 125(4). This provides that:

> '(4) where the notice states provisions which would enable the landlord to recover from the tenant –
>
> (a) service charges, or
>
> (b) improvement contributions
>
> the notice shall also contain the estimates and other information required by s 125A (service charges) or 125B (improvement contributions).'

Section 125(4A) is also interesting: it requires details to be given of 'any structural defects known to the landlord affecting the dwelling-house or the building in which it is situated or any other building over which the tenant will have rights under the conveyance or lease'. This could, of course, affect future repair and maintenance costs, and is helpful information for a tenant in deciding whether to proceed with the right to buy or not. The section is varied in circumstances concerning extension of the right to buy and preservation of that right. Details are in the Housing (Extension of Right to Buy) Orders 1987 and 1983, and Housing (Preservation of Right to Buy) Regulations 1989 and 1993. These are called below the 'Extension Orders' and the 'Preservation Regulations'.

Section 125A of the Housing Act 1985

Estimates and information about service charges

10.87   This section is the crucial section for service charge purposes. It does not mirror or in any way reflect any statutory provisions affecting tenants of private landlords. The important point is that the landlord is obliged to give a tenant exercising the right to buy an estimate of service charges for each of the following five years, and the aggregate figure. This enables the tenant, when considering the offer to buy, to do so with full knowledge of material financial commitments for a reasonably full period in the future. In cases where the Extension Orders apply, s 125A is modified and ss 125(2) and (3) are omitted. Section 125 is also modified where the Preservation Regulations apply.

10.88   The section provides (s 125A(1)) that the landlord's notice in respect of a house is to include 'the landlord's estimate of the average annual amount (at current prices) which would be payable in respect of each head of charge in the reference period (under s 125C the reference period is effectively five years from the date of the conveyance of the house or the lease of a flat) and ... the aggregate of those estimated amounts'. Where the premises are a flat there is slightly different information (s 125A(2)).

10.89 For a flat the landlord's notice has to include the estimates of service charges and repairs '(including works for the making good of structural defects)' mentioned in s 125A(3), and a statement of the effect of para 16B of Sch 6 (see at **10.93** below), as well as information concerning a loan for service charge purposes. Section 125A(3) sets out the estimates which are to be for works 'in respect of which the landlord considers that costs may be incurred in the reference period'. The reference period is, in effect, five years (see at **10.88** above). Where the Extension Orders affect the purchase, s 125B does not apply. The estimates which have to be given for flats are:

'(a) for works itemised in the notice, estimates of the amount (at current prices) of the likely cost of, and of the tenant's likely contribution in respect of each item, and the aggregate amounts of the costs and contributions, and

(b) for works not so itemised, an estimate of the average annual amount (at current prices) which the landlord considers is likely to be payable by the tenant.'

10.90 The effect of the above for both flats and houses is that the tenant intending to buy a freehold or take a lease has to be given information, based on current figures, of the maximum service charge costs for the next five years. The position is improved even more from the point of view of the tenant of a flat by para 16B of Sch 6 to the Housing Act 1985, which provides that the tenant's liability for service charges is restricted. The tenant is 'not required to pay in respect of works itemised in the estimates contained in the landlord's notice under section 125 any more than the amount shown as his estimated contribution in respect of that item, together with an allowance for inflation'. There is a muddled but similar provision (Sch 6 paras 16B (2) and (3)), where the landlord has given an average figure for service charge costs rather than itemised figures. Paragraph 16B shows how the initial period for the calculations is worked out, on the assumption that the service charge year is unlikely to be the same as the date on which the lease is granted, which is the trigger date for the five-year period.

10.91 Paragraph 16 of Sch 6 to the Housing Act 1985 is varied in some cases. Additional paras 16D and 16E apply when the Preservation Regulations apply. Paragraph 16D gives the Secretary of State the right to create regulations calculating the inflation allowance, and para 16E covers a formula to restrict the tenant's contribution to service charges and improvements in the case of an acquisition on rent to mortgage terms.

10.92 The Court of Appeal considered a right to buy purchase in *Sheffield City Council v Jackson* [1998] 3 All ER 260. The notice to the tenants/proposed purchasers made it clear there were arrears of service charge owing. The court held that the tenant could not challenge the arrears after completing the freehold purchase. This was in part because the price was assessed on the information in the notice, and further in part as the court did not see how a tenant could be released from his covenant to pay service charge and at the same time affirm the remainder of the transaction.

Section 125B of the Housing Act 1985

Contributions to improvements re flats

10.93   As well as giving service charge forecasts as outlined in the previous section, the landlord's counter notice to the tenant's right to buy request has to include information concerning improvements in the case of flats, but not houses. (This section does not apply in the circumstances specified in the Extension Orders.) The information is similar to that for service charges under s 125A, namely the landlord must give itemised estimates of those works for which the landlord considers improvements may be made within the five-year 'reference period'. The estimates have to give details of the works and the likely cost (at current prices) and the tenant's likely contribution for each item and the aggregate of those costs. The notice must also refer the tenant to para 16C of Sch 6 and the statement therein. The latter paragraph is somewhat different to the equivalent for service charges. (Paragraph 16B of Sch 6: see at **10.90**.) Paragraph 16C(2) of Sch 6 says that the tenant 'is not required to make any payment in respect of works for which no estimate was given in the landlord's notice under section 125'. Therefore, if the landlord's notice fails to mention improvements at all, the tenant has no obligation to pay for any improvements carried out within the first five years. Sub-para (3) says that the tenant 'is not required to pay in respect of works for which an estimate was given in that notice any more than the amount shown as his estimated contribution in respect of that item together with an allowance for inflation'. Paragraph 16C(4) sets out the position for improvements in the initial period of the lease and the period prior to the grant of the lease etc.

10.94   Flats are often in a building where improvements to one part may be material to the remainder. In the case of houses the likelihood of parties other than the occupier needing to consider improvements to which the occupier is to contribute is smaller, although as the purchaser of the freehold is only affected where he is to pay service charges the point could arise.

10.95   The 1980 equivalent of the above provisions were material in the case of *Sutton (Hastoe) Housing Association v Williams* [1988] 1 EGLR 56 (see also at **5.202**) where the landlords sought to recover the cost of replacement windows from the tenants, some of whom were reluctant to pay. The windows had been mentioned in Part III of Schedule 6 to the lease, which set out anticipated repairs and improvements for the succeeding ten-year period. (The 1980 provisions did not refer to improvements, but the Court of Appeal commented that repair and improvement are 'not mutually exclusive'.) The landlords were entitled to recover the costs during the relevant reference period.

Criticism

10.96   These provisions are a fascinating extension of the service charge statutory provisions, and restrictions on tenants' liabilities. The main point is, perhaps, that they arise in limited circumstances, ie only when a tenant exercises a right to buy, and are therefore not applicable for general use. The landlord needs to rely on his advisers for estimates of what is needed for houses and flats, and what might be wanted by way of improvements for flats.

10.97   The separate reference to improvements is interesting. Improvements were only brought into the general definition of service charges for tenants of private landlords by the Commonhold Act of 2002. It can be hard to distinguish between repairs and improvements, and where something needs to be replaced an element of improvement can appear because of newer methods of manufacture etc. Having to cover both types of items ensures that the tenant is fully informed, and cannot be caught out by unexpected expenses where, for example, the landlord genuinely considers the items to be improvements rather than repair and, without the need to mention improvements, would not have specified them. There was some doubt in the *Sutton (Hastoe)* case (at **10.95** above) whether the replacement of the windows was repair or improvement (single glazed windows were being replaced with double glazed windows) but it was held that the terms were not mutually exclusive.

10.98   A five-year period gives the tenant a very good period to start the new arrangements with reasonable certainty of his outgoings. A longer period would be even harder for the authority to assess with any reasonable degree of accuracy. From the point of view of the landlord the difficulty is to cover the unexpected items. This means that the landlord must be as sure as possible that the estimated figures, or the specified items, are the only ones that are going to be needed, and it would surely not be unfair also to include a normal and reasonable figure for contingencies. As the landlord has restricted ability to recover the costs during the five-year period, it can, of course, leave repairs and improvements to be carried out until after that period has expired.

10.99   A tenant who is taking a lease from a private landlord can try to negotiate a limitation on his liability for the first few years of the lease in similar terms (a service charge cap). Depending on the state of the property market and the relative negotiating strengths of the parties such a provision could be a real boon to the ingoing tenant. Provided the landlord has reasonable faith in his managing agents and a good five- or ten-year plan he may feel able to agree, although he would be well advised to put in some qualification for unexpected expenses, eg where a roof which is expected to last 15 years needs major repairs within five years. The big difficulty is really to gauge trends in costs – will they be up or down? The Act puts a compulsory service charge cap on the amount recoverable by a public sector landlord, who may not be particularly willing.

Section 125C of the Housing Act 1985

'The reference period'

10.100   This section defines the reference period during which the service charges and charges for improvements in right to buy cases are frozen, subject only to inflation. The period begins on 'such date not more than six months after the notice is given as the landlord may reasonably specify as being a date by which the conveyance will have been made or the lease granted'. The reference period ends 'five years after that date, or where the notice specifies that the conveyance or lease will provide for a service charge or improvement to be calculated by reference to a specified annual period, with the end of the fifth such period beginning after that date'. (Section 125C(1) and (2) of the Housing Act 1985.)

Section 450 of the Housing Act 1985

Loans for service charges

10.101 The three parts of s 450 contain rights relating to loans for repairs or improvements of flats. Improvements were added by Sch 9 to the Commonhold and Leasehold Reform Act 2002. Under the first part (s 450A), the Secretary of State can make regulations to permit a tenant who has exercised his right to buy the lease of a flat (the right does not apply to a freehold purchase) and whose landlord is the housing authority who granted the lease or another housing authority, to call for a loan towards service charge costs or improvements payable during the first ten years of the lease. Section 450(2); regulations are in the Housing (Service Charge Loans) Regulations 1992. The regulations can cover the amount of the intended loan by relation to a maximum or minimum amount. The regulations can also allow for the service charge to be left outstanding. The loan is only in relation to service charges for repairs or improvements (ie not other services such as cleaning, lighting or gardening), whether the repairs were to the flat or the building or any other building. The reference to service charges for repairs to the flat seems at first sight rather odd, but is presumably intended to apply to those repairs to the flat itself (such as external maintenance) which the landlord carries out and charges to the tenant. Under s 450A(6) 'repairs' is specifically defined to include 'works for making good a structural defect'. Section 450(6) also says that 'housing authority' for the purposes of s 450A 'includes any registered housing association other than a co-operative housing association, and any unregistered housing association which is a co-operative housing association'. Sections 450B and 450C relate to loans for other purposes and supplementary provisions.

Housing Act 1985, Sch 6

Terms of leases after exercise of right to buy

10.102 Paragraphs 16A and 16B of Sch 6 (see at **10.90** et seq above) concern the limit on service charges payable for a five-year period. For the purposes of this book those provisions are the most significant parts of Sch 6.

10.103 Schedule 6 covers matters to be included in the Conveyance or lease following the exercise of the right to buy. Paragraphs 1 to 7 cover both freeholds and leaseholds, while paras 8-10 cover conveyances of freeholds. Part III of Sch 6 (paras 11-19) contains other provisions which have a bearing on service charges affecting leases, in those cases where a right to buy tenant has to take a long lease rather than a freehold. Paragraph 12 says the lease is to be for 125 years (or five days less than the landlord's leasehold interest if that is less) and under para 11 the rent is not to exceed £10 per year. (Although the landlord can grant leases to expire at the same time as other similar leases granted after 8 August 1980.) Paragraph 13 provides that the lease of a flat must grant the same rights the tenant enjoyed before exercising the right to buy, unless the parties agree otherwise.

10.104 Apart from paras 16B and 16C (see at **10.90** and **10.93** above), the crucial paragraphs for service charges are paras 14 and 15. In para 14 (affecting flats only) are implied obligations on the landlord 'to keep in repair the structure and exterior of the dwelling house and of the building in which it is situated (including drains, gutters and external pipes) and to make good any defects affecting that structure'. In addition there is an implied covenant by the landlord 'to maintain any other property over or in respect of which the tenant has rights by virtue of this schedule'. Services provided are to be 'maintained at a reasonable level' and the landlord is 'to keep in repair any installation connected with the provision of those services'. (Paragraph 14(2) of Sch 6.) There is a right for a county court to make an order excluding or modifying these implied covenants 'if it appears to the court that it is reasonable to do so'. (Paragraph 14(4); this is the only case in service charge law where contracting out is possible, and, of course, only applies for public sector landlords in these limited circumstances.) No guidance is given, but no doubt the probable life of the building would be among the material factors. Apart from the obligation to freeze service charges to the estimated amount for five years, this (limited) right to contract out of some obligations is perhaps the most important difference between the ordinary service charge statutory arrangements set out in Chapter 9 and the 'right to buy' service charge provisions set out in this part of this Chapter. The implied covenants are helpful, as they clarify the obligation of the landlord in respect of major items, and in the absence of a contracting-out order the landlord will not be able to seek to change its repairing obligations.

10.105 Finally, para 15 applies where the landlord itself holds a leasehold interest. It implies a covenant by the landlord to pay the head rent and observe the head lease covenants save to the extent that the tenant is liable to do so. There is also provision under which in effect the landlord agrees to use its 'best endeavours' to ensure that the superior landlord complies with its obligations.

10.106 *Coventry City Council v Cole* [1994] 1 All ER 997 discusses payments by tenants in the context of right to buy leases in useful detail. It is discussed in detail at **8.23**.

PART 5 – RIGHTS ONLY FOR RECOGNISED TENANTS' ASSOCIATIONS

Section 84 and Schedule 4 of the Housing Act 1996

10.107 The 1996 introduced a new right which is largely a mixture of rights granted before, but, in this case, is only given to recognised tenants' associations as defined in s 29 of the Landlord and Tenant Act 1985. (See at **9.214** et seq.) At first sight it hardly seems to need statutory authority for them to appoint a surveyor to advise themselves, but by the appointment the surveyor is given statutory rights to inspect vouchers etc, and, more importantly, to inspect common parts of the building, and to have his rights enforced by court order.

10.108 Section 84 of the Housing Act 1996 gives a recognised tenants' association ('RTA') the right to appoint a surveyor 'to advise on any matters relating to, or which may give rise to, service charges payable to a landlord by one or more members of the association'. This phraseology covers charges that have been made and also where a charge is anticipated. It also suggests the RTA can exercise the rights even if only one of its members is affected by the issue.

10.109 The surveyor has to be a 'qualified surveyor', who has to have the same qualifications as the person qualified to carry out a management audit under s 78(4) of the Leasehold Reform, Housing and Urban Development Act 1993. (See at **10.15** and **10.22** above.) The point of s 84 is to give the surveyor the powers contained in Sch 4 to the Act.

10.110 The RTA has to notify the landlord of the appointment and thereupon the powers come into play. The notice (s 84(3)) has to tell the landlord who the surveyor is, and also 'the duration of his appointment and the matters in respect of which he is appointed'. The RTA can notify the landlord that the appointment has ended, and this could either indicate the end of the job, or allow the RTA to appoint a new surveyor.

10.111 Schedule 4 sets out the powers of the surveyor. He has a right to appoint people to assist him. This could cover, for example, structural engineers, or mechanical and electrical engineers, or similar professionals.

10.112 Paragraph 3 of the Schedule gives the surveyor the right to require the landlord to afford the surveyor 'reasonable facilities for inspecting any documents sight of which is reasonably required by him for the purposes of his functions', and for taking copies. The landlord is required to respond to the request within only one week, either agreeing or giving reasons why he objects to doing so. Under para 5(1) the surveyor can call for a court order to enforce the right of inspection if the landlord has not complied within one month of the request.

10.113 The appointed surveyor has the major right under para 4 of Sch 4 to 'inspect any common parts comprised in the relevant premises or any appurtenant property'. There are definitions (para 4(2)) of areas the inspection can cover, but these are basically those areas over which management functions are discharged. Again, the right is exercised by notice and again, on default, the surveyor can seek a court order. In this case the court order can be requested if access is not permitted 'within a reasonable period', and the court can 'make an order requiring the landlord to do so on such date as is specified in the order'. (Paragraph 5(2).) Inspection of the common parts was first introduced in the management audit provisions of the Leasehold Reform, Housing and Urban Development Act 1993. (See above, at **10.15**.) The 1993 right only applies to qualifying tenants holding long leases, and the 1996 right only applies where there is a recognised tenants' association. The major difference is the 1996 ability to enforce the right by court order.

10.114   None of the earlier provisions specifically confirm the right of the court to grant a mandatory injunction. Although criminal penalties are available in some cases for failure to comply this does not help the tenant who has suffered as a result of that failure: the right to enforce the provisions through the court is clearly most useful to a tenant. The application to court has to be within four months of the service by the surveyor of the notice requiring inspection of the paperwork or the building as the case may be. (Paragraph 5(3) of Sch 4 to the Housing Act 1996.)

10.115   The Schedule has consequential provisions where the reversion has been assigned and dealing with superior landlords. These are largely on the same lines as the earlier legislation.

Comment

10.116   The rights granted by the Housing Act 1996 are one of the best reasons for tenants to form a recognised tenants' association. The provisions are silent on cost and it would not seem that there is any right for the tenants to recover from the landlords the cost of appointing the surveyor. The 1985 Act creates various criminal offences, but the court orders envisaged by the 1996 Act could have a more direct benefit and impact for the tenants who are able to call on them. The provisions do not directly say what the result is if the summary or inspection reveals an unsatisfactory state of affairs. Perhaps there are too many possible permutations, but the RTA has to go through quite a few procedures to take advantage of this – first of all being formed, then appointing a surveyor, then the surveyor has to serve notice, and then if there is a default court proceedings are needed to enforce the right, all before the tenants are able to have direct benefit. The results of the inspections will, however, be useful evidence to enable the tenants to exercise any of the further remedies open to them after taking the above steps.

PART 6 – MISCELLANEOUS

Housing benefit

10.117   In *R v Beverley Borough Council Housing Benefits Review Board, ex p Hare* (1995) 27 HLR 637, it was decided that when comparing rent payable for suitable alternative accommodation under the Housing Benefit (General) Regulations 1971, regard should be had to service charges, so that, in effect, references to rent in reg 11 includes references to service charges. Regulation 10(1) permits payment of housing benefit to cover, inter alia, service charges. Benefit can be reduced if comparable rents are lower.

10.118 In *R v Housing Benefit Review Board for Swansea, ex parte Littler* (1998) Times, 9 September, it was held that the only service charges covered by the housing benefit were those related to the provision of adequate accommodation. It did not include counselling and similar support services.

The Unfair Contract Terms Act 1977

10.119 This Act does not apply to contracts for the creation or transfer of an interest in land (s 13), and *Electricity Supply Nominees Ltd v IAF Group plc* [1993] 3 All ER 372 confirms that the Act does not apply to leases. The 1993 case revolved around whether or not a provision excluding the tenant's right to set off was unfair, and thus ineffective under the 1977 Act. It was held that the Act, which only applies to exclusion clauses, does not apply to leases. There had previously been doubt about whether the Act could apply to leases if the actual creation of the lease could be severed from other (allegedly unsatisfactory) provisions that were in the nature of exclusion clauses. Accordingly, a tenant charged with service charges cannot rely on the 1977 Act to enable him to set off against the service charge any claim he might have against the landlord for breach of covenant by the landlord.

Unfair Terms in Consumer Contract Regulations 1999

10.120 Where they apply, the Unfair Terms in Consumer Contract Regulations 1999 ('the Regulations') cause 'unfair' terms not to bind the 'consumer'. (Compare the Unfair Contract Terms Act 1977 which, as stated above, only applies to exclusion clauses.) The Regulations apply to contracts between a seller and a 'consumer'. A consumer is a natural person (ie it cannot be a company) who, in contracts covered by the Regulations, is acting for purposes which are outside his trade, business or profession. The seller or supplier is someone, in such contracts, who is 'acting for purposes related to his trade, business or profession, whether publicly owned or privately owned'. The Law Commission Report, *Renting Homes* (November 2003) states in para 3.3 that the 1999 Regulations apply to 'tenancy agreements'. Accordingly, the Regulations apply to tenancy agreements where the landlord is letting in the course of his trade, and the tenant takes as an individual. For the purposes of this text, of course, the Regulations are only material if such a tenancy agreement includes service charge provisions. One suspects this would actually be rare. Where it does apply, the statutory protection of the Landlord and Tenant Act 1985 etc described in Chapter 9 would also apply. The Regulations in such a case would merely add another layer (regs 3 and 4).

10.121 A contract term which is not 'individually negotiated shall be regarded as unfair if contrary to the requirement of good faith, it causes a significant imbalance in the parties' rights and obligations arising under the contract to the detriment of the consumer'. A term is treated as not individually negotiated where it has been drafted in advance (eg 'our standard form') and 'the consumer has therefore not been able to influence the substance of the term'. This could give rise to the unsatisfactory possibility of a private tenant who simply accepts a printed form without advice being able to have unfair terms later treated as not binding on him, whereas his more cautious neighbour who had taken legal advice and negotiated his tenancy agreement separately, cannot do so! The protection is that the unfair term is not binding on the 'consumer'. The latter term is not, perhaps, a sensible alternative name for a tenant. The Law Commission Report mentioned above recommends, in para 4.20, that the Regulations are modified to make it clear they apply to all 'landlords and occupiers'. In addition, clauses are liable to be set aside if they are not written in 'plain intelligible language'. In case of doubt the term is to be construed in favour of the 'consumer'. (Regulations 7 and 8.)

10.122 The regulations (Sch 2) give details of items that are considered unfair. These include exclusion of liability for non-performance or inadequate performance, provisions entitling the supplier to terminate the agreement but not the consumer, rights to increase the price without the consumer being entitled to terminate, and provisions excluding the consumer's right to have disputes settled by the court or arbitration. It will be noted that these are virtually all matters that can appear in some form or other in many leases and can affect service charge arrangements. These provisions are much wider than the provisions of s 27A(6) of the Landlord and Tenant Act 1985 which, in effect, makes void provisions in the agreement setting out means of resolving service charge disputes other than by way of the courts, leasehold valuations tribunal or arbitration.

10.123 It remains to be seen how these Regulations will actually affect leases of non-business premises. Probably, very little so far as service charges are concerned, as residential tenants already have a huge raft of statutory protection in all sorts of ways, and not just those explored in Chapters 9 and 10 of this book. The Law Commission Report proposes that tenancies are to fall into two types, one somewhat similar to shorthold tenancies for private landlords and the other with security of tenure granted by social landlords. If their proposals come to pass tenancies for up to 21 years will be subject to consumer laws rather than property laws. If these proposals become law then there may be tenancies subject to service charges, perhaps for terms of between five and 20 years, to which the Unfair Terms in Consumer Contracts Regulations 1999 will apply. It is likely to be some years before this happens, but when it does, those considering such contracts will have to look at them through consumer protection eyes, rather than construing the documents under property law. This seems unsatisfactory. Property law is made for property transactions, and, for example, granting an underlease of part of a building with service charge provisions, concerns over use, alienation and rent reviews, is totally different to buying a pair of shoes. In the latter case only the retailer and the customer are involved – the example given the transaction not only impinges on quite a few parties (undertenant, intermediate landlord, superior landlord, possibly guarantors and/or management companies and/or mortgagees, as well as other tenants in the building), but it is an ongoing arrangement, not a single event.

Supply of Goods and Services Act 1982

10.124 This Act covers various aspects of services provided in the course of business. Under s 13 the skill and care employed in running services should be 'reasonable', and under s 14 any services to be provided should be provided within a reasonable time. Section 15 provides that where no price for a service is agreed in advance the charge made must be no more than is reasonable. However, the Court of Appeal in *Havenridge Ltd v Boston Dyers Ltd* [1994] 2 EGLR 73 said where the parties to a lease agree as to the allocation of risk and responsibilities between them it was 'unrealistic to describe the arrangement as 'the supply of services' by one party to the other'. The case turned on problems about insurance in a commercial matter, but the judge said that s 15 did not create an implied term in that case, and it would seem unlikely that there would be any real difference in this connection between service charges and insurance.

CHAPTER 11

The Codes of Practice

*There is more ado to interpret interpretation, than to interpret things; and
more books upon books than upon any other subject.*

Michel de Montaigne

PART I – INTRODUCTION

11.1   As this book keeps reiterating, there is a huge difference between residential and commercial property so far as service charges are concerned. This has give rise, inter alia, to two separate Codes of Practice. They are both excellent publications and are recommended as useful guides in the fields they address. They are relevant to service charges both directly, where they encourage practices that affect the amount of costs payable, and indirectly in encouraging working methods that can influence, explain and record those costs. The Residential Code currently contains out-of-date references, but presumably these will be revised shortly to take account of the changes to residential service charges introduced by the Commonhold and Leasehold Reform Act 2002 (eg on consultation, designated accounts etc) when these are all in force. In the meantime it is still a very useful tool. Both Codes are introduced below, and some interesting contrasts in the approach of the two are discussed. The Codes are too long to be included in the Appendix.

The Residential Code

11.2   The Residential Code is undated but was copyrighted in 1997, following publication of the Housing Act 1996, and was published by the Royal Institution of Chartered Surveyors. Its title is '"Service Charge" Residential Management Code' and it has been approved by the Secretary of State for England and Wales under s 87 of the Leasehold Reform, Housing and Urban Development Act 1993. (For s 87 see at **9.281** et seq.)

11.3   The Code is primarily directed at RICS members who manage residential property, and it gives detailed practical advice about how to deal with a range of matters. (It is the companion to a similar Code affecting management of residential property that does not have service charges.) The Foreword says it 'has been prepared in the hope that it will promote desirable practices in respect of the management of residential property'. It goes on the say that most of the Code is 'aimed directly at the Manager of residential property'. The Code does not apply, according to the Foreword, where the landlord is a public sector authority or a registered social landlord, but it does apply where a social landlord is an agent for a private sector owner.

11.4   The whole tenor of the Code is to assist the managing agent to manage in a reasonable, proper and methodical manner. It contains some useful marginal notes citing relevant statutory provisions. It covers many aspects of management, including in particular items relating to holding money which virtually amount to a 'designated account' procedure. (See proposed s 42A of the Landlord and Tenant Act 1987, at **9.260** et seq), as well as comments on managing agents' charges.

11.5   It defines service charges as in s 18 of the Landlord and Tenant Act 1985, although as it was printed before the Commonhold and Leasehold Reform Act 2002, it does not mention improvements in the definition. For the same reason it does not reflect the current consultation procedure or the requirement for designated accounts introduced by the 2002 Act, but not yet in force. There are limited provisions referring to improvements, although the Commercial Code covers this aspect extremely well.

11.6   The Foreword to the Code reminds readers that factors to be considered when making management decisions include 'the age and location of the property, the terms of occupation, the level of payment for services and the management fee'.

The Commercial Code

11.7   By contrast, the Commercial Code (which is for commercial premises, not just non-residential premises) sets out what is good practice, without including the detailed basic 'how to' information contained in the Residential Code. It concentrates on service charges, rather than management generally.

11.8   The Commercial Code is called *The RICS Code of Practice – Service Charges in Commercial Property*. It was published in June 2006 following work by a steering group representing various bodies concerned with property. They were The Royal Institution of Chartered Surveyors, British Retail Consortium, British Council for Offices, Property Managers Association, British Property Federation, and British Council for Shopping Centres. In addition, there was legal input. It was the third edition and is much more user friendly than the first (1996) one (which was much shorter and had no paragraph numbers or even page numbers, making any reference to contents laborious), although it is divided into parts A–E and the numbering of paragraphs in the Code itself (section C) could usefully have been shown as C1, C2 etc. This is done below, for clarity. The new edition, unlike its predecessors, does not say that individual clauses should not be interpreted in isolation, but should be read in context with the Guide as a whole.

11.9   It has the good standing of a guide produced on behalf of a group of major organisations in the field representing the viewpoints of landlords, tenants and property professionals. It talks of owners and occupiers rather than landlords and tenants. The Introduction (Part B) starts by saying:

> 'The recommendations contained in this Code represent the property industry's view of the most desirable structure for service charges, which will be appropriately implemented in new leases. Existing leases may contain service charge provisions which differ from the latest thinking within this Code. Where this is the case, existing service charge clauses will be interpreted as far as possible in line with the principles and practices as set out here, unless the lease specifically stipulates a different approach, which therefore has legal force.
>
> At lease renewal, leases will (as far as is permitted by law) be brought up to the standard as set out in this Code. Best practice requires owners and occupiers to ensure their advisers have done this. If it is required, both to meet best practice and in the interests of compatibility with other occupiers, that an occupier is required to pay for services not previously included in his or her lease, adjustment may be made to the rent to reflect this.'

11.10   The Code introduces the slogan 'not for profit, not for loss' to reflect the desired even-handed position as between landlord and tenants. The Introduction also says the steering group is considering business lease renewals under the Landlord and Tenant Act 1954 in the hope that by 'practice direction, pre and post action protocols or common practice, the norm will be to fully modernise leases at renewal in terms of full service charge clauses that allow for appropriate revision, and alternative dispute resolution (ADR) to the benefit of owners and occupiers alike'. The steering group is also consulting to see whether mezzanine floors distort service charge apportionments.

11.11   The Commercial Code also seeks to press for service charge accounts to use industry standard descriptions, to enable more accurate comparison of like for like, and it also recommends use of the RICS dispute resolution service.

11.12   The Commercial Code covers only commercial property and therefore it is not one that is required by statute to be officially approved. At the time of writing it has no statutory backing but it is authoritative evidence of what is accepted as good practice in relation to commercial service charges. The government has been threatening that if the separate Code of Practice for Commercial Leases in England and Wales (which does not deal with service charges) is not followed, then it may introduce legislation. The separate Code of Practice was introduced in an attempt to prevent a threatened government ban on upward-only rent reviews. It concentrates on the terms to be offered when leases of commercial premises are being negotiated. The government was concerned about upward-only rent reviews. The Reading University study of the effect of that Code showed that upward-only rent reviews were of less concern to tenants than restrictions on assignment and sub-letting. Some major property organisations have since indicated their intention to be more flexible on the latter point. It remains to be seen whether legislation on this or any other aspect of commercial leases will ensue. If legislation is brought in to deal with rent reviews or alienation for commercial property it may perhaps include provisions affecting service charges while the subject is under consideration. For example, it may suggest using the Commercial Code as evidence of good practice. Any legislation might also include provisions similar to some of those affecting residential premises, in particular an implication of reasonableness, an automatic trust of money received, rights to inspect vouchers and perhaps designated accounts. If such legislation is brought in and includes consultation provisions let us hope that it reflects more the original single version of s 20 of the Landlord and Tenant Act 1985, rather than the cumbersome five alternative schemes for consultation in the new regulations.

The two Codes

11.13   Part 2 of this chapter compares the two Codes in respect of service charges. As a matter of convenience, we will follow the order of the provisions in the Residential Code, and then mention those items that are either particularly noteworthy or exclusive to the Commercial Code.

PART 2 – COMPARING THE CODES

Preliminary

11.14   The aims of the two Codes are set out in the Forewords quoted above at **11.3** and **11.9**. The Residential Code commences with definitions which are not particularly critical. The Commercial Code also has a definitions section (Part A), which includes 'not for profit, not for loss,' as well as some technical terms used for comparing service charges in different locations, and 'rebranding' and 'refurbishing'.

Managing agents

11.15   As was mentioned in the introduction to this chapter the Residential Code is a guide for managing agents, particularly those who are members of the RICS. Paragraphs 2–4 cover in great detail aspects of the position of the managing agent. These include appointment and charges and his duties and conduct. For example, para 2.5 has sub-paras (a)–(o) outlining the normal duties of a manager, and para 2.6 has a similar number of subparagraphs on additional items that could be included in the agent's specification, possibly at an additional cost. The Residential Code (para 2.4) comments that fees for residential management are usually quoted per unit of accommodation rather than as a percentage of outgoings or income. Paragraph 2.7 says that insurance commission and all other sources of income to the managing agents arising out of the management should be declared to the landlord and, if requested, to the tenant. Commission is not mentioned in the Commercial Code, although several paragraphs (eg C64) of that Code indicate that interest earned on the service charge fund should be identified and credited to the account. Paragraphs 5.6(b), 5.10 and 11.9 of the Residential Code all say that interest belongs to the fund. The Commercial Code discusses management in paras C1–C8, recording that a duty of care is owed to occupiers and owners (C1), management should be monitored, and operated under 'sound management procedures' (C5). Management fees should be the 'reasonable price for the total cost of managing the services at the location'. (This appears under the heading Administration, leading to para C38.) It also says the management costs should not be limited to a percentage of expenditure. Management services should be 'regularly tendered or benchmarked against the market unless the parties are happy with the service benchmark'. (Paragraph C38.)

11.16 Because the Residential Code is aimed mainly at managing agents and RICS members the duties of the manager and his conduct are set out in considerable detail in paras 4.1–4.37. These emphasise the need to respond to tenants' queries 'promptly and suitably' (para 4.3). Best practice in communication is discussed in the Commercial Code in paras C9–C17. Paragraph C14 recommends owners and/or managing agents should hold regular meetings with occupiers. It also urges the occupiers to co-operate and, for example, recommends the parties give contact details (C14) and keep details up to date (C8).

Dispute resolution

11.17 The Residential Code has a few paras (4.27–4.29) on dispute resolution, and in para 11.5 records the tenants' right to apply to the Leasehold Valuation Tribunal before or after the event. Reference to the Leasehold Valuation Tribunal is not, of course, applicable to commercial property. The Commercial Code deals with dispute resolution in section D8, where it highlights what it sees as the benefits of Alternative Dispute Resolution over court proceedings. Perhaps not surprisingly, it recommends the RICS procedure, where there can be consensual mediation and expert determination. Paragraph C52 recommends that the tenant has a reasonable period (eg four months) from receiving the accounts in which to raise enquiries. In addition, it refers to PACT (Professional Arbitration on Court Terms) for seeking to agree lease terms on business lease renewal.

Accounts, rent deposits and rent

11.18 Paragraph 5 of the Residential Code is headed 'Accounting for Other Peoples Money'. It is largely advice and includes a section, for example on opening a client bank account. The suggestions in paras 5.6–5.8 are very similar to the arrangements for holding service charge money in a designated account under s 42A of the Landlord and Tenant Act 1987, introduced by the 2002 Commonhold Act, but not yet in force. (See at **9.260** et seq.) The Commercial Code, para C58, also recommends service charge payments, sinking funds replacement funds and reserve funds are kept in a separately identified account. Paragraphs C68–C70 discuss holding service charge money, emphasising that if there is to be an obligation on the landlord to hold the money in a separate account this should be clearly stated in the lease. The Commercial Code provides that the interest on the account should be credited to the account (C19 and C64). Paragraph 6 of the Residential Code relates to rent deposits and does not affect service charges, and rent deposits are not addressed in the Commercial Code.

Services

11.19   The Residential Code refers to services as in the original version of s 18 of the Landlord and Tenant Act 1985, thus not including improvements. By contrast, the Commercial Code has excellent provisions (C28 and C29) describing chargeable and non-chargeable services. Paragraph C28 says that service charge costs are to be 'restricted to charges and associated administration costs properly incurred by the owner in the operational management of the property. This will include reasonable costs of maintenance, repair and replacement (where beyond economic repair) of the fabric, plant, equipment and materials necessary for the property's operation'. Paragraph 29 usefully sets out items which the service charge costs 'will not' include. These are (briefly) initial costs of design and construction of fabric, plant or equipment; development setting up costs; 'improvement costs above the costs of normal maintenance, repair or replacement;' future redevelopment costs; costs which are matters between the owner and an individual occupier (such as enforcement costs for collection of rent, costs of letting units, consent for assignments, rent reviews, 'additional opening hours' etc), and costs arising from the failure/negligence of the manager or owner.

11.20   In para 8 of the Residential Code is a useful summary of the main statutory and similar obligations affecting the provision of services to dwellings. These include references to health and safety issues, environmental protection, water supplies, electricity equipment, statutory repairing obligations for dwellings in leases for up to seven years, etc. Obviously, these are not reflected in the Commercial Code. Paragraph 8.2 of the Residential Code says the managing agent 'should routinely monitor the cost effectiveness of contracts, aiming always to maintain services that provide value for money'. The Commercial Code reflects the same sentiment in para C32: 'The owner will procure quality service standards to ensure that value for money is achieved at all times.' Paragraph 8.4 of the Residential Code briefly refers to requests for new services, and cases where the service is no longer required. New services or plant are covered extremely well in section D2 to the Commercial Code. This covers improvements, replacement with enhancement, innovation and refurbishment. C30 also records that the costs of enhancement can be charged when it can be 'justified following the analysis of reasonable options and alternatives'. Consulting tenants over the choice of contractor for regular repairs is recommended in para 8.14 of the Residential Code, although this has been overtaken by the revised statutory obligations on a landlord introduced by the Commonhold Act. The Commercial Code suggests tendering and benchmarking and that the owner can use procurement specialists to achieve greater value for money (C31–C37), and section D2 deals with improvements and refurbishing of equipment. It does not suggest consulting tenants over the choice of contractors as such, although the Commercial Code does emphasise communication generally. The Residential Code says (para 8.15), that where accommodation is provided for staff or ancillary to the provision of the services 'any rent charged should be reasonable'. The Commercial Code, para C44, says the owner should bear a 'fair proportion of costs attributable to his or her use of the property' (eg where a centre management suite is used in part as the owners regional office).

Budgeting/estimating

11.21   This is discussed in detail in para 9 of the Residential Code. Much of it is advice to managing agents. The advice is fairly obvious and straightforward and para 9 includes mention of rights for tenants of dwellings to apply for the appointment of a manager, to apply to a Leasehold Valuation Tribunal if service charges are unreasonable, and to apply for lease variation (eg if payments in advance are not permitted in the lease). It says budgets should be prepared carefully and that it is better to 'estimate prudently and to include a contingency sum' (para 9.7). It also says (para 9.12) that tenants should be notified of significant departures from budget. Budgeting is mentioned in the Commercial Code, at paras C48–C51. This recommends (C48) providing the estimate one month before the start of the service charge year, and using standard descriptions of services, to assist comparison between different service charge centres (Section D7 and Appendix E1). Neither Code gives examples of a budget statement.

Reserve Funds and sinking funds

11.22   Paragraph 10 of the Residential Code discusses what it calls Reserve Funds, but which are actually a mixture of reserve and sinking funds. It is quite a useful summary. The Commercial Code, paras C58–C63, mentions sinking funds briefly. It gives a summary in section D6 (where it explains the difference between sinking funds and reserve funds) and indicates that sinking, reserve and depreciation funds are rare in commercial premises 'despite offering advantages … due mainly to the associated tax and administrative issues'.

Accounting for service charges

11.23   Paragraph 11 of the Residential Code is a detailed summary largely covering statutory matters affecting leases of dwellings. The comments about the rights of tenants to apply to a Leasehold Valuation Tribunal etc are repeated in paras 11.5–11.7. It repeats that money should be in a separate bank account (para 11.8) and that interest should be added to the account (para 11.9). It refers (paras 11.16–11.20) to the provisions of s 21 of the Landlord and Tenant Act 1985 under which a tenant can call for a summary of costs, although this section is

likely to be replaced in a different form. Paragraph 9 does not give any more particular comment about the accounts, but in Appendix V are some examples of
accounts. By contrast, the Commercial Code has very useful details about
preparing accounts (C49–C55) and it also has sections covering different examples. These are D5 (apportionment schedules); D7 (cost code analysis); E1
(industry standard cost headings); E2 (example of landlord's surveyor' service
charge certificate); E3 (example of service charge detailed expenditure report);
and E4 (example of service charge variance report).

Auditing

11.24   The Residential Code (para 12) briefly mentions auditing. Paragraph
12.1 says the accounts should be audited by a suitably qualified accountant
'unless the costs of the audit cannot be recovered'. There may at some time be a
statutory obligation on the landlord to provide audited accounts to the tenant of a
dwelling if the proposed changes to s 21 of the Landlord and Tenant Act 1985 in
the Commonhold and Leasehold Reform Act 2002 are brought into force.
(Currently a change to the primary legislation is being considered.) If legislation
requires the accounts to be audited, even for a single tenant, the cost of complying with that statutory obligation must be recoverable. Paragraph C53 of the
Commercial Code says that 'if the account is certified by an auditor, such costs
will be charged to the service charge account'. The following paragraph says that
if the occupier 'requests an independent audit, the owner will agree and the audit
fee will be charged to the occupier'. Paragraph C55 then refers to the case where
the lease requires the accounts to be 'independently' certified and (perhaps surprisingly) says that 'an appropriately qualified person from the owner or managing agent will issue the certificate', and the costs will be paid through the service
charge. It says that for transparency the 'status of the person issuing the certificate' should be made clear.

Contractors

11.25   Managing agents should pay attention to 'economy, efficiency, quality
of service and speed,' and in accordance with the landlord's instructions when
dealing with contractors (the Residential Code, para 13.1). The Code then goes
on to refer to the original consultation procedure that has been replaced by the
Commonhold Act. The Code proposes choosing suitable contractors (para 13.4),
defining their duties, and monitoring their actions (para 13.5). The managing
agent should require all contactors to comply with health and safety legislation,
and to have public liability insurance (paras 13.6 and 13.7). The paragraph also
advises only using contractors who have the appropriate tax exemption certificate, because otherwise tax has to be deducted from payments and the agent has
to account to the revenue (para 13.8). The Commercial Code covers dealing with
contractors in para C21, saying that contractors and suppliers 'will be required to
perform according to written performance standards,' and in para C22 saying
that performance should be regularly measured and reviewed against defined

performance standards. Section D1 gives helpful comments on 'performance contracts', which concentrate on setting out what is to be achieved rather than what is to be done. It does not refer to the need for tax exemption certificates.

Repairs

11.26 In the Residential Code, para 14 deals with aspects of repairs. It includes comments on various statutory obligations relating to different types of tenancy and consultation (based on the original version of s 20 of the Landlord and Tenant Act 1985) as well as comments on aspects of communication with the tenants. The latter is somewhat similar to the Commercial Code (C9 – C17). Planned maintenance is also mentioned in para 14.12 (and something similar in para C25 in the Commercial Code). The Residential Code comments on the standard of repair, a requirement for it to be 'cost effective,' and records that replacement sometimes is more cost effective than repair (14.13). The repair/replacement angle is clearly covered in section D2 of the Commercial Code, and instead of being cost effective the Commercial Code says 'the aim is to achieve value for money and effective services rather than lowest price' (C24).

Development works

11.27 The Residential Code is concerned (para 15) to ensure that new construction works cause as little disruption to the tenant as possible. It recommends consultation with tenants about details of the programme. This is somewhat similar to C17 in the Commercial Code. Paragraph 15.3 reminds the agent to consider re-apportioning the service charge percentages after new works: in the Commercial Code, section D4 talks about apportionment and says 'best practice requires regular reviews to be undertaken to ensure that the apportionment matrix remains fair given any changes to the occupation or use of the property'. In other words it suggests that where there are changes it may be appropriate to reconsider the method of apportionment, and not just the percentages, to achieve fairness.

Insurance

11.28 Paragraph 16 of the Residential Code deals with insurance. It largely covers practical advice on arranging insurance to reflect the lease terms, and some aspects of insurance claims. It mentions the statutory provisions in the Schedule to the Landlord and Tenant Act 1985, which have since been slightly amended by the Commonhold Act. Paragraph 16.14 discusses the excess on a policy – that part of the amount claimed that the insured person has to pay. It points out that as the insurance would cost more if there was no excess then the amount of the excess should be charged to the service charge account, except where the claim arises from the negligence of the tenant, in which case the agent should consider whether the excess could be recovered from the negligent tenant. The Commercial Code does not deal with insurance.

Information, residents' associations, consultation and disputes

11.29 Paragraphs 17–21 of the Residential Code cover the above. None of them specifically relates to service charges and they are largely advice and comment on the statutory provisions. The Commercial Code does not cover these items, except in respect of communication (paras C9 to C17).

Arrears, termination and renewal of tenancies

11.30 Paragraphs 22–24 of the Residential Code deal with these issues. Again the paragraphs are largely general advice and comment on statute. Arrears and termination are not discussed in the Commercial Code, but there is a section (D8) on dispute resolution which, inter alia, highlights the RICS dispute resolution service, and the PACT scheme (Professional Arbitration on Court Terms). PACT aims to assist lease renewals under the Landlord and Tenant Act 1985.

Appendices to the Residential Code

11.31 The Residential Code ends with Additional Advice and a Further Note to RICS members. Before those end pieces are some Appendices as follows:

Appendix 1 – Lease Variations Details of the Landlord and Tenant Act 1987 rights (see Chapter 10).

Appendix 11 – Statutory Rights of Leaseholders/Tenants This outlines the rights of appointment of a manager, acquisition of the landlord's interest, and rights of first refusal on sale of a block of flats (all in Landlord and Tenant Act 1987 as they then stood), and rights to a management audit, rights to enfranchise and rights to new leases of dwellings (Leasehold Reform Housing and Urban Development Act 1993). It does not mention Right to Manage, which was introduced by the Commonhold Act.

Appendix 111 – Regulations, Health and Safety Codes and Guidance Documents A useful summary of the major regulations extant in 1997, but with a warning that the list is not complete!

Appendix 1V – Tenancies without implied obligations to repair.

Appendix V – Example of a Summary of Costs under s 21 of the Landlord and Tenant Act 1985.

[As all the above apply only to residential property they have no equivalent in the Commercial Code.]

The Commercial Code – other items

11.32   Many of the items in the Residential Code are covered in a different fashion in the Commercial Code as recorded above. The following are items in the Commercial Code which are either not in the Residential Code or are worth recording for other reasons.

Performance contracts

11.33   The emphasis on arranging performance contracts criteria, rather than a specification of what is to be done (paras C21–C22 and section D1) is very interesting and is not mentioned in the Residential Code.

Value for money and transparency

11.34   Paragraphs C31–C37 concentrate on value for money, supplemented by C18 to C20 pressing the need for transparency, such as having separate bank accounts. Paragraph C18 mentions service charges reserved as rent, but seems to miss the point about the reason for doing so.

Service charge costs

11.35   Paragraphs C28–C 29 (quoted at **11.19** above) are a really good summary of what service charges should include and what they should not. In addition, there is a good section (D2) which deals with (a) initial provision, improvement and refurbishment of equipment, (b) improvement to existing equipment, (c) replacement with enhancement, (d) innovation and (e) refurbishment, coupled with an obligation to consult on improvements. It says the owner should provide the facts and figures to justify the expense of improvements.

Communications

11.36   There is considerable concentration on the benefits and need for consultation between owners and occupiers, notably in paras C9 to C17.

Promotions

11.37   Promotional budgets usually affect mostly retail centres and leisure parks. Paragraphs C77 to C82 of the Commercial Code say the costs should be shared between owner and occupier (it recommends 50:50 sharing in C77), and that promotions should be subject to prior consultation, monitoring and review. It also says pedestrian flow data should be collected and issued to all owners and occupiers as a matter of course (C80). This subject is not material for residential premises.

Income

11.38   Paragraphs C83 to C86 and section D3 deal with income from such sources as vending machines, selling recyclable waste, promotional space, children's rides etc. The Code says there should be a clear statement of policy on how such income is allocated, although it is not clear if this should be in the lease or in the accounts. If the provision of a service involves expenditure which is debited to the service charge account the income should be paid to it, and income from promotions should be credited to a marketing expenditure budget. If the landlord is to keep the income from some activity on the common parts the Code (C85) seeks to have a sum representing a suitable proportion of service charges credited to the service charge account. This is an aspect that does not usually affect residential premises, and the Residential Code does not deal with it.

Apportionment

11.39   Paragraphs C41–C47 of the Commercial Code are useful comments on the apportionment of service charges, and section D4 is an excellent summary of the usual methods of apportionment, including an example of weighting. Appendix E3 gives examples of schedules where different costs are applicable to different premises. The Residential Code does not deal with apportionment.

Budget/accounts

11.40   The Commercial Code gives greater detail of what accounts should cover (C48–C51) and there are detailed examples of a certificate, an expenditure report and a service charge variance report in sections E2–E4. One area that is new, and not reflected in the Residential Code, is an emphasis on trying to achieve standard descriptions of chargeable items to enable meaningful comparisons to be made with other service charge centres (sections D7 and E1), and the section on Transparency following C17. The author would urge lease draftsmen to be careful of simply using standard wording – the lease should fit the property, not simply a standard list of possible chargeable items. Descriptions used in accounts are of course a different matter.

Sinking funds

11.41   These are the subject of C58–C63, and with a good summary in section D6. Although not legally necessary for commercial property, the Code (C58) recommends the sinking fund is held in an 'interest-bearing account, held in trust for the occupiers, and separate from the owner's own monies'. It also (C62) says the budget and year end accounts should 'state clearly contributions to and expenditure from the sinking fund account together with the account opening and closing balances and the amount of interest earned and tax paid in the relevant period'. In addition, it points out that on a sale (of the reversion, although it only mentions a sale) the sinking fund money and accrued interest should be passed to the purchaser (C63). The Residential Code covers sinking funds in para 10, but not in the same way.

Lease renewal and dispute resolution

11.42   There is considerable emphasis in the notes in the Commercial Code trying to ensure that on lease renewal the leases are amended to reflect best practice as in the Code. It recognises that this is not easily done, but seems to be trying to encourage standardisation of service charge conditions in leases, and the use of 'industry standard cost headings'. In addition, it is pressing for more use of the RICS dispute resolution service to settle disputes.

Appendices to the Commercial Code

11.43   Some of the sections at the end of the Commercial Code have already been mentioned: the full list is as follows:

D Technical support

Section D1 – Performance contacts.

Section D2 – Initial provision, improvement and refurbishment of equipment

Section D3 – Treatment of non-core income

Section D4 – Common methods of apportionment

Section D5 – Apportionment schedules

Section D6 – Sinking and reserve funds

Section D7 – Cost code analysis

Section D8 – Dispute resolution

Section D9 – Management charges

E Appendices

E1 – Industry standard cost headings

E2 – Example of landlord's surveyor's service charge certificate

E3 – Example of service charge detailed expenditure report

E4 – Example of service charge variance report

Conclusion

11.44   Let us repeat our welcome for the two Codes. They are both excellent in their different approaches. The Residential Code is much wider in range, as it

includes most aspects of management, but clearly highlights the numerous obligations affecting residential premises created by statute as they were before the
Commonhold Act changes. It is aimed in particular at those involved in management of residential premises although its use as a general guide for landlords,
tenants and their advisers is much greater. By contrast, the Commercial Code is
much more specific to service charges alone, and it does not need to comment on
statutory aspects because there are virtually none.

11.45   Subject to being aware that quite a few of the major statutory provisions
have been replaced (as indicated in Chapters 9 and 10) the Residential Code will
give an extremely helpful and detailed approach to anyone wanting to be
involved in management of a residential leasehold property, or just looking for a
good guide to good practice. The practical tips about the way to deal with management matters are good. There have been recent reports of major firms of
agents withdrawing from residential management because the complications
make management less attractive financially. There are also some companies,
new to the field, who use call centres for management purposes. It is hard to see
this as satisfactory. Such call centres are likely to be a long way away, covering
lots of premises. Accordingly, a phone call is likely to be taken by someone who
does not know the property, making explaining the problem accurately difficult.
As the call centre will not know details of the property and will have to pass the
problem on to someone local to deal with, there would seem plenty of scope for
crossed wires and delay. Management of residential property is full of pitfalls
and the Code gives very great help in highlighting the complex requirements in
different circumstances.

11.46   The approach of the Commercial Code is totally different. Obviously, it
does not at present need to deal with statutory requirements, as there are none,
and it is thus able to concentrate on a few areas of difficulty for commercial
service charges. It deals very well with such matters as improvements, what
should be included in accounts, and methods of apportionment. It deals with a
smaller number of topics in greater detail.

11.47   Both Codes emphasise value for money, recommendations for obtaining
estimates on a regular basis, and consultation. They both have useful pointers to
items that should be included in accounts. The Residential Code is of course
available for any landlord, tenant or manager as evidence of what is or is not
good management. This is because it is officially approved under a statutory
power.

11.48   Should a tenant negotiating a commercial lease seek to require the landlord to comply with the Commercial Code? The answer is probably 'yes,' but the
landlord should be very wary of agreeing, and only prepared to agree if he is satisfied he will be complying with the Code in full. He should also restrict any
covenant to complying with the Commercial Code in its form at the date of the
lease, ie not committing himself to future codes containing different provisions.
A landlord who has any doubt should refuse to give any warranty or covenant to
that effect, or make any representation himself or through his solicitors or agents,

because a warranty or representation can give rise to a claim for damages if the landlord fails to comply. (See eg *Connswater Properties Ltd v Wilson* (1986) 16 CSW 928.) The position would obviously change if the government brings in legislation on commercial leases that includes some reference to a code. In such a case, and depending on how such legislation is worded, the landlord may need to consider whether he should specifically provide that he is not obliged to abide by such a code if he is entitled to do so.

11.49   For either residential or commercial premises, it is suggested that, if the lease requires matters to be dealt with in accordance with 'good estate management', the provisions of the relevant code could be used as evidence. This is clearly the case with residential premises as the Residential Code has been approved under s 87 of the Leasehold Reform Housing and Urban Development Act 1993. For commercial property if the landlord and tenant disagree whether something done or omitted is good estate management or not, then the Commercial Code should be available as authoritative evidence on the point.

11.50   There may well be pressure (from managing agents) over the next few years for commercial leases to be standardised so far as service charge provisions are concerned, to reflect the views of the Commercial Code, either initially or on renewal. Lawyers must be careful of simply including items because the Code recommends particular forms of words. The lease needs to reflect the property and the management strategy of the landlord or his managing agents, and drafting should not be driven simply by a desire for uniformity, or because it may seem easier. Leases are individual deeds for individual premises.

CHAPTER 12

Management companies and similar bodies

The world is disgracefully managed, One hardly knows to whom to complain.

R Firbank

PART I – GENERAL

12.1   This chapter discusses some aspects of those companies that can be material for service charge purposes. Most of the points apply primarily to companies formed in relation to residential blocks, but there is no reason why the same principles should not be considered when dealing with an office block or other entity where there are many tenants with the same interests and who, between them, are liable to maintain the block. Perhaps more common on the commercial front is the management company formed by tenants to hold and manage common parts, such as roadways on industrial estates and retail parks.

12.2   In many residential blocks the landlords have sold the flats to individuals at a premium and a nominal rent: once they have received the premium the landlord has less interest in the block and its maintenance than before. The tenants are concerned about the premises in which they live and for which they often have a long lease that may be their principal asset. By contrast, offices are usually let at full rents where there are rent reviews, often to business organisations whose main concern is running their own business. At the end of the term of a business lease the landlord will want to let again but will rarely be able to obtain a premium. For retail or industrial parks occasionally the common access road (or sometimes a common service yard or car park) is transferred to a company, the members of which are the owners, or sometimes lessees, of the premises that have the right to use those areas.

The usual schemes

12.3   There are a number of possibilities:

(a)   *Tenants buy freehold* When all the units (flats or offices) have been let the landlord may be prepared to consider letting the tenants between them buy the freehold. The tenants would thus have both control and also the obligation for maintenance. The advantage to the tenants is that they can decide to carry out maintenance at a standard, pace, and time to suit themselves,

355

rather than being bound by the landlord's timetable. In such a case the tenants will often form a company to acquire the freehold and the tenants will become shareholders and/or directors. This is very rare for non-residential property.

(b) *Tenants to hold common parts* In some residential premises the landlord lets the flats on leases at a premium and has then transferred merely the common parts, eg stairs, corridors, and lifts, to a management company run by the tenants, with the landlord keeping the freehold of the flats himself. The transfer of common parts to the management company would normally be by way of lease, as transfers of part of freeholds currently give rise to problems of enforceability of positive covenants, which notably include repairing covenants, see eg *Rhone v Stephens* [1994] 2 AC 310. This scheme is less satisfactory for a number of reasons, but is more attractive to some landlords who prefer to remain landlord of the profitable part of the property, namely the flats. The tenants (again) would become shareholders/directors of the common parts company. The same type of scheme can apply to accesses etc for industrial or retail areas.

(c) *Intermediate lease* A third possibility is for the landlord to retain the freehold of the site but to grant to a management company an intermediate head lease, ie a lease interposed between the freehold and the occupational leases of the individual flats. The management company could be either run by the tenants themselves or by a third party. The management company is then the immediate landlord of the occupying tenants. Such a company is responsible to the freeholder for payment of the rent payable under its own lease (the head lease), which is commonly an amount similar to the total of the rents payable for the individual flats. The management company is similarly responsible to the tenants for maintenance of the building and collection of rents of the flats and the service charge. The landlord is thus free of the direct obligation for maintenance. It has been mentioned elsewhere (at **3.78**) that the tenants should insist that the landlord accepts a liability to repair if the management company fails to do so, as there is no obligation on the landlord to repair unless he has covenanted to do so and only has one rent to collect – a much more satisfactory and simple affair from his point of view than having to recover smaller sums from separate tenants. (*Alton House Holdings Ltd v Calflane (Management) Ltd* [1987] 2 EGLR 52.) There is an exception where the landlord has a statutory repairing obligation under s 11 of the Landlord and Tenant Act 1985, but the latter only applies to leases granted for seven years or less and so does not affect long leases of flats where the question of management companies is most likely to arise. The landlord/freeholder is also protected from shortfalls where flats are vacant or individual tenants default unless the head lease rent is geared to match the rents actually received.

(d) *Freehold of block of flats acquired by tenants under statute* In addition to 'normal' blocks of flats, there are cases where the freehold is acquired by the tenants either under the right of first refusal given by Pt 1 of the Landlord and Tenant Act 1987, or by enfranchisement (acquiring the

356

freehold compulsorily) under the Leasehold Reform, Housing and Urban Development Act 1993. The position will then be similar to that outlined at (a) above.

(e) *Commonhold* At present it is not possible for tenants to compel a change from leasehold to commonhold. However, when a commonhold is set up the effect is somewhat similar to the case of tenants buying the freehold, to the extent that the owners of the units are automatically entitled to be members of the Commonhold Association, which is the company responsible for management, but which is not a landlord. Commonhold is discussed in Chapter 17.

(f) *Joint ownership* For the sake of good order, readers are reminded that, in addition to management companies, it is perfectly possible and sensible to provide for the freehold or intermediate leasehold to be held by up to four individuals (or companies) as joint tenants. This is the most practical and cheapest arrangement where the premises are a small block of up to four flats (or a house divided into up to four flats), and can work well for up to say seven or eight flats where the tenants are prepared to agree to four of their number acting as trustees on behalf of them all. The legal title is held by the trustees jointly and there need to be suitable provisions to ensure that if one sells his flat the new owner will be substituted as a trustee in place of the selling tenant. These arrangements can fall down where tenants die or become insolvent. The above alternatives are no longer available where the tenants of flats exercise the right of collective enfranchisement. The purchase now has to be by an 'RTE Company', rather than by a 'nominated purchaser' as before.

(g) *Maintenance trustee* In the above cases the landlord transfers a legal interest to the tenants. There is another method, which is arranging for maintenance by a company other than the landlord which is usually known as the maintenance trustee route. In that case the landlord grants a lease to the tenant and provides that the maintenance will be carried out not by himself but by a separate company. The maintenance trustee is not given a legal estate, and often simply has the right to collect service charges and to hold the receipts on trust to carry out repairs. It has no further rights, and it is worth repeating that if there is no express obligation on the landlord to carry out maintenance in default by the maintenance trustee no such obligation will be implied. (*Alton House Holdings Ltd v Calflane (Management) Ltd* [1987] 2 EGLR 52, see at **3.78** and **9.52**.) In maintenance trustee cases sometimes, but not always, the tenants are shareholders in the maintenance trustee company. In some other cases the maintenance trustee is an entirely independent company, although some are the landlord's creature.

12.4   An example of the way the trustee arrangement works appears, *Nell Gwynn House Maintenance Fund Trustees v Commissioners of Customs & Excise* [1994] EGCS 163 . In a large block of flats in Sloane Avenue, London SW3, some leases had been granted direct by the freeholder who then granted a lease of the remainder to the maintenance trustee. The maintenance trustee managed the block, being reimbursed costs by way of (1) direct contributions from the undertenants to whom it had granted leases (2) payments from tenants who had themselves underlet, and (3) payments from the landlord in respect of the flats it had let direct.

12.5 The Court of Appeal in *Adami v Lincoln Grange Management Ltd* [1998] 1 EGLR 58 decided a case where the maintenance trustee was in effect the landlord. The tenant was under an obligation to repair the flats and also to insure. Although the tenant should have insured, in practice the maintenance trustee did so. The building included a flat which suffered subsidence damage, but unfortunately the insurance company was in financial difficulties and was unable to meet the claim. The tenant repaired the damage and claimed from the maintenance trustee. It was held there was no implied covenant by the maintenance trustee to repair: it was only liable to lay out the money it actually received.

Getting the Memorandum and Articles right

12.6 In 1992 the Court of Appeal considered the case of a management company set up in relation to a freehold residential development in *Bratton Seymour Service Co Ltd v Oxborough* [1992] EGCS 28. On the development site near Wincanton the intention was for the 24 residential units to be sold to individuals with the common parts being transferred to a company formed to manage the common parts. The common parts were the drive, water supply and drainage ('the utilities'), and the gardens and grounds ('the amenities'). The conveyances to purchasers required the purchasers to contribute to the costs of the utilities. The utilities and the grounds were transferred to the management company, and the 24 shares were divided among the purchasers. The defendant, as owner of two shares, paid his contributions under the conveyances for the maintenance of the utilities. At a meeting of the management company it was agreed that the shareholders should pay £12 per month to the management company to fund its activities. The defendant paid for a while but became dissatisfied and thereafter only paid, as per his conveyance, towards the utilities. The company and the defendant sought declarations as to whether or not the defendant was obliged to contribute to the costs of the amenities. The lower court held that there must be a term implied in the Articles of Association of the management company that shareholders should contribute to the amenity costs because that was what the management company had been set up to do: the implication was needed for business efficacy. The Court of Appeal disagreed. In particular the Articles, once registered at Companies House, were binding on the company and its members (Companies Act 1985, s 14(1)) and were a public record open to inspection. A company could not alter its Articles (Companies Act 1985, s 16(2)) so as to impose an extra burden on a member who had not voted for the change. The effect was that, in the absence of an express provision requiring payment towards the amenity costs in either the conveyance or the Articles of Association, the purchaser/shareholder was under no legal liability to contribute. As usual the moral seems to be to ensure that the documents, whether they be the conveyance/lease or the Articles of Association, should say what is intended clearly and unambiguously.

Companies House Guidance

12.7   At this point it is worth quoting from the 'Notes for Guidance in respect of Flat Management and Similar Companies'. (CHN14 published by Companies House in March 1993; this does not seem to be published any more, but there is a lot of useful information on the Companies House website.) The notes apply to 'flat management companies owned by the tenants and other similar bodies, such as residents' and tenants' associations incorporated under the Companies Act'. After pointing out that if the company owns property and ceases to exist 'you could find that you cannot sell your flat', the Notes continue:

> 'If your company does not own property and simply collects money for repairs and maintenance and pays bills when they come, think about whether you need a company. Have a word with your solicitor or accountant. It may be that a less formal arrangement such as a residents' or tenants' association would serve you just as well without the responsibilities of a company.'

(See at **12.13** et seq as to various responsibilities and costs associated with companies. See at **12.3** (d) and (f) as to companies for collective enfranchisement.)

PART 2 – TYPES OF COMPANY

12.8   There are three types of company likely to be material for service charge properties. The first is a private company limited by shares, the second is a private company limited by guarantee, and the third is a private unlimited company. The fourth type of company is a public limited company, but it is unlikely that a management company would be a public limited company. Apart from any other consideration a public limited company needs an authorised share capital of at least £50,000 (Companies Act 1985, s 11 and, s 117).

12.9   The main differences between the three types of company mentioned above are:

(a)   The private company limited by shares is one where the liability of its members, ie the shareholders, is limited to the amount, if any, unpaid on the shares held by them. Thus shares are often described as '£1 fully paid ordinary shares', clarifying that the shareholder has no further direct liability for the debts of the company.

(b)   In the case of a company limited by guarantee the limit of liability of a member of the company is the amount which the members have agreed to contribute in the case of a winding up. The amount to be contributed has to be specified in the Memorandum, which is a document of record which can be inspected at Companies House (Companies Act 1985, s 2(4)). For collective enfranchisement of flats there is a special type of company limited by guarantee (see at **12.3**).

(c)   In the case of a private unlimited company, there is no limit to the members' liability. An unlimited company does not always have to file accounts and can thus be cheaper to run than either a limited company or one limited by guarantee, although the members of an unlimited company do not have the protection of limitation on their liability.

Points to watch out for in relation to companies

12.10   One major point is to ensure that the costs of keeping the company in existence are recoverable. These can include audit fees, and fees for filing annual returns. For example, in *Broadwater Court Management Co Ltd v Jackson-Mann* [1997] EGCS 145 leases of flats in Tunbridge Wells had been granted. The landlord then sold the freehold to the tenants, who formed a management company for the purpose. The Court of Appeal held the leases did not entitle the management company (the new landlord) to recover the audit fee and company registration fee. As the lease had been granted before the company was formed the absence of reference to such fees is not surprising. Apparently, the court did not see fit to allow recovery on the grounds of business efficacy (as the Court of Appeal did in *Embassy Court Residents' Association Ltd v Lipman* [1984] 2 EGLR 60, at **12.35** below; see also *Bratton Seymour Service Co Ltd v Oxborough* [1992] EGCS 28, at **12.6** above, where the Court of Appeal refused to imply a provision in the Memorandum and Articles.) The moral is to agree a variation to the leases when setting up such a company. If not, in cases where it applies, then the management company (ie the tenants) could seek an order for variation of the lease under the Landlord and Tenant Act 1987 (see at **10.2** et seq). Until such a variation was in place, the management company would either be in breach of the statutory obligations for keeping the company in existence or it would be (in practice) subsidised by some of the tenants.

12.11   Most of the companies used as management companies will be either limited companies or companies limited by guarantee which are 'shelf companies'. Specialist company formation agents form companies in advance like ready-made suits on shop racks, and those who want one buy the company from the agents. The company formation agents will have complied with all the practical formalities, and so, normally, the only matters for the new proprietors of the company to consider are the following (which the company formation agents will arrange on receipt of instructions):

(a)   changing the name (eg to Gordon Mansions (Management) Ltd);

(b)   ensuring that the Memorandum and Articles of Association are suitable for a management company (it may be necessary to pass resolutions to change the Memorandum and Articles: the agents know what is needed and are usually very helpful);

(c) those matters described below as legal requirements, being such matters as appointment of directors, shareholdings and voting rights.

12.12 As ever in matters affecting property, taxes need to be considered at various stages. When a landlord transfers an interest to a company, for example either the freehold or on the creation of a new lease, this will have tax consequences and these should be worked out in advance. Forming the company involves various fees. A further consideration is whether the company, when formed, needs to be registered for Value Added Tax purposes.

12.13 Aside from tax matters are those relating to the constitution of companies. Companies normally need at least one director and a secretary and must hold various meetings. The members of the company (normally leaseholders of the various flats) need to decide who shall be the directors, voting rights, and the proportions in which they should hold shares. In addition, and at least as importantly, most companies have a duty to file audited accounts, and even those which do not need to file audited accounts need to have accounts which are certified to supply to the members. There are various fees for filing, although the major expense may well be that for annual certification of accounts. There are penalties for failing to file annual returns and other notices in time, and many duties for directors. The position of director is one of responsibility backed by penal sanctions for failure, and so becoming a director is not something to be taken on lightly. (See, for example, the Company Directors Disqualification Act 1986 as to prohibition on bankrupts or other disqualified people acting as directors. In addition, there are many provisions in the Companies Act 1985 containing penalties for various unlawful acts by directors as well as potential penalties relating to service charges under ss 25 and 33 of the Landlord and Tenant Act 1985, as discussed at **9.186** et seq.)

12.14 A very critical point to remember is that if the formalities (notably filing annual returns) are not met, the company can be struck off the register of companies, leaving the position of the landlord and tenant very awkward.

PART 3 – PHYSICAL MANAGEMENT

12.15 Once the tenants acquire the freehold or superior leasehold interest they are likely to be responsible for management. It is important that they should recognise this at an early stage. At the initial meetings (eg, as soon as the decision is made to buy the freehold or form a company), the question of future management needs to be addressed. For larger blocks it is best to employ managing agents, although for the very small blocks the tenants may prefer to manage by themselves, particularly if some of the tenants have suitable surveying or building knowledge or skills, or other useful attributes, such as knowledge of accounts or even property law.

12.16 If tenants are enfranchising largely to control the repairs, the tenants will have management in mind, but the cost of necessary major repairs needs to be taken into account when budgeting for the acquisition. If the tenants would be liable to pay for specific necessary repairs through the service charge they will still have to pay for those repairs in some way: they may find themselves paying twice if they seek to force the landlord to carry out the repairs before the purchase – once through the service charge and once through a higher price for a building in better repair!

PART 4 – LEGAL MANAGEMENT

12.17   This heading is to remind readers that the tenants forming a company need to decide at an early stage the form of the legal arrangements for management. This normally involves consideration of the way to deal with voting rights, shareholding and the appropriate quorum for meetings.

Voting

12.18   The author's own preference is for voting to be on the basis of one vote per flat, although some people prefer voting to be based on either shareholding or on the percentage of service charge paid by the individual tenant. Under the author's preferred method, each flat has a similar vote, regardless of size or outgoings associated with it. Under other schemes the votes reflect the actual service charge percentages payable by tenants or the original capital value, as reflected in the number of shares issued. One hesitates to recommend either of those methods because they give a fair reflection of only a limited aspect of the management of a flat, whereas one vote per flat gives each flat owner an equal say. However, each of these ways is perfectly valid.

Shareholding and guarantees

12.19   The second aspect of legal management is shareholding for those companies that have shares. For companies limited by guarantee similar thought is needed for the amount to be guaranteed. (For RTE Companies it is £1.) Normally, each tenant will be required by his lease to hold a share or number of shares, and will be obliged to transfer the share or shares when assigning the lease of the flat. For sensible management it is most important that there should be such provisions. It is clearly unsatisfactory for such shares to be held by people other than the current tenants.

12.20   The amount of shares held can either be one per flat or they could reflect the amounts paid by the tenants, perhaps based on premiums paid for the leases or, in enfranchisement cases, based on proportions of contributions to the total purchase price for the freehold. Remember that shareholding proportions are significant for division of income (in some cases, this would include rent from tenants who did not participate) and of capital (eg if the premises are destroyed and if the insurance proceeds can pass to the shareholders, such as where the tenants own the freehold of property which cannot be rebuilt, or which all concerned decide not to rebuild.) The distribution has other hurdles, of course, such as satisfying mortgagees. In enfranchisement cases where a flat becomes vacant and the RTE Company is able to grant a new lease to a new tenant at a premium the latter can be distributed among the shareholders.

12.21 If shareholding is to reflect the premium paid the tenants should recognise that this fixes for the life of the lease a comparative value that may not reflect the value at a later date. For example, if two flats in a block were bought at the same time with flat A having a premium of £75,000 and flat B £85,000 it may be that the shareholdings would be, say 75 and 85 respectively. At the commencement such an apportionment would be reasonable, and it could be said that the shareholdings should reflect the original investment of the first tenant. However, in ten years time the original tenants may have assigned to new tenants. Tenants on purchasing will pay a price reflecting the perceived value at the time of purchase. If flat A was improved with double glazing, new kitchen fittings, central heating and fitted wardrobes, it might have increased in value despite being smaller, and the assignee might have paid £85,000. If, by contrast, flat B had been left untouched the price might only be £85,000 or even £82,000. Therefore, if the idea of apportioning the shares according to the original cost of the flat is followed, subsequent tenants may feel their proportion of the capital is not fair, because at a later date it does not bear the same proportion to total value as the price they paid bore to the total value of the block.

Directors

12.22 A company has to have directors. There is power in the Companies Act 1985, s 1(3A) to have a company with a single director but this is unlikely to be suitable for a management company, or indeed acceptable to the tenants. Being a director of a company running a block of flats can be a good way to make new friends, although it can also be a way to lose friends!

12.23 The tenants will need to decide who will be the directors and what is to be the quorum for their meetings. The number of flats is material for this, but whatever is decided should be as fair as possible. Where there are few flats it may be appropriate for all the tenants to be directors. The tenants will be running the show themselves. Except in those few cases where the landlord reserves the right to hold a share the tenants will be the only actors and the person sometimes seen as the villain (the previous landlord) will be off-stage. Finding tenants willing to act as directors can be a problem, but where a company is formed they are necessary.

12.24 Directors need to be aware of the obligations they have for accounting and calling meetings etc. Where a company is running smoothly informality can be suitable and indeed helpful. Where there are problems, or where there are a large number of tenants, the directors need to treat the directorship very seriously and to ensure that proper minutes are kept, and that all tenants entitled to notice of meetings are notified. For any company the legal formalities of filing notices, annual returns and audited accounts must be complied with. (There are numerous obligations on directors and secretaries under the Companies Act 1985 (as amended) which are outside the scope of this book. It is possible for companies to take out Directors and Officers Insurance to cover some possible claims.)

Directors' remuneration

12.25 In many cases tenants accept the post of director without payment and as a service to fellow tenants. There can be a great deal of work involved for the willing few, and other tenants should recognise this and be prepared, in suitable cases, to offer remuneration to the directors and, of course, the secretary. The lease and/or the Memorandum and Articles of Association should specifically permit payment of salaries to directors and the secretary. This is important where, for example on a large development, the tenants want to have an external professional such a surveyor, accountant or even a solicitor as a director.

Meetings

12.26 It is normally a requirement for a company to have an annual general meeting (ie once a year) at which all shareholders (in this case, all tenants) are entitled to attend and to question the directors as to pertinent matters. (Companies Act 1985, s 366.) Under s 366A (introduced by s 115(2) of the Companies Act 1989), a private company can dispense with the need for an annual general meeting. In some cases, no meetings will be needed except an annual general meeting and perhaps another to consider the auditor's report, but where there are major works to be carried out it is likely that the directors should consider more frequent meetings.

Warning to residential tenants becoming landlords

12.27 Whichever way the tenants of dwellings decide to manage the block, they must remember that the statutory provisions of the Landlord and Tenant 1985 etc (see Chapter 9) apply to them as landlord of the residential tenants. This is the case even where the tenants are the directors or shareholders of the company which is the landlord of those flats: for enfranchisement it applies to the RTE Company. This is particularly important to remember in respect of the consultation for major works which must still be given to all tenants (Landlord and Tenant Act 1985, s 20; see **9.82** et seq) and, in future, the obligation to use a designated account. (See proposed s 42A of the Landlord and Tenant Act 1987, at **9.260**.) A 1991 Report by The Department of the Environment entitled *The Landlord and Tenant Act 1987: Awareness, Experience and Impact* records that the requirement to comply with statutory provisions after acquiring the freehold is widely misunderstood by tenants.

12.28   Consultation is perhaps particularly important for those tenants who did not participate in the enfranchisement, but must be carried out for all the residential tenants, even those who are directors and shareholders of a management company. Failure to comply can make the amounts in question irrecoverable, and that is contrary to the interests of the company.

PART 5 – MANAGEMENT COMPANIES IN COURT

12.29   There follow some cases in which management companies were material parties, to show the nature of disputes that can arise and some matters of principle affecting them.

Cases on repair

12.30   *Alton House Holdings Ltd v Calflane (Management) Ltd* [1987] 2 EGLR 52 was a case which revolved around a slightly unusual set of leases of premises in London NW8 where there was a landlord, a tenant and a maintenance company. The maintenance company was separate from the landlord, but originally had the same directors and shareholders. The leases were drafted so that the landlord had no obligation to repair, and the maintenance company was only obliged to collect certain payments from tenants and apply the receipts in carrying out repairs. The landlord's premises included flats, garages and showrooms and later included a medical centre. The tenants of the flats and the offices were obliged to pay fixed percentages of expenditure estimated in advance and adjusted later in the usual way. The medical centre, however, had negotiated a fixed payment. After a while the payments from the tenants (including the limited contribution from the medical centre) became insufficient to cover the cost of necessary repairs in full. The tenants sought a declaration that there was an implied term (based on s 19 of the Landlord and Tenant Act 1985) that the landlord would make up any shortfall. This was rejected by the court. The judge said: 'There is no covenant by the maintenance company to do repairs at its own expense. In those circumstances, there being no obligation on the maintenance company to put its hand into its own coffers, there can be no implied covenant by the landlord to fill that coffer up again.' The maintenance company therefore could not look to the landlord for help. Anyone becoming a director or shareholder of such a company needs to check whether there may be this type of problem.

12.31   In *Holding and Management Ltd v Property Holding and Investment Trust plc* [1990] 1 All ER 938 (see at **5.193**), the relevant premises were a block of flats in London SW7. Substantial defects were discovered in the exterior walls. The tenants paid service charges to a maintenance trustee, on the same lines as in the *Alton House* case above, where the receipts were placed in a trust account to use for repair. Because of the extent of the damage various estimates were obtained for remedying the problem. The first scheme would have cost about £1m. A second scheme was prepared which would have cost about £500,000. The tenants put forward a third scheme that would have cost about £250,000, and during the court hearing a variation of the third scheme was agreed. The court held that the first scheme had been for work that, in effect, went beyond the scope of repair. The Court of Appeal agreed with the court below which disallowed the costs of engineers and legal fees relating to the first scheme for the period after the cost became known to the maintenance trustee. Therefore, the maintenance trustee company could not recover the costs from the tenants. The final issue in the case related to the costs to the maintenance trustee of the proceedings themselves. The maintenance trustee tried to recover those costs through the maintenance fund and failed. The maintenance trustee had adopted an adversarial course towards the tenants, and, although trustees are normally entitled to claim their costs from the trust fund, this type of case was not the same as those where a trust fund was kept on foot for the benefit of future beneficiaries. Similarly, in *Iperion Investments Corporation v Broadwalk House Residents Ltd* [1995] 2 EGLR 47, at **9.145** above, the landlord who was unable to obtain legal costs of action against a defaulting tenant via the service charge, was also a company owned by the tenants.

12.32 The moral is that where a maintenance trustee or other trustee company is used it should seek an indemnity from the landlord in respect of expenses that cannot be claimed from the tenants before accepting the position.

12.33 The third case is *Hafton Properties Ltd v Camp* [1994] 1 EGLR 6. The tenants of a block of flats in Thornton Heath, Surrey were concerned about repair. They held long leases at a low rent but with an obligation to pay a service charge to a management company. The management company was one in which each tenant was obliged, under his lease, to hold a share. The tenants said the management company had failed to carry out necessary repairs. Accordingly, they refused to pay and the landlords sought possession on the grounds of non-payment. Non-payment of rent was ground for forfeiture, but at the hearing it was realised that as the service charge had to be paid to the management company, not the landlord, the landlord could not claim for non-payment. In the lease the landlord was under no express obligation to repair. It was held that lack of repair by the management company was not a breach of the landlord's covenant for quiet enjoyment. The tenants sought to have a term implied that in such circumstances the landlord was obliged to carry out repairs if the management company did not. Again this claim failed. It was pointed out that the tenants could have applied to have a receiver appointed of the management company if thought fit.

12.34 Another case of interest is *Gordon v Selico Co Ltd* [1986] 1 EGLR 71, where a landlord and a maintenance trustee company in effect acted in a way that deceived a person intending to take a lease of a flat. Works (effectively covering up dry rot rather than removing it) were carried out by a builder at the request of the maintenance trustee, which was run by the same people as ran the landlord company. The landlord was held vicariously liable for the actions of the builder in these circumstances. There are further details of this case at **6.40**.

12.35   In *Embassy Court Residents' Association Ltd v Lipman* [1984] 2 EGLR 60, a tenant had a lease of a flat in London E18. The lease had been granted by a landlord who then granted an intermediate lease to the residents' association. The tenant was asked to pay a management fee and objected that this was not in his original lease. After argument the Court of Appeal held that to give business efficacy to the various transactions there should be implied in the leases to the individual tenants a term that the residents' association could properly incur expenditure to carry out the obligations imposed on it, and that expenditure could be recovered from the tenants. This went as far as entitling the residents' association to appoint managing agents and to charge to the tenants the management fee. The case was heard before those at **12.30** and **12.31**. While this case can assist as authority for the charging of management fees it may well be of limited authority in relation to more general aspects.

12.36   The landlord company, owned by the tenants, used an unusual way to obtain payment in the recent case of *Morshead Mansions Ltd v Mactra Properties Ltd* [2006] EWCA Civ 492, which could give assistance to some management companies where it applies. Here there were 104 flats and one lessee (Mactra) owned 23 of these. Each tenant held a share in the landlord company, and Mactra owned 25. There had been some problems between the landlord and Mactra over a period, and the landlord eventually commenced forfeiture proceedings. The latter were compromised with a consent order, which was to be in full and final settlement of all the claims. The order (inter alia) provided that the sum in question (nearly £180,000) could not be recovered from the tenant. However, the articles of association of the landlord company contained an article (article 16), that entitled the landlord, by resolution at a general meeting, to set up a recovery fund and levy contributions from the tenants. The landlord company passed a resolution under article 16 the day after the court decision. The resolution required Mactra to pay the contribution. Mactra said that this was a matter the consent order had settled. The judge disagreed, and on appeal the Court of Appeal also held the resolution entitled the landlord to recover the sum. The consent order had settled matters as between landlord and tenant: the resolution was between company and shareholder. Although there was some overlap between the position of the parties as landlord and tenant on the one hand, and as company and shareholder on the other, there were real differences. The order did not preclude claims as between company and shareholders. It was not possible to construe the consent order as precluding claims under a resolution that was passed later.

Miscellaneous

12.37   The decisions in *New Pinehurst Residents Association (Cambridge) Ltd v Silow* [1988] 1 EGLR 227, at **5.148** above and *Berrycroft Management Co Ltd v Sinclair Gardens Investments (Kensington) Ltd* [1997] 1 EGLR 47 (at **9.51**) also show aspects of the landlord, tenant, management company relationship.

Insolvency of management company

12.38   In *Re Cranley Mansions Ltd, Saigol v Goldstein* [1994] 1 WLR 1610 tenants owned the freehold of flats in London SW7 through a company. The company decided to carry out major works. One of the tenants (Mrs G) decided to appoint the same builders to carry out works for herself at the same time. Mrs G was to pay 19% of the cost of the main works as well as the whole of the cost of the works to her own flat. Inevitably problems arose. Mrs G claimed that the work had not been satisfactorily carried out and refused to pay. The effect was that the management company became insolvent. The case turned on technical interpretation of insolvency rules, in particular in regard to voting. Mrs G was held not entitled to vote in matters relating to the insolvency, as her claim was an unliquidated claim, but as the voluntary arrangement had been created by the votes of tenants who were entitled to vote the arrangement with creditors was allowed to stand. (The relevant provisions were s 6 of the Insolvency Act 1986 and r 1.17 of the Insolvency Rules 1986.)

12.39   This case illustrates a disadvantage of tenants owning the freehold. An insolvent management company would be unable to carry out its functions and thus necessary works and services would not be carried out. Presumably, the tenants could seek the appointment of a receiver and manager under the Landlord and Tenant Act 1987, or, (if they and the building qualify), the right to manage, but apart from being an admission of failure this course would inevitably add to the costs which one way or another would inevitably come from the pockets of the tenants.

Recognised Tenants' Associations

12.40   This is a brief reminder for the sake of completeness of a topic covered in Chapter 9 under ss 29 and 30B of the Landlord and Tenant Act 1985 (see at **9.214** and **9.226**). A recognised tenants' association is a group of tenants. The benefits include the right to be consulted about managing agents, and to have a management audit under the Leasehold Reform, Housing and Urban Development Act 1993.

12.41   They do not have to be companies, but they could be. Usually, they merely hold a watching brief for the tenants, and make representations on their behalf. As a contrast, most management companies have legal obligations to carry out services etc.

12.42   The Residential Code (see Chapter 11) has a useful section, para 18, on recognised tenant's associations, summarising the benefits, although the Commonhold and Leasehold Reform Act 2002 changes mean that some benefits mentioned in the Code, which were formerly only available to such associations, are now available to all tenants.

Comment

12.43   One prominent management surveyor has commented that management of a property is not the problem: the difficulty is the management of the people involved. Management companies often start with a group of enthusiasts who want to make things work. While they are still there, and assuming a reasonable level of competence, such management can work well. Problems can arise when (a) the original group of enthusiasts move out, or (b) there are personality clashes among the management company's directors and one or more tenants, either on a personal level or in respect of property matters, or (c) no-one is prepared to act as director.

12.44   This is really just a warning so that those considering forming a management company or asked to become directors of a management company are aware that it is not the solution to all problems. An old building with a leaking roof remains an old building with a leaking roof, whatever legal system of management is in place.

12.45   For commercial premises there is a different problem. Take a company with headquarters in London and branches all over the country. If there is a branch in Liverpool with a management company of which the main company is a shareholder, the actual management needs to be agreed. If the company has a property director and finance director working, normally, in London, and a branch manager in Liverpool, who should be representative of the company on the management company? If it is the branch manager in Liverpool he needs to have suitable authority. If he is given authority to agree expenditure up to £2,000 what happens if the management company wants to spend £10,000? Should the property director or the finance director be authorised to attend on such occasions? The latter would, one suspects, be unwilling to attend AGMs all over the country on what the head office may think of as small beer. It may be that the position will have to be reviewed annually. Each company will have to form its own plan of campaign, but the above points should be thought about.

CHAPTER 13

Apportionments on sale and surrender

We think in generalities, but we live in detail.

Alfred North Whitehead

STANDARD CONDITIONS

13.1   There are many options for apportioning service charges when properties are sold or a lease is surrendered. Apportionments should be considered when the heads of term are negotiated, and ideally, and certainly in the case of the sale of a reversion, an agreed basis of dealing with them notified to the solicitors to incorporate in the contact.

13.2   The most usual conditions used for straightforward contracts of single dwellings are the Standard Conditions of Sale, fourth edition. Standard Condition 6.3.5 of these deals with apportionments of service charges in a brief fashion. (See at **13.3**.) The National Conditions of Sale and the Law Society's Conditions of Sale, which have both been superseded by the Standard Conditions of Sale, had basically similar provisions. The main defect is that the condition is in very general terms and does not take account of different types of sale or of payment. The Standard Condition is the same regardless whether the sale is of a reversionary interest subject to multiple tenancies or the assignment of a single lease by an individual tenant. The condition also takes no account of whether the service charges are payable in advance or in arrear. In a case on apportionment on sale of a block of flats, *Laimond Property Investment Ltd v Arlington Park Mansions Ltd* [1989] 1 EGLR 208, Dillon LJ said: 'As I see it, sub-clause (5) of condition 6 of the National Conditions of Sale applies naturally to a sale by the lessee to an assign of the leasehold interest under a lease. It does not apply at all easily to a sale of the freehold reversion on leases under which service charges are payable.' In the event, the court's decision was that an express contractual term overrode the National Condition in question. (See at **13.23**.)

13.3   Standard Condition 6.3.5 requires the parties to make a provisional apportionment on completion, based on the 'best estimate available'. There is then to be a balancing payment following the finalisation of the figures. For service charges this means the year end adjustment. The adjusted figure is to be paid to whoever is entitled to it no more than ten working days after the final apportionment is made. The condition also provides for payment of interest if there is delay in paying the adjustment. Using this condition entails costs in professional time if the solicitors or the agents (or both) are required to open up their files, perhaps a year after the sale, to assess what had been charged and make the adjustment. Unless the amount is likely to be reasonably substantial there is a lot to be said for the parties agreeing to make an adjustment on completion without any requirement for another bite at the cherry later.

13.4 The Standard Commercial Property Conditions (2nd edn), condition 8.3.5, which is obviously more commonly used for commercial property and is more suitable where there is more than one property, is virtually the same. It goes on, specifically in relation to service charges, in condition 8.3.6, to say that where a lease requires a tenant to reimburse the landlord for expenditure on goods or services:

> '(a)   the buyer is to pay the seller the amount of any expenditure already incurred by the seller but not yet due from the tenant and in respect of which the seller provides the buyer with the information and vouchers required for its recovery from the tenant, and
>
> (b)   the seller is to credit the buyer with payments already recovered from the tenant but not yet incurred by the seller.'

These seem a very practical approach to service charges, and covers the position about whether payments are in advance or arrears by referring to sums 'not yet due from the tenant'. Conditions 8.3.7 and 8.3.8 have further provisions about apportionment, and 8.3.4 sensibly provides for apportionments of annual sums to be based on a 365-day year.

13.5 There are special conditions used for auctions, namely the Common Auction Conditions (1 May 2002). Condition 22 is specifically about service charges – the only one of the conditions with a specific reference to them, and it approaches the topic in a different way to the others, which is comprehensive and practical. It applies where a lot is sold subject to tenancies that include service charge provisions. It specifically says that no apportionment is to be made on completion for service charges. It goes on in condition 22.3 to provide that within two months of completion the seller must give the buyer a detailed service charge account for the service charge year current on the completion date. This is to show (a) payments on account received from each tenant, (b) service charge expenditure 'attributable to each tenancy', and (c) any irrecoverable service charge expenditure. Condition 22.4 says in respect of each tenancy if the service charge account shows payments on account exceed 'attributable service charge expenditure', the seller must pay the buyer the excess when it provides the service charge account. Where attributable expenditure exceeds the payments on account the buyer is to use reasonable endeavours to recover the shortfall from the tenant at the next reconciliation date, and pay the amount so recovered to the buyer within five business days of receipt of cleared funds. The author knows of one auctioneer who makes a standard change to the latter provision by omitting the obligation on the buyer to seek to recover the shortfall, and requiring the payment within ten business days of receipt of the service charge account. Condition 22.5 says that the seller must bear any irrecoverable service charge expenditure incurred before completion (apportioned to actual completion), and the buyer is to bear any incurred after the actual completion date. Adjustments are to be made again, within five business days of the seller providing the service charge account to the buyer. Sinking funds are covered by condition 22.6, which says that if the seller holds any reserve or sinking find on account of future service charge expenditure the seller must assign it, including accrued interest, to the buyer on completion, and the buyer must covenant with the seller to hold it in accordance with the terms of the tenancies and to indemnify the seller if it does not.

ALTERNATIVES

13.6 The following section sets out the alternative ways in which service charge apportionments can be treated in various types of transaction.

PART I – ASSIGNMENT OF A SINGLE LEASE

WHERE THE TENANT MAKES ADVANCE PAYMENTS

13.7 Using the Standard Condition unamended in the contract, the parties and their advisers will therefore need to do one apportionment on completion and another later.

Example I

Assume completion is on 15 November 2007 and the service charge year runs from 25 March to 24 March. The vendor has paid £1,100 in advance for each of the March, June and September quarters. After the year end the landlord notifies the purchaser that a further £270 is payable.

(1) ON COMPLETION
The vendor has already paid for the quarter up to 15.11.07 to 24.12.07 and will want to recover from the purchaser for the period after the completion date.

Calculation on completion
Service charge paid in advance –15.11.07 to 24.12.07
(40 days) at £9.04 per day –

Add to completion figure   £361.60

(2) AFTER THE YEAR END ADJUSTMENT
The figures show that the total service charge for the year should be £4,670, being £4,400 paid plus £270 shortfall. Apportioning this on a time basis the vendor should pay for the period 25.3.07 to 14.11.07 (204 days) and the

purchaser should pay for the period 15 November 2007 to 24 March 2008 (161 days). Using the above figures, the vendor should have paid £2,610.08 and the purchaser should have paid £2,059.92, a total of £4,670. The vendor had paid three quarters totalling £3,300 and had been given an allowance of £361.60, so his actual payment amounted to £3,300 less £361.60, namely £2,938.40. As recalculated, the vendor should only have paid £2,610.08 and therefore has to pay the purchaser a further £328.32 being the difference between what he had paid and what the adjustment shows.

The Law Society has published a recommended method of calculating apportionments. It seems very complicated. The following calculations are based on the way such apportionments are normally made, namely by taking the period in question as a fraction of the whole year. If the Law Society method or some other type of calculation is desired then that can be set out in the contract.

Calculation after year end adjustment

		£
Full year's service charge paid	4 at £1,100.00	4,400.00
Add year end balance payable		270.00
Full year's service charge		£4,670.00
Proportion of whole year payable by vendor	£4,670 for period 25.3.07 to 14.11.07 (204 days)	£2,610.08
Proportion payable by purchaser	£4,670 for period 15.11.07 to 24.3.08 (161 days)	£2,059.92
		4,670.00
Already paid by the vendor	(3 quarters at £1,100 each)	3,300.00
Less refund received from purchaser on completion		361.60
Vendor's net payment		2,938.40
Deduct proportion properly payable by vendor		2,610.08
Balance repayable to the vendor		£328.32
As a check it can be seen that the purchaser will have paid:		
December quarter		1,100.00
Year end adjustment		270.00
Apportionment on completion		361.60
Apportionment after year end		328.32
Total payable by the purchaser		£2,059.92

13.8   The second alternative is to apportion the service charge solely on the basis of the advance payments made paid by the tenant up to the completion date with no later adjustment. The calculation is based on the payments made in advance being apportioned by an allowance being given to the purchaser representing the number of days after the completion date for which the advance payment has been made. The line would be drawn at that point and the professionals could put their files away. In the above example only the first calculation would be made, and the purchaser would pay an additional £361.60 with the completion money and there would be no later adjustment. On relatively small figures, this is probably the most appropriate method.

13.9 The third method, and the one which is in the author's view the most satisfactory, is to base the apportionment on the payment made in advance adjusted by any further information that the managing agents can provide about actual expenses made, or to be made, up to the completion date, without a later adjustment. Using the above example (at **13.7**), the managing agents might be able to anticipate, from budget forecasts, that there would be a further £270 to pay. In that case, the final amount of the apportionment would have the same effect as both the original and adjusted figures at **13.7**.

Example 2

	£
PRIVATE Estimated amount payable for whole year	4,670.00
Estimated amount payable for whole year	4,670.00
Paid by the vendor – three quarters	3,300.00
Payable by the vendor – proportion from 25.3.07 to 14.11.07 (204 days)	2,610.08
Additional amount payable by the purchaser on completion	689.92

It will be noted that the apportionment requires the purchaser to pay £689.92 which is the total of the two figures (£328.32 and £361.60) which the apportionment in Example 1 above shows, but does it in a single calculation.

13.10 If the agents anticipated an increase at the year end of approximately £250 the calculation would be:

Example 3

	£
Service charge for the year 25.3.07 to 24.3.08	
Four instalments at £1,100	4,400.00
Add estimated adjustment	250.00
Total	4,650.00
Proportion payable by the vendor (204 days at £4,650 pa)	2,598.90
Actually paid (three quarters)	3,300.00
Less amount payable as above	2,598.90
Therefore deduction to be allowed to purchaser	£ 701.10

While this is a few pounds more than the result of an exact recalculation it would cost more in professional time to recalculate and write about than the amount concerned.

WHERE THERE ARE NO ADVANCE PAYMENTS

13.11 Where there has been no advance payment the purchaser will seek a reduction in the sale price equivalent to the proportion of service charge that the current tenant should have paid for the period from his last payment to the completion date.

ALTERNATIVES

13.12 The Standard Conditions could be used: this would require an apportionment based on an estimate followed by a later adjustment.

Example 4

As in 13.07 the tenant pays £1,100 per quarter for the service charge year which runs from 25.3.07 to 24.3.08. As the tenant pays in arrears by the completion date (15.11.07) the tenant will only have paid £2,200 representing the quarters due on 24.6.07 and 29.9.07. The apportionment on completion will therefore need to be a deduction from the total payable by the purchaser representing the period 29.9.07 to 15.11.07 (the completion date). This is the period for which the vendor is liable but has not paid.

Apportionment on completion

Proportion at £4,400.00 pa payable for the period 29.11.07 to 15.11.07 (48 days)	£578.63

(To be deducted from the completion money)

After the year end adjustment is made the figures are recalculated as follows:

Apportionment after year end

	£
(Assume an extra £270 is payable as well as the quarterly payments of £1,100).	
Total for the year	4,670.00
Paid by vendor –	
Two quarters	2,200.00
Allowance on completion	578.63
	2,778.63
Payable by the vendor 25.3.07 to 15.11.07 (204 days)	2,598.90
Amount overpaid and recoverable	179.73

13.13   Again, the second alternative is for the parties to agree to an apportionment based simply on the figures as at completion. In the above case the apportionment would simply mean that the purchaser would be given an allowance of £578.63 as shown in the first calculation. There would be no further apportionment. Again, in the case of relatively small figures this has a lot to recommend it.

13.14   The third alternative is to base the single apportionment to be made on completion on the managing agent's assessment of the probable service charge liability for the period up to the completion date with no further adjustment. This is similar to **13.9** but, as in the previous example, would have a single more accurate assessment.

Where there is a sinking fund

13.15   Both parties need to take account of the presence of a sinking fund or reserve fund when considering service charge apportionments. In a very buoyant market a tenant might ask the assignee to refund to him the amount the selling tenant has contributed to the fund. It is unlikely that a purchaser will be willing to do so, but it must be recognised as a possibility. If a refund of this nature is agreed the contract provisions must make this clear.

13.16   Since the money or assets representing the sinking fund are not held by the tenant there is no apportionment to be made when a lease is assigned, except in the extremely rare case of a purchaser refunding the vendor's contribution. The purchase, of course, is a suitable time to check the amount of the tenant's share of the sinking fund.

13.17   If the tenant who is assigning has been given a waiver from contributing to the sinking fund the landlord should check whether the waiver was on the basis that the tenant had to pay into the fund on assignment, and should give consent in such cases conditional on the payment to the fund being made (with interest if the waiver so provides). (See Part 12 of Chapter 7 (at **7.60** et seq) as to waivers for sinking funds.) A landlord, in addition, should check whether the waiver was personal to the named tenant: if it was then arrangements need to be made to ensure later service charge demands reflect the change.

Retentions

13.18   When there is an apportionment on completion with a later adjustment the parties should consider whether it is appropriate (a) for the purchaser to make a retention from the purchase money or (b) place some money on deposit towards the possible amount payable when the final figure is known. Such retentions or deposits are rare except where the amount is likely to be substantial. The important aspect is that after the completion takes place it could be difficult to contact the other party. The former tenant may leave the area after the assignment. The purchaser may well still be in possession when the year end adjustment is made, but sometimes purchasers are, for example, either UK companies or foreign companies, or trusts rather than the person who is to occupy the premises. A further aspect is the possible insolvency of the person who may be under an obligation to make a further payment. The permutations where one party or another could stand not to recover an apportionment in these circumstances are a particularly strong argument for seeking agreement in all straightforward cases for provisions whereby there is no adjustment after completion. One suspects that many parties forget the provisions of the contract where there is a requirement for later apportionment. That is another reason for agreeing a simple cut-off provision without a later recalculation. Any such provisions need to be included in the contract.

PART 2 – ASSIGNMENT OF THE REVERSION

13.19 Different considerations apply in the context of apportionments where the landlord is selling his interest. In that case the purchaser is concerned to ensure:

(a) That there are suitable apportionments of moneys paid out and moneys received.

(b) That the money received from tenants and any investments representing such money which constitutes the money needed for payment of future service charge works and services is transferred to the purchaser.

(c) That the records are handed over so that the new managing agents can manage the future service charge and resolve all the accounting problems for the year. This is a practical point rather than an apportionment matter. It is sometimes best to retain the same managing agents, at least until the end of the financial year.

(d) The contract should also contain provisions concerning the assignment (or not) of the benefit of maintenance contracts for cleaning, lift maintenance, gardening etc and, of course, as to dealing with any arrears outstanding at the date of completion. The parties in such cases need to consider whether the Transfer of Undertaking regulations (T'UPE') apply.

(e) A landlord assigning the reversion is entitled to seek a release from the tenants under the Landlord and Tenant (Covenants) Act 1995 (at **9.22**). This is done by notice, and should be considered particularly where there are a lot of tenants and substantial service charge obligations being passed to the assignee of the reversion, or the landlord is to insure.

(f) Any other provisions relevant to ensure smooth handover of management.

13.20 An aspect that applies on the sale of a reversion but not on assignment of an individual lease is the timing. There is a lot to be said for trying to arrange completion of a complex reversionary interest on the year end date, or at least on a day for payment of service charge contributions. This not only makes it much easier to cover apportionments but also assists in removing arguments about dealing with arrears because the debt is clearly related to a significant date.

13.21 Section 141 of the Law of Property Act 1925 contains provisions relevant to collection of arrears of rent etc from tenants under pre-1996 leases. In effect, s 141 provides that the arrears pass to the purchaser of the reversion and a former landlord cannot pursue a claim for those arrears unless he has the benefit assigned back to him by the purchaser. This was varied by s 30 of the Landlord and Tenant (Covenants) Act 1995 under which claims for arrears against former tenants of post-1995 leases are restricted to six months after the notice is given. (See at **9.9** et seq.)

13.22 The manner of dealing with VAT on apportioned figures also needs to be addressed. Basically for properties where the landlord has elected to waive the exemption (ie has decided to charge VAT) apportionments should relate to the net figure, and not the charge plus VAT. Where the landlord has not opted (and thus is not charging VAT), the figure to apportion is the gross figure.

13.23 The purchaser should seek a contract provision that the seller/landlord will not spend on service charge matters, between exchange of contracts and completion, any sum in excess of that disclosed in the planned maintenance programme previously agreed with the purchaser, or, alternatively, will not spend any sum for service charge expenses in excess of a specified amount without the purchaser's prior approval. This will avoid the risk of the purchaser having to find a larger sum for completion than he expected, after which he would have to face the wrath of the tenants when he seeks to collect! This would avoid the type of problem which arose in *Laimond Property Investment Ltd v Arlington Park Mansions Ltd* [1989] 1 EGLR 208. The contract for sale of a freehold block of flats at Chiswick incorporated the *National Conditions of Sale* (20th edn) but also contained express conditions re apportionments. After completion the purchasers were sent a bill for over £6,000 as costs of the landlord's surveyors for a survey and specifications of works needed to eliminate defects. The purchasers had not been given any intimation that such a bill was on its way. (National Condition 6(5), had it applied, would have required the purchasers to pay an adjustment after completion when the final figures were known.) In the event, the purchaser succeeded in its objection, but if the contract had required the vendor only to pay in accordance with an agreed budget this problem would not have arisen or the bill would have been disclosed earlier.

13.24 A further alternative is to prohibit any payments on services between exchange and completion, although this well could cause the landlord to be in breach of covenant with the tenants and thus cannot be recommended.

13.25 In *Linkproud Ltd v Ballard* [1997] 26 EG 156, a landlord sold the reversion of a house divided into flats, without the tenants having been given the right of first refusal under Pt 1 of the Landlord and Tenant Act 1987. The contract provided for the purchaser to pay the price of £2,100 plus about £6,400 arrears of rent and service charge. The tenants wanted to buy the freehold, and the Lands

Tribunal held that the price they had to pay was the total of the two above sums – the sale contract was a disposal of the freehold and the right to the arrears. A few years later, in *Castlegroom Ltd v Enoch* [2003] 2 EGLR 54, a county court judge held that the fact that the service charge had not been agreed or determined did not prevent the tenants from calling for the title. The outstanding balance would be subject to the vendor's lien under s 32(2)(a) of the Leasehold Reform, Housing and Urban Development Act 1993.

APPORTIONMENT ON SALE OF REVERSION

Where there are advance payments

13.26 Where there is full recovery of service charges by the landlord then all that is needed is for an account to be taken at the date of completion. The procedure in the Common Auction Conditions (at **13.5** above) is worth considering for such premises. This will show the amounts spent on service charge items to that date and the receipts by the tenants, and an addition or allowance can be made on completion based on that figure which will need no further adjustment.

Example 5

Assume the sale is not on a quarter day or year end, but is on 15 May, with the service charge year being from 1 January. The landlord has 100% recovery of all costs. The total receipts from the tenants by 15 May, being the advance payments for the quarter commencing 25 March, are £13,688.00. On the same date the payments actually made by the landlord on service charge expenses amount to £11,943.38. The landlord has therefore received £1,744.62 more than he has spent and should reduce the sale price by this sum accordingly.

	£
Amount received from tenants	13,688.00
Sums spent on services	11,943.83
Balance to be credited to purchaser	1,744.62

All receipts and payments after that date will be for the purchaser.

13.27 Where the landlord does not have full recovery of service charges from the tenants then the apportionment can be on a similar basis to that in **13.26** above, but the figures will need to include a notional sum representing the proportion of service charge costs that the landlord himself normally bears. This percentage (apportioned for the relevant period) will be included as if the landlord had made payment of that amount into the fund.

Example 6

Using the same dates and figures as at **13.26** above, we assume in addition that the landlord has to bear some of the costs (either because the specified percentages payable by tenants in the leases do not add up to 100% or because some expenditure is not recoverable):

(i) If the percentages do not add up then the calculation is simply mathematical – thus if the landlord has to find 6.3% of the outgoings the calculation should be as follows:

		£
Amount paid out		11,943.83
What the landlord contributes:	6.3% of £11,943.83	752.46
Add what the tenants contribute		13,688.00
Total assumed income		14,440.46
Deduct amount paid out		11,943.83
Net balance to be allowed to purchaser		2,496.63

(ii) If the imbalance is because some of the expenditure is not chargeable to tenants then the non-chargeable amount is simply deducted from the amount paid, and the landlord accounts to the purchaser for the difference.

	£
Amount paid out	11,943.83
Deduct cost of items not chargeable to tenants	2,629.50
Net balance to be charged to the tenants by the purchaser	9,314.33

Where the tenants do not pay in advance

13.28 The buyer needs to pay to the seller the amounts paid out on service charge expenses up to the date of completion, as it will be the purchaser who will recover the sums from the tenants in arrear.

Example 7

	£
Total expenses paid by landlord	11,943.83
Deduct payments by tenants on account	9,750.00
Net amount to be added to completion money payable by the purchaser	2,193.83

As at **13.23**, it is probably appropriate for a purchaser to seek to restrict the amount the seller can spend between exchange and completion to the amount of budget costs, or to a specified figure, except with the consent of the purchaser.

13.29 If the landlord is paid in arrear and is not entitled to recover the whole of his service charge expenses the provisions just mentioned will be inadequate. In addition to apportioning actual payments made on service charge expenditure the purchaser should seek to ensure that the completion figures reflect the percentage of the total costs that the landlord would have born for that period.

Example 8

Assume that the landlord has paid £11,943.83 and has received from tenants £9,750.00. Assume also that the landlord in practice is able to recover through the service charge 90% of the total of what he spends.

		£	£
Actual amount paid by the landlord			11,943.83
Less	(1) Amount received from tenants	9,750.00	
	(2) 10% of sums paid (which landlord would normally bear)	1,194.38	10,944.38
Balance to be added to the sum payable on completion			999.45

13.30   Occasionally, a property is sold with the 'benefit' of the right to collect arrears of rent, service charge or rentcharge which are 'sold' to the purchaser at a discounted rate. The discount obviously reflects the probability (or not) of recovery of the individual amounts. If this course is adopted the parties need to consider the value added tax element (if VAT is charged) in relation to the discount.

13.31   Where it is suggested that apportionments are estimated at completion with an adjustment later the parties should consider the practical risk involved. If the seller is likely to have to pay more in, say, ten months time, after the year end, will the seller still be traceable, or indeed in existence (a single asset company may be wound up) and solvent? The sale may have been because the seller is having to raise money. Doubt about the probability of recovery of a sum in the future is another good reason for seeking to avoid a two-stage apportionment. Alternatively, the parties could require retentions or deposits, depending on who is likely to have to pay more following the year end re-assessment. Where there is a lot at stake it may even be appropriate for both parties to deposit money in a joint account so that, whoever is liable to pay, the cash is available for the other.

Where there is a sinking fund

13.32   The contract for sale of the reversion should contain provisions for the sinking fund, or reserve fund, money to be transferred to the purchaser or the managing agents of the purchaser, together with any securities representing the fund. The parties will need to take careful tax advice about the effect of the sinking fund (eg, whether the transfer might trigger a tax liability such as inheritance tax) and the purchaser should seek detailed accounts showing all sums paid into the sinking fund and what payments have been made from it, as well as what proportion of the fund is notionally held for each of the tenants. The contract could usefully contain a provision requiring the purchaser to nominate the trustee(s) for the sinking fund where this is applicable, and it should contain an indemnity by the purchaser in favour of the seller against any future liability in respect of the sinking fund. The whole of the fund should be handed over: this is not a case for apportionment. The Common Auction Conditions provide the only Standard Conditions that address this issue (see at **13.5** above).

PART 3 – SURRENDER

13.33   The principles as to apportionment discussed above are material when a lease is surrendered. In respect of a surrender the apportionments are between landlord and tenant, rather than seller and buyer, but normally relate to one lease and thus the possible permutations are much as in Part 1 above. Depending on which party is most concerned to achieve the surrender, special terms relating to service charges may be negotiated.

13.34   If the service charge has been paid in advance, there could be an apportionment to the date of completion, either with no further adjustment or with an adjustment when the year end figures are known. The latter would need a binding obligation on the parties, preferably by deed, because the lease itself ceases to exist as a result of the surrender and the landlord often gives the tenant a specific release. The landlord should have the precise details of income and expenditure and so should be able to make an exact apportionment as at the date of surrender: if this is not possible for some reason, or the parties decide to require an adjustment later, then retentions and deposits may be applicable as in the case of the earlier examples. As in the case of assignment of a lease, apportionments by way of a single final payment on completion of the surrender are recommended, unless there are very good reasons otherwise (eg where a major expense has been incurred but for which the figures are uncertain). While not strictly material for the purposes of this book, readers are reminded that there are several points that need to be considered when dealing with a surrender. For example, surrenders by deed can involve payment of stamp duty land tax; value added tax may be payable on surrender money for non-residential premises in some cases; an agreement for surrender of a business lease may be unenforceable without a court order, although the surrender itself can be valid, and where a lease is registered the parties should ensure documents enable the land registry to close the tenant's title, or remove a note of the lease from the landlord's title.

13.35   If the service charge is paid in arrear the same apportionments could be made as above. In such cases they will usually result in a payment by the tenant to the landlord. Again, the payment could be with or without a subsequent adjustment.

13.36   If there is a sinking fund and all the leases subject to the same sinking fund are being surrendered together, perhaps to facilitate redevelopment, then the tenant may be entitled to a refund of his proportion of the sinking fund. Except in such limited cases there would normally not be any right for the tenant to seek recovery of a proportion of the sinking fund which would continue to exist for the benefit of the premises for which it was created. The position would of course be different if there was some special arrangement.

PART 4 – TERMINATION OF A LEASE

13.37   Leases can end by the passing of time, or the exercise of a break clause, or by surrender or even by forfeiture. On termination, normally a tenant is liable for the service charge apportioned to the date on which the lease actually terminated or the date on which the tenant ceases to occupy, whichever is later. The landlord may be entitled to seek a year end adjustment, again, apportioned to the date of termination, but it seems fairly rare for a landlord to do so.

13.38   The issue of what costs can be charged to the tenant tends to revolve around whether or not the costs were 'incurred' before the date of termination. If the costs were incurred prior to the termination date the landlord can charge the tenant. See eg *Electricity Supply Nominees Ltd v Thorn EMI Retail Ltd and British Telecommunications plc* [1991] 2 EGLR 46, where the superior landlord of commercial premises charged the tenant for service charge for the period to the date of termination of the head lease, and the tenant recovered those costs from the undertenant (who held over under the Landlord and Tenant Act 1954) even though the head lease had terminated. This was proper reimbursement under the principle in *Moule v Garrett* (1872) LR Exch 101, but if they were incurred after termination then they cannot be recovered. For example, in *Capital and Counties Freehold Equity Trust Ltd v BL plc* [1987] 2 EGLR 49, the landlord had entered into contracts for work to be done but none had been started prior to the end of the lease term. Costs 'incurred' (in the words of the lease) did not add anything to the expressions 'expended' or 'become payable' (which were other expressions in the lease), and the costs in question had neither been expended nor become payable. The judge said if he had to give a meaning to the word 'incurred' it referred to 'future or contingent payments'. He also said: 'Looking at the scheme of the lease as a whole, the obligation of the landlord to provide the services and the tenant's obligation to pay for them or contribute towards them are coterminous, and therefore it is only services which are provided during the lease which are chargeable.'

13.39   A few recent cases have considered aspects of termination:

(a)   The tenant is not entitled to a refund of his sinking find contributions at the end of the term – *Secretary of State for the Environment v Possfund (North West) Ltd* [1997] 2 EGLR 56 (see at **7.13**).

(b)   Where major roof repairs were completed at the end of a short-term lease the tenant was able to persuade a court that it was not reasonable for the tenant to pay a full percentage, particularly as the works seemed at least to some extent intended for the benefit of the proposed next occupier – *Scottish Mutual Assurance plc v Jardine Public Relations Ltd* [1999] EGCS 43 (see at **5.41**).

(c) Where the anticipated life expectancy of an item (air conditioning) had arrived but it was not in disrepair, the landlord could not charge the tenant for renewing it – *Fluor Daniel Properties Ltd v Shortlands Investments Ltd* [2001] EGCS 8 (see at **5.134**).

(d) For the suspension of the obligation to pay service charges (or not) when the premise, are destroyed see *P & O Property Holdings Ltd v International Computers Ltd* [1999] 2 EGLR 17 (see at **8.18**).

CHAPTER 14

Maximising service charge recovery for leases

It is a socialist idea that making profits is a vice; I consider the real vice is making losses.

Winston Churchill

14.1   This chapter brings together the general points to assist a landlord to recover as much of his service charge costs as he can. Many of the points have been mentioned before, but are set out together in this chapter as a matter of convenience. The guidance can be divided into four aspects namely:

(a)   getting the lease right;

(b)   managing the property sensibly;

(c)   using a good accounting system; and

(d)   using company law.

(There are general service charge negotiating tips for landlords at **3.82** et seq. Different considerations apply to service charges in commonholds: see Chapter 17.)

PART I – GETTING THE LEASE RIGHT

Inspect and agree the scheme

14.2   It is usually best for the definitions in the lease (whether of premises or of services, to be agreed in advance with the landlord and the managing agents. A site inspection by the solicitors drafting the lease can pay handsome dividends in ensuring that the lease is as correct and complete as possible to enable full recovery.

14.3   Express mention of specific items (eg 'the common parts (including for the avoidance of doubt the lifts and escalators)…,' or 'maintenance of the clocks statues and architectural features of the common parts') is better than hoping that general words will be construed to cover particular items. If in doubt, it is better to mention something than to leave it out. If an item is mentioned in the lease there is a prospect of recovering costs relating to it: if it is not mentioned the landlord may be obliged to try to persuade a court that it is covered under some other reference. For some cases which illustrate this, see *Rapid Results College Ltd v Angell* [1986] 1 EGLR 53 (at **2.9**); *Campden Hill Towers Ltd v Gardner* [1977] QB 823 (at **5.21**); *Embassy Court Residents' Association Ltd v Lipman* [1984] 2 EGLR 60 (at **5.22**); *Twyman v Charrington* [1994] 1 EGLR 243 (at **3.22**); *Hallisey v Petmoor Developments Ltd* [2000] EGCS 124 (at **3.22**); *Petersson v Pitt Place (Epsom) Ltd* [2001] EWCA Civ 86, [2001] EGCS 13 (at **3.22**); *Ibrahim v Dovecorn Reversions Ltd* [2001] 2 EGLR 46 (at **3.22**); *Stapel (Ernst) v Bellshore Property Investments Ltd* [2001] 2 EGLR 7 (at **3.25**); and *Alton House Holdings Ltd v Calflane (Management) Ltd* [1987] 2 EGLR 52 (at **12.30**).

Definitions of property

14.4   The most important aspect is getting the definitions as precise as possible. The definitions are (a) of that which is to be let to the tenant, (b) of the property which the landlord is to maintain and (c) of the works and services which the landlord is to provide and for which he intends to charge.

14.5   The property to be let should be clearly defined (remember the parapet! – see at **2.9**) and the lease should not leave any doubt about whether any part is actually within the demise or outside (discussed at **3.12** et seq).

14.6   For example, in the case of a property at the top of a multi-let building is the roof included or not? (See at **3.22**.) (Similarly, with foundations.) The point is that if it is in the demise then it is, normally, the tenant's liability to repair, but if it is the landlord's responsibility the lease needs to be carefully drawn to make this clear, and also whether or not it is an item for which service charges can be recovered. If either of these points is in doubt the landlord may have difficulty. From the tenant's point of view, a lacuna of this sort is equally unsatisfactory: if the roof is not clearly within the landlord's responsibility the tenant will not be able to oblige the landlord to carry out repairs which may become necessary, and thus the demised premises may suffer. The tenant may have the benefit of self help, eg as in *Loria v Hammer* [1989] 2 EGLR 249 (see at **5.43**), or implied covenants on the part of the landlord, as in *Barrett v Lounova* [1990] 1 QB 348 (see at **5.26**). However, it is best for both parties not to have to rely on such aids.

14.7   The definition of the landlord's property should be as precise as possible but should allow for changes. If gardening, landscaping, window cleaning, etc are to be carried out then there could be an objection by the tenant if the grounds were physically changed, for example, where some road was altered and the shape of the garden was affected. This should not be controversial, provided that it is clear that the premises over which the landlord's services are to be performed are substantially the same, and that the landlord cannot seek to add to a building in one place a building or grounds which have no genuine connection with the original site. It is more difficult where a landlord expands a site, for example, where a parade of six shops is increased and becomes a parade of twelve shops. However, tenants should not be prejudiced provided the new tenants are treated in the same way and (assuming the landlord wants to treat the whole area as one) that any service charge percentages are adjusted to reflect the change. This means the fixed service charge percentages must be capable of variation where necessary, as well as the extent of the landlord's property. See *Pole Properties Ltd v Feinberg* [1981] 2 EGLR 38 (at **4.25**). The site should not remain ossified for ever simply because of the way leases have been drawn, particularly in the case of premises subject to long leases. (See also the cases at **14.3**.)

Definitions of services

14.8   On the same point the definition of the services to be provided is vital and, again, can be assisted by a site visit and the detailed input of the managing agents and landlord (discussed at **3.10** et seq). It is best to mention as fully as possible the actual services that are intended or expected to be provided. If there is a garden and the landlord is to maintain it – make sure gardening is covered, but it also helps to avoid doubt if the lease covers peripherals such as purchase and replacement of gardening tools, and the ability to enter into contracts either in general (which can then cover various items) or at least for the gardening. Some tenants object to references to 'providing' such items as garden tools, on the basis that the landlord should provide them in the first case and the tenant should only pay through the service charge for replacement when needed. There is some merit in this, but it is not entirely satisfactory because (a) it may be found after some years that a new tool, not used before, would be more efficient or would save costs, perhaps by cutting down time spent, and yet the tenants who would benefit are reluctant to pay for the item if it was not used before, and (b) sometimes new equipment is invented that has great benefits but was not available at the time the lease was granted. Continuing the gardening theme, this could well apply to a sit down mower replacing an electric hand pushed mower. On that basis, the landlord should resist attempts to prevent the service charge covering new items, but may have to compromise by including a reference to items agreed by the tenants, or which save the service charge fund money. For material cases see *Frobisher (Second Investments) Ltd v Killoran Trust Co Ltd* [1980] 1 All ER 488 (at **3.88**); *Papworth v Linthaven* [1988] EGCS 54 (at **2.7**); *Lloyds Bank plc v Bowker Orford* [1992] 2 EGLR 44 (at **5.203** et seq); and *Riverlate Properties Ltd v Paul* [1975] Ch 133 (at **2.5**). The replacement of items need not be identical to what it replaces – see eg *New England Properties v Portsmouth New Shops* [1993] 1 EGLR 84 (at **5.40**).

Sweeping-up clauses

14.9   While the need to ensure that the definitions are as complete as possible cannot be emphasised too forcefully, it should also be stressed that the list of services should also include a sweeping-up clause in an attempt to ensure that any service which is not expressly mentioned is included as far as possible within the recovery provisions. It has been indicated above that the sweeping-up clause is not one to rely on, but it should be included in the hope that it will help in case of need. If a standard clause has been left out a sweeping-up clause may give the landlord a flimsy lifebelt to use. (See at **5.196** et seq and the cases therein mentioned.)

System for recovery

14.10 The other vital item which needs to be clear in the lease is the mechanism for recovery of service charge costs (discussed in Chapter 4). This is another critical matter to be agreed with the landlord and the managing agents. The lease should make it clear if advance payments are required, and the basis of those payments – in other words, is the payment to be made following an estimate and on the usual quarter days? If there is to be an estimate, make it clear who is to give it. If the recovery is by way of a fixed percentage ensure the landlord has the right to vary it if circumstances change (see at **14.7**). In such cases does the landlord want the lease to indicate the basis of calculation (floor area, rateable value, etc)? If so, it should be stated to relate to the floor area, or other criteria, once every year, to avoid the need for numerous recalculations.

14.11 Another item to clarify is the method of accounting and whether there is to be a certificate given to the tenant of the amount due, and, if so, what is it to cover (eg just the total costs, or the total costs and also the amount payable by the tenant), and who is to give it. In addition, check with the landlord if he has a preference for the date of the financial year end. Many of these points are (for solicitors and managing agents) good client relations, and are easy to include in leases. Certificates are discussed at **4.78** et seq.

14.12 In the case of commercial properties it may be as well to have a disputes procedure. Under typical systems the tenant is entitled to dispute charges provided he has made the advance payments and provided also that he raises his objection within a specified period after the certificate is given, with time to be of the essence. Such a system can be useful to ensure any dispute is raised reasonably promptly, when the facts and information are fresh. Statute provides a scheme for service charges for dwellings. (See at **6.69** et seq.)

Sinking funds

14.13 The final aspect of getting the lease right is to include, if the landlord so requires, the right for the landlord to set up a sinking fund or reserve fund, at least in those cases where the current tenants, or potential future tenants, are such as may have difficulty in finding a large amount at one time when, for example, a lift or roof needs urgent replacement. Actually operating the sinking fund has its complications as outlined previously (in Chapter 7) but, despite the difficulties, such a fund can be helpful to tenants who can pay on a regular basis but would be unable to find what might be a substantial figure in one year. If it is primarily intended to be for a particular item it is recommended that is says so in the lease.

PART 2 – MANAGE THE PROPERTY SENSIBLY

14.14   This is aimed at reminding readers of what should be obvious, but is sometimes lost in the day-to-day bustle of management. That is that the landlord should manage the property in a sensible fashion. A landlord who wants to obtain maximum reimbursement of service charges is far more likely to achieve that result if the tenants are happy with the way things are run than otherwise. Where the tenants feel the landlord is acting too autocratically they will be more disposed to challenge the costs. If they feel the landlord is acting reasonably and fairly he is more likely to be given the benefit of the doubt. See, for example, *Holding and Management Ltd v Property Holding and Investment Trust plc* [1990] 1 All ER 938 (at **5.193**); *Concorde Graphics Ltd v Andromeda Investments SA* [1983] 1 EGLR 53 (at **4.85**); *Finchbourne Ltd v Rodrigues* [1976] 3 All ER 581 (at **2.15**); and *Martin v Maryland Estates Ltd* [1998] 25 EG 169 (at **9.72**).

14.15   Examples of sensible management are employing suitable managing agents; keeping the tenants informed of what is happening; suitable treatment of interest earned on receipts; following the statutory requirements affecting dwellings; monitoring works done; having a system for regular consultation or meetings with the tenants, and ensuring that costs are correctly allocated. Most of these matters are addressed in the two codes of practice discussed in Chapter 11.

Employing suitable managing agents

14.16   My recommendation is that the landlord should not just make sure that the agents employed for those properties where a managing agent is needed are suitably qualified (eg members of the RICS) but are also experienced in managing the actual type of property concerned. Many agents concentrate on either commercial or residential property: clearly it is not ideal for a commercial agent to manage a residential block. As with so many other aspects of life, personal recommendation is the best way to choose an agent, but (a) make sure the agent is qualified, and (b) make sure the person recommending the agent has experienced the agent's handling of similar premises. Even if the agent specialises in residential property, running a 200-flat mansion block is a far cry from managing a three-storey house divided into three flats. There may at some time be a requirement for agents who want to manage dwellings to hold a licence or be regulated. Obviously, if such a requirement is introduced, the landlord should ensure that his agent has the necessary licence or registration.

Keep the tenants informed

14.17   Information is perhaps the most useful tool for showing the tenants that the landlord is acting sensibly. This includes in particular notifying the tenants in advance of matters physically affecting the premises, such as the intended dates for decoration or significant repairs. The statutory obligations are mentioned below, but there are also such matters as periodic circulars to the tenants from the managing agents on matters currently affecting the premises. In addition, the accounts and estimates should be as full as reasonably possible with explanatory notes, rather than kept brief, to ensure that the tenants have been notified of all pertinent matters. Arranging for regular tenants' meetings can aid pleasant relations and ensure that the landlord is seen to be at least aware of what the tenants have to say. Obviously, there are times when regular meetings might be needed frequently (eg during major works) and other times when the management is running smoothly meetings are only rarely needed, but the point is to show the tenants that the landlord is at least giving the tenants the opportunity of putting forward matters that concern the tenants.

14.18   Landlords of both residential and commercial property should now also bear in mind the guidance set out in the two codes of practice, discussed in Chapter 11.

Statutory provisions and codes of practice for residential premises

14.19   Landlords of residential property need to comply with the Landlord and Tenant Act 1985 and the other parts of the statutory code, as outlined in Chapters 9 and 10, or they will be unable to recover in full. (See, eg, *Martin v Maryland Estates Ltd* [1998] 25 EG 169, at **9.67**.) Readers are reminded that this applies even (a) where the residential element is a small part of the whole, and (b) when the landlord is a company controlled by the tenants (see at **12.27** et seq). A landlord who fails to comply will not only in many cases be unable to recover all his service charge costs, but can also be liable for criminal proceedings. The most important practical statutory element is consulting on proposed works, or on long-term agreements. (Landlord and Tenant Act 1985, s 20; see at **9.56** et seq.) In addition, the tenant is entitled to the landlord's co-operation in response to enquiries under various statutory provisions, for example allowing inspection of vouchers, passing on requests for information to superior landlords and providing insurance details under ss 22 and 23 and the Schedule to the Landlord and Tenant Act 1985. (For s 22, see at **9.170**, for s 23 see at **9.178**, and for the Schedule see at **9.236**.) The Residential Code described in Chapter 11 can be used as evidence of good practice under s 87 of the Leasehold Reform, Housing and Urban Development Act 1993. Where a landlord of dwellings intends to carry out any works and (following either formal consultation under s 20 of the Landlord and Tenant Act 1985 or informal consultation) finds there may be objection to his proposals, he can seek approval in anticipation from the Leasehold Valuation Tribunal under s 27A(3) of the Landlord and Tenant Act 1985 (see at **9.201**). Similarly, the landlord can apply to the LVT, when tenants object to a demand, for a ruling that it was reasonable to incur the service charge. (Landlord and Tenant Act 1985, s 27A(1); see at **9.201**.)

Monitoring

14.20   The landlord should ensure a good monitoring system covering at least two major aspects. First the landlord should ensure that work or other services for which a contract in force is actually done, and done to a suitable standard. The standard is important in all leasehold cases, but for residential tenants a failure to ensure the work is of a reasonable standard could be in breach of s 19(1)(b) of the Landlord and Tenant Act 1985 and, apart from any other consideration, could result in the landlord being unable to recover part of the cost. There is also a question of value for the money the contractor wants the landlord to pay, as well as good relations with the tenant. The landlord should be satisfied for his own benefit, apart from the interests of the tenants, that works are done in a satisfactory manner. This will also assist the landlord in deciding whether or not to employ the contractor on other jobs. The managing agent should monitor all regular contracts, such as cleaning, gardening, security etc, to see that they are run well, and should consider whether or not to put those services out to tender periodically. This should be done as a matter of good practice, whether or not the landlord has covenanted to have regular tenders. (This is covered in both Codes of Practice.)

14.21   The other aspect of monitoring works and services is to ensure that money which has to be spent is charged to the service charge account only where such a charge is a proper charge within the lease terms. It creates considerable distrust and ill will if a landlord seeks to include in the service charge the cost of something which is not properly payable by the tenants.

Comply with conditions precedent

14.22   If the lease sets out conditions precedent for the recovery of sums from the tenant, the landlord must comply or will be unable to recoup the money in question. It is best not to include conditions precedent in the lease, but, if there is one, the landlord must follow the arrangement or he will have real difficulty. A classic example is *CIN Properties Ltd v Barclays Bank plc* [1986] 1 EGLR 59. It concerned a lease of part of a large block of offices in Regent Street in the West End of London. In addition to the lease there was a separate deed, although nothing turned on the deed being separate from the lease. In effect the deed provided for the landlord to be responsible for main structural repairs with a right to recover a proportion of those costs from the tenants. The deed put the onus on the landlord to obtain estimates or tenders for the work, and went on to say: 'Provided that (the Landlord) shall not accept any tender or estimate or enter into any contract or place any order for the carrying out of any such repairs or works without first submitting the same (together with plans and specifications…) to [the Tenant] for approval (such approval not to be unreasonably withheld or delayed).' Extensive works were required, costing in all some £6 million, of which the tenant's share would have been about £166,000. The tenant was never asked to approve tenders, estimates, orders or contracts. The Court of Appeal overturned the decision at first instance (where the judge had been persuaded that the prior submission of estimates was mere machinery), and held that the obligation to seek approval was a condition precedent, and as the landlord had not complied with that condition precedent it could not recover the relevant proportion from the tenant. (Conditions precedent are mentioned at **3.90** and **3.91**.)

Operate a complaints system

14.23 Many leases have provisions for either arbitration or for some other method of dealing with complaints from tenants, for example, that decisions are to be made by the landlord's surveyor. If the lease has such a system then it should be used, but for good client relations a landlord should be prepared to deal with complaints and criticism in an informal way to defuse potential problems and seek to ensure smooth running of the management. It should at all times be remembered that a landlord and tenant relationship is one that is intended, by its nature, to last for a period of time. Where there is a complaints system and the tenant requires it to be operated formally the landlord should ensure that he does so, and thus complies with the terms of his own lease. In particular where the lease requires the tenants to put forward a note of any objection to the accounts or certificates within a limited time the landlord should ensure that the procedure is dealt with promptly and not unreasonably delayed by the landlord. For residential property disputes, provisions are less important because of the tenant's right to apply to the Leasehold Valuation Tribunal, but sometimes there are matters that are more suitable for some less formal approach.

PART 3 – USE A GOOD ACCOUNTING SYSTEM

14.24 The third element of maximising recovery of service charge costs is a good accounting system. Traditionally managing agents kept records in ledgers and various paper forms. More recently, computers have been used to assist. There are several computerised systems on the market. Any agent choosing one should ensure that it is suitable for the use intended – ie a residential package is unlikely to be suitable for commercial property etc.

14.25 The accounting system breaks down into the following basic elements:

(a) ensuring the cash position is known at all times;

(b) making sure that receipts and payments are consistent with the required cash flow;

(c) sending accounts and certificates as soon as practicable; and

(d) ensuring the details in the accounts etc are correct.

There should also be a system for checking that payments required from tenants have been made and that concessions to individual tenants (or waivers) are catered for.

Checking the cash position

14.26 The landlord should be able to ascertain at all times how much is in hand. Effectively, the landlord should be able to tell what money has been received from tenants, what bills have been received and either have been paid or are to be paid, and what bills are expected to be received. This is basic cash flow information, but should be known at all times:

(a) There is always the possibility of an unexpected heavy item of expenditure occurring suddenly: the landlord should have the information available so that he is aware of how much money the service charge fund has in hand to cope with the emergency, and his other service charge commitments.

(b) This information is needed to ensure that work and payments are timed so that the income is at all times receivable before payments are due to be made.

(c) There is always the possibility of an offer being made for the landlord's property. If the accounts are apparently in a muddle this could put off a purchaser and might delay a sale. It will certainly not impress either the landlord or the purchaser.

Make sure the details are right

14.27 When accounts are prepared the landlord should seek to ensure that all details are correct; for example, such matters as correct treatment of value added tax and charging the correct percentages. (See *Universities Superannuation Fund Scheme Ltd v Marks & Spencer Ltd* [1999] 04 EG 158 at **4.6**.) Simple clerical errors in addition can cause considerable irritation, but even more importantly can cause extra work in having to revise the accounts and circulate the new accounts to all the tenants with an explanation. Ensure that the records are correct and that the demands are sent to the current tenant, not one who assigned a year ago. The landlord should also ensure that wherever possible there is a record in his records, if nowhere else, of how any unusual items are calculated.

14.28 On the same point, a landlord of residential premises should remember that:

(a) The demand must comply with s 47 of the Landlord and Tenant Act 1987 and should therefore have details of the landlord's name and address and (if the address is not in England or Wales) also an address for service in England and Wales for service (see at **9.275** et seq).

(b) The landlord is not entitled to charge for works costing any tenant more than £250 for ordinary works or £100 for works under a long-term agreement (or to enter into a non-excluded long term agreement) unless he carries out proper consultation under s 20 of the Landlord and Tenant Act 1985 (see at **9.56** et seq).

(c) The receipts from tenants are trust money under s 42 of the Landlord and Tenant Act 1987 (see at **9.250** et seq).

14.29 Where a tenant has been given a concession in the lease, or by a side letter, the demands or accounts should reflect this. For example, where a lease contains a provision that the tenant of a specific unit is not liable for any costs relating to roof repairs then where there has been a roof repair the demand to the tenant should reflect the concession. It may be that the details of the costs of work can be adjusted to show the total paid and then simply deduct the relevant proportion of the cost of roof works for the unit, or alternatively the certificate should show that the charge should be £X on the same basis as the other tenants but is £Y (a smaller figure!) because of the concession. This sort of adjustment is easier in those cases where the different costs are split up in table form, in which case the actual figure may be easy to identify. It is obviously more difficult in cases where the concession relates to some matter in general terms, for example inherent defects, but a concession should be given where it is applicable, and the managing agent or landlord should be in a position to satisfy the tenant that the concession has been applied.

Explanatory notes in accounts

14.30 The importance of giving suitable information to the tenants is mentioned above. This includes ensuring that the accounts have relevant notes to clarify matters that might need explanation. Leaving out such notes can give the tenant an excuse to ask questions and thus delay payment. Both codes of practice emphasise the importance of communication with the tenants (see Chapter 11).

14.31 Matters which could helpfully be mentioned in notes to accounts include:

(a) If for some years the tenant whose lease obliges him to pay 'a fair proportion' of the total costs has actually been paying 17% of the costs, and the 17% becomes 21% in one year the tenant is reasonably entitled to an explanation of why the percentage has changed. It is best to record this in the accounts for all tenants to see.

(b) It is very helpful, and a recommendation of the Commercial Code, that the accounts should include a comparison with the budget figure and also the former year's figures so that tenants can see the increase or decrease. This also helps the landlord to see if his agents and contractors are acting efficiently or not.

(c) Where a new item of charge appears it is of help to mention in the accounts why it is shown. If it is simply that there have been no costs for the item in previous years, a mention of this should make tenants recognise that the landlord is acting responsibly and not simply seeking to charge for something he is not entitled to recover.

Collection, checking and enforcement

14.32   A landlord needs to have a system for checking that when demands are sent out payment is received in good time, and, if not, that procedures are followed for recovery. This is one of the most important aspects for the landlord and of course for the service charge fund generally. If some tenants are a few quarters behind this will affect the money in hand to pay the bills, and either the landlord will have to pay (and he has ordered the work and will normally be responsible), or the work will not be done and (a) the (landlord's) property will suffer and (b) the tenants will complain.

14.33   The usual system involves a demand being sent prior to the due date. There is then a check to see what payments are received on or about the actual date on which payment is due. There should next be a reminder, except perhaps for persistent defaulters. Where the lease permits charging interest this should be pointed out to the defaulter. A further check is then needed, and if the reminder does not result in payment within, say, a week or 14 days of the due date sometimes a personal call, to the premises or by telephone, can bring in the balance due. If this fails then the landlord will have to consider the remedies open to him.

14.34   The normal remedies (discussed at **4.90** et seq) can be broken down into the following categories:

(a)   Suing the tenant. This can take some time and the landlord is unlikely to be able to recover all his costs. A landlord may be able to obtain a charging order (like a mortgage) after obtaining judgment, but this only helps when the tenant finds someone willing to pay money for the lease, and provided that amount is more than any mortgage which has priority over the charging order.

(b)   For an individual or company a landlord could issue a statutory notice. When this notice is served, if payment is not made within the due period the individual can be made bankrupt or a company can be put into liquidation. This is more of use in cases where the landlord thinks the tenant can pay but is simply delaying, than in cases where the tenant is insolvent – in the latter case there is little the landlord can do except to forfeit the lease as soon as possible and seek a new tenant. He can claim under insolvency rules, but will often not receive the total sum, and it takes time.

(c)   Distraint can help in some commercial cases, but is not available for arrears of service charge for residential properties. (See at **4.91**. Being trust money it cannot be rent.) This remedy only applies where the service charge is reserved as rent, and is not available where there is a genuine dispute over the service charges.

(d)   If the tenant has a sub-tenant the landlord can invoke the Law of Distress Amendment Act 1908 and can call on the sub-tenant to pay sums direct to the superior landlord until all arrears are cleared.

(e)   In cases where the tenant has a genuine cash flow problem but can convince the landlord that he will be able to pay in full over a period the landlord can consider re-scheduling the payments. Payments monthly in advance rather than quarterly may assist a tenant, or even payment monthly or quarterly in arrears. (See *D'Jan v Bond Street Estates plc* [1993] EGCS 43, at **4.4**.) In cases where the property may be difficult to relet there is much to be recommended in helping a tenant who is likely to be able to come through a difficult patch, and who may appreciate the help the landlord has given – aiding good landlord/tenant relations.

(f)   If the current tenant is unable to pay a landlord can consider claims against any previous tenant who may still be liable, or against any guarantors of the present tenant or former tenants who may also still be liable. (See at **4.101**.) The six-month limit and other provisions of the Landlord and Tenant (Covenants) Act 1995 needs to be kept firmly in mind in this context. (See at **9.10** et seq.)

(g)   The landlord may be able to forfeit the lease on the basis of breach of covenant. If the breach, in the case of a dwelling, is non-payment of a service charge, the landlord will need to have the breach agreed by the tenant or determined by a court or arbitration before forfeiture proceedings can be started. (Housing Act 1996, s 81, at **9.288** et seq.) If the lease is forfeited, the landlord will be left with the property but without a tenant. Accordingly this remedy is always considered as a last resort unless the market is buoyant and re-letting would not be difficult.

PART 4 – USING COMPANY LAW

14.35   A different approach was used in *Morshead Mansions Ltd v Mactra Properties Ltd* [2006] EWCA Civ 492 (see at **12.36**), which may assist some management companies. There, the landlord company was able to pass a resolution to recover service charge money from a tenant who was also a shareholder of the company, where it was unable to recover the sum from the tenant as tenant.

CHAPTER 15

Challenging a service charge demand

The quarrel is a very pretty quarrel as it stands; we shall only spoil it by trying to explain it.

Richard Brinsley Sheridan

15.1   In the previous chapter, notes of the significant points to assist a landlord to achieve maximum service charge recovery were gathered together. This chapter deals in similar fashion with the various aspects that may assist a tenant who receives a service charge demand he feels unduly high, to keep the tenant's liability down.

THE FOUR CHALLENGES

15.2   The four basic forms of challenge to a service charge demand are described below. In many cases there are several of the four elements combined:

(a)   the lease does not permit the landlord to charge for the item in question;

(b)   the landlord failed to comply with statutory requirements (affecting residential tenants only);

(c)   the work or service was not necessary; and/or

(d)   the works or services were too expensive.

15.3   If the first point applies the landlord will be unable to recover: this is the tenant's most effective weapon. In the second case the landlord's ability to recover may be excluded or at least limited to the statutory amount. The third and fourth alternatives require proving the point in a practical way. As the two final challenges have similar approaches, they will be dealt with together below. Some other aspects are mentioned at the end of this chapter.

PART I – GENERAL ASPECTS OF CHALLENGING

Read the lease

15.4   There are a number of basic points, but the first and probably most important one is to read the lease when an unsatisfactorily high demand is received. The main points to look out for are:

(a) Remember that the provisions relevant to service charges may appear in many parts of the lease, and not just the service charge schedule. In addition there may be material provisions in Deeds of Variation, Licences, waivers or side letters. (See at **2.28**.)

(b) Is there a disputes procedure? If there is, the tenant must make sure he follows the procedure correctly. (Action through the courts is always possible, unless there is a binding arbitration agreement, but can be expensive and slow; see at **15.10** et seq, where the lease is of a dwelling.) Of particular importance are any time limits. If there is a time limit for objecting, make a diary note to ensure it is not missed. If there is a time limit and it has been missed by the time professional help is sought then consider whether time is of the essence, or whether there are legal grounds for seeking an extension of time. (For a recent case discussing applying to appoint an arbitrator out of time (in a rent review context), see *Monella v Pizza Express (Restaurants) Ltd* [2003] EWHC 2966 (Ch), [2004] 1 EGLR 43.)

(c) If the lease requires reasons to be given for objections then those reasons should be marshalled. If necessary a preliminary objection should be sent within the time limit, even if not all the reasons or other information are to hand.

(d) Check that the lease permits the landlord to charge for the work or services referred to in the demand. If the demand refers to decoration of common parts, is this a proper item? For example, is there a limit to the frequency in which such decoration can be carried out, or has it been done immediately after a previous redecoration? See eg *Riverlate Properties Ltd v Paul* [1975] Ch 133 (at **2.5**); *Frobisher (Second Investments) Ltd v Killoran Trust Co Ltd* [1980] 1 All ER 488 (at **3.88**); *Lloyds Bank plc v Bowker Orford* [1992] 2 EGLR 44 (at **5.203** et seq); *Yorkbrook Investments Ltd v Batten* (1985) 52 P & CR 51, and other cases mentioned at **14.3**.

(e) Check carefully any exclusions or waivers that may apply. For example, is there is an exclusion for capital items, or for refurbishment costs, if either of these is included in the demand? In some leases or side letters there may be a maximum contribution payable by the tenant, either generally or for some specific aspect. (For waivers see at **7.60** et seq.)

(f) For major items, particularly on residential properties, see if there is a reserve or sinking fund which is intended to be used for the item in question. If so, can the tenant require the landlord to use the sinking fund or reserve for the item in question before claiming further service charge contributions for the same thing? If the landlord is liable to contribute to the sinking fund do the accounts reflect this? (For sinking funds and reserve funds see Chapter 7.)

Check the demand and the accounts

15.5 Check that the demand complies with the lease.

(a) Is it certified if the lease so requires, and, if so, is it certified by the correct person? If it has to be by the landlord's surveyor make sure that it is not by the landlord's accountant: if the person giving the certificate is an employee of the landlord does the lease permit this? Is the certificate a certificate of the aspects required by the lease? – in other words, if it is to be a certificate of the percentage payable by the tenant then a certificate of the total cost of works has no validity. (Discussed at **4.78** et seq.)

(b) Does the demand clearly show the period covered, and is that period the correct one? For example, if the service charge year is from 25 March to 24 March – is that what the certificate covers? If it is for less than a year – why? Are there any notes to explain any inconsistency? Does the demand cover a period for which a demand has already been received?

(c) Is the demand wholly or partly for a period before the current tenant became the tenant? If it is then the current tenant may be able to avoid liability in the absence of a direct covenant with the landlord to pay the arrears. (See eg *Wharfland Ltd v South London Co-operative Building Co Ltd* [1995] 2 EGLR 21, at **4.109**.) If the demand covers a year during which the current tenant acquired the lease there may be an apportionment to be considered. (See Chapter 13 for apportionments on sale.)

(d) If the claim is against a former tenant bear in mind the six-month time limit under s 17 of the Landlord and Tenant (Covenants) Act 1995, and the effect of lease variations under s 18 of the same Act. If the demand is sent to a former tenant and is not in accordance with s 17 of the 1995 Act the former tenant need not pay. (See at **9.10** et seq.)

(e) Does the demand give other information, such as details of the costs of the services, and the balance carried forward from the preceding year? If not, it may be appropriate to ask for further details so that the tenant can assess whether the sum claimed is both properly within the lease and reasonable in amount. The codes of practice (Chapter 11), both recommend giving information to tenants, and the tenant is entitled to require the landlord to justify what the landlord wants to charge for.

(f) If the demand shows a percentage of the total, is that the correct percentage? If the lease does not specify the percentage to be charged, is the percentage the same as before, and, if not, has the landlord justified any change? (Discussed further below at **15.6**.)

(g) If the lease requires copies of accounts or estimates to be produced with the demands have they been produced?

(h) Does the demand cover costs of replacement or improvements? If so, does the lease permit the landlord to charge for such items? This is a matter of interpretation, but the point can be very important. (See eg at **5.38** et seq.)

Check the percentage charged

15.6 In cases where the lease states that the tenant is liable to pay X% of the total service costs, or Y% of some services and Z% of others, check that the demand shows the correct percentage(s). Where the lease provides for payment of 'a fair proportion' checking is not so easy. If the tenant has consistently been charged a similar percentage before then, subject to challenge on the cost of the works, it may be difficult to challenge the percentage. If the percentage is different to the percentage charged previously the tenant may have grounds for objection. Certainly, if the 'fair proportion' of one year is changed the following year to the detriment of the tenant he is entitled to require the landlord to justify the change. The courts seem reasonably content to allow the landlord to assess the 'fair proportion' on various different bases, eg floor area or rateable value, provided that the landlord treats all the tenants in the same way so that the proportion is fair. Courts have limited power to change a fixed proportion in a lease: see *Pole Properties Ltd v Feinberg* [1981] 2 EGLR 38 (at **4.25**) and *Jollybird Ltd v Fairzone Ltd* [1990] 2 EGLR 55 (at **4.26**), and lease variations under the Landlord and Tenant Act 1987 (at **10.2** et seq).

Was the work done?

15.7   One of the tenant's complaints may be that the landlord is making a charge for works or services which were not actually done or provided. For example, if there has been a charge for grass cutting or regular window cleaning sometimes a tenant can show that it was simply not done, whatever the contractor's records might say. (See *Yorkbrook Investments Ltd v Batten* (1985) 52 P & CR 51 (at **5.133**) and also *Gordon v Selico Co Ltd* [1986] 1 EGLR 71 (at **6.40**). In the latter case, the landlord's builders had done work which covered up wet rot and dry rot.) If a tenant has reason to doubt the accounts it is obviously helpful if he can provide some written record of what was done and what was not done. For example, if a tenant knows gardening should be done once every month it would be of great assistance in a dispute if he could make a record of every time the gardeners visited, or, if easier, a record of every first Saturday in the month showing whether the gardeners came or not. The author has, for example, come across a case where a landlord was charged by a cleaning company for weekly visits which they never made. (The Report by the Department of the Environment in 1991, *The Landlord and Tenant Act 1987, Awareness, Experience and Impact*, quotes similar unsatisfactory cases.)

15.8   The key is that if there is a dispute and the matter comes to court the tenant who wants to obtain satisfaction needs to be able to provide evidence for the judge. Copies of contemporaneous correspondence with the landlord or the landlord's agent, explaining about an unsatisfactory state of affairs are probably the most useful aid. This is because not only does it set out the facts as the tenant sees them, but it gives the landlord an opportunity to put matters right and to resolve a problem, rather than simply being a defensive way of seeking to avoid payment. It is also evidence that the landlord was put on notice. If the landlord agrees in writing, this can be shown to the court. If he fails to reply this can be the subject of comment in court.

15.9   Tenants of dwellings have rights to inspect vouchers under s 22 of the Landlord and Tenant Act 1985 (see **9.170** et seq) and some non-residential leases give express rights to inspect various papers. Exercising such rights can assist to check what is being charged. If matters come to litigation, there is always a right of disclosure, and in any event it is in the interest of the landlord to provide paperwork to back up his claim.

PART 2 – NOT MEETING STATUTORY REQUIREMENTS FOR DWELLINGS

15.10   It will be remembered that, for residential leases, there is statutory protection for tenants and disputes provisions, such as arbitration clauses, are ineffective. Disputes are normally referred to the Leasehold Valuation Tribunal (see Landlord and Tenant Act 1985, s 27A at **9.201** et seq.). Where it is alleged that:

(a)   a landlord is claiming for works without having given the required estimates (Landlord and Tenant Act 1985, s 20; see at **9.56** et seq); or

(b)   where the tenant considers the amount to be more than a reasonable sum, or that the work has not been carried out to a reasonable standard (Landlord and Tenant Act 1985, s 19; see at **9.38** et seq); or

(c)   where the works were carried out more than 18 months before the demand without prior notice to the tenant (Landlord and Tenant Act 1985, s 20B; see at **9.130** et seq),

an objection should be stated as soon as possible after receipt of the demand. (See at **15.5** on demands generally, and at **15.11** for demands for service charges for dwellings.)

15.11   If the property is residential, has the landlord given previous notice of his name and address for service (Landlord and Tenant Act 1987, s 48; see at **9.278**) and does the demand itself comply with the Landlord and Tenant Act 1987 (s 47; at **9.276**) by showing the name and address for service of the landlord?

15.12   Residential tenants have the right to inspect accounts, receipts etc under s 22 of the Landlord and Tenant Act 1985 (see at **9.170** et seq).

15.13   Residential tenants who have formed a recognised tenants' association also have the right in some cases to have their own management audit (under s 84 of the Leasehold Reform, Housing and Urban Development Act 1993; see at **10.107** et seq), which may help where there is serious doubt about the accounts or the demand. In particular it allows a surveyor to inspect the common parts, backed up by the ability to obtain a court order.

15.14   Again, for residential tenancies, an application to a Leasehold Valuation Tribunal could be made under s 27A of the Landlord and Tenant Act 1985 (see at **9.201**) for a declaration that the costs charged are not reasonable.

15.15   Residential tenants have specific rights to withhold payment in certain cases. These include:

(a)   where the landlord has not provided a written summary of costs (certified by an accountant if more than four tenants contribute) under s 21 of the Landlord and Tenant Act 1985 (see at **9.149** et seq); and

(b)   where the demand does not include a name and address for service (Landlord and Tenant Act 1987, s 47).

15.16   In residential cases there is power for tenants (or indeed landlords) of long leases of flats to apply to the court for variation to leases where the total recoverable service charges are either more or less than 100%. (Landlord and Tenant Act 1987, s 35; see at **10.2** et seq.)

15.17   In cases of dispute as to whether or not a landlord has acted reasonably, either party can refer to the Residential Code (see Chapter 11), as evidence of good practice under s 87 of the Leasehold Reform, Housing and Urban Development Act 1993. A party to a non-residential lease could refer similarly to the Commercial Code for evidence of good practice, although the latter has no statutory backing.

PART 3 – WORKS NOT NECESSARY OR TOO COSTLY

15.18   These are sometimes the most important questions, but also one of the most difficult. In the case of residential properties reasonableness is implied under the provisions of s 19 of the Landlord and Tenant Act 1985. For all properties the case of *Finchbourne Ltd v Rodrigues* [1976] 3 All ER 581 (at **2.14** and **2.15**) should have virtually the same effect. Clearly, if the lease is qualified by references to 'reasonable' costs or 'economic' costs or some similar qualification the tenant can seek to rely on these express qualifications, although it was held in *Havenridge Ltd v Boston Dyers Ltd* [1994] 2 EGLR 73 (at **2.16**) that 'reasonable' was not implied where the lease used the expression 'proper'.

15.19   Unfortunately, although the principle is clear the problem is translating the principle into reality: 'is this figure more than is reasonable for this service or that work?' Where there is a dispute, the parties will need to obtain expert evidence of an appropriate charge for what was done. This can be expensive, but some of the following suggestions may assist. Inevitably each case depends on its own facts but it is worth considering (a) estimates, (b) historical comparisons, (c) comparisons with other properties, and (d) length of term. These possibilities are explored below:

Estimates

15.20   Were there competing estimates? If there were:

(a)   was the charge in accordance with the estimate; and

(b) if it was not the lowest estimate, was there a good reason for accepting one other than the lowest?

15.21 For residential premises a summary of estimates must be produced to the tenant for consultation in advance for major works. (Landlord and Tenant Act 1985, s 20; see eg at **9.81**.) It is more rare for the tenant of commercial property to be entitled to see estimates in advance, but for major works some landlords make a practise of providing estimates and inviting comments in advance, partly as a public relations exercise and partly because this can make objections at a later (and more costly) stage less likely.

15.22 If there were several genuine and independent estimates and the charge is in accordance with the estimates it is unlikely that the landlord will have too much difficulty supporting his claim, providing of course that the work is properly chargeable.

15.23 If there were estimates and yet the charge is substantially higher than the estimated figure the tenant can ask the landlord why this is so. The usual reasons are variations to the works for which the estimate was given, or extra costs arising from circumstances discovered after the work has started:

(a) If there were no variations then the tenant may have grounds for suggesting the charge is excessive. Where costs have been added for items discovered during the works the tenant should see if the original estimate contained the usual contingency figure.

(b) Where extra works, likely to cost above the minimum cost, are found to be needed during the works the landlord of residential property needs to consult again (see *Martin v Maryland Estates Ltd* [1998] 25 EG 169 at **9.72**).

(c) If there were variations to the work for which the estimate was given the tenant should ascertain what they were and (in particular) ensure that the cost of such additional work was a proper charge under the terms of the lease. They might have related to work outside the landlord's premises for which the service charge is payable, or be for works which are the responsibility of another tenant, or items which could have been recovered through the insurers, or even irrecoverable improvements. Again, if the amount of those variations would cause any residential tenant to pay more than the minimum figure, consultation should take place.

(d) If the landlord should have consulted under s 20 and did not do so he has the ability to apply to the Leasehold Valuations Tribunal for a dispensation if he can show he has acted reasonably. (Landlord and Tenant Act 1985, s 27A(6) at **9.209**).

Historical comparison

15.24 This subheading is intended to suggest that the service charge history of the property may be material. For example:

(a)   If the costs of the service in question have been rising gently for the last seven years why did they increase sharply this year?

(b)   Has the work itself, eg lift replacement or external decoration, been done more than once in the recent past?

(c)   Is this an item for which a charge has been made before, or is it the first time? If it is done frequently, this may indicate that it has not been done correctly, or that the maintenance, for which the tenant is probably paying, has not been properly carried out.

Comparison with other property

15.25   Seeking comparisons with other property is another means of trying to see if the charge is excessive, but it is difficult for such comparisons to have much weight unless the two sets of premises are very similar. Different centres have different services and sometimes different average wages costs, and so it is hard to compare them.

15.26   Some people try to see how service charges compare as a rate per square foot. This may have some use, if there is a great deal of consistency in all the examples, but such consistency is rare and this method is regrettably rarely of practical use accordingly. Loughborough University Business School carried out a study over several years on various commercial properties, and tried to make comparisons based on a fairly wide set of categories of services. In an article about the study, Dr John R Calvert (*Estates Gazette*, 12 November 2005) it was claimed that:

(a)   The cost per square foot is a meaningful ratio, and that the service charge costs seem to vary lineally with the area of a building, and so there 'are no economies of scale'.

(b)   It expressed concern that there is no enforceable code of practice (see Chapter 11). (The new Commercial Code of Practice recommends using standard descriptions to enable comparisons to be made on a similar basis.)

(c)   The study also showed, worryingly, that least 25% of all certificates arrived more than a year after the end of the service charge year, and that no budget, in their survey, arrived more than three months before the period, and at least 45% after the year had started, with at least 13% arriving more than one year late. Budgets arriving late make it difficult for a tenant to budget suitably, and this is probably unhelpful for both landlord and tenant.

(d)   The study produced a monitoring limit of £4.76 per square foot, and recommended that certificates showing above that figure should be monitored over time. It also recommended that if the figure was over £7.45 per square foot that the certificate should be immediately investigated.

15.27   One may be somewhat sceptical about the use of such tables. For example, at the Jolly Trolley Shopping Centre the rate may be 5 pence per square foot and at the Roof Top Shop Concourse it may be £7.50. However, there may be virtually no services to be done by the landlord at the Jolly Trolley Shopping Centre, or the landlord may simply fail to comply with his obligations and thus keep the costs down, but to the detriment of the Centre. At the Roof Top Shop Concourse the figures may reflect a refurbishment, applicable only once every 10 or 20 years. The use of comparables of individual types of service, ie only security, or only repair and decoration, may make comparisons of more help. The Loughborough study was hoping that an agreed set of descriptions could be accepted throughout the industry so that meaningful comparisons could be made, but there was evidently difficulty with this. Again, the author is a little sceptical, as a 'one size fits all' approach is somewhat doubtful, particularly where there are so many potential permutations of buildings and services and general circumstances.

Length of term

15.28   For cases where a tenant was able to reduce the landlord's charge because only a short period of the term was left see *Scottish Mutual Assurance plc v Jardine Public Relations Ltd* [1999] EGCS 43 (at **5.41**) and for a case where the relevant item had reached the end of its estimated life but was not out of repair see *Fluor Daniel Properties Ltd v Shortlands Investments Ltd* [2001] EGCS 8 (at **5.134**).

PART 4 – TENANT'S POSSIBLE SELF HELP

Banding together

15.29   Clearly, if there is a lot at stake the tenant will have to consider seeking independent advice from a chartered surveyor, quantity surveyor, or engineer, depending on the type of charge at issue. One of the biggest problems of this, as with obtaining legal advice, is that the cost of such advice can easily be out of proportion to the amount genuinely at issue. However, such advice may be affordable if the tenants get together to object to a particular item. If a tenant thinks the charge for advice of £2,000 is too high for himself, dividing it among five tenants would be more manageable. Tenants considering banding together may have encouragement from the case of *Woodtrek Ltd v Jezek* (1981) 261 EG 571 (see at **2.25**).

Withholding part of the sum demanded

15.30   If sensible negotiation or valuer's advice fails to convince a landlord that the charge is too high the tenant is left with the further option of self help. This is often most effectively done by the tenants acting jointly, but unless the tenants can properly say that the landlord has carried out no service whatsoever (a rare occurrence) it is best for the tenant(s) to tender such sum as they consider reflects a reasonable sum for the services provided and keep back the balance. If all the tenants pay, for example, 80% of the landlord's demand, if that is the amount they agree is due, accompanied by a letter saying that they consider the demand excessive and giving reasons if they have not already been put in writing, it would be a brave and thick-skinned landlord who took action against them all, knowing he had a contested dispute.

15.31   Residential tenants could also make an application to the court for a declaration under s 19(4) of the Landlord and Tenant Act 1985 or could call for their own management audit under ss 76–84 of the Leasehold Reform, Housing and Urban Development Act 1993, see at **9.38** and **10.13** above. They also have specific rights to withhold payment in some cases (see at **15.15** above). In such cases landlords sometimes sue one of the smaller tenants: any such unlucky tenant should try to arrange in advance for the other tenants to back his case financially for the general benefit of all the tenants.

Set-off

15.32   The tenant has one advantage in that he can refuse to pay if the total cost is more than is reasonable, except perhaps where set-off is expressly excluded. See, for example, *Connaught Restaurants Ltd v Indoor Leisure Ltd* [1994] 4 All ER 834, where it was held, in effect, that to exclude a tenant's right to set-off the lease more or less had to use those words. For a case of set-off claimed successfully by a landlord (arrears of service charge set-off against damages for breach by the landlord of a repairing covenant), see *Filross Securities Ltd v Midgeley* [1998] 3 EGLR 43. In *Unchained Growth III plc v Granby Village (Manchester) Management Co Ltd* [2000] 1 WLR 739, the Court of Appeal threw out an unmeritorious claim for set-off. The court also stated that the Unfair Contract Terms Act 1997 did not render the express provision against set-off invalid: it was within the exception to reasonableness contained in para 1 of Sch 1 to the Act. Set-off of sums claimed from a landlord by a tenant was not allowed against a manager appointed under the Landlord and Tenant Act 1987 in *Taylor v Blaquiere* [2002] EWCA Civ 1633, [2003] 1 WLR 379 (see at **10.50**). In *Muscat v Smith* [2003] EWCA Civ 962, [2003] 1 WLR 2853, a tenant was able to set off an unliquidated claim for damages for breach of covenant against the current landlord where the breach had been by the previous landlord. This was a form of equitable set-off. The Court of Appeal discussed normal (legal) set-off which they said did not apply as the breach was by a prior landlord, not the current landlord. They also held that s 141 of the Law of Property Act 1925 (under which, at least for pre-1996 leases, the right to recover rent passes to the purchaser of the reversion), the tenant could set off as a form of equitable set-off, as opposed to general set-off. See also *Bluestorm Ltd v Portvale Holdings Ltd* [2004] EWCA Civ 289, [2004] 2 EGLR 38(at **6.41** above), where the tenant tried unsuccessfully to set off against a service charge liability the loss of value of its interest arising from the state of repair of the block.

15.33   See also at **5.43** and **5.71**, where tenants took direct action: *Loria v Hammer* [1989] 2 EGLR 249; *Marenco v Jacromel Co Ltd* [1964] 191 EG 433; and *Elmcroft Developments Ltd v Tankersley-Sawyer* [1984] 1 EGLR 47. However, direct action does not always save the tenant money: see eg *Broomleigh Housing Association Ltd v Hughes* [1999] EGCS 134 (at **4.8**).

PART 5 – OTHER ASPECTS

Concealment of intention to charge

15.34   In a unique case, *R (on the application of Rowe) v Vale of White Horse District Council* [2003] EWHC 388 (Admin), [2003] 11 EGCS 153, a council which should have been entitled to charge sewerage charges under right to buy conveyances was unable to recover. By an administrative error no charges were made between 1982 and 1995, and between 1995 and 2001 no charges were made as a result of a deliberate policy following legal advice. In 2001 house-holders were informed that the council would be charging, backdated to 1995 (six years). The court considered four elements relating to restitution where a supplier supplies services to another and there was no contractual relationship. The only relevant element to be decided in this case was whether it was legally unjust for the householder to retain the benefit of the services without payment. It was held that the council had forfeited its right to charge for the services. 'They had been under a duty, in dealing with the users of their services, to be transparent and to disclose from the beginning what might be in store, rather than springing a surprise and later claiming payment of arrears.' The report is not clear on the point, but one assumes that the householder was a successor in title to a right to buy purchaser of a freehold. If so, this is an example of a successor in title to freehold property not being liable for performance of positive covenants. If the householder had been a (residential) tenant then s 20B of the Landlord and Tenant Act 1985 would have prevented a claim for costs incurred more than 18 months previously without notice. In either event, what seems to be a deliberate concealment may be another ground for a challenge to service charge demand.

Consultation

15.35   Where a landlord consults with a tenant, whether under the statutory provisions or otherwise, the tenant can help himself by responding to the consultation in good time and making his views known. If the detail is not clear the tenant can ask for more information so that he can understand what is being done and why. If the landlord wants to replace something, does the tenant think it needs replacing now, or at all? If it is significant, it may be worth asking a builder or architect to look at the proposals so their comments can be included in the response, but the tenant must act within the timescale required.

15.36   Conversely, a tenant could point out to the landlord or his managing agent where something could usefully be done to save heavier costs in the future: consultation should be a two-way matter.

Negotiating the lease

15.37   There are negotiating tips for tenants at **3.56–3.81**. These include trying to include a declaration that the landlord is to use prudent economy in carrying out the works, and provisions excluding certain items from the charge.

15.38   Readers are reminded that on renewal of a business lease there is House of Lords authority for the proposition that a landlord cannot insist on replacing a lease without a service charge by a new lease with a service charge against the tenant's wishes. (*O'May v City of London Real Property Co Ltd* [1983] 2 AC 726 (at **3.102**).)

CHAPTER 16

Freehold equivalents of service charges

Laws should be like clothes.

They should be made to fit the people they are meant to serve.

Clarence Darrow

PART 1 – INTRODUCTION

16.1   There are major problems about enforcement of positive covenants against successors in title of freehold property. It is material for this book because a covenant to carry out services or works is a positive covenant, as is a covenant to pay for those works or services. This chapter investigates various means by which the obligation to carry out services and the obligation to pay for them can be made to be effective for freeholds against successors to those who entered into the covenants in the first case.

PART 2 – PERPETUAL YEARLY RENTCHARGES

16.2   Perpetual yearly rentcharges are well known in only a few areas (such as Bath, Bristol and Manchester). Many of the eighteenth-century properties in such cities are freeholds, but subject to payment of a perpetual yearly rentcharge. These are different from leases, where a tenant held a property for a specified period and paid a rent to a landlord during that term. The rentcharge is paid for ever and ever. Some owners/freeholders arrange to buy out their rentcharges, but many are unable or unwilling to do so. The amount of the rentcharge is not financially very significant.

What they were

16.3   One big drawback of the rentcharges from the point of view of the owner of the premises was that the rentcharge was usually supported by covenants. These had been imposed to ensure that the property was kept in good repair, so that the property was always of sufficient value to support payment of the rentcharge. Nowadays, a vacant site is likely to be worth £5 a year, but in the eighteenth century that was obviously not so. Such covenants seemed inconsistent with freehold ownership, and are the reverse of leasehold service charges where the landlord does the work and the tenant pays – for perpetual yearly rentcharges the person doing the work and the payer are the same.

16.4   The perpetual yearly rentcharge was thus simply a means for the original seller and his successors in title to receive an annual income in perpetuity. The rentcharge was a charge on the property, and although the rentcharge owner was not a landlord he had rights of distress to recover the rentcharge, and power to appoint a receiver of the rentcharge. As the amounts are small, the cost of exercising these remedies is out of proportion to the amount concerned.

16.5   Rentcharges tended to be in respect of a whole building. If, as in Bath, the whole building had later been divided into flats let on long leases, the question arose as to how to deal with the rentcharge. There were many cases where rentcharges were split and subdivided. This created extra problems in investigating the title to the rentcharge on a purchase or sale of the rentcharge.

16.6   Apart from buying the rentcharge, it could cease in other ways such as non-payment for 12 years (see ss 15(1), 17 and 38(1) of the Limitation Act 1980) or by merger if the freeholder acquired the interest of the rentcharge owner. Occasionally, rentcharges were released, as in the case of a rentcharge originally charged out of a pair of houses which later became charged in whole out of one of them, leaving the other free. If the rentcharge owner agreed to the arrangement this was a legal apportionment and enforceable against the rentcharge owner. (Law of Property Act 1925, s 70 and *Price v John* [1905] 1 Ch 744.) If the rentcharge owner had not consented, this was called an equitable apportionment and was not binding on the rentcharge owner, who had the right to enforce payment out of any part of the property on which the rentcharge had been originally imposed.

Rentcharges Act 1977

16.7   The Rentcharges Act 1977 was intended to remove rentcharges over a period, with a few exceptions. To that end the Act prohibited the creation of new rentcharges except in certain very limited circumstances. After the Act came into force (22 August 1977) the only new rentcharges permitted (under s 2 of the Rentcharges Act 1977) are:

(a)   a rentcharge which has the effect of making the land on which the rent is charged settled land (under s 1 of the Settled Land Act 1925 land charged voluntarily, in consideration of marriage, or by way of family settlement, with the payment of a rentcharge for the life of any person, or even for a shorter period, is settled land);

(b)   a rentcharge which would have the same effect, but for the fact that the land charged is already settled land or is held on trust for sale;

(c)   estate rentcharges (this is the most important exception and is discussed below);

(d)   rentcharges created under statute in connection with works on land (eg repairs or improvements); and

(e)   rentcharges created by court order.

16.8   The 1977 Act also provided (s 3) for perpetual yearly rentcharges to be extinguished at the end of 60 years from 22 August 1977 or 60 years from when the rentcharge first became payable, whichever is later. There is also a procedure (ss 8-10), under which the freeholder can obtain from the Secretary of State a figure on payment of which the rentcharge can be compulsorily redeemed.

16.9   As no new perpetual yearly rentcharges can be created in normal circumstances, we will not comment further on such rentcharges, and will turn to the most important modern rentcharges which can and are being created, namely estate rentcharges, and which are the freehold equivalent of the leasehold service charge.

PART 3 – ESTATE RENTCHARGES

The statutory definition

16.10   Section 2(4) of the Rentcharges Act 1977 defines an estate rentcharge as a rentcharge created for the purpose:

> '(a)   of making covenants to be performed by the owner of the land affected by the rentcharge enforceable by the rent owner against the owner for the time being of the land; or
>
> (b)   of meeting, or contributing towards, the cost of the performance by the rent owner of covenants for the provision of services, the carrying out of maintenance or repairs, the effecting of insurance or the making of any payment by him for the benefit of the land affected by the rentcharge or for the benefit of that and other land.'

Section 2(5) goes on to say that:

> 'a rentcharge of more than a nominal amount shall not be treated as an estate rentcharge for the purposes of this section unless it represents a payment for the performance by the rent owner of any such covenant as is mentioned in subsection (4)(b) above [ie the provision of services, etc], which is reasonable in relation to that covenant.'

16.11   This brings us back to familiar territory with a payment by A for services or works carried out by B.

The problem

16.12   The reason why the Rentcharges Act 1977 was passed was twofold:

(a)   One was the difficulty that so many rentcharge owners and freeholders were having because the change in the value of money made both (i) the cost to the payee of collecting a small sum and (ii) the cost to the freeholder of buying the rentcharge, out of proportion.

413

(b) The second problem was more technical. It was to provide a formal framework to enable the person with the benefit of a positive covenant to enforce that covenant against a successor in title of a freehold estate. (The latter is now also possible through commonhold, see Chapter 17.)

16.13 The enforcement point is very serious. Although the burden of a restrictive (negative) covenant passes when the freehold of the burdened land is transferred, the burden of positive covenants does not.

Example

16.14 Take an obvious example. Mr Sherwood, owner of two adjoining freehold properties known New Chancery and Old Chancery, sells Old Chancery to Mr King. In the transfer of the freehold the purchaser, Mr King, enters into two covenants. One is that he will not use Old Chancery for business purposes. The other covenant is to pay one half of the cost of maintenance, lighting and cleaning of the common driveway leading to Old Chancery and New Chancery. The covenant not to use for business purposes is a restrictive covenant, and the covenant to contribute to costs is a positive covenant.

(a) As Mr King has entered into the covenants, he is clearly bound by them both. It is assumed that they are in valid form and are expressed to be binding on the property and to show which property has the benefit. If Mr King starts using the property as a toyshop he will be in breach, and the vendor, Mr Sherwood, can seek an injunction to stop retail selling, or can claim damages. If the drive needs repair Mr King similarly will be liable for his share, and Mr Sherwood can sue for recovery.

(b) The problem arises when Mr King sells Old Chancery to a purchaser, whom we shall call Mr Westgarth. After that date the restrictive covenant can be enforced but not the positive covenant. So if the new purchaser Mr Westgarth decided to use Old Chancery for the sale of shoes or ships or sealing wax then Mr Sherwood could take effective action, but if Mr Sherwood repaired the common driveway Mr Westgarth could simply refuse to pay his share. As a successor in title he is only bound by restrictive covenants, not the positive covenant to pay.

Enforceability of positive covenants

16.15 The position was confirmed in 1994 by the House of Lords in the case of *Rhone v Stephens* [1994] 2 AC 310. That was a case on repair of roofs, but it applies equally to other positive covenants. Lord Templeman giving the leading judgment gave a useful summary of many authorities, going back as far as 1540 (the Grantees of Reversions Act 1540) and 1583 (*Spencer's Case* (1583) 5 Co Rep 16a). The effect of all of these is to confirm that although the benefit of restrictive covenants can run with the land (ie they can be enforced) the same is not true of positive covenants. Even the case of *Halsall v Brizell* [1957] Ch 169, which purported to show that a person could not have the benefit of a right without the burdens attached to that right, was not sufficient to assist in the case of simple repair covenants.

16.16   In the *Halsall* case the exercise of the right (of drainage) was said to be conditional on payment of a proportion of the cost. In *Rhone v Stephens* Lord Templeman wholeheartedly agreed with the *Halsall* decision but said 'it does not follow that any condition can be rendered enforceable by attaching to it a right, nor does it follow that every burden imposed by a conveyance may be enforced by depriving the covenantor's successor in title of every benefit which he enjoyed thereunder'. Lord Templeman also referred to various Law Commission Reports which have been highly critical of the lack of enforceability of positive covenants against the successors in title.

16.17   More recently, the Court of Appeal, in *Thamesmead Town Ltd v Allotey* [1998] 3 EGLR 97, considered covenants to contribute to communal parts of a residential estate. The purchaser, who had bought under the right to buy legislation, covenanted to contribute to the cost of repair, cleaning etc of paths, drains etc and landscaped areas. The transfer contained an obligation on the purchaser to ensure that subsequent purchasers entered into a deed of covenant in similar terms. (This itself may have been a positive covenant.) The tenant had no specific rights under the transfer over the landscaped areas, nor did the vendor council covenant to maintain the landscaped areas. The property was transferred by the original purchasers, but the second purchasers did not enter into a deed of covenant. They would not pay and the council took them to court. There were arguments about not taking the benefit without accepting the burden (as in *Halsall v Brizell* above), but the court made it clear that you cannot make a positive covenant enforceable simply by attaching a right to it. The court also said that to make a positive covenant enforceable against a successor the condition of discharging the burden (ie the payment) must be relevant to the exercise of the benefit: here the purchaser could not use the landscaped areas, and thus had no benefit. In the event the claim for payment was rejected. (The amount in dispute was effectively only £6.34, but the decision affected the whole estate in perpetuity.)

16.18   For the case of a freehold where there were no repairing covenants see *Abbahall Ltd v Smee* [2002] EWCA Civ 1831, [2003] 1 All ER 465. It was held that an owner who acquired title by adverse possession, and thus had not entered in to any covenants, was liable for a proportion of the costs of maintenance of items used in common. This seems to be an exception to the position outlined above, although clearly the court did not want to allow someone who had acquired property without using the proper channels to be able to benefit from his own default. No doubt part of the reason was that, if the squatter had bought the property in the normal way, the documents would have contained some obligations about repair.

16.19   There is no doubt that positive covenants cannot always be enforced against a freehold successor in title. In the case of leaseholds there is always privity of estate between landlord and tenant so that positive covenants are enforceable. Section 3(7) of the Landlord and Tenant (Covenants) Act 1995 provides that for leases granted after the commencement of the Act all lease covenants are enforceable, whether they 'touch and concern' the land or not.

16.20 In due course, some government will no doubt bring in legislation to make positive covenants affecting freeholds enforceable against successors. The Law Commission drafted a Bill in the 1980s to this effect, but there seems reluctance for the government to bring in such a bill. This is, in the author's view, partly because of concern that it will affect existing arrangements where people have bought freehold properties and received (correct) advice that they are not bound by certain covenants which apparently affect their property. If the law is changed, people who had been told that certain covenants were unenforceable could find them being enforced. This hardly seems a good reason for doing nothing – it is easy for Parliament to provide that the Act only applies to covenants entered into after the Act became law, or after a specified date, or phased for covenants when they have existed for a specified period. Until such a law is passed practitioners will have to do their best make arrangements work. At present the best way is using estate rentcharges. (An alternative is commonhold (see Chapter 17).)

The solutions

16.21 Conveyancers have tried several means of making positive covenants enforceable against successors in title of the person who entered into the covenant. With such a heavy emphasis on professional negligence these days the point needs careful consideration – a dissatisfied client who is unable to recover expenses may seek to claim against professional advisers who did not achieve the desired result. Commonhold property is freehold, but it has its own system for services and works and payment for them, as set out in Chapter 17. The three most usual ways of dealing with services and payment, in the order of effectiveness, are set out below.

Estate rentcharges

16.22 These are the subject of the next section of this chapter.

Requiring a purchaser to covenant

16.23 This entails providing in the documents that a purchaser cannot register a transfer of the freehold at the Land Registry without ensuring that the transferee enters into a direct covenant with the party who has the obligation to carry out the services. The covenant is to observe the positive covenants, coupled with an obligation to ensure that successors enter into similar covenants. This is reasonably successful provided it is carefully worded, but can fail in some cases where the chain of ownership is broken, such as on death or insolvency. This is because the executors or a trustee in bankruptcy etc have acquired their interest by operation of law, and did not have to enter into the (positive) covenant to obtain a new covenant from the purchaser. Accordingly, they can transfer the property without having to comply. In most cases they will seek a suitable covenant, but if the purchaser refuses the executors or trustee may be unable to insist.

16.24   In the modern form of the arrangement the parties include in the documents a request for the Land Registry to include a restriction that no new proprietor can be registered without a certificate from the person to benefit, or his solicitor, that the covenant has been provided. (For example, Form L from the recommended forms of notice in the Land Registration Rules 2003.) This is, of course, helpful, but, strictly, the obligation to carry out works, or the obligation to pay cannot be enforced against an executor or trustee in bankruptcy of the person who entered into the covenant, during the period when they are estate owner by operation of law. Of course, when they come to sell, as they usually do at some time, the restriction on the register will come into play, and the purchaser from the executor or trustee will need to comply with the restriction or will be unable to be registered as the proprietor of the land.

16.25   This scheme is often used for items such as access roads and unadopted drains. For such cases expenses are not incurred regularly, and many are on the basis of payment in arrear. Occasionally, some are in advance, where estimates are to be produced and agreed. This would then be a condition precedent, and the person seeking payment would have to comply. If the works are more extensive, and include eg security, landscaping, lighting, maintenance of signs, marking out of common parking areas etc, then the provisions are likely to resemble those of a leasehold service charge, with estimates, payments on account and annual adjustments.

16.26   Whether the scheme is limited or more extensive, many of the concerns highlighted above in relation to drafting and negotiating leasehold service charges, mentioned in Chapter 3, are equally relevant to freeholds. In particular is the need to ensure that the services to be provided are clearly identified, and also which of the services or works the payer is to pay for.

Making the benefit conditional on payment

16.27   In other words, providing that the use of the services, eg the use of the road, is conditional on payment of a proportion of the cost of maintenance, ie as in *Halsall v Brizell* [1957] Ch 169 (above at **16.15**). This has the disadvantage that in reality it is usually impossible to prevent the one party who has not paid from using, eg the road, without also stopping others who have paid using it. The same point applies to joint drainage. While such a provision is clearly more likely to have effect than a simple positive covenant to pay a proportion of cost, it is a poor third as a choice.

PART 4 – ESTATE RENTCHARGES SCHEME

16.28   As mentioned above (at **16.10**), estate rentcharges can be lawfully created, and are not subject to automatic termination like perpetual yearly rentcharges. Section 2(4) of the Rentcharges Act 1977 specifically refers to estate rentcharges as being created for the purpose '(a) of making covenants to be performed by the owner of the land affected by the rentcharge enforceable by the rent owner against the owner for the time being of the land or (b) of meeting, or contributing towards … the cost of … the provision of services'. In practice many estate rentcharges are both.

16.29   The estate rentcharge can be supported by a right of re-entry if it is unpaid for 40 days. (Law of Property Act 1925, s 121(3).) It can also be enforced by distress if it is 21 days in arrear (Law of Property Act 1925, s 121(2).) These two rights can be more useful in some cases than rights to sue for breach of covenant, although the right to sue is obviously also available to the rentcharge owner. Distress, however, may not be generally available much longer, as it seems likely to be phased out over the next few years. The rent owner can also create a demise of the land to recover the arrears and costs, and such demise can be used to raise money by mortgage or sale, or receipt of income from the land. (Law of Property Act 1925, s 121(4).) The latter remedy may be most useful where the property has been let.

16.30   The rentcharge is recoverable against 'the owner for the time being of the land' (Rentcharges Act 1977, s 2(4)) but it may be sensible to ensure that the cost of work is collected in advance.

16.31   It is not uncommon for a freehold property to be sold subject to a double rentcharge. One is a fixed annual amount (intended to cover the first limb of s 2(4)) and the other rentcharge (the second limb) is similar to a service charge. The fixed sum is usually fairly small, particularly bearing in mind the provisions of s 2(5) which states that a more than nominal rentcharge (other than as reimbursement of costs) cannot be an estate rentcharge, and would thus be likely to be subject to compulsory redemption.

16.32   Although s 2(4) refers to a rentcharge for securing performance of a covenant 'or' one for service charge recovery it appears in practice to be accepted that both can be side by side. There is an advantage in having an annual sum payable. It means that the existence of the obligation is before the parties on a regular basis. For example, assume that the estate rentcharge is used to ensure that successors in title to the purchaser of a freehold warehouse unit contribute to the costs of maintaining the road. It would not be surprising to find that the road only needs repair every ten years. During that period the freeholder could easily forget that he has any obligation to pay towards repairs: the annual estate rentcharge demand for the nominal sum is a reminder of that continuing responsibility to others. It also helps ensure that the rentcharge owner is kept up to date with the names of the purchasers.

Single estate rentcharge

16.33   There can be a straightforward reservation of a single estate rentcharge. This can be one of an unspecified amount equal to the appropriate share of the costs of services which are to be borne by the property in question. It is usually payable on demand or in advance.

Double estate rentcharges

16.34   There can be a double estate rentcharge comprising both the elements mentioned at **16.28**.

Estate rentcharges to a management company

16.35   Sometimes when an estate is developed the developer will transfer the freehold plots of land or units (houses, warehouses, etc) to purchasers, and will transfer the freehold of the road or other common areas over which services are to be performed to a management company. The purchaser of the unit will be required to enter into the estate rentcharge, or rentcharges, with the management company. As in the case of leaseholds, the management company is often the creature of the purchasers who are required to become shareholders and who are also required to transfer their shares in the company when they transfer their own freehold. (See Chapter 12 for management companies.)

16.36   For a case relating to a management company set up to run the common parts of a freehold development under which various payments were made, see *Bratton Seymour Service Co Ltd v Oxborough* [1992] EGCS 28 (at **12.6**).

Drafting points

16.37   There are no statutory words required to create an estate rentcharge. What is needed is for the relevant document to show it clearly intends to create a charge over a parcel of land as security for payment to the estate rentcharge owner. The transfer usually contains words such as '... ALL THAT property comprised in the above mentioned title charged with the payment to the Transferor [or the Management Company] of the estate rentcharge hereinafter referred to ...' That is clear and sufficient.

16.38   The deed creating the rentcharge should also contain an express right of re-entry by the estate rentcharge owner in case there is a default by the rentcharge payer. The estate rentcharge payer has a right to apply for relief from forfeiture under s 146 of the Law of Property Act 1925.

16.39   Where the estate rentcharge is to be paid to a management company that company should be a party to the transfer creating the rentcharge, or there should be a separate deed between the purchaser and the management company complying with s 2 of the Law of Property (Miscellaneous Provisions) Act 1989. The purchaser should ensure that the management company agrees to comply with the repairing obligations for which the rentcharge is reserved. A cautious purchaser might seek a fallback position under which either the vendor agrees to carry out repairs if the management company defaults (although this is unlikely to be agreed). Better still, the purchaser could have rights to enter to carry out the repairs himself with rights to recover from those sharing the facilities. Where the various purchasers are to be shareholders in a company, any purchaser should seek information about shareholding levels and voting rights, appointment of directors, and provisions requiring the purchaser to transfer his shares when transferring the freehold.

Definitions

16.40   Inspection before drafting is recommended whenever possible (see at **3.6** et seq). The points about leasehold service charges are equally valid in nearly all particulars when considering drafting estate rentcharges, although the range of services is often very much more limited than for leases (see Chapter 3 generally).

16.41   The definitions of premises are vital (see at **3.12** et seq). The property over which services are to be carried out needs to be defined with precision, but also, where possible, with a degree of flexibility. This is perhaps more difficult to agree with a purchaser of a freehold than of a lease, but it is in a way even more important. After all, it is more likely that a freehold development will change over the decades than a leasehold development which may only operate for 15 years. Certainly, buildings and equipment become out of date and from time to time need replacing, and thus the parties should accept that the freehold development will change.

16.42   For the same reason definitions of services (see at **3.35** et seq) need to be reasonably flexible, although the seller should be careful not to make the range of services for which a charge could be made too wide or he could (a) discourage potential buyers or (b) run the risk of finding that a court would hold that the services are too indefinite to be the subject of enforcement. Estate rentcharges do not always have a sweeping-up clause.

16.43   Estate rentcharges are encountered mostly in the context of repair and maintenance of estate roads and drainage systems. These are not too hard to cover, in that the drafting should cover the existing road and the existing drains and replacements of them, including the cost of replacement. It is also not too hard to cover the cost of maintenance of roads or drains which still serve the property, even if they are in a different layout from that which existed when the development was laid out. Where it becomes much more difficult is where the layout is changed drastically, particularly to enable further users to use the facilities. The best protection to the parties here is to provide:

(a) that the estate rentcharge covers repairs and replacement of the road and drains in their position at the date of the transfer; and

(b) that it also covers repairs and replacement of the roads and drains which in the future serve the premises even if they are in a different position, but where the change is such that the roads and drains also serve premises which were not served when the estate rentcharge was entered into, that the estate rentcharge payer is only responsible for a proportion of the costs reflecting an appropriate proportion of the changed use. In other words, if three units originally benefited and a further three units were connected to the road the estate rentcharge percentage of the original covenanting parties should be halved, as they are now one of six instead of one of three.

It would also be worth trying to agree that before any new premises can be allowed to use the same facilities the parties should agree (i) that the capacity is adequate and (ii) that any percentages for the estate rentcharge are revised.

The Orchard Trading case

16.44 The Court of Appeal recently considered estate rentcharges in the very useful case of *Orchard Trading Estate Management Ltd v Johnson Security Ltd* [2002] EWCA Civ 406, [2002] 18 EG 155. The court reviewed estate rentcharges generally and the 1977 Act. Two points are particularly worth recording:

(a) The payer argued that the estate rentcharge in question was invalid as it did not expressly say it was limited to a 'reasonable' amount, and was thus outside s 2(5) of the 1977 Act. (See at **16.10** above for s 2(4) and (5).) The court rejected this argument. The costs were to reimburse the full expenditure (on sewerage works), and the deed also referred to recovery of various professional fees in relation to that expenditure. The judge in the lower court, approved by the Court of Appeal, said that the purpose of the deed was to meet in full the expenditure and, 'given that no more than 100% of the expenditure is recoverable, then the payment must in my judgment be reasonable in relation to that covenant. The mischief attacked by subsection (5) is, I think, in the circumstances where a fixed sum is provided for in the rentcharge which bears no proportion [sic] to the actual expenditure, and that is not the present case.' The Court of Appeal said the appeal was based on a challenge to the validity of the rentcharge, not whether the charge itself was reasonable. The court went on to say: 'I cannot accept that the absence of an express limitation of reasonableness in the deed renders the deed void.'

(b) The payers also challenged the demand so far as it related to the payment of rates which were not mentioned in the document. That claim was also struck out. The Court of Appeal agreed with the trial judge that the roadways and sewerage works were held to enable the rent owner to perform its obligations for the benefit of the unit owners.

16.45 It will be seen that this case confirms that the word 'reasonable' does not need to be used in the estate rentcharge part of the deed. It also seems to provide that the obligation to pay may not be restricted to the exact wording of the deed – obviously rates were not mentioned, but in the circumstances the Court of Appeal deemed it appropriate to imply that they were payable. My usual plea to those drafting to include everything – do not rely on the court implying further items, although this case may give comfort in a case where there has been some obvious omission.

Recovery provisions

16.46 The provisions for payment tend to be more brief than for a service charge, because the normal estate rentcharge to cover costs is recoverable in arrear rather than in advance, although this is not universally so. They are often similar to the 'common parts' recovery clause used in conveyances, whereby the covenantor agrees to pay a fair proportion of the expenses of items such as drains or party walls used in common between the property he is buying and adjoining properties. In those cases where the estate rentcharge payer is asked to pay in advance it sometimes follows an agreement between the parties concerned as to the cost – in other words the carrying out of the work is conditional on agreement of estimates. Since the estate rentcharge is often for repair of a private roadway, the costs can often be high, and thus such a provision is reasonable. It is to be remembered that if the documents contain a provision to the effect that recovery is conditional on prior agreement the person seeking to recover must comply with the condition or he will not be able to recover. (See eg *CIN Properties Ltd v Barclays Bank* plc [1986] 1 EGLR 59 (at **14.22**), and *Northways Flats Management Co (Camden) Ltd v Wimpey Pension Trustees Ltd* [1992] 2 EGLR 42 (at **6.42**).)

16.47 It is useful to record the percentage of costs which the property is to bear, but with flexibility as above. There are often provisions for arbitration in case of dispute, and such provisions are useful if the parties feel that this would be cheaper or quicker (or both) than court proceedings. (See below for dividing up the property.)

16.48 There are no statutory provisions requiring prior estimates etc as in the case of the Landlord and Tenant Act 1985, s 20, and so if there are no provisions for consultation with the estate rentcharge payer prior to the request for payment then no such consultation is needed, but it is usually sensible, to achieve recovery of the amounts required (as in service charge cases) to consult with the payers, at least in relation to major items or unusual items.

16.49 Draftsmen need to remember that the person who wants to be paid needs to know who is to pay. In the case of leases often the landlord's consent is needed before a tenant can assign. In other leases, particularly long leases, it is only necessary for the tenant to notify the landlord that the assignment has taken place. It is clearly inappropriate for an estate rentcharge payer to have to seek consent to sell his freehold. So that the estate rentcharge owner has the relevant information to be able to collect the estate rentcharge when it is due, the transfer should ideally contain provisions to ensure that the estate rentcharge owner (the payee) is notified of changes. One of the most effective ways is to provide that the payer remains liable for payment unless and until he notifies the payee of changes of ownership. It is therefore in the interest of the original payer to make sure that any sale is duly notified. It is good practice for the deeds to require a transferee to enter into a direct covenant with the rent owner when purchasing.

Records

16.50 Records should be kept of expenditure as well as vouchers, and it can be helpful for such items as estimates and tenders to be available for the estate rentcharge payers to inspect. Apart from any other consideration, these will be of assistance should a dispute come to litigation. It gives the payer much more confidence that what is being requested is reasonable and genuine when the papers are readily available for inspection. A purchaser should seek a provision permitting inspection of the vouchers and the vendor should not object.

Sale

16.51 Purchasers of property subject to rentcharges, or the benefit of the right to receive them, should adapt the contract provisions appropriately.

16.52 The points made in Chapter 13 as to suitable provisions are relevant for estate rentcharges.

Property subject to payment of an estate rentcharge

16.53 The purchaser of a property subject to a rentcharge needs:

(a) to make enquiries as to the level of payment, and whether any particularly large expenditure is anticipated in the near future (this is perhaps of particular importance for estate rentcharges where there may be no payment for many years and then a large payment);

(b) to check if there are arrears (they should be cleared by the vendor or an allowance made to the purchaser); and

(c) to find if there have been problems, and, if so, the nature of them.

16.54 The vendor of a property from which a rentcharge is payable needs to ensure that the contract:

(a) discloses the rentcharge and commits the purchaser to taking on the responsibility, including any necessary obligation to give notice to the estate rentcharge owner; and

(b) provides for the purchaser to pay any relevant apportionment where the estate rentcharge is on an annual basis. If the estate rentcharge is for works that have been carried out the vendor should pay: if they are for works still to be carried out then it may be appropriate for the purchaser to pay.

The right to receive the estate rentcharge

16.55 The more difficult provisions are in relation to the sale of a property which has the benefit of the right to receive estate rentcharges. Again, the provisions for sale of a property subject to a number of leases where the tenants pay service charges are similar. (See at **13.19** et seq.) The main points are:

(a) Obligations to disclose the accounts and details of work done and payments received.

(b) Obligations to hand over the records and vouchers.

(c) Clear provisions for apportionment. These will vary depending on whether the estate rentcharge payers pay in advance or in arrear. Provision will also need to be made for cases where the estate rentcharge is outstanding.

(d) The contract should be clear on the payment for work done for which no bill has been received – are these to be paid by the vendor or the purchaser?

(e) The purchaser may well seek confirmation that no payments should be made between exchange of contracts and completion for which an estate rentcharge payer is to be asked to pay, or perhaps not in excess of an agreed budget figure.

Division of property and apportionment

16.56 Many estate rentcharges are for large warehouse or factory units on commercial developments. After a period the units concerned may be altered and split up. In such a case it is perfectly possible for the estate rentcharge to be divided among the constituent parts. Where that happens the normal practice is for the part being sold to be charged with (sold subject to the payment of) X% of the original estate rentcharge payable under the provisions of a specified transfer, and the property retained is to stand charged with the payment of the balance of the original estate rentcharge. It is also possible to provide for the whole of the rentcharge to be paid out of the part being sold, or the part retained.

16.57 As mentioned above (at **16.6**), if the estate rentcharge owner consents to the division then it will be effective against the rentcharge owner. In those cases the estate rentcharge owner will only be able to recover the X% from the part sold off and the balance from the remainder of the original site. It is hard to see a benefit for the estate rentcharge owner to agree: he has to send out two demands instead of one and keep two records instead of one, and if one part is unpaid there is a smaller (and thus proportionately more expensive) part to claim from the defaulter. Paragraph 2 of Sch 1 to the Landlord and Tenant (Covenants) Act 1995 makes a minor change to s 77 of the Law of Property Act 1925 in respect of implied covenants where part of land affected by a rentcharge is transferred. There is, however, a statutory procedure as indicated in the next paragraph which can affect the position.

16.58   If the estate rentcharge owner will not agree to a legal apportionment the estate rentcharge payer can seek an order from the Secretary of State apportioning the rentcharge under ss 4 and 5 of the Rentcharges Act 1977. The procedure involves notifying the Secretary of State of the suggested apportionment, and the Secretary will prepare a draft order giving effect to an apportionment. The draft Order is served on the estate rentcharge owner who is entitled to make objections and representations. After time for objections, usually 21 days under s 5(5), an order is made (s 5(10)) and served on the estate rentcharge owner. There is a right of appeal by any party affected to the Lands Tribunal (s 6). For very small apportionments (under £5 per year), the apportionment is treated as having effect only for the purpose of redemption of that part of the rentcharge under the compulsory redemption provisions described at **16.8** above (s 7).

16.59   The provisions above, as to redemption for a small apportionment, might apply where, for example, the part sold off is a very tiny part of the original, such as the sale of the site of a private car garage out of a large warehouse unit.

PART 5 – OTHER FREEHOLD SERVICE CHARGES

16.60   Readers are reminded that there can be service charges which affect freeholds in respect of flats which are acquired by the tenants either:

(a)   under the Landlord and Tenant Act 1987, where (i) the tenants buy the freehold under the right of first refusal or (ii) the landlord's interest is acquired compulsorily following his serious default in complying with his obligations; or

(b)   under the Leasehold Reform, Housing and Urban Development Act 1993, where the tenants collectively enfranchise.

Estate management schemes

16.61   On similar lines, Chapter V of Pt 1 of the Leasehold Reform, Housing and Urban Development Act 1993 should be mentioned. This permits landlords to set up and obtain approval of the Lands Tribunal to an estate management scheme. This is needed so that in an area which was formerly run on a leasehold basis by landlords, and which becomes partly leasehold and partly freehold following enfranchisement of some of the premises, can still be managed as a whole. There is a similar provision under the Leasehold Reform Act 1967.

16.62   The Lands Tribunal decision in *Re Grosvenor Estate (Mayfair) London's Application* [1995] 2 EGLR 202 concerned the estate management scheme for Mayfair. The scheme provided for continued control by the former landlords over premises no longer let by them in respect of decoration, alteration etc. Those interested are referred to the report, but one item is relevant for this book. Clause 19 of the scheme provided for payment of a management charge, so that the former landlords would not be responsible for all the costs of management of the area after some properties ceased to be held from them on lease. The tribunal approved the right of the landlord to include such a charge in the estate management scheme. Apparently, the charge was index linked.

16.63   Finally, commonhold has now been introduced. It can affect residential, commercial or mixed premises. Commonhold units are held on a freehold basis, but are always subject to payment of a charge loosely similar to service charges. Commonhold is the subject of the next chapter.

CHAPTER 17

Commonhold

When concluded, this will be one of the finest Bills to go through both Houses.

Baroness Scotland of Asthal (in the House of Lords debate on the Commons amendments to the Commonhold and Leasehold Reform Bill, 15 April 2002)

PREFACE

Personal note from the author

I have been interested in commonhold since I first heard about it as a Law Commission proposal in the 1980s. When the proposal was revived in about 2000 I became interested again, and was privileged to be invited to join a working party formed by the Department for Constitutional Affairs to assist in the preparation of the Regulations, and also some guidance notes. It was a most interesting and satisfying experience.

The two types of charge

Since the end of 2004 commonhold has been available as a third means of holding property, alongside freehold and leasehold. The purpose of this Preface is to say that there are two separate aspects of service charges which relate to commonhold property, and they must not be confused.

1. First, there are the charges to be made for running the commonhold (called the 'commonhold assessment') which are payable by the holder of a commonhold unit. They are the subject of this chapter.

2. It is also possible for a unit-holder to let his unit, and, if he does, it is possible he may charge his tenant service charges. This is the second aspect. However, there is a big difference between this and a normal landlord and tenant relationship. This is because the commonhold unit-holder only holds the unit – he does not hold any of the common parts. All he can let is the unit, and so any services he carries out are to the unit, and not to common areas. The scope for normal service charges within a lease of a commonhold unit is therefore limited.

INTRODUCTION

Why have commonhold?

17.1   Commonhold was introduced to England in 2004 by virtue of the Commonhold and Leasehold Reform Act 2002. The Act is supplemented by the Commonhold Regulations 2004 ('the Regulations') and the Commonhold (Land Registration) Rules 2004. The commonhold scheme is set out in general terms in the Act, but the two sets of Regulations provide the details to make it work. One cannot understand commonhold without taking account of both the Act and the Regulations. Indeed, the Regulations amend the Act in one or two minor cases. The Act was introduced for the reasons mentioned in the next paragraph. It is recorded here because there must be a percentage allocated to each commonhold unit for costs, and the commonhold equivalent of service charges, the 'commonhold assessment', bears no resemblance to either service charges in leaseholds or estate rentcharges. Leasehold service charge considerations can apply in limited circumstance as between commonhold unit-holders and any tenant they may have.

17.2   The main reasons for introducing commonhold are:

1.   *Enforcement of positive covenants*

    (a)   English law does not entitle a freeholder to enforce a positive covenant against a successor in title of the person who made the original commitment. (See eg *Rhone v Stephens* [1994] 2 AC 310, mentioned at **16.15**.) Since positive covenants include, in particular, both covenants to repair items and covenants to pay a contribution for repair, this is a considerable problem. There have been some attempts to get round this problem (see Chapter 16, at **16.21** et seq) but they often fail when there is insolvency or death, and an estate passes by operation of law. Leaseholds do not have the same difficulty because landlord and tenant covenants (positive and negative) subsist during the whole of the term.

2.   *Problems with leases*

    (b)   There are cases where tenants feel landlords take advantage of them, which is the reason for the extensive statutory protection for residential tenants. Some problems in this context arise from service charges, where there is scope for tension because A is carrying out services that he wants B and C to pay for, and also because occupiers or other tenants often feel they have little control over what is being done to their building. The 2002 Act introduces the Right to Manage which enables tenants of dwellings to take over management (see at **10.34** et seq), and there are rights for tenants of flats to appoint a manager under the Landlord and Tenant Act 1987 (see at **10.44** et seq), but there are qualifications in both cases and so these remedies are not available for all leasehold premises. Mind you, not every building can be converted to a commonhold (see at **17.11**).

(c) A lease is a reducing asset. A lease becomes less valuable and more difficult to mortgage or sell as it gets shorter.

(d) Management can be more difficult, and thus more expensive, where the leases are inconsistent.

The commonhold solution

17.3   Commonhold was introduced to address all the above problems. A commonhold can be commercial or residential or mixed. It enables those who hold a commonhold unit to enforce positive obligations against other unit-holders, or against the commonhold association which is responsible for management.

(a) The right to enforce obligations applies while the (freehold) commonhold subsists, in the same way as the right to enforce leasehold covenants subsists while the lease is in being.

(b) Dissatisfaction with the leasehold system is less material, as unit-holders have a freehold interest in their own unit, and they manage the premises between themselves through the commonhold association, which is the company of the unit-holders. (See at **17.8** et seq, below for the scheme.) Where there are joint unit-holders the first named or the person nominated will be the member for that unit and thus able to exercise voting rights etc – s 13 of the Act and reg 2 (which, incidentally, amends s 13 of the Act).

(c) Because the unit-holders have a freehold, the reducing length of a lease is not a problem for a commonhold unit-holder.

(d) The system of commonhold is within one master document, the 'commonhold community statement' (the 'CCS'), rather than lots of different, and possibly inconsistent, leases.

Use of commonhold in practice

17.4   It is likely that the main use of commonhold, at least initially, will be for new blocks of flats. However, commonhold is not restricted to residential premises, and can be either wholly residential, wholly non-residential, or a combination of the two.

17.5   Apart from blocks of flats, commonhold could be used, for example, for a parade of shops with flats over, where there are common areas such as stairs and corridors and parking areas or service yards. Equally, there could be a residential housing development where the roads or drainage for some reason are not adopted and where arrangements will be needed for repair.

17.6   Commonhold could also be used for a commercial development such as an industrial park where the roads or services are not adopted but the occupiers prefer to hold a freehold. For comments on specific aspects of commercial commonholds see at **17.106** et seq.

17.7 Much will depend on the wishes of the parties and how well the scheme is seen to work. The success of the scheme may well depend on how parties value the benefit of having a freehold and being in control, as opposed to having a reducing lease and a landlord.

THE COMMONHOLD SCHEME

17.8 A commonhold is a set of premises held in common under its own set of rules. The individual parts ('the commonhold units') are held by 'unit-holders'. The commonhold units are held as freeholds. All of the commonhold which is not part of any unit is 'common parts', and the common parts are held by the 'commonhold association'. Since, apart from an initial phase, the only people entitled to be members of the commonhold association are unit-holders, the effect is that all parts of the commonhold are held either (a) by unit-holders or (b) by the commonhold association, which is the company of the unit-holders. The key point is that the commonhold is managed under its own local rules, 'the commonhold community statement'. The Department for Constitutional Affairs has published a Non-Statutory Guide to the Regulations, which is fairly helpful.

17.9 The difference between the leasehold system and the commonhold system can be seen as the difference between a kingdom and a republic. In the one case there are parties with different interests (superior and inferior), and in the other case all parties are equal. The point about equality is one that highlights one factor of commonhold – namely that the unit-holders have to be involved in management because there is no landlord to do it. There may well be an active set of unit-holders who are happy to shoulder the burden. If they do that is fine, so long as they do not oppress the others. What can be a problem (and it applies also to leaseholds where the tenants acquire the freehold) is that when the active parties move on someone else has to take up the baton. It may not always be easy to find people willing to do so. (Management is mentioned below at **17.12** et seq.) Its closest analogy is those cases where tenants have bought the freehold between them. In such a case the landlord and tenant relationship continues, whereas there is no landlord for a commonhold.

The main differences between service charges in commonhold and leasehold

17.10 Apart from the consequences that flow from there being no landlord the following are the major differences between service charges in leaseholds and a commonhold assessment within a commonhold:

(a) Service charges are a matter of choice for leaseholds: commonhold assessment is compulsory for commonhold. (Section 38(2)(c) of the Act.)

(b) A lease normally sets out the works or services for which the landlord is entitled to charge by way of service charge. By contrast, the commonhold community statement does not go into detail of works or services for which charges are to be made: the commonhold assessment will be based on the cost of whatever the unit-holders decide to do, on an annual basis.

(c) The commonhold assessment arrangements effectively appear in one document, the CCS. For leases there can be various management arrangements contained in the leases of different parts of the development. For example, where there are shops with flats above, the shops and flats may well have different service charge provisions and, of course, the statutory provisions only affect the flats, meaning they have to be treated differently.

(d) Service charge schemes can vary from lease to lease within a development, but the commonhold arrangements are a single (prescribed) arrangement, covering three types of payment which have to be considered in each case. These are an annual sum, additional charges in emergency, and the equivalent of a sinking fund. (See at **17.23** et seq.) There is scope to amplify the commonhold provisions, but the form of the CCS in the Regulations must be used.

(e) Commonhold assessment is based on fixed percentages for each unit, and those percentages must add up to 100%. (Section 38(2) of the Act.) In the case of leasehold service charges the tenant's proportion can be a fixed percentage or a 'fair proportion' or some similar expression. (See at **4.18** et seq.) In addition, it is not unlawful for the total percentage in leaseholds to add up to either more or less than 100%.

(f) The statutory provisions affecting residential leases mentioned in Chapters 9 and 10 relating to reasonableness, consultation, proposed designated accounts etc do not apply to the commonhold assessment, whether residential or commercial. This is because there is no lease or landlord. The statutory provisions apply to the lease by a unit-holder of a residential commonhold unit, but will have a very limited effect (see at **17.96**).

(g) A unit-holder is prohibited from providing in the lease of a residential unit that his tenant is to pay the commonhold assessment. (reg 11(1)(f).) This does not apply to commercial leases unless an additional provision to this effect is added to the commonhold community statement. The author has not seen a similar restriction in a lease, prohibiting the tenant requiring an undertenant to pay the service charge.

(h) There is a unique right for the commonhold association to be able to require the tenant to divert his rent to the commonhold association to pay the commonhold assessment if the unit-holder is in arrears. With leaseholds there is limited right for a superior landlord to call on an undertenant to pay his rent to the superior landlord under the Law of Distress (Amendment) Act 1908, but this diversion is a different arrangement. (See at **17.51** et seq.)

(i) There is limited scope for the first unit-holder to negotiate the terms of the arrangement, as would be the case with the first tenant. This is because the first unit-holder will be buying a (freehold) title that is already registered. Such negotiation on aspects affecting charging is, in any event, not so important in commonhold cases, as the details of what the unit-holder is to be charged for do not appear in the CCS.

(j)   For commercial tenants there is no statutory obligation on a landlord to consult with the tenant. For leases of dwellings the tenant has a right to be consulted on service charge works under s 20 of the Landlord and Tenant Act 1985. (See at **9.56** et seq.) There is a limited procedure for consultation on the commonhold assessment which applies to all unit-holders, whatever the use of the unit (see at **17.25**, and **17.34**).

(k)   There are differences about liability for successors and predecessors in title. For commonhold the unit-holder is never liable for his successors, but is liable for his predecessors. (See at **17.113**.)

(l)   The commonhold association has no power to distrain or forfeit to recover arrears of commonhold assessment, in contrast to a landlord who has these rights in relation to rent and (sometimes) for service charges.

(m)   A unit-holder, or one of joint unit-holders, is a member of the commonhold association, and thus can automatically have a say in management. That is by no means always the case for leaseholds.

Creating a commonhold

17.11   The scheme applies where the freehold of property that qualifies is registered at HM Land Registry as a freehold in commonhold land. (Commonhold and Leasehold Reform Act 2002, s 1.) On the completion of registration at HM Land Registry of the first transfer of a commonhold unit the commonhold rights and obligations arise. (Commonhold and Leasehold Reform Act 2002, ss 7(3) and 9(3).) This is not the place to discuss the details of what properties can be made into commonhold. Effectively, however, it needs at least two parcels of freehold (there must be more than one, so they can be held in common) and must include ground level. There cannot be a flying freehold within the commonhold. The details appear in s 1 of and Sch 2 to the Act, although it may be worth mentioning that as matters stand:

(a)   the underlying interest must be a freehold, not a leasehold;

(b)   leases existing when the commonhold is created become extinguished; and

(c)   there is no current way for tenants to compel the freehold to be converted to a commonhold.

Land Registry Practice Note 60 is helpful in relation to practice on registration etc of commonholds.

Management of the commonhold

17.12   Once the commonhold is set up the commonhold association (comprising, in effect, only the unit-holders) manages the commonhold (Commonhold and Leasehold Reform Act 2002, s 35) and thus the only people concerned with it are the unit-holders. There can be an initial phase where the person who applies to register the freehold as a freehold in commonhold land (called in the Act 'the developer') also has an interest, but this interest ceases after a time – Commonhold Act, s 58 and Sch 4, and regs 14(8), (9) and 15(10). (See at **17.65**.) There are no leases and no landlord. The scheme is material for this volume because the commonhold association, which has to manage the commonhold, must set an annual budget, which is called the 'commonhold assessment' (s 38 of the Act), and collect it from the unit-holders. The CCS, which is the blueprint for the commonhold in question, also has to set out the percentages of the commonhold assessment payable for each unit. The service charge percentages must add up to 100%, although a unit can be shown with a 0% contribution (Commonhold and Leasehold Reform Act 2002, s 38(1)(c) and (2)).

17.13   The commonhold association has an obligation to maintain and insure all common parts. (Commonhold and Leasehold Reform Act 2002, s 26.) As the common parts include every part of the commonhold that is not comprised within a unit (Commonhold and Leasehold Reform Act 2002, s 25(1)) there can be no part of the commonhold that is neither a unit nor part of the common parts. Compare, for example, the leasehold cases at **3.22**.

17.14   The obligation for maintenance etc of commonhold units (as opposed to the common parts) can be split in the CCS as desired between the commonhold association and the unit-holders.

17.15   The commonhold association is responsible for maintenance and insurance of the common parts and, as in the preceding paragraph, it may be responsible for other parts as well. In the case of a self-contained building or a self-contained part of a building containing only one commonhold unit (such as industrial units or detached houses) the CCS may, but does not have to, exclude from the definition of the unit the 'structure and exterior'. In all other cases (ie where there is more than one unit in a building), the CCS excludes the structure and exterior from the definition of any unit, thus ensuring that repair and insurance of the structure and exterior for such premises are the responsibility of the commonhold association (regs 9 and 15(7)). This means that, for example, for blocks of offices or flats, the commonhold association will be responsible for the structure and exterior as well as other common parts, leaving the unit-holder only liable for internal repairs (s 14 of the Act).

17.16   There can be, within a commonhold, areas called 'limited use areas' (s 25(2) of the Act). Such areas are common parts, which only some unit-holders are entitled to enjoy. For example, if there are balconies attached to flats it may well be that the commonhold association would retain the obligation to maintain and decorate them so that they are kept in the same style. The balcony would then be a limited use area, shown in the CCS as being only for the use of the unit adjoining it. There could be other limited use areas such as some parking spaces, service yards for the use of commercial units only, parts of the grounds, fire escapes for the benefit of upper floors, or eg the lift in one wing. Limited use areas could also, in a mixed use development, include the leisure facilities (eg tennis courts or swimming pool) intended for use only of the residents and their invitees. For such areas costs of maintenance, insurance etc are material and will need to be included within the commonhold assessment.

THE COMMONHOLD COMMUNITY STATEMENT

17.17 The basis of management of the commonhold is set out in the commonhold community statement (the 'CCS'). (Commonhold and Leasehold Reform Act 2002, ss 1(1) and 31.) The CCS is one of the documents which need to be registered at the Land Registry when the commonhold is first set up (s 2 of and Sch 1 to the Act). The Land Registry will create one title per unit and one for the common parts when the commonhold is first registered. Therefore, a purchaser will take an existing registered title.

17.18 It is the critical document for any commonhold. It will cover much of the facets included in a complete set of leases for the block. (Commonhold and Leasehold Reform Act 2002, ss 11 and 31.)

17.19 The CCS is to be in the form set out in Sch 3 to the Commonhold Regulations 2004, with blanks to be filled in for the practical details and with plans showing the commonhold as a whole and the individual units. The published version must be used and not changed, except that items can be added at the end of the prescribed sections or at the end of the Annexes. Any such alteration, called 'local rules' in the Regulations, must be highlighted by incorporating headings to show these are 'additional provisions specific to this commonhold' (reg 15).

17.20 Commonhold community statements are to be similar, so that the unitholder of a commonhold unit in Plymouth will see much the same if he buys a commonhold unit in Peterborough, Preston or Ponteland. Anything non-standard must be specified, making it easy for those familiar with commonholds to identify such additions. Obviously, parts added to the CCS cannot be valid if they conflict with the Act or the Regulations (s 31(9) of the Act).

17.21 The CCS consists of:

(a) A 'health warning', to the effect that the document creates legally binding rights and duties, and recommending anyone affected to take appropriate advice.

(b) This is followed by Part 1, which is a general Introduction and explains about the CCS, the commonhold association, the structure of the commonhold community statement, and it also includes useful definitions. This is linked to Annex 1, which has spaces to be completed for the names of the commonhold and the commonhold association, and the company number of the commonhold association.

(c)   Part 2 describes the commonhold in greater detail by reference to Annex 2, which is where the units are described and other details such as rights for units appear.

(d)   Part 3 is very short but important, as it refers to Annex 3 which sets out the allocation of the commonhold assessment and reserve fund levy, as well as voting rights. The Annex shows the percentages payable out of the various units.

(e)   Part 4 is the Rules of the commonhold. Paragraph 4.2, which runs to 42 sub-sections, shows the detailed arrangements for assessment and collection of the commonhold assessment, and is discussed below (at **17.23** et seq). Part 4 also covers other significant matters such as the permitted use of the units; insurance; repair and maintenance; alteration of common parts; dealings with the units (including transfers and leases); amendments to the CCS; notices; the registers that need to be kept by the commonhold association, and the disputes resolution procedure. This is mirrored by Annex 4, which gives practical details of some of these items, eg required insurance risks can be included, if desired.

(f)   If there are to be development rights (see at **17.66** et seq), these will be added as a final Annex.

(g)   Finally, there is a signature page.

17.22   There are some suggestions for drafting a CCS at **17.60** et seq, and some precedents in Appendix 2 to this volume. There are official guidance notes published by the Department for Constitutional Affairs with some suggestions.

COMMONHOLD ASSESSMENT

Part 1 – Collection from the unit-holder

17.23   Paragraph 4.2 of Part 4 of the CCS (paras 4.2.1–4.2.42) sets out the system in so far as it covers the assessment of the amount payable and the obligation of the unit-holder and (in case of default only) the tenant of a unit, to pay. It sets out the three types of sums payable under the general umbrella of commonhold assessment:

(a)   the annual amount;

(b)   an additional levy needed in case of emergency; and

(c)   a reserve fund payment (following a 'reserve study').

See at **17.29** for the reserve study.

The ordinary annual amount

17. 24   The directors of the commonhold association are required to prepare an estimate of the income the commonhold association needs (ie the commonhold assessment) to meet its obligations, eg repair and maintenance and insurance of the common parts, and the cost of complying with formalities at Companies House, at least once a year, or oftener if necessary. (CCS, para 4.2.1.) Companies Act compliance is not mentioned but this seems a necessary expenditure: see *Embassy Court Residents' Association Ltd v Lipman* [1984] 2 EGLR 60 (at **12.10** and **12.35** above).

17.25   The estimated sum is to be notified to the unit-holder in a prescribed notice. (Form 1 to the Regulations; CCS, para 4.2.2.) It sets out the total cost and the percentage applicable to the unit in question (the latter is set out in Annex 3 to the CCS) and the amount that would thus be payable. The notice gives the unit-holders at least one month in which to make written representations. (CCS, para 4.2.3.)

17.26   The directors are required to consider any representations made to them (CCS, para 4.2.4) and thereafter must serve a demand on the unit-holder for the amount due, using Form 2 from the Regulations. The demand gives the unit-holder not less than 14 days to pay. There is nothing preventing the directors from including in the demand for payment a provision permitting payment of the amount due by instalments. This will presumably lead to quarterly payments in advance in suitable cases.

17.27   The unit-holder is under an obligation to pay the demand. (CCS, para 4.2.15.)

The emergency levy

17.28   The directors can require an additional payment in case of emergency. (CCS, para 4.2.5.) This is demanded by a notice in Form 3. It sets out the amount payable and the percentage, in a similar fashion to the demand for the annual commonhold assessment, but in addition it has to set out why the emergency assessment is necessary. Again, the unit-holder is under an obligation to pay. (CCS, para 4.2.15.) The notice sets out the date on which payment is to be made, although the CCS does not, in this case, specify a minimum period. This is presumably because the circumstances are such that the sum may be needed immediately, or it may be for something that arose just after the annual demand which will need to be paid before the next annual demand is due. In this case there is no right for the unit-holder to make observations.

The reserve fund Levy

17.29   Paragraphs 4.2.6–4.2.14 of the CCS set out the obligation of the commonhold association to have a reserve study to review potential future financial commitments, and to consider setting a reserve fund levy. A 'reserve study' is defined in para 1.4.5 of the CCS as 'an inspection of the common parts to advise the directors whether or not it is appropriate to establish or maintain a reserve fund'. The 'reserve fund' is defined, in the same paragraph, as 'a fund set up by the directors of the commonhold association to which unit-holders contribute to finance the repair and maintenance of the common parts or commonhold units'. The reference to units is to cover those cases where the commonhold association is responsible for maintenance of units as well as the common parts.

17.30 The directors must consider whether to commission a reserve study in the first year of the commonhold. (CCS, para 4.2.6.) This unlikely to be important in the case of new property, although it may be if there are such items as lifts or generators and boilers which may need replacement in due course. It could be very important where an existing building is converted to commonhold. It might be best to consider such a study before going to the expense and work involved in setting up a commonhold – if the results are too bad the parties may not wish to proceed, although those concerned may be considering setting up a commonhold largely to enable major items to come under their control.

17.31 The more important provision is para 4.2.7 of the CCS which requires the directors to commission a reserve study by an 'appropriately qualified person' at least once in every ten years. There is no definition of an appropriately qualified person, but qualifications could be added as local rules if desired.

17.32 The directors are to consider the reserve study and must in particular decide whether it is appropriate in the light of what is shown in the reserve study to set up 'a reserve fund and/or maintain any existing fund, and if it is appropriate to establish a reserve fund then the directors must do so'. (CCS, para 4.2.8.) Directors are also directed 'at appropriate intervals' to review the decision as whether to establish and maintain one or more reserve funds. (CCS, para 4.2.9.) The directors are under a very useful obligation (CCS, para 4.2.11) to 'try to ensure that unnecessary reserves are not accumulated'. (This is a useful expression for tenants negotiating a lease with a sinking fund.)

17.33 It is worth noting that the unit-holders have a specific right (CCS, para 4.2.10) by ordinary resolution, to require the directors to establish a reserve fund. Thus although the primary liability is on the directors the unit-holders can call on them to take action if they fail to do so.

17.34 If a reserve fund is set up a preliminary notice must be sent in Form 4 attached to the Regulations. This, in the same way as an estimate for the annual commonhold assessment, gives the unit-holder one month in which to make representations. The directors are required to consider the representations and must then send out a demand in prescribed Form 5. The demand must give at least 14 days for payment. (CCS, paras 4.2.12–4.2.14.)

17.35 It is to be noted that, other than in the first year, this is a compulsory requirement. The directors must have a reserve study every ten years, and they are given power to set up what is in effect a sinking fund to remedy whatever the study shows. The Rules do not comment as to how the money is to be held – eg it does not say it is held on trust, but of course the commonhold association is the company of the unit-holders and thus it is not a third party arrangement, as in the case of money paid by tenants to a landlord towards a sinking fund. It is a burden the directors need to recognise when accepting office, but it does give strength to their hand when seeking to ensure the building is kept in good order.

17.36   It must be made clear that it seems that the 'reserve fund' defined in the CCS is intended to be what is called a sinking fund in relation to leaseholds. Despite the author's representations to the working party of the Department for Constitutional Affairs that the CCS refers to a reserve fund when it really means a sinking fund, the description remains, and, to be fair, it is the wording used in s 39 of the Act. It needs to be emphasised that, as far as the author is concerned, what is called a 'reserve fund' in the Act and the CCS are more equivalent to a sinking fund than to a reserve fund, in so far as those expressions appear in Chapter 7 relating to leaseholds, and in the commercial Code, Chapter 11 above.

17.37   While the Regulations were being drafted one proposal was for the CCS to contain details of the matters to be considered in a reserve study, and a definition of a suitable person to carry out the study. Both items were dropped from the final version, leaving the onus on the directors to decide what is appropriate at the time, but readers might be interested to know that one time it was intended that the CCS should provide for the reserve study to consider:

(a)   the estimated remaining life of the building and/or plant;

(b)   the costs of maintaining and replacing the item; and

(c)   the annual contribution required to reflect such costs.

There is nothing to stop such provisions being included as local rules, if desired.

Late payment

17.38   If payment of any of the three types of commonhold assessment is late the unit-holder is liable for interest. (CCS, para 4.2.16.) An interest rate can be specified in Annex 4, but if it is not specified there is no default interest rate. It could presumably be covered by a resolution of the commonhold association from time to time, although the rate will not then be immediately apparent to anyone looking at the CCS.

17.39   In addition, in cases where the unit has been let, the commonhold association can call on the tenant to pay the rent to the association instead of the tenant. (See at **17.42** as to diversion of rent.)

Comment

17.40   The ability of unit-holders to be able to make observations on proposed charges is an improvement to the original provisions, but the effect is still that the commonhold assessment could be one proposed by the directors, not approved by a majority of unit-holders, but still binding on all the unit-holders. There is no implication of reasonableness, and some unit-holders could find that they are always outvoted. A person buying a commonhold unit must be aware that if the commonhold association decides it wants to carry out certain works and passes a resolution to that effect the unit-holder must pay his percentage, even if the proposal is one that could (for a leasehold dwelling) be challenged as not being reasonable. (See at **17.119** for some limited possible challenges.)

17.41   These are aspects that a draftsman may wish to consider covering by local rules. There are some suggested precedents in Appendix 2.

Part 2 – Diversion of rent from tenants

Unit-holder's right to let the unit

17.42   A unit-holder is entitled to let his unit subject to some basic restrictions. The Act and the CCS and the Regulations refer to a 'tenancy' but the provisions are intended to apply equally to a lease.

Non-residential units

17.43   A unit for which the permitted use is non-residential can let the unit subject only to any restriction there may be in the CCS. (Section 18 of the Act.) It remains to be seen what restrictions are likely to be used. One suspects that the main restrictions will be in the case of mixed use buildings where the non-residential units will have certain uses prohibited. As the unit will be freehold it will be unwise, where retail use is intended, to say the use will be eg as a bookshop, but the CCS may perhaps refer to 'retail use' but with some anti-social uses not allowed, at least in the case of mixed use premises. So perhaps use as a hot takeaway food shop, or a sex shop or a betting shop may be prohibited. In the absence of anything in the CCS there is no restriction on the length of term or any restriction on premiums or rent for non-residential leases.

Residential units

17.44   For a unit where the permitted use is residential any letting has to be subject to the Regulations. This is much more restrictive.

17.45   There cannot be a letting of a residential unit at a premium (reg 11(1)(a)). This provision was included because there was concern that if a unit was bought and then let on a long lease at premium and a low rent there would be little rent to be diverted to the commonhold association if the unit-holder defaulted.

17.46   In normal cases the letting of a residential unit cannot be for more than seven years, and provisions which include options to extend or renew etc, taking the lease over seven years, are barred (reg 11(1)(b)–(e)). The exceptions to the seven-year limit are set out in reg 11(2), but at present only apply in cases where the tenant had previously held a lease of the same unit which was extinguished when the commonhold was created. There are qualifications about some lease provisions for these longer leases, but basically they must be granted on similar terms (subject to the term not being more than 21 years), and again provisions extending or giving an option to renew taking it over the 21-year period are prohibited.

17.47 The third qualification for residential units, the most important for this book, is that the tenancy must not be granted on terms under which the tenant is required to pay the commonhold assessment to the commonhold association in the place of the unit-holder (reg 11(1)(f)). The reason is that it is intended that the unit-holder of a residential unit will have a real interest in the premises. He will be able to let the premises if eg he has a job away for a few years, or in buy to let cases, but he cannot sell by way of a long lease at a premium, leaving the commonhold with a lot of people with legal interests but being absentee landlords who are not concerned about complying with the obligations.

Letting: general

17.48 Letting is the only aspect of commonhold where there is a difference between the residential and non-residential parts as at **17.42–17.47** above. The only aspect where this has a material effect is in the type of tenancy that can be granted. Otherwise, the provisions about letting apply regardless of use.

17.49 The CCS provides that the unit-holder must let the proposed tenant have a copy of the CCS before the tenancy is granted, with Form 13. (CCS, para 4.7.12.) Form 13 points out that the tenant will be bound by some of the duties in the CCS 'irrespective of the terms of the tenancy agreement'. If the unit-holder does not serve the notice the tenant can claim against the unit-holder for any loss arising and the unit-holder is under an obligation to make good that loss within 14 days of notice. (CCS, paras 4.7.13 and 4.7.14.) In addition, the CCS provides in para 4.7.20 that if the commonhold association has suffered a loss because a tenant has not complied with his duties under the CCS then the tenant is liable to the commonhold association for that loss.

17.50 There is no obligation in the Act or the Regulations for a unit-holder to seek the consent of the commonhold association for letting. Indeed, s 20(1) of the Act says a CCS 'may not prevent or restrict the creation, grant or transfer of (a) an interest in the whole or part of his unit ...' This would seem to prevent a change to a CCS requiring consent as a condition of creating a lease. (Notice of the lease must be given to the commonhold association (CCS, para 4.7.15). The form is Form 14.)

Diversion of rent

17.51 'Diversion of rent' is the name given in the CCS to the process under which the commonhold association can call on the tenant (whether residential or non-residential) to pay his rent to it in cases where the unit-holder has failed to pay the commonhold assessment. It is somewhat similar to the provisions in the Law of Distress (Amendment) Act 1908 under which a superior landlord can call on a sub-tenant to pay his rent direct to the superior landlord where the intermediate landlord has not done so.

17.52   The method is set out in detail in paras 4.2.17–4.2.40 of the CCS. These are backed up by a right under paras 4.2.41 and 4.2.42 for the commonhold association to call for details of a tenancy granted (using Form 8) if details have not been properly given to it. The information is to be given within 14 days.

17.53   The system for diversion of rent is fairly straightforward. If the unit-holder fails to pay any of the three types of commonhold assessment (see at **7.23** above) within the time required and he has let the unit then the diversion of rent can be used. If the unit-holder has let the unit (the commonhold association should be given details of all lettings: para 4.7.15 of the CCS) and the commonhold association has not been given details but is aware a letting has occurred it can require details of the letting to be given by serving notice in Form 8 to 'one or all of the parties' to the tenancy agreement. (CCS, para 4.2.41.) In other words, it can require the information from the tenant if the unit-holder is not responding.

17.54   Where the unit-holder has defaulted the commonhold association can serve notice in Form 6 on the tenant requiring him to pay all or part of his rent to the commonhold association instead of to the unit-holder. (CCS, para 4.2.18.) The tenant is only required to pay to the association what he has to pay to his landlord and on the same days. Hence the objection to leases of residential units at a premium, where there may well be only a small rent payable. (CCS, para 4.2.19.) A copy of the notice has to go to the unit-holder, although there is no requirement to notify any mortgagee. The tenant is obliged to pay in accordance with the notice (CCS, paras 4.2.18 and 4.2.20) but the CCS makes it clear that such payment is treated as satisfaction of what the tenant owed the unit-holder, who cannot enforce the lease for non-payment in such circumstances. The payment also discharges the unit-holder from his liability to the commonhold association for the sum paid. The CCS prohibits the tenant from exercising against the commonhold association any right of set-off that he has against the unit-holder. If the tenant pays late, then interest can be charged. (CCS, paras 4.2.23–4.2.26.)

17.55   There are similar provisions enabling the commonhold association to call on a sub-tenant to divert his rent where both the unit-holder and the tenant have defaulted. (CCS, paras 4.2.28–4.2.38.) The commonhold association has to notify the unit-holder and the tenant when the diversion is no longer needed. (CCS, para 4.2.22.)

Comment

17.56 Diversion of rent is an extremely useful string to a commonhold associ-ation's bow. How much it can recover will of course depend on the amount of the rent, but the prohibition on premiums for residential tenancies means that the rent for such tenancies should normally be a market rent. It is not common for commercial leases to be at a premium and a low rent, but there is no prohibition on premiums for them in the Regulations or CCS. The CCS can include provi-sions about non-residential leases, and so there is nothing to stop local rules pro-hibiting non-residential leases at a premium, if that is thought appropriate. While diversion does not guarantee that the rent will suffice to pay the amount out-standing, it will help.

17.57 The scheme seems well thought out and should work. The obligation on the unit-holder to provide a copy of the CCS to each tenant means that tenants should be aware of the scheme. A tenant should have no concern (if he is given notice), because he will lawfully be able to pay rent to the commonhold associa-tion and the unit-holder will not be entitled to take action against the tenant for breach of the lease in this respect. In addition, there are provisions under which anyone suffering as a result of the failure to operate the procedure ensuring that tenants are made aware of the CCS provisions can call for the defaulter to make good the loss. The unit-holder will be aware of the provisions of the CCS as to letting and rent diversion, and as a tenant is supposed to be provided with a copy of the CCS he should also be aware of it. If the unit-holder owes £2,000 and the diverted rent is only £1,000 there will be a shortfall, but it will be less than if the rent could not be diverted. It is always a problem for any building if the occupiers do not pay the costs of maintenance. Diversion of rent is an extra means the com-monhold association can call on. The prohibition on a tenant exercising against the commonhold association those rights of set-off he might have against his landlord is a, very minor, point a tenant should be aware of when considering taking a tenancy of a commonhold unit.

17.58 If a unit-holder defaults, the commonhold association has no power to forfeit or distrain, as in a leasehold case. If necessary a commonhold association will have to sue and (eventually) obtain a charging order and enforce payment that way. While this is slow, and, to many people, unsatisfactory, it is worth com-menting that for leaseholds, where a tenant fails or refuses to pay, it can be a long period before, if at all, a landlord is repaid in full. A landlord has the right to forfeit, but the tenant can apply for relief from forfeiture.

17.59 It is not clear what would happen if there was a conflict between a supe-rior landlord claiming from an undertenant under the Law of Distress (Amendment) Act 1908, and a commonhold association requiring the rent to be diverted. One suspects that the commonhold association would have priority, as the tenancy and sub-tenancy are both held under the terms of the CCS, and the CCS obligations would be first in time. This is posed as one of those questions which may be more useful as an exam question than a real problem.

PART 3 – DRAFTING

Commonhold community statement

17.60   Most of what has been said in this book about the importance of clarity and definitions of property in relation to leaseholds applies to commonholds. Much of the Commonhold Community Statement (see at **17.17** et seq above) is somewhat like a compilation of many of the terms normally seen in leases, and the provisions need to reflect much the same points. It looks as if, at least initially, the CCS may provide only brief details of the property and none at all of the works or services to be provided, other than very general references to repair maintenance and insurance. The detail could be amplified, if desired (see at **17.19**), or could, for example, indicate the expected standard of repair etc desired. This is, of course, in marked contrast to the way service charges are covered in a lease.

17.61   As there is only one guiding document for the whole commonhold, there should not be inconsistencies. This is to be compared to a set of leases which may have been negotiated by different solicitors and/or created over several decades.

17.62   The other main point is that the CCS defines individual units and every other part of the commonhold is part of the common parts (s 25(1) of the Act). Accordingly, there is less scope for doubt about the area over which the commonhold association has responsibilities – it is responsible for the common parts, including limited use areas, plus those parts of units which the CCS states are its responsibility.

17.63   Although drafting is, as ever, critical, there is little scope for negotiation. A lease is normally negotiated between the landlord and the initial tenant: the CCS is likely to be drafted by the 'developer's' solicitors in conjunction with the developer and the managing or selling agents, without the involvement of solicitors for any other party. Once the commonhold is set up the CCS is in place and is registered at HM Land Registry. The Land Registry will create a new title for each unit at that point, as well as for the common parts. (Commonhold (Land Registration) Regulations, r 28(1).) The purchaser of a unit will therefore take a transfer of that new title – ie a transfer of title number AB12345 with the benefit of whatever rights that unit has, and subject to whatever applies to it. Save in the case of a commonhold where there are lots of units still to be sold for the first time, a transferee will have the greatest difficulty in being able to change any terms, because that will need a change to the CCS which will then need to be re-registered at the Land Registry (s 33(3) of the 2002 Act). Any change to the CCS needs agreement of the unit-holders, and this may be expensive and time consuming. (See reg 15 and CCS, para 4.8 for details of what can be changed and how.)

17.64   The rights and obligations need to be set out in Annex 2. Either Annex 2 or Annex 4 could also include details of the services for which a charge is to be made, but this is not the intention. The scheme simply envisages that the commonhold association through its directors will decide from time to time on items for which money is to be spent and paid for by the commonhold association. This avoids the need to check whether specific items are chargeable or not, and also avoids the need to change the CCS where there are changes or improvements, for example by the installation of new features such as CCTV cameras or a new leisure facility. However, if desired, further details could be included as local rules in the CCS on this point, either initially or by way of a later change to the CCS. (There are some precedents in Appendix 2.)

'The developer'

17.65 There is some ability for a change of the CCS at an early stage if the person who first registered the commonhold (called 'the developer' in s 58 of the Act) has retained the right to carry out development business ('development rights'), which can include a right to change the CCS.

17.66 Schedule 4 to the Act sets out what can be development rights. Briefly they are:

(a) completion of works;

(b) 'transactions in commonhold units' and marketing;

(c) addition or removal of land from the commonhold;

(d) amendment of the CCS; and

(e) appointment and removal of directors of the commonhold association.

The development rights mostly cease when the works are completed (reg 18(5)) and rights to appoint and remove directors cease when the developer ceases to be the owner of at least one quarter of the total number of units (reg 14(8)(f)) and so these rights should be only temporary in most cases. The purchaser of a unit needs to be aware of the development rights, as the ability to make changes could affect (inter alia) the commonhold assessment payable, or increase the areas for which the commonhold association has responsibility.

17.67 Development rights cannot be used to interfere with 'the enjoyment by each unit-holder of the freehold estate in his unit, and ... the exercise by any unit-holder or tenant of his rights under the commonhold community statement' (reg 18(2)). The right for a developer to change the CCS is likely to be used where there is an obvious error such as a unit not being given any rights of access, or where, perhaps because of poor sales of units, the design of unsold units is changed to make them more marketable. This could include, for example, redesigning two bedroom flats to become three bedroom flats if that is what the market is looking for. If so, there may be a different number of units, and clearly a need to change the commonhold assessment percentages.

17.68   Although Sch 4 to the Act permits a developer to remove land from a commonhold, reg 18(3) makes it clear that he cannot do so in the case of land that has been transferred to a unit-holder (ie it is part of a unit) without the prior consent of the unit-holder. There is no requirement that the unit-holder will not act unreasonably, and it will be a matter of agreement, unless the contract leading to the transfer contains material provisions. A prior agreement is needed: a provision in the contract would seem to be a prior agreement. A unit-holder who has been asked to give up part of his unit could not be expected to agree without some payment by the developer and an adjustment to the commonhold assessment percentage if the area removed is substantial, although see at **17.70** below concerning changes.

Comment on commonhold assessment

17.69   The scheme for collection and payments on account appears in the CCS, see at **17.23** above. There seems little latitude for variation of the basic collection system. Details of what is needed are left to be decided by the unit-holders at the appropriate time. This is perhaps sensible, as the unit-holders will be able to decide among themselves what arrangements they think best suit the commonhold, and these could change over the years. For example, if there is a commonhold covering a house divided into two flats (it is difficult to see the advantage of a commonhold where there are only two units, generally) the commonhold assessment may well be simply the equivalent of amounts claimed under a 'common parts' lease provision where payment is only requested when needed, although the commonhold association must still make its annual assessment (s 38(1)(a)). By contrast, a block of 20 flats would almost certainly need to be run on the basis of quarterly payments in advance. As the CCS leaves the dates for payment to be decided by the unit-holders they can make arrangements that reflect a suitable scheme for the commonhold at the time.

17.70   As the money received belongs to the unit-holders, as members of the commonhold association, there is no real need to include provisions about the money being held on trust, but some commonholds may wish to include in the CCS provisions about the means of holding or investing money collected for the reserve, eg in a specified bank, or as to who is to be entitled to sign cheques (by reference to the office held). These items could quite properly be included in minutes of the directors from time to time, but there is something to be said for including them in the CCS – it means that anyone wanting to become a unit-holder would be able to see these arrangements in advance, and they could not be changed without a change to the CCS, thus needing a resolution of the commonhold association and re-registering at the Land Registry.

17.71   The CCS has to identify all the units, and anything else is common parts. (Section 25(1) of the Act and CCS, para 1.4.5.) Therefore, common parts do not need to be defined. The commonhold association has to maintain and insure the common parts, but it can also be responsible for maintenance of parts of units. The CCS has to 'make provision imposing duties in respect of the insurance, repair and maintenance of each commonhold unit' (s 14(2) of the Act). The commonhold association is also responsible for the structure and exterior of a building occupied as a number of units (such as in a normal block of offices or shops) (reg 9). Care must be taken to complete Annex 4, paras 6 and 7 of the CCS accurately to reflect this. Where units are detached it is likely that the commonhold association and proposed unit-holder would both prefer the unit-holder to have the responsibility for structural repair and insurance of his unit. It is hard to see a commonhold association wanting to be responsible for internal repairs and decoration of units, whether detached or part of a block.

17.72 Because the common parts are what is left when all the units are taken out of account (s 25(1) of the Act, and CCS, para 1.4.5) it is not essential to define common parts. However, there would seem no harm in a brief description in the CCS to say that '(for the avoidance of doubt) the common parts include [for example] the structure and exterior of the building and the corridors stairs gardens and limited use areas'. This could be helpful as a general guide to someone reading the CCS, and may save having to compare lots of plans, provided it is clear that it is not intended to be an exhaustive definition. (Hence the word 'include'.) It helps to remind the directors of the areas of responsibility. Clearly, if something on these lines is included it needs to be correct, and not contrary to the Act or Regulations.

17.73 Obviously, all costs the Commonhold Association has to bear need to be recovered. It has no other income – no rent. The CCS in the Regulations leaves details to be decided annually by the members. However, if there are any special items they can be usefully mentioned in the Annexes. For example, if a building includes a leisure club or swimming pool available for the use of the public as well as the members of the commonhold it would be helpful to mention this in the CCS and set out what is to happen to the income arising from use by the public, and the expenditure. The same point applies to a shopping mall in which temporary displays are to be given. Is any surplus to be put back into repair (which, in the author's opinion, it should be), or is there a possibility of the members of the commonhold from time to time having dividends from the income?

Commonhold assessment percentages

17.74 Commonhold assessment is based on fixed percentages (Commonhold Act, s 38). The Act does not say how the percentages are to be arrived at and presumably floor area will be used normally, but the percentages could be weighted. There is no need to say in the CCS how the percentage is assessed: a commonhold is intended to be run as the unit-holders wish. The commonhold assessment proportions can therefore be whatever the parties setting it up wish, for example a unit can have a nil percentage allocated to it, subject to the requirement for the percentages to be set out in the CCS and to add up to 100% (s 38(2) of the Act). The nil rate might well apply, for example, to a caretaker's flat within the block.

17.75 It would be open to the person setting up the commonhold in a mixed use building to provide that 100% of the commonhold assessment is payable out of the non-residential parts, leaving each residential unit with a 0% allocation (or vice versa). Such an approach would probably make it much more difficult to sell the units from which the commonhold assessment has to be paid, and so such a scheme is perhaps unlikely. See also at **17.76** et seq below for restriction on changes. Because of the requirement for fixed percentages there is no option of having a 'fair proportion' as the fraction payable. In the case of more complex commonholds it is likely that the commonhold assessment percentages for different aspects would be set out, so that rather than a single figure per unit there would be different percentages for the units for individual aspects of the services. Thus unit 1 might be responsible for 8.63% of costs relating to the block it is in, but 2.29% for expenses relating to common grounds shared by the blocks. The form of CCS does not contemplate this, but it is, the author believes, permissible, provided the service charge for each of the elements adds up to 100%. Alternatively, variable figures could be achieved by using percentages for reserve fund levies relating to specific items. The Articles of Association (arts 27–37 in the form set out in Sch 2 to the Regulations) contemplate one vote per unit. Although reg 14 permits some specific amendments to the Articles changes to the voting rights are not among those permissible changes.

Changing the percentage

17.76 It is difficult, as stated elsewhere, to change a fixed service charge percentage in a lease. (See **4.24** et seq.) It is probably at least as difficult and expensive for commonhold. The CCS, which must set out the percentages, can only be changed by agreement of all concerned. These are likely in practice to include mortgagees as well as unit-holders. (See s 33 of the Act and CCS, para 4.8.)

17.77 Paragraph 4.8.11 of the CCS provides that changes to the percentages need a special resolution of the commonhold association. Paragraph 4.8.12 has an extremely useful protection to a unit-holder. It states that this ability to change is subject to the right of a unit-holder not to have the 'percentage of the commonhold assessment or levy allocated to his, or any other, commonhold unit altered if the effect of the alteration, taking into account all the circumstances of the case, would be to allocate a significantly disproportionate percentage of the commonhold assessment or levy to his commonhold unit'. (Paragraph 4.8.13 has similar provisions regarding the number of votes.) This is, of course, a considerable help to a unit-holder against having his commonhold assessment unreasonably increased.

17.78 A revised CCS needs to be re-registered at the Land Registry so that anyone investigating the legal provisions will see the up-to-date position. Until registered the amendment is of no effect (s 33(3) of the Act). Accordingly, changing fixed percentages is likely to be fairly rare, and perhaps unlikely to be formalised unless the commonhold is changed by the addition of more land or buildings, or the removal of part of what is included, or perhaps changes to the sizes of some of the units (eg by three units becoming two). Perhaps changes to percentages may occur once the development rights cease to be effective if the developer has put unreasonably high percentages on the units being sold first to aid the sale of the remainder. The right to change the percentage of course only relates to the percentage of the total: it does not give any right to challenge a specific demand. (See at **17.119** for a few suggestions of possible challenges.)

17.79 It may be that if there are only a few commonhold unit-holders a change would not be too expensive to document. As a temporary measure it could be dealt with informally, perhaps by a resolution of the commonhold association, for example that the percentages to be collected from units 6 and 8 were reversed. (They could not change the percentages so that the total was other than 100%.) This may be acceptable while the unit-holder remains a unit-holder, although the purchaser of a unit, and his mortgagee, will want to have the matter corrected by a formal change to the CCS and re-registration. A purchaser may be prepared to accept the position, perhaps with a new resolution confirming that the informal arrangement will apply to him when he becomes the new unit-holder. However, he would be well advised to insist on a formal change (particularly where it reduces his liability), although he would probably be required to pay the costs involved. These may include those of lawyers and surveyors for a number of unit-holders.

17.80 When re-registering a revised CCS at the Land Registry consents are needed as before eg from unit-holders and their mortgages (ss 3 and 33 of the Act and reg 3).

Part 4 – Remedies for breach

17.81 One aspect of management that has been the subject of concern in some quarters is that the commonhold association has no power to forfeit the commonhold unit if the unit-holder does not pay his commonhold assessment. A landlord of a lease can forfeit the lease in such circumstances, although there are safeguards for the tenants. (See eg the comments about s 81 of the Housing Act 1996 in Chapter 9.) It must be remembered that for leaseholds the premises remains the property of the landlord while being let to the tenant for a defined period. By contrast, there is no landlord in a commonhold. The unit-holder holds a freehold, and there are few freeholds which are subject to early termination. There seems to be a trend towards removing the right of forfeiture generally, or certainly making it less attractive as a remedy, and so the lack of such a right may not be particularly disadvantageous as compared to leaseholds. The Law Commission proposals for termination of tenancies involve the need for a court order to terminate a tenancy in virtually every case. It is proposed that such termination would not be possible for a lease with over 21 years to run. These are simply proposals at present, but with such a philosophy it is hard to see any exception being made to introduce forfeiture of a freehold commonhold unit.

17.82 Although in case of default, the commonhold association will not be able to forfeit or distrain, it can exercise most of the remedies open to a landlord and mentioned in previous chapters (see eg **4.90** et seq). It does have one additional useful right, namely the ability to call for the tenant of a unit to divert his rent to the commonhold association where the unit-holder is in default. (See at **17.42** et seq.) This can be helpful, particularly as in the case of residential units the unit-holder cannot let at a premium, and so the rent payable should be a proper rent. Commercial leases tend to be let at a full rent.

17.83 The CCS sets out a disputes procedure that may be followed before resort to litigation. (See at **17.84** et seq.) In a bad case the commonhold association would presumably, after following the disputes procedure, be able to obtain judgment for an amount owing and then obtain a charging order. It could also make the relevant unit-holder bankrupt, or put it into liquidation, if a company. The charging order is likely to be the most effective remedy where the unit-holder defaults, although obviously no money is received until the unit is sold, and even then it would be subject to the claims of any prior chargees. In the meantime the commonhold association would be out of pocket. If forfeiture is not available in a leasehold case the landlord would be in much the same position. Forfeiture is becoming less useful for leaseholds.

Part 5 – Dispute resolution

Complaints against the commonhold association

17.84 The Commonhold Community Statement has a dispute resolution procedure which must be followed. The procedure appears in para 4.11. Paragraph 4.11.1 of the CCS states that the procedure applies only to the enforcement of rights and duties arising from the CCS or provisions in or under the Act, and includes enforcing the conditions to which a right is subject.

17.85 Originally, it was intended to be compulsory, but there is now an exception (where the disputes procedure does not need to be used), when (a) a unit-holder or tenant is seeking to enforce a right or duty of the commonhold association to pay money or to enforce a right or duty in emergency, or (b) where the commonhold association is seeking to enforce such rights against a unit-holder or tenant. In such cases the party making the claim can either (a) use the disputes procedure or (b) (if the commonhold association is a member of an approved ombudsman scheme) refer the dispute directly to the ombudsman, or (c) bring legal proceedings. (CCS, paras 4.11.3 and 4.11.11.)

17.86 Enforcement by a unit-holder or tenant against the commonhold association is covered in paras 4.11.2–4.11.9. Subject to the qualifications at **17.85** the unit-holder or tenant must use the procedure when seeking to enforce a right or duty contained in the CCS or a provision of the Act. However, consideration must first be given to resolving the dispute (a) by negotiation with the commonhold association, or (b) by using 'arbitration, mediation, conciliation, or any other form of dispute resolution procedure involving a third party, other than legal proceedings'. (CCS, para 4.11.4.) So a unit-holder can go to court, but is required to consider alternative dispute resolution first. Since court applications these days ask a person seeking to issue proceedings if they have considered ADR, this may not add much, but clarifies that the government seems to prefer people to try to resolve disputes without resort to the courts unless really necessary.

17.87   To start the procedure the unit-holder or tenant gives a complaint notice to the commonhold association. (CCS, para 4.11.5.) This is a notice in Form 17 in the Regulations. The notice must set out details of the complaint and the action the unit-holder requires the commonhold association to take. The notice does not set out a time within which a response is required. The commonhold association can respond (CCS, para 4.11.6) with Form 18 which sets out three alternatives, namely that the commonhold association (a) needs further information, (b) accepts the validity of the complaint, or (c) disputes the matter complained of.

17.88   Paragraph 4.11.7 provides that either upon receipt of the reply to the complaints notice, or when 21 days have passed (whichever is earlier), if the complainant wants to take the matter further he must consider, again, whether the problem could be resolved by (a) negotiating with the commonhold association or (b) by using arbitration, mediation etc. The response on Form 18 may indicate that some form of ADR would be appropriate. The CCS (para 4.11.8) then goes on to say that, subject to that obligation to consider negotiation, arbitration etc again, the complainant may, if the commonhold association is a member of an approved ombudsman scheme, refer the matter to the ombudsman. Paragraph 4.11.9 says that if the commonhold association is a member of an approved ombudsman scheme legal proceedings can only be brought once the ombudsman has investigated and determined the matter and notified the parties of his decision. Where the commonhold association is not a member of an approved ombudsman scheme then legal proceedings can be brought following completion of the disputes resolution procedure.

17.89   This part of the procedure relates to complaints by unit-holders against the commonhold association other than a duty to pay money (perhaps a refund of commonhold assessment), or enforcing a right in emergency (perhaps where a unit-holder is prevented from using a limited use area to which the CCS gives his unit rights). Other claims under the disputes procedure would presumably include, for example, complaints that the commonhold association has not set an annual budget, or has not set up a reserve fund despite being required to do so by the members, or where there is a reserve levy on which unnecessary reserves are being accumulated. One assumes it would also cover such matters as the directors acting otherwise than in accordance with the Memorandum and Articles of Association – for example, holding meetings without a suitable quorum or on insufficient notice.

Complaints by the commonhold association

17.90   Paragraphs 4.11.10–4.11.16 of the CCS include somewhat similar provisions where the commonhold association seeks to enforce rights or duties in the CCS or provisions of the Act against a unit-holder or tenant. A 'duty' would obviously include the duty under paras 4.2.15 (for the unit-holder), and 4.2.20 (for a tenant) and 4.2.30 (for a sub-tenant) to pay the commonhold assessment.

17.91   When seeking to enforce a duty to pay money or a right or duty in an emergency, the commonhold association may either (a) use the dispute resolution procedure, or (b) refer the dispute directly to the ombudsman, if the association is a member of an approved ombudsman scheme, or (c) bring legal proceedings. (CCS, para 4.11.11.) This seems very practical: if a unit-holder has been sent a demand for the commonhold assessment and simply fails or refuses to pay there seems little point in delaying before issuing proceedings.

17.92   The commonhold association is under an obligation to consider negotiating or using ADR, as in the case of a complaint by a unit-holder. In addition the commonhold association has to consider 'taking no action if it reasonably thinks that inaction is in the best interests of establishing or maintaining harmonious relationships between all the unit-holders, and that it will not cause any unit-holder (other than the alleged defaulter) significant loss or significant disadvantage'. (CCS, para 4.11.12; this final provision echoes s 35(3) of the Act.)

17.93   If the commonhold association decides to proceed with the dispute resolution it needs to give a default notice to the unit-holder (Form 17) or tenant (Form 19). The alleged defaulter can respond using Form 20. Again, if there is a reply or after 21 days have gone by, whichever is sooner, the commonhold association 'if it wishes take further action to enforce the right or duty', must first consider (again) whether the matter could be resolved by negotiation or using ADR. Subject to considering ADR the commonhold association may either (if it is a member of an ombudsman scheme) refer the matter to the ombudsman or, 'if it is satisfied that the interests of the commonhold require it' bring proceedings. (CCS, paras 4.11.13–4.11.16.)

Disputes between unit-holders

17.94   There is a separate procedure for disputes between unit-holders, but this is unlikely to be material in relation to commonhold assessments. Again, for enforcing a duty to pay money or a right in an emergency the unit-holder or tenant may use the disputes resolution procedure or issue proceedings. If the unit-holder wants to use the procedure for other things (say, an argument about allowing pets, or perhaps the use of a unit), he gives notice to the commonhold association in Form 21 requesting the commonhold association to take action. The commonhold association have to decide whether it should take up the matter, or whether to take no action (where it thinks this will be in the best interests of harmonious relationships). If it is to take no action it must decide whether to allow the complainant to 'enforce the right or duty against the alleged defaulter directly'. It will be interesting to see how this aspect is used. It seems to allow the commonhold association to prevent one unit-holder taking action against another. The procedure involves a series of notices, consideration of ADR and a final, seemingly reluctant, right to allow legal proceedings. (CCS, paras 4.11.17–4.11.30.)

Lack of statutory protection re the commonhold assessment

17.95 The commonhold association has to collect the commonhold assessment. In practice the costs will be for the same sort of items for which a leasehold service charge normally arises. The main differences are the lack of (a) a landlord and (b) a specification of chargeable items as in a lease, but apart from this the system is perhaps nearest to those cases where the tenants have acquired the freehold through a management company. The biggest difference, which is very important, is that as there is no landlord and no lease in commonhold, the statutory provisions for dwellings (notably as to reasonableness and consultation under the Landlord and Tenant Act 1985) simply do not apply to the commonhold assessment.

17.96 Clearly, a unit-holder can let his unit, but the reference in the preceding paragraph is to the commonhold assessment. The unit-holder of a single residential unit who lets that unit would be unlikely to be carrying out services and so would not be charging leasehold service charges to his tenant – in any event he cannot own any common parts on which the services could be performed. If he lets on the basis that eg he carries out internal decoration and charges the tenant, that is a matter only for the unit-holder and his tenant – it does not affect the remainder of the commonhold. As between the unit-holder and his (residential) tenant the statutory provisions affecting dwellings would apply, but not to the commonhold assessment.

17.97 Obviously, as the commonhold unit-holders are also members of the commonhold association they have the right to be involved in management. There is still the possibility that the active members of the commonhold could ride roughshod over those who take less interest, but they have the protection of the provision mentioned at **17.77**, which is not one reflected in leasehold law. The unit-holders can of course call meetings of the commonhold association under the terms of the Memorandum and Articles of Association, but by then the damage may well be done.

17.98 What is the difference between (a) a commonhold block of flats and (b) a leasehold block of flats where tenants have acquired the freehold and a caucus in reality manages that freehold? It is that, although the latter have a share of the freehold, they are also tenants, and so (as tenants) will have the protection of the provisions, notably for reasonableness, under s 19 of the Landlord and Tenant Act 1985 and consultation under s 20. Those rights can be exercised by the tenant who will have a remedy if there has been unreasonable action: the commonhold unit-holder will not have that benefit.

17.99 The CCS does not require the directors to obtain estimates for major works or any consultation other than the one-month period after the provisional figures are put forward. (See at **17.24** et seq.)

17.100 It would be open to a commonhold association to pass a resolution that there should be X number of estimates obtained for all works costing more than £Z or (if desired) a provision on theses lines could be added to the CCS, perhaps at the end of para 4.5 as an additional local rule. Any addition must be highlighted by a heading showing it is an 'additional provision specific to this commonhold' (reg 15(11)). Such additions can be included either in the body of the CCS, continuing the numbering system, or all additions could be included together in a further Annex. My preference is for additions to be in the main text so that it all the provisions (eg about the commonhold assessment) are together, but the draftsman has the choice, and wherever there are changes they must be highlighted as mentioned at **17.19** above.

17.101 The real protection for unit-holders is to attend meetings and make their views known when decisions on future expenditure are being made. In case of doubt they can see about calling the directors to hold a general meeting under the relevant provisions of the Articles.

Part 6 – Management

17.102 If there are only, say, four or five units in a commonhold it may be that the unit-holders will carry out management themselves. In the case of larger commonholds one would expect the unit-holders to seek the help of managing agents. The position would be reasonably similar to the case where the tenants have acquired the freehold, although (a) the managing agents would take instructions from the commonhold association, rather than the company formed by the tenants as a joint freehold purchaser in the leasehold case, and (b) the agents would not need (as in a leasehold case) to ensure that the leases permitted recovery of the costs the commonhold association want to expend. The objects to be achieved are the same, namely to manage the premises so that the tenants or unit-holders can enjoy their beneficial ownership.

17.103 The managing agents should obviously be aware of the provisions of the CCS and thus the scheme. They will not have a landlord to deal with, only the commonhold association. The managing agents should advise the commonhold association about the necessary expenditure for the succeeding year, and will presumably serve the various notices (estimates and demands), and advise the directors on the action to take following any responses to the budget figures, and to notice of the results of any reserve study. They will presumably also be involved in consultation on other matters such as the schemes for internal or external decoration, or the scope of major refurbishment works.

Contractors

17.104 One point of concern is in relation to contractors carrying out work for a commonhold association. The association will instruct the contractor to replace the roof or whatever it is. If the cost is high the contractor needs to be careful about the payment. The commonhold association is the owner of the common parts, but as these are likely to consist of corridors and stairs and pipes, possibly a shell structure and perhaps communal gardens, the value is likely to be limited and thus not really good as a mortgage security. The commonhold association can mortgage the common parts subject to a prior unanimous resolution (ss 28 and 29 of the Act). The commonhold association is of course entitled, and indeed obliged, to collect the commonhold assessment and perhaps could assign the benefit, but again this seems poor security. If the contractor sues he may find the commonhold association does not have much money. It may not want to be put into liquidation and thus may make an effort to avoid liquidation.

17.105 The point is that a contractor might do well to seek security, or payment in advance, or have money placed on deposit. If the contractor sued the association and was able to recover from the unit-holders under their guarantees, because it is a company limited by guarantee, the guarantee is only one pound for each unit-holder and so that is unlikely to be of any practical assistance for a large bill. The same point can apply where management is by a maintenance trustee. If there is a landlord who has ordered the work the contractor can call on the landlord, but there is no landlord for a commonhold.

Part 7 – Commonhold for commercial units

17.106 Commonhold is associated in many minds with residential blocks of flats and this is, indeed, likely to be the main initial use. There are cases, however, where it may be used for commercial purposes, perhaps particularly for offices and industrial units and mixed blocks.

17.107 Some commercial organisations prefer to have a freehold rather than a lease because they feel they have fewer restrictions and they cannot be forced to move at the end or sooner determination of a lease term. In addition, they often face rent reviews and the need for consent from a landlord for various activities. On the other hand, a freehold does use up capital, and some companies consider this could be more usefully used in the business. Those who want to have a freehold but keep some capital can of course buy the freehold and mortgage it. This could be done either for a freehold subject to an estate rentcharge or a commonhold unit. As an alternative, it could arrange the purchase of a commonhold unit by a funder followed by a lease to the company. The commonhold will be a freehold, although it is not free of conditions: it will be subject to the CCS and its Rules.

17.108 A development of industrial units which share a road or other facilities that are not maintained at public expense could be turned into a commonhold.

Maintenance of the common parts would be covered by the CCS and, because commonhold unit-holders will be able to enforce obligations against each other, including successors in title, the provisions for repair and for payment for that repair will be workable. The CCS will set out the obligations and the unit-holders will be members of the commonhold association. It would have the enforceability of the estate rentcharge scheme, but the owners of the units concerned would all be involved in the management, which is not necessarily the case for estate rentcharge schemes.

17.109 One disadvantage is that if the development is a commonhold, then changes may be more difficult to arrange than for estate rentcharge cases. (See s 33 of the Act and CCS, para 4.8.)

(a) If a factory is held as a freehold subject to an estate rentcharge it can usually be divided up if desired without needing consent. For example, if the factory becomes too large it might be desirable to demolish it and divide the plot into two. One part could then be sold. The owner can do so and he may be able to persuade the estate rentcharge owner to agree to send two demands instead of one. (See at **16.6** and **16.56** above.) Subject to this, and anything special in the deeds, he can deal with his freehold as he chooses.

(b) By contrast, in a similar situation where the factory is a commonhold unit the unit-holder will need to obtain the consent of the commonhold association and the CCS will need to be changed and re-registered. (See ss 21(2) and 33 of the Act and CCS, paras 4.8.8–4.8.10.) This is thus likely to be more expensive and, if the factory owner was unable to persuade the rest of the commonhold association to agree then he would be unable to proceed.

It is worth commenting that leases usually prohibit assignment of part, and a change to the freehold estate rentcharge property may need deeds of variation etc to cover changed rights of way or for services.

17.110 For commercial property, the point about representation at meetings of the commonhold association mentioned at **12.45** in respect of management companies is equally valid for commercial commonholds.

17.111 A commercial organisation also needs to put a management scheme in place to ensure it checks the commonhold assessment consultation quickly so that it can make any necessary representations within the one-month period.

Part 8 –Alienation

Transfers

17.112 Section 15(2) of the Act makes it clear that the CCS cannot 'prevent or restrict the transfer of a commonhold unit'. This applies to complete units – for part units consent is needed under s 21(2)(c).

17.113 The Act provides that the unit-holder is liable for the obligations mentioned in the CCS while he is the unit-holder, but not otherwise. Section 16 makes it clear that a former unit-holder cannot be made liable for the arrears of his successor. The Act does not specifically say that a successor can be made liable for the default of the person who transfers to him, but the commonhold community statement contains such a provision at para 4.7, as described at **17.117** below.

Procedure on buying

17.114 On buying a commonhold unit the purchaser should carry out similar searches and enquiries to those made when acquiring any other freehold or indeed leasehold property. Accordingly, he should make the usual preliminary enquiries and a local land charge search and any environmental searches he requires. He should inspect the entries on the register for the unit (and also the register for the common parts for which the commonhold association has specific responsibility). He should also look at the Memorandum and Articles of Association of the commonhold association as he will become a member of it.

17.115 The main document will, of course, be the CCS setting out the scheme, and this needs particular attention. A purchaser will need to see he has the necessary rights and what the obligations are. As the CCS has to be in a standard form, those dealing with commonholds regularly will find that they can simply concentrate on the details in the various Annexes and any items added as 'local rules'. For these purposes, he will also need to see the commonhold assessment provisions.

17.116 The CCS must set out the percentages payable from his unit or units. It is quite likely that if a flat is sold with a garage the two will be treated as separate units. Apart from any other consideration this means they could be sold separately without needing to change the CCS, because otherwise to sell separately would be selling part of a unit, which needs consent and a change to the CCS. The standard CCS provisions are in para 4.2, as described above at **17.21** et seq, but it is important to see if they have been amplified, for example by adding further requirements for consultation, or implying reasonableness etc. The purchaser should also, as on any other purchase, inspect the commonhold assessment accounts for recent years, and check whether there is any large expenditure anticipated. The budget figures for the current year and the comparison with previous year will be useful information.

Certificates of amount due

17.117 The CCS has a helpful section (CCS, para 4.7) to enable a purchaser to check whether the vendor has arrears. The procedure is that the unit-holder can call on the commonhold association to provide a 'commonhold unit information certificate' relating to the unit. Within 14 days the commonhold association is to provide the certificate in Form 9. There are three reasons for a purchaser to require a unit-holder to obtain a certificate:

(a) The purchaser is liable (CCS, para 4.7.3) to pay 'the debts under paragraphs 4.2.15 and 4.2.16 [these are (a) the three types of commonhold assessment and (b) interest: see at **17.23**] by any former unit-holder in respect of that commonhold unit'. (Note that this refers to *'any'* former unit-holder.)

(b) Provided that the purchaser pays the amount so certified the commonhold association cannot call on the purchaser to pay any more in respect of arrears, even if the certificate is wrong. (CCS, para 4.7.4.)

(c) If arrears are disclosed the contract can be adjusted to provide for them to be paid before completion, or a retention agreed, or some other arrangement to be made.

17.118 Within 14 days of the transfer the purchaser must give notice to the commonhold association in Form 11. Where there are arrears the commonhold association can call on the transferee, after 14 days, to pay the arrears, up to the amount specified in the certificate. Interest is also payable. (CCS, paras 4.7.3, 4.7.5 and 4.7.9.) If no certificate is obtained the transferee will be liable for whatever is owing: it would presumably be negligent for a purchaser's solicitor not to require the unit-holder to call for a certificate.

Part 9 – Possible challenges

17.119 The principles for interpreting commonhold assessment matters for a commonhold will be different to leasehold service charges, because, instead of interpreting a lease and applying that to the facts, for commonholds the amounts to be spent are agreed by the directors of the commonhold association, subject only to a limited consultation. The following limited lines of objection could be raised by an unhappy unit-holder:

(a) The demand was in error mathematically, eg by using the wrong percentage.

(b) There was no consultation period for the commonhold assessment or reserve levy.

(c) When consulting the directors did not use the prescribed form, or the consultation period was less than one month.

(d) The decision of the relevant directors' meeting was ultra vires, eg there was some procedural irregularity such as no proper notice, or no quorum.

(e) The works or services carried out were not those approved by the relevant meeting.

(f) The works were forced through by a majority of unit-holders to the prejudice of the minority who objected.

(g) The works to be charged for included works outside the commonhold.

CHAPTER 18

Service charges under various regimes

By different methods different men excel;
But where is he who can do all things well?

Charles Churchill

INTRODUCTION

18.1   This chapter contrasts aspects of service charges in various circumstances. The circumstances are:

(a)   under a normal lease;

(b)   where management is by a tenants' management company (which will usually only be the case for residential premises);

(c)   where management is by a manager appointed under Pt II of the Landlord and Tenant Act 1987;

(d)   where management is by the tenants by way of an RTM Company under the Right to Manage contained in ss 71–113 of the Commonhold and Leasehold Reform Act 2002 (see at **10.34** et seq);

(e)   where an estate rentcharge is payable under the Rentcharges Act 1977 (see Chapter 16); and

(f)   commonhold assessments in a commonhold (see Chapter 17).

18.2   The following comparison may assist, in some cases, when deciding what form of management should be used for particular premises. However, service charges are only one element, and there are many others, notably tax, and whether the owner wants to retain an interest or not. Some of the alternatives only apply where the premises or the occupiers fit certain criteria. In some cases there are further qualifications too specific to be mentioned in a general summary of this type, but the following is intended to give a general overview of the possibilities.

THE PREMISES AND QUALIFYING TENANTS

18.3   Leaseholds and property managed by a tenants' management company can arise out of any premises, but not all properties can have the benefit of all the above schemes. For example commonhold and right to manage can only arise out of property that fits certain (differing) criteria, and commonhold property must be freehold. (Commonhold and Leasehold Reform Act, ss 1 and 4 and 71, and Sch 2.) The Right to Manage can only arise where a certain proportion of the premises is occupied by qualifying tenants (s 72(1)). A 1987 Act receiver can only be appointed, and the Right to Manage can only arise where the tenants are tenants of flats. In the case of RTM the tenants must also hold long leases. (Landlord and Tenant Act 1987, s 21 and Commonhold and Leasehold Reform Act 2002, s 75.) Estate rentcharges are usually created out of freeholds, although there seems nothing to prevent them being created out of leaseholds.

18.4 There are slightly different statutory rules for service charges of dwellings where the landlord is a local authority – see at **10.65** et seq. The right to appoint a manager under the Landlord and Tenant Act 1987 does not apply to a local authority, or where there is a resident landlord. (Landlord and Tenant Act 1987, s 21(3).) Similarly, the Right to Manage cannot be exercised where there is a local authority landlord, and there is a resident landlord exemption. (Commonhold and Leasehold Reform Act 2002, s 72 and Sch 6, paras 3 and 4.)

The payers and payees

18.5 Where there is a lease and management is by a landlord or a management company then the obligation to pay is determined by the terms of the lease. If there is a service charge then almost invariably it is the tenant who is liable to pay, usually to the landlord.

18.6 If a 1987 Act receiver has been appointed then the obligation to pay is still in accordance with the lease, but the payment will usually be to the receiver appointed by the Leasehold Valuation Tribunal. In some cases the receiver may have a more limited obligation.

18.7 Where tenants have exercised the Right to Manage collection of the service charge from qualifying tenants is by the RTM Company (s 96(2) of the 2002 Act). It is entitled to claim service charges from the landlord in respect of those areas not held by qualifying tenants, ie not held by tenants holding long leases of flats. Under the Right to Manage, in effect, the qualifying tenants pay what their leases provide they should pay, and the landlord is to pay the balance of any service costs. The amount the landlord pays is (at least notionally) divided among the (non-qualifying) tenants in accordance with floor area, regardless of the provisions of their lease (s 103). The RTM Company is also entitled to receive the balance of service charge receipts held by the landlord when the RTM Company takes over, (the sum received less any amounts which the landlord has to pay out (s 94).

18.8 For an estate rentcharge the payee is usually the person who carries out the work, and the payer is the person on whose land the rentcharge is charged. (Rentcharges Act 1977, s 11.)

18.9 A commonhold service charge (the *'commonhold assessment'*) is collected by the commonhold association and is usually payable by the unit-holder, but the rent payable by a tenant of a let unit can be used towards the liability for commonhold assessment by a defaulting unit-holder, by diversion of rent. (Commonhold and Leasehold Reform Act 2002, ss 38 and 19(2), and for diversion of rent see at **17.42** et seq.) If a commonhold unit-holder lets a commercial unit he can include a provision in the lease requiring the tenant to pay the commonhold assessment direct to the commonhold association: this is prohibited for residential units. (Commonhold Regulations 2004, reg 11(1)(f).)

The service charge schemes

Leases

18.10 In virtually all cases where there is a lease with service charges the details are set out in the lease. Occasionally, the provisions are in a separate deed. The lease usually entitles the landlord to recover the costs arising from certain services which are set out, in greater or lesser detail, in the lease. The landlord is only entitled to charge in accordance with the lease provisions. The lease will usually also detail the collection arrangement, often on the basis of the tenant paying quarterly in advance against an estimate, and with an adjustment of some sort at the year end. There are often provisions about production of accounts, and sometimes about certificates of cost or of the proportion to be paid.

Estate rentcharges

18.11 Where there is an estate rentcharge the provisions are slightly different, although on the same lines. The idea is for the person who carries out the works or services (the rent owner) to be able to call for payment towards those services that are set out in the documents. The estate rentcharge is usually created by separate documents for each property (in a similar fashion to leases), although there is sometimes a single deed into which all the affected parties enter. Often, the estate rentcharge is collected in arrear on demand rather than quarterly in advance, as the payments are frequently for works that are not regular but only arise when repairs are needed. The range of works and services tends to be much less than in leasehold cases.

Commonhold assessment

18.12 The commonhold assessment is totally different. Although the Commonhold Community Statement ('CCS') will set out the basic obligations of the commonhold association which manages the commonhold, the services to be carried out are unlikely to be described in the CCS. What is to be done and charged for is actually decided annually by the directors of the commonhold association. The directors send estimates (using a prescribed form), to which unit-holders have had an opportunity to respond. They then send demands, also in prescribed form, for all units (residential and non-residential). The common-hold association can employ managing agents who may run it rather like the leasehold equivalent, but the directors of the commonhold association (the company of the unit-holders) decide what needs to be done and then call for payment: this is radically different to the case of a landlord who decides what to do and imposes that decision on the tenants, although the landlord can only charge for what is permitted by the lease. It is closer (but not identical) to cases where tenants have acquired the freehold and retain leases of their parts of the premises.

Limit on the amount recoverable

18.13   In the case of any lease of a dwelling the amount recoverable is limited by reference to 'reasonableness' and to the compliance by the landlord with numerous statutory obligations affecting dwellings (see Chapters 9 and 10). It is worth repeating that these provisions apply even where the tenants manage the premises, as well as where management is by the landlord. These provisions also apply to the 1987 Act manager and the RTM Company. The statutory provisions do not apply to leases of commercial premises.

18.14   An estate rentcharge has to be 'reasonable in relation to that covenant' (ie the covenant to do work) under s 2(5) of the Rentcharges Act 1977.

18.15   For commonhold there is a difference between the commonhold assess-ment (for the freehold unit) and a service charge payable under the lease of a unit:

(a)   The holder of a commonhold unit (whether residential or non-residential) has no direct protection against an unreasonable commonhold assessment for a commonhold. The commonhold association is obliged to serve esti-mates on all unit-holders and give them one month in which to make repre-sentations before the demands for payment can be sent. The directors must have regard to the responses. That is the only protection for a unit-holder. He will, however, have had the opportunity to be involved in management, because the commonhold assessment is set by the commonhold association of which he will be a member. This is somewhat similar to the position where the tenants manage the block. If the unit-holder is outvoted he has no ability to challenge the necessity for the work or its cost, unless he can use a challenge such as one of those suggested in Chapter 17, eg that the works were not those on which consultation took place. (See at **17.119**.) It remains to be seen how the courts will deal with the disputes that will undoubtedly arise in such matters.

(b)   The statutory provisions affecting leases will apply where a commonhold unit-holder has let a residential unit. The statutory provisions will apply as between the unit-holder and his residential tenant, although it is difficult to see this arising often as the unit-holder only owns the unit and not the common parts: the statutory provisions could thus presumably only relate to internal matters within the unit and not the common parts of the commonhold. (See at **17.95** et seq.)

18.16   The only other similar restriction I am aware of relates to service charges by a local authority under right to buy leases. The amount is restricted during the first five years to the amount estimated by the landlord when the right to buy was exercised. (See at **10.88** et seq.)

Arrears

18.17   In the case of leaseholds the position is that strictly a tenant is not liable for the arrears owing by a former tenant. (See eg *Wharfland Ltd v South London Co-operative Building Co Ltd* [1995] 2 EGLR 21.) This applies to all the leasehold cases. The landlord must claim the arrears before an assignment, or make payment of arrears a condition of the assignment where consent is needed.

18.18   There can be recovery from former tenants of a limited amount of arrears (up to six months) under the Landlord and Tenant (Covenants) Act 1995 by serving notice under s 17. This applies to the immediately preceding tenant of a *'new lease'*, ie one granted after 1995, who has entered into an authorised guarantee agreement: in the case of leases granted before 1996 the landlord may also be able to claim against former tenants. This is discussed in Chapter 4 (at **4.103** et seq) and Chapter 9 (at **9.9** et seq).

18.19   In the case of rentcharges the liability is that of the 'owner for the time being of the land' (Rentcharges Act 1977, s 2(4)), and so it would not seem that the rent owner can claim against anyone other than the owner of the land at the time the expense was incurred. (Rentcharges are discussed in Chapter 16.)

18.20   For commonhold the position is that the transferee of a commonhold unit is liable for the arrears of his predecessor(s). He can obtain a certificate of the amount due, which can be used in contract negotiations. (See Chapter 17, at **17.112–17.118**.) Readers are reminded that the commonhold association cannot control the transfer of units: its consent is not needed, in contrast to the common position with leaseholds. Section 16 of the Commonhold and Leasehold Reform Act 2002 makes clear that a former unit-holder cannot be liable for the default of his successor.

Remedies for recovery

18.21   In nearly all cases a person entitled to a service charge can sue for it. However, proceedings for arrears of leasehold service charge for dwellings cannot proceed unless the amount has been determined by a Leasehold Valuation Tribunal or post-dispute arbitration or agreed by the tenant. (See Chapters 9 and 10.) These points apply to landlords, management companies, 1987 Act receivers and RTM Companies. For an estate rentcharge, suing is allowed. The commonhold association is urged to use the dispute resolution procedure in the CCS, and to consider alternative dispute resolution before issuing proceedings. (Commonhold and Leasehold Reform Act, s 35(3).)

18.22   The person collecting the service charge can distrain by sending in certificated bailiffs in all cases except:

(a)   commonhold, and

(b)   leases where

　　(i)   the service charge is not reserved as rent, or

　　(ii)   the premises are a dwelling, or

　　(iii)   where the Right to Manage is being exercised.

Distraint is likely to be made less useful to a landlord for its purposes under proposals for change. A rent owner can also distrain for arrears of an estate rentcharge.

18.23   A landlord can usually forfeit a lease, by going through the necessary hoops. As they are not landlords none of the following can forfeit: a 1987 Act manager, or an RTM Company (s 100(3)) or the rentcharge owner, or a commonhold association (s 31(8)).

The percentages payable

18.24   It is only in the case of commonhold that there is a statutory requirement to have a service charge (the 'commonhold assessment'), and in that case the units must each have a percentage allocated to them, and the percentages must add up to 100% (s 38).

18.25   In the case of long leases there are provisions in the Landlord and Tenant Act 1987 under which parties can apply to have a lease or leases varied and these can possibly affect the percentage payable. (See at **10.2** et seq.)

18.26   For a Right to Manage property the landlord may be liable to pay the service charge costs not allocated to the qualifying tenants, ie those residential tenants holding long leases. At least where the total service charge percentages do not amount to 100% the landlord is liable for the balance, which is supposed to be divided notionally among his tenants (ie the non-qualifying tenants) on the floor area basis. (See at **18.7** above.)

18.27   In the case of rentcharges there is no statutory provision for varying a percentage, although for non-estate rentcharges there can be compulsory redemption. (See Chapter 16.)

APPENDIX 1

Checklist

This is a brief note of some matters that may be relevant to answer a query in a hurry.

MAIN CHAPTERS

For drafting and negotiating see Chapter 3.
For specific items of charge see Chapters 5 and 6.
For maximising recovery see Chapter 14.
For challenging a high demand see Chapter 15.
For Contract factors see Chapter 13.
For estate rentcharges and similar freehold service charges see Chapter 16.
For commonhold see Chapter 17.

GENERAL SERVICE CHARGES IN LEASES

1 Residential or commercial?

2 Check the lease, Deeds of Variation, licences, and side letters/waivers.

3 Are the works and services clearly defined?

4 Are both the demised property and the landlord's property clearly defined?

5 Can the landlord vary the services?

6 Are there qualifications to the landlord's obligation to provide the services?

7 How is the service charge paid? – Quarterly in advance?

8 How do the year end adjustments work? – repayment of excess, or only credit for following year?

9 Is the service charge reserved as rent?

10 Is the service charge included as such in the rent abatement provision following destruction?

11 Does the tenant pay a fixed percentage or a fair proportion? If the latter – does the lease show how it is calculated?

12 Is there power to vary a fixed percentage?

13   Is there a weighted service charge?

14   If tenant pays on estimates, does the lease say who gives the estimates?

15   Who gives certificates at the year end?

16   Is there any special requirement for certificates (as to timing or form etc)?

17   What are the terms of any waivers?

18   Does the lease provide for interest on late payment?

19   If there is a management company –

   (i)   Does it carry out the services?

   (ii)   Does the landlord have a right/obligation to do works in default?

   (iii) Does the tenant have to be a member?

   (iv)   Does the tenant have voting rights, or rights to be a director?

20   Is there a tenants' association? If so, for residential, is it a recognised tenants' association?

21   Are any particular items excluded from the service charge (eg initial construction costs, inherent defects)?

22   Is there a sinking fund? If so, does the lease say what it is intended to cover, and how much of the fund is credited to each tenant? Is the landlord obliged to use the fund?

23   Is the service charge money invested?

24   (For residential) – Has there been proper consultation on the works at issue? (See Chapter 9 at **9.56** et seq).

25   Is there a sweeping up clause? Is it relevant for the works in dispute?

26   What exclusions are there for the landlord's obligations?

27   Is there a disputes clause? If so, what are the time limits?

28   Has the tenant got copies of the accounts and estimates for the last few years?

29   Check the notes to the accounts to see if they justify the matters of concern.

FOR ESTATE RENTCHARGES

30   See 3 and 4 above re definitions of works and premises.

31   What is the payment system?

32   Have circumstances changed to justify a change to the percentage?

33   Is the payee obliged to produce estimates as condition of payment?

34   Has the payer a material waiver?

35   Is there a disputes procedure, and if so what are the time limits?

COMMONHOLD

36 Check the current version of the Commonhold Community Statement and the Memorandum and Articles.

37 Was there proper consultation prior to demands? (See Chapter 17 at **17.23** et seq.)

38 See copy of any relevant resolution of the Commonhold Association/Directors as to the works to be done.

39 Are there any grounds for challenging the validity of such resolutions?

40 Is there a study reserve?

41 Is the unit let?

(a) If so is the tenant of the unit liable to pay the commonhold assessment? If so, on what basis?

(b) If no proper notice of letting has been given the commonhold association should require the details.

(c) Is diversion of rent needed?

Precedent 1
Full service charge provisions for a lease

1   *This precedent, like Precedent 2, only covers matters directly affecting the service charge. Precedent 1 is for a shop ('the Shop') within a shopping centre ('the Centre'). Included are some alternative provisions which may be suitable for other leases of other types of premises. Precedent 2 is for a lease of a flat where there is a management company.*

2   *This precedent is very full to indicate how the service charge can be covered in a lease. Accordingly, it refers to many parts of the lease. It is basically drawn from a landlord's point of view, although there are a few benefits for the tenant, such as the obligation to hold the Service Rent in an interest bearing account.*

3   *For the shop lease the 'Centre' comprises a number of blocks of shops and, the Shop is within one of the blocks ('the Block'). The definition of Common Parts is in two parts – the general common parts and the common parts of the Block. The landlord covenants to provide the services to the Block, but only to use reasonable endeavours to provide services in respect of the remainder of the Centre.*

4   *A range of services is shown in Precedent 3. These can be used as a guide, and can be incorporated on a pick and mix basis, although there may be other items for any particular property, and details of the actual services to be provided must be checked with the landlord and the managing agent for each property before drafting.*

5   *In the shop lease the service charge is reserved as rent and to emphasise this is called, in this precedent, 'the Service Rent'. Some prefer to call the payment a 'Service Charge' or 'Maintenance Charge' or a 'Maintenance Contribution'.*

6   *The Service Rent is payable quarterly is advance. Any shortfall is payable within 14 days of the year end adjustment. Any excess is carried forward unless it exceeds a specified amount, in which case it is to be refunded to the tenant.*

7   *The tenant is to pay a fair proportion of the total costs, as assessed by the landlord's surveyor, rather than a fixed percentage. In Precedent 2 the*

*tenant pays fixed percentages, and Precedent 4 shows how to apply differ-
ent percentages for different services). There is power to vary the percentage.*

8   *The tenant has two months from receipt of details of the amount due in
which to raise objections and have them referred to an independent source.
Such a provision is not valid for leases of dwellings.*

9   *The precedent permits the landlord to set up a reserve fund.*

10   *The landlord can charge for promotional activities.*

11   *The commercial Code recommends that estimates are sent out one month
before the start of the service charge year, and accounts within four months
of the end: some draftsmen may like to incorporate these (on instructions)
if these time limits are thought practical. If so, they would appear in the
Fourth Schedule, paragraphs 4(1) and (2) below.*

PRECEDENT I

A1.01

[Definitions]
The following expressions have the following meanings:

'Accounting Year' (subject to paragraph 5(2) of the Fourth Schedule) means a
period of 12 months ending on the 24th day of December in each year of the term

'The Block' means ALL THAT building known as Rainy Parade shown edged
in green on the Lease Plan forming part of the Centre together with such alterations additions extensions and additions and subject to such reductions as may
from time to time be made thereto

'The Centre' means ALL THAT land and buildings for the time being known
as The Jolly Trolley Shopping Centre Newtown Westshire All Which said
premises are registered with title absolute under title number WS 123456 shown
edged in blue on the Lease Plan together with such other land and buildings
adjoining or reasonably adjacent thereto as may from time to time be added to or
form part of The Jolly Trolley Shopping Centre or such smaller area as may
result from a disposal of part or parts thereof from time to time[1]

'The Common Parts' means (a) the roadways service yards forecourts malls
car parks ramps sub-ways bridges canopies ornamental structures and features
footpaths pedestrian precincts and covers thereover bus stops and bus waiting
areas open areas landscaped areas and children's playing areas within the Centre
from time to time provided for the Tenant and other tenants and occupiers of the
Centre and/or their respective customers and invitees or members of the public
and (b) all entrances halls atriums passages staircases lifts balconies toilets and
other facilities within or forming part of the Block and which are provided or
available for the use of the Tenant in common with others and (c) all other parts
of the Estate not intended to be let[2]

'Demand' means a demand for payment of a proportion of the Service Costs
in accordance with paragraph 4(2) of the Fourth Schedule

'Estimate' means an estimate of the Service Costs in accordance with paragraph 4(1) of the Fourth Schedule

'Expert' means a chartered surveyor agreed upon by the Landlord and the Tenant or in default of agreement appointed by the President [Provided That where an Expert has been previously agreed or appointed in relation to a dispute concerning Service Costs affecting a letting of any part of the Centre on terms similar to those of this Lease in relation to the Service Costs the Landlord shall be entitled to require that the same Expert be appointed for the purposes of any matter required to be dealt with by an Expert under this Lease][3]

'Landlord's Surveyor' means any person or firm appointed by the Landlord to perform any of the functions of the Landlord's Surveyor under this Lease (which expression can include an employee of the Landlord or a company in the same group as the Landlord)

'The perpetuity period' applicable to this Lease shall be a period of 80 years from the date hereof

'The President' means the President for the time being of the Royal Institution of Chartered Surveyors or his duly appointed deputy or nominee

'Rents' means the rents firstly secondly and thirdly reserved herein

'Reserve' means the total of the sums (if any) held by the Landlord in respect of the matters referred to in paragraph 2(2) of the Fourth Schedule

'Services' means the services or any of them and other items described in paragraph 3 of the Fourth Schedule

'Service Costs' means the costs to the Landlord computed under paragraph 2 of the Fourth Schedule of providing services to the Centre and includes where appropriate a Reserve

'Service Rent' means the proportion or proportions of the Service Costs attributable to the Shop from time to time properly determined by the Landlord's Surveyor acting reasonably and who shall have the right from time to time to allocate or assess different proportions in respect of different services[4]

'The Shop' means the ground floor shop unit known as 33 Rainy Parade in the Centre shown on the Lease Plan edged in red together with all additions and improvements thereto and all landlord's fixtures and fittings together with the shop front and fascia and internal non-load bearing walls and the screed floors and the interior surfaces of all structural walls and the ceilings (but not the beams or joists from which the ceiling is suspended) and the surface of the floors (but not the joists or base supporting the top surface of the floor) the windows and window frames and the doors and door frames together with all the service conduits solely serving the Shop (but not those which also serve other premises) and excluding from the definition of the Shop any structural part of the Block[5]

---

1 In some leases there may be a need for definitions for other premises such 'the Estate' or 'the Development', or 'Block A and Block B'.

2 This may be the most important definition for service charge purposes and needs careful consideration. If the premises being let are, eg, part of a building such as third floor offices, or a first-floor flat, then the definition of common parts will need to include references to entrances and corridors and stairs, and may also need to mention lifts or escalators. There may also be areas such as a common area for refuse storage, or for washing or drying clothes, and there may be leisure facilities available for tenants such a gymnasium or swimming pool or tennis court or cafeteria. There may be a specific parking area for visitors. If there are such items which are

common parts they should be specifically mentioned if the costs for maintenance of them are to be recoverable, unless they appear as a separate head of charge (eg 'the pool'.).

3 This can save costs if an expert has already seen the leases and accounts for the development.

4 The final phrase is needed as the tenant is not paying a fixed percentage. If the tenant pays a fixed percentage there should be a right to vary the percentage, such as paragraph (d) in the Agreements and Declarations in Precedent 2. There are some examples of setting out how the service charge percentage is to be calculated in Precedent 7, Part 1. As mentioned in the head notes, some people prefer to call the payment by a different name.

5 This is the definition of the demised premises. It needs careful attention to avoid any gaps between what is let and the common parts. The premises being let may be called by some other name such as 'the Premises' or 'the demised premises' or 'the Unit' or 'the Flat'.

A1.02

[Demise]

The Landlord demises to the Tenant the Shop Together With the rights set out in the First Schedule but except and reserving to the Landlord the rights set out in the Second Schedule TO HOLD unto the Tenant for the term of 15 years commencing on the 25th day of December 2008 PAYING during the term

FIRST the rent of £20,000 per year (subject to review in accordance with the provisions of the Third Schedule) such rent to be paid in advance without any deduction or set-off by equal quarterly payments on the usual quarter days in each year

AND SECONDLY a yearly rent equal to the appropriate proportion of the insurance premium paid by the Landlord in accordance with the Landlord's covenant hereinafter contained

AND THIRDLY the yearly rent being the Service Rent ascertained and paid in accordance with the provisions of the Fourth Schedule[1]

1 If the service charge is not being reserved as rent then the item thirdly described above will not apply. Similarly, if the tenant either does not pay the insurance premium or if it is included in the service charge the second item will not apply.

A1.03

[Tenants' covenants affecting the service charge]

(To pay the Rents)

(a) To pay the Rents at the times and in manner aforesaid[1]

(To repair)

(b) To keep in good repair and condition throughout the term the Shop and the interior and exterior of the shop front and fascia together with any glass within or forming part of the Shop and the Landlord's fixtures and fittings Provided That save in the case of the shop front the Tenant shall not be liable to carry out any work to any part of the main structure of the Building (which expression for the purpose of this clause shall be deemed not to

472

include internal non load-bearing walls) and [exclusion of damage from Insured Risks]

(c) [Shop front decoration]

(d) [To decorate internally in every fifth year]

(To pay costs of party items)

(e) So far as the same is not included in the Service Rent to pay on demand a fair proportion (to be conclusively determined by the Landlord's Surveyor) of the costs incurred in respect of repairing cleaning inspecting and replacing any party walls fences sewers drains channels pipes wires passageways stairways entrance ways roads pavements and other things the use of which is common to the Centre and adjoining premises[2]

(f) [To pay Value added tax]

(g) [To pay interest on sums in arrear which should include the Service Rent]

1 The definition of Rents above includes the Service Rent. If the service charge is not reserved as rent there needs to be a covenant such as 'To pay the Rent at the times and in the manner aforesaid and the Service Charge at the times and in the manner described in [the Fourth Schedule]'.
2 This clarifies the position: work on party property might not be carried out by the landlord and would thus not be within the Service Costs.

A1.04

[Landlord's covenants affecting service charges]

(a) [To insure the Centre against Insured Risks]

(To provide the services)

(b) Subject as herein provided and to the due payment by the Tenant of the Service Rent and unless prevented by strikes lockouts or other causes beyond the Landlord's control:

(i) to provide the Services referred to in paragraph 3(1) of the Fourth Schedule and

(ii) to use all reasonable endeavours to provide the services referred to in paragraphs 3(2) to 3(20) of the Fourth Schedule[1]

1 It is assumed from the above wording that the two final items in paragraph 3 of the Fourth Schedule are not services the landlord is obliged to perform, eg VAT. In this precedent the services are to be set out in the Fourth Schedule. In some leases (particularly residential leases) the landlord covenants to carry out services which are set out in the clause, and so the obligation to pay therefore refers to the landlord's covenant.

A1.05

[Agreements and declarations]

(No obligation to continue the Services)

(a)   The provision of any of the Services shall not create or imply any obligation on the part of the Landlord to continue to provide or maintain any such Service save in so far as the Landlord expressly covenants to do so under clause 4 hereof

(No liability for interruption to Services)

(b)   The Landlord shall not be liable to the Tenant in respect of any interruption occasioned to any of the Services or any loss or damage in consequence thereof by reason of any necessary repair or maintenance of the Common Parts or any other parts of the Centre (provided that reasonable means of access to the Shop is maintained at all times during normal trading hours) or by reason of any damage thereto or destruction of any part of the Centre or of any other cause beyond the Landlord's control

(Notice of disrepair)

(c)   The Landlord shall not be liable for delay in carrying out any repairs for which the Landlord is liable hereunder unless it has been given notice of disrepair by the Tenant and has failed to carry out any necessary repair within a reasonable time of receiving such notice[1]

(Rights to alter the Centre)

(d)   If at any time in its absolute discretion the Landlord desires to alter or divert or stop up any of the roadways service yards forecourts malls car parks ramps subways bridges pedestrian precincts open areas or landscaped areas comprised within the Common Parts the Landlord shall have full right and liberty to do so subject to leaving available for the Tenant and its servants and customers and members of the public reasonable means of access to the Shop[2]

(Cesser of rent)

(e)   [If the cesser of rent is to apply to the Service Rent this will appear here and the cesser clause should refer to the 'rents firstly [secondly] and thirdly herein reserved' or 'the rent first herein reserved and the Service Rent', as the case may be.]

1   This is not a clause included in all leases, but is recommended.
2   For leases other than for the shop the definitions in this clause will need adjustment.

[Fourth Schedule]

(Service Rent provisions)

A1.06

(Definitions)[1]

1   [If the specific service charge definitions mentioned above are not included in the main body of the lease they would normally appear here.]

A1.07

(The Service Costs)

2   The Service Costs shall be the total of:

(Costs of services)

(1)   the costs in any Accounting Year to the Landlord of the provision of such of the Services as are provided or incurred including the costs of any inspections in connection therewith

(The Reserve)

(2)   an amount (to be revised annually by the Landlord at its discretion) to be charged in any Accounting Year as a contribution to the establishment of a Reserve towards the estimated cost to the Landlord of the provision of the Services or any of them and in particular the replacement of substantial items of plant or equipment needed for providing the Services (including without prejudice to the generality of that expression lifts escalators and boilers) such amount to be ascertained on the assumptions inter alia

(i)   that the cost of replacement of items of plant machinery and other equipment and other capital items is calculated on such life expectancy of the said items as the Landlord's Surveyor may from time to time reasonably determine to the intent that a fund shall be accumulated sufficient to cover the cost of replacement of the said items by the end of their anticipated life and

(ii)   that the decoration of or other treatment to the outside of the Block and/or the Common Parts for which the Landlord is responsible will be carried out in every third year of the term

PROVIDED THAT the costs relating to any item in respect of which any sum or sums shall have been included in the Reserve during an Accounting Year shall at the Landlord's discretion as to the amount thereof (if any) be met out of the Reserve and if and to the extent that any such expenditure is made out of the Reserve the same expenditure shall not also be charged to the Tenant by way of Service Rent
    AND PROVIDED FURTHER THAT nothing herein contained shall oblige the Landlord to establish or to maintain a Reserve[1]
    (Additional sums)

(3)   [If the Landlord is to have the right to call for additional payments during the year the provision can be inserted here: see Miscellaneous Lease Clauses – Precedent 7, Part 17.]

1   Not all leases include a reserve or sinking fund, but if the ability to set up such a fund is required wording on these lines is suitable. Specific items are mentioned in the provision and there is an obligation to use the money received towards the items they are intended for. If a sinking fund is desired for a specific object, such as a roof, this should ideally be mentioned in (2) above.

A1.08

(The Services to be provided)

3 The Services shall comprise the following namely:

(Services)

(a) [Suggestions for numerous items that might appear in a service charge Schedule appear in Precedent 3, and the relevant ones can be incorporated, checking that the definitions are consistent.]

(Sweeping-up clause)

(b) The cost of providing such other services as the Landlord shall consider ought reasonably to be provided for the benefit of the Centre or for the proper maintenance and servicing of any part or parts thereof

A1.08

(Payment of the Service Rent)

4 The Service Rent shall be payable as follows: –

(1) Before each Accounting Year or as soon as possible after the start thereof the Landlord shall serve on the Tenant an Estimate prepared by the Landlord's Surveyor of the amount of the Service Costs expected to be incurred during the Accounting Year and of the Service Rent expected to be payable by the Tenant and the Tenant shall pay on account of the Service Rent one quarter of the sum so estimated in advance on each of the usual quarter days [And It Is Agreed That the Service Rent payable during the first Accounting Year of the term shall be £XXX or the due proportion thereof for the relevant part of the Accounting Year and such initial sum shall *[shall not]* be subject to variation as set out in this paragraph 4]

(2) As soon as practicable after the end of each Accounting Year the Landlord shall cause to be prepared and served on the Tenant an account of the Service Costs for that Accounting Year which shall be certified by a chartered surveyor or a chartered accountant as true and correct together with a calculation of the Service Rent ('the Demand') in accordance with such certified account and thereupon the amount of the Service Rent for that Accounting Year shall be final and binding upon the Landlord and the Tenant subject only to the provisions of paragraph 6 of this Schedule

(3) (a) If the Service Rent for any Accounting Year exceeds the amount shown on the Estimate the amount of the excess payable shall be paid by the Tenant to the Landlord within 14 days after receipt of the Demand by the Tenant or within 28 days of the end of the Term as the case may be

(b)   If the Service Rent for any Accounting Year shall be less than the amount paid following the giving of the Estimate the amount of the overpayment repayable

   (i)   if more than [£500] shall be repaid by the Landlord to the Tenant within 14 days of the date of the Demand [and if paid after that date the Landlord shall pay interest at the interest rate on such sum from the date 14 days after the date of the Demand until the date of receipt by the Tenant] and

   (ii)   if [£500] or less shall be credited to the Tenant against the next succeeding payment or payments of Service Rent after the date of the Demand or in the case of the last year of the term shall be refunded within 14 days [as in sub-paragraph (i)]

A1.09

(Miscellaneous matters)

5   It is hereby agreed that:

(Receipts to earn interest)

(1)   The Service Rent paid by the Tenant and the other tenants of the Centre shall be placed in an interest bearing account and the interest earned thereon shall be used as a credit towards the Service Costs but the Landlord shall not be obliged to apportion the interest earned among the individual tenants[1]

(Change of Accounting Year)

(2)   The Landlord shall be entitled to change the Accounting Year by giving to the Tenant not less than (3 months') notice whenever the Landlord shall deem desirable but not more than once in any period of 18 months and on the occasion of each such change the Landlord shall make any necessary and proper adjustments resulting from the change[2]

[Alterations to the premises]

(3)   The fair proportion of the Service Rent payable by the Tenant is not subject to increase by reason of the construction of a mezzanine floor within the Shop or any alteration to the Shop (made where needed with the consent of the Landlord) which does not extend the Shop beyond the external floor area at the date hereof Provided That the Landlord shall have the right to change the fair proportion of the Service Rent payable by the Tenant to reflect any change in the external floor area of the Shop or any other unit in the Centre[3]

(Alterations to the Common Parts)

(4) The Landlord shall be entitled to make such alterations as the Landlord thinks fit

    (i) to the Common Parts (provided that this shall not entitle the Landlord to derogate from its grant) and/or

    (ii) as may be necessary to comply with any Act of Parliament and/or with the Landlord's obligation to supply the Services and/or

    (iii) to all or any plant and equipment (including if the Landlord reasonably deems necessary the installation of plant machinery and equipment of a different type) and to suspend any Services while the works of alteration or installation are being carried out or in the event of an emergency[4]

(Unlet parts)

(5) If any part of the Centre intended to be let is for the time being unlet a sum equal to the Service Rent attributable to the unlet part shall be borne by the Landlord[5]

(Reserve to be held on trust)[6]

(6) (i) All sums received by the Landlord in respect of the Reserve (if any) shall be held by the Landlord upon trust to apply the same and any interest accruing thereon for the purposes for which the same were collected and subject thereto upon trust for the persons who at the expiry of that period shall be the tenants of the Centre in shares equal to the proportion which the Service Rent payable by them respectively bears to 100% of all the Service Rents

    (ii) The power of appointing a new trustee of the trust referred to in this sub-paragraph (5) is vested in the Landlord from time to time

    (iii) The trustee of the fund shall have full power to invest in all securities authorised for investment of trust funds including those authorised under section 42 of the Landlord and Tenant Act 1987

    (iv) If the Centre is destroyed by an insured risk the Reserve shall be distributed among all the tenants of the Centre in proportion to the amount of Service Rent which each is liable to pay (subject to the deduction of any arrears at the relevant time)

1   This provision is aimed at commercial leases. For residential leases the statutory obligations must be remembered, and, when it is bought into force, the obligation to hold service charge receipts in a designated account. As the regulations are still not available it is not certain whether there may be rules on interest or a prohibition on not apportioning interest.

2   For residential leases changing the accounting year may be restricted to changing to a date not more than 12 months ahead (ie 11 months is OK but 13 months is not) if replacement section 21(9) of the Landlord and Tenant Act 1985 is brought into force as envisaged in section 152 of the Commonhold and Leasehold Reform Act 2002.

3   This provision is perhaps more often found in leases of industrial units, but could be helpful here.

4 The definitions will need changing if this provision is used for properties other than the shop lease.
5 See the note to (4).
6 This provision should be omitted for leases of residential property (Section 42 Landlord and Tenant Act 1987). The definitions will need to be reconsidered if the lease if not for the shop.

A1.10

(Settlement of disputes)[1]

6(1) If the Tenant disputes whether any item in an Estimate or a Demand is properly payable under the terms of this Lease the Tenant shall serve on the Landlord within two months of receipt of the Estimate or Demand as the case may be a notice specifying the disputed item or items and in the case of a Demand the time for service of such notice shall be of the essence

(2) If the Tenant and the Landlord fail to reach agreement on the said dispute within two months of the service of the Tenant's said notice either party shall be entitled to refer the dispute to an Expert (in the case of the Tenant provided that the Tenant has paid the Service Rent) and the dispute shall be determined by the Expert who shall act as an Expert and not as an arbitrator and whose fees shall be borne as the Expert directs or in the absence of a direction shall be payable in equal shares by the Tenant and the Landlord

(3) The Tenant shall not be entitled to dispute the cost of any work or Service comprised in the Service Costs solely on the ground that the work or Service could have been performed or provided for or cost less than that incurred by the Landlord provided that the said cost was incurred following reasonable advice on the point from a suitably qualified person or was a sum estimated in good faith by the Landlord's Surveyor

(4) Until the Expert's determination has been given payment of the Service Rent by the Tenant in accordance with the Estimate or the Demand shall be deemed to be without prejudice to the determination of the dispute

(5) If the Expert's determination shows that the Tenant has made an overpayment of Service Rent the Landlord shall either credit the next payment of Service Rent or shall refund to the Tenant the amount in question in accordance with the provisions of paragraph 4(4) of this Schedule

1 This provision should be omitted for residential premises, as such clauses are ineffective for dwellings – s 27A(6) Landlord and Tenant Act 1985.

Precedent 2

LEASE OF FLAT (WITH MANAGEMENT COMPANY)

1   This precedent only includes matters relative to service charges. The Management Company is a party as well as the landlord and the tenant. The tenants are assumed to be members of the management company. This is likely to be suitable for a large block.

2   The service charge is not reserved as rent (it is trust money).

3   In this precedent the tenant pays different specified percentages ('the Tenant's Contribution') of the costs relating (a) to the Building and (b) to the remainder of the Estate, and there is a right to change the percentages in case of need. There is no specified right to charge different percentages for tenants who use different facilities, but it is assumed that the percentages are calculated on a reasonable basis to take account of such factors initially.

4   The Tenant's Contribution is payable half yearly in advance and adjusted annually. The Management Company can call for a top-up if needed (clause 3(f)).

5   There is no disputes procedure, nor is there a reserve.

6   The service charge year is that of the management company rather than the landlord.

7   The Tenant's Contribution is suspended if the premises are destroyed for the period of the loss of rent/service charge insurance.

8   The final provision is a statement that the provisions are intended to enable the Management Company to recover all its expenditure. This is declaratory of the intention, but cannot override the statutory implication of reasonableness.

9   The statutory provisions affecting dwellings covered in Chapters 9 and 10 apply to this lease.

PRECEDENT 2

A2.01

[Definitions]

1 [The following definitions will be needed for service charge purposes:

'The Flat' [excluding reference to the garden] ; 'The Building' [not including the grounds round the building] ; 'The Common Parts' ; 'The Service Charge' [ie the cost of providing services]

2 In addition the following definitions will be needed:

'The Accounting Year of the Management Company' means the year from the 25th day of March to the 24th day of March in the following year or such other accounting year as may in future be adopted by the Management Company

'The Auditors' Certificate' means a certificate prepared by a member of the Royal Institution of Chartered Surveyors or a chartered accountant certifying the amount of the total expenditure on the Service Obligations made or incurred by the Management Company or (as the case may be) by the Landlord under clause 5(e)

'The Due Dates' means 25th March and 29th September in each year

'The Estate' means the Landlord's property shown edged in blue on plan 2 on part of which the Building is situated

'The Service Obligations' means the obligations undertaken by the Management Company to provide the services and other items specified in clause 4

'The Tenant's Contribution' (subject to the provisions of clause 6(e)) means the following percentages of the Service Charge:

(i) 12.275% of the Service Charge relating to the Building and

(ii) 3.5% of the Service Charge relating to the Estate except such parts thereof as consist of buildings divided into flats

A2.02

[Tenant's covenants]

3(a) [To pay rent]

(b) [To repair the Flat]

(c) (i) Not to assign underlet or part with possession of part the Flat (as opposed to the whole thereof)

(ii) Not to assign the whole of the Flat without the prior consent of the Landlord (such consent not to be unreasonably withheld or delayed) and without

(1)   first obtaining a deed in a form approved by the Landlord's solicitors at the expense of the Tenant containing a covenant by the assignee with the Landlord and the Management Company to pay the rent and the Tenant's Contribution and otherwise to comply with all the provisions on the Tenant's part herein contained and

(2)   procuring the transfer to the assignee of the Tenant's share in the Management Company[1]

(iii)   Not to underlet the whole of the Flat except with the prior written consent of the Landlord which shall not be unreasonably withheld but the Landlord shall not be treated as acting unreasonably if (in the case of lettings for [seven] or more years) the Landlord requires as a condition of giving consent that the underlessee enters into a direct covenant with the Landlord and the Management Company to observe the covenants contained herein (other than the covenant for payment of rent) [and that the Tenant's share in the Management Company is transferred to the underlessee for the period of the under-lease][2]

(d)   On the Due Dates to pay to the Management Company such sums on account of the Tenant's Contribution as the Management Company or its agents may reasonably consider sufficient together with the contributions payable by other tenants of the Estate and by the Landlord under clause 5(b) to meet the Service Charge for the period until the next Due Date Provided That if the Landlord is carrying out the Service Obligations under clause 5(e) the Tenant shall pay to the Landlord the Tenant's Contribution and also the Tenant's Proportion of the costs of the Management Company in respect of complying with formalities under the Companies Acts (including costs relating to preparing and auditing accounts of the Management Company and filing annual returns and other documents at Companies House)

(e)   Within 14 days of receipt of a copy of the Auditor's Certificate to pay to the Management Company (or to the Landlord if the Landlord is carrying out the Service Obligations under clause 5(e)) the amount shown therein as due from the Tenant for the relevant year less any amount which the Tenant has paid in advance

(f)   Within 14 days of demand to pay to the Management Company (or to the Landlord as the case may be) the same percentages as the Tenant's Contribution of any sum or sums actually and properly expended by the Management Company or the Landlord as the case may be or which it might be necessary to expend in performance of the Service Obligations which expenditure the Management Company cannot meet from money in hand

(g)   To allow the Management Company and the Landlord and all others duly authorised by either of them to have access to the Flat on reasonable notice (save in emergency) if necessary for the due performance of the Service Obligations

1 Landlord's consent is mentioned to ensure that there is some chance of checking that the assignee can afford the Tenant's Contributions. Some people consider such a provision unnecessary because of the Landlord and Tenant (Covenants) Act 1995, but a covenant is preferable in view of the involvement of the Management Company.

2 There may be other conditions for consent, but the ones mentioned here are those particularly applicable to service charges.

A2.03

[Covenants by the Management Company]

4 The Management Company covenants with the Tenant and as a separate covenant with the Landlord that provided the Tenant makes the payments referred to in clause 3(d) the Management Company will:

    (a) Pay all outgoings in respect of the Common Parts and of the Estate except those outgoings which are the responsibility of tenants of any flats on the Estate under the terms of their leases

    (b) Keep the Common Parts and the service conduits in the Building in repair and rebuild or replace any parts that cannot be repaired or where rebuilding or replacement is economically appropriate [and any other services, such as the relevant services set out in Precedent 3]

A2.04

[Landlord's service charge covenants]

5 The Landlord covenants with the Tenant and as a separate covenant with the Management Company as follows:

    (a) To ensure that any Lease of a flat on the Estate granted for a term of [seven] years or more will contain provisions as to payment towards the Service Charge in substantially the same form as in this Lease

    (b) To pay a proper proportion of the Service Charge in respect of such flats on the Estate as may from time to time not be let on leases under which the tenant thereof is liable to contribute to the Service Charge

    (c) At the reasonable request of and at the cost of the Tenant to enforce against the tenant of any other flat on the Estate covenants entered into similar to those in this Lease Provided That the Landlord shall seek to recover the costs from the tenant in breach first and the liability for costs on the part of the Tenant is restricted to those costs which the Landlord is unable to recover from the defaulting tenant

    (d) To permit the Management Company to have access to the Building and any part of the Estate on reasonable prior notice (save in cases of emergency when no notice is required) for the purpose of carrying out the Service Obligations

(e) In the event of the Management Company failing to carry out the Service Obligations in a satisfactory manner then at the request of the Tenant in writing the Landlord shall be entitled to carry out the Service Obligations (or those which the Management Company has failed to carry out satisfactorily) in place of the Management Company and in such case the Tenant's Contribution or an appropriate proportion thereof shall be paid to the Landlord

A2.05

[Agreements and declarations]

6 (a) All internal non-structural walls ceilings and floors separating the Flat from other flats in the Building shall be party walls and repaired and maintained as such

(b) If the Flat becomes uninhabitable or access thereto becomes impossible as a result of the happening of an insured risk then unless the policy becomes vitiated as the result of an act or omission of the Tenant the rent and the Tenant's Contribution shall cease to be payable until the later of (i) the Flat being again habitable or access thereto being available (as the case may be) or (ii) the end of the period during which any insurance policy in respect of loss of rent and Tenant's Contribution in is force and such sums can be claimed[1]

(c) Neither the Management Company nor the Landlord shall be liable to the Tenant for any interruption in the performance of the Service Obligations caused by mechanical breakdown shortage of materials labour disputes or any other matter beyond the reasonable control of the Management Company or the Landlord

(d) The Landlord's Surveyor shall have the right to vary the percentages of the Tenant's Obligation from time to time if it shall be reasonable to do so as a result of changes in circumstances and in particular if the number of flats on the Estate shall increase or decrease or if part of the property belonging to the Landlord and reasonably treated as part of the Estate shall increase or decrease resulting in an increase or decrease in the obligations of the Management Company or the Landlord[2]

(e) The parties hereto acknowledge that the purpose of the provisions relating to the Service Charge and the Tenant's Obligation are to enable the Management Company to recover all the money for which the Management Company may be liable in respect of the outgoings of the Estate and the Building so that there is no residual liability on the Landlord[3]

1 Many landlords will not agree to the rent cesser clause also covering the service charge.
2 Where there is a fixed service charge percentage the lease needs to contain a power for the percentage to be varied in case of change.
3 A declaration of this type is useful. If the landlord carries out the services the clause would simply refer to the landlord rather than the management company.

Precedent 3

NON-EXHAUSTIVE LIST OF SERVICES

1   *This is a list of services that could be used for a service charge schedule. The services need to be considered individually to see which (if any) are material. They are grouped under headings for convenience, although the headings are not essential. Several of these services could come under more than one heading – there is no right or wrong way, provided services to be provided are covered.*

2   *In a number of cases alternatives are given for what are much the same services. In such cases it is recommended that the precedent which reflects the general style of the rest of the precedent will be best, eg some are more expansive than others, and of course the defined terms need to be consistent with the rest of the lease. For example, the clause may need to refer to the Management Company rather than the Landlord, or the Block rather than the Building. It may be appropriate to include items from more than one clause under any heading to achieve the collection desired.*

3   *This list is not complete: there may well services not covered within the clauses below. If so a suitable reference must be included if the landlord is to recover costs for them.*

A3.01

Repair/decoration of the building incorporating the demised premises

Repairing maintaining renewing (where repair is not reasonably practicable or economic) cleaning painting decorating or otherwise treating as the Landlord shall reasonably consider appropriate the Block (including all plate glass in and forming part of the Block which is not the responsibility of individual tenants) and including the structure of the Block and all plant machinery and equipment of whatever nature in and about or forming part of the Block (including for the avoidance of doubt the roof load-bearing walls and foundations) including the lift and escalators and electronically controlled doors and including repairs and works carried out in the course of making good any damage caused by or necessarily incidental to the exercise by the Landlord of any right reserved in this Lease or any other lease of any part of the Centre but so that this provision shall only relate to those part or parts of the Block which are not designed to be let

OR When necessary to repair decorate clean and treat the foundations roofs and structural parts of the Building and the external parts of the Building (including all fire escapes canopies balconies balustrades parapets decorative features and other items attached to the exterior of the Building but excluding the windows and window frames and external doors and doorframes of the Premises)

OR Keep the service conduits in the Building in repair and rebuild or renew or replace any parts that need to be repaired renewed or replaced including (where reasonably appropriate) provision for energy conservation and noise insulation

A3.02

Repair/decoration of the Common Parts

Repairing maintaining renewing (where repair is not reasonably practical or economic) cleaning painting decorating or otherwise treating as the Landlord shall in its reasonable discretion consider appropriate the Common Parts

OR At such intervals as the Landlord's Surveyor shall consider reasonable redecorate or paint or treat as appropriate the Common Parts and the exterior surfaces of the window frames and of the window sills and the exterior of the external doors of the Flat and any balconies

OR Keep the Common Parts and the service conduits in the Building in repair and rebuild or replace any parts that cannot be repaired or where rebuilding or replacement is economically appropriate

OR Periodically inspecting examining decorating maintaining repairing overhauling resurfacing and where necessary replacing every part of the Common Parts including but without prejudice to the generality of the foregoing the plant machinery and engineering services therein and also the Estate Road and the Parking Spaces and including sums properly and reasonably payable under maintenance contracts covering the same

OR Keep the Common Parts properly clean and free of rubbish and adequately lit

A3.03

Lighting, heating, cleaning and hot water

To provide and maintain at all times:

(i)   appropriate lighting in the Common Parts

(ii)   an adequate supply of hot and cold water to the toilets within the Common Parts and the Premises

(iii) climate control for the Building

(iv) heat to the radiators in the Building between 1st October and 30th April (inclusive) each year between the hours of 8.00 a.m. and 1.00 p.m. on Saturdays and 8.00 a.m. and 7.00 p.m. on other days but not on Sundays or Bank Holidays [such heat being sufficient to maintain an average air temperature in the Premises of 65 degrees Fahrenheit where the temperature outside the Building does not fall below 32 degrees Fahrenheit and the doors and windows of the Premises are closed]

(v) Porters caretakers and other staff necessary for the good management of the Building and the security of the Tenants or the Building

(vi) Cleaning the Common Parts

(vii) Cleaning the outside of the windows of the Building once in every month

OR Lighting such parts of the Common Parts as the Landlord may reasonably deem desirable or necessary and the repair (where repair is not reasonably practical or economic) and maintenance of such lighting including the fittings cables and wires relating thereto

OR Keep the Common Parts (and in particular all corridors and stairs) properly cleaned and suitably lit

OR Cleaning all windows and glass in the Common Parts (other than any such windows or glass which are the responsibility of a tenant) as often as is necessary

OR The provision of water to the Common Parts and each and every part thereof together with water rates standing charges and any other costs or outgoings in relation to such supply

OR The provision of hot water for heating to such parts of the Common Parts as are designed to receive the same

A3.04

External areas

Landscaping planting and cultivation of such part or parts of the Common Parts as are from time to time allocated or designated for such purpose

OR Maintain in a neat and tidy condition and properly cultivated all the gardens of the Estate

OR The provision within the Common Parts and the maintenance renewal and replacement as occasion shall require and as the Landlord shall reasonably deem appropriate in the interests of good estate management of seating directional signs notices display boards litter bins street furniture children's play equipment public telephones and other facilities

OR Maintaining cleaning replacing and updating as necessary name signs on the Estate and marking out and lining the Estate Road and the Parking Spaces

OR Maintenance of the lawns gardens and landscaped areas within the curtilage of the Building and cultivation and tending and where necessary replacing the plants within the Common Parts

OR Keeping the Landscaping Areas tidy and suitably planted and tended and generally complying with the requirements of the planning permission concerning the same and replacing plants and shrubs which die

A3.05

Refuse/pest control

The disposal of refuse from the Centre including the collection thereof and the replacement where necessary of receptacles bottle banks recycling containers compactors and other equipment and plant needed or reasonably considered desirable by the Landlord or the local authority and including complying with statutory obligations in relation to waste management

OR Arranging for the periodic removal of refuse from the Refuse Area and providing appropriate receptacles for use therein including skips recycling containers compactors and bottle banks

OR The cost of maintenance contracts for the repair replacement (where repair is not reasonably practical or economic) and maintenance of the plant and equipment used for carrying out the Services to the Common Parts or any part or parts thereof and contracts for landscaping and cultivation and pest control

A3.06

Plant and equipment (including computers and carpets)

The costs of purchasing renting operating maintaining repairing and when necessary replacing the lifts generators boilers the telephone telex computing systems broadband internet connection facsimile and communicating systems serving the Centre as a whole or any part or parts of the Common Parts and including any optical fibre or other cables satellite dishes antennae aerials and all wiring and fixings for the same [and to include upgrading the computer systems when the same need replacing and in any event when they are no longer supported by the supplier]

OR To repair and if and whenever reasonably necessary to replace and maintain in good working order all plant machinery apparatus and equipment comprising or serving the lifts and for providing and use of water heating central heating (including boilers and generators) and climate control systems within the Common Parts or the Building (save only where such plant machinery apparatus and equipment is not a landlord's fixture) the lighting in the Common Parts the sprinkler system and fire alarm system and smoke detectors and fire fighting equipment and all service conduits and appliances in the Building and which serve the Building other than those which exclusively serve the Premises or other areas designed to be let

OR The provision and replacement in the Common Parts where appropriate or necessary of toilet requisites and hygiene services including the supply maintenance repair and cleaning of receptacles plant and equipment in connection therewith

OR Maintain clean and treat all flooring and carpeting in the Common Parts and replacing (where beyond economic repair) the carpet or any part thereof with carpet of suitable quality

OR Maintain and where necessary replace furnishings to the entrance lobby halls and staircase

OR Maintain repair and (where necessary) renew the carpeting to the corridors hall and stairs of the Building Provided That should it be necessary to replace the carpeting the Landlord's Agent will consult with the tenants of the Building as to the type and design and colour of the replacement but the Landlord shall not be bound by any particular proposals[1]

OR Maintain an automatic door-opening system and the communication system from the front access to the Flat and (where thought suitable) arrange a maintenance contract for the same

OR Maintaining and marking out and updating as necessary the noticeboard in the Common Parts and (where beyond economic repair) replacing the same

OR Re-carpeting or otherwise covering the floors of such parts of the Common Parts as the Landlord may reasonably deem desirable or necessary

OR Enter into service contracts for the maintenance and repair of the lifts boilers and other plant in the Building and to insure the same against normal risks

OR Provide maintain and where necessary replace all equipment tools and materials necessary for the performance of the Service Obligations and for the security and safety of the Building and its occupiers

1   For residential premises the landlord may well have to consult with the tenants because of the estimated cost, but this provision entitles the tenants to be consulted also as to colour and style, and not just as to the cost.

A3.07

Security/fire precautions

The provision and maintenance of security at the Centre including the employment of security personnel and the provision maintenance repair insurance and replacement (where necessary) of all such gates fences cameras computer systems for operating and monitoring the security cameras loudspeakers or communications and other security devices as the Landlord shall reasonably deem necessary

OR Periodically installing maintaining inspecting overhauling repairing and where necessary or where required by the fire officer or insurers replacing any fire detecting fire prevention and/or fire fighting equipment and any fire escape and any sprinkler system

OR Provide and maintain and where necessary replace fire fighting equipment and a suitable servicing contract for regular inspection and maintenance thereof

OR Provide maintain and where necessary renew and enter into contracts for the maintenance of fire fighting equipment (including smoke alarms) and other equipment reasonably needed for the safety or security of the Building

A3.08

General management

The general management of the Centre
   OR Supervising and managing the Common Parts

OR Employ such managing agents surveyors accountants architects and contractors as may be necessary for the reasonable performance of the Service Obligations and for the collection and recovery of [the rents and] the Service Charge

OR Fees charges expenses and commissions payable to any surveyor valuer architect engineer solicitor accountant or managing agent whom the Landlord shall from time to time employ in connection with the management or maintenance and repair of the Development and the Common Parts

OR All payments whether direct or indirect made by the Landlord to or in respect of any consultant or agent or to any local or public authority towards or in connection with the carrying out of the Services or any of them

A3.09

Management costs

If the Landlord does not appoint managing agents to assist with management of the Development (but not otherwise) a sum equal to [10%] of the aggregate costs expenses and outgoings referred to in clause 3(4) of this Lease (but excluding this paragraph) shall be added thereto to reimburse the Landlord for the general administration and management of the Development

OR The proper fees and expenses of the Landlord's managing agents accountants and other professional advisers in performing and carrying out the general management of the Centre and (if the Landlord shall not employ such professional advisers) the expenses of management incurred by the Landlord together with a reasonable management charge not exceeding [5%] of the total Service Costs excluding value added tax from such calculation

A3.10

Contracts

The employment of such independent contractors agents consultants professional workmen porters and other personnel as in the reasonable opinion of the Landlord may be required in respect of the provision or carrying out of any one or more Services to the Common Parts or any part thereof

OR Employ such managing agents surveyors solicitors accountants or others as may be necessary for the reasonable performance and supervision of the Management Company's obligations under this Lease and for the collection of the Service Charge

OR Enter into such contracts as are appropriate and reasonable for the maintenance checking repair and (where necessary) replacement of the automatic front door of the Building and the entry phone system and the security lights

A3.11

Costs of accounts

All fees and costs incurred in respect of the yearly statements and certificates prepared for the purpose of the Service Costs the Service Rent and the general management of the Centre

OR Procure that the Service Charge is audited by qualified auditors independent of the Landlord and that the Auditors Certificate shall be served on the tenants of the flats on the Estate

OR Arrange for the Service Charge to be properly audited and for the Auditor's Certificate to be sent to the Tenant[1]

1   Inspection of vouchers could be mentioned here, but is omitted as all tenants of dwellings now have this right.

A3.12

Outgoings (including notional rent)

All outgoings of each and every part of the Centre utilised or set aside to accommodate the Services or used in connection with the provision thereof and/or the accommodation of all personnel employed in connection therewith together with the actual rents or reasonable notional rental value (if lower) of any such premises whether or not forming part of the Centre for the occupation by or use of any such personnel as aforesaid such rent or rents to be ascertained or determined annually by the Landlord's Surveyor [Provided That any such notional rent for residential accommodation shall be no more than a rent for an assured tenancy of the premises in question under the provisions of the Housing Act 1988 and any such notional rent for any commercial premises shall be no more than would be determined for a new lease of such premises for a term of normal length for similar premises determined under the provisions of the Landlord and Tenant Act 1954]

OR The provision of fuel oil gas and electricity or other energy supplies or power sources from time to time used in running or operating any Service to the Common Parts and/or any part or parts thereof and including equipment designed to achieve energy saving

OR Charges for electricity or gas telephone and fuel consumed on the Common Parts and payable by the Landlord and also water rates and uniform business rates

OR All charges assessments and other outgoings (if any) payable by the Landlord in respect of any part or parts of the Common Parts including uniform business rates and water rates and standing charges assessed upon the Landlord and council tax in respect of any residential accommodation provided for the use of personnel under paragraph [ ] of this Schedule

OR Pay all outgoings in respect of the Common Parts and of the Building except outgoings as are the responsibility of any of the tenants of the flats in the Building under their respective leases

A3.13

Enforcement of covenants

The enforcement of any covenant condition or provision contained in any lease underlease licence or agreement relating to the Centre or part or parts thereof where in the reasonable opinion of the Landlord such enforcement would be in the interests of good estate management Provided That the Landlord shall not be entitled by reason of this provision to recover as part of the Service Rent any costs incurred in proceedings so far as such proceedings are for recovery of rent payable under any lease of a part of the Centre And Provided Further That the Landlord shall first use all reasonable endeavours to recover such costs from the defaulting tenant or other person responsible for the breach

OR All costs relating to making regulations in respect of the proper use of the Common Parts (and in particular the Car Spaces and the Refuse Area and the Landscaped Area) and the enforcement of those regulations

A3.14

Employment of staff

The salaries wages pensions and pension contributions and other proper emoluments and the employer's social security contributions or other statutory levies of all personnel directly employed by the Landlord or its managing agents on duties at the Centre or a fair and reasonable proportion of such expenses in the case of personnel employed by the Landlord to work partly at the Centre and partly elsewhere

OR Employing staff in connection with the performance of the Landlord's obligations hereunder and the provision of services to the Common Parts and all other incidental expenditure in relation to such employment including but without prejudice to the generality of the foregoing the payment of statutory and such other insurance health pension welfare and other payments contributions and premiums that the Landlord is obliged to pay or may in its reasonable discretion consider desirable or necessary to pay to or for staff and the cost of provision and replacement of uniforms working tools appliances storage facilities cleaning any other materials and any other equipment reasonably needed for the proper performance of their duties

OR The provision and supply of any necessary uniform protective clothing footwear glasses headgear gloves tools appliances equipment and materials as the Landlord may in its reasonable discretion deem necessary or desirable for use in the provision and execution of any Service which the Landlord is to provide or maintain or which is required by law

A3.15

Secretarial expenses

Secretarial services for the tenants of the Building including a telephone answering service photocopying facsimile transmission correspondence word processing scanning plan copying the receiving and posting of letters and parcels and the receiving and passing on of messages

Provided That it is agreed

(A) that such services will only be provided for the benefit of tenants between the hours of 9.00 a.m. and 5.30 p.m. on weekdays and

(B) that requests by tenants for the provision of such services will be dealt with strictly in order of receipt of requests and otherwise at the discretion of the office manager for the Building and

(C) that each tenant shall pay for stamps and other disbursements associated with his own use of the secretarial services monthly in arrear and a fair proportion of the expenses of the telephone facsimile and photocopying costs according to use

A3.16

Insurance

Such third party public liability insurance relating to the Centre or to plant and equipment used for providing services to the Centre as the Landlord's Surveyor considers appropriate or desirable to effect

OR All costs and expenses whatsoever incurred by the Landlord in and about the discharge of the obligations on the part of the Landlord set out in clause [ ] of this Lease [the insurance obligation][1]

OR Professional fees for valuations for insurance purposes not more than once in any Accounting Year

1   If the insurance premium is to be treated as part of the service charge it should be mentioned here: It is preferable to keep service charges and insurance separate.

A3.17

Statutory requirements

Complying with all statutory requirements in relation to the Centre

OR All such other acts and things as may be reasonably necessary or desirable for the maintenance of the Building or for the comfort and convenience of the occupiers or to comply with statutory obligations

OR Carrying out any works required to comply with the provisions and requirements of any statute already passed or hereafter to be passed (including but without prejudice to the generality of the foregoing the Town and Country Planning Acts the Public Health Acts and the Environmental Protection Act 1990) and any notices directions regulations bye-laws rules or conditions under any such statute

A3.18

Value added tax

Any value added tax payable by the Landlord in respect of the matters referred to in this Schedule

A3.19

Landlord's covenant about other leases and vacant units

The Landlord covenants with the Tenant that provided the Tenant makes the payments referred to in clause [ ] hereof the Landlord will:

(a)   Ensure that any lease of any flat in the Building granted for a term of [five] years or more contains obligations on the part of the tenant thereof to pay a tenant's contribution on terms substantially in the same form as in this Lease and

(b)   Pay a proper proportion of the Service Charge in respect of any flat or flats in the Building which is or are for the time being not let on terms as to contribution to the Service Charge substantially in the same form as in this Lease

A3.20

Bank charges

The actual cost to the Landlord by way of interest commission bank charges or otherwise of borrowing any sums necessary to provide the Services or any of them Provided That such interest shall be no more than a normal and reasonable rate of interest charged by clearing banks for loans for similar purposes and for similar periods And Provided Further That such borrowings shall be taken up only in respect of unanticipated major expenses and shall be repaid as soon as reasonably practical

A3.21

Promotional expenses

The costs incurred in providing and maintaining in respect of the Centre or a substantial part thereof trading promotion advertising public relations and general publicity (but not the costs incurred by the Landlord in seeking new tenants for vacant units in the Centre) Provided That the proposed budget for such promotional expenses shall be notified in advance to the tenants of the Centre and the Landlord shall be entitled to expend on such matters an amount not exceeding such proposed budget figure unless a majority in number of the tenants of the Centre *[or tenants of the Centre paying between them at least [70%] of the Service Costs]* notify the Landlord in writing within 28 days of receipt of such proposed budget that they object to the proposed budget figure

A3.22

Sweeping-up clauses

The cost of providing such other services as the Landlord shall consider ought reasonably to be provided for the benefit of the Centre or for the proper maintenance and servicing of any part or parts thereof

OR Do such other acts and things as may be reasonably necessary or desirable for the maintenance of the Estate and for the safety comfort security or convenience of the tenants

OR The Service Costs shall include the costs of providing such other services as the Landlord shall consider ought properly and reasonably to be provided for the benefit of the Building or for the proper maintenance and servicing of any part thereof

Precedent 4

SPECIFIED PERCENTAGES FOR DIFFERENT SERVICES

1   *This precedent concentrates only on those aspects of service charge provisions where there are a series of specific percentages for different services and for different parts of the landlord's property.*

2   *The precedent assumes a shop development. The development consists of a large supermarket with a separate block of six approximately equal ground-floor shops above which the first floor is let as offices. Each shop has rights to use the access ways and service yard, and the tenants have the use of their own portion of a common car park. The common parts exclude the landlord's supermarket and it is assumed that the tenant of the supermarket is responsible for all maintenance of the supermarket, but will contribute to expenses of common parts such as the access road.*

3   *The service charge schedule in this precedent specifies the services and charges a different percentage for each, based on a pre-assessment of the use of the services in question by the particular shop. Two alternative methods of achieving this type of arrangement are shown. In the first the percentages are set out, the initial items reflecting percentages of costs relating to the centre as a whole, and the subsequent percentages are those affecting only the building in which the shops are situated. The alternative style sets out the services in the usual detail (which are omitted here because the services will basically be as in the first alternative). This definition of the services is followed by a second part of the schedule splitting the costs among the services in tabular form. Obviously either precedent could be expanded to cover many more services, where relevant. It could also be adapted for use where there are more than two different areas (eg services affecting the northern, southern and eastern malls, or ground floor, first floor and second floor, or shops, offices and the supermarket all separately).*

4   *This is a useful system but needs to be very carefully worked out to ensure that the percentages charged add up to 100% (if that is intended). This could be done by including reference to the percentages charged to each unit on the development if desired.*

5   *A provision for changing the percentages is not given here, but it is recommended that one is included (as in earlier precedents). Clearly, it will need
to be used in all the leases, because if one is changed all the others are
likely to be affected.*

6   *The usual provisions concerning collection, accounting, disputes, etc are
not given here, but these will need to be included in a suitable form.*

PRECEDENT 4

A4.01

[Landlord's covenant]

1   The Landlord shall unless prevented by circumstance beyond its control
provide and carry out or procure (so far as the Landlord considers necessary
in the interests of good estate management) the provision and carrying out
of the Services described in the Schedule so far as they may be necessary
for the reasonable use and enjoyment of the demised premises Provided
That

(a)   in performing its obligations hereunder the Landlord shall be entitled
to employ agents contractors and such other persons as the Landlord
may from time to time think fit and

(b)   the Landlord may temporarily withdraw any of the Services if in its
opinion such withdrawal is in the interests of good estate management

A4.02

[Tenant's covenant]

2   To pay by way of further rent such percentage or percentages as is set out
in the Schedule of the total cost of each of the Services

PRECEDENT 4A

A4.03

[Service Charge Schedule – Alternative 1]

1	Maintaining repairing and renewing the service road and footpaths and the service area –	5.60%
2	Maintaining repairing and renewing the Shops' Car Park –	12.00%
3	Providing and tending all plants shrubs and garden areas in the Common Parts and keeping the same properly planted and free from weeds –	2.75%
4	Providing security and an alarm system for the Common Parts –	2.75%

5	Any special charges made by the local authority affecting the Centre as a whole –	1.85%
6	Charges of the managing agents and the salaries and other emoluments of porters security staff and other staff employed at the Centre –	2.75%
7	Costs of maintaining and replacing the equipment used for providing services to the Centre –	2.75%
8	The provision of other reasonable or requisite matters which the Landlord may at any time reasonably provide for the benefit of the tenants of the Centre or for the benefit of the Centre as a whole –	2.75%
9	Maintaining renewing and repairing the conducting media serving the Building ('the Building') in which the demised premises are situated-	5.50%
10	Insurance against third party risks and damage to property in respect of the Centre –	2.75%
11	Fuel and supply costs for the common parts of the Building –	8.50%
12	Maintaining decorating lighting and cleaning the main structure of the Building and the Common Parts within the Building –	8.50%

PRECEDENT 4B

A4.04

[The Service Charge Schedule – Alternative 2]

Part 1

(The Services)

[Description of the services – this will be much the same as above but without the percentages]

Part 2

(The Percentages)

Item	Building	Centre
Service road repairs	–	2.75%
Shops' car park repairs	–	12.00%
Gardening	–	2.75%
Local authority costs	5.50%	1.85%
Managing agents' costs	6.88%	2.75%
Equipment costs	6.88%	2.75%
Repairs etc to conducting media	5.50%	2.75%
Insurance	6.88%	2.75%
Fuel costs	8.50%	–
Maintenance of the Building	6.88%	–
Decoration of common parts	6.88%	–
Lighting	6.88%	2.75%
Cleaning	6.88%	2.75%
Miscellaneous costs	6.88%	2.75%

Precedent 5

PRECEDENT SHOWING TENANT'S REVISIONS

1   This precedent simply shows various parts of the lease showing where and how substantial amendments by a tenant's solicitor can be made. This is based on a lease with which the author was involved. The amendments shown are, mostly, based on the initial amendments by the tenant's solicitors, which were subsequently the subject of lengthy negotiations. The precedent does not show the finished form of the lease, and is for illustration only. The tenant's solicitor, in the author's view, went over the top in seeking to change the system and (in terms of negotiation) put up the back of the landlord's solicitor by making far more changes than might have been needed simply to protect his client.

*2   Pieces added on behalf of the tenant are shown in **bold,** and parts deleted by the tenant are shown in* ~~*[italics, in square brackets and struck through].*~~

3   The lease is of a shop ('the Premises') in a parade of shops ('the Development'), where the draft provided (originally) for the tenant to pay a fixed percentage of the cost of the landlord's services.

4   As in other cases only aspects reflecting service charges are shown. All the service charge parts of the lease have not been shown, only the more important amendments. For example, it is not shown that the tenants wished to delete the provision that the service charge is reserved as rent, or many cases where the word 'reasonably' was inserted. The amendments shown are specific amendments seen by the author, but adjusted to make them of general assistance. Not all the services and the amendments are given, as many are repeated phrases, but the precedent is intended to show the way a tenant seeking to amend a draft can incorporate his provisions. Comment on some points has been added.

PRECEDENT 5

A5.01

[Amended definitions]

1   'The Common Parts' means **All parts of the Development save for the Lettable units** [substituted for a full definition referring to the service road ramps forecourts pedestrian precincts etc][1]

~~[*'The Service Charge Percentage' means 24%]*~~ – replaced by the tenant in full to refer to **'The Due Proportion' means the proportion which the gross internal ground floor area of the Premises bears to the total gross internal ground floor area of the Lettable Units from time to time'**[2]

1   A compromise would be to use the tenant's wording with the landlord's wording, so that after the tenant's wording is added 'and includes the service road' etc.

2   This has the advantage of ensuring that the service charge is based on ground floor area but (a) specifically excludes areas above or below the ground floor and (b) prevents the use of weighted floor areas, at least for this unit and (c) would need amendment to refer to the area at the commencement of the Accounting Year, rather than 'from time to time' (see *Moorcroft v Doxford*). It also prevents the landlord being able to use different percentages for different services, or to make no charge for the same services.

A5.02

[Revised landlord's covenant]

The Landlord covenants with the Tenant that unless prevented by strikes lock-outs or other causes beyond the Landlord's reasonable control **save where such events arise as a result of an act or omission on the part of the Landlord or any person under its control** and subject as herein provided [and to the due payment of the Service Charge by the Tenant]

(a)   to provide the services referred to in paragraphs 3(1) and 3(2) of the Schedule

(b)   to use all reasonable endeavours to provide the services referred to in paragraphs 3(3) to 3(12) of the Schedule

and to comply with its obligations in the Schedule in an efficient and cost-effective manner [or effectively efficiently and economically] in the interests of the tenants of the Lettable Units as a whole and shall use all reasonable endeavours to maintain the Service Costs at the lowest figure consistent with the due performance of the Landlord's obligations in the said Schedule and insofar as the carrying out of the said services involves the carrying out of any works the Landlord shall procure that the same are carried out in a good and workmanlike manner with good sound and suitable materials of their several types and in accordance with good building practice and the Landlord shall at reasonable intervals review and where appropriate put out all principle maintenance and management contracts to competitive tender.[1]

1   From a landlord's point of view several of these additional provisions, while on the face of it a good thing for the tenant, are simply a recipe for dispute. What if something needs to be done quickly? Is it 'efficient and cost effective' to do it within one week at a cost of £2,000 or within three weeks at a cost of £1,500? What if the works or services are basically for the benefit of the tenants at the south end of the Development but have no direct benefit for the northern end – can such work, which ex hypothesi is beneficial for part of the Development, be the subject of a charge where the tenant's amendment refers to the interests of the 'Lettable Units as a whole'?

A5.03

[An alternative]

A covenant by the Landlord **'To use its best endeavours to maintain the Service Charge at the lowest reasonable figure Provided That the Tenant**

shall not be entitled to object to the amount of a Service Charge cost solely on the ground that the service could have been provided at a lower cost'.

A5.04

[Revised agreements and declarations]

3(a)   [Cesser of rent amended to ensure that the service charge as well as rent ceases when the Premises are damaged or destroyed.]

(b)   [The provision that the decision of the landlord's surveyor on any matter he is called on to decide shall be final and binding so far as it is on matters of fact, leaving disputes on matters of law to be decided by the courts – deleted by the tenant].[1]

(c)   That the Landlord shall not be liable to the Tenant for any interruption occasioned to any of the services in the Schedule or any loss or damage by reason of any necessary repair or maintenance of the Common Parts ~~for any other part of the Development~~ (provided reasonable access to the Premises is maintained at all times) or by reason of damage to or destruction thereof by an Insured Risk or Act of God or other reason beyond the Landlord's control **unless such an event arises as a result of an act or omission of the Landlord or another person on its behalf**[2]

1   This is not a critical omission from the landlord's point of view, but where included the clause can lead to a degree of certainty for both landlord and tenant.
2   The addition at the end is relatively harmless, but the omission of the words in the middle can create management problems where tenants are making alterations to their premises.

A5.05

[Amendment to the rent review schedule]

An additional disregard:

4   (Disregarding) **any increases in rent attributable to an improvement the cost of which forms part of the Service Costs**[1]

1   This amendment is too wide – the tenant is seeking 100% disregard for something where he may only have contributed a tiny proportion of the cost of an improvement and where the landlord may have actually contributed part of the cost. It would seem appropriate as an amendment only in those cases where the tenants between them have contributed the full cost, or otherwise amended as suggested in the main text.

A5.06

[Amended service charge schedule]

1   [Definitions – amended to reflect the 'Due Proportion' if that is agreed.]
2   Service costs – showing significant amendments

The Service Costs shall be the total of:

(1)   the **reasonable and proper** costs in any Accounting Year **reasonably and proper** incurred by the Landlord ~~[off]~~-**in** the provision of the Services ~~[and items set out and/or referred to in paragraph 3]~~-**but for the avoidance of doubt the Service Costs shall not include any of the following:**[1]

   (i)   **any expenditure occasioned as part of the construction of the Development [or its improvement or refurbishment]**

   (ii)   **the repair of any part of the Development damaged or destroyed by an insured risk where the policy has not been vitiated or the recovery reduced by any act or omission of the Tenant**

   (iii) **any expenditure necessitated** solely **by the wrongful act or default of the Landlord or its servant or agents**

   (iv)   **any expenditure in respect of which the Landlord actually recovers the cost thereof from any party (other than by way of Service Charge) or to secure repair or maintenance work from any party including (without limitation) by way of warranty claims or claims under guarantees** Provided that the cost of recovering such expenditure shall be part of the Service Costs

   (v)   **any capital expenditure (including both purchases and equipment leasing)**

   (vi)   **any promotional or advertising costs**

   (vii) **any management expenses (a) in relation to the collection of rent or service charge or licence fees or any arrears or other monies due from any tenant or occupier of any part of the Development (b) in connection with the enforcement against any such tenant or occupier of the terms of any lease under which such tenant has a liability in respect of any part of the Development and (c) in connection with any rent review or lease renewal**

   (viii) any expenditure incurred in maintaining or repairing and/or replacing any part of the Common Parts which was not extant at the date of this Lease and the provision of which was not necessary[2]

(2)   [The tenants sought to delete the right for the landlord to set up a reserve fund, which is the subject of clause 2(2) of the Schedule.]

---

1   (All the following proposed excluded items are similar to the Tenant's proposals. The words which are not in bold below are suggested re-amendments to those provisions which may otherwise be acceptable. The parts in square brackets are the tenant's suggestions which do not seem acceptable.)

2   The author's views on those amendments are indicated. The start of additional point (i) is really only suitable for a reasonably new property: the second part of (i) is too wide to be acceptable to most landlords. In additional point (iv) the amendment (showing it relates to matters actually recovered) is to avoid disputes about items that the landlord may or may not be able to recover being treated by the tenant as a reason for not paying in full. Additional point (vi) is not deleted but should be where promotional costs are among those the landlord wishes to recover. Point (v) seems far too wide to be acceptable. It would, for example, seem to exclude recovery costs for

buying a new broom to sweep the Common Parts when the old one has worn out. The management costs as the first part of item (vii) are normally recovered in a service charge (except the cost of collection of rent). Costs of enforcement of covenants is a matter that may be in the interests of the tenants. Item (viii) would prevent recovery of costs affecting any extension to the Development. In a 25-year lease this seems unrealistic and the landlord should not be restricted from increasing (or indeed reducing) the Development and the service charge provisions should cover this.

A5.07

The services

3   The services and items aforesaid shall comprise the following:[1]

(1)   Maintaining repairing *[renewing]* cleaning lighting repainting redecorating or otherwise treating as the Landlord shall **reasonably** consider appropriate the Common Parts

(2)   *[Resurfacing or otherwise treating and]* marking out from time to time as the Landlord shall *[in its absolute discretion]* **acting reasonably** consider appropriate all parts of the Common Parts

(3)-   *[Supervising and]* managing the Common Parts which cost shall not exceed 10% of the Service Costs (including such fees)

(4)   the *[provision and/or]* hire or leasing and where necessary replacement of security for the Common Parts including cameras (etc) and/or other security measures required *[or recommended]* by the insurers *[or the police]* including contracting for the provision of security at the Development and/or the employment **on reasonable terms** of security personnel and the salaries wages **state** pension **contributions** and **pension contributions and other emoluments** and social security contributions **or other statutory levies** of all personnel directly employed at the Development by the Landlord or its managing agents on security duties or general duties at the Development or a fair and reasonable proportion of such expenses in the case of personnel employed by the Landlord to work partly at the Development and partly elsewhere

(5)   the general management of the Development including:

(a)   periodically *[installing inspecting]* maintaining overhauling and repairing and (where necessary **in order to comply with the obligation to repair and where more economic than repairing**) replacing any fire detector and/or fire fighting equipment

(b)   the employment **on reasonable terms** of such independent contractors consultants and other personnel as in the **reasonable** opinion of the Landlord may be requisite for the provision or carrying out of any service to the Common Parts **in the interests of the tenants of the Lettable Units as a whole**

(6)   the disposal of refuse from the *[Development]* **Common Parts** *[including the collection thereof and the provision of receptacles and bottle banks and compactors and other plant and equipment in connection therewith]*

(7) maintaining repairing **and (where in the nature of and more economic than repair)** renewing cleaning repainting or otherwise treating any name board on the Common Parts **for displaying the names of the tenants or occupiers of the Development**

(8) [deleted – provision for payment of rates on those parts of the Development not let to tenants]

(9) [deleted – provision for the costs of enforcement of covenants where this is in the interests of good estate management and excluding costs of recovering rent and which had an obligation on the landlord to seek recovery first from the party in breach]

(10) [deleted – provision for third party insurance]

(11) [deleted – provision of signs and directional notices, litter bins and street furniture]

(12) [deleted – the sweeping-up clause]

1   This an abbreviated version of the Schedule – many of the amendments and re-amendments are repetitive, and the above are illustrative).

Accounting procedure – showing significant amendments

(1) [Preparation of estimates – no significant amendments.]

(2) As soon as practicable **but in any event within one month** after the end of each Accounting Year the Landlord shall cause to be prepared and sent to the Tenant an account of the Service Costs to be certified by a chartered accountant (who may be an employee of the Landlord **who shall in any event act fairly and impartially**) as true and correct and a calculation of the Service Charge for that Accounting Year and thereupon the amount of the Service Charge shall ~~(subject only to the provisions of the disputes clause)~~-**in the absence of manifest error** be ~~(final and binding on the Tenant)~~-**paid in accordance with the provisions of this paragraph**

(3) If the Service Charge for any Accounting Year shall exceed or be less than the sum estimated above the amount of the underpayment or the excess shall be paid by the Tenant to the Landlord or by the Landlord to the Tenant (as the case may be) within 14 days after receipt of the account by the Tenant **(in the case of sums due to the Landlord) or within 14 days of production of the account (in the case of sums due to the Tenant** and in the case of the last year on demand **and in any event if such sums are not paid within 14 days of the due date to pay interest on unpaid sums at the Interest Rate from the due date to the date upon which such unpaid sums are actually paid**

508

Agreements and declarations showing significant amendments

(1)   [The tenants deleted the right of the landlord to change percentages when a change was justified. They replaced it with a rider including a provision on the following lines.]

> **All monies paid by the Tenant and other tenants of the Lettable Units by way of service charge and any income received by the use of the Common Parts (including parking fees and fees from parties using the Common Parts for display or promotional activities and income from recycling projects) which has not been paid in providing the services shall be placed in a separate interest bearing trust account until such monies are required for disbursement in the provision of the services and interest earned on such account (less any tax payable) shall be credited to such account at regular intervals and until actual disbursement shall be held by the Landlord for the benefit of the Lettable Units as a class**

(2)   The Landlord shall be entitled to make such alterations as ~~[the Landlord thinks fit (i) to the pipes wires and other service installations and the Common Parts and/or]~~ as may be necessary to comply with any Act of Parliament or order deriving its validity therefrom ~~[or with the Landlord's obligations to supply services and to all or any plant machinery or equipment including if the Landlord thinks fit the installation of plant machinery and/or equipment of a different type]~~ or to suspend any services while the work of alteration or installation is being carried out or in the event of an emergency **Provided That there shall be available at all times a reasonable alternative for all tenants of the Lettable Units and the Landlord shall use all reasonable endeavours to procure that any inconvenience to such Tenants is kept as brief as practicable**

(3)   [In relation to the Reserve there was one significant amendment as follows]

> The power of appointing a new trustee of the trust (of the Reserve) is **jointly** vested in the Landlord **and the Tenant**[1]

(4)   (In relation to the provision for disputes to be referred to an expert) the only material amendments were:

   (a)   to remove the time limit (originally the Tenant could apply for expert determination provided he objected within two months).

   (b)   to amend the provision that the Tenant was not entitled to object to a cost on the ground that it could have been 'performed or provided ~~[for or cost less]~~ **at marginally lower cost**' than the actual cost or that estimated in good faith on behalf of the Landlord

   (c)   In relation to the provision for payment to the Tenant if the expert found there had been an overpayment the tenants were seeking interest from the date of determination until payment to the Tenant.

---

1   This is inappropriate where there is more than one tenant.

Precedent 6

UNDERLEASES

1   The precedents already produced are for cases where the landlord carries out works and services and charges the tenant. For such purposes it does not matter greatly whether the lease charging the service charge is granted out of a freehold or out of a leasehold interest, although in both cases any material covenants, restrictions and easements need to be reflected in the leases. This set of precedents envisages those cases where a tenant holds a lease ('the Head Lease') under which he is liable to pay a service charge, and he grants an underlease.

2   If the tenant does not want to recover the service charge he pays from the undertenant then he can simply omit any provisions for recovery when he drafts the underlease. He will need to be careful to make consequential amendments, particularly if the underlease is granted by reference to the terms of the Head Lease, but otherwise there is no need for a specific precedent.

3   Where the undertenant is to contribute to service charges there are a few material points to be taken into account in drafting. These are:

(a)   Is the undertenant simply to be obliged to reimburse his landlord what is paid, or is the undertenant to have some say in the disputes procedure (if any) under the Head Lease?

(b)   If the undertenant is taking a lease of part only is the undertenant to pay a fixed percentage of the service charge imposed on his landlord, or is it to be 'a fair proportion', or some similar formula? The fixed percentage is usual and is adopted here.

4   In the first two alternatives (6A and 6B) it is assumed that an underlease of the whole of the property is comprised in the Head Lease. In the first alternative (6A) the tenant simply reimburses what the landlord pays. In the second alternative the undertenant is given a right to press for the disputes procedure to be implemented. This is at the cost of the tenant and with the tenant depositing the amount in dispute. It seems right for the tenant to pay the costs: the landlord will become involved in management time and expense for a matter which does not really affect him since the undertenant has to pay all the service charge. It is thus the undertenant who is really the

511

party primarily concerned. The disputed sum should be placed on deposit so that before becoming embroiled in the dispute on behalf of the under-tenant the landlord will know the money is actually available and readily recovered, and it may discourage opportunist objections.

5   *The third and fourth alternatives (6C and 6D) are for underleases of only part of the property let to the landlord. They are on the same basis – alternative 6C being for simple reimbursement of an agreed percentage of what the landlord pays, and precedent 6D being similar but with the undertenant having an opportunity to call on the landlord to invoke the dispute procedure. For the case of a tenant of part where the tenant has a chance to object to the amount payable (6D) an indemnity in case the result of the dispute is that other tenants of the landlord have to pay more and the landlord is unable to recover it is included. Again, it seems the tenant who wants to cause the dispute should accept the financial consequences.*

6   *As in the case of Head Leases the service charge payable by an undertenant can be reserved as rent if desired. In the precedents for underleases of the whole, it has been assumed that they are so reserved: in the precedent for underleases of part, this is not assumed.*

7   *In the precedents custom is followed and the parties to the underlease are called 'the Landlord' and the 'Tenant'. Where the superior landlord is mentioned he is called the 'Superior Landlord' and it is assumed there is a separate definition recording that the superior landlord is the landlord for the time being of the Head Lease.*

PRECEDENT 6A

A6.01

[First alternative – Underlease of the whole where the undertenant simply reimburses his landlord]

(In the reddendum) –

PAYING FIRST the yearly rent of [£20,000] on the usual quarter days in advance AND PAYING SECONDLY within 7 days of demand by way of further rent a sum equal to the Service Charge from time to time paid by the Landlord to the Superior Landlord under the terms of the Head Lease

PRECEDENT 6B

A6.02

[Second alternative – Underlease of whole, but tenant has some dispute rights]

(In the reddendum)

FIRST the yearly rent of [£20,000] on the usual quarter days in advance AND PAYING SECONDLY by way of further rent such sum in each year as the

Landlord shall pay to the Superior Landlord by way of Service Charge under the provisions of the Head Lease such sums to be paid (subject to clause (X) hereof) within 14 days of demand

(Landlord's covenant)

The Landlord covenants:

(i)   *(To observe the terms of the Head Lease including paying the service charge)*

(ii) If requested by the Tenant (and at the cost of the Tenant) to make such representations to the Superior Landlord as to the Service Charge payable under the terms of the Head Lease and to take such other action in respect thereof as the Tenant shall reasonably require under the provisions of clause (X) hereof

(Agreements and declarations)

(X) (a) If the Tenant considers that the Service Charge payable under the terms of the Head Lease is unreasonably high or includes items which should not properly be included within the Service Charge ('an Objection') the Tenant shall be entitled to call on the Landlord to make such representations as the Tenant reasonably requires and otherwise to take such steps as are open to the Landlord under the terms of the Head Lease in respect of the Objection subject to the Tenant paying into an interest bearing account ('the Deposit Account') in the joint names of the Landlord and the Tenant the amount of the Service Charge or the relevant proportion thereof which is the subject of the Objection

(b) On receipt of evidence of the opening of the Deposit Account the Landlord shall take such steps or make such representations as aforesaid and shall supply to the Tenant within 5 days a copy of all notices to and by and correspondence with the Superior Landlord or the Superior Landlord's agent or any independent third party appointed under the terms of the Head Lease to determine such disputes and the Landlord shall take notice of all representations by the Tenant in relation to such correspondence and notices but shall not be bound by such representations

(c) Within 7 days of the settlement of the Objection the Landlord shall notify the Tenant of the result and the Deposit Account shall be closed and the balance distributed so that such part as represents any amount payable by the Landlord to the Superior Landlord as a result of the settlement of the Objection (including the interest earned thereon) shall be paid to the Landlord and the balance (if any) including interest but after deduction of any bank charges shall be repaid to the Tenant

PRECEDENT 6C

A6.03

[Third alternative – Uunderlease of part where the undertenant reimburses a percentage to his landlord]

(In the reddendum) –

PAYING the yearly rent of [£20,000] on the usual quarter days in advance AND ALSO PAYING within 7 days of demand a sum equal to [8.5%] the Service Charge from time to time paid by the Landlord to the Superior Landlord under the terms of the Head Lease

[There should be a covenant by the Landlord to pay the Head Lease rent and service charge.]

PRECEDENT 6D

A6.04

[Fourth alternative – similar Underlease of part where the undertenant has some disputes rights]

(In the reddendum) –

PAYING the yearly rent of [£20,000] on the usual quarter days in advance AND ALSO PAYING [8.5%] of such sum as the Landlord shall pay to the Superior Landlord from time to time by way of Service Charge under the provisions of the Head Lease such sums to be paid (subject to clause (X) hereof) within 14 days of demand

(Landlord's covenant)

The Landlord covenants … at the request and cost of the Tenant to make such representations to the Superior Landlord as to the Service Charge payable by the Landlord under the terms of the Head Lease as the Tenant shall reasonably require under the provisions of clause (X) hereof

(Agreements and declarations)

(X) (a) If the Tenant considers that the Service Charge payable by the Landlord under the terms of the Head Lease is unreasonably high or that such charge includes items which should not properly be included within the Service Charge ('an Objection') the Tenant shall be entitled to call on the Landlord to make such representations and take such steps as are open to the Landlord under the terms of the Head Lease in respect of the Objection as the Tenant reasonably requires subject to the Tenant paying into an interest bearing account ('the Deposit Account') in the joint names of the Landlord and the Tenant the amount of the Service Charge which is the subject of the Objection [together with a further sum of [£1000] as a contribution towards the Landlord's costs of taking up the Objection]

(b) On receipt of evidence of opening of the Deposit Account (and provided that this is paid within sufficient time for the Landlord to act within the period for objections allowed within the Head Lease) the Landlord shall take such steps or make such representations as aforesaid and shall supply to the Tenant within 5 days a copy of all notices and correspondence with the Superior Landlord or the Superior Landlord's agent [or any independent third party appointed under the terms of the Head Lease to determine such disputes] and the Landlord shall take notice of all representations by the Tenant in relation to such correspondence and notices but shall not be bound by such representations

(c) On the settlement of the Objection the Landlord shall notify the Tenant of the result and the Deposit Account shall be closed and the balance including interest distributed so that such part as represents any amount payable by the Landlord to the Superior Landlord as a result of the settlement of the Objection (including the interest earned thereon) shall be paid to the Landlord [together with the amount allocated therein for the landlord's costs] and the balance (including interest) shall be repaid to the Tenant

(d) If on the determination of the Objection it is found that the Tenant and other tenants of the Landlord have to pay a higher amount of Service Charge than before the Objection the Tenant will indemnify the Landlord against any loss arising to the Landlord as a result of the Landlord being unable to recover from any other tenant of the Building the amount found to be payable following the resolution of the Objection

Precedent 7

MISCELLANEOUS LEASE CLAUSES

This is a set of miscellaneous provisions that may be of use to readers. Some are better expressed than others. There are many other precedents in this volume and some of the precedents here are different examples of clauses that appear elsewhere. Different wording has been used in all the clauses and so those looking for specific provisions may find them here or as part of the full precedents at the start of this Appendix. The wording reflects, in the author's view, that what is said is the important thing, rather than the way it is said – in other words the point of each provision is to make its point unambiguously, and to cover the ground intended. It is hoped that these provisions will illustrate some ways of achieving what is wanted, rather than necessarily providing ideal exact wording for each of the various circumstances.

The clauses are intended to be a mix and match bunch of provisions that could be used in a lease whether by a landlord or a tenant. The definitions are deliberately different and, as with all other precedents, must be adapted to fit the circumstances. They are set out in approximately the order in which they would be likely to appear in a lease. The names and addresses are only to make some items easier to follow, and are not from real documents. Brief notes are included in some places.

PART I

CALCULATING SERVICE CHARGE PERCENTAGES[1]

1 These are three clauses for showing, in the Lease, how the tenant's percentage of the service charge is to be assessed. The first two are based on floor area and the third on rateable value. None of them envisages weighted percentages. The rateable value calculations to provide for appeals by using only the assessment at a specified date avoid recalculations of all the service charges, even if the rateable value is later changed with the change being backdated.

A7.01

[First version – floor area with a formula]

(a)   'The Tenant's Percentage' is that percentage of the Service Costs represented by the formula:

$$\frac{A \times 100}{B} \text{ where:}$$

'A' is the total floor area of the Premises in square metres measured on the outside of the external walls and

'B' is the total floor area in square metres of the floor area of all the buildings on the Development measured on the outside of the external walls thereof

(b)   The Tenant's Percentage' is to be calculated on the last day of each Accounting Year and in the event of a change from the Tenant's Percentage used in the previous Accounting Year the accounts shall include details of the revised calculation

(c)   It is agreed that the Tenant's Percentage at the date of this Lease is 12.55%

A7.02

[Second version – floor area]

(a)   The 'Tenant's Proportion' means the proportion which the 'Internal Area of the Demised Premises' bears to the 'Total Internal Area' and for these purposes:

(i)   'the Internal Area of the Demised Premises' is the net internal area of the Demised Premises measured in accordance with the relevant current Code of Measuring Practice issued by the Royal Institution of Chartered Surveyors ('the RICS') and

(ii)   'the Total Internal Area' is the aggregate net internal area of all the premises within the Development which are either let or intended to be let (including for the avoidance of doubt the Demised Premises) and

(iii)   the 'Tenant's Proportion' is to be assessed on the first day of each Accounting Year and if on any such date there has been a change in the Total Internal Area or in the Internal Area of the Demised Premises from the previous Accounting Year the Landlord shall notify the Tenant in writing and Tenant's Proportion shall be recalculated using the then relevant current issue of the Code of Measuring Practice of the RICS and shall be agreed between the parties or in default of agreement within two months of the notification from the Landlord either party may refer the dispute to the decision of a

Surveyor ('the Surveyor') who shall be a Fellow or Associate of the RICS agreed by the parties or nominated on the application of either party by the President of the RICS and the Surveyor shall act as an arbitrator within the meaning of the Arbitration Act 1996

A7.03

[Third version – rateable value][1]

[Tenant's Covenant]

To pay to the Landlord from time to time in manner hereinafter provided the proportion properly attributable to the Premises (meaning thereby that proportion which the rateable value of the Premises bears to the aggregate rateable value of the Premises and the other Lettable Units in the Shopping Centre on the 24th day of June in each year) of the total outgoings and expenditure adjusted if necessary in accordance with proper provision made in respect of sub-clauses (c) and (d) hereof (the aggregate amount of which outgoings and expenditure is hereinafter referred to as the 'Service Cost') paid incurred or borne by the Landlord in discharging the obligations executing the works and providing the services amenities and facilities specified in the Schedule hereto or any of them respectively and the amount of the Service Cost and the proportion thereof aforesaid shall be determined and notified in writing in manner hereinafter provided by the Landlord's Surveyor

Provided Nevertheless:

(a)   that if at any time there shall not be in force any determination of rateable value by the relevant rating authority in respect of the Premises or in respect of any of the other Lettable Units in the Shopping Centre then either:

   (i)   the gross yearly rent (not being merely a nominal or concessionary rent) for the time being payable to the Landlord in respect of the Premises or the other Lettable Units respectively or

   (ii)   in the case of any other Lettable Unit in respect of which no yearly rent or only a nominal or concessionary rent is payable to the Landlord such yearly sum as in reasonable the opinion of the Landlord's Surveyor represents the then current market rent of the Lettable Unit

   shall for the purpose of provisional apportionment be treated as the rateable value thereof until the actual rateable value thereof has been determined and assessed when any necessary adjustment or correction shall be made

(b)   that if on the 24th day of June in any year there is current an appeal against the assessment of the rateable value for the Premises or of any other Lettable Unit the rateable value for the premises in question shall be treated for the purposes of the calculation of the Service Charge as the amount against which the appeal has been made and shall not be subject to adjustment for that Accounting Year even if the appeal is successful and a new rateable value is determined which for rating purposes is backdated to an earlier date

(c) that if the system or method of rating buildings and premises in operation at the commencement of the term shall hereafter be changed or abrogated so as to render the apportionment of and contribution to the Service Cost according to rateable value inoperable or manifestly inequitable to either the Tenant or any other occupier of a Lettable Unit then such apportionment and the proportion of the Service Cost to be attributed to and paid in respect of the Premises shall be calculated as at the next following 24th June by some other just and equitable method to be conclusively determined by the Landlord's Surveyor

1 As mentioned elsewhere, the author does not recommend using rateable values for apportionment purposes. This assumes there is a definition of Lettable Units.

PART 2

PERCENTAGE PAYABLE

A7.04

[First version – where services are not needed]

Where it is shown to the reasonable satisfaction of the Landlord's Surveyor in respect of any specified service amenity or facility that neither the Tenant nor the Premises nor the occupiers or users thereof derive any benefit or advantage directly or indirectly from the provision of such service amenity or facility by the Landlord such adjustment shall be made in the proportion of the Service Cost attributable to the Premises as the Landlord's Surveyor shall consider to be appropriate

A7.05

[Second version – changes to premises]

In the event of the Estate being altered added to or re-developed or if in the reasonable opinion of the Landlord the Service Charge Percentage becomes manifestly inequitable then the Service Charge Percentage shall be adjusted by the Landlord in such manner as shall be just and equitable

A7.06

[Third version – services not used by tenant]

The 'Tenant's Proportion' shall mean such proportion of the Service Costs having regard inter alia to the area and nature and use of the Demised Premises and the Services enjoyed or capable of being enjoyed by it from time to time as shall reasonably and properly be attributed to the Demised Premises by the Landlord's Surveyor or in accordance with the gross internal area of the Demised

Premises expressed as a proportion of the gross internal area of the whole of the Building save those expenses exclusively attributable to any other part of the Building

PART 3

A7.07

[Service charge based on floor area to be revised periodically][1]

1   The Tenant's Contribution until the first rent review date shall be calculated as a charge at the rate of [£2.25] per square foot per annum and the extent of the demised premises is hereby agreed to be [824] square feet

2   The rate at which the Tenant's Contribution is charged shall be reviewed at the same time as the review of the principal rent payable hereunder

3   Upon every such review the Landlord shall be entitled to increase the rate of charge by such amount as is reasonable in all the circumstances to reflect the anticipated expenditure for the period to the succeeding rent review taking into account:

   (a)   The actual costs incurred by the Landlord on an annual basis over each of the preceding five years

   (b)   Liabilities which will or are likely to become payable during the next succeeding five years

   (c)   The increase in the Index of Retail Prices published by H M Government from the date hereof or the date of the last rent review (as the case may be) to the relevant review date

   (d)   Any other matters which are relevant to the costs of the Landlord for provision of the Services specified in the Fourth Schedule hereto

4   Following every such review the Landlord shall notify the Tenant as soon as practicable of the revised figure for Tenant's Contribution which shall thenceforth become payable in substitution for the Tenant's Contribution rate figure previously applicable

5   It is hereby agreed that the Landlord shall be entitled to increase the rate of the Tenant's Contribution with effect from a rent review date even if there is no increase in the principal rent

---

1   This is an unusual provision, but not unknown. The tenant pays service charge based on a fixed rate (here shown as a rate per square foot). The fixed rate is adjusted at the same time as the rent is reviewed. The main disadvantage of such a provision is that it is very artificial and (except possibly in the first few years) does not satisfactorily represent the true cost of the services. It should not be used for residential purposes for that reason (it will be open to challenge under section 19 of the Landlord and Tenant Act 1985), and because of its inaccuracy it is not recommended for commercial property. Its only advantage is to give a tenant certainty as to the amount of service charges for a fixed period, while permitting adjustment at five-yearly intervals rather than yearly. This clause has no mechanism for appeal against the adjusted figure, and only a generalised indication of the factors to be used on review.

PART 4

A7.08

[Obligation on landlord to consult on major works][1]

(1)   Before carrying out any works to the Common Parts or other works or services towards which the Tenant is to contribute by way of the Service Charge (except in the case of works which have to be carried out quickly in emergency) and which are estimated to cost more than [£4,000] [in any of the first five years of the term or [£5,000] in any of the next five years of the term or [£6,000] in any of the next five years of the term] the Landlord will send to the Tenant a Works Notice in accordance with sub-clause (2) of this clause[2]

(2)   The Works Notice shall refer to this clause and shall be accompanied by a specification and/or plans and/or other information sufficient to enable the Tenant to see what works or services are proposed together with not less than two estimates of the cost thereof

(3)   (a)   If the Tenant receives a Works Notice from the Landlord the Tenant shall be entitled to request the Landlord to obtain an estimate for the work from another contractor

    (b)   If the tenant desires such an estimate the Tenant shall within ten working days of receipt of the Works Notice notify the Landlord of such requirement and the name and address of its nominated contractor and the Landlord shall request an estimate from such other contractor as soon as reasonably practicable

    (c)   Provided that the contractor nominated by the Tenant is prepared to give an estimate the Landlord shall produce to the Tenant a copy of the estimate from the nominated contractor

    (d)   Within ten working days of receipt by the Tenant of such estimate the Tenant shall be entitled to make representations to the Landlord as to which of the estimates shall be accepted having regard to the other terms of this Lease and the Landlord shall have regard to the Tenant's representations but shall not be bound by them

    (e)   The Landlord shall not commence the works before the end of 15 working days from service of the Works Notice or 20 working days from the date of receipt of an estimate from the nominated contractor of the Tenant whichever is later

(4)   If the Tenant does not serve on the Landlord notice within ten working days of receipt of the Works Notice either (a) a notice in accordance with sub-clause (3)(b) of this clause requesting an estimate from a nominated contractor or (b) a notice objecting to the carrying out of the works or services or the cost thereof the Tenant shall be deemed to have agreed to the carrying out of the works or services [and the cost thereof]

[(5) If the Landlord does not serve a Works Notice in any case where it is required by this Lease the liability of the Tenant under the Service Charge in respect of the work or services in question shall be limited to the amounts set out in sub-clause (1) of this clause]

1 Note: these clauses are based on the original form of the provisions of the Landlord and Tenant Act 1985 which are implied in leases of dwellings. The clauses are therefore intended for commercial leases to give the tenant protection, by way of consultation on proposed major works or services, roughly similar to that which a residential tenant enjoys.
2 An alternative to the phrase in brackets could be – [or more than [10%] of the total service costs in the previous Accounting Year].

PART 5

[COST OF WORKS]¹

A7.09

The Lessor will use [its best] [reasonable] endeavours to maintain the Service Costs at the lowest figure consistent with due performance and observance of its obligations hereunder but the Lessee shall not be entitled to object to any item comprised therein by reason only that the materials work or service in question might have been provided or performed at a lower cost.

A7.10

[1st Alternative]

To ensure that all works for which the Tenant is to contribute towards the costs are effected as cheaply as possible consistent with the proper maintenance of the Building.

A7.11

[2nd Alternative]

To carry out the works and services described in this Schedule in as economical a manner as is practicable consistent with the Landlord's obligations herein.

A7.12

[3rd Alternative]

The Landlord shall carry out the works and services in a prudent and economical manner.

A7.13

[4th Alternative]

The works shall be carried out in as cost effective a manner as is practical.

A7.14

[5th Alternative]

The Landlord shall have regard to obtaining value for money in carrying out the works and accepting estimates.

1 These are various versions of a provision to be included as a general statement, usually within the service charge schedule, in which the landlord agrees to keep the cost of services as low as reasonably practicable. The 5th alternative refers to value for money, the phrase used in the Commercial Code of Practice.

PART 6

A7.15

[Form of certificate set out in lease]

The Certificate shall be substantially in the form set out in the Schedule hereto
    Schedule
    (Form of Certificate)
    To: The Landlord and to the Tenants
    re: [The Darlhi Excentrics Centre, Magreet, Surreal]
As landlord's surveyors WE HEREBY CERTIFY that the total Service Charge Expenditure (as defined in the leases of premises at the above Centre and in accordance with the provisions of those leases) for the year to [25th March 2010] amounts to [£43,752] as shown on the attached accounts.

We HEREBY FURTHER CERTIFY that the amount payable for the year to [25th March 2010] by each of the tenants of the said Centre is as set out in the List attached to the said accounts.

    Dated [24th April 2010]

    Signed by [P. Casso on behalf of Mondrian & Co of Lobster Exchange Buildings, Unreal Road, Phantasyshire,] for and on behalf of [Ernst Miro Limited], landlord of the [Darlhi Excentrics Centre]

    Accounts are to be attached with a list of the contributions of each tenant.

1 Providing in the lease for the form of the certificate can be helpful. It can make it easier for the surveyor to be sure that the certificate is in an acceptable form. The objection to such a provision is that what might otherwise be a perfectly good certificate could be invalid if it is not in the right form, and it could make it impossible for a certificate to be given if the surveyor has a need to qualify the certificate in some way. Names and addresses are included to show how the certificate would actually appear: in the lease the certificate would of course be blank.

PART 7

A7.16

[Apportionments of interest to be excluded]

Provided That the interest to be credited to the Service Charge as above shall be added to the fund as a whole and the amounts received shall not be apportioned for the credit of individual tenants on the basis of the date of receipt from particular tenants or otherwise.

PART 8

A7.17

[Right to inspect vouchers][1]

(1) The Tenant will have the right to inspect vouchers receipts and estimates ('the Vouchers') relating to all amounts charged to the Service Charge by giving to the Landlord or the Landlord's Managing Agent not less than two weeks' notice within one month of receipt by the Tenant of the certificate of the amount due for the Accounting Year

(2) The Landlord shall make the Vouchers available for inspection by prior appointment at the offices of the Landlord or the Landlord's managing agent within 21 days of receipt of the notice from the Tenant.

(3) The Tenant shall not be obliged to pay any excess charge shown in the said certificate until 14 days after the said inspection

1   This is not needed in leases of dwellings.

PART 9

[EXCLUSIONS FROM SERVICE CHARGE][1]

A7.18

Capital costs

Provided That notwithstanding the provisions set out above the Landlord shall not be entitled to include in the Service Charge any of the costs

(a)   of the construction of the Building or

(b)   of the initial decorating or fitting out of the Building or the Common Parts or

(c) of the installation or provision by the Landlord of any plant or machinery in the Building or the Common Parts prior to the date of this Lease.

1 Note: The most effective protection for a tenant against unfair service charges is to qualify the service charge provisions by specifying items for which the landlord cannot charge. This is a series of clauses that can be used individually or in groups by a tenant seeking to restrict the amount of service charge the landlord might otherwise be entitled to recover. They are grouped under headings. Several can be used jointly, and the opening words of the first example (suitable adapted) could be used as an introduction to a series of exclusions.

A7.19

Refurbishment costs

Provided That the costs of decorating and renewal and maintenance of the Common Parts shall not exceed the proper and reasonable cost of necessary repair maintenance and decoration in the course of normal wear and tear of any such items [and the costs recoverable from the Tenant shall not include any costs representing improvement of the Development or the installation therein of any new plant or furniture or equipment which does not replace similar items needing replacement where repair is not economically practical.][1]

1 [**Alternative to the ending**] [and the costs recoverable from the Tenant shall exclude the costs of maintenance and decoration to the extent that the costs of such maintenance and decoration exceed the necessary costs of maintenance and decoration of the Common Parts as existing at the date of this Lease].

A7.20

Environmental expenses re contaminated land

Provided That the Landlord shall not be entitled by virtue of the above provisions to include in the Service Charge any part of the costs of remediation action taken under the provisions of the Environmental Protection Act 1990 in respect of contaminated land [where such contamination arose prior to the date of this Lease].

A7.21

Inherent defects

Provided That the Landlord shall not by virtue of the above provisions be entitled to include in the Service Costs the costs of any works needed to repair or replace or make good any defects in any part of the Development arising as a result of defective construction or defective design or defective or unsuitable materials used in the construction of the Development [within 12 years of the commencement of the Term].

A7.22

Good estate management

Provided That the Services shall be carried out in accordance with the principles of good estate management

A7.23

Excluding costs recoverable from others

Provided That the Service Costs will not include any sums which the Landlord is entitled to recover from any insurers or other tenant or any other third party and the Landlord will pursue all commercially prudent remedies against any insurers or third parties where the Service Costs would increase in the absence of the recovery of any monies pursuant to such remedies

ITEMS NOT BENEFITING TENANTS

This is primarily suitable for leases where the tenant does not pay a fixed percentage.

A7.24

[Alternative 1]

Provided That the Landlord shall not be entitled by reason of the above provisions to include within the Service Charge the cost of providing maintaining decorating or replacing any items from which the tenants of the Demised Premises derive no benefit.

A7.25

[Alternative 2]

Provided That where any costs incurred by the Landlord in relation to the Services are incurred only in relation to some of the premises on the Estate let or designed to be let then the proportion of the Service Costs to be payable by the Tenant shall be calculated excluding all such costs where the Demised Premises are not among those premises to benefit from such costs

A7.26

Restricting frequency of regular works

Provided That notwithstanding the above provisions the Landlord shall not be entitled to charge in the Service Costs (i) for decoration of the exterior of the

Building and the interior of the Common Parts more than once in every [four] years and (ii) for the cost of cleaning the interior of the Common Parts and staircases and landings more than [once in each week] and (iii) for the cost of cleaning the windows of the Common Parts more than [once in each month] and (d) for the cost of inspections of the Development for the purposes of insurance valuations more than [once in every two years].

A7.27

Fees on Landlord's matters

Any fees or expenses attributable (a) to disputes with other tenants or occupiers of the Development not relating to the Common Parts or (b) attributable to any action or proceedings relating to the Landlord's title to the Development or any superior title

A7.28

Unusual expenses

Any expense which under generally accepted accounting principles and practices in relation to similar types of premises would not be considered a normal maintenance or operating expense to be charged to a tenant pursuant to some term or provision of a lease

A7.29

Promotional expenses

Promotional advertising or publicity costs [save those approved by the Tenant (such approval not to be unreasonably withheld or delayed) [save those approved by a majority in number of the tenants of the Centre] [in excess of a budget figure agreed in advance by tenants of the Centre who are liable to pay [in excess of 70% of] the estimated costs] other than in the form and style agreed by the tenants of the Centre and not to include any costs relating to advertising of units for letting or sale.

PART 10

[THE SERVICE CHARGE CAP][1]

1   Note: This shows four alternative ways in which the level of service charge can be limited.

A7.30

[1st alternative]

Provided That the Service Charge payable by the Tenant shall not exceed [£5,000] in any Accounting Year [for each of the first five Accounting Years during the term].

A7.31

[2nd alternative]

Provided That the Service Charge payable by the Tenant in any Accounting Year shall not exceed the amount payable by the Tenant in the preceding Accounting Year by more than [5%]

A7.32

[3rd alternative]

Provided That the Service Charge payable by the Tenant for any Accounting Year shall not be increased by a greater percentage over the amount payable for the preceding Accounting Year than the increase over the same period in the Retail Prices Index

A7.33

[4th alternative]

Provided That the Service Charge payable by the Tenant in any financial year shall not exceed [25%] [130%] of the rent first reserved herein.

PART II

[SWEEPING-UP CLAUSES][1]

1   Note: These are three versions of sweeping-up clauses. The second and third have a family resemblance but significant differences, including notably the use of the conjunction 'and' in one case and 'or' in the other.

A7.34

[1st alternative]

The cost of providing such other services as the Landlord shall consider ought reasonably to be provided for the benefit of the Centre or for the proper maintenance and servicing of any part or parts thereof.

A7.35

[2nd alternative]

Any other service or expenditure including insurance not expressly hereinbefore referred to which the Landlord may in its reasonable discretion decide shall be proper and reasonable to provide for the Centre and which shall be:

(i)   capable of being enjoyed by the Tenant and its employees or invitees and

(ii)   reasonably calculated to be for the benefit of the Tenant and other tenants of the Centre or be reasonably necessary for the maintenance upkeep or cleanliness of the Centre and

(iii) in keeping with the principles of good estate management

A7.36

[3rd alternative]

To provide any other service that is:

(i)   capable of being used or enjoyed by the occupier or occupiers of the Demised Premises or

(ii)   reasonably calculated to be for the benefit of the Tenant and other lessees of the Centre and/or the Common Parts or reasonably necessary for the maintenance upkeep or cleanliness of the Centre and/or the Common Parts or

(iii) is in keeping with the principles of good estate management or

(iv)   has been previously agreed with the Tenant and other lessees of the Centre and/or the Building

PART 12

A7.37

[Landlord to observe Code of Practice][1]

The Landlord agrees that in managing the Development it will act in accordance with the Code of Practice called 'Service Charges in Commercial Properties – A Guide to Good Practice' issued by the British Council of Shopping Centres and other organisations in August 2000 [Provided That in case of any difference between the terms of this Lease and the provisions of the said Code the terms of this Lease shall prevail].

1   For commercial property only.

PART 13

[SUNDAY OPENING BY SOME TENANTS ONLY][1]

A7.38

(a)   To pay towards the costs to the Landlord ('the Sunday Costs') for opening the Centre on Sundays (including the extra costs for staff energy costs and additional cleaning lighting and heating) for each Sunday on which the Tenant opens for trading

(b)   The Sunday Costs shall be paid by all those tenants of the Centre who open for trading on any Sunday in the Accounting Year in the proportions which their respective Service Charge Proportions bear to the Service Charge Proportions of all those Tenants of the Centre who open for trading on the Sunday in question

1   This is for leases of shops in a centre where some shops open on Sundays and some do not. It provides for the costs incurred to be divided among those tenants who open, based on their relative service charge proportions. It does not directly contemplate changes to the sinking fund contributions, although there will obviously be more wear and tear on equipment etc by reason of extra use. There is also no direct differentiation between tenants of large shops (only entitled to open for six hours) and tenants of smaller shops (who can open for longer periods). Normally one would expect the tenant of a larger shop to have a larger service charge proportion, but changes would be needed if the length of opening is to be addressed.

PART 14

A7.39

[Keeping reserve/sinking fund to a minimum][1]

1   The Landlord agrees that when assessing sums needed for the Reserve Fund/Sinking Fund he shall ensure that unnecessary reserves are not accumulated.

2   If the Reserve Fund/Sinking Fund is found to be more than reasonably necessary the Landlord will repay to the tenants of the Building the excess in proportion to the amount which each tenant is liable to contribute.

1   This is based on paragraph 4.2.11 of the standard form of Commonhold Community Statement.

PART 15

A7.40

[Tenant to repair part of common parts][1]

(a)   [The Tenant hereby covenants with the Landlord] at all times to keep the mall and walkways shown edged in green on the plan in good repair and condition and clean and suitably lit and open and available for use by the tenants of the Shopping Centre (the 'Tenant's External Works') it being agreed that the obligation of the Tenant herein in respect of the said mall and walkways is for the better management of the Shopping Centre Provided That if at any time the Tenant fails to carry out the Tenant's

External Works the Landlord shall (without prejudice to any other rights and remedies of the Landlord) be entitled (but not obliged) to carry out the Tenant's External Works

(b)   [The Landlord hereby covenants with the Tenant] to pay to the Tenant within 28 days of receipt from the Tenant of suitable evidence of such cost [a fair proportion of] the whole of the costs actually incurred by the Tenant in carrying out the Tenant's External Works

(c)   If the Landlord carries out the Tenant's External Works following default by the Tenant the cost of so doing shall be included in the Service Costs

1   This is the reverse of the normal service charge case. It is for those few cases where the lease provides for a tenant to be responsible for part of the landlord's property outside the area actually let to the tenant. It normally applies to car parks adjoining a major unit in a shopping centre or occasionally a part of the common parts such as an area of a mall adjoining the shop. This clause provides for this and for the landlord to have step-in rights and also to contribute to the costs. If the landlord carries out the works the costs become part of the normal service charge costs.

PART 16

[WEIGHTING SCHEME WITHIN THE LEASE]

1   These precedents for inclusion within the Lease (which is unusual but could be helpful) show two approaches to treating weighting. The relevant parts could be used as the basis of a written weighting scheme – perhaps in notes for tenants on the scheme for the development generally. The two examples are both for shop leases on a shopping development.

2   The first alternative bases the service charge on a figure calculated on the ratio of the floor area of the shop to that of the other shops, with a scale of weighting which adjusts that floor area. Only the service charge provisions relating to weighting are included. The precedent is fairly short.

3   In the second alternative the service charge payable is a fixed percentage, but there is a provision for adjusting the percentage, if circumstances change, on the basis that the adjustment takes account of a defined weighting system. Only provisions concerning collection are provided. The weighting is much more sophisticated and envisages allowances for upper floors etc. There are some signs of tenant's amendments. These include references to prudent economy and a provision excluding the tenant from liability to pay for items which do not benefit him. It also provides for income from the car park to be credited to the service charge fund. The service charge is set out as a figure initially, and the amount in the following years is based on that figure.

4   The areas are shown in square feet: it could be in square metres. The square footage and percentages are for illustration only. Each scheme needs to be worked out for the development in question.

5   *In both versions the shop which is let is 'the Premises', the development is called 'the Shopping Centre', and the money paid out by the landlord is called 'the Service Cost'.*

[THE FIRST ALTERNATIVE – THE TENANT PAYING FAIR PROPORTION]

A7.41

[Service charge schedule]

Part 1
    [Collection arrangements]
    Part 2
    (Weighting)
The proportionate part of the Service Costs referred to in paragraph 1 of Part 1 of this Schedule will be determined as at the Year End in each year according to the ratio which the notional net internal area of each of the units in the Shopping Centre designed for retail use bears to the notional aggregate net internal floor area and shall be calculated as follows (measured in each case under the relevant RICS code then current):

(i)   For the first 10,000 square feet of any unit at 100%

(ii) For the next 10,000 square feet at 75%

(iii) For the remainder of the net internal floor area of each unit at 50%

[The net internal floor areas for the purposes of this Schedule will be calculated to the nearest 100 square feet] .
    Part 3
    [The Services]
    [Second alternative – tenant having fixed percentage]

A7.42

1.1   The Service Charge payable by the Tenant shall be calculated as follows:

    1.1.1 subject to clauses 1.1.4 hereof [8.42%] [or 7.25% of those costs relating to the cost of items relating to the Parade and 2.44% of the costs of items relating to the Common Parts] ('the Service Charge Proportion') of the Service Costs

    1.1.2 provided that in the calculation of the Service Charge in clause 1.1.1 hereof if any Lettable Units shall at any time be vacant the Service Costs for such Lettable Units shall be borne and paid by the Landlord for the period during which such Lettable Units shall remain vacant

    1.1.3 provided also that if in the Landlord's reasonable discretion it shall deem that any part of the Service Costs shall be for the particular benefit of a particular tenant or number of tenants in the Shopping

Centre and of no or less benefit to the other tenants or tenant then (notwithstanding the provisions of clause 1.1.1 and 1.1.2 hereof) the Landlord shall be entitled to re-charge the whole or such apportioned part as may be fair and reasonable of such Service Costs expenses to that tenant or group of tenants so as to achieve a fair and equitable apportionment of the Service Costs as between all tenants and occupiers who contribute thereto

1.1.4 provided always and it is hereby agreed that in effecting any adjustment of the Service Charge Percentage in accordance with the authority conferred on it by clause 1.1.2 and 1.1.3 hereof the Landlord will ensure that the tenants of the Shopping Centre continue to benefit from a weighted Service Charge apportionment of at least as favourable a basis as follows (based on calculating the notional net internal floor area of each unit at the Shopping Centre on the date of such adjustment and calculating the proportion of Service Costs on the basis of such notional net internal areas):

1,500 square feet at ground floor by a factor of 1 (0 to 1,500 square feet)

1,000 square feet at ground floor by a factor of 0.8 (1,501 to 2,500 square feet)

1,500 square feet at ground floor by a factor of 0.6 (2,501 to 4,000 square feet)

6,000 square feet at ground floor by a factor of 0.5 (4,001 to 10,000 square feet)

The remainder at ground floor by a factor of 0.4 (over 10,001 square feet)

First floor shops and areas at first floor level ancillary to ground floor shops by a factor of 0.5%

Basement units ancillary to ground floor shops by a factor of 0.5%

Accommodation at second floor level ancillary to ground floor units and office accommodation located at first second or third floors by a factor of 0.25%

PART 17

[SUPPLEMENTAL PAYMENTS DURING THE YEAR]

A7.43

[Alternative 1]

During any Accounting Year the Landlord may revise the contribution payable by the Tenant to the Service Charge for that Accounting Year so as to take into account any actual or expected increase in expenditure and as soon as practicable after such revision the Landlord's Surveyor must certify the amount of the revised contribution and the Tenant shall pay the balance within 14 days of receipt of the certificate thereof.

A7.44

[Alternative 2]

If the Landlord shall incur expenditure in respect of an item of repair maintenance or renewal which is within the definition of the Service Costs and the amount of which exceeds [one half] of the current year's estimated Service Rent the Tenant shall pay to the Landlord the Tenant's Proportion thereof within 14 days of demand in addition to any sums paid or payable under the preceding provisions [of this Schedule].

PART 18

A7.45

[Items omitted from one year's accounts]

An omission by the Landlord to include in any statement or estimate of Service Costs for any Lease Year a sum expended or a liability incurred in that year shall not preclude him from including such sum or the amount of such liability in the statement or estimate for any subsequent Lease Year.

PART 19

A7.46

[Limit on Landlord's obligation to contribute]

The Landlord shall have no liability to contribute to the Service Costs except in relation to any other Lettable Unit for which no contribution is payable by a tenant occupier or other person.

PART 20

A7.47

[Income from common parts]

(a) In the relevant Accounting Period the Landlord shall credit [50%] of the net income after deduction of any tax and/or any other lawful imposition made by any competent authority from any such event as is mentioned in paragraph (b) hereof

(b) The preceding clause shall relate to income from promotional events leasing or licensing of exhibitions or displays income from cash telephones coin operated children's' rides and other machines for which payment is made by members of the public or other use of the Common Parts.

Precedent 8

FORMS OF CERTIFICATE

1   Under this heading some suggestions are put forward for certificates for use in service charge matters. There is a suggested form of certificate within a lease at A9.15 above.

2   The first certificate is a certificate given by auditors showing the amount of costs incurred during the year by the landlord for service charge purposes.

3   The second certificate is a certificate of the amount payable by the tenant (based on the figures in a certificate such as certificate 1).

4   The third certificate (and probably the most useful, provided that it reflects the lease terms) is a combination of 1 and 2.

5   To show the alternatives Certificate 2 assumes that the tenant has overpaid (with the excess carried forward), and Certificate 3 assumes an underpayment.

CERTIFICATE I

[Certificate of landlord's expenses]

A8.01
[From Love & Co, Chartered Accountants]
To: Valentine Limited
7 Wedding Lane,
Hartstown,
Middlesex
(Landlords of the property named below)
And To: the tenants of the property named below
Our reference: CUP/ID
Your Reference: Arrow   14th February 2008
Re The Ring Shopping Centre, Aisletown, Southshire
We, as auditors to Valentine Limited HEREBY CERTIFY:

1   that we have audited the accounts relating to the above Shopping Centre in accordance with the provisions of clause 4(5) of each of the leases of the shop units, and

2   that the total expenditure properly paid or incurred by or on behalf of Valentine Limited in fulfilling the obligations of the landlord under the terms of the said leases for the year to 24th December 2007 amounted to £249,776.82 (exclusive of the 10% management charge under clause 4(8) of each of the said leases) and

3   that the attached summary is a true and complete summary of the said expenditure.

....

(Signed by A. Cupid on behalf
of Love & Co).
[Attached would be a copy of the accounts.]

CERTIFICATE 2

[Certificate of what the tenant pays]

A8.02

[From Love & Co, Chartered Accountants]
To: Mr. and Mrs Truelove,
Unit 3,
The Ring Shopping Centre,
Aisletown,
Southshire
(The tenants of the property named below)
Our reference: CUP/ID
Your Reference: 14th February 2008
Re Unit 3, The Ring Shopping Centre,
Aisletown, Southshire

We, as auditors to Valentine Limited, the landlords of the above property, HEREBY CERTIFY that the Service Charge payable by you for the year to 24th December 2007 in accordance with the attached Certificate of Landlord's Expenses amounts to £2,771.87 under the terms of your lease.

We hereby further certify that as you have paid £2,820 in advance for the said period the sum of £48.13 is to be carried forward as a credit for you for the year commencing 25th December 2007.

....

(Signed by A. Cupid on behalf
of Love & Co).

CERTIFICATE 3

[Combined certificate]

A8.03

[From Love & Co, Chartered Accountants]
To: Mr. and Mrs Truelove,
Unit 3,
The Ring Shopping Centre,
Aisletown,
Southshire
(The tenants of the property named below)
Our reference: CUP/ID
Your Reference: 14th February 2008
Re The Ring Shopping Centre, Aisletown, Southshire
We, as auditors to Valentine Limited, the landlords of the above property,
HEREBY CERTIFY

1   that we have audited the accounts relating to the above Shopping Centre in
     accordance with the provisions of clause 4(5) of each of the leases of the
     shop units, and

2   that the total expenditure properly paid or incurred by or on behalf of
     Valentine Limited in fulfilling the obligations of the landlord under the
     terms of the said leases, for the year to 24th December 2007 amounted to
     £249,776.82 (exclusive of the 10% management charge under clause 4(8)
     of each of the said leases) and

3   that the attached summary is a true and complete summary of the said
     expenditure, and

4   that the Service Charge payable by you for the year to 24th December 2007
     amounts to £2,771.87 under the terms of your lease.

We hereby further certify that as you have paid £2,685 in advance for the said
period there is a balance due from you of £86.87 which is payable to the landlord
within 14 days of the date of this certificate under clause 4(28) of your lease.
Interest is payable if the payment is delayed.

....
(Signed by A. Cupid on behalf
of Love & Co).

Precedent 9

FORMS OF WAIVER

*1   As part of lease negotiations tenants sometimes seek agreement from the
      landlord that the tenant in question is not to be liable for some part or other
      of the lease obligations which apply to other tenants. Whether or not the
      landlord should agree is a matter for instructions, and will to a large extent
      depend on the bargaining power of the parties.*

*2   These are precedents of waivers to a named tenant as this is the usual
      arrangement. (If all tenants of the property were to have the same benefits
      the better course would be to change the lease). The waiver is usually
      intended to cease to apply when the tenant assigns (or in one case where the
      tenant requests consent to assign, and thus indicates a wish to cease to be
      the occupying tenant). A phrase near the beginning of the first precedent is
      put in square brackets, and if these words are omitted the waiver will apply
      to each tenant while the lease subsists. This could be of use, for example,
      for the letting of the last unit, to encourage a letting but keep the lease basi-
      cally the same as other leases. For a business lease which has rights to
      renew at the end of the term the draftsman will wish to include the second
      proviso (that the waiver is not intended to apply on renewal).*

*3   The first precedent is a very brief but complete waiver within the lease in
      respect of any payment for specified items of charge. In brackets are alter-
      natives making it personal to a named tenant. If the precedent is not limited
      to a named tenant then the second proviso is recommended. It is unusual
      but could be of use. The other precedents are all waivers in respect of
      sinking fund contributions, which is the more normal use of such waivers.
      They are by side letter and lease clauses respectively.*

*4   The sinking fund waivers are given specifically on the basis that the tenant
      makes a payment (a) when it is needed or (b) when he ceases to occupy.
      This is done by providing that where money has to be spent on the items for
      which the sinking fund was set up the tenant will contribute what he would
      have paid over the years but for his waiver, and that in any event if the
      tenant ceases to occupy the premises he will pay into the fund what should
      have been paid. The second precedent also requires repayment in the event*

541

of the tenant seeking consent to assign. The landlord can raise the payment to the fund as a condition of licence for assignment.

5   *The appropriate place to include a waiver in a lease is normally at the end of the provision allowing the landlord to set up the sinking fund, although it could equally appear in any section of the Lease containing agreements and declarations, or any other part where there are specific exclusions of liability. In the case of the third and fourth precedents the waiver is not only personal to the tenant but also to the landlord.*

6   *There are provisions in the second and third precedents for payment of interest. This is to reflect the point that if the tenant had paid towards the reserve in the same way as other tenants the fund would have accrued interest and thus would have been larger.*

PRECEDENT

A9.01

[First alternative – lease waiver against particular charges]

Provided That [while Misanthrope Ltd is the tenant under this Lease and is trading from and occupying the demised premises for the purposes of the use permitted in this Lease but not otherwise] this Lease shall be interpreted as if the above provisions were varied in the following manner:[1]

---

1   Include details of the variations, such as a cap on the service charge such as one of those in A9.30 – A9.33, or exclusions of specific capital items such as those in A9.18 – A9.29 below.

A9.02

[Second alternative – lease provision waiving sinking fund obligations]

The Service Costs are:

(1)   *[The costs of providing the Services]* and

(2)   (i)   the amount (if any) (to be reviewed annually by the Landlord at her discretion) to be charged in any Accounting Year as a contribution towards a reserve ('the Reserve') to provide for the estimated cost to the Landlord of the provision of the Services

       (ii)   The Reserve is to be ascertained on the assumption that the cost of replacement of items of plant and machinery equipment roofs canopies car park resurfacing and other capital items is calculated on such life expectancy of the said items as the Landlord may from time to time reasonably determine

(iii) The parties agree that the intent is that a fund shall be accumulated sufficient to cover the cost of replacement of the said items by the end of their anticipated life

PROVIDED THAT

(a) nothing herein contained shall oblige the Landlord to establish or maintain a Reserve sufficient in whole or in part to cover such cost of replacement and

(b) the replacement or repair costs of any items in respect of which any sum or sums shall have been included in the Reserve during an Accounting Year shall first be met out of the Reserve and

(c) if and to the extent that any such expenditure is made out of the Reserve the same expenditure shall not also be charged to the Tenant by way of Service Charge

AND PROVIDED FURTHER THAT while Arthur Gride is the Tenant he shall not be liable to make any contributions to the Reserve except as follows:

(a) on each occasion when it is necessary to spend money on a matter for which the Reserve has been set up the Landlord will give to Arthur Gride details of the cost in question and shall require payment

(b) Arthur Gride shall pay to the Landlord within 10 days of such written demand such sum as shall represent the Tenant's Percentage of such cost and

(c) If Arthur Gride shall cease to trade from the Premises or shall request consent to assign or underlet or otherwise part with possession of the whole or any part of the Premises Arthur Gride shall pay to the Landlord within 21 days of receipt of a written demand containing full details of how such sum is calculated the sum representing the amount of the Reserve which would have been payable by Arthur Gride for the period up to the date of the said demand but for this Proviso

[(d) The sum payable under the preceding sub-clause shall be calculated:

(i) to include provision for payment by Arthur Gride of a sum equal to the interest that would have been earned on such amount had Arthur Gride paid the Reserve in accordance with the provisions of this Schedule and

(ii) giving credit for any payments made under sub-clause (a) of this Proviso].

A9.03

[Third alternative – Side letter waiving sinking fund obligation]
Crummles Cottage,
Browdie Lane,
Squeers,
Beds
1st June 2008
Dear Mr Gride,
<u>Cheeryble Buildings, Bray Drive, Linkinwater</u>
This letter is intended to be a side letter to the lease ('the Lease') of the above property between me as landlord and you as tenant relating to the above premises dated with today's date.

I confirm that while you are the tenant under the Lease and for so long only as I am landlord, you will not be liable to make any contributions to the Reserve mentioned in the Schedule thereto except as follows:

(a) on each occasion when it is necessary to spend money on a matter for which the Reserve has been set up you will pay to me within 10 days of written demand such sum as shall represent the Tenant's Percentage (as defined in the Lease) of such cost and

(b) If you cease to trade from the Premises [or request consent to] assign or underlet or otherwise part with possession of the whole or any part of the Premises you will pay to me within 21 days of receipt of a written demand containing full details of how such sum is calculated such sum as shall represent the amount of the Reserve which would have been payable by you under the Lease for the period up to the date of the said demand but for this letter of waiver

(c) The sum payable under paragraph (b) of this letter shall be calculated to include a sum equal to the interest that would have been earned on such amount had you paid the Reserve in accordance with the provisions of the Schedule to the Lease, but giving credit for any payments made under paragraph (a) above.

For the avoidance of doubt this waiver is personal to you and only applies for so long as I am the landlord.

Please sign and return the attached copy of this letter by way of acknowledgement of the terms of this waiver.

Yours sincerely,
Peg Sliderskew (Mrs).

A9.04

[Fourth alternative – Waiver in lease of sinking fund obligation]

1   Provided That while Scrooge Limited is the Tenant it shall not be liable to make any contribution to the Sinking Fund except as follows:

(i)   In the event of it being necessary to replace any item for which the Sinking Fund has been set up Scrooge Limited shall pay to the Landlord within 10 days of written demand such sum as shall represent the Service Charge Percentage of the cost of such item and

(ii) If Scrooge Limited shall cease to trade from the Premises or shall [request consent to] assign underlet or otherwise part with possession of the Premises then Scrooge Limited shall pay to the Landlord within 10 days of written demand such sum as shall represent the amount of the Sinking Fund that would have been paid for the period from the commencement of the Term to the date of receipt by the Landlord in respect of the Premises but for this proviso

(iii) If any payments are payable under clauses (i) or (ii) above there shall in addition be paid interest at the Interest Rate from the date of demand to the date of receipt by the Landlord if the payment shall not be made within 10 days of the written request and in the case of payment under clause (ii) shall also be paid with interest representing the interest that would have been earned on such amount had Scrooge Limited paid contributions to the Sinking Fund on the usual days in advance in accordance with the provisions of this Schedule but credit being given for any payments made under clause (i) hereof

2   The provisions of this waiver will apply only while Scrooge Limited are the Tenant and Cratchett Enterprises PLC are the Landlord.

A9.05

[Fifth alternative – waiver of sinking fund obligations by letter]
Dated 26th March 2007
LJ LAW LIMITED
20 Upper Ground,
Irving,
Lairgs
Dear Bill,
Re 23 Purlewent Drive, Old Windsor, Kent
This letter is a side letter to today's lease of the above. In consideration of the completion of the Lease we hereby agree that for so long as you are the tenant and occupy the Premises we will not enforce the provisions of paragraph 2 of the Fourth Schedule to the Lease requiring you to contribute to a reserve fund or sinking fund.
This agreement is solely on the understanding that:

(a) while you are the Tenant you will contribute to the repair and maintenance and replacement of the items for which the said reserve fund and sinking fund are intended to apply when the same need repair maintenance or replacement, and

(b) in the event of you ceasing to occupy the premises or assigning the Lease or on its termination in any manner you will pay to the managing agents the amount which would otherwise have been payable by you in respect of the Premises for the whole of the period up to date of such ceasing of occupation, assignment or termination.

The concession in this letter is personal to you.

Please confirm your acceptance of the above conditions of waiver by signing and returning one copy of this letter.

Yours sincerely,

Signed by SJS duly authorised for and on behalf of the Landlord.

Accepted and agreed.

Dated ....

To be signed by Bill Turner as tenant.

Precedent 10

ENQUIRIES BEFORE CONTRACT

1   These precedents are four sets of enquiries for four circumstances. Stationers have several types of enquiries and many solicitors have their own. The purpose of these is to provide a comprehensive set of enquiries with a view to practitioners considering including any relevant enquiries from these that are not in their own sets for the particular circumstances.

2   The first two are for a tenant who intends to take a new lease. The first is for a new property. In such a case there is obviously no history, and the enquiries are accordingly limited in scope. The second set is for a new lease of premises that have previously been let, and so enquiries about the service charge history are material.

3   The third set of enquiries is on the purchase of an existing leasehold interest. In such case the main object is to find as much information as practical of the history of the service charge as they affect the property being acquired, together with future predictions.

4   The final set of enquiries is for the purchase of a property with the benefit of leases which contain service charges – in other words on the purchase of the reversion. In that case the purchaser again needs information, but in this case about the whole of the property and not just a single unit. The purchaser needs information about the running of the service charge in general, the recovery record, and so on.

5   Since a residential property has statutory connotations for such matters as consultation, some extra questions that apply only in residential cases have been added to the end of some of the enquiries.

6   The enquiries have been drafted with the aim of giving rise to a positive response. Using shorter questions makes it more difficult for a general or ambiguous response to be given.

7   As in the other precedents, we are only dealing here with enquiries affecting service charges.

ALTERNATIVE I

A10.01

[Enquiries before taking a new lease of a new property]

Re Unit 3, The Willow Estate, Glance Place,
Slip. ('The Property')
Grace to Warner
Service Charges

1 Please provide a copy of the initial service charge budget.

2 Please provide an estimate of the anticipated service charge for the Property for the first accounting year.

3 If the lease does not specify the percentage of the service charge payable for the Property please specify what this is to be.

4 Please confirm that the landlord will not be seeking to recover through the service charge:

    (a) any capital costs of the construction, site works, or plant and equipment, or

    (b) the cost of making good any defects covered by the building contract.

5 Please confirm the landlord will pay service charge for empty units:

    (a) during the period until they are all let, and

    (b) thereafter.

6 (1) Is the landlord intending to set up a Sinking Fund?

    (2) If so –

        (a) For what items is the fund to be used?

        (b) (i) What is the current estimate of the replacement cost of each of the items for which the fund is to be set up, and

            (ii) what is the estimated life of each of the items in question?

        (c) (i) Please confirm that there will be no waivers in respect of service charges or sinking funds given to other tenants, or otherwise that arrangements will be made for all tenants to contribute to the Sinking Fund on the same basis.

            (ii) If this cannot be confirmed please confirm the landlord is responsible for the amounts concerned.

        (d) (i) Please confirm that the Sinking Fund will be invested in an interest bearing account.

            (ii) Please confirm that all interest earned on the Sinking Fund moneys will be credited to the Sinking Fund.

7 Who will be the managing agents?

[For residential only]

8 Are you aware of any proposal for setting up a Recognised Tenant's Association? If so please provide contact details.

ALTERNATIVE 2

A10.02

[Enquiries on taking a new lease of an existing property]

re The Pad, Off Street, Box, Wilts
Hammond to Voce
Service Charges

1   Please supply copies of the last three year's service charge accounts.

2   Please supply a copy of any formal or informal estimate of the service charge for the coming year.

3   Please give the name and address of the managing agents. (The buyer may wish to approach the agents if the seller is unable to provide some of the information requested below.)

4   (a)   Has any former tenant of the Property disputed any service charge amount or item during his ownership?

    (b)   If so, please give details.

5   (a)   Is the seller aware of any dispute by any other of the landlord's tenants about any aspect of service charges?

    (b)   If so, please give details.

6   Is the landlord proposing to carry out major works or refurbishment within the next few years which would have an effect on the amount of the service charge? If so please give such details as are available.

7   (1)   Is there a sinking fund or a reserve fund?

    (2)   If so –

        (a)   (Unless stated in the lease) please state what items the sinking fund is intended to be for.

        (b)   Please state how much has been contributed to the fund in respect of the Property.

        (c)   Please state how the fund is held (eg in a separate interest earning account in the name of the managing agents or the landlord).

        (d)   Is any item for which the fund has been set up expected to need replacing in the next three years?

        (e)   Please confirm that there are no waivers given to other tenants, or otherwise that arrangements have been made for all tenants to contribute to the Sinking Fund on the same basis.

8   Is there a tenants' or residents' association?

    If so, please provide the name and address of the secretary or other contact.

    [For residential premises only]

9   (a)   Please provide evidence that the service charge money is being held in a 'designated account'.

    (b)   Please give details of the bank, the name of the account and the account number.[1]

10   Please provide copies of all details sent to former tenants of the Property (by way of consultation under the Landlord and Tenant Act 1985) for works to be carried out which have either not yet been paid for in full or which have not yet been carried out, and the response to the consultation.

11   If there is a residents' association – is it a Recognised Tenants' Association within the meaning in section 29 of the Landlord and Tenant 1985?

12   If there is a tenants' association which is not a recognised tenants' association, has the association applied to be recognised?

13   (a)   If there is a Recognised Tenants' Association has it made representations about the managing agents?

       (b)   If so, please give details.

1   The designated account provisions are not yet in force.

ALTERNATIVE 3

A10.03

[Enquiries on purchasing a single existing leasehold interest]

33, Keeper Parade, Cover Square, Seam ('the Property')
Underwood to Evans
Service Charges

1   Please supply copies of the last three years' service charge accounts.

2   Please supply a copy of any formal or informal estimate of the service charge for the coming year.

3   (a)   Is the seller aware of any proposal for carrying out major works or refurbishment within the next few years which would have an effect on the amount of the service charge?

      (b)   If so, please give such details as are available.

4   Please give the name and address of the managing agents. (The buyer may wish to approach the agents if the seller is unable to provide some of the information requested below.)

5   Has the seller disputed any items of service charge during his ownership? If so please give details.

6   Is the seller aware of any disputes by other tenants of the landlord about any aspect of service charges? If so, please give details.

7   Please confirm that there are no arrears of service charge owing by the seller.

8   (1)   Is there a sinking fund or a reserve fund?

      (2)   If so –

            (a)   Please state what items the sinking fund is intended to be for.

            (b)   Please state how much has been contributed to the fund in respect of the Property.

            (c)   Please state how the fund is held (eg in a separate interest earning account by the managing agents, or by the landlord).

            (d)   Is any item for which the fund has been set up expected to need replacing in the next three years?

            (e)   Please confirm the fund is held on trust for the tenants.

            (f)   Is the amount in the fund considered to be adequate for its purposes by the managing agents?

9 (a) Does the seller have the benefit of any waiver (other than as disclosed in the lease) the benefit of which can or might be passed to the buyer?

(b) If so please give details.

10 Is there a tenants' or residents' association? If so, please provide the name and address of the secretary or other contact.

[For residential premises only]

11 (a) Please provide evidence that the service charge fund is held in a 'designated account'.[1]

(b) Please provide details of the bank, account name and account number.

12 Please provide copies of all details received by the seller from the landlord by way of consultation under the Landlord and Tenant Act 1985 for works which have either not yet been paid for in full or not yet carried out, and the response to such consultation.

13 If there is a residents' association – is it a Recognised Tenants' Association within the meaning in section 29 of the Landlord and Tenant 1985?

14 If there is a tenants' association which is not a Recognised Tenants' Association does the seller know whether the association has sought to be recognised?

15 (a) If there is a Recognised Tenants' Association, has it made representations about the managing agents?

(b) If so, please give details.

16 (a) Has the vendor made representations in relation to consultation by the landlord on works in either of the last two years?

(b) If so, please provide details of the representation and the response.

1 See the note to enquiry 9 in the precedent at **12.2**.

A10.04

[Enquiries on buying a reversion with the benefit of service charge leases]

The Stump Centre, Maiden Vale, Bail
Seam Properties Ltd to Test Invest plc
Service Charges

1 Please give authority to the managing agents to allow the purchaser's agents to inspect the vouchers and papers relating to the service charge.

2 Please supply a copy of the service charge accounts submitted to tenants for each of the last five years with any associated notes.

3 Please supply a schedule for each of the last three years showing the recovery from each of the tenants of the service charge costs, with dates.

4 Please confirm that none of the tenants is currently in arrears, or provide details of all current arrears.

5 (a) If not apparent from the leases please state the percentage service charge recoverable from each of the tenants.

(b) Have any of the fixed service charge percentages in the leases been changed? If so (unless this appears from documents already supplied) please provide details and reasons.

6   (a) Please confirm there is no shortfall between the service costs paid by the landlord and the amounts recoverable by the tenants.

       (b) If not, please give details of the shortfall.

7   (a) Have any of the tenants complained of the manner in which the seller (as landlord) has complied with its obligations to provide services? If so, please give full details.

       (b) Are there any such complaints which have not yet been resolved? Please specify.

8   Is there a sinking fund or reserve fund? If so –

       (a) Please specify what items the fund has been set up to provide for.

       (b) How is the fund held? (eg is it in a separate interest earning account and, if so, please give details of the account including the name of the bank, account number and account title).

       (c) Please specify how much of the fund is held on behalf of each individual tenant.

       (d) Please specify the anticipated remaining life of each item for which the fund has been set up.

       (e) On completion any such account must be transferred to the buyer, and appropriate notices to the bank and forms for changing signatures must be provided.

9   (a) Have any tenants been given a waiver of any service charge obligations (as to sinking funds or otherwise) other than any set out in the copy leases already supplied?

       (b) If so, please provide a copy of each.

10   (a) The purchaser will require to agree the service charge budget for the period between exchange of contracts and completion, and will require a contract provision that only items referred to in the budget will be paid out during that period without the previous consent of the purchaser.

       (b) Please give details of the anticipated payments for the probable period between exchange and completion.

11   Is there a tenants' association? If so please give the name and address of the secretary or other proper officer.

    [Where there are residential tenants]

12   (a) Please give details of the 'designated account' in which the service charge fund is held.[1] .

       (b) Please provide evidence that all tenants have been given evidence that the service charge payments made have been paid into the designated account

13   Please supply a copy of each service or hiring agreements relating to the provision of services or any equipment in the premises including eg fire prevention equipment, lifts, security services, cleaning or maintenance contracts.

14   Please confirm in relation to all such agreements

       (a) that they are in force

       (b) that there are no payments outstanding,

       (c) that there have been no complaints from the tenants about the performance of the contacts,

       (d) that the seller is happy with the performance of the contracts.

       (e) that the seller will agree to transfer them to the buyer if so requested and if the agreement so permits.

15   (a)   If there is a tenants' association is it a recognised tenants' association as defined in the Landlord and Tenant Act 1985?

      (b)   If the answer to 15(a) is 'Yes' please provide copies of any information given to the Association in response to all questions they have raised.

16   (a)   If any works to be carried out during the current accounting year are in excess of the statutory minimum please supply a copy

            (i)   of the notices to tenants consulting with them under the 1985 Act and

            (ii)   all responses from tenants.

      (b)   If any of the tenants has nominated a contractor to give an estimate for works:

            (i)   has such estimate been requested?

            (ii)   if requested from contactors has such an estimate been given?

            (iii) If so, please provide copies

      (c)   If any tenants made representations in the current accounting year during consultation please provide a copy of the response by the landlord, including (where applicable) reasons given to the tenants for the landlord's choice of contractor.

1   See the note to enquiry 9 in the precedent at **12.2.**

Precedent 11

CONTRACT PROVISIONS

1   As explained in the text the usual contract provisions (the Standard Conditions of Sale and the Standard Commercial Property Conditions) each contain a provision which is reasonably satisfactory in a contract for assignment of a single lease provided the parties are content to complete and then make an adjustment after the year end figure becomes known. Following are various alternatives for a contract for assignment of a single lease, and two full sets of clauses regarding apportionments on the sale of the reversion.

2   For the contract for sale of a single lease, alternatives have been provided (a) for no subsequent apportionment (A11.01); (b) for the apportionment on completion to be based on the managing agent's estimate at the time of completion (A11.02); (c) for a case similar to (b) but with a right for either party to call for a recalculation if a recalculation based on the re-assessed service charge figure would result in a payment of more than a particular figure, ie apportionment to be reworked if the difference is of substance (A11.03), and (d) a similar provision whereby either party (A13.04) or the purchaser alone (A11.05) can call for such an apportionment.

4   For the sale of the reversion two precedents have been provided which are intended to cover all the most usual provisions needed for such a sale so far as service charges and rent are concerned. They are in differing styles. In both versions it is assumed that the sale is of property subject to residential as well as commercial premises and included a warranty that proper consultation on works with residential tenant has taken place. (If the warranty is untrue it could lead to an action for damages by the buyer). The precedents do not deal with any aspect other than those affecting service charges and (as a similar matter) apportionments also of rent. The first precedent (A11.06) does not apportion service charge or rent for the period before the quarter current at completion, ie the Buyer does not pay arrears. The main point is that in the first version service charge apportionments are made on a simple cash received/cash paid basis as at completion so that there is no need for further apportionments.

5   The second precedent for sale of a reversion (A11.07) assumes completing based on an estimate and revising the figure after the year end. In both cases it is provided that the seller shall produce an estimate of the expected outgoings and will not exceed expenditure from that estimate without the buyer's agreement. This is obviously more important where completion is to be long deferred than for a short completion. It is even more important where the formal estimate has not been prepared for the current year: the purchaser will need to know what is expected and to exercise a degree of financial control.

6   As service charges and rent are similar for apportionment in many ways, rent in the apportionment clauses has been included. No provision covering the possibility of rent reviews not being implemented before completion date has been included: such a provision will be needed for some contracts (and is included in the Standard Commercial Property Conditions). As a matter of importance, different provisions requiring the seller to manage the property pending completion have been included, and a requirement for an indemnity provision in the transfer.

7   The subheadings should be sufficiently self-explanatory. In each case it has been assumed that the Standard Conditions of Sale (4th Edition) are used. That is the edition current at the time of drafting.

SALE OF SINGLE LEASE

A11.01

[Alternative 1]

[Sale of lease – No subsequent apportionment]

[1]   Standard Condition 3.5.3 shall be amended so that service charges payable under the Lease shall be apportioned at the completion date on the basis of the best estimate then available and there shall be no subsequent recalculation of the service charge apportionment

A11.02

[Alternative 2]

[Sale of lease – single apportionment based on agent's estimates]

[1.1] Standard Condition 3.5.3 shall be amended so that the service charge payable under the Lease shall be apportioned at the completion date and there shall be no subsequent recalculation of the service charge apportionment

[1.2] The service charge apportionment on completion shall be based on the best estimate by the Landlord's managing agents of the service charge payable for the relevant service charge year and the Seller will use reasonable endeavours to obtain such estimate prior to completion

A11.03

[Alternative 3]

[Sale of lease – later adjustment only if the apportionment would exceed a particular figure]

[1.1] Standard Condition 3.5.3 shall be amended so that the service charge payable under the Lease shall be apportioned in accordance with clause 1.2 at the completion date and subject to clause 1.3 there shall be no subsequent recalculation of the service charge apportionment

[1.2] The service charge apportionment on completion shall be based on the best estimate of the Landlord's managing agents of the service charge payable for the relevant service charge year and the Seller will use reasonable endeavours to obtain such estimate prior to completion

A11.04

[First alternative clause 1.3 – either party to call for recalculation if apportionment would exceed a stated figure]

[1.3] Either party shall have the right to call for the said service charge apportionment to be recalculated if after the service charge for the year current at the Completion Date has been re-assessed at the end of the service charge year a recalculation of the apportionment to the date of actual completion would show that either party should have paid or been given an allowance (as the case may be) of [£500] or more than was shown in the completion statement and in such case the Seller shall pay to the Buyer or the Buyer shall pay to the Seller as the case may be within 10 days of the recalculation being made the difference between the amount shown on the original completion statement and the amount shown following the revision together with interest on such difference at the interest rate from the date of recalculation to the date of payment if payment is not made within that period

A11.05

[Second alternative clause 1.3 – buyer alone able to call for recalculation if the apportionment would exceed a stated figure]

[1.3] (a) The Buyer shall have the right to call for the said service charge apportionment to be recalculated if, when the service charge for the current year has been re-assessed at the end of the service charge year, a recalculation of the apportionment to the date of actual completion would show that the Buyer should have been given an allowance of at least [£500] more than he was given in the completion statement

(b) The Seller shall pay to the Buyer, within 10 days of notice being given by the Buyer to the Seller of the revised figures being known, the difference between the amount shown on the original completion statement and the amount shown following the revision, and, if payment is not made within that period, together with interest at the interest rate 10 days from the date on which the Buyer gives to the Seller notice until the date of payment.

SALE OF THE REVERSION TO LEASES

A11.06

[First alternative]

[Apportionment on completion without later adjustment]

Definitions[1]

1 In this clause the following expressions shall have the following meanings:

'The Leases'	the Leases set out in the Schedule being leases of parts of the Property
'Services'	the services to be provided by the landlord under the Leases to the cost of which the tenants of the Leases contribute
'Service Charges'	the payments due from the tenants of the Leases in respect of the costs of the Services
'Service Charge Costs'	all costs expenses outgoings and financial liabilities actually paid to the Seller in respect of the Services up to and including the Date of Actual Completion
'Advance Payments'	all payments received by the Seller before the Date of Actual Completion from the tenants of the Leases on account of Service Charges (whether or not reserved as rent in the Leases)
'Current Service Charge Year'	in relation to each of the Leases the accounting period for Service Charge in which the Date of Actual Completion falls
'the New Budget'	the estimated statement of the Service Charge Costs for the Service Charge Year after the Current Service Charge Year estimated by the Seller details of which have

been provided to the Buyer before the date hereof [or which the Seller will have prepared within 14 working days of the date hereof for agreement by the Buyer such agreement not to be unreasonably withheld or delayed]

'the Date of Actual Completion'	the date on which the sale and purchase hereby agreed is actually completed
'Rent Days'	the quarter day or other day on which rents and other payments reserved as rent in the Leases are payable to the landlord thereof
'Rents'	all rent and other sums reserved as rent in the Leases other than Service Charges
'The Statement'	the statement of actual Service Charge Costs and Advance Payments referred to in clause 2 hereof

Service Charges

2.1 Five working days before the Date of Actual Completion the Seller shall give to the Buyer a statement showing (a) the aggregate of Service Charge Costs in the Current Service Charge Year to the date of the Statement and (b) all Advance Payments made by the tenants of the Leases for the Current Service Charge Year to the same date and on completion the Seller shall allow to the Buyer any excess of (b) over (a) or the Buyer shall pay to the Seller any excess of (a) over (b) as the case may be

2.2 On the Date of Actual Completion the Seller shall pay or allow to the Buyer the amount held by the Seller on account of the sinking fund for the Building with details of the amount of such fund held for each of the tenants who contribute to it

2.3 The Seller agrees not to make any payment towards the Service Charge Costs after the preparation of the Statement and before the Date of Actual Completion except in emergency and in the latter case will provide to the Buyer full details of the items and the reason for payment as soon as possible after the Date of Actual Completion and the Buyer shall repay such sums to the Seller within 14 days of receipt of such details

3.1 The Seller hereby agrees that [it will procure to be prepared the New Budget within 14 days of the date hereof and that] it will not make any payments in respect of Service Charge Costs between the date of this Contract and the intended Completion Date which are either in excess of the amount for the item in question in the New Budget or which are not included in the New Budget except with the prior consent of the Buyer which will not be unreasonably withheld or delayed and which shall not be needed in case of emergency

3.2 If the Seller has to make payments of Service Charge Costs in emergency it will provide full particulars of the works done to the Buyer within five working days of the start of the works and the reason for the works and the estimated costs thereof

4 If the Seller receives any Advance Payments from tenants of the Leases for the Current Service Charge Year after the Date of Actual Completion it shall pay the same to the Buyer within five working days of each such Advance Payment becoming cleared funds

5 The Seller shall on completion hand to the Buyer duly completed and executed forms to enable the transfer to the Buyer or the nominee of the Buyer of all accounts holding reserves or sinking funds or investments representing the same in respect of future Service Charge Costs together with any accrued interest thereon (less tax for which the Seller is accountable)

6 The Seller shall within one month of the Date of Actual Completion allow the Buyer to inspect and take copies of all vouchers and accounts on reasonable prior appointment made to substantiate the amount of the Service Charge Costs for the Current Service Charge Year and shall thereafter assist the Buyer to answer enquiries from tenants about the Service Charge Costs for the period to the Date of Actual Completion

Rent

7 If the Date of Actual Completion is a day other than a Rent Day the Rents shall be apportioned between the Seller and the Buyer as follows:

7.1
$$\frac{A \times Rents}{365} = B \text{ where:}$$

'A' is the total number of days between the Date of Actual Completion and the day before the next Rent Day (both days inclusive) and

'B' is the amount due to the Buyer unless the calculation results in a negative figure in which case the same shall be the amount due to the Seller

BUT no Rents shall be apportioned or payable by the Buyer in respect of any period before the Rent Day prior to the Date of Actual Completion

7.2 If the Date of Actual Completion is later than the intended Completion Date referred to in the Schedule hereto as a result of any neglect or default of the Buyer then in addition to any other remedy which the Seller may have the Seller shall be entitled (but not obliged) to require that the Rents are apportioned at the said intended Completion Date in accordance with the formula in clause 7.1 and not the Date of Actual Completion

General

8 The Seller hereby agrees to manage the Property until the Date of Actual Completion in accordance with the principles of good estate management

and not to give any notices or enter into any binding agreements or conclude any rent reviews or grant any new lease or tenancy or vary or accept a surrender of any of the Leases or agree to do so without in any such case obtaining the previous approval of the Buyer which shall not be unreasonably withheld or delayed and which shall be deemed to be given if no representations are made within 10 working days after the request for approval

9   The Buyer shall in the Transfer to the Buyer covenant with the Seller that the Buyer and the Buyer's successors in title will from the date of the assurance and during the residue of the respective terms created by the Leases [including any statutory continuance thereof] indemnify the Seller against any breach of the covenants and conditions on the part of the landlord contained or referred to in each of the Leases occurring after the date of the Transfer

[10 The Seller warrants that it has duly consulted with the tenants of the Leases of dwellings under the provisions of section 20 of the Landlord and Tenant Act 1985 to enable recovery of the Service Charge Costs for the Current Service Charge Year]

1   Some of the definitions below may appear elsewhere in the contract and thus can be omitted from this provision.

A11.07

[Second Alternative]

[Adjustment after year end]

Definitions

1   In this clause the following expressions shall have the following meanings:

'The Leases'	the Leases set out in the Schedule being leases of parts of the Property
'Services'	the services to be provided by the landlord under the Leases to which the tenants of the Leases contribute
'Service Charge Costs'	all costs expenses outgoings and financial liabilities incurred by the Seller (whether or not the same have become payable or been paid) in respect of or in connection with the management insurance and/or maintenance of the Property and the provision of the Services in relation thereto including where any such amount is not finally ascertained before the date of actual completion the Seller's reasonable estimate thereof

'Advance Payments'	all payments received by the Seller from the tenant of any of the Leases on account of Service Charge Costs (whether before or after the Date of Actual Completion)
'Current Service Charge Year'	in relation to each of the Leases the Service Charge Accounting Period in which the Date of Actual Completion falls and any earlier accounting period for which service charge costs have not been finalised and/or in respect of which sums will be or are due to the Seller in respect of Service Charge Costs
'the New Budget'	the amount of the Service Charge Costs already estimated by the Seller for the Service Charge Year after the Current Service Charge Year or which the Seller will have prepared within 14 days of the date hereof for agreement by the Buyer which agreement will not be unreasonably withheld or delayed
'the Date of Actual Completion'	the date on which the sale and purchase hereby agreed is actually completed
'Rent Days'	the quarter day or other day on which rents and other payments reserved as rent in the Leases are payable to the landlord thereof

2.1   On completion the parties shall apportion the Service Charges on the basis of the best estimate then available and in accordance with clause 2.2 and the rent in accordance with the formula in paragraph 8

2.2   On completion the Buyer shall pay to the Seller any sums (other than rent) due to the Seller under the provisions of any of the Leases but unpaid for which the Seller is entitled to be reimbursed under the provisions of the Leases and which have been:

2.2.1 paid by the Seller since the commencement of the Current Service Charge Year (or otherwise not included in the last Service Charge accounts) but not demanded pursuant to the provisions of the Leases at the Date of Actual Completion

2.2.2 invoiced to the Seller after the commencement of the Current Service Charge Year but not paid by the Seller prior to the Date of Actual Completion

2.2.3 invoiced to and paid for by the Seller but not received from tenants pursuant to the provisions of the Leases at the Date of Actual Completion

3.1   Within one month after the end of the Current Service Charge Year the Seller shall give to the Buyer a statement ('the Statement') showing (a) the aggregate of Service Charge Costs in the Current Service Charge Year and (b) all advance payments made by the tenants of the Leases for the Current Service Charge Year and within 10 working days of delivery of the Statement the Seller shall pay to the Buyer any excess of (b) over (a) or the Buyer shall pay to the Seller any excess of (a) over (b) as the case may be together with interest at the interest rate on such excess from the date one month after the end of the Current Service Charge Year to the date of payment

A11.08

[Alternative for adjustment only above an agreed figure]

3.1   Within one month after the end of the Current Service Charge Year the Seller shall give to the Buyer a statement ('the Statement') showing (a) the aggregate of Service Charge Costs in the Current Service Charge Year and (b) all advance payments made by the tenants of the Leases for the Current Service Charge Year and if the Statement shows a difference exceeding [£2,500 plus value added tax in total] between the amount of the Service Charge apportionments on completion and the Statement that difference shall be paid by the Seller to the Buyer or vice versa within ten working days after (in the case of the Seller) knowledge of the difference and (in the case of the Buyer) written demand

3.2   If the Seller receives any Advance Payments from tenants of the Lease for the Current Service Charge Year after the Date of Actual Completion it shall pay the same to the Buyer within ten working days of receipt of cleared funds for each such advance payment and such payment shall take into account in the Statement

4   The Seller shall if so requested by the Buyer within three months of the Date of Actual Completion permit the Buyer to inspect and take copies of all vouchers and accounts needed to substantiate the amount of the Service Charge Costs for the Current Service Charge Year and shall use all reasonable endeavours to assist the Buyer to answer questions or objections from tenants as to Service Charge matters for the period prior to the Date of Actual Completion

5   The Seller shall hand to the Buyer on the Date of Actual Completion all forms or other authorities needed to transfer to the Buyer all accounts or investments (if any) holding reserves or sinking funds in respect of future Service Charge Costs together with any accrued interest (less tax for which the Seller is accountable)

6   The Seller agrees that it will procure to be prepared the New Budget and that it will not make any payments between the date of this Contract and the

intended Completion Date which are either in excess of the amount for the item in question in the New Budget or which are not in the New Budget except with the prior consent of the Buyer which will not be unreasonably withheld or delayed and which shall not be needed in cases of emergency and where payments are made in emergency the Seller will provide details to the Buyer within five working days

7   The Buyer shall in the assurance to the Buyer covenant with the Seller that the Buyer and the Buyer's successors in title will from the date of the assurance and during the residue of the respective terms created by the Leases (including any statutory continuance thereof) indemnify the Seller against any breach of the covenants and conditions on the part of the landlord contained or referred to in the Leases occurring after that date

8   If the Date of Actual Completion is a day other than a Rent Day the rents shall be apportioned between the Seller and the Buyer as follows:

8.1

$$\frac{Rents \times A}{365} = B \text{ where:}$$

'A' is the total number of days between the Date of Actual Completion and date before the next Rent Day (both days inclusive) and

'B' is the amount due to the Buyer unless the calculation results in a negative figure in which case the same shall be the amount due to the Seller

8.2 If the Date of Actual Completion is later than the intended Completion Date otherwise than as a result of any neglect or default of the Seller then in addition to any other remedy which the Seller may have the Seller shall be entitled (but not obliged) to require that the Rents are apportioned at the intended Completion Date and not at the Date of Actual Completion in accordance with the formula in clause 8.1

9   The Seller hereby agrees to manage the Property until the Date of Actual Completion in accordance with the principles of good estate management and to notify the Buyer of all notices received from the tenants and not to enter into any binding agreements or conclude any rent reviews or grant any new lease or tenancy or vary or accept a surrender of any of the Leases or agree to do so without giving ten working days' notice to the Buyer and the Seller shall take account of any representations made by the Buyer about any such matters but shall not be bound by those representations

[10 The Seller warrants that it has carried out all necessary consultation required under section 20 of the Landlord and Tenant Act 1985 to enable recovery of the Service Charge Costs for the Current Service Charge Year shown in the Statement from the tenants of Leases of dwellings]

Precedent 12

FORMS OF NOTICE

These are a set of notices for different purposes. For ease of reference there are separate notes immediately before each notice. The names and places are simply to make the precedents easier to follow and are not intended to represent real people or places.

Notice 1

Section 146 notice

1   *If a landlord wants to forfeit a lease for breach of covenant other than non-payment of rent he must first serve a notice under section 146 of the Law of Property Act 1925. If the alleged breach is that service charge has not been paid then a section 146 notice is needed before forfeiture can arise, unless the service charge is reserved as rent.*

2   *A section 146 notice must identify the breach complained of, and must give the tenant a reasonable time within which to remedy the breach. On the assumption that the lease probably gives a date for payment which has obviously gone by, a fairly short period in the draft below is given.*

3   *In practice it is rare for a section 146 notice simply to refer to non-payment of service charge. If there are other breaches they can all be covered in one notice, remembering that there has to be a reasonable period given for compliance.*

4   *Landlords need to be aware of the need for a section 146 notice before forfeiting: they must also decide whether or not forfeiture is a sensible remedy in the case in question.*

5   *Before serving any notice the landlord should check whether the lease has any specific provisions as to service (eg Registered Post or recorded delivery, or occasionally specific addresses for particular parties).*

6   *If the breach is solely non-payment of service charges (as in this example) and the premises are a dwelling, the section 146 notice cannot be served until 14 days after the agreement or determination of the service charge liability (see the comments in Chapter 9 on section 81 Housing Act 1996, paragraph 9.288 et seq).*

A12.01

Notice 1

NOTICE PURSUANT TO SECTION 146 OF THE LAW OF PROPERTY ACT 1925

To: Mr. A Head
99 Neck Street,
Foote,
Digitshire

With reference to the Lease dated 1st January 1986 made between John Legge (1) and Philip Cheek (2) ('the Lease') relating to 99 Neck Street, Foote, Digitshire ('the Premises')

Legge Limited whose registered office is at 3 Vein Street, Petella, Digitshire ('the Landlord') HEREBY GIVE YOU (AS THE CURRENT TENANT OF THE LEASE) NOTICE as follows:

1   Under clause 3(2) of the Lease the tenant covenanted to pay to the landlord the 'Service Charge' as therein defined in advance on the usual quarter days in each year.

2   The Service Charge payable for the Premises under the Lease has been assessed at £6,883.40 for the year to 24th December 2007 and a certificate of the amount due was sent to you in accordance with the terms of the Lease on the 3rd February 2008.

3   Despite requests for payment the quarterly payments of £1,720.85 for the quarters commencing on 25th March 2007 and 24th June 2007 (totalling £3,441.70) remain unpaid and you have thereby committed a breach of the said covenant 3(2) of the Lease.

4   The liability for you to pay of £3,441.70 arrears of service charge to Legge Limited was confirmed an Order ('the Order') of the Digitshire Leasehold Valuation Tribunal dated 1st July 2008 in proceedings number GLVT/28 but the payment has not been made.

5   The covenant in the Lease for payment has therefore been broken and you are required to remedy the breach complained of by payment in accordance with the Order within 7 days of the date of service of this Notice of the said sum of £3,441.70 together with interest thereon at 4% above the base rate of Blood Bank plc in accordance with the terms of the Lease and also to pay all reasonable costs and expenses associated with this notice.

6   If you fail to remedy the breach as required Legge Limited shall exercise the right of re-entry under the Lease and also claim damages.

Dated this 21st day of July 2008.
(Signed) (L. Bow)
Femur & Co.,
66 Brow Street,
Shin,
Herts.
Solicitors for and on behalf of Legge Limited

A12.02

Notice 2

NOTICE BY TENANT OF LANDLORD'S DISREPAIR

1 This notice is not necessary, in the way that a section 146 notice is necessary. However there are advantages in giving notice in a formal way. The main one is that the landlord will recognise that the tenant is serious, and that failure to act could lead either to court action or at least withholding of service charge. In addition a formal notice provides ideal evidence of the time by which the landlord had become aware of the problem, if it is later to be alleged that he has been slow in acting.

2 The following notice assumes that the landlord is responsible for repairs to the common parts and has failed to carry out some repairs. The tenant has pointed out the lack of repair (by letter or telephone) and no action has been taken. This notice is addressed jointly to the managing agents and the landlord and should be served on each.

3 If the service charge has been paid in advance for intended work, mentioned in estimates, which has not been done this notice may help, but if it seems there is fraud then proceedings should be instituted.

4 The tenant serving such a notice will of course need to be aware that where service charges are concerned he is likely to have to pay towards the cost when the work is done. Most tenants who want action taken are prepared to pay, but they should also be aware that other tenants may not. It could well be best not to serve such a notice without first consulting with those other tenants who may also be affected. At the least this could avoid criticism from the other tenants when they receive a larger bill than they had hoped for.

5 As in the case of other notices the terms of the lease should be considered in case there are special requirements as to the place or manner of service.

To: Rowan Limited,
2 The Oaks,
Burnham Beeches,
Bucks
(The Landlord)
And To: Ash & Willow,
Woodside Way,
Appleton,
Bucks
(The Managing Agents)

As the current tenant of the Lease ('the Lease') of Flat 8 Sumac Mansions, Redwood Way, Appleton dated 29th May 1983 made between Alder Limited (1) and John Pear (2) I HEREBY GIVE YOU NOTICE THAT I require you to comply with the terms of covenant 4(3) of the Lease by putting into repair or otherwise remedying or making good the defects specified in the Schedule hereto within a reasonable period of today, and in any event before 30th July 2008.

Dated this 1st day of April 2008
The Schedule
(List of defects to the common parts of Sumac Mansions)

1   Make good the rotten window sills on the landing windows and redecorate.

2   Strip off peeling paint from the ceiling of the corridors and redecorate.

3   Make good the carpet on the second floor corridor.

3   Overhaul the lift to avoid the constant breakdowns.
(etc)
(Signed) J. Pine

A12.03

Notice 3

NOTICE OF ADDRESS OF LANDLORD
UNDER SECTION 48 LANDLORD AND TENANT ACT 1987

This notice is the type of notice that must be given to the tenant of residential premises so that he has a name and address for his landlord.

Liverpool and Everton
24 Port Vale,
Sheffield
Managing agents
To:
Mr and Mrs Ranger,
24 Queens Park,
Halifax, Yorks.
Re 24 Queens Park, Halifax

As agents for and on behalf of your landlords of the above premises WE HEREBY GIVE YOU NOTICE that the landlords of the above are West Ham Limited, whose address is 25 The Valley, Charlton, London.

WE HEREBY FURTHER GIVE YOU NOTICE THAT the address for service of any notices on West Ham Limited is care of Full, Back & Co, solicitors, of 1966 Tottenham Spur Road, Colchester, Essex.

(Signed) B Fulham for Liverpool and Everton.

Wednesday 24th June 2007

A12.04

Notice 4

NOTICE OF LANDLORD'S ADDRESS FOR SERVICE
UNDER SECTION 47 LANDLORD & TENANT ACT 1987

1   This is the section that requires that written demands for rent, service charge or administration charges in respect of residential premises to give details of the landlord's address, and, if different, the address for service.

2   *Where the demand is for the rent for a long lease of a dwelling, (but not for a service charge or an administration charge) it must comply with the notice provisions of section 166 of the Commonhold and Leasehold Reform Act 2002. Details of those requirements appear in The Landlord and Tenant (Notice of Rent) (England) Regulations 2004. As they are basically concerned with rent they are outside the scope of this book. The draft below is thus for rent and service charge for a lease of a dwelling that is not one granted for more than 21 years.*

Austen and Bronte,
Mansfield Hall,
Wickham,
Literashire
To Mr. A. Rochester,
Wildfell Hall,
Bingley,
West Yorkshire 1st June 2008
Re Wildfell Hall, Bingley

We hereby apply for payment of the rent and service charge for the above premises for the half year commencing 1st July 2007 as set out in the attached statement.

We hereby give you notice that the landlord of the above property is Branwell Limited of P.O. Box 22, Emma Chambers, Panama, and whose address for service of proceedings in the United Kingdom is Suite 88, Northanger Abbey, Haworth, North Yorkshire.

(Signed) Currer Bell for Austen and Bronte.

A12.05

Notice 5

NOTICE OF CHANGE OF ACCOUNTING YEAR

1   *This precedent can be used for commercial or residential premises where the landlord wishes to change the accounting year.*

2   *Such information is sometimes given in notes to the accounts. This is on the basis of a single notice by way of letter, a copy of which is sent to each tenant. It is in an informal style and sets out the interim arrangements.*

Impressionists Ltd,
Monet House,
Turner Street,
Gainsborough,
Rutland. 2nd February 2008
To: All tenants of Constable House, Lowry.
Dear
Leases of Constable House

I write to let you know that the Accounting Year as defined in all the leases at Constable House is being changed. This follows the merger of this company with its associated company Degas, Morisot & Co. Ltd. The companies in the group consider it more efficient for the financial periods for all companies they own to be the same.

Accordingly it has been decided that instead of the Accounting Year being to 6th April in each year, as set out in the Leases, from now on it will be for the year to 23rd June. The Leases permit a change.

An estimate will be prepared for service charges for the period from 6th April to 23rd June 2008. After that estimates will be prepared in the usual way for the year starting on 24th June 2008 (and subsequent years), and the tenants will pay service charge for the revised year from 24th June in four equal instalments in advance.

If you have any questions about the change please do not hesitate to ask me.
Yours faithfully,
(Signed) C Renoir for and on behalf of Impressionists Ltd.

A12.06

Notice 6

NOTICE OF CHANGE OF PERCENTAGES

1   This is a suggested approach to notifying the tenants of a change of fixed percentages following a change of circumstances.

2   Where there are a series of leases all with fixed service charge percentages it is likely that if there is some major change (eg the sale, destruction, or change of use of a material part) there would be changes needed to all the percentages. The draft assumes that this is the case, and so the easiest way is to provide a list of all the percentages, preferably showing old and new.

3   If the service charge is based on a weighted floor area the same system can be used but with an extra column. There should be columns for 'Actual floor area' and also for 'Adjusted floor area'. The new percentages would of course be based on the latter.

4   As in the previous precedent, an informal approach is taken.

Edwin Drood & Associates,
Bleak House,
Dombey Way,
Copperfield,
Kent
7th February 2008

To:
   All tenants of Nickleby Parade, Carton Terrace, Wardle.

As you may be aware, on 1st February the block comprising numbers 38 to 46 Nickleby Parade was sold. The purchasers have responsibility for repair of the premises sold to them. Accordingly the service charge percentages on the premises remaining in the ownership of the landlord, Mr. J. Marley, need to be adjusted. We attach a list showing the effect of the changes. Although your percentage is being increased this percentage relates to a smaller property, and we do not anticipate significant changes to the amount of service charge you will be paying.

The changes take effect from 1st February 2008 and we will provide an apportionment in the estimates covering the period up to the end of the current service charge year.

We will be happy to answer any questions about the changes.
(Signed) P. Pirrip for Edwin Drood & Associates.
(Attached list)
Revised percentages for Nickleby Parade,
from 1st February 2007

Premises	Area in Square feet	2006%	2007%
1–4	1,600	8%	10%
2–8	1,600	8%	10%
9–12	1,600	8%	10%
13/14	1,000	5%	6.25%
15/18	1,600	8%	10%
19/20	1,000	5%	6.25%
21–24	1,400	7%	8.75%
25/26	1,200	6%	7.5%
27–30	1,600	8%	10%
31/32	1,200	6%	7.5%
33–35	1,200	6%	7.5%
36/37	1,000	5%	6.25%
	16,000		
(38–46)	(4,000)	(20%)	–
	20,000	100%	100%

Precedent 13

CONSULTATION ON WORKS (RESIDENTIAL)

1   The statutory reference is the Landlord and Tenant Act 1985 section 20 in the form replaced by section 151 of the Commonhold and Leasehold Reform Act 2002. (See paragraph 9.56 et seq above). The detailed requirements appear in The Service Charges (Consultation Requirements) (England) Regulations 2003.

2   These provisions, and consequently the precedents, are in respect of residential premises only. In those cases the landlord is under an obligation to consult with the tenants in three main cases. They are:

(a)   before carrying out works which will cost any tenant more than £250

(b)   before entering into a long-term agreement and

(c)   before carrying out works under a long-term agreement for which any tenant has to pay more than £100.

The other two cases are (a) transitional provisions (which, in effect, are no longer material) and (b) cases where the landlord has to give 'public notice' of costs. As these are unlikely to be material except in rare cases, precedents are not provided, except for the three main cases.

3   The notices in this precedent (in the absence of prescribed forms) are intended to comply with the statutory obligations. The different types of consultation each have subtle differences. These are reflected in the precedents.

4   A version for each of the three above types of consultation has been drafted. Consultation is usually in several stages: Notices have been prepared for the first two stages for the first two types of consultation. The third stage, where it applies, is only to notify the tenants of the appointment that has been made and to justify that appointment. The final precedent may assist in drafting reasons either at the first two stages or in the third stage, where that is material.

5   The final precedent consists of a few suggested reasons for making the choice that the landlord has made (needed where any tenant has made representations or nominated someone to give a quotation). (See eg para 9.86 above).

6   *The second precedent is in the form of formal notice addressed to the secretary of a Recognised Tenants' Association. It has to be given to all the tenants as well, even if they are all members of the association.*

7   *The Act refers to a 'notice' being given to the tenants. The first is drafted by way of letter from the managing agents, and the second as a formal notice. Provided that the letter is either expressed to be a notice or clearly complies with the section there would seem to be no reason why a letter is not sufficient. If in doubt a formal notice may be better.*

8   *The second stage has to be accompanied by summaries of at least two estimates. Three are suggested in the precedents, as this seems fairly common. At least one of the estimates must be from someone not connected with the landlord. In A13.01 is a comment that one of the estimates is from a company associated with the landlord. This is not strictly necessary, but it seems good practice to avoid any suggestion that the tenants were unaware that one of the estimates was not from an independent source.*

9   *The regulations refer to a notice being 'given' to the tenants. It is clearly easiest to have a set of notices or letters prepared and delivered at the same time by hand to each flat (which are inevitably all together). If the letters are to be posted then the lease should be consulted to see if there are special provisions about how or where notices are to be served: there may be special requirements, in particular where a company is the tenant, or the tenant allows the premises to be occupied by someone who is not responsible for paying the service charge.*

[Consultation on Works costing any tenant more than £250][1]

A13.01

[First stage]

Shepherd Ltd,
3 Apple Avenue,
Pecan,
Cumberland
Managing agents
To each of the tenants.   26th March 2008

Dear Sir/Madam,
<u>re Mince Mansion, Pigeon Place, Blueberry</u>

As you know, last year there were some leaks in the roof of the western wing of Mince Mansion. The problem has been examined and the landlord has been advised that the only way to ensure that the leaks are not repeated with increasing frequency and seriousness is to replace the felting and broken or missing tiles. Your landlords, Stargazy Limited, accordingly propose to follow that advice and to carry out roof repairs.

As the damage arises simply because of the age of the building and not from any storm damage or other insured risk the cost cannot be recovered through the insurance.

The work to be done is stripping the tiles and the existing felting and completely replacing the felting with new felting, as well as replacing any damaged battens, and then re-setting the tiles, and replacing the missing or broken tiles. Under present legislation the landlord has to give notice to the tenants of its intention to carry out such works if any of the tenants is likely to have to pay £250 or more. It seems probable that this is the case, and this letter is intended as such a notice.

Particulars of the work are set out in the specification prepared for the purpose. You have the right to inspect the specification if you wish at these offices between 9.00 a.m. and 6.00 p.m. Monday to Friday. If you do, please telephone in advance, so that the papers can be made available without delay. We do not have a copier at the premises, but can provide a copy of the specification if you wish.

We propose to obtain estimates from:

1   Stargazy (Fish) Ltd (a subsidiary company of the landlord)

2   Rabbit Brothers

3   Pumpkin Roofs Ltd

You have the right to forward any comments you may have on the proposal to us at our Pecan address. Any such comments must be received by us no later than 30th April 2008. In addition to the right to make comments you have the right within the same period, if you wish, to notify us of the name of a contractor who you would like the landlord to ask to quote for the work. If there is more than one nominated contractor the rules set out a system of preferences to decide who the landlord should approach. The work is not emergency work and will not be started before the consultation period has ended.

If you need any further comments from me as to the proposals please let me know as soon as possible, and I will endeavour to assist.

Yours sincerely,

R. Crust for Shepherd Ltd.

---

1   This includes the requirements set out in Schedule 4 Part 2 of the 2003 Regulations. If there is a recognised tenants' association that association also needs to be notified (as is done in the second set of precedents).

A13.02

[Second stage]
Shepherd Ltd,
3 Apple Avenue,
Pecan,
Cumberland
Managing agents
To each of the tenants.   23rd July 2008

Dear Sir/Madam,
re Mince Mansion, Pigeon Place, Blueberry

We refer to our letter of 26th March setting out details of the proposals relating to proposed roof works. We have had some responses from tenants and the specification has been adjusted to take account of these comments by omitting the reference to replacing broken tiles. We have obtained quotations from the three contractors mentioned in our letter, and also from Steak (Ayle) Limited. The latter was the contractor who was nominated by most of the tenants.

We enclose copies of the four estimates which are, briefly, as follows:

1   Stargazy (Fish) Ltd (a subsidiary company of the landlord) – £23,438.70 (plus VAT)

2   Rabbit Brothers – £24,150.00 (plus VAT)

3   Pumpkin Roofs Ltd – £27,775.00 (plus VAT)

4   Steak (Ayle) Limited – £25,620 (plus VAT).

As the estimate from Stargazy (Fish) Ltd is the lowest the landlord proposes to carry out the works using that company as the contractor.

Each of the estimates includes certain provisional quantities and costs which will be measured and calculated during the course of the works. The final figure (to be charged to the service charge) may therefore be slightly different. We are of course, however, concerned to maintain strict financial control over the works.

I shall of course endeavour to ensure that the work is carried out with the least inconvenience to residents, and I will write to notify you of the actual date for the start of the work as soon as the date is known.

Yours sincerely,
R. Crust for Shepherd Ltd.

[Consultation with tenants and Recognised Tenants' Association on entering into a long-term agreement][1]

A13.03

[First stage]

FIRST NOTICE UNDER SECTION 20 OF THE LANDLORD AND TENANT ACT 1985
and
Schedule 1 to The Service Charge (Consultation Requirements) (England) Regulations 2003
To: Mrs Mary Read,
Secretary of the Morgan Mansion Residents' Association
Flat 8, Morgan Mansion,
Dampier Street,
Kidd,
Oxford
AND to all the tenants
Re Morgan Mansion, Dampier Street, Kidd

As Agents for and on behalf of Woodes Rogers Limited, the landlord of the above property, WE HEREBY GIVE YOU NOTICE THAT:

1   The Landlord proposes to employ a contractor on a contract lasting more than one year to carry out works ('the Works') brief details of which appear in Part 1 of the Schedule to this Notice. [(1)   The Works are more particularly described in the job specification dated 23rd April 2008 of Calico, Rackham & Co, a copy of which is attached to this notice.] [(2) A copy of the job specification can be inspected before the end of the period specified in Part 2 of the Schedule below between 2.00 p.m. and 5.30 p.m. at our offices at 66 Marque Street, Boucan, Huntingdon. You have the right to take copies of it, if you wish, by prior appointment.][2]

2   Under section 20 of the Landlord and Tenant Act 1985 the landlord is obliged to notify the tenants of the intention to enter into a long-term contract which is not an exempt contract. The proposal in paragraph 1 is for a long-term contract which is not exempt. [The proposal is for the appointment of managing agents and Part 5 of the Schedule below applies.][3]

3   Under the said section 20 the landlord is obliged to give reasons for entering into a long-term agreement. The reasons are set out in Part 3 of the Schedule below.

4   Under the said section the recognised tenants' association and also the tenants are entitled within 30 days of the date of this notice:

(a)   to make representations about the proposal, and

(b)   to nominate a contractor from whom an estimate is to be sought.

You are hereby notified of this right.

5   The landlord is proposing to seek quotations for the Works from the companies named in Part 4 of the Schedule below. If you wish quotations for the same work to be requested from another company or person please send details to us within the said time limit. The 2003 Regulations set out a procedure under which the landlord must seek quotation(s) where more than one nomination is received from the recognised tenants' association and/or the tenants.

6   Any observations on the proposal and/or any nominations under paragraph 5 must be submitted in writing to us at our address at Boucan within the period specified in Part 2 of the Schedule below.

Schedule

Part 1 – Brief details of the Works
Cleaning the windows of the common parts inside and out every two weeks, and cleaning the entrance doorway, halls, corridors and stairways on a regular cycle with a deep clean every two years.

Part 2 – Expiration of period for the tenants' response
31st July 2008

Part 3 – Reasons
The landlord is under an obligation in the leases to carry out the works in Part 1, and believes that it can achieve costs savings by entering into a long-term agreement as compared to a shorter-term agreement.

Part 4 – Contractors being approached for quotations
Calico, Rackham. & Co.
Bartholomew Sharpe & Associates

Part 5 – Details of the appointment of managing agents
[Not applicable]
[Captain, Tew & Co of Boucan are chartered surveyors who are experienced in managing residential premises. Several members of the firms are either fellows or associates of the Royal Institute of Chartered surveyors. The firm tries to abide by the Code of practice for residential property approved by the Secretary of State as far as it is practical to do so consistent with the terms of Leases.][4]

Dated 1st July 2008

(Signed) Anne Bonney for and on behalf of Woodes Rogers Limited, of 66, Marque Street, Boucan, Huntingdon, Managing Agents for the landlord.

1   This is based on the requirements of Schedule 1 to the 2003 Regulations relating to proposals to enter into a long-term agreement which is not the subject of public notice. It must be sent to the recognised tenants' association and also to all tenants. The Regulations require special provisions about managing agents and options to try to cover the requirements have been included.
2   Delete (1) or (2) as appropriate.
3   Delete as appropriate.
4   Delete as appropriate.

A13.04

[Second stage]

SECOND NOTICE UNDER SECTION 20 OF THE LANDLORD AND TENANT ACT 1985
and
Schedule 1 to The Service Charge (Consultation Requirements) (England) Regulations 2003

To: Mrs Mary Read,
Secretary of the Morgan Mansion Residents' Association
Flat 8, Morgan Mansion,
Dampier Street,
Kidd,
Oxford
AND to all tenants

Re Morgan Mansion, Dampier Street, Kidd
This Notice follows the notice relating to a proposal to enter into a long-term contract sent to you on 1st July 2008.

[2   No representations or nominations have been received from you within the time limit given by the said Notice.]

[2   In accordance with your nomination an estimate has been obtained from Alexander Selkirk Ltd]

[2   In accordance with your nomination we endeavoured to obtain a quotation for the Works from Alexander Selkirk Ltd but that company was unable or unwilling to give a quotation.]¹

3 We have obtained four estimates for the Works. The estimates are as follows:

(a)   Bartholomew Sharpe & Associates – £3,841.93 per year (plus VAT) for a 3-year agreement.

(b)   Calico, Rackham & Co – £3,950.00 per year (plus VAT) (for a 3-year agreement)

(c)   Alexander Selkirk Ltd – £4,280.00 per year (VAT not being payable) (2-year agreement)

(d)   W.E. Teach Limited (See paragraph 6 below)

[None of the quotations was from a company connected with the landlord.]

[Bartholomew Sharpe & Associates is a company connected with the landlord under the provisions of the 2003 Regulations.]²

4   [None of the estimates contains provisions for adjusting the costs.] [The estimate of Calico Rackham & Co was given on the basis that the figures would be increased annually by the equivalent of the increase in the retail prices index. W.E. Teach Limited require their hourly rate to be reviewed annually.]³

5   The landlord [has taken note of the representations made on behalf of the residents' association in your letter of 14th July 2008 and] proposes to accept the estimate of Bartholomew Sharpe & Associates [which is the cheapest quotation] and to carry out the works starting on 12th September 2008.[4]

6   [Under the leases the tenants are liable to contribute fixed percentages of the cost. As each tenant pays 10% it is estimated each tenant will pay £451.42 (10% of £3,841.93 plus £672.34 VAT) towards the costs under the long-term agreement.] [The accompanying summary sets out the share of the costs of these works payable by each tenant.] [The costs of W. E. Teach Limited are based on an 8-year agreement at an initial hourly rate of £8.40 and accordingly it is not possible to give a precise estimate of the cost to each tenant for the year.]

Dated 1st July 2008

(Signed) Anne Bonney for and on behalf of Woodes Rogers & Co, of 66, Marque Street, Boucan, Huntingdon, Managing Agents for the landlord.

1   Delete as applicable.
2   Delete as applicable.
3   Delete as applicable.
4   Delete as appropriate.

A13.05

[Consultation on works to be carried out under a long-term agreement]

This is based on the requirements in Schedule 3 of the 2003 Regulations.
Fairbanks Managing Agents
Flynn House,
Chaplin Walk,
Bogart.
4th July 2008
To: the tenants of Garson Mansions
Dear Sir/Madam,
Gardening contract at Garson Mansions, Lancaster

As you know, following consultation in 2006 we appointed Clara (Bow) Nurseries to carry out gardening works under a five-year contract. We are obliged to give notice to tenants where works proposed are going to cost any tenant more than £100 in one year. For the year from 29th September 2007 the landlords propose that Clara (Bow) Nurseries shall carry out the gardening works set out in the specification which we sent to you with the original notice. It is anticipated that the works will cost some tenants more than £100 in the coming financial year. The obligations to carry our gardening works as set out in the consultation remains, and the landlord is satisfied the costs are still competitive.

We are obliged to give notice to the tenants and to give them the opportunity to make any observations they wish on the works within 30 days of the date of this letter, which is intended to be such a notice. You have the right to see the specification again, and it can be inspected during the 30-day period (which ends on 3rd August 2008) at our offices during normal business hours on prior appointment being made. As the total cost for the works in the year from 29th September 2007 is estimated to be £2,800 (with no VAT payable), in accordance with the original estimate, the share of the costs payable by each tenant for these works will be £200.

If you have any comments you must let us know within the 30-day period.

Yours faithfully,

B Keaton for Fairbanks Managing Agents.

A13.06

[Examples of reasons to be given where needed]

During the first phase of consultation the landlord has to say why the work is needed. In addition, if the tenants either make representations or nominate a contractor the landlord may be obliged to give reasons for his choice at later stages, as indicated in the general text. In A13.02 and A13.04 above suggested reasons were included in the second notice. The following may be helpful suggestions for some cases.

1   Although the estimate from [A] is slightly higher than the estimate from [B] it has been decided to accept the estimate from [A] as they are able to start the work at the time required by the landlord, whereas [B] were unable to give a starting date.

2   The landlord has decided to accept the estimate from [C]. Although the cost is marginally higher than the estimates from [D] and [E], it is considered that [C] will do a better quality job which should last longer and thus not need further work so soon.

3   The landlord has been advised that because of their standard of workmanship and their general level of customer care the estimate of [F] should be accepted.

4   Although [G] gave an estimate as requested by the tenants and it is one of the cheapest the landlord has decided not to accept their estimate. [G] were unable to provide confirmation that they have proper third party liability insurance, and they are not members of any of the usual trade organisations. In addition they could not provide a certificate from the Inland Revenue to show that they do not need to deduct tax from sub-contractors. They were also unable to confirm that they had sufficient permanent staff to be able to return to carry out remedial work if there is a problem. Accordingly the landlord has decided to accept the slightly higher estimate of [H], where the problems just mentioned do not arise.

5   The landlord has noted the comments made by the tenants in response to the notices consulting on the works. The landlord has had regard to the comments, and has decided to accept the quotation of [I].

6 The landlord has followed the suggestion of the majority of the tenants and accordingly has appointed [J].

7 Several tenants have stated that they do not consider the replacement of the windows on the second floor necessary. The landlord has noted these comments by the tenants, but has been advised by his surveyor that the work should be done this year because if it is left for another year the costs will then be proportionately higher, as the windows will have deteriorated further.

8 Following representations from a number of the tenants to the original notices it has been decided not to replace the carpet on the fourth floor this year, and the quotations now given accordingly do not include any cost for that item.

Precedent 14

ESTATE RENTCHARGE PROVISIONS

1   Rentcharges are discussed in Chapter 16. Included in this part are some precedents for the creation of rentcharges, and the sale of a rentcharge.

2   The first precedent is a transfer creating a single estate rentcharge, to cover simple costs. The second version is a much more full version with a double rentcharge. Both will need to be adapted to fit the Land Registry prescribed forms. The third precedent comprises clauses from the contract for the sale of the benefit of a rentcharge.

3   The first transfer is simple and has been kept to a minimum. It assumes two houses sharing a joint driveway, for the maintenance of which the owners of the two houses are to pay in equal shares. It has been assumed that the owner of one house is selling the adjoining house (probably following its construction) to a purchaser, granting mutual rights of way over the driveway. It is necessary either for one party to be responsible for all maintenance or for each to be responsible for that part of the drive which is on their property. To ensure that both halves of the drive are kept in equally good order, it has been provided for the vendor to be responsible for maintenance of the whole of the drive with a right of recovery by way of a rentcharge. The rentcharge is an estate rentcharge, and it is only payable to enable the transferor to recover costs of maintenance etc for the joint access. There is provision for prior consultation on cost, and for the payer to be able to nominate a contractor to give an estimate. The costs are likely to arise only on an irregular basis and so the provision for notification of changes of ownership is important. This precedent also includes a right for re-entry on breach.

4   The second precedent (the more full version) is more like the service charges in a lease, and fairly full details of services the estate rentcharge is to cover have been included, as it is likely that these are the type of items most commonly seen. (Others could include a common drainage system or a common car park). For these purposes the example of an industrial unit where there are common roads, refuse areas and landscaped areas etc has been used. The draft provides for the services to be carried out by a man-

agement company, which would in practice be owned by the individual freehold owners of the units. This saves the vendor from a continuing liability. There are strict provisions designed to ensure that the management company is notified of transfers and that shares held by the purchaser in the management company are transferred when the freehold is transferred on. There is a double rentcharge – one being an annual payment of a (nominal) fixed amount, and the other the contribution to services. For the non-fixed rentcharge there is a disputes clause, and within the services is a sweeping-up clause.

5   Thirdly is a set of clauses for a contract for the sale of a rentcharge. They are not particularly complex but may assist. Contract provisions for the sale of a property which is subject to a rentcharge have not been drafted, because there is nothing special about such a contract except that the parties should make sure there are provisions for apportionment, either by reference to the standard conditions or with a separate provision. The provisions in Precedent 13 could be easily adapted if desired.

A14.01

[Transfer with single estate rentcharge]

TRANSFER OF PART Land Registry TP1

1   **Stamp duty**

2   **Title number out of which the Property is transferred** BK1066

3   **Other title numbers against which matters contained in this transfer are to be registered** None

4   **Property transferred** 23 Edward Villas, Andrew Road, Charleston, Royal County of Berkshire

5   **Date** 23rd April 2007

6   **Transfereror** Charles Edward Stuart of 24 Edward Villas Andrew Road Charleston

7   **Transferee** Henry Tudor of 6 Hampton Court Kingston Upon Thames Surrey

8   **Transferee's intended address for service** 23 Edward Villas, Andrew Road, Charleston, Royal County of Berkshire

9   **The Transferor transfers the Property to the Transferee**

10   **Consideration**

     The Transferor has received from the Transferee for the Property the sum of £100,000 and the Transfer is further in consideration of the payment of the Rentcharge hereinafter defined

11   **The Transferee transfers with** full title guarantee

12   **Declaration of Trust**

     The Transferees hold the Property on trust for ……..

13   **Additional provisions**

     Definitions

Rights granted for the benefit of the Property

A right of way with or without vehicles at all times and for all purposes in common with the Transferor and the Transferor's successors in title over that part of the joint driveway ('the Joint Driveway') shown edged in green on the said plan

Rights reserved for the benefit of other land

(1) a right of way for the Transferor and his successors in title at all times and for all purposes in common with the Transferee and the Transferee's successors in title with or without vehicles over that part of the Joint Driveway which is within the Property and is shown on the plan edged in blue and

(2) reserving out of the Property to the Transferor as owner of 24 Edward Villas aforesaid and his successors in title in fee simple the rentcharge ('the Rentcharge') hereinafter described to be forever charged on and issuing out of the Property and

(3) reserving to the Transferor and his successors in title a right of entry onto the Property for the purpose of complying with his obligations herein set out

(4) reserving to the Transferor or his successors in title owner or owners of the Rentcharge (in addition to any other remedy statutory or otherwise open to them) the right at any time or times to enter the Property or any part thereof in the name of the whole and to have and repossess the same as if this Transfer had not been made if there is a failure by the Transferee or his successors in title to pay the Rentcharge in whole or in part for two months after the date on which any payment is due or to perform any of the positive covenants contained in this Transfer for the security of the Rentcharge[1]

Restrictive covenants by the Transferee

Restrictive covenants by the Transferor

Additional provisions to be added in para 13

Positive covenants by the Transferor

1 (a) In consideration of and subject to payment of the Rentcharge the Transferor hereby covenants with the Transferee and his successors that the Transferor and his successors in title will at all times hereafter keep in good repair and condition the Joint Driveway (including where necessary resurfacing the same)

Provided That

(i) where any item of repair or resurfacing is likely to cost more than [£500] in total including Value Added Tax (or such larger sum as the parties or their successors shall from time to time agree) the Transferor or his successors in title as the case may be shall first notify the Transferee or his successors in title as the case may be of the nature and extent of the proposed works and the estimated cost thereof and before commencing such work shall have regard to any representations made in respect thereof

(ii) if the Transferee or his successors in title as the case may be considers that the necessary works could be done equally satisfactorily for a lesser cost the Transferor or his successors in title as the case may be shall obtain more than one estimate for the works (including an estimate if so requested from a contractor proposed by the Transferee or his successors in title as the case may be) before commencing the works (except where such works are needed in an emergency) subject to the overriding condition that the parties agree that the Joint Driveway is to be kept in a good state of repair to avoid accidents and damage to persons or vehicles

2 (b) The Transferee hereby gives to the Transferor licence to enter on to the Property at all times on reasonable notice (except in emergency) to carry

out repairs and other works to the Joint Driveway and the Transferor covenants to carry out such works in such manner as to cause as little disturbance and inconvenience as possible to the Transferee

Positive covenants by the Transferee

To pay the rentcharge referred to in paragraph 4 hereof at the times and in the manner therein stated

Rentcharge

3   (a)   The Rentcharge shall be a sum equal to one half of the cost (including the cost of all labour materials and taxes payable) of keeping in repair and good condition and where necessary resurfacing or relaying the Joint Driveway including its drainage and any lighting or marking out

       (b)   The Rentcharge shall be paid by the Transferee or his successors in title to the Transferor or his successors in title as the case may be within seven days of written demand which demand shall be accompanied by evidence of the cost in question

       (c)   If the Rentcharge is not paid within the said period of seven days from written demand the Transferor or his successors in title shall have the right (in addition to any other right) to interest on the amount due at the rate of 5% per annum above the base rate at the time of Royal Bank of Scotland plc or if that rate is no longer used then some equivalent rate

       (d)   The Transferee for himself and his successors in title hereby agrees that the Property shall henceforth stand charged with the payment of the Rentcharge

       (e)   The parties hereto apply to note on the register of the title to 24 Edward Villas namely BK 1066 the provisions of this clause

[Any other provisions needed on other aspects]

Execution

1   Note that this right of re-entry may be subject to perpetuity problems so far as it concerns matters other than non-payment of the rentcharge. (Law of Property Act 1925, s 1(2)(e)). If this is a concern the clause could omit reference to performance of the positive covenants, or a definition could be added including a reference to a perpetuity period and this clause could refer to that perpetuity period.

A14.02

[Transfer of part imposing double rentcharge]

TRANSFER OF PART Land Registry TP1

1	**Stamp duty**	
2	**Title number out of which the Property is transferred**	SP1212
3	**Other title numbers against which matters contained in the this transfer are to be registered**	SP1213, SP12114, SP1215, and SP7654
4	**Property Transferred**	Unit 6, Median Corner, Angle Industrial Estate, Edge, Shropshire
5	**Date**	29th February 2008

6	**Transfereror**	CURVED CONCRETE CREATION CORPORATION LIMITED (Company registration number 1234321)
7	**Transferee**	JINKING JOINERS LIMITED (Company registration number 4321234)
8	**Transferee's intended address for service**	(Registered office) 99 Horseshoe Crescent Hook East Anglia

9 **The Transferor transfers the Property to the Transferee**

10 **Consideration**

The Transferor has received from the Transferee for the Property the sum of two hundred thousand pounds and of the covenants hereinafter contained and the obligation for payment of the Fixed Rentcharge and the Services Rentcharge

11 **The Transferee transfers with** full title guarantee

12 **Declaration of Trust**

The Transferees hold the Property on trust for ……..

13 **Additional provisions**

Definitions

13.1	'Transferee'	Includes its successors in title to the Property and each and every part thereof
	'Property'	The property hereby transferred being unit 6 on the Estate as hereinafter defined and as shown edged in red on the plan
	'the Management Company'	ANGLE MANAGEMENT COMPANY LIMITED whose registered office is at Linear House Median Corner Angle Industrial Estate Edge Shropshire (Company registration number 987654)
	'Estate'	The Angle Industrial Estate Edge Shropshire shown for identification edged in blue on the plan
	'Estate Road'	The roads or footpaths within the Estate

'Common Parts'	All parts of the Estate other than those parts transferred to purchasers or designed and intended to be so transferred and which Common Parts are for identification shown hatched in green on the plan attached hereto
'Expenditure'	The total expenses incurred by the Management Company in the provision of the Services as defined in the Third Schedule hereto and in respect of the accounting for and collection of the Services Rentcharge
'the Fixed	A perpetual yearly rentcharge of five pounds per annum
'the Services	A perpetual yearly estate rentcharge calculated as hereinafter set out being
Rentcharge'	a payment towards the Expenditure

13.2   (a)   Words importing the singular number include the plural number and vice versa

(b)   Words importing the masculine or neuter genders include the masculine feminine or neuter genders and words importing individuals shall include companies

(c)   Where any party hereto includes two or more persons all obligations express or implied herein on the part of such party shall be joint and several obligations

(d)   References to a statute shall include any statutory modification or re-enactment thereof as well as any orders directions or regulations made under the authority thereof

Rights granted for the benefit of the Property

13.3   *[These will include rights for electricity, water etc through the Estate, rights of way in common over the Estate road, rights to use any common parking area, to use the common refuse area, and rights to have its name on the notice board at the entrance as well as any other necessary rights.]*

Rights reserved for the benefit of other land

13.4   *[These will be any necessary rights over the Property for the benefit of the remainder of the Estate such as rights for pipes and cables to pass under the Property and for access for repair]*

13.5   And Also Reserving out of the Property in fee simple the Fixed Rentcharge and the Services Rentcharge to be forever charged upon and issuing out of the Property and to be paid without any deduction or set-off whatsoever in manner hereinafter appearing

13.6   The right is reserved to the Management Company to enter the Property with or without workmen or others at all reasonable times on reasonable prior notice (save in emergency when as much notice as practical shall be given) so far as is necessary for the purpose of fulfilling any of their obligations under this Transfer including inspecting and testing

Restrictive covenants by the Transferee

13.7   The transferee covenants with the Management Company and the Transferor for the benefit of the Estate and each and every part thereof:

(c)   (i)   Not to transfer the Property or any part of the Property without at the same time transferring to the intended transferee the shares held by the Transferee in the Management Company in accordance with the articles of association of the Management Company and in the case of the transfer of less than the whole of the Property the person transferring such part of the Property shall transfer to the person to whom it shall so transfer such part of the Property a number of the shares in the Management Company reasonably reflecting the relative values at the time of the part of the Property being so transferred compared to the part being retained

(ii)   If the Transferor shall fail to transfer such shares the Management Company shall have the right to claim all amounts due under this Transfer (and in particular the Fixed Rentcharge and Services Rentcharge) from the person registered as holder of the shares in the Management Company until the shares are so transferred

(d)   (i)   Not to transfer the Property (or any part thereof) without including in the Transfer a covenant by the Transferee in favour of the person so transferring and the Management Company:

(A)   To observe and perform the covenants and conditions on the part of the Transferee herein contained including (without prejudice to the generality of the foregoing) the payment of the Fixed Rentcharge and the Services Rentcharge or (in the case of a transfer of only part of the Property) a suitable specified proportion thereof

589

(B)   To forward to the Management Company for registration a certified copy of each Transfer of the Property or any part thereof within 21 days of the date of each and every transfer or (in the case of transfer arising from the death of an individual or insolvency) to forward to the Management Company a certified copy of the grant of probate or letters of administration or of the authority of the trustee in bankruptcy receiver or liquidator as the case may be within two months of the issue thereof

(C)   To accept the share or shares in the Management Company held by the Transferee (or a suitable proportion of those shares based on the comparative values of the part of the Property transferred and the part retained in the case of a transfer of part only of the Property)

Restrictive covenants by the Transferor

13.8   *[Add as necessary]*

Covenants by the Transferee

13.9   The Transferee covenants with the Management Company as follows:

(a)   To pay the Fixed Rentcharge to the Management Company on the 25th day of March in each year whether or not a formal demand is sent and to pay the Services Rentcharge in the manner set out in clause 13.2 hereof

(b)   *[Covenants such as indemnity covenants for existing obligations, restrictions on use, or alterations, as to nuisance etc]*

Management Company covenants

13.10 The Management Company covenants with the Transferee and as a separate covenant with the Transferor subject to payment of the Services Rentcharge to use reasonable endeavours to supply the Services described in paragraph 13.11 in accordance with the provisions therein contained

Services

13.11 The following are the Services which the Management Company is to provide in respect of the Common Parts

PROVIDED THAT

(i)   the Management Company shall not be liable for any disruption in any of the Services caused by matters beyond its reasonable control nor for failure to carry out any repairs unless it has been notified in writing of the lack of repair and has failed to carry out the necessary work within a reasonable period and

(ii)   the Expenditure for which the Service
Rentcharge is payable shall include (in addition
to the cost of the Services indicated below):

> any water rates and general or uniform
> business rates or similar outgoings payable
> in respect of the Common Parts and

> the reasonable and proper costs of any
> managing agents or contractors reasonably
> appointed by the Management Company
> for the purposes of providing the Services
> and

> the costs of maintaining and managing the
> Management Company (including the
> cost of preparing accounts having the
> accounts audited and filing notices and
> annual returns and all other matters needed
> to comply with the requirements of the
> Companies Acts) and

> the costs of preparing accounts for the
> purposes of the Services Rentcharge and
> the collection thereof

(a)   Repairing cleaning sweeping marking out and
(where necessary or more economic than repair)
resurfacing the Estate road

(b)   Lighting the Estate road as necessary including
providing the energy supply therefor and the
repair and replacement of bulbs and where
necessary and more economic than repair
replacing the light fittings and lamp standards
with suitable replacements

(c)   Repairing maintaining inspecting and where
necessary relaying and connecting to such of
the pipes wires cables and other conduits as
pass under or through any part of the Common
Parts for the benefit of any of the Units on
the Estate

(d)   Repairing maintaining cleaning and decorating
or otherwise treating and (where necessary and
more economic than repair) replacing the
entrance gates to the Estate and the name
boards adjacent to the gates and any equipment
reasonably required for fire prevention or
fire fighting

(e)   Tending and maintaining the landscaped areas
of the Common Parts including grass cutting
pruning and where appropriate replacing
plants shrubs and trees

(f)   Security

(g)   The removal of refuse from the Refuse Area
shown edged in orange on the plan as often as
shall reasonably be required in accordance with
all relevant statutory requirements

(h) Insuring against third party liability and other proper risks in respect of the Common Parts

(i) Any other works or services needed for the Common Parts to comply with any Act of Parliament or the proper requirements of any local authority or statutory undertaking or the proper requirements of the insurers

(j) Carrying out such other services to the Common Parts as shall reasonably considered to be for the benefit of the occupiers of the Estate or as shall be required by a majority in number of the occupiers of the Units on the Estate

Rentcharges

13.12.1 **The Fixed Rentcharge**

The Fixed Rentcharge shall be payable by the Transferee to the Management Company in advance on the 25th day of March in each year and the first payment (which shall not be apportioned) shall be paid on the date of this Transfer

13.12.2 **The Services Rentcharge**

The Services Rentcharge shall be 8% of the Expenditure as certified in the Certificate mentioned in sub-paragraph 13.12.2(b) hereof and shall be payable:

(a) by equal quarterly payments in advance on the usual quarter days in each year based on the Management Company's reasonable estimate of the Expenditure expected to be needed for the year ('the Accounting Year') from 25th March in each year (or from such other date as the Management Company shall from time to time determine)

(b) as soon as possible after the end of the Accounting Year the Management Company shall cause to be prepared accounts showing the Expenditure for that year and such accounts shall be certified by a chartered surveyor or other suitable person who shall prepare a certificate ('the Certificate') of the total of such costs and the amount payable by each occupier of the Units on the Estate and the Management Company shall send a copy of the Certificate to the Transferee

(c) If the amount paid on account of the Expenditure is less than the amount shown to be payable by the Certificate the Transferee or its successors in title shall pay to the Management Company within

21 days of the delivery of a copy of the Certificate to the Transferee the difference between the amount actually paid in advance and the amount shown in the Certificate to be due and if such difference is not paid within the said period of 21 days the Transferee or its said successors in title shall pay interest at the rate of 4% over the base rate of Midland Bank plc from the date of delivery of the Certificate until the date of receipt by the Management Company of the amount due

(d) If the amount paid on account of the Expenditure is more than the amount shown to be payable by the Certificate the excess shall be carried forward towards the amount due for the next Accounting Year unless such excess exceeds 10% of the sum shown to be properly payable in the Certificate for the said Accounting Year in which case the whole amount overpaid shall be repaid to the Transferee or its successors in title within 21 days of the date of the certificate

Registration

13.13 The parties hereto apply to the Land Registry to enter a restriction on the register of the title to the Property that no disposition of the registered estate (other than a charge) by the proprietor of the registered estate or of any part thereof is to be registered without a certificate signed by the person to whom the Property (or part thereof) is transferred that the provisions of clause 13.7 of this Transfer have been complied with

Disputes

13.14 If the Transferee should at any time dispute the amount properly payable under the Certificate it shall give notice to the Management Company of the dispute within two months of the date of the Certificate (time to be of the essence) and in the absence of agreement within three months of the date of the Certificate either party shall be at liberty to refer the dispute to a single arbitrator to be agreed by the parties or in default of agreement nominated by the President of the Royal Institution of Chartered Surveyors and such arbitrator shall act as an arbitrator within the provisions of the Arbitration Act 1995 and not as an expert

Executed by all three parties

CLAUSES FOR CONTRACT FOR SALE OF THE BENEFIT OF RENTCHARGES

A14.03

Only specific rentcharge provisions are included below, and it is assumed that the Standard Conditions of Sale or other conditions are included by reference

1   The Seller will sell All That estate rentcharge ('the Rentcharge') created by the Transfer [Conveyance] [Deed] of which details are set out in the Schedule hereto affecting the property described in the Schedule for the annual amount therein mentioned Together With all powers and remedies for securing and compelling payment of the rentcharge conferred by law or by the said Transfer [Conveyance] [Deed] so far as such powers are valid and enforceable

2   The title to the Rentcharge shall consist of an office copy of the entries on the register and filed plan of title number AB 12345 and a copy of the Transfer

    or – The title to the Rentcharge shall commence with the [Conveyance] [Deed]

3   The Buyer having been given details of the name and address of the last person to pay the Rentcharge shall not be entitled to evidence of the title of that person to the premises out of which the Rentcharge issues

    [Apportionment provisions may be needed as in the various versions of Precedent 14 if it is desired either to apportion on completion without a further apportionment after the year end (which is only material for estate rentcharges which vary with the cost of services), or eg if there is to be an apportionment if the year end adjustment shows a figure larger than a specified amount.]

THE SCHEDULE

Details of the Transfer/ Conveyance	Premises out of which the Rentcharge issues	Annual amount
12.3.45	67 Last Street,	£50.
F. Inis (1)	Very End,	[or – An amount based on the cost of services]
T. Ermine (2)	Conclude.	

Precedent 15

COMMONHOLD RULES, ENQUIRIES, CONTRACT AND LEASE CLAUSES

1   *Commonhold is discussed in Chapter 17. There is official guidance on the website of the Department of Constitutional Affairs –DCA.GSI.GOV.UK- ('Guidance on the Drafting of a Commonhold Community Statement including Specimen Local Rules'.) There are also some precedents appearing in the usual precedent books and some new books on commonhold.*

2   *The precedents below cover matters that the rules of the Commonhold Community Statement ('CCS'), enquiries before contract, contracts for sale of a unit and leases of units might usefully address. Even if such provisions for a CCS as are mentioned below are not in the CCS initially, members may wish to consider including some at a later date if they are amending the CCS and re-registering it, where any of these items are thought likely to assist problems that have arisen, or when a change is necessary for some reason.*

3   *The standard CCS from the regulations must be used, but can be expanded. Items to be added to the CCS must be added (a) in that part of the CCS where they apply (after the earlier provisions and continuing the numbering) or (b) in a separate Annex which includes all the amendments. The changes need to be flagged by using a heading 'Additional provisions specific to this commonhold'. These additional items are known as 'local rules'.*

4   *The provisions affecting the commonhold assessment (the commonhold equivalent of the service charge) are, as explained in Chapter 17, very different to those in leases or rentcharge deeds. In particular the works or services do not need to be defined, as they are decided annually. However, the CCS could include some provisions covering such matters as the standard of work, a requirement for maintenance contracts for some items, and perhaps for obtaining estimates for more expensive items. Precedents for such matters appear below.*

5   *In the descriptions of the various units the points about clarity of definitions as regards leases applies. The clearer the definition the less chance there is*

595

of any dispute over what is included in the unit. As the common parts of a commonhold are anything that is not described as part of a unit (and as the definition of each unit appears in the CCS) the definition of the extent of the common parts is not so important as in leases, where there is scope for omission or duplication among a set of different documents. Indeed it is not really necessary to define the common parts at all.

6   *Part 1 below contains some suggested local (additional) rules for the CCS.*

7   *In Part 2 are suggested preliminary enquiries to be made for the proposed purchaser of a commonhold unit. The enquiries relate only to the commonhold assessment aspects, and other enquiries have not been included.*

8   *Part 3 has some suggested contract provisions (relating only to the commonhold assessment aspects) on the sale of a commonhold unit. These revolve round an obligation on the seller to obtain a Commonhold Unit Information Certificate from the commonhold association, which gives details of arrears owing.*

9   *Finally in Part 4 are some provisions for a lease of a unit, covering three alternatives depending on whether the landlord pays the commonhold assessment and the tenant refunds it or does not, and those cases where the tenant agrees to pay the commonhold assessment direct (the last alternative not being available for leases of residential units).*

Part 1

Additional provisions for the CCS

1   *The following are suggested as possible additional local rules to be included in the CCS to assist with collection of the commonhold assessment.*

2   *The first precedents below are to imply an element of reasonableness for estimates. Note that including such a provision will make the collection of commonhold assessment more difficult, as amounts will be subject to challenge, whereas without this provision the directors can charge what they think appropriate and unit-holders have very limited grounds for objecting. The second precedent (which it is suggested is the most appropriate) requires the directors to hold a general meeting if more than a specified percentage of unit-holders (or those with votes totalling a certain percentage) require one. That gives an opportunity for the directors to support their proposals and the unit-holders to challenge them.*

3   *Other precedents require the directors to obtain estimates for major items, specify a standard for works, and a provision requiring the commonhold assessment money to be held in a particular type of account. The final precedent for the CCS is an example showing the commonhold assessment proportions being split into various categories (each of which must add up to 100%).*

4   *The precedents, when used, need the heading (showing they are additional provisions) and the conditions must be numbered following from the previous standard provision they follow. The numbering below is illustrative and needs to be considered for each individual CCS.*

A15.01

Suggestions implying reasonableness for cost
Note that this has the disadvantage to the commonhold association that it removes the certainty provided by the standard provision, which does not imply reasonableness. The use of a provision such as this could accordingly lead to disputes over whether what was done, or the cost of it, is reasonable.

Additional provision specific to this commonhold[1]

4.2.43   The word 'reasonable' shall be added before the word 'expenses' in paragraph 4.2.1

[or]

4.2.43   The directors of the commonhold association must have regard to prudent economy when assessing the annual estimate of income required and when considering what works or services are to be provided for the commonhold.

1   Note that if more than one provision is to be added after the same part of the standard provisions there need only be one heading, which can refer to 'additional provisions specific to this commonhold'.

A15.02

Obligation to hold a general meeting if the costs are high. *These are a few suggestions to give unit-holders an automatic chance to have the proposals for charges tested at a general meeting of unit-holders.*

Additional provision specific to this commonhold

4.2.44   If, in response to an estimate of annual income served in Form 1 under paragraph 4.2.2 or to an estimate of a proposed Levy served in Form 4 under paragraph 4.2.12, or to a request in Form 3 for an emergency payment under paragraph 4.2.5 [more than (70%) of the unit-holders who respond] [unit-holders with a total of (70%) of the voting rights] object to the amount estimated the secretary shall call a general meeting of the commonhold association to discuss the proposals to be held no later than 14 days after the end of the period for representations and the directors shall defer issuing demands for payment until 7 days after the date of such general meeting.

[or]

4.2.44   If, after the directors have served a notice in Form 1 under paragraph
           4.2.2 of the estimated amount of the commonhold assessment
           payable by the unit-holders, [70%] of the unit-holders (based on the
           amount of their contributions to the total commonhold assessment)
           so require the directors will call a special general meeting to discuss
           the estimate no later than 21 days from the date of the end of the con-
           sultation period and the directors will not issue demands for payment
           until 7 days after the date of the special general meeting.

[or]

4.2.44   If the estimate for the commonhold assessment for any year shows
           that unit-holders are to be required to pay [25%] more than in the
           previous year the directors shall (with Form 1) give reasons why the
           cost is being increased.

A15.03

Obligation to obtain estimates. *If this is used the directors must comply with its
terms or the estimates in Form 1 may be held to be invalid. The first alternative
is preferable, as it means the commonhold association can take advantage of the
protection given by the provision or not as the unit-holders prefer.*

Additional provision specific to this commonhold

4.2.46   The directors shall ensure that at least three estimates are sought for
           any item within the proposed commonhold assessment expenditure
           [exceeding such amount as shall from time to be time be decided by
           a general meeting] [exceeding 10% of the estimated total of the cost
           for the year estimates] .

A15.04

Standard of works. *This gives scope for the property to be kept up to a good
standard or (for a building of lesser quality) for costs to be kept down. The directors will need to bear this in mind when assessing what works or services are
required. If such a provision is used it should follow the repair provisions of the
CCS.*

Additional provision specific to this commonhold

4.5.3   The works to be carried out by the Commonhold Association shall be
           done to a standard [suitable for a property of the age and type of the
           buildings within the commonhold and maintenance of the grounds
           shall similarly be carried out to a suitable standard] [appropriate for
           a high class block of flats of the age of the buildings comprised in the
           commonhold.]

A15.05

Holding money. *The CCS does not include provisions about how commonhold assessment money is to be held. The following may be of use, although this can, of course, otherwise be dealt with by decisions of the directors from time to time. The advantage of such provisions in the CCS is that the terms are apparent for all to see. The suggested numbering reflects that they are added after the finance provisions in paragraph 4.2 of the CCS.*

Additional provisions specific to this commonhold[1]

4.2.47   Money paid by unit-holders towards the commonhold assessment shall be held in an account in the name of the commonhold association and any money in a reserve fund shall be held in an interest bearing account including the word 'reserve ' in the title as well as the name of the commonhold association

4.2.48   Cheques or other instructions relating to the said account or accounts shall be signed or otherwise authorised by a minimum of two directors of the commonhold association [one of whom must be the treasurer except in cases of emergency].

1   Note that if more than one provision is to be added after the same part of the standard provisions there need only be one heading, which can refer to 'additional provisions specific to this commonhold'.

A15.06

Obligation to use a maintenance contract for a specific item. *Although this is not necessary, there may be some merit in clarifying in the CCS that a particular item is one for which a maintenance contract must be used. The rule must not, of course, suggest that the named item is the only item needing a maintenance contract. It could be of use as a reminder to all reading the document that such facility exists, whether it is a lift or swimming pool or refuse disposal unit, or some other item which will need maintenance or replacement at some time. With such a provision there can be no question about whether the cost of such a contract is recoverable, although no doubt there may be complaints about the actual cost from time to time. Such a rule should appear after the provisions relating to repair.*

Additional provisions specific to this commonhold

4.3.45   Without prejudice to the generality of the obligation of the commonhold association to maintain and repair the common parts it is expressly provided that the directors shall ensure that the [lifts in the Building] [the air conditioning / climate control system] [the swimming pool] are/is are maintained under a service contract with a suitably qualified person or company.[1]

1   For further assistance with drafting see the Department for Constitutional Affairs Guidance Notes 92 to 96 and 101–102, as well as the worked examples in the Guidance Notes starting at page 48.

A15.07

Multiple percentages

1   The Guidance Notes from the Department of Constitutional Affairs indicate (in paragraph 59) that it is possible to have different percentages for different parts of the commonhold assessment. Below is a further alternative for a slightly more sophisticated apportionment of costs. It must be noted that each of the sets of percentages must add up to 100%.

2   This can be as complicated as desired, and is based on the type of slightly more sophisticated apportionments of service charges shown in some leases, particularly of office blocks. The general headings mentioned below may give rise to some questions of definition, but they should give a reasonable indication of the areas of charge for which specific percentages can be charged. Other differences could well be applied in a mixed use building, for example for the service yard for the shops and the lift for the flats above. These provisions are perhaps most likely to be of use for a mixed use building.

3   It is critical to have a sweeping-up clause on the lines of the final part: if not and a charge arises which is not within the other items mentioned, then the CCS would be defective and there would of course be a question over the percentage properly payable.

ANNEX 3

1 Allocation of Commonhold Assessment

	Commonhold unit number	Percentage allocation (total 100%)
Building maintenance, repair and insurance	1	25%
	2	30%
	3	15%
	4	30%
		100%
Repair maintenance and replacement of lifts	1	0%
	2	20%
	3	40%
	4	40%
		100%
Maintenance of the grounds	1	25%
	2	25%
	3	25%
	4	25%
		100%

Cleaning, security, complying with statutory
requirements, decoration, replacement of
plant and equipment (other than lifts)

1	10%
2	20%
3	30%
4	40%
	100%

Any other payments for which the commonhold association
is entitled to charge unit-holders

1	20%
2	20%
3	30%
4	30%
	100%

Part 2

A15.08

Enquiries before purchasing a commonhold unit

As recorded above, these notes only refer to the commonhold assessment elements of the Enquiries.

1   Please supply copies of the last three years' accounts for the commonhold assessment.

2   (a)   Please supply a copy of the estimated budget figure for the commonhold assessment for the current accounting year.

   (b)   Please supply a copy of any emergency levies estimate in Form 3 for the current accounting year.

   (c)   Please supply a copy of any notice of a proposed reserve fund levy in Form 4 for the current accounting year.

3   If there is a reserve, please state what it has been set up for.

4   Have any general meetings of the Commonhold Association during the Seller's ownership of the unit passed any resolutions affecting future liability for commonhold assessment? If so, please provide a copy.

5   Is the Seller aware of any disputes in regard to:

   (a)   the budget for the commonhold assessment,

   (b)   collection of commonhold assessment from the Seller,

   (c)   collection of commonhold assessment from any other unit-holders,

   (d)   the works proposed to be carried out by the Commonhold Association,

   (e)   works that have been carried out and for which a charge has been made within the last three years,

   (f)   the rights or obligations of unit-holders in respect of the commonhold,

(g)   any claims that decisions of the directors of the commonhold (or decisions of a general meeting) were invalid or ultra vires?

If so, please provide details and copies of any relevant notices or letters.

6   (a)   Has there been a reserve study?

(b)   If there has, please provide a copy of the latest survey or any other information the Seller may have.

7   If there are managing agents please provide details of their name, address and, if possible, reference.

8   Are all the directors of the Commonhold Association members of the Association?

9   (a)   Is the Seller aware of any proposal for a change or any need to change the provisions of the Commonhold Community Statement?

(b)   If so, please give details.

(c)   Is any such proposed change likely to result in a change to the percentage of the commonhold assessment payable in respect of the unit?

Part 3

Contract provisions

1   The Contract could usefully contain provisions as to apportionment of the commonhold assessment similar to those in Precedent 13 – eg either providing for no adjustment after the year end, or perhaps an adjustment if the amount would be more than a particular figure. The previous provisions can be used apart from referring to the commonhold assessment rather than the service charge.

2   A provision on the lines below is recommended in all contracts for the sale of a commonhold unit. The procedure is in the CCS and the purchaser should be encouraged to use it. It requires the seller to request a certificate – the CCS only entitles the unit-holder to call for the certificate.

A15.09

Requirement for a Commonhold Unit Information Certificate

1   (a)   The Seller shall, [within 5 working days of the date of this Contract] [no later than 21 days before the Completion Date] request from the Commonhold Association a Commonhold Unit Information Certificate in Form 9 under paragraph 4.7.1 of the Commonhold Community Statement, and shall provide a copy thereof to the Buyer [the Buyer's solicitors] within 2 working days of its receipt.

(b) The Seller will pay to the Commonhold Association the balance shown in Form 9 prior to the Completion Date and will produce to the Buyer evidence of such payment.

2 (a) If the Seller is unable to obtain Form 9 prior to the date for completion the Buyer shall be entitled to retain from the amount payable on completion such sum ('the Retention') as shall be a reasonable assessment of the amount that is or may be outstanding (being not less than [one quarter's payment]) and the Retention shall be placed on deposit in the joint names of the Seller's Solicitors and the Buyer's Solicitors and shall be held on the basis set out in the following sub-paragraphs.

(b) The Retention shall be held in the account until the solicitors for the Seller and the Buyer have received satisfactory evidence either that no commonhold assessment is outstanding for the period to the date of actual completion or evidence of the amount that is outstanding to that period.

(c) Once evidence as in sub clause (b) is obtained the Seller's Solicitors and the Buyer's Solicitors shall account from the Retention to the Commonhold Association for any commonhold assessment then outstanding and shall account to the Seller for the balance (if any) in the account (including interest earned thereon) less the reasonable and proper costs of the solicitors for the parties incurred in relation to the Retention. If the amount in the account shall be less than the amount of commonhold assessment owing at the date of actual completion ('the shortfall') the Seller shall pay to the Buyer the balance within five working days of the shortfall becoming known and if such payment is not made within the said period the Seller shall pay the shortfall together with interest at the Interest Rate for the period from the date of the shortfall becoming known by both parties to the date of receipt by the Buyer.

(d) If there shall be a dispute over any of the provisions in this clause as to the Retention or the evidence of the sum outstanding the dispute shall be referred to the arbitration of a single arbitrator whose decision shall be final and binding on the parties [in accordance with clause X of this Contract] and the fees of such arbitrator shall be borne equally by the Seller and the Buyer unless the arbitrator shall determine otherwise.

Part 4

Lease provisions

These are provisions primarily to cover the three alternatives – (a) where the landlord pays the commonhold assessment and the tenant does not refund it, (b) where the landlord pays and the tenant does refund it, and (c) where the tenant pays the commonhold assessment direct to the commonhold association (not available for leases of residential units). A provision that both parties will abide by the rules of the commonhold is not included, as this is covered in the CCS.

A15.10

The landlord paying the commonhold assessment – no repayment
[Covenant by the Landlord]

The Landlord will at all times during the term pay to the Commonhold Association the commonhold assessment for the demised premises in accordance with the provisions of the Commonhold Community Statement and will indemnify the Tenant against all or any claims in respect thereof.

A15.11

Tenant to repay the commonhold assessment to the landlord

As explained in the text, Regulation 11(1)(f) prohibits a provision making the tenant liable for payment of the commonhold assessment to the commonhold association for a lease of residential premises. However, this precedent is for reimbursement to the landlord, which is different, and so it is not prohibited. Note, however, that such a tenant can claim the benefit of the 'reasonableness' provisions of the Landlord and Tenant Act 1985 as against his landlord, and will be able to apply to the Leasehold Valuation Tribunal. There is nothing the landlord can do about this, as it is not possible to contract out (in the absence of special regulations, which seems unlikely). The landlord must remember that he may find himself with a shortfall if the LVT says the amount payable is more than is reasonable. He cannot raise this against the Commonhold Association.

[Covenant by the Landlord]

At all times during the term pay to the Commonhold Association the commonhold assessment for the demised premises.

[Covenant by the Tenant]

To repay to the Landlord the commonhold assessment paid by the Landlord for the demised premises without any deduction within 14 days of receipt of a written demand from the Landlord.

A15.12

Tenant of non-residential unit paying the commonhold assessment direct

Following from the head note to the previous precedent, a residential tenant cannot be called on (in the lease) to pay the commonhold assessment direct to the Commonhold Association. Accordingly this can only be used for commercial commonhold units.

[Covenant by the tenant]

1   To pay to the Commonhold Association the commonhold assessment in accordance with proper demands therefor at all times during the term

2   If the Tenant shall fail to pay the commonhold assessment in accordance with clause 1 and the Landlord is obliged to pay the commonhold assessment the Tenant shall refund to the Landlord on demand all amounts paid by the Landlord in respect thereof (including any interest and costs) and in default such sum shall be recoverable from the Tenant as rent in arrear.

Index

[all references are to paragraph number]